Jessup Whitehead

Cooking for Profit

A New American cCookbook Adapted for the Use of All...

Jessup Whitehead

Cooking for Profit
A New American cCookbook Adapted for the Use of All...

ISBN/EAN: 9783744785044

Printed in Europe, USA, Canada, Australia, Japan

Cover: Foto ©Andreas Hilbeck / pixelio.de

More available books at **www.hansebooks.com**

COOKING FOR PROFIT.

A NEW AMERICAN COOK BOOK

ADAPTED FOR THE USE OF ALL

WHO SERVE MEALS FOR A PRICE.

BY

JESSUP WHITEHEAD.

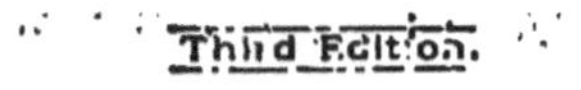

CHICAGO.
JESSUP WHITEHEAD & Co., Publishers
1893.

CONTENTS.

THE CONTENTS ALSO INCLUDE:

PREFACE.

This book is in many respects a continuation of the preceding volumes in the series, it fulfills the designs that were intended but not finished before, more particularly in the second part which deals with the cost of keeping up a table. It is not an argument either for or against high prices, but it embodies in print for the first time the methods of close-cutting management which a million of successful boarding-house and hotel-keepers are already practising, in order that another million who are not successful may learn, if they will, wherein their competitors have the advantage. At the time when the following introduction was written, which was about four years before the finish, I was just setting out, while indulging a rambling propensity, to find out why it was that my hotel books which were proving admirably adapted to the use of the ten hotels of a resort town were voted "too rich for the blood" of the four hundred boarding-houses; also, it was a question how so many of these houses running at low prices are enabled to make money as easily as the hotels which have a much larger income. At the same time some statistician published a statement that attracted attention showing that the vast majority of the people of this land have to live on an income of less than fifty cents a day. At the same time also an English author published a little book, which, however, I have not seen and did not need, with the title of "How to live on sixpence a day," (twelve cents) which was presumptive evidence that it could be done. In quest of information on these points I went around considerably and found a good many "Mrs. Tingees" who were not keeping boarding-houses, and I honor them for the surpassing skill that makes the fifty cents a day do such wonders; but the right vein was not struck until the opportunity occurred to do both the buying and using of provisions from the very first meal in a Summer Boarding House.

In reference to unfinished work I take the liberty here of saying that the bills of fare in this book with the quantities and proportions and relative cost from the continuation and complete illustration of an article entitled "The Art of Catering" in *Hotel Meat Cooking*. Knowing how much to cook, how much to charge, how to pre-vent waste and all such questions raised there are carried out to an answer in these pages. In regard to the use of French names for dishes it is necessary that a statement should be made. A great reform has taken place in the last ten years in the composition of hotel bills of fare, and the subject matter of these books having been widely diffused by publication in the hotel newspapers, has undoubtedly had much to do with the improvement that is now observable. My own design was, however, to explain French terms, give their origin and proper spelling, and to that end I had a mass of anecdotes, historical mention and other such material collected to make the explanations interesting. As a preliminary, I began exposing the absurdities committed by ignorant cooks and others trying to write French, and before this had proceeded far the newspapers took up and advocated the idea that French terms should be abolished altogether. If that was to be the way the knot of misspelling and misnaming dishes was to be cut, there was no use for my dictionary work and the material was thrown away; I followed the new path and it proves a plain and sensible one. At the same time there is an aspect of the subject which cooks seeking situations perceive and editors of newspapers may never think of, and that is that there are many employers whom the reform has not reached who will pay a hundred dollars for a cook who can give his dishes imposing foreign names more willingly than fifty dollars to a better cook who can only write United States. First class hotels which have all the good things that come to market avoid French terms. They that have turkey and lamb, chicken, peas and asparagus, oysters and turtle and cream want them shown up in the plainest reading; to cover them up with French names would be injudicious; but if we have but the same beef and mutton every day, the aid that a few ornamental terms can give is not to be despised. First of all it is requisite that those who use such terms should know what they are intended to indicate and how they should be spelled and then they can be taken or left according to the intelligent judgment of those concerned

I. W

Cooking for Profit.

INTRODUCTORY.

The pleasing discovery has recently been made by the writer, in the pursuit of a new business, that the interest in the subject of cookery is universal and only wants the proper sort of instructors, the right kind of books and some way of making it known that they are the right kind to set everybody to trying their capabilities in this at once the most useful and most ornamental art. True, there are cook books already by the hundreds, but that is not all that is required, a greater difficulty than to write and compile a book on the subject is to get people to read it, and certain pages or even certain items that might be veritable jewels of knowledge at times to the possessors of the books lie there undiscovered.

We have already tried the conversational style in writing about cooking, and have reason to be satisfied with the results of the experiment as far as it has gone. We have the satisfaction at least of finding that what has been written has been read, and what we have learned of our subject has in that manner been made plain to such readers as had need of the knowledge.

Amongst all the commendations of our published hotel book, the "American Pastry Cook," received from the workers who have tried and know, and some of whom have even written gratefully for the help they found in it, we have met no harsher adverse criticism than that of a fashionable caterer of prominence in his own city, who said that it was too good; that if the author could make the articles in it, and as good as described, he ought to be in a certain famous hotel, "where the best they can get is not good enough for them."

This though not intended for praise, certainly was praise of the highest kind, for the book having the ambitious title of *American Pastry Cook*, and the volume next to come being the *American Cook*, ought not to show American cookery and the American table to be in any repect inferior to that of any other nation or people whatsoever. That book does, and the whole work will when completed contain the cheapest and best articles as well as the costlier kinds, but cheapness is not put in the foreground.

It is now proposed to run serially in the HOTEL GAZETTE a book with some original features, having the cost of each article carefully counted and all superfluities that are set down as optional in other books left out of this altogether. It is to be a book that will show how to make money by cooking; a book suited to the wants of an immense number who live by boarding others at the lowest rate compatible with respectability of appearances, and a book that shall be on the same plane of everyday life with the people in the smaller hotels and in private houses that the writer meets with every day. They do not run bills of fare, nor plan nor reckon up their meals at from fifty cents to one dollar each person.

A book of this character must recognize the great fact that there are infinitely more women engaged or interested in cooking than men; it is hardly too much to say that every woman is interested, and they do not need to be told that they ought to know how to cook, that is acknowledged in advance, but, "oh dear! the toil! the dry uninteresting study of the incomprehensible cook books!"

Said a lady laughingly, the other day in a parlor full of friends—a lady of wealth and position, the daughter of a prominent judge, and the wife of a leading lawyer of that section—"When we were married my husband said he would give me a fifty-dollar bill if I would learn to make good bread. We have been married five years and I have not learned yet, but I think I can out of this book. I am going to try to secure that greenback yet!"

Said another one the same day, and this one was extremely poor, the only worker in the family, having a sick husband—"Now I find I can make things from my book that sell well in the windows, we will give up trying to keep boarders, that is killing us both and paying nothing, almost."

To meet the wants of thousands such, it is necessary to adopt the household cup and spoon measures where measures are wanted. Curious as it may seem to workmen these people in small hotels find one of the greatest difficulties of life in having to weigh and measure,

very few possess scales and they do not realize generally that absolute success, and success every time depends upon the exact proportions of their ingredients. As it is impossible for us to give exact proportions without a better standard than the variable size of the cups in use we shall have to give a double set of measures, one by the cup and the other by pint and pound.

Persons who practice from this book can find which cup holds half a pint, which is half a pound of water, and the standard, and always using the same can soon learn to measure as many ounces as they want in it by observing the difference of the specific gravity of each article used. Thus:

No. 1—Cup and Spoon Measure.

A cup means the common size of white cup generally used in hotels and restaurants that holds $\frac{1}{2}$ pint of liquid.

WATER.—A pint is a pound, a cup is $\frac{1}{2}$ pint, therefore a cup of water is 8 oz.

MILK.—A cup of milk is $\frac{1}{2}$ pint, or 8 oz.

EGGS BY MEASURE.—A cup of yolks or whites or of both mixed is $\frac{1}{2}$ pound, equal in weight to five large eggs. It takes 9 whites to fill a cup. It takes 13 yolks to fill a cup. When you have yolks left over, it is near enough to count 2 yolks equal to one egg, or a cup of yolks as good as 7 eggs because richer than whole ones. Water should be added to them to increase the bulk and make them capable of being beaten light.

EGGS BY COUNT.—10 eggs average a pound: 5 eggs fill a cup. When there are duck, goose, turkey, bantam or guinea-fowl eggs to be used, instead of counting they can be measured after breaking for cooking purposes by the above rule—i e, a cup of eggs is equal to 5 ordinary hen's eggs.

BUTTER.—A cup of cold butter is $7\frac{1}{2}$ ounces, if pressed in quite solid. A cup of melted butter is $\frac{1}{2}$ oz lighter. It is usually near enough for cooking to call a cup ½ pound. Butter size of an egg is 1½ ounces.

Lard.—Same as butter.

Sugar.—A level cup of granulated sugar is 7 ounces—2 cups is 2 ounces less than a pound. Although sugar by the grain is heavier than water, and will sink instantly the air spaces between the grains make a cupful weigh less than so much liquid. ½ pound of granulated sugar is a cup rounded up. The powdered sugar that is known as fine granulated weighs the same, icing sugar or flour of sugar is lighter, a cup is but 6 ounces. All that can be scooped up in a cup out of a barrel of any grade weighs 9 ounces. Brown sugar a level cup is 6 ounces. Up in the mountains the cake receipts people have been used to, fail. It is all because of the sugar. So much sugar cannot be used at great elevations as at sea-level, hence the reason for being particular about the weights.

Molasses.—A cup of thick molasses weighs 12 ounces—that is three-quarters of a pound—half as much as water and 5 ounces more than so much sugar. Thin syrups, however, do not weigh quite so much.

Flour.—A level cup of flour is 4 ounces. A cup heaped up with all that can be dipped with it out of a barrel is 7 ounces, nearly twice as much as the level. A quart of flour just rounded over is a pound.

Bread-crumbs.—A cup of bread is 4 ounces pressed in rather solid. A pound of bread is a pressed-in quart.

Corn-meal.—A cup of corn-meal is 5 ounces, 3 rounded cups are a pound, or a pound of corn-meal is a little less than a level quart.

Oatmeal.—A level cup of oatmeal is 6 ounces. All that can be dipped up with a cup weighs 7 ounces—nearly ½ pound.

Corn Starch.—A level cup of starch flour or cooking starch is 6 ounces, the same as corn-meal. All that can be heaped in a cup weighs 7 ounces.

Farina.—The same as starch.

Rice.—A level cup weighs 7 ounces. All that can be heaped in a cup weighs 9 ounces.

Light Bread Dough.—A rounded cup is ½ pound.

A Basting-spoon means the pressed iron spoon about half as long as one's arm. The bowl of most of them of different lengths of handle holds the same. Six basting-spoons of liquid are ½ pint or a cup. It is the most useful measure for molasses. A full spoon of molasses is 2 ounces. A basting spoon of melted butter or lard not quite full is 1 ounce, 6 spoons brim-full will be ½ pound of butter.

A Table-spoon 14 times full is a cup or ½ pint of water, 2 tablespoons of melted butter is 1 ounce. It is near enough to count a tablespoonful ½ ounce of any fluid except molasses of which a tablespoon may be made to take up an ounce. A heaping tablespoon of sugar is 1 ounce, 6 or 7 will fill a cup. A heaping tablespoon of starch is 1 ounce, 4 will fill a cup—starch can be heaped so much higher than sugar. A moderately heaped tablespoon of flour is 1 ounce, three fully heaped will fill a cup—4 ounces. Of eggs broken in a cup, 3 tablespoons are equal to 1 egg.

A teaspoon is ½ a table spoon. When baking powder, cream tartar, sugar, starch and the like is to be measured a rounded teaspoon is meant. It is near enough in most cases to count a teaspoonful ½ ounce.

In the absence of such a table as the foregoing ready prepared we have found such questions the most perplexing of any that have been given us to answer. It looks now as if any of those who are opposed to scales and weights, might so well acquaint themselves with the capacities of one cup as to become accurate cooks, and safe from the discouraging effects of culinary failures.

SOME ARTICLES FOR THE SHOW CASE.

2—Angel Food or White Sponge Cake

WHITEST AND FINEST CAKE MADE.

5 whites of eggs—or six if small.
5 ounces fine granulated sugar—½ cup large.
2½ ounces flour—½ cup large.
1 rounded teaspoon cream tartar.
1 teaspoon vanilla or lemon extract.

Mix the cream tartar in the flour by sifting them together. Whip the whites firm, put in the sugar and beat a few seconds, add the flavoring, then stir in the flour lightly without beating. As soon as mixed put the cake in the oven. It needs careful baking like a meringue, in a slack oven and should stay in from 20 to 30 minutes. A small, deep, smooth mold is the best and should not be greased. When the cake is done turn it upside down and leave it to get cold in the mold before trying to take it out.

When you have pure cream tartar from a drug store use only half as much as of the common lest the cake taste of it.

3—Plain Glaze or Icing for the Above.

4 tablespoons powdered sugar.
1 white of an egg.

Put the sugar in a cup and mix it with the white of egg. As soon as the sugar is fairly wetted it is ready. It dries pearl white; takes but a minute to make. Spread it all over the bottom and sides of "angel food."

Cost of material 15c., size 1 quart; weight 15 oz.

The rule for the foregoing in large quantities is an ounce of sugar to each ounce of white of eggs and half as much flour. Those who deal in it largely say it is, or at least was before they got it into a regular routine, the most troublesome cake they made, the tendency being always to fall in the middle. They now use plain deep molds having centre tubes of unusually large size. There is no difficulty with small cakes. But the whites must be whipped quite dry in a cold place.

4—Lady-Fingers.

7 ounces granulated sugar—1 cup.
4 eggs.
3 tablespoons water.
6 ounces flour—1 heaping cup.
1 ounce sugar to dredge.

Separate the eggs, the whites in a bowl, the yolks in the mixing pan. Put the sugar to the yolks and stir up, then add the water and beat with a bunch of wire 10 minutes. Have the flour ready. Whip the whites with the wire egg whisk till they are firm enough to bear up an egg. Mix the flour in the yolks and stir in the white of eggs last.

Put the batter into a large paper cornet with the point clipped off, or into a lady-finger sack and tube, and press out finger lengths in regular order on a sheet of manilla paper. When the sheet is full dredge fine sugar over, catch up two corners of the sheet and shake off the surplus, and lay it on a baking-pan. Bake a light yellow-brown in about 6 minutes. Take off by wetting the paper under side and stick the two cakes together while they are still moist.

Cost of material 14c.; number of cakes 6 dozen pairs, weight 18 oz.

5—Star Kisses.

8 ounces fine granulated sugar—rounded cup.
4 whites of eggs.
1 teaspoon flavoring.

Whip the whites with a bunch of wire, in a cold place until they are firm enough to bear up an egg, add the sugar and flavor and beat a few seconds longer. Put the meringue paste thus made into a sack and star-pointed tube or else into a stiff paper cornet having the point cut like saw teeth and press out portions size of walnuts on to pans slightly greased and then wiped clean. Bake in a very slack oven about 10 minutes or till the kisses are of a light fawn color and swelled partially hollow. They slip off easily when cold.

Cost of material 10c; number of cakes 5 doz., or according to size.

6—Fairy Gingerbread, or Ginger Wafers.

This appears to have originated in Boston where it is held in high favor and it is a sort of social duty to know how to make it. No eggs needed.

1 cup butter—7 oz.
2 cups light brown sugar—13 oz.
1 cup milk—½ pint.
4 cups flour—1 pound.
1 teaspoon ground ginger.

Warm the butter and sugar slightly and rub them together to a cream. Add the milk, ginger and flour. It makes a paste like very thick cream. Spread a thin coating of butter on the baking pans, let it get quite cold and set, then spread the paste on it no thicker than a visiting card, barely covering the pan from sight. Bake in a slack oven, and when done cut the sheets immediately into the shape and size of common cards. This is also known as euchre gingerbread. Is served in packs and eaten between games.

Do it up in paper packages to prevent breakage, with one sheet outside.

Cost of material 23c; weight 2¼ pounds; cakes innumerable.

7—Jelly Roll.

1 cup sugar—7 ounces.
4 eggs.
1 cup water small.
2 cups flour—9 ounces.
1 large teaspoon baking powder.
½ cup fruit jelly or thin marmalade.

Separate the eggs, the whites in a good-sized bowl, the yolks in the mixing pan. Put the sugar to the yolks, stir up, then add the water and beat up till they are light and thick. Mix the powder in the flour, whip the whites to a very firm froth. When they are ready stir the flour into the yolk mixture and mix in the whipped whites last.

Cut sheets of blank paper the size of your baking pans, spread the batter on them, without previous greasing, as thin as can be, and bake in a quick oven about 6 minutes. Brush over the under side of the paper with water, the cake laid flat on the table, and take it off. Spread the cake with thin jelly and roll up.

It makes it rounder and smoother to roll it in a fresh sheet of paper and keep it so until wanted, care being taken that the cake is sufficiently baked not to stick. It shoul t be observed that this and number 4 can both be used for the same purposes, this is the cheaper.

Cost of material 19 or 20c.; weight over 1½ pounds; light and large.

8—Cocoanut Gems, Cakes or Caramels.

These very quickly and easily made cream candy drops we learned to consider worth having in our show case through observing how rapidly they sold at two rival fruit and confectionary stands in a western city. They were freshly stacked up in sight close to the sidewalk every morning, about a bushel in each place as it seemed, and were all or nearly all sold by night. They may be found in most confectionaries under different names.

1 pound granulated sugar—2 cups.
8 ounces grated cocoanut 2 cups.
⅓ cup of water.

Set the sugar and water over the fire in a small, bright kettle and boil about five minutes, or till the syrup bubbles up and ropes from the spoon, and do not stir it. Then put in the cocoanut, stir to mix, and begin at once and drop the candy by tablespoonfuls on a buttered baking pan. The dry dessicated cocoanut is the easier kind to work with. With the moist, fresh graten more time should be given for the sugar to boil to the candy point.

Leave a little in the kettle and color it pink with a few drops of cochineal, adding water if necessary. Drop a spot of the pink on each white cake.

Cost of material 20 or 22c. Number according to size. They sell at 2½c each.

9—Pound Fruit Cake.

Yellow but spotted with fruit.

The staple every day sort of plum cake. The fruit does not sink to the bottom in this mixture.

14 ounces sugar—2 cups.
14 ounces butter—2 cups.
11 eggs.
18 ounces flour—4 rounded cups.

Mix the above the same as pound cake, then add to it,

1 pound raisins.
1 pound currants.
8 ounces citron.
1 teaspoonful baking powder.

Use seedless raisins. Nothing is good made full of raisin seeds. Mix the fruit together and dust it with flour before stirring it into the batter. The cakes require from 1 to 1½ hours to bake.

2 teaspoonfuls of mixed ground spices, cinnamon, mace, and alspice, can be added to the above if so desired. It changes the appearance of the cake, however, and renders it perhaps less saleable. But either way it is an excellent cake.

Cost of material—sugar 10, butter 20, eggs 18, flour and powder 4, raisins 20, currants 10, citron 15—97c.; weight over six pounds, size a five pint cake mold full.

Preserving Corn with Salt.

Cut green corn off the cob and pack it in jars in layers with salt enough between each layer to form a brine that will cover the corn. Place a plate or board on top of the corn, cover the jar and keep in a cool place.

When to be used soak the required quantity in fresh water for 24 hours, changing the water once or twice, then boil and season with milk and butter, or make into corn pudding, or fritters.

The above method used to be universally followed before canning, became so common. The corn is not so well-flavored, yet serves a purpose in some places.

Kossuth Cakes.

Make sponge drops large and thick, hollow out the bottoms, fill the hollow with whipped cream sweetened and flavored, and place two together. Dip them in melted sweet chocolate or chocolate icing and place on an oiled dish to dry. They are a Baltimore specialty, are generally made to order, only for parties; the price about a dollar a dozen.

Cheese Fondue, a la Savarin.

It is one form of cheese omelet. Take equal weights of cheese and eggs and one fourth as much butter—that would be 3 eggs, 4 ounces cheese, butter size of a guinea egg. Grate the cheese, mix the butter with it in a pan over the fire, break in the eggs, season with pepper, scramble all together same as scrambled eggs, but not too hard, as the cheese becomes tough and ropy if cooked too much.

Cheese Ramequins.

Roll out pie paste, cover it with grated cheese, fold up and roll out twice more. Cut out like thin biscuits, wash over with egg and bake. For luncheons and teas.

THE LUNCH COUNTER.

10—Alamode Beef Soup.

There is a well established favorite soup sold in the large cities under this name; whether any relation to beef-a-la-mode or not makes no difference whatever. It is especially adapted for a lunch, or to be made a meal of, being simply made thick and of course nutritious with beef boiled to shreds in it.

To make 12 quarts soup take,

5 gallons water.

5 pounds soup beef.

Shanks and bones, all the water will cover.

An onion, a carrot, a turnip.

12 cloves, 1 bayleaf.

1 tablespoon salt.

1 teaspoonful black pepper.

Break up the shanks and bones, wash off in cold water, put them into the boiler with the meat not touching the bottom, boil gently for 6 hours, then take out the piece of beef. Add to the stock the cloves and bayleaf and continue boiling until the water is reduced to three gallons, and the remaining meat is well dissolved, which may be three or four hours longer. Strain off the stock through a gravy strainer, skim free from fat, set it on the fire again in the soup pot; cut the vegetables or chop them and throw them in, and mince the piece of beef without any fat and add that likewise. Boil ½ hour, thicken slightly with flour-and-water, season with the salt and pepper and skim off the particles of fat that rise from the minced beef. It is thick with meat and minced vegetables.

It is not much detriment to such a soup to have the fat remaining in it, except the crumbs of fat meat that rise from the mince and spoil its smooth appearance, but it is needed for other uses in the kitchen.

To make soup every day as easily as possible there must be a regular time for setting on the first boiler—the stock boiler—and a routine something like this:

In the morning when preparing breakfast and dinner, get the soup pieces of meat together. After dinner as soon as possible set the boiler full of these pieces and the complement of water on the range and let it slowly simmer as long as there is a fire at night. Then the last thing at night, if warm weather, strain off the stock and set in a cool place till morning. But if cold weather and the stock cannot spoil in the boiler during the night it will be better to leave it and draw it off quite clear before the morning fire is started under it.

Good soup can be made by setting the prepared boiler on early in the morning and drawing off the stock at about 11 o'clock, but it is not the best way for obvious reasons.

Cost of material—rough beef at 5, bones at 2, vegetables etc, 5, 12c per pound gall.

11—Cold Baked Ham.

Scrape and carefully shave off the outside of a ham and saw off the rank end of the knuckle bone. It is an improvement to soak the ham in water 12 hours before cooking.

Boil it in the salt meat boiler from 2½ to 3½ hours, according to size. Take out, remove the rind, trim a little and bake it brown and shining—about ½ hour.

12—Roast Ham Bread-crumbed.

Boil and trim the ham as heretofore directed. Mix 3 cupfuls of the sifted crumbs of dried and crushed bread with 1 cupful of grated cheese. Brown the ham in the oven only very slightly, take it out and press upon it all the bread crumb mixture that can be made to stick. Put back in the pan and brown it in the oven carefully all over alike, basting the dry places with a little clear fat from the pan. The cheese mixed with the crumbs acts as a cement for the coating, gives a rich color and a good flavor. A ham done this way is good either for hot or cold.

Cost—A 16 pound ham at 12½c $2,00. Loss by shrinkage, rind, bone, waste 6 pounds, 10 pounds nett salcable ham for $2,00 costs 20c per pound. 1 pound of ham makes from 4 to 8 plates, or 12 sandwiches.

13—Fried Oysters.

1 dozen oysters.
1 cup cracker-meal or crumbs.
½ cup milk batter.
Lard to fry.
Lemon to garnish.

Spread the oysters on a clean napkin and wipe them dry.

Mix in a small bowl 2 rounded tablespoons flour with 6 tablespoons milk, gradually free from lumps and like cream. Be particular to measure; and use milk because it takes on a finer color in frying than if water is used. Dip the oysters into the batter then into the cracker-meal or bread crumbs and let them lie well covered for a while. If so preferred double bread them by dipping the second time in the batter and then in the cracker-meal again.

Fry in hot lard about 3 or 4 minutes or until brown. Drain in a strainer, serve heaped in a hot dish and quarters of lemon at each end.

14—Fried Oysters in Haste.

Where there is not time to dry the oysters take
6 tablespoons cracker-meal.
2 large tablespoons flour.
Some oyster liquor in a small pan.

Mix the cracker-meal and flour thoroughly together dry. Dip the oysters out of their own liquor into the meal, out of the meal into the extra pan of oyster liquor and out of that into the meal again. Do not rub the oysters as the bread-

ing will not stick a second time, but press them in singly. Fry brown in 3 or 4 minutes, garnish with parsley and lemon.

Cost of material—with bulk oysters at 60c per quart of 4 doz. oysters 15, breading 1, lemon 1, 17c. Lard to fry, 2 oz for each dozen oysters either consumed or damaged 2c—total 19c.

15—Oyster Fritters.

Mix one-fourth flour with three-fourths cracker meal dry, and have some oyster liquor or milk or both mixed in a pan. Put in a good pinch of salt. Dip the oysters out of their own liquor into the mixed meal, out of that into the oyster liquor then into the meal again, and do so twice more, giving the oysters 4 coats. Fry in hot lard crisp and brown in 5 minutes. Serve in circular order in a dish and garnish. These keep the perfect shape of the oyster and the oyster flavor in the crust much better than if made by dipping into thick fritter batter.

Cost—the same as fried oysters.

16—Oysters Sauteed in Butter.

Mix one-fourth flour with three-fourths cracker meal (or sifted crumbs of dried bread) dry. Dip the oysters out of their own liquor into the meal, press down without rubbing and give them a good coating.

Put 1 ounce of butter into a frying-pan and melt it. Lay one dozen oysters in close enough to stick together by the edges. Fry carefully as butter easily burns, until the under side is nicely browned, then lay a plate upside down upon them, turn over and slide them back into the pan again and brown the other side. Serve them still caked together on a hot plate.

Cost of material—oysters 15, breading and lemon 1, butter 2, 18c per doz.

17—Oyster Pies—Individual..

These are covered pies of the usual

well-known form containing from 12 to 18 small oysters. They are served in a deep plate with a soup ladleful of oyster-stew liquor poured around. The pies are about the size of a large saucer.

To make 10 such pies take for the crust,

    20 ounces flour—5 cups.
    8 ounces lard or suet—1 rounded cup.
    1 cup water.
    1 teaspoon salt.

Rub the lard into the flour dry, pour the water into the middle and stir up to soft dough. Spread the flour that remains unwetted on the table, pat the dough smooth in it, roll it out 2 or 3 times and fold it up and it is ready for use. Cut pieces, roll out very thin and cover 10 pie pans.

Then put into each 18 small oysters and the liquor belonging. Dredge in a little salt and pepper and a little dust of flour rubbed through a seive with the fingers. Put a top crust on and cut off the surplus by pressing the hands against the edge of the pie pan all around. Bake about 10 minutes, serve hot as above stated.

Cost of material—flour 3, lard 7, cost of crust 10c. With bulk small oysters at 50c per quart of 15 dozen—oysters 50c. 3 pints milk and oyster liquor seasoned 12c—total 10 pies 72c—say, 7½c each.

18—Oyster Pot-Pie.

Sells well in the restaurant.—
2 quarts small oysters.
1 ounce butter.
1 cup milk.
Salt and pepper.
    Crust made of
1 pound flour—4 cups.
3 teaspoons baking powder.
1 cup water.
Drain the oysters pretty well from their liquor and put them into a 3-quart bright milk pan. Mix the crust like making biscuit, but without shortening, and have it as soft as possible to be han-

dled. Pat it out flat with the hands and cover the oysters. Bake 15 minutes and then introduce at one side a seasoning of salt and pepper—a teaspoonful of each—a small piece of butter, a cup of milk and a bastingspoon of flour-and-water thickening. Stir about, replace the piece of dough that was raised up and bake a short time longer. The crust should be as light as a sponge and lightly browned, but the oysters not cooked hard.

Cost of material—with bulk small oysters at $180 gall.—oysters 90, butter 2, milk 2, flour 3, powder 2. seasonings 1, $1,00. Contains about 16 doz oysters, or according to grade, and crust to correspond.

19—Chow-Chow—Domestic.

-----

12 large green tomatoes.
12 cucumbers.
12 onions.
1 head cabbage.
There should be about twice as much cabbage when all are chopped as of any one of the others.
Chop them small, mix, sprinkle with salt and let stand over night.
Then drain off and cover with weak vinegar and let stand 2 days. Drain again and add to it
    3 quarts cider vinegar.
    1 cup grated horseradish.
    4 ounces white mustard seed.
    ½ ounce celery seed.
    1½ ounces ground cinnamon.
    2 tablespoons turmeric.
    4 tablespoons dry mustard.
    ½ pound sugar.
    4 green peppers minced.
When well mixed set it on the range in a bright kettle and boil up. When cold it is ready for use. The above makes something over 2 gallons. It is a fine relish for the lunch table. Keep in glass jars.

Cost—too variable for estimate. To people with gardens very little. Probable average 50c per gall.

20—Plain Pie Paste.

1 level cup lard—7 ounces.
4 level cups flour—1 pound.
1 teaspoon salt.
Water to mix—½ cup.

Drop the lard into the flour and rub them together until well mixed. Pour a small cup of cold water in the middle and stir around gradually. Take the paste out while quite soft, pat out smooth on the table with plenty of flour under; roll it out, fold up in three roll, out and fold up twice more, and it is ready for use. The rolling and folding makes the paste flaky and better than it otherwise would be, although this is not intended to be real puff paste.

21—Suet Pie Paste.

2 pressed in cups minced suet.
4 cups flour.
1 teaspoon salt.
Warm water to mix.

Make the suet as fine as possible by first shaving in thin slices and then mincing very small with a little flour mixed in while mincing, to prevent sticking to the knife. Rub the suet into the dry flour, add salt, mix up gradually from the middle with water slightly warm. Take the dough out of the pan and roll out to a sheet on the table, fold over in three and roll out twice more. Pie paste made as above, then allowed to become very cold and rolled twice again is almost as good as puff paste in flakiness.

The time may be shortened by having the suet, pretty well chopped, in a warm room to soften, then pounding it smooth, throwing it into the flour and mixing up and rolling out without stopping to rub it in the flour first, which is a tedious operation.

Cost of material—average for both suet and lard 12c; makes 3 or 4 covered pies large enough to quarter, if rolled thin.

22—The Covered Lemon Pie of the Great Bakeries.

NO EGGS NEEDED.

8 ounces sugar—1 large cup.
3 ounces flour—1 small cup.
1 lemon.
1 pint water—2 cups.

Grate rind of lemon into a small saucepan, using a tin grater and scraping off with a fork what adheres. Squeeze in the juice, scrape out the pulp, chop it, put in the water and boil. Mix the sugar and flour together dry and stir them into the boiling liquor. When half thickened take it off and let finish in the pies.

The above makes two large pies or three small. It is necessary to be particular to get the right amount of flour. The mixture is pale yellow from the rind and sugar.

Put top crust as well as bottom on these pies.

Cost of material 10c—pies each 8 or 9 cents. Cut in 4.

There are some immense bakeries in the city of Chicago and one of them is peculiar in that it turns out nothing but pies. It has grown up to its present dimensions from being a mere corner pie shop, and even yet one of the firm, the working partner, bakes all the pies himself, indeed he says that so close is the margin of profit in the business that when once he was laid up by a spell of sickness the loss during his absence amounted to about three hundred dollars per week. Hotel keepers and others who have to hire inefficient help and who see things burnt up and wasted will understand how that might be; and then there is the important matter of buying cheaply and well.

The people of the present time are actuated by all sorts of queer desires and ambitions. Some want to go around the world in eighty days, some want to walk a thousand miles in so many hours, and the grand goal in view that the owners of this great pie factory have set themselves the task of reaching or die in the attempt is the production of a million pies in a year. Two years ago the number turned out in the course of twelve months had reached to eight hundred and thirty thousand, and it did seem as though the remaining trifle of one hundred and seventy thousand pies might be compassed in the succeeding year, making it a round million in twelve months, however it was not to be. Whether somebody had a corner on pumpkins that year, or whether apples were high through increased shipments to Europe where pies cannot go, or whether pies had begun to go out of fashion, or strong rivalry with this firm had sprung up so it was that the sales actually fell twenty-five thousand pies short of the greatest pie year. Still the prospect is good for the firm to achieve the object of their ambition. The population of the city is still increasing and no new or alarming accusations against pie have been started of late. This establishment possesses six carrying vans, five of which are of the capacity of omnibusses and are as finely painted. They cost five hundred dollars each, have horses to match and each van takes out five hundred pies at every trip. The customers are lunch counter keepers and restaurants, hotels and boarding houses, bakeries, groceries and private houses, all over the city. They run five huge rotary ovens of which the doors are never closed, but the pies put in at the front pass around the interior on the revolving floor and come to the door again done and ready to taken out. Of course their pies are good or they could never hope to sell a million a year, and the sorts they make are quite numerous in variety. Still they are cheap.

23—Lemon Cream Pie.

Cover the pie pans with a single crust but with a thicker edge than common, and bake it slack done. Take out and fill with lemon cream, cover with me-

ringue and bake again but only until the meringue or frosting has a light color on top.

The lemon cream filling.

2 cups milk—1 pint.
¼ cup sugar—4 ounces.
½ cup flour—2 ounces.
1 tablepoon butter—1 ounce.

Few drops oil lemon, or extract or grated rind.

Put a spoonful of sugar in the milk and set on to boil. The sugar prevents the milk from burning on the bottom. Mix the flour and rest of sugar very thoroughly together dry, drop them into boiling milk and stir rapidly with the wire egg beater. Throw in the butter. Let cook at the back of the range 10 minutes. Flavor before spreading in the pie crusts.

For the frosting take whites of eggs, 3 tablespoons sugar, whip the whites quite firm, beat in the sugar a few moments, spread over the pies and dry bake in a slsack oven.

At the great bakeries mentioned the frosting is placed around in a pattern with a star kiss tube, as named at No. 5.

Save the yolks of eggs to make custard pies.

Cost of material—crust for 2 pies 6c; filling and frosting 13c, 19c—cut each in 4.

24—Pumpkin or Squash Pie.

6 cups cooked pumpkin or squash,— or 3 pints or pounds, or a can.
1 cup light brown sugar—7 ounces.
1 cup flour—4 ounces.
1 cup milk ½ pint.
1 teaspoon ground ginger—½ ounce.
½ teaspoon salt.

Have the pumpkin drained dry after cooking, and mashed smooth. Mix in the sugar, ginger and pinch of salt. Mix the flour with the milk in a bowl gradually, perfectly free from lumps, and stir that well into the pumpkin.

Cover 3 large pie pans with thin

crusts of short paste made of a small cup of lard rubbed into 4 cups of flour and mixed up with water and a little salt and rolled. Fill them to the brim with the pumpkin, bake ½ hour in a slack oven. Eat cold.

Cost of material—4½ lbs raw pumpkin or squash at 2c, one-third waste—pumpkin 9, sugar 5, flour 1, milk 2, ginger 1; 18c for filling. Crust average 3c each, total each pie 9c. Large dinner plate size, full. Cut in 4. A 3 lb. can pumpkin or squash costs 20c by the dozen.

25—Apple Pie.

7 or 8 average apples—2 pounds.
Short paste for 2 covered pies.

Buy sweet, ripe apples that need no sugar, have a care, however that they are of a good cooking sort. Pare and slice them thinly off the cores.

Spread thin bottom crusts on 2 large pie pans, put in the sliced apples raw, cover with a top crust, bake ½ hour in a slack oven.

A grating of nutmeg can be added if desired to improve the flavor, and with some kinds of apples it is an advantage to put in a spoonful or two of water and dredge a little flour on top of the fruit before covering.

When puting on the top crust the quickest and best way instead of cutting around is to press both hands against the edge of the pie pan, turning it around on the table and so cutting off the paste. It closes the edges together and takes off all the surplus.

Cost of material—apples 6, double crusts for 2 pies 8; 14c. Large dinner plate size, full. Cut each in 4.

Sound apples lose one-third their weight by paring and coring, unsound apples, of course, are an indefinite proposition. A bushel of apples is 48 lbs; it contains from 150 to 200 apples, according to size, average, say 175. A bushel

of apples makes 48 pies, dinner plate size.

26—Mince Pie—No 1.

Cover large pie pans with a bottom crust of plain pie paste and put into each a heaped ½ pint of the following mincemeat. Cover with a top crust and bake ½ hour. Keep warm until served.

Cost of material—crust each 4, mincemeat 6, 10c. Large size cut in 4.

27—Mincemeat—No. 1

8 cups minced beef—2 pounds.
12 cups minced suet—3 pounds.
12 cups currants—4 pounds.
12 cups chopped apples—3 pounds.
2 heaped cups raisins—1 pound.
2 heaped cups brown sugar—1 pound.
2 heaped tablespoons mixed ground spices—cinnamon, alspice and cloves.
4 cups orange and lemon rinds boiled tender and chopped—1½ pounds.
2 cups common brandy—1 pint.
14 cups cider—3½ quarts.

Season the chopped meat and suet with salt and black pepper, then mix all and keep in a jar or keg a week or two or longer, before using.

Cost of material—Meat loses one-third in boiling, buy 3 lbs beef, heart or tongue at average 8c., beef 24, suet 24, currants 40, apples 9, raisins 20, sugar 10, spice 10, orange peel 8, brandy 50, cider 45; $2,40c. Amount 3 galls., 80c gall. Heaping ½ pint to each large pie makes 40 at cost of 6c each.

28—Mince Pie—No. 2.

Cover pie pans with plain pie paste rolled very thin and put into each pie a full large cup of the following mincemeat. Cover with a thin top crust and bake in a slack oven about 20 minutes.

Cost of material—crust for each pie 3½, filling 3½; 7c each. Large size, full. Cut in 4.

29—Mincemeat—No 2.

1 ox heart boiled tender and minced.
6 cups minced suet—$1\frac{1}{2}$ pounds.
4 cups black molasses—1 quart.
4 heaped cups brown sugar—2 pounds.
2 heaped cups raisins—1 pound.
3 heaped cups currants—1 pound.
3 heaped tablespoons ground spices—allspice, cinnamon and cloves mixed.
1 heaped tablespoon black pepper.
2 cups vinegar—1 pint.
4 cups orange and lemon peel boiled tender and minced.
6 heaped cups raw dried apples—$1\frac{1}{2}$ pounds.
6 pressed-in cups bread crumbs—$1\frac{1}{2}$ pounds.
16 cups water—4 quarts.

Boil the dried apples in 2 quarts of the water and before they become too soft take them out and chop them and put them with the liquor in a large jar. Pour 2 quarts water over the bread and add that, then all the other ingredients as named. Season the meat and suet with salt. It is ready for present use.

Cost of material—$1,40. Amount 3 galls.; 47c gall. Makes 40 pies, large size.

Cheese Pudding.

Line a small shallow dish with good pastry, beat up two eggs, add half a pound of grated cheese, one quarter ounze of butter, and a seasoning of pepper and salt; mix well, and pour into the lined dish.

Cheese Straws.

Take equal portions of flour, grated cheese, and butter — one quarter or half a pound of each, according to the number of "straws" required. Add a slight seasoning of salt and pepper; make the whole into a paste, roll out, cut into strips or straws, and bake in a quick oven.

Cheese Pounded.

Cut up one pound of cheese that has become too dry for the table, into small pieces; add three ounzes of butter and a teaspoonful of made mustard. Put in a mortar and pound it until smooth; press it into glass or earthen pots such as are used for potted meats. Use it by spreading on thin bread and butter or toast.

Cheese Souffle.

Mix a quarter of a pint of milk with about a dessert-spoonful of flour and a pinch of salt. Put in a sauce-pan, and stir over the fire until it thickens. Add one quarter pound of cheese, fine grated, and the yolks of two eggs. Beat all together, and then, having beaten the whites of the eggs into a stiff froth, add them to the rest, and bake in a quick oven.

Cheese Scallops.

Soak three ounzes of breadcrumbs in some milk, add two beaten eggs, one ounze of butter, one quarter pound of grated cheese, and pepper and salt. Mix thoroughly, pour into scallop shells, and cover with breadcrumbs. Bake until brown.

RESTAURANT BREAKFAST.

30—Coffee.

More coffee is consumed in this country than in any other under the sun; its value is understood, its power as a stimulant to bodily and mental activity is appreciated and no other article of general consumption can be named of which the public are so careful to guard against adulteration as this. Packages of ready-ground articles are generally shunned; the merchants must keep the sacks of coffee, ready browned but of different grades in sight and a mill for it to be ground in before the buyer's eyes, and these straightforward methods are the outgrowth of more than mere personal solicitudes or defences against the small frauds of imitation or substitution which in the case of innumerable other articles are submitted to with careless indifference, they result from the feeling that the active business of the community cannot be carried on in the fast way to which the New World cities have become habituated without the stimulating aid of good coffee, that is to say of genuine coffee. For the potency of the berry to refresh and impel to new exertion is not to any considerable degree dependent upon the method of preparing it for the table. Coffee causes wakefulness when eaten raw, or drawn by long steeping in cold water, its effects are rather deadened than increased when it is made into the pleasant breakfast beverage with cream and sugar. Its energy is most expansive in the out door camp where, boiled in a camp kettle it is drunk by the pint or quart without milk and the drowsy hunters or travelers spring up and start off singing.

There are the best of reasons therefore why no great success should be expected for any eating house that depends upon boarders who are free to change, until it is made a special matter of care first, to provide genuine coffee of good qaulity, and second, to have it made strong, clear, fresh and furnished with cream, pleasant to the sight, to the sense of cleanliness and purity and to the taste. Some drink coffee for the sake of the coffee, some, Rip Van Winkle's, for the cream and sugar, but the latter, if not already past work when they begin, come over at last to the ranks of the active multitude.

The stimulation afforded by the coffee berry having become an absolute necessity it is a question only whether the coffee made is to be of such a sort that it must be gulped down like a medicine and a second draught avoided if possible, or whether sipped with the utmost enjoyment of both its flavor and fragrance, and this is a matter that rests mostly with the maker who in turn is dependent for success upon the vessel that keeps it for him after it is made, for an improper urn will spoil the best coffee ever concocted in the course of an hour or two. The most important improvement in coffee urns is that of fitting the inside with a stone jar which holds the coffee and keeps it free from metallic taint. It is practically impossible to make coffee to order as wanted, neither can coffee bought of good quality and made strong be thrown away when left over from a meal, but if kept in a metal pot or urn turns black and bitter, discolors milk and cream like a dye and has none of the fine aroma it had when first made. The substitution of a bright new tin vessel for the old and cankerous one will remedy the matter for a short time but rust spots form inside the new one within a week and the coffee gradually becomes as bad as before. If the makers of stoneware or some harmless unglazed pottery would put upon the market coffee urns with faucets, and an inner rim to hold the hoop of a muslin filtering bag a remedy would be furnished for much bad coffee within the reach of those who cannot buy the costly plated urns with the stone-ware linings. When a good way of keeping the coffee so that it will not change to ink between one meal and the next has been adopted it will become worth while to lay a stress upon the selection of the best kinds. Good Rio coffee is the most servicable, the cheapest, and in nine cases out of ten is good enough if well made, but those who can distinguish between the flavors will prefer Java, and a mixture of Java and Rio is generally satisfactory. The fancy kinds such as Mocha, African, or whatever new names may be given are generally peculiar only in being the produce of young trees which after awhile bear the same old sort of coffee as other plantations. It is said that there is no more of what used to be known as Mocha coffee; nothing remains but a name.

31—To Make Coffee—Family.

1 heaping cup ground coffee—4 ounces.

8 cups water—2 quarts.

The most people who do cooking for profit cannot afford to make coffee without boiling, the full strength is not extracted until the boiling point is reached and to make it otherwise more coffee is required or less water. However, it need not keep on boiling after the first heat.

Have the coffee ground coarse like oatmeal, put it on in cold water and let come to a boil, then immediately remove it to the stove hearth or some place to keep hot without boiling and a few minutes before it is to be poured off add ½ cup of cold water. Coffee made this way half an hour before the meal will pour off quite clear without anything added to clearify it.

32—French Coffee.

Put a large cup of coarsely ground coffee shaken in and heaped up (4 ounces) into the perforated top of a coffee pot and pour over it 6 cups of boiling water. Keep the pot at boiling heat without actual boiling. When the water has run through, pour it off into another vessel and pour it through again and then once or twice more. Whatever sediment may have passed through in spite of the repeated filtering through the coarse coffee will remain at the bottom if never disturbed by boiling, and the coffee will pour off clear and strong. But very bad coffee is often made by careless people by this method.

33—To Make Coffee—Restaurant.

If there is no properly constructed coffee urn, provide a tin one having a faucet near the bottom, and a muslin bag running down to a point hanging inside from a hoop that rests on the rim of the urn and is covered by the lid. Put in the coarse ground coffee—½ pound to 4 quarts of water. Keep a coffee pot specially to boil the water in, you will know how much it holds, and use it for nothing else. Pour the boiling water upon the coffee in the bag, draw it off at the faucet and pour it through again and again. Keep the urn where it will be at boiling heat almost, yet not boil. This is often very hard to manage where there is no steam-heated stand, but some way must be found if the coffee is to be good.

Where there is a regular-built coffee urn kept hot either by steam or gas that can be regulated at will, the way is to put into the urn the proper amount of water and the coffee tied securely in a muslin or canvas sack and there let it draw.

The addition of eggs to the raw coffee if not postitively necessary to make the coffee clear seems to give it a mild taste like the addition of milk. It is most useful when the coffee is ground too fine.

If eggs are to be used put the coffee in a pan, mix 1 or 2 eggs with a cup or two of cold water, wet the coffee with it, then put on in the big coffee pot and boil before pouring it into the filtering bag in the urn.

34—Cream For Coffee.

Use the very small individual cream-pitchers that hold only 2 tablespoonfuls and serve one with each cup of coffee.

With this careful apportionment it is often found practicable to procure cream enough for the purpose where otherwise the serving of real cream could not be attempted.

Cost of coffee with cream and sugar—with coffee at 20c., and ½ ounce or a tablespoon to each cup, and 2 teaspoons or 1 ounce sugar and 2 tablespoons cream to each cup, and cream 90c., gall.—coffee 5, cream ½ pt, 6., sugar 5; 16c., for 8 cups or 2c. a cup for material.

35—Tea.

1 teaspoonful makes 1 large cup.

4 teaspoonfuls make a quart of tea.

1 heaping cupful is 14 teaspoonfuls, and makes 1 gallon of tea if mixed tea is used and allowed some time to draw.

2 heaping cupfuls of tea is a quarter of a pound, and makes 2 gallons, or the same number of cups as a pound of coffee, or about 30 as cups are filled.

There are many who claim to make 2½ gallons of coffee from a pound, and the same will increase the quantity of tea to the pound but it must be at a disadvantage to the good quality of the articles. It is probable that where a business is successful in spite of a poor quality of tea and coffee provided, it would be still more successful with that point upheld.

On the other hand a great deal of dissatisfaction is caused in hotels through an unsystematic way of making the tea; because there is really scarcely anything to be done that little is slighted; a quantity of tea much too large is thrown into water that does not boil, in the hope to obtain tea the quicker, which is bad at first; but afterwards the tea becomes so strong that nobody can drink it. There should be a measure of some sort always in the tea box, that there may be no excuse for dipping it up by uncounted handfuls.

When the tea becomes so that it looks like coffee in the cups, yet has neither strength nor fragrance and of course is unfit to drink, it may be partly due to the use of black tea, but it is the certain result of allowing the tea to stand and boil too long, no matter what kind of tea may be provided.

The best way to make tea for a larger quantity than can be supplied from the family tea-pot is to put the measured amount required into a box made like a quart measure, of perforated tin, having a lid to fasten on, and drop it into an urn of boiling water, containing the right proportion, and then stop the boiling and allow ½ hour for the tea to draw. The box must be large enough to allow the tea to swell and the water to circulate through it. Before all the tea is drawn off add more boiling water—a fourth as much as was used at the first—for the second drawing. On an average each person takes 2 teaspoonfuls of sugar to each cup of tea—that is 1 ounce. In some good restaurants the plan adopted is to give with each cup three lumps of sugar in a butter-chip or very small saucer; and a correspondingly small individual pitcher with 2 tablespoonfuls of cream.

Cost of material—4 ounces tea 20, sugar 20, cream 30; 70c—35 cups tea for 70c, 2c a cup.

36—Chocolate.

Common unsweetened chocolate is to be used as the sweet chocolate being ½ sugar is not strong.

1 ounce common chocolate makes 4 cups.

1 heaping cupful of grated common chocolate, is 3 ounces and makes 3 quarts; it contains 7 tablespoonfuls.

1 heaping tablespoonful of grated common makes 2 cups as cups are filled.

Chocolate must be cold to grate; it melts and runs when made hot. The ounces are marked on the cakes.

To make chocolate take:

3 cups milk.

1 cup water.

2 heaping tablespoons grated chocolate.

Boil the milk and water in a saucepan, drop in the chocolate and beat with the wire egg-whisk until the chocolate is all dissolved and it boils. It should be made to order whenever practicable, the milk and water being kept ready boiling, but if made beforehand should be kept in a sink of the steam chest or double kettle and not allowed to boil again.

Cost of material by gallon—4 ounces chocolate 10, 3 quarts milk 21, sugar 10; 41c for 18 cups 2¼c a cup—single cups cost 2½c.

37—A Restaurant Pot of Coffee, Tea or Choclate.

A pot is a pint silver or crockery-ware coffee pot that a person may order instead of 2 cups; the restaurants that charge 10c per cup furnish a pot of 2 cups for 15c or a pot for 2 of 4 cups for 25c of either coffee or tea, but 5c higher per pot for chocolate.

French coffee, meaning coffee of double the common strength, dripped and not boiled is 25c per pot of 2 cups.

French coffee with cognac per pot of 2 cups, 3-fourths coffee and 1-fourth brandy 50c.

Some Necessary Explanations.

As we are starting out to furnish a ready-reckoning book that may in the course of time show the average or probable cost of everything from a pie to a grand banquet and as the selling prices of many dishes in the restaurants and elsewhere will often have to be quoted, for sufficient reasons, we wish to caution all readers against forming hasty conclusions as to the profits made in any case. There is not the least intention on our part of setting the buying and selling prices side by side for comparison, for in fact the cost of material is very often a very small part of the expenses of serving meals. What those expenses are made up of beside the cost of material it is outside of our present business to inquire and these remarks are made for fear of any false ideas being formed by some readers who have never been in business but think they ought to be, and by others who may not know the difference between gross receipts and net profits.

As regards the accuracy of our estimates it is necessary to mention that great differences in the prices of raw provisions will be found to exist in different parts of the country, coffee is cheaper in San Francisco than in the east, salmon is not half the price of halibut, being only about 12c per pound when in Chicago it costs 40c and halibut only 20; eggs and butter take a wide range in prices, and so forth. Still as our prices are always stated upon which the estimates of cost are based each individual can change them and arrive at the result in his own locality. To cooks in particular who seldom trouble themselves about the cost of materials and who proverbially are sure to fail when they go into business alone through deficiency of that kind of knowledge, we hope to be of great use by showing the necessity of being exact in weights and measures if they would not double the cost of articles made and render profit impossible.

38—Tenderloin Steak For One.

Price in first-class restaurants 55c, including bread, butter, potatoes and condiments.

Cut a slice from the filet rather over than under ½ pound, and in thickness according to the size of the filet, notch through the outside skin with the point of the knife, flatten the steak with a blow of the cleaver to rather less than an inch thick, lay it on a plate and brush over both sides with a slight touch of butter, broil over clear coals about 5 minutes, or as ordered, and season with a dredging of salt and pepper while it is cooking. Serve in a hot dish; pour over it 2 tablespoonfuls of melted fresh butter, garnish with a few sprigs of parsley and place ½ a lemon at the edges.

Serve potatoes as ordered; if chips or French-fried they may be in the dish as a border, other kinds in a separate dish.

Cost of material—steak 18, butter to sauce 2, potatoes 1, lemon 1, condiments 2, bread 2, butter 3; 29c.

39—Double Tenderloin.

The difference or deduction commonly made when steak for two, of the other descriptions is ordered is not observed with tenderloins, but when a person requires a double one it is simply cut accordingly and so charged for. A steak to weigh a pound will take a fourth of the entire filet. Having cut it off the requisite length shave off two or three narrow strips of the skin that partly encircles it, to allow it to spread, and setting it on end on the block flatten it with the cleaver. Broil and serve as usual.

The filet consists of a lot of strings of meat loosely held together and to be at the best the steaks must be cut straight up and down, as a slanting cut makes course meat. At the thin end it is better as regards good eating to cut the slices not quite through, open and flatten them to make the usual size. This however does not answer for an unusually large or double sized steak, but the fineness of texture has to be sacrificed for the dimensions.

40—Tenderloin or Filet Steaks—Their Cost.

The filet of beef is the long strip of solid lean meat that runs along the whole length of the loin under the back bone and between it and the kidney fat. When the loin is cut and sawn straight down to make porterhouse and sirloin steaks each one of such steaks contains a piece of the filet from 2 to 4 ounces in weight, according to where it is cut and the thickness. It is the smaller lean portion that has the suet upon it. To make the tenderloin steaks of the restaurants the filet is taken out all in one piece. This cannot be obtained of all butchers but some, having a certain class of trade will sell tenderloins at from 25 to 30c per pound. Those who buy beef

by the loin or hind quarter, and having sale for all the different grades of meat, also take out the filet entire should still count it at about 30c, per pound as the following calculation shows. An even weight is taken to make the estimate easy to change when the price of beef is different.

300 pounds of loin at 12c costs $36. 1-third of it is bone; 1-third is coarse meat and fat; 1-third is fine clear steak, including the tenderloin and the rest nearly equal to it.

The bone is worth 2c per pound for soup—$2,

The coarse meat and fat is worth 8c per pound—$8. Take these amounts from $36. the first price of the beef, and the fine steaks will be found to cost 26c per pound. As the tenderloin is accounted a little better than the rest and is in greater request it may be properly reckoned at 30c per pound cost price raw.

41—Filet a la Chateaubriand.

Price $1,25, or indefinite according to style of house.

It is a large tenderloin steak broiled between two thin steaks over a slow charcoal fire until done through, with all the gravy of the three carefully preserved. The outside steaks removed when done only their gravy squeezed over the other. Common thin steaks answer for the outside. Have them wide enough and fasten the edges together with small skewers before placing on the gridiron. Pour sauce of hot butter with salt and pepper in it around the steak, add parisienne potatoes and cut lemon. Truffle sauce instead of the butter, if desired.

42—Potatoes Free With All Meat Orders—Their Cost.

Two average potatoes, or ½ pound raw make a dish.

Potatoes at $1,00 per 100 are 60c per bushel and 4 middling potatoes cost 1c. The cheapest way, as a matter of course, is to serve them with their jackets on or, as the French say and sometimes print in their *menus, en chemise.* The next cheapest is the saute potatoes, boiled first, peeled when cold and sliced into a frying pan with a little fat and browned more or less. Those pared raw and fried by immersion in hot lard cost the most.

In counting the cost of potatoes as an article of food it is necessary to estimate that they loose half. their weight by paring raw, 100 pounds bought for $1 will be only 50 pounds after pairing—that is to say if pared by the help, and the potatoes of a rough sort with deep eyes. Smooth potato·s like the rose or snowball, pared by the person who pays for them may lose only a third of their weight.

But potatoes boiled or steamed with the skins on will only lose 15 pounds out of 100 by peeling when done, or 2 or 3 ounces out of a pound instead of 6 or 8. Where potatoes are used by the wagon load these differences are of great consequence.

Taking the orders at a restaurant as they come for plain boiled or baked or the forms in which potatoes are boiled before paring, and the fried and chips and perhaps broiled, and sweet potatoes it is a fair average count of $\frac{1}{2}$c per dish for potatoes and $\frac{1}{2}$c for lard to fry, or 100 dishes potatoes free with meat orders for $1.

43—Porterhouse Steak For One.

Price in first-class restaurants 65c, including bread, butter, potatoes and condiments.

The porterhouse cut is the middle or best part of the loin beginning an inch or two from where the filet begins near the last rib and extending back till the round bone at the point of the hip is struck. The porterhouse steaks are slices sawn clear through, taking both bone, upper loin and tenderloin. They cannot well be cut weighing less than a pound and gene-

rally run from that to a pound and a half according to size of beef. A loin yields from 8 to 12 such steaks depending upon the thickness. The butchers sell such steaks at 25c per pound retail.

Having cut the steak from the loin about an inch thick cut off part of the thin strip of the flank so as to leave about 3 inches length attached, chop off half the depth of the back bone to give a neat appearance without taking all the bone away, and carefully sever the outside edge to prevent drawing up while broiling. Brush over with the butter brush and broil from 6 to 10 minutes or as ordered. Serve with a border of chip or fried potatoes.

Cost of material—$1\frac{1}{4}$ lbs meat (by the loin) 25c, butter to sauce 2, potatoes 1, condiments 2, bread 2, butter, 3; 35 to 40c as the meat may cut.

44—Condiments With Meat Orders— Their Cost.

The greatest expense is for· the table sauces and ketchups—Worcestershire, Halford, London Club sauces and the like and tomato ketchup, and the next for olive oil, french mustard, and horseradish, while the cost of the fillings of the cruet stands is merely nominal. One half the expense of the costlier articles may be saved by judicious management, by keeping the sauces shaken up, setting them out to each order and then moving them to a back shelf, not inviting promiscuous waste. In a business of moderate dimensions the expense of table sauces alone will easily run up to $25, per month. Cucumber pickles are generally included in the free list of condiments but dearer kinds are charged extra.

45—Butter With Meat Orders—Its Cost.

With fine butter ranging in price from 30c per pound at the lowest to 60c and even to 75c at times, there is no protection against loss on every meal served except in serving the butter in individual allowances in small butter chips. The neat way of doing this is to make the butter in individual prints, using for the purpose a butter stamp precisely like the pound size in common use by the farmers only these hold but ½ ounce. They are in general use in city restaurants. They are like toy butter stamps in size and are imported along with other wood carvings from Switzerland. To make the prints, dip the wooden stamp in hot water, press in the tablespoonful of butter that fills it, and push it out with the moveable inside.

A person at table who has not enough butter will call for more but such requests are not very frequent, and the plan effectually prevents the eating of slices of high-priced butter and slices of bread in equal proportions. Fine creamry butter at 48c per pound is 3c an ounce. We calculate at 2 or 3c per order.

46—Porterhouse Steak for Two.

Price in first-class restaurants $1,20, including 2 dishes of potatoes, bread, butter and condiments.

This is 2 steaks on one dish and one may be cut a little shorter than the other so that with the broad part of the steaks at each end the one dish on which they are served will have a neat and even appearance; the 3 inches of the flank end being seldom eaten, but necessa.y to make a large dish of a single steak.

47—Sirloin Steak.

Price in first-class restaurants 45c including potatoes, bread, butter and condiments,

Either "a steak with a bone in it" cut from the end of the rib roast down to the first good porterhouse steak, or from the loin thick end beyond the last porterhouse. Cut to weigh nearly a pound. Broil and serve with a spoonful of butter poured over, and potatoes.

Cost of material—steak 15, butter to sauce 2, potatoes 1, condiments 2, bread 2, butter 3; 25c.

48—Mushrooms With Steak Orders.

Price in first-class restaurants 20 to 25c additional each person.

About half a can with each beefsteak. Drain the mushrooms from their liquor and fry (saute) them in a small frying pan with a little butter. Add pepper and salt. When they have acquired a slight color draw them to one side of the pan, put in a heaping teaspoonful of flour and rub it smooth in the hot butter, still keeping the pan over the fire, and when the flour has become slightly browned pour in the mushroom liquor gradually and a few spoonfuls of water. Shake in the mushrooms, let all boil up, squeeze in the juice of a quarter of a lemon and pour over the beefsteak in the dish.

Cost of mushrooms. Canned mushrooms are all imported. There are artificial caves near Paris where the cultivated mushroom beds are over seven miles long. Several different grades of the canned goods are on the market ranging in price from about $25 to $33 per case of 100 cans (tins they are called by the English). The low priced article is made up largely of mushroom stalks and large open mushrooms. These have to be cut in pieces to serve with steaks. They do well to mince for mushroom sauce. The finer goods are mostly small buttons and are white, beside being more solidly packed. A third of a can of the best goods will generally make a better dish than half a can of the low grade. Retail price from 30c to 40c per can. Cost of mushrooms with beefsteak as above should be 15c, or according to buying rate.

49—Oysters with Steak Orders.

Price in first-class restaurants 20c to 25c, additional each person.

The oysters, ½ dozen if large or a larger number of small are in a brown oyster sauce prepared the same as the mushrooms in preceeding article or in detail.

A heaping tablespoon of flour will thicken a cupful of liquor; only 2-thirds of that amount is wanted, therefore, put a rounded spoonful of flour and the same of butter together in a small frying pan and stir them over the fire until they are light brown and not in the slightest degree burnt. Then pour in gradually nearly a cupful of oyster liquor and water, stir to mix and season with salt and pepper, then put in the ½ dozen or more of oysters and when they are at boiling heat pour them over the steak.

Cost of material—oysters 6, butter 3, flour and seasonings 1, 10c.

50—French Pease with Steak Orders.

Price in first-class restaurants 20c to 25c additional each person.

About ½ can of pease with each beefsteak. Throw away the water and put the pease into a small saucepan with an ounce of butter and little salt, shake them over the fire until hot and pour over and around the steak.

For pease *a la Francaise* the difference is that a little cream sauce must be made first with a spoonful of flour and the same of butter stirred together over the fire but not browned, and a half cup of milk added; then put in the pease and let it get hot.

Cost of pease—French pease range in price from $25 to $33 per case of 100 cans (tins), the quality varying from large mature pease apparently artificially colored, to the "petits pois extra fins," which are very small and sweet. It takes a third of a can for a sirloin steak and ½ can for a porterhouse. Pease retail at 30c to 40c per can. Cost with butter average 15c. There are home packed pease to be had as good as the French at much less cost. The French articles are made green by the addition of a little vichy salt to the water they are canned in.

51—Tomato Sauce With Meat Orders.

Price in first-class restaurants 10c additional each person.

Throw 4 tomatoes into boiling water; in three or four minutes take them out peel and cut off the green around the stem, mash them in a little saucepan over the fire and let simmer in their own juice. In another pan put an ounce of butter with a scrap of raw ham and a teaspoon of minced onion and when they have fried a minute add a small tablespoon of flour and stir until light brown. Add ½ cup of water or stock and then the stewed tomatoes. Salt and pepper slightly. Press the sauce through a gravy strainer. Pour it over the meat in the dish.

Cost of material per order 5c—A cheaper quality for low-priced dishes can be made without butter; and also by simply stewing down strained tomatoes and their liquor until thick enough, and adding salt and pepper. The last is probably the best of all but must be prepared before wanted, needing slow stewing down at the back of the range.

52—Onions With Meat Orders.

Price in first-class restaurants 10c to 15c additional each person.

Slice thinly enough onions to fill such a dish as is used to serve fried potatoes in. Put them into a small frying pan with a spoonful of lard or drippings, shut down with a plate or good lid and let cook in that manner until tender—5 to 10 minutes—then take off the plate and let the onions get light brown. Sprinkle with salt. Drain away the grease, if any left, and serve the onions on the meat in the dish.

Cost of material—the price of the onions and the detriment caused by the odor that prevades the establishment.

53—Small Steak.

The common term for a steak of no particular cut. Price in restaurants from

25c down to 15c, including baked, boiled or saute potatoes, bread, butter and seasonings.

A pound of round steak as cut by the butchers divided in three makes 5-ounce steaks, all meat, of a size sufficient for an ordinary meal. Beat them out a little with the side of the cleaver and fry instead of broiling them with the scraps of fat in the same pan.

COST of material—with round steak at 12c—meat 4, 1 potatoe ½c cruet condiments ½c bread 2, butter 2; 9c. With rough steak at 8c, 1c per order less, or a large steak of 2 orders to the pound.

54—Cheap Beefsteak.

After purchasers have been found willing to pay 25c to 30c per pound for selected portions there remains a large amount of every carcass that will rate either at the 12½ cent rate of round of beef or as skirt or flank and buttock worth about 8c or of a cheaper grade yet, the neck and brisket. This may be bought at 5c, but it is half bone If 150 pounds costs $7,50 at 5c, when the bone is taken out it will be 75 pounds of clear meat costing 10c per pound. If the bone be worth 2c per pound for soup—as doubtless it is, the 75 pounds is worth $1,50, making the clear meat cost only 8c per pound. This meat is equally nutritious with the selected portions but is not fit for broiling, as it takes a longer time to make it tender.

To make it good, slice it and lay it in a deep baking pan and fry it with drippings or some of the brisket fat pieces in the usual manner, with a strong seasoning of pepper and salt and a small allowance of onion and when it is brown on both sides fill up the pan with water and let it bake in that manner in the oven for an hour or two. The water will be reduced to brown gravy by that time. Add a teaspoonful of flour thickening.

COST of material—½ pound of meat with gravy and seasonings 3½, 1 large boiled potatoe ½, bread 2, the meal 6c.

Chicken and Rice a la Valenciana.

Take a fresh killed fowl. Cut in small pieces, braise for twenty minutes in a saucepan. Chop very fine two onions, with two dants garlic and a fagot of parsley; add to the chicken and braise for five minutes over a slow fire Then add one pint of tomato sauce and a quart of soup stock and two heads of cloves. When the stock comes to boil, add a pound of rice and season to taste. Let it cook over a slow fire till done.

Ladies' Lunches.

For ladies' lunches a truce has been sounded to the expensive decorations of dinner cards, painted ribbons and bags for bonbons. The *menu* has been simplified. Chops with pease, a Spanish omelet (a delicious dish this), birds broiled, fried potatoes, mushrooms on toast, artichokes, salads, champagne, coffee and fruit: this is now deemed a very stylish lunch for ladies, and is not overloaded. Roasted almonds, salted, make a very good relish after the sweets.

Spanish Omelet.

Place in a sauté-pan one clove of a garlic, a quarter of a can of tomatoes, chopped mushrooms and chopped ham; season with salt, pepper and cook. Break three eggs into a bowl and beat thoroughly; add a half a cup of milk, salt and pepper and make an omelette in the usual way and place in the middle the thick part of the foregoing preparation; roll your omelette on a side dish and pour the remainder around the omelette and serve.

RESTAURANT DINNER DISHES.

55—Rich Beef Soup.

Price in first-class restaurants 15c large bowl, with bread.

To make a gallon of soup put into a boiler a pailful of soup meat and soup bones broken up—about 10 or 12 pounds by weight—and the same measure of water—which will be 2½ gallons or 20 pounds—and slowly boil until it is reduced to about half, or 5 quarts. Then strain it off through a fine gravy strainer or seive into the soup-pot and skim off the fat, probably a pint or pound. If convenient and the vegetables are at hand a small bunch of various kinds should be boiled along with the soup bones, it is of more consequence, however, to get the stock to boiling early, that it may have 6 or 8 hours time, as the seasoning can be done afterwards. Then take the

4 quarts of soup stock.
2 cups cold cooked beef cut in dice.
2 cups raw vegetables same way—turnip, ruta-baga, carrot, onion, celery, a little of each to make the amount.
1 clove of garlic.
½ a bayleaf.
8 cloves.
4 heaping tablespoons browned flour.
2 tablespoons salt.
1 tablespoon pepper.

Shave all the dark outside from the piece of cooked beef and cut it into clean squares, boil them and the cut vegetables in the soup ½ hour, cut the garlic small and add with the other seasonings. Mix the browned flour with some of the soup and thicken with it. The bayleaf can be taken out again with the skimmings. Browned flour is flour baked dry in a pan in the oven.

Cost of material—soup bones 25, cooked beef 5—(seasonings paid for by frying fat from stock)—30c gall. Add bread or crackers and castor condiments 8 bowls 12c; 5 or 6c a bowl.

56—Boiled Fresh Codfish, Egg Sauce.

Price in first-class restaurants per dish of 1 pound 35c, including bread, butter, potatoes and condiments.

Clean a fresh codfish—the head is considered a delicacy in some countries, and it makes good chowder, but if not wanted for that boil it in the same vessel with the fish to enrich the liquor—have the water ready boiling in the fish kettle, throw in a handful of salt, put in the fish and boil gently at the side of the range about ½ hour or until the flesh will leave the backbone when tried. Then lift out the drainer or false bottom with the fish upon it and keep it hot.

57—Egg Sauce.

4 cups clear broth or water.
½ cup butter.
3 hard-boiled eggs.
3 rounded tablespoons flour.
1 tablespoon salt.

Boil 3 cups of the water with ½ the butter in it and the salt. Mix the flour with the rest of the water and add it for thickening. When boiled up add rest of butter and beat till all melted chop the eggs coarse and stir them in.

Cost of egg sauce—butter 8, eggs 5, flour and salt 1, 14c for 8 orders.

Cost of boiled codfish—10 lbs gross $1,00; loss and shrinkage 4 lbs—8 12-oz dishes with 4 oz sauce 15c dish. Add bread, butter and potatoes to cost.

Note—The size of the dishes here mentioned is enough for 3 or 4 hotel dinner dishes.

58—Salmon Steak Maitre d' Hotel.

Price 50 cents.

Have ready some potatoes with the skins on cooked in a steamer and hot as they keep a better shape for restaurant dishes managed this way than if pared and stewed.

Pepper and salt a 12-ounce salmon steak, rub the bars of the hinged wire broiler with butter and broil the steak either over or before a clear fire about 6 or 8 minutes, loosen it from the wires by pushing with a brush dipped in butter and place on a hot dish of large size.

Peel and cut 2 or 3 potatoes in quarters and shake them up in a little hot butter with salt; place them around the steak.

Chop a lump of butter size of an egg in a frying pan, throw in a large teaspoon of chopped parsley, pour it hot over the salmon. Cut a lemon, sqeeze half over the salmon and garnish with the other quarters, and sprigs of parsley.

Cost of material—salmon steak average 25, lemon and parsley 2, butter 4, potatoes, 1, 32c.

Note—Salmon steak varies in price from 10c to $1,50 per pound raw in market according to place and season, and restaurant prices accordingly.

59—New England Boiled Dinner.

Price in first-class restaurants 30c, including bread, butter, and condiments. Boil 3 or 4 pounds corned beef for 3 hours or longer. Also 1½ pounds salt pork about 1 hour.

Cook, either by boiling or steaming, 1 head of cabbage, 8 small onions, 8 pieces each of carrots, turnips, parsnips, and beets, and 8 potatoes.

To serve, put a portion of every kind of vegetable in orderly shape in an 8-inch flat platter and a 4-oz slice of corned beef and 2-oz slice of salt pork on top.

Cost of material—4 lbs corned beef at 7c will lose one-half by bone and shrinkage—8 4-oz dishes 28c. Salt pork 8 dishes 20c, vegetables, nearly a pound weight in each dish, equal to 1½ lbs gross raw at average 2c, lb for all kinds, 8 dishes, 12 lbs, 24c—total 72c for 8 dishes, 9c per dish. Add bread, butter and condiments to cost. Save the frying fat from the meat boiler.

Note. Cheap restaurants serve the above dinner for 15c, perhaps for less. The quantities can be cut down somewhat, the beef served with some bone in it, the vegetables often bought for less than half the quoted average or the dearer sorts left out.

60—Irish Stew With Vegetables.

Price 20c.

It should be observed that this dish which is very popular if properly cooked is utterly worthless when the meat is not stewed tender.

2 breasts of mutton—4½ lbs.
8 potatoes cut, or 16 small—4 lbs.
8 small onions.
2 turnips.
A bunch of parsley and thyme.
Salt and pepper and thickening.

Saw the mutton briskets in two places lengthwise across the bones and divide them in neat lengths. Put them on in 3 or 4 quarts of water and let stew 3 hours. Parboil all the vegetables in another saucepan, then drain away the water and put them in with the mutton and let cook about an hour longer. It may be necessary to keep out the potatoes if they are of a kind that break when done and steam them separately. Thicken the stew with 2 tablespoons flour, salt and pepper to taste and add the parsley chopped.

Dish the meat equivalent to ½ lb raw weight, and a potato, onion and piece of turnip around, and plenty of the sauce.

Cost of material—meat 22, potatoes 4, onions and turnips 4, seasonings and flour 2, 32c for 8 dishes or about 4c a dish. Add bread, butter and condiments to cost.

61—Roast Turkey.

Price 35c; with cranberry or oyster sauce 40c.

As a rule a turkey that weighs 10 lbs. raw, drawn, should make 10 restaurant dishes of the price—2 sidebones, 2 drumsticks, 2 second joints, 2 tail pieces, 2 neck pieces, all split through and divided as necessary, with a slice of the breast upon each and dressing in the dish. This proportion can only be kept up with plump turkeys of medium size large and very fat ones having a considerable weight about the crop and neck that cannot be utilized, and the bone cuts being too large and coarse. Young and light turkeys, sometimes no larger than common hens although not fat are good for restaurant use, sometimes admitting of being served in 4 or 5 portions only; light, but a dishful.

Pick over and singe the turkey, take off the wing pinions if a number are to be cooked together as they make a good stewed dish and are but little cared for when roasted. Wash, and stuff the turkey with bread dressing, truss the legs in the body. Put it in a baking pan with a handful of salt, the fat from the gizzard and some toppings of the stock boiler and a cup of water. Roast it in the oven about 2 hours. At the beginning of the cooking keep a greased sheet of paper over it to prevent blistering the skin and remove it later to baste and brown the turkey. When done take it up, pour off the grease and make gravy in the baking pan.

62—Stuffing For Turkey.

8 solid cups fine minced bread crumbs.
1 heaping teaspoon salt.
1 heaping teaspoon black pepper.
1 heaping teaspoon ground sage.
2 cups warm water.
1 heaping cup finely minced suet.
Mix all together but not mash it to paste, and stuff the turkey with it.

Cost of stuffing—2 lbs stale bread 10, 5 oz suet 4 seasonings 1; 15c.

Cost of roast turkey stuffed—10 lbs turkey $1:80, stuffing 15, gravey 5; $2:00 for 10 dishes, 20c dish.

63—Minced Turkey with a Poached Egg.

Price 35 cents including bread, butter, potatoes and condiments.
One 8 lb turkey.
2 cups fine bread crumbs—6 oz.
3 pints broth.
3 heaping tablespoons browned flour.
1 small onion.
1 large teaspoonful black pepper.
2 of salt,
12 eggs.
Either boil or roast the turkey, boiling is the better way when the turkey is old but roasting gives the better flavor. Pick all the meat from the bones and cut it in very small dice, mix in the bread minced extremely fine. An 8 lb turkey only yields 3 lbs clear meat—6 pressed cupfuls. Put the turkey bone, skin and pieces of fat and piece of onion on to boil in 3 quarts of broth and boil it down to 3 pints. Strain off, add the pepper and salt, thicken with the browned flour and when it has boiled put in the turkey meat and stir until quite hot through. Dish a cupful—$\frac{1}{2}$ lb—in a platter, flatten the top and place one poached egg upon it.

Cost of material—turkey at 18c 8 lbs $1,44, bread and seasonings 5, eggs 20, $1,69 for 12 dishes about 14c dish. Add bread, butter and potatoes to cost.

Note—A smaller amount can be made with one fowl or a part of a turkey left over, by observing the same proportions. When no poultry fat a little butter should be used in its place. A chicken makes 3 or 4 large dishes.

64—Rabbit Pot Pie.

Price in first-class restaurants 30 cents dish of about 1 pound.
4 pounds rabbit—1 jack or 4 common.
10 ounces salt pork.
1 small onion and some parsley.
1 tablespoon black pepper.
2 tablespoons of salt.

3 tablespoons of flour.

2 pounds flour for crust.

Cut up the rabbits; chop of the thin part of the ribs and throw them away, divide down the back and make 4 pieces of it and divide the legs into 2 if large. Steep in cold water to whiten the meat and cleanse thoroughly. Boil 3 hours in 4 quarts water, or until reduced to 2½ quarts. Cut the pork into strips and fry them partially, the onion cut up in the fat, and as soon as they begin to brown add them to the stew. Season and thicken, pour the stew into a baking pan and cover with soft pot pie crust (No 18) made of 2 pounds flour, 6 teaspoons powder, 3 cups water and salt. Bake 20 or 30 minutes basting the crust with the stew liquor at last. Dish rabbit equivalent to ½ pound in dish with gravy and light spongy crust on top.

Cost of material—rabbits 40, pork 10, seasonings 2, flour 7, powder 3 oz 6c; 65c for 8 dishes or about 8c dish.

65—Macaroni and Tomatoes, Italienne.

Price in first-class restaurants 15c—a vegetable side dish of less than ½ pound.

½ pound macaroni—½ a package.

½ cup grated cheese.

1 cup thick stewed tomatoes.

1 cup brown meat gravy.

Pepper.

This is the favorite way with the Italians. The dish need not be baked. They simply boil the macaroni and then make it rich, not to say greasy, with the other articles and gravy from the meat dishes.

Break the macaroni into three-inch lengths, throw it into boiling water and let cook twenty minutes. Drain it, put it into a baking pan, mix in the grated cheese, the tomatoes, the gravy, salt and pepper and, if necessary, a lump of butter. Mix up and let simmer together about half an hour, either in a slack oven or on the stove hearth. It will be all eaten if not made too strong flavored with tomatoes or too salt—the common mistakes.

Cost of material—macaroni 10, tomatoes a pint stewed down 8, cheese 2, gravy 2; 22c for 6 or 8 dishes.

66—Asparagus on Toast.

Price 15c. An extra vegetable side dish where potatoes are given free.

Trim off the ends of the stalks of asparagus, let it lie in cold water awhile. Have the water ready boiling, put in a little salt and a pinch of baking soda size of a bean, to keep the asparagus of good color, drop in the asparagus tied in bunches and boil gently until the green end is tender, from 15 minutes to 45 minutes according to age and thickness. Drain without breaking off the heads. Serve 8 to 12 in a dish with a slice of buttered toast under the white ends and a spoonful of melted butter poured over the heads in the dish.

Cost—According to the market and season. When canned asparagus, a can makes 3 orders—asparagus 8, toast and butter 2, 10c dish—restaurant size.

67—Plain Fritters With Sauce.

Price served as a pudding dish 10c.

4 cups flour—1 pound.

1 large teaspoon baking powder.

2 cups water slightly warm.

3 eggs.

3 tablespoons melted lard.

1 of molasses.

Pinch of salt.

Lard to fry.

Sift the flour into a pan and throw in the powder, make a hollow in middle, put in all the rest—the water not quite cold enough to set the shortening—and stir up thoroughly into a soft fritter dough. It may need another basting spoon of water. Beat well. Fry large spoonfuls in hot lard or good fat from the meat pans. Serve 2 in a dish with ¼ cup of sauce. Makes 24 fritters or according to size and how light the dough is made by beating.

Cost of material—flour 3, powder 1, eggs 5, shortening 1, molasses 1, lard consumed or damaged in frying 8; 19c for 24 fritters—sauce 15—34 cents for 12 dishes, 3c dish.

68—Sauce for Fritters.

4 cups water—a quart.
Lemon peel, blade of mace, few cloves.
2 cups sugar.
½ cup corn starch.
Boil the water with the flavoring in it. Mix the starch in the sugar dry, drop it into the water quickly and beat with the egg whisk. Strain into another saucepan and simmer at the side of the range until it becomes clear like syrup.

Cost of sauce—3 pints cost 15c.

69—Baked Apple Dumplings With Sauce.

Price as pudding 10c.
For large restaurant dish make the dumpling of a whole apple but of a size that run 4 to a pound. Make the plain paste as for pies at Nos. 20 and 21.

Pare and core the apples, roll the paste out to a large, thin sheet on the table, slip an apple under the edge, gather the paste around and pinch it off underneath. Bake placed close together in a moderate oven until the apples are done when tried with a fork—generally 30 to 45 minutes. Serve with sauce.

Cost of material—crust each 2, apples (at 4c lb) each 1, 3c dish—with sauce 1, 4c dish.

70—Apple Dumpling Sauce.

1½ cups boiling water.
1 cup light brown sugar.
½ cup butter.
Nutmeg.
1 tablespoon flour, large.
Mix flour and sugar together in a saucepan dry, pour the boiling water to them, add butter and grate in some nutmeg, stir over the fire until it boils.

Cost of sauce—14 bastingspoons or orders 14c.

Scrapple

is made thus: Select a young pig's head, slit the ears and clean them and the mouth thoroughly and remove the eyes, cut out the tongue, scald and skin it. Put the head into three gallons of cold water and boil slowly until the flesh is easily removed from the bones. Remove the scum and take out the head; reduce the meat to a mince, return it to the liquid and season moderately with salt and pepper; mix together a teaspoonful each of powdered sage, sweet marjoram and thyme, and add to the meat. Mix together a quart each of Indian meal and buck-wheat flour, and add it slowly to the liquid, stirring as in the making of ordinary mush. Should the fire be too hot, remove the pot to the back of the range, where it will boil very moderately for half an hour. Stir until ready to pour it into greased pans, where it is to remain until solid. Should the water have evaporated too much all of the meal may not be required, and on the contrary, you may require more meal if it has not evaporated sufficiently. Cut in slices about one-quarter of an inch thick, dredge the slices with fine meal, and fry crisp in a liberal quantity of smoking fat. Some prefer it fried plain, with very little fat, and browned nicely on both sides.

RESTAURANT SUPPER DISHES.

71—Soft-Shell Crabs Fried.

Two crabs to an order, common price 50c including bread, butter, potatoes and condiments.

Every part is eatable except the sand pouch underneath, which pull off and wash the crab in cold water. Dry on a cloth, bread it by dipping in beaten egg with a little water in it and then in cracker meal and fry in hot lard until the claws are crisp and the crab is light brown. Garnish with fried parsley.

Cost of material—crabs 12½c each, lard 2, breading 3, accompaniments 6; 36c.

72—Soft-Shell Crabs Boiled.

Pull off the small claws and the sand pouch and wash. Drop the crabs into boiling salted water and cook about 10 minutes. Serve with butter sauce, parsley sauce, cream sauce or mayonaise, as ordered.

Cost—2 crabs 25, sauce 2, bread, butter, etc. 6; 35c.

73—Pork Tenderloin Broiled or Fried.

Price in first-class restaurants 35 cts. including the usual accessories.

Pork tenderloins weigh from 6 ounces to a pound each. The large ones should be split part way and opened out and flattened; the small take two to an order not split. Season and broil same as beefsteak well done, or saute in a frying pan. Serve with a spoonful of butter over and a border of fried potatoes.

Cost of material—pork tenderloin 12, potatoes 1, bread and butter 5, condiments 2; 20c.

74—Pork Tenderloin With Fried Apples.

The tenderloin cooked by broiling or frying. The apples instead of potatoes.

Slice two apples across the core without pairing or coring; dip the slices in flour and lay them in a large fryingpan in which is a little hot drippings or lard. Fry one side brown then turn them over with a broad knife. This is one of the things that is done right only in a few places, unskillful hands get the apples "mussed up" and greasy. Some kinds of apples fry well enough without flour.

Dish up on the edge of the hot dish around the tenderloin, chop or salt pork.

Cost—apples at 4c pound 2 apples weigh ½ pound, frying-fat 1c, 2 or 3 cents a dish.

75—Honeycomb Tripe Broiled or Fried.

Price 35 cents, including bread, butter, potatoes and condiments.

Quite a specialty in some restaurants. Cut pieces of about 12 ounces, they are nearly twice as large as the open hand, dip both sides in flour, broil in the hinged wire broiler, brush liberally with butter and serve the honeycomb side upwards with the butter in a froth upon it. Serve potatoes either around it or in a separate dish, according to kind. Can be fried (sawteed) in a frying-pan in a little butter after flouring in the same way without breading, but will not brown very well without the butter.

Cost of material—tripe 12, butter to sauce 2, extras 6; 20c.

76—Ham and Eggs—Restaurant.

First-class price 45 cents, including bread, butter, potatoes and condiments.

Medium-sized hams should be selected, the very small ones being too lean, salt and hard, and the very large not making handsome cuts. Shave off the outside, cut slices clear across, very thin, down to the bone, drive a skewer into the block down by the bone to steady it and saw through with a small sharp saw kept for the purpose. This is a difficult and trying job with a soft ham unless good tools are kept to work with, and the ham is very liable to be torn and hacked in a very wasteful manner. The slices of ham weigh from 5 or 6 ounces to 12 ounces according as cut.

Broil the ham about 6 minutes, lay it in a hot dish. Fry 3 eggs, half turned over and dish them side by side with the ham.

———

Cost of material—(allowing for waste, butt and shank) ham 12, eggs 6. potatoes 1, bread and butter 5, condiments 1; 25c.

———

77—Omelet With Jelly.

———

First-class price, omelet with 3 eggs 25 cents.

Break 3 eggs into a bowl, put in with them 3 tablespoons milk. Beat to mix but not to make it too light. Put a bastingspoonful of the clear part of melted butter, into the frying pan, pour in the omelet without waiting for the butter to get hot and discolored, let cook gradually, shaking it frequently to the further side of the pan until the thin edge, forced upward, falls over into the middle. When it is nicely browned and the upper side just set, put current jelly or other fruit jelly in a long line in the middle that is made hollow in the further side of the pan for the purpose. Roll so as to shut in the jelly, slide it smooth side up on to a hot dish, dredge powdered sugar on top and mark it with slanting cross-bars by touching the sugar with a red-hot wire or spoon handle.

———

Cost of material—eggs 8, butter to fry 3, jelly 5, sugar 1; 17c.

———

78—Omelet With Oysters.

———

Frist-class price 50 cents, made with ½ dozen large oysters.
3 eggs.
Milk, butter, seasonings.
Cook the oysters rare done in a little saucepan separately, with a spoonful of milk, scrap of butter and thickening to make white sauce of the liquor.

Break the eggs in a bowl, put in a spoonful of milk and beat with the wire egg whisk. Add a pinch of salt.

Shake a tablespoonful of melted lard or clear butter about in the omelet frying pan and before it gets very hot pour in the omelet and let it cook rather slowly.

Properly made omelets are not exactly rolled up, but there is a knack to be learned of shaping them in the pan by shaking while cooking into one side of it, the side farthest from you, while you keep the handle toward you raised higher. Loosen the edges with a knife when it is nearly cooked enough to shake.

When the omelet is nearly done to the center place the oysters with a spoon in the hollow middle and pull over the further edge to cover them in. Slide on to the dish, smooth side up. Garnish with parsley and lemon.

One reason of omelets and all fried eggs sticking to the frying pan is allowing the pan to get too hot. They seldom stick when poured into a pan that is only kept warm till wanted. The pans should be kept for no other purpose, and be rubbed smooth after using, if not bright.

———

Cost of material—oysters 10, eggs 8, butter, sauce, seasonings 4, garnish 2, table extras 6; 30c.

———

79—Oyster Omelet.

———

Make the omelet according to directions preceding and pour over it when done and in the dish the oysters cut in pieces in a brown sauce as follows.

Put a large ½ cup of oysters into a frying-pan with their liquor, and salt and pepper and keep them in motion by shaking over the fire until they are soft-cooked. Take up with a skimmer and cut them in pieces.

Stir a heaping teaspoon of sifted flour and twice the measure of butter together in a very small saucepan over the fire until light brown, add ½ cup milk and the cooked oyster liquor, if any, and when it has boiled up put in the cut oysters.   Add the juice of a quarter of lemon.

The above brown oyster sauce should be prepared before the omelet is cooked as omelets are not good unless eaten as soon as done.

Cost, the same as omelet with oysters preceding.   ½ cup oysters is ½ doz large.

80—Liver and Bacon Broiled..

First-class price 35 cents, including potatoes, bread, butter and condiments.
½ pound slice of calf's liver.
3 ounces breakfast bacon.

Cut the liver broad and thin, pepper and salt, dip both sides in flour, broil and while it is cooking brush it over with soft butter.

Fry the 2 slices of bacon first, then finish on the gridiron.   Serve the liver with the butter frothing upon it, the bacon on top and potatoes around in the dish.

Cost of material.   The supply of calf's liver is never equal to the demand and the butchers easily get 25c per pound. Beef liver has to be the main reliance for this dish and can be had much cheaper.   Liver average 10, bacon (allowing for waste in cutting) 6, butter 1, potatoes 1, bread, butter, etc. 5; 23c.

81—Welsh Rarebit or Canapes au Fromage.

First-class price 40 cents.
4 to 6 ounces good cheese.
Butter size of an egg—2 ounces.
¼ cup of ale.
2 yolks of eggs.
Little cayenne and salt.
4 thin pieces of toast.

Chop the cheese small, throw it and the butter into a little saucepan and as they get warm mash them together. When softened add the yolks and ale and pinch of cayenne and salt.   Stir till it is creamy, but do not let it boil, for that would spoil it.   Place the slices of toast on a dish, pour the creamed cheese upon them and set inside the oven about two minutes.   The ale only heightens the flavor, and some prefer to use milk.

The simplest form of Welsh rarebit is a slice of cheese placed on a slice of bread and baked in the oven.   It depends upon the quality of the cheese a good deal whether it will prove satisfactory.

And an addition to canapes au fromage is sometimes made in the form of a nicely-poached egg on the top of each canape, in the hot cheese.   This dish then goes by the fanciful name of the "golden buck"—at least it has been so named in a few places where price was no object and specialties paid.

Cost of material—cheese 8, butter 4, ale 4, eggs 5, toast 1, table extras 4; 26c.
With poached eggs on top, cost increased and price indefinite.

82—Minced Potatoes.

This likewise has been a restaurant specialty and has been known as of great effect in drawing trade.   It ought to be observed, however, that it takes a considerable allowance of butter in the pan to give the potatoes the fine yellow-brown, and appetizing flavor that will draw the people from a distance of many blocks to breakfast or supper.

Chop cold boiled potatoes quite fine and season with salt.   Spread a spoonful of drippings or butter in an omelet-pan or small frying-pan and place the minced potatoes about an inch deep. Cook on top of the range like a cake, without stirring.   Invert a plate that just fits the pan over the potatoes.   Let them brown nicely and slowly, then turn over on to the plate.   Push in the edge a little all around and serve on the same plate with the brown on top.   There are oval shaped pans that make these suitable for a platter, and even in the round frying-pan it can be managed to give the cake the platter shape.

83—Corn Meal Mush and Milk.

One of the floating paragraphs of the day is concerning a noted British journalist who cannot bring himself to like corn meal and says unfavorable things about it such as saying it is nothing but oatmeal with a flavor of mice. He has evidently been trying yellow meal, and probably that not properly cooked. An early training "down south" convinced the writer of these lines that there is much more in corn meal than is generally supposed, and various people who have tried his methods have expressed a pleased surprise. It is no use, however, to try to gain favor for yellow corn meal. Its strong flavor may be agreeable to such as have been accustomed to it since childhood, but their preferences will not be shared by many. Always use white corn meal, coarsely ground and free from flour, make the mush with all the water it will take up, have it as soft and jelly-like to fry as it can well be cut and handled when cold; be careful to salt it right and fry it handsomely and you will find corn meal in its different forms of mush and milk, fried mush, corn bread, muffins, batter-cakes, corn meal puddings, and others, an article so pleasant to the palate that it soon comes to be regarded as one of the indispensibles. While it is true the negro cooks of the south have had almost the monopoly of the art of cooking corn meal it will not do to admit that what they accomplish through the simple habit of doing, cannot as well be done by the exercise of intelligent judgement. Take

2 heaping cups white corn meal.
8 cups water.
1 rounded tablespoon salt.

Where the mush has to be made on a cook stove, a cast pot with feet, to raise the bottom an inch from the fire, is the best vessel to use. It lessens the tendency to burn and reduces the waste if the inside is brushed over with a touch of lard or drippings. Put the salt in the water, boil, and sprinkle the dry meal in with one hand while you beat with an egg-beater or spoon in the other. Put on the lid, and let simmer with the steam shut in for about three hours.

If carefully cooked *with a lid on* and not burnt there will be as much mush as there was water put in, that is two quarts.

Double the quantity needed for one meal should be made and half put away to become cold to fry. For this purpose very slightly grease a pan, press the mush in evenly, and slightly brush over with melted lard again. No matter how little the grease, it prevents the formation of a crust by drying on top.

Each quart of cold mush will cut into about ten slices or blocks for frying.

Cost of mush and milk—corn meal 4, milk 2 quarts 16—20 cents for 8 half pints milk and 8 half pints mush or 2½c each pint bowl.

Note—mush and milk served as a first course for supper or breakfast in hotels is but a spoonful in each bowl; perhaps a third, or less, of the restaurant bowl above specified.

Hominy Muffins.

Pound one pint of cold boiled hominy to a smooth paste, add to it half a pint of flour, one teaspoonful of salt, a heaping tablespoonful of baking powder. Beat the yolks and whites of two eggs separately, add to the yolks two ounces of butter, same of sugar, and a scant pint of lukewarm milk. Mix these ingredients together and stir into the flour, mix quickly, pour the batter into hot, well-buttered muffin rings, and bake in a quick oven.

HOTEL BREAKFAST DISHES.

84—"Old-Fashioned" Broiled Beefsteak and Gravy.

Take a whole sirloin or other steak as cut by the butcher, notch the edges to prevent curling up on the gridiron and beat it out on the block more or less according to its thickness or the greater or less tenderness of the meat, for the experienced cook is ble to improve a poor steak considerably.

Put a shovelful of charcoal in the ash pan of the range and some live coals from the fire on that, cover with a pan or other means of making a draft over the coals. Rub the bars of the gridiron with a piece of bacon rind, lay the whole steak upon it and cook medium well done over the charcoal when it has burned clear. Have a piece of butter ready in a tin pan with a heaping teaspoon of good black pepper and two of salt, put in the hot steak and press it into the butter, making the gravy run out, add half a cup of hot water, set the pan and contents over the coals and when it begins to simmer the gravy and pepper will have thickened the water and made a good gravy.

Dish up on a large hot platter, carve in pieces about the size of two or three fingers and serve a spoonful of the gravy with each cut.

The next thing to broiling for that kind of beefsteak is frying over the fire, but a little piece in a pan does not come out natural-looking, but burns around the edges—it must be a full pan or nothing.

Good broiling can be done in a hinged wire broiler set over the open hole of a stove, but forethought is required to let the fire burn down to a bed of glowing coals in time for it, and to turn the damper so that the draft will be strong enough to carry the smoke up the chimney. Some families and others are made miserable by having their so-called broiled meats always tasting of smoke and coal smoke at that. This is something that calls for the exercise of common sense.

Cost of family beefsteak and gravy— 2 pounds steak at 12c loses one-fourth bone, fat and cooking, 24 ounces costs 24 cents,—butter and seasoning 8—3 ounces of meat to each order, 32 cents for 8 orders or 4c each person.

85—Individual Beefsteaks.

This method practiced by a domestic cook has been known to give extreme satisfaction to a large houseful of people when a so-called first-class cook had utterly failed to fill the requirements of the place.

Order the steak from the butcher cut thin, and divide it in pieces weighing 2 ounces—about the size of 4 fingers. Lay your steak on a board of hard wood and pound it down thin with the *back* edge of a heavy knife. Fry the steaks as wanted in frying pans slightly greased and let cook only 2 or 3 minutes and send in hot without gravy. All the merit of this plan is in the sort of blunt chopping with the knife-back, that spreads out the meat, gristle and all as thin as the edge of a dinner plate.

86—Minced Beefsteak.

4½ cups lean beef minced
1½ cups beef fat minced.
½ cup cold water.
1 heaping teaspoon salt.
Same of black pepper.
Or, 3 pounds meat, one fourth of it fat, chopped and seasoned like sausage and a little water added.

Take the thick part of beef flank or any that is tender but that looks too stringy and rough for steaks, cut both lean and fat clear of such skin and gristle as will not chop nicely. Mince it in a bowl and when finished and seasoned press it in a 2 quart pan and when to be cooked cut in slices like beefsteaks and fry on both sides, and serve with its own gravy poured over it. It should be made fresh every day.

Cost—indefinite. It is an expedient for using up the best part of an unhandy piece of meat in a way that saves buying perhaps a first-class steak, while the pieces that cannot be minced are used to make soup or stew.

87—Plain Omelet.

Two eggs and one teaspoonful of milk. Add a pinch of salt, beat in a bowl enough to thoroughly mix but not make it too light, as if the omelet rises like a souffle it will go down again, so much the worse.

Pour into a small frying pan, or omelet pan, in which is one tablespoonful of the clear part of melted butter, and fry like fried eggs. But when partly set run a knife point around to loosen it and begin to shake the omelet over to the further side of the pan until the thin further edge forced upward falls back into the omelet. When the under side has a good color, and the middle is nearly set, roll the brown side uppermost, with a knife to help, and slide the omelet on to a hot dish. Serve immediately while it is light and soft.

88—Omelet with Parsley.

Mix a tablespoonful of minced parsley with the omelet mixture while beating it up. Make as directed in the preceding article.

89—Omelet with Onions and Parsley.

Mince two tablespoonfuls of onion and fry it in a little lard in a frying-pan with a plate inverted upon it. In five minutes take up the minced onion without grease and add it to the omelet mixture made ready with parsley in it; stir up and fry as directed in plain omelet.

90—Omelet With Ham.

Have ready on the table some grated or minced lean ham in a dish. Pour a plain omelet of two eggs into the frying-pan and strew over the surface about a tablespoonful of the grated ham.

91—Omelet with Cheese.

Make in the same manner as ham omelet, with grated cheese instead of ham.

92—Omelet with Tomatoes.

Stew tomatoes down nearly dry, season with butter, pepper and salt. Inclose a spoonful in the middle of an omelet according to the preceeding examples.

Cost of omelets. Omelets are kept off the bill of fare more on account of the time and attention required to cook them properly than because of their cost which is only from $\frac{1}{2}$c to 1c more than the eggs alone would be. This is speaking of hotel and family orders where the added seasonings is but about a tablespoonful, and not of omelets with asparagus, points or other rarities. Eggs vary in price from 6 cents per dozen in country places to 60 cents in the cities at midwinter.

93—Scrambled Eggs.

Not to be beaten up like an omelet but only stirred about. Put a spoonful of melted butter or butter and lard into the small frying-pan, and then two eggs, sprinkle pepper and salt. Stir the eggs about a dozen times around with a fork. Pile in the middle of a little flat dish before they get cooked too hard.

Note. The *oeufs* (eggs) *brouilles aux truffles,* or *aux pointes d' asperges,* often named in *menus* are scrambled eggs with truffles and asparagus and similar accessories, the word brouille being of the same derivation as our broil, signifying a row, being in a tumult, stirred up.

94—Shirred Eggs.

Some people keep little yellow ware dishes for this purpose, or other dishes that cannot be damaged by baking. Spread with a teaspoon a slight coating of soft butter over the inside of the dish, drop in two eggs, not beaten, and set them inside the oven, or, perhaps, on the top of the range on one side. Try by shaking, and take them from the fire when the whites are quite cooked. Send in the same dish set in a flat one.

95—Fried Eggs.

These are the most called-for of any form in which eggs are cooked and there is the widest possible difference between the work of a skilful and unskilful cook in this particular. The fried eggs that are a disgrace to any table are broken as to the yolks before they go in the pan, then they have black grease simmering up all around the edges and running over their surface, they are cooked nearly as hard as leather, they stick to the pan and cannot be turned over and finally when they are forcibly pushed into a dish the same smoky, black grease flows around them like gravy. That it should happen so sometimes is nothing to be remarked, but these lines are prompted by amazement that some will go on frying eggs that way always and habitually and do not seem to know that anything is wrong.

To fry the eggs cleanly and handsomely, keep the small frying pans always rubbed clean, if not bright, and never set them empty upon the range but keep them warm on the bar along the front of it or on a hot shelf or a row of bricks at the back.

96—Poached Eggs.

Also called dropped eggs.

It is no trouble to poach eggs handsomely if two or three rules are observed.

Have a roomy vessel with plenty of water, the frying-pan shape is good, but it is not deep enough. Have a little salt in the water. Never let the water boil furiously after the eggs are in, as that breaks them; keep it gently simmering at the sides.

The eggs break and are wasted because when first dropped they go heavily to the hot bottom and there stick, to prevent which set the water in motion by stirring it around with a spoon. The eggs dropped in are carried around a moment and the white cooks sufficiently to prevent adhesion.

Break the eggs carefully into little dishes and drop into the water one at a time. Take them out with a perforated ladle.

Serve either well drained in a small deep dish and a speck of butter on top or else laid neatly on a trimmed slice of buttered toast.

97—Boiled Eggs.

The best furnished hotel kitchens have a kettle much like a long fish kettle in appearance, and a number of tin baskets, each with its handle, that fit in side by side. The kettle is full of boiling water, and the baskets with different orders of eggs, can be withdrawn without disturbing the others. One hand is detailed to attend to the egg boiling, and he has sand glasses to time them by, or a clock, or both. At ordinary levels two or three minutes for soft-boiled and four or five for hard-boiled is the rule, but at great altitudes in the Rocky Mountains as much as eight minutes is the least time for hard-boiled eggs. The low point at which water boils is the reason for the difference.

98—Fried Mush.

Take the pan of cold mush that was set away over night, hold over the fire a minute and shake it on the table. Cut a quart of mush into 8 pieces. Roll them in cracker meal mixed with flour, then in milk, then in the cracker meal mixture again, let them lie in it to get a good coating. Drop into a frying pan half full of clear drippings made very hot first, and let fry light brown.

Cost—Mush 3, breading 4, fat or lard 4; 11 cents, or from 1 to 1½c each person.

99—Fried Mush Egged and Breaded.

1 quart cooked mush.
1 pound cracker meal.
2 eggs.
¼ pound fat to fry.
Mix 3 tablespoonfuls milk or water with the eggs and beat up. Roll the pieces of mush in it and then in the cracker meal and fry a handsome brown in hot lard in a sauce pan deep enough to immerse them.

COST of material—Neither the cracker meal nor the lard will be all used but an allowance should be made for waste or deterioration of what is left over. Mush 3, eggs 4, cracker-meal 8, lard 8; 23c for 8 to 12 orders—say 2½c each person.

100—Corned-Beef Hash.

Some of the worst blunders the half-made cooks commit are in making hash. Corned-beef hash can be made a real delicacy, good to look at with no appearance of mystery about it, the pink meat fair and cleanly in the smooth and clean potato, and good to taste being more tempting to a fickle appetite than solid beefsteak. It is not necessarily a very cheap dish although it is convenient as a means of using a remainder of corned beef to make room for a fresh boiling. The attempt to make hash very cheap by making it the general receptacle for all sorts of pieces is a penny wise and pound-foolish proceeding, for nobody wants it and it is thrown away at last and through that and other blunders it has come to be at last that hash cannot even be given away at a free lunch. The writer of these lines has seen the officers of the finest vessels afloat send a special request to the kitchen for dishes of the deck hands' fresh made hot and savory corned-beef hash for their breakfast in preference to all that was upon the table, and the passengers who had made its acquaintance followed up the hint and found out the place where hash was good.

There is no elaborate receipt to follow these remarks, the necessity in the case is not to put things in, but to keep things out. Keep out the cold turnips. Keep out the cold mashed potatoes even, if they are not uncommonly good and fresh. It has been shown a little way back in regard to the cost of potatoes, that two large ones are worth less than half a cent, and the water added when they are mashed cheapens them still more. Mashed turnip it still more worthless. Keep out the black and hard scraps and ends of meat, they will give a color and appearance and stale taste that will cause the mess to be thrown out, the good to be lost with the bad. Keep out the onions. This is the last thing that will be agreed to. Cooks of hotels have been known to quit the house rather than they would leave the onions out of the hash. But the people who live in the expensive class of hotels will leave the dish alone if you do not, and if they despise it who else is going to bring hash in fashion again? It is in the interest of true economy to make hash popular, because it uses up corned beef, which is too plentiful. To make "dry hash" that will be eaten and enjoyed, take:

1 pressed-in cup minced corned beef.
4 medium potatoes—1 pound.
½ a level teaspoon good black pepper.
1 level teaspoon salt.
1 ounce fresh butter.
A spoonful of hot water.

Shave off all discolored outside of meat. Chop as fine as pepper-corns or wheat in a wooden bowl with a chopping knife, add the pepper, salt and butter to it. Pare the potatoes raw, steam or boil them, put them to the meat boiling hot and mash together. It is not of much consequence whether it is to be baked or not but it looks better browned over and can be served hottest that way. Leave out the butter when there is plenty of fat to the meat. Those who study to make this almost forgotten dish good take care to corn fat pieces of brisket and calves udder for the purpose.

Cost of material—½ pound selected cooked meat equal to 1½ pound raw9 , potatoes 1, butter 2; 12c a quart or 8 family or hotel orders.

101—Pork Brown Stew.

1 pound coarse cut of fresh pork.

4 medium potatoes.

1 tablespoonful minced onion.

2 or three leaves green sage or a pinch of ground herbs.

1 level teaspoon minced red pepper.

2 of salt.

1 cup fresh roast meat fat for frying.

3 tablespoons flour.

The fat to fry in is only used temporarily and does not lose anything. Let it be especially saved from the roast meat pan for the brown breakfast stews, and have no unpleasant taste about it. Put it on in a small deep sauce pan to get hot. Cut the meat in pieces, throw two or three at a time into the fat when it is hot enough to hiss, let them get the same sort of brown outside that roast meat has, but quickly; take out with a skimmer. When all the pieces are browned in that way, pour the fat back in your jar, put the pieces of meat back in the same saucepan, add 3 cups of water, the potatoes pared and cut in halves, and the seasoning, and stew until the potatoes are done. Mix the flour in a cup with water and thicken the stew with it.

Cost of material—Pork 10, potatoes 1, flour and seasonings 1; 12c for 8 family portions.

102—Wheat Muffins—Best.

2 rounded-up cups light bread dough—little over a pound.

4 tablespoons melted butter—2 ounces.

Same of milk or cream.

1 teaspoon sugar.

3 yolks of eggs—or 1 yolk and 1 egg.

Pinch of salt.

½ cup of flour.

Take the piece of dough from your light bread or rolls that was set to rise

over night. Two hours before breakfast work the butter, sugar and milk in and set in a warm place a few minutes. Then beat in eggs and flour and keep beating against the side of the pan until the batter is very elastic and smooth. Let rise in a warm place about an hour.

The muffin rings should be two inches across and one inch deep. Grease them, set in a greased pan, half fill with the batter, which should be thin enough to settle down smooth, but thick enough not to run under the rings; let rise half an hour, bake ten minutes in a hot oven.

103—Muffins from the Beginning.

When there is no dough set for other purposes the muffins can be made from the beginning with:

3 level cups flour.

1 cup warm water and yeast mixed.

5 tablespoons melted butter.

1 teaspoon sugar.

Same of salt.

3 yolks or 1 yolk and 1 egg.

Mix up too soft to handle yet not thin enough to run; beat well and set in a warm corner to rise. Beat extremely well in the morning, use in muffin rings and bake.

Cost of material—Flour and yeast 3, eggs, sugar and salt 4; 7 cents for 12 muffins.

104—Buckwheat Cakes.

2 cups buckwheat flour.

2 cups water and yeast mixed.

1 level teaspoon salt.

1 tablespoon golden syrup.

2 tablespoons melted lard.

Make a sponge or batter over night of the warm water, yeast and flour. In the morning add the enriching ingredients; beat up well, and bake thin cakes on a griddle.

Most people like buckwheat cakes with a little cornmeal mixed in the batter. Eggs are not needed except when accidentally the batter ferments too much, when an egg will bind and make the cakes easier to bake. Serve with butter and syrup.

After the first mixing with yeast some of the batter may be saved and used instead of yeast for several succeeding days. A pinch of carbonate of soda may then be needed to be mixed in the batter in the morning, but cakes made that way, for some reason, are more palatable than with sweet yeast—care being taken to proportion the soda to the degree of slight sourness.

COST of material—Buckwheat 2, yeast 1, syrup 1, lard 1; 5 cents for 1 quart batter or 24 cakes or 8 plates. To eat with them, 8 ounces butter 20, ½ pint syrup 6; 28 cents total 33 cents 8 plates.

NOTE.—As it is seen the cost of the buckwheat is next to nothing, but as the butter and syrup is nearly all, it is obvious that to whatever extent the lavish use of butter can be checked, a saving will be effected. The alleged indigestibility of buckwheat should be laid to the common extravagance in butter and syrup. To such as are proof against dyspepsia, the poeple who lead active out-door lives,the fat from fried sausages is more relishing than butter with buckwheat cakes.

These and all other batter cakes are made more costly than they ought to be, as well as unhealthy in many places, by the wasteful way of ladling great spoonfuls of melted lard on to the griddle to bake, or rather fry, the cakes in. A pound of lard does not last long that way and it is unnecessary. Cakes can be baked on any sort of a griddle if it is only rubbed and polished with a cloth every baking, but if greased at all a piece of bacon or ham rind or of suet answers every purpose and the cost is scarcely appreciable.

Sweet Tomato Pickle.

Seven pounds ripe tomatoes, peeled and sliced; three and one half pounds sugar; one ounce cinnamon and mace mixed; one ounce cloves; one quart of vinegar. Mix all together and stew one hour.

Picklette.

Four large crisp cabbages, cut fine; one quart onions, chopped fine; two of vinegar, or enough to cover the cabbage; two pounds brown sugar, two tablespoonfuls of ground mustard, two tablespoonfuls of black pepper, two tablespoonfuls turmeric, two tablespoonsfuls celery seed, one tablespoonful allspice, one tablespoonful of mace, one of alum, pulverized. Pack the cabbage and onions in alternate layers, with a little salt between them. Let them stand until next day. Then scald the vinegar, sugar, and spice together, and pour over the cabbage and onions. Do this three mornings in succession. On the fourth put all together over the fire and heat to a boil. Let them boil five minutes. When cold pack them in small jars. It is fit for use as soon as cool and keeps well.

Turnovers.

Roll out some puff-paste and cut in oblongshaped pieces. Put some finely cut cheese on the paste, turn over, and pinch down the edges and bake.

HOTEL DINNER.

105—Ox Tail Soup.

2½ quarts of soup stock.
1 ox tail.
1 small carrot.
1 turnip.
1 onion.
Celery, bay leaf, cloves, salt and pepper.

Make the stock by boiling a beef shank in 6 quarts of water several hours, until it is reduced one-half.

While the stock is boiling take a carrot, turnip, onion and stalk of celery, and, with any kind of a round cutter or an apple-corer and knife, cut enough lozenge shapes to fill a cup with the mixed sorts. Throw a few of the remaining scraps into the boiling stock for seasoning, and ½ a bay leaf and 3 cloves.

Saw or chop the ox tail into thin round slices and steep them an hour in cold water. The ox tail must stew at least 2 or 3 hours to be eatable and so far dissolved as to enrich the soup, and it may be done either in the stock boiler, and the pieces picked out afterward to go in the soup plates, or may be stewed in some of the stock in a separate saucepan, whichever way may be most convenient.

At last strain the specified amount of stock clear into the soup pot. Boil the shapes of vegetables in water by themselves ½ hour, then drain off and put them into the soup, also the ox tail slices. Add brown butter and flour thickening in small quantity, let the soup simmer slowly until it becomes smooth and clear again, and skim until all the fat is removed. Season with salt and cayenne.

Serve a slice or two of the ox tail and some of the vegetables in each plate.

When a soup like the foregoing has not a clear syrup-like sort of thickness or body, but is dull, like flour gravy, it may be cleared by longer simmering and adding more stock with some cold tomato juice, or lemon juice or even cold water, and skimming from the side

If not already light brown add a spoonful of burnt sugar caramel.

Cost of material—Beef shank for stock 10, oxtail 8, vegetables, seasonings, thickening 4; 22 cents for 10 half pint plates, or say, 2c plate or 4c pint bowl.

106—Fried Bass With Bacon.

Scale and clean the fish, chop off the fins, and if small cook them without cutting; if large, split them lengthwise and cut across making four.

Pepper and salt the pieces, roll them in flour and let lie in it until the last; drop them into a pan of hot lard and let fry from five minutes upwards according to size.

Fry a slice of breakfast bacon for each piece of fish in another pan and send in the bacon on the fish and a garnish of parsley and plain boiled potatoes.

Note—There are several varieties of bass and for some reason hardly to be explained hotel stewards seem to be proudest of displaying striped bass in their best *menus*. The black bass is, however, the favorite with restaurant customers and it seems fair to infer that it has some good qualities which make it so. It is certainly the favorite with anglers. In weight it ranges from one pound to five. Only from 2 to 4 ounces need to be served as a dinner order of the cooked fish, and a spoonful of potatoes in some form should go in on the same plate. For a restaurant order a fish weighing just one pound is the most satisfactory all around.

Cost—bass 24c for 2 pounds, 8 ounces bacon 8, potatoes 8 orders 2, lard to fry 2; 36c for 8 dishes or 4½ cents each; hotel size.

107—Boiled Beef with Horseradish.

A fat, unctuous, gristly piece of the brisket or "plate" is the best for this, or the rib ends that are sawed off a rib roast. Boil it slowly for at least three hours; have a little salt in the water (which is afterwards to be used to make soup.) Grate or finely scrape down a stick of horseradish, put it in a bowl with vinegar and water enough to cover, and use it for sauce.

COST of material—Beef 2 pounds 12, loses one-third—horseradish 2, mashed potatoes 2; 16c for 8 dishes, 2c per dish.

108—Roast Sucking Pig.

The pig will be ready trussed when it comes from the butcher's, with the toes inserted in slits cut in the skin. Lay it on its back and drive the point of a sharp knife down through the bone of the back, dividing it convenient for carving, and also detach the ribs along one side, and loosen the inner joints of the hips and legs, which can be done without spoiling the outside appearance of the pig. Wash and wipe it dry, stuff with bread dressing containing sage and onions, and sew up with twine. Roast about two hours, covered with a sheet of greased paper for part of the time, and baste with butter to get a fine transparent brown color on the skin at last. Make gravy in the pan to pour around the pig in the dish. Serve apple sauce separately in a sauce dish. It is a time honored custom to insert a small apple in the mouth of the pig before sending it to table.

NOTE—Pigs weighing from 30 to 40 pounds are more frequently furnished to hotels than the very small ones, and, as they are not sent to table whole are considered more satisfactory. They are too large to be cooked whole but are split in halves, carefully hacked through the bones inside according to the directions for sucking pig, and basted and crisped light brown in the same manner. Serve with apple sauce.

109—Apple Sauce for Meats.

Pare good ripe apples and slice them into a bright saucepan. Add water enough to come up level with the apples and stew with a lid on till done—about thirty minutes. While they are stewing throw in a littlte butter. Mash at last with the back of a spoon. No sugar.

COST of material—10 pound pig $2,00, stuffing 10, apple sauce 7; $2,17—say for 20 to 25 orders not less than 10c per dish.

NOTE—Pigs often cost a much larger amount than their weight at 20c per pound would be, five dollars being often obtained at Christmas and other holiday seasons. The number of dishes is somewhat dependent upon skill in carving. In any case, however, this is an expensive dish.

110—Chicken Pie, Plain.

When chicken pie or any similar dish is written in a *menu* as of some particular style, it, of course, carries the implication that there are more ways than one. A very small variation or addition of vegetables, mushrooms or eggs and wine may suffice to change the name. It is only necessary to say here that one way by which young chickens, squirrels, rabbits etc., are partly fried in butter before being covered with a crust, and the gravy in the pan is made rich and light brown, may be found detailed elsewhere for pigeon pie, and the following is the other principal method, or country style.

1 large fowl or 2 chickens.
1 slice of fat salt pork—2 ounces.
1 large potato.
1 teaspoonful of minced onion.
1 of black pepper.
1 of salt.
1 pound of pie crust.
2 tablespoonfuls of flour.
A little parsely.
The salt pork is only a seasoning, and may be dispensed with or substituted with butter or the fat of the fowls.

Cut the fowl in 8 pieces if large, first dividing it in half through the back and breast, chop each side in 4, taking a piece out between the leg and the wing. Cook the gizzard and heart with the fowl, but leave out the liver, which is apt to impart its flavor to the whole dish. Boil the meat till tender, which may take anywhere from 1 hour to 4, according to the kind of fowl. It does not make much difference how old the fowl is if it be boiled accordingly with seasonings added. It will make the liquor rich as jelly after a while.

Half an hour before taking the fowl from the fire put in the potato, cut in pieces, and afterward thicken the liquor with flour and water and mix in some chopped parsley.

Turn it into a baking pan, dredge a little more black pepper over the top and a little flour over that, and then cover with plain pie paste and bake it ½ hour.

Cost of material—Fowl 40, pork 3, vegetables and seasonings 1, paste 5, 49 cents for 8 dishes, or 6 or 7c per dish.

111—Boiled Kale or Seakale.

Wash free from grit, tie it in bunches, trim off the root end and boil it in salted, water, like winter spinach, about twenty minutes. Drain in a colander. Pour a spoonful of butter sauce over each bunch in the dish.

112—Mashed Potatoes.

Being such a common and easy article it is often the most neglected and goes to the table dark and full of lumps, when it ought to be as smooth as if pressed through a sieve. Butter and milk to mash with are good additions in their way, but vigorous pounding of the potatoes with a little salt and hot water or perhaps the clear fat from the top of the soup will make very fine mashed potatoes when neither of those luxuries can be afforded. The longer the mashing is continued provided the potato is kept

hot at the same time, the whiter it becomes. It is an improvement, to bake the mashed potato in a pie pan, brushing the top over with milk to cause it to brown easily.

113—Bread Custard Pudding.

2 cups-pressed in-fine bread crumbs.

2 cups milk.

1 ounce butter—small egg size.

1 tablespoon sugar.

Nutmeg or grated or minced lemon peel.

1 egg

Crumble the bread fine either by chopping or grating; grate half of the rind of a lemon into it or a little nutmeg. Mix the milk with the egg and sugar; melt the butter and mix in and pour the mixture over the bread crumbs in a buttered pudding-pan or bowl and bake about twenty-five minutes. Various changes can be made by adding raisins, currants or citron to this pudding. The fruit must be sprinkled in after the pudding is in the baking pan. It will sink if stirred. Serve a sauce with the pudding.

Cost of material—11 cents for one quart or 8 portions. With sauce 2c each order.

114—Rhubarb Pie.

Rhubarb should be peeled and cut in two-inch lengths, and cooked with only water enough to cover the bottom of the kettle, with half a pound of brown sugar to each pound spread over the top and the steam shut in. It burns easily, and should be cooked at the side of the range or set upon a brick, till the sugar dissolves with the juice to form a syrup.

Line the pie pans with puff paste, made not very rich, fill with the stewed rhubarb and place broad strips of paste, cut with a paste jagger across and bake; or use the plain pie paste and bake with a top crust.

Cost of material—Rhubarb 5, sugar 5, crust 5: 15c. for 2 pies, cut in 8 or 10.

115—The Stock Boiler.

Where the best management prevails and the work goes on like machinery, one wheel within another, there is a regular time of day to set the stock boiler on, it may be in the evening to simmer till the last, and then the liquor strained off is set away till the next day, or it may be early in the morning. The boiler should be larger than the ordinary stove pots. Put into it a gallon of clear cold water.

The meats to be cooked during the day are trimmed of all the tough and gristley ends, such as are sure to be thrown away if fried, broiled or roasted, and all the bones are taken from the meat that can be without detriment to the joint, and these scraps, after washing in clear water, are put into the boiler. Then, if there is a soup bone beside, or a chicken to be boiled, or a leg of mutton it will be so much the richer stock. Some days there will be reason to choose which kind of soup to make, according to the contents of the stock boiler, which is a more economical way to look at it than if the boiler was to be furnished to suit the soup. A cream soup, for example, may be made when the stock is thin, and when it is rich as jelly make beef gravy soup or mock turtle.

The available meat being in next, throw in a little vegetable seasoning. such as a small onion and piece of turnip and carrot. But these are not indispensible, for the soup will be seasoned afterwards.

Let the boiler heat slowly and when at last it boils, skim carefully two or three times, put the lid on and let simmer 4 or 5 hours, when there will probably be 2 quarts of rich stock ready when strained, to be used in soup or to make gravies and sauces.

The strainer fine enough for ordinary use is made of perforated tin, or a pan with a perforated tin bottom. Strike the edge of the pan rapidly to make the soup go through.

116—Celery Cream Soup.

3 pints soup stock.
1 pint rich milk.
Outside stalks of celery, about 4.
1 small onion, minced.
Small piece of lean cooked ham.
1 tablespoon flour.
Butter size of an egg.
Salt and white pepper.

Boil the soup stock with the onion and scrap of ham in it for flavor. Cut up the celery—about enough to fill a large cup—in dice shapes, and boil it ten minutes in water; then strain the water away. Mix the butter and flour together, and stir them into the boiling stock to thicken it slighty, then strain it into another saucepan and put in the parboiled celery and the pint of milk. Season with pepper and salt to taste. Let it simmer ten minutes or more after the celery is in.

Mince a piece of green leaf of celery very fine, and sprinkle it from a knife point into the soup. This makes six or seven plates.

Butter and flour for thickening is the orthodox article (roux), but should the butter fail to arrive punctually at the time the flour can be mixed with a little water instead. The stock used should have been skimmed free from fat, if not the soup must be.

Cost—21c for 2 quarts, or 3c per plate.

117—Boiled Red Snapper—Shrimp Sauce.

There should be a proper fish kettle for boiling a fish whole, having a perforated false bottom or drainer, that can be lifted out with the fish upon it when done. Where there is no such article the best substitute is a common milk pan of large size. Cover it with another pan that the fish may get steamed if not quite covered.

Choose a small fish, scale it, draw, chop off the fins, wash and wipe it dry on a cloth.

Half fill the pan with water and put in a little salt, vinegar, a small onion and four cloves stuck in it and half a bay leaf. When it boils put in the fish and simmer it at the side of the range about half an hour. Then pour off the water, take the skin off the upper side, slide the fish on to its dish, if to be served whole, and pour over it some shrimp sauce. But if served individually it may be divided with a fish slice in the pan and sauce poured over in the plates. Small and tender fish, like fresh mackerel, are best rolled up in a pudding cloth and boiled in plain salted water, then carefully unrolled onto the dish.

118—Shrimp Sauce.

1 pint of clear broth or water.
Butter size of an egg.
1 tablespoonful of flour—rather large.
Yolk of 1 egg.
Salt and pepper.
½ can Barataria shrimps.
Stir the flour and most of the butter together over the fire. When they bubble begin adding the hot broth or water, and stir it till cooked and thick—about two minutes longer. Then drop in the egg yolk and beat, and next the remaining small piece of butter and beat till it is melted. Season slightly and put in the shrimps. They are already cooked.

119—Duchesse Potatoes.

Usually served with fish, on the same plate. They are little cakes of mashed potatoes, in fancy shapes or plain. Take four steamed potatoes and mash them with an ounce of butter, the yolk of an egg and salt. Spread on a pie plate, brush over with the yolk of an egg mixed with a spoonful of milk, cut in pieces of any shape, take up the pieces with a knife

point, place them on a greased baking pan and bake a nice color on top.

Cost of fish with sauce etc.—2 pounds fish 40, seasoning 1, shrimps 15, butter eggs and seasonings 3, potatoes 8 portions 2—61 cents for 8 to 12 portions, or about 7c an order.

120—Larded Filet of Beef.

This is nothing if not neat, uniform, precise and workmanlike in appearance. There must be a pound of fat bacon for larding, cold and firm, so that it can be cut aright. Cut the slices a quarter inch thick, cut these in lengths of 1½ inches and then into strips all precisely alike and as thick as a common pencil.

Procure the filet or tenderloin of beef with the fat on it, that is with the coating of suet that covers the upper side of it, and shave that down until the covering of fat is about as thick as a beefsteak all over it. Then raise the edge of the fat at one side, skinning the filet, so to speak, and lay the sheet of fat over on the other side without cutting it off. This is to have the sheet of fat attached ready to cover over the filet again after it is larded with strips of bacon. Draw the point of a sharp knife across and across the skin inside the fat, to score it so that it will not draw up in cooking. Trim off the thin end of the filet and round off the thick end. Commence at the thick end with the larding. Insert a piece of bacon in the end of the larding needle and draw it through the top parts of the meat pinched up with the left thumb and finger for the purpose, one end of the strip of bacon so inserted will be left leaning backward, the other forward, on the surface. Insert 6 or more of these strips in a row across. Begin the next row so that the strips will come alternately between those of the first, and the exposed ends will cross the others, and so continue, with the regularity of stitching cloth, to the other end. Cover the larded filet with the sheet of fat. Make a long and uarrow baking pan hot in the oven, with a tablespoonful of salt and a cup of drippings in it, and enough water to keep the bottom from burning. Put in also a slice of turnip, carrot and onion, and a piece of celery. Have the oven hot, put in the filet, and roast it with the fat, covering it half an hour; then take off the fat, baste the filet with the contents of the pan, and let cook fifteen minutes longer, by which time the surface of the meat should be brown, and bacon strips brown too, without being burnt at the ends.

Filets of beef vary in weight and thickness, and the time above given is only a guide to the average. Unless specially ordered otherwise, the thick part of the filet should cut slightly rare in the middle, while the thinner portion is well done.

In carving, the filet should be sliced across vertically because it is a mass of strings of meat lying side by side, and if cut slantingly the slices begin to be stringy and coarse. A filet that is to be braised along with herbs, spices, vegetables, wine, etc., is larded with strips of bacon or fat pork that pass clear through from one side to the other diagonally, so that the slices cut across when done, show the larding all through the meat.

Cost of filet—4 pounds $1,20, pork 15 (not all used but culled and spoiled), seasonings paid for with drippings; $1.35 for 3 pounds net, or 15 to 20 slices or 7c an order

---

121—Mushrooms Stewed in Wine.

Larded filet of beef with mushrooms or, *aux champignons*, is the almost universal dish at small party dinners. The common method of preparing the mushrooms has been described at No. 48, but if a finished sauce is required use half brown beef gravy and half mushroom sauce, add a bastingspoon of wine and simmer at the side of the range and skim until clear, then if not thick enough boil it down rapidly, and after that add the mushrooms, cayenne, and a spoonful of sherry.

122—Brown Gravy.

Before serving the filet, or any roast meat let the gravy in the pan dry down until the grease can be poured off clear, while the glaze remains adhering to the pan; pour in water to dissolve it, and when it has boiled add a trifle of brown flour thickening if it seems to need it; strain through a fine strainer; serve some in the dish with the filet, the rest in a sauceboat.

123—Brown Flour for Thickening.

While butter and flour mixed in equal parts and baked brown makes the best thickening for gravies, plain browned flour does nearly as well and is more desirable when the butter is not very good. Put some sifted flour dry into a frying pan and bake deep brown in the oven. Use it at the rate of a tablespoonful to a cupful of liquid. Wet with water the same as raw flour, before stirring it in. It may be kept in a can always ready.

124—Stuffed Tomatoes.

6 or 8 large tomatoes.
1 cupful fine bread crumbs.
1 rounded tablespoonful of minced onion.
1 heaping tablespoonful minced fat bacon, or butter in equal amount.
Slight grating of nutmeg.
Cayenne and salt.

Do not peel the tomatoes, but take a slice off the rough stem side and scoop out the inside with a tablespoon into a colander, so that the juice may partly drain away. Cut a thin slice or two of bread and mince across to make a cupful. Mix the crumbs and tomato pulp together, bacon, onion, very little salt, if any, pepper, and touch of nutmeg or mace.

Fill the tomatoes with the mixture rounded up on top, bake in a small pan well buttered, with a greased sheet of paper over, one-half hour. Then moisten over the tops with the back of a spoon dipped in butter, dredge fine crumbs on top and bake again without cover until they are well browned.

Cost—1 to 2 cents each according to season. One of the best substitutes for mushrooms with filet of beef.

125—Egg Plant Plain Fried-(Sauteed.)

Slice the egg plant, without paring. into five or six, throwing away only the end parings. Boil the slices in salted water a few minutes to extract the strong taste, drain them, and while still moist dip both sides in flour, then fry brown in a frying pan with a little drippings. They are served as a vegetable, like fried parsnips, etc.

Cost—1c each person.

126—Chicken Croquettes.

1 young hen lightly roasted.
½ cup mushrooms.
1 small cup butter.
Same of flour.
1 cup cream.
Same of broth or water.
A slight grating of nutmeg.
A little lemon juice.
Pepper and salt.

Cut the meat of the roast fowl into the smallest possible dice, mince the mushrooms and add, sprinkle with a teaspoonful of mixed pepper and salt, grate a little nutmeg and squeeze a lemon over it.

Make cream sauce by stirring the butter and flour together in a sauce pan and adding the broth and cream when it begins to bubble, and when the sauce is ready moisten the meat with it, stir it up well and set it away to become cold. Then make out in rolls about the size of a finger, roll in flour, then egg, then in cracker crumbs and fry in hot lard. Pile in the dish and garnish with fried parsley.

Cost of material—fowl 50, butter 8, mushrooms 10, cream 6, seasonings 2 eggs, breading and frying 6, 82; 16 to 20 croquettes cost 4c to 5c each.

Note—The above is the way to make croquettes of the best quality, but a much cheaper will be found elsewhere described, and half the quantity can be made with the remains of fowl left over.

127—Stewed Cucumbers.

Pare three or four young and good cucumbers, and cut them in thick slices, boil these in water, with a little salt and vinegar in it—the same as for egg-plant—for about fifteen minutes, then pour away the water. Make a cupful of cream sauce in another saucepan, and, when ready, beat in the yolks of two eggs and a tablespoonful of vinegar. Pour this yellow sauce over the slices of cucumber, after they have been placed neatly in their dish.

128—Angelica Punch.

2 cups California angelica wine.
2 cups hot water—a pint.
1 cup sugar ½ pound.
1 cup stemmed raisins—½ pound.
1 lemon.
2 whites of eggs and 2 tablespoonful of powdered sugar to beat in.

Chop the raisins, grate half the rind the lemon, squeeze in all of the juice, pour the hot water to them, add the sugar, and stir until it is all dissolved. Strain the flavored syrup thus obtained into a freezer, and rub the most of the raisin pulp through as well. Add the wine and freeze. When nearly frozen whip the two whites and the powdered sugar together till thick, add them to the punch and finish freezing. It is like cream. Serve in stem glasses.

Cost of material—wine 25, sugar 5, raisins 10, lemon 2, whites and sugar 3, ice and salt 12; 57 cents for 2 quarts (when beaten) of punch, or 16 glasses or more—3 cents a glass.

129—Boiled Young Ducks.

Having picked and singed them, split them down the back and draw them. Cut off the neck and feet. Wash them quickly in cold water and wipe dry, and flatten them slightly to broiling shape with a tap of the cleaver. Lay the duck on a plate, dredge with salt and pepper and brush over both sides with butter. Broil on the gridiron over clear coals, the inside first, about 15 minutes. Serve on a hot dish, with a border of small pieces of toast or green peas with currant jelly or a quartered lemon, or with the following sauce.

130 Orange Sauce For Meats.

1 orange.
1 cupful of brown sauce.
½ cupful of claret.
A little cayenne.

Shave off very thinly the yellow rind of about a quarter of the orange and boil it in the brown sauce about 10 minutes. Cut half the orange into small slices and remove the pith and seeds.

Strain the brown sauce from the peel, throw into it the orange slices, squeeze in the juice of the remaining half, add the claret and cayenne, let it boil up and skim off the film that will rise.

If there is no brown sauce on hand soup stock can be used and thickened with a spoonful of flour worked in a small piece of soft butter. Pour the sauce under the ducks in the dish and dispose the pieces of orange around them.

Cost.—4 young ducks, $1; 1 can peas or sauce equivalent, 20—8 persons, 15 cents each.

131---Crab Salad.

6 boiled crabs, common size.
1 cup finely minced white cabbage.
½ cup salad dressing.

Pick the meat out of the crabs, cut all that can be cut into pieces of even size and rub the rest smooth in salad dressing, adding a little mustard. Mix cabbage and dressing thoroughly, and the crab meat mix in lightly, without breaking the pieces. Fill 8 crab shells with the salad and place them on a dish previously prepared with a bed of cress or other green.

Cost.—6 crabs, 30; dressing, 4; 34 cents for 8 orders.

132 Apple Turnovers.

Sometimes served as a "sweet entree;" more suitable to put in place of pie; best for luncheon, pic-nic parties, and for sale; a favorite form of pastry everywhere.

Make the flaky pie paste with about 12 ounces of butter to a pound of flour, roll it out to a thin sheet and cut out flats nearly as large as saucers, with the lid of a baking powder can or similar cutter.

Place a good spoonful of dry stewed apple in the middle of each piece of paste and double over in half-moon shape. Press the two edges together and crimp them with the thumb and finger. When the baking pan is full of the turnovers, brush them over with egg-and-water, and dredge granulated sugar on top. Bake slowly till they are crisp, glazed and of a fine reddish brown color. These large sizes have generally to be cut in two. They contain more fruit and are better eating when made small.

Cost of Material.—Four turnovers —crust 4, apple marmalade, 2, egg and sugar glaze, 2; 8 c. or 1 cent each order.

133---Puff Paste.

1 pound of cold flour.
15 ounces of cold butter.
1 cupful of ice water.

Get quite ready to make the paste before you begin, that it may be done quickly. It will not, perhaps, be light and good if allowed to stand long in a warm room. Leave out a handful of flour to dust with. Make a hollow in the middle of the rest in a pan, pour in the ice-water and mix up gradually with the fingers. Turn the paste on the table double and press a little to make it, smooth. Roll it out to half an inch thickness, pound the butter with a potato masher to make it pliable, drop half of it in lumps all over the sheet of paste, sift a very little flour over, press down the lumps of butter, fold over in three and turn the broad side toward you. Roll out again, drop the rest of the butter as before, fold in three and count that one. Roll out evenly with plenty of flour to prevent sticking, fold over in three and count that two. Do the same four times more, making six folds (beside the first one not counted) and it is ready for use, but should be allowed to stand awhile in the refrigerator to lose the tendency it has when first made to draw up out of shape.

If you have a good refrigerator at hand the puff paste will be the better for being set in it after the third folding and allowed to remain $\frac{1}{2}$ hour and then taken out and finished rolling, but, if not, the only way to have the paste good is to start with cold material and make it and bake it so quickly that it has not time to warm and melt in the meantime.

Cost of material—butter 23, flour 3; 26 cents for $2\frac{1}{2}$ pounds. Makes 5 pies with single bottom crusts, or 3 covered—depending upon the size or 20 turnovers or 20 to 25 tarts in patty pans, or 10 to 16 tartlets like the following.

Note—Lard of a solid, firm sort will make puff paste that is quite as good as that made with butter, and that rises nearly as high in the baking; and the cost is reduced according to the difference in price per pound. But soft lard cannot be used for this purpose. The best common flaky paste is made with half lard and half butter, with salt sprinkled over the lard, the butter put into the dough first, and the whole of the ingredients kept as cold as possible.

134—Cherry Tartlets.

1 heaping cup ripe cherries.
I level cup light brown sugar.
$1\frac{1}{2}$ pounds puff paste.

Set the cherries on to cook in a small saucepan with a bastingspoon of water, and sugar spread over the top. Put on the lid and let simmer slowly then set them away to become cold. The fruit for this purpose should be rich with a thick strong syrup, because only a small quantity is used and it should not run out of the tartlets.

Roll the puff paste to $\frac{1}{4}$ inch thick, cut out with a biscuit cutter, and cut the middle of each part way through with a smaller cutter. Put them in a hot oven and when they are risen open the door partly and let them dry well done. Take out the middle piece with a knife point and fill the tarttets with the stewed fruit.

Cost—about 2c each, or according to whether fresh or cannnd frut is used and the price.

135—Tipsy Pudding.

Sheets of sponge cake partly saturated with rum and set in a pan of cold boiled custard, For the cake make this:
$\frac{1}{2}$ cupful of sugar 4 ounces.
2 eggs.
6 tablespoonfuls of water.
1 cup of flour—4 ounces.
1 teaspoonful baking powder.

Separate the eggs—the whites in a bowl or dish, the yolks in the mixing pan. Put the sugar and water in with the yolks, and beat them till they are a thick yellow froth. Mix the powder in the flour, add that and stir up well. Whip the whites firm, add them last.

Grease and flour 2 jelly cake pans, divide the mixture into them and bake of a very light color. When done place the sheets of cake one on the other in a pan and pour $\frac{1}{2}$ cup of rum or brandy into them with a teaspoon. Have ready 2 cups of custard and pour around. Cut in 8 and serve like pudding and sauce.

Cost of material—sugar and flour 3, eggs 4, powder 1, rum 12, custard 9, 29c, for 8 dishes 3 or 4 cents an order.

136—Boiled Custard.

2 cups milk.

2 eggs.

2 heaping tablespoons sugar.

Flavoring of nutmeg or stick cinnamon. Boil the milk with half the sugar in it to prevent burning on the bottom. Beat the two eggs in a cup with the rest of the sugar and a spoonful of milk added. When the milk boils pour a little to the eggs, then turn all into the saucepan and stir until it thickens and shows signs of boiling. Too much cooking will spoil it.

137—Caramel Ice Cream.

3 cups rich milk.

1 cup cream.

6 yolks of eggs.

2 tablespoons sugar for caramel

8 tablespoons sugar to sweeten

¼ cup curacoa.

Set the 2 ounces of sugar over the fire in a little saucepan, without water, and let it melt and brown to the color of maple syrup, then add to it a few spoonsfuls of water and set it at the side to dissolve and make liquid caramel.

Boil the 3 cups of milk with half the sugar in it, beat the yolks with the rest of the sugar and a spoonful of milk added, pour them and the milk together and cook a minute carefully to make smooth yellow custard. Add the caramel to it and strain it into the freezer, pour in the curacoa when cold and whip the cup of cream and add that and freeze with rapid beating.

Cost of material—milk and cream 10, eggs 8, sugar 7, curacoa 20, ice and salt 10, 55 cents for about 2 quarts after freezing.

138—Clams on the Half Shell.

The smallest clams are preferred. Wash the outside thoroughly before opening. Loosen the clams from shell they are served in and retain all the liquor the shell will hold. Place 4 or 5 in each plate and half a lemon in the middle.

Cost—depends on locality. The further from the sea shore the more of a variety to serve at a fine diner.

139—Consomme Royal.

We have no word in English for consomme but broth, and that is not an equivalent, but only a substitute. French cooks understand by consomme a clear soup as rich as melted jelly. Consomme royal is of the color of brandy, with little egg custards floating in it.

Simmer a large fowl and two or more shanks of veal in a gallon of water for three or four hours, and while it is cooking add the vegetables and seasonings. These should be the usual soup bunch (without parsnips or green onion tops, however), together with a stalk of celery, half a bay leaf, a teaspoonful of bruised pepper-corns and a sprig of green thyme or marjoram.

When it has boiled long enough strain the broth into a saucepan.

To clarify the consomme, chop a pound of lean beef fine, mix with it two whites of eggs and a cup of cold water. Then pour the broth to the beef, stir up and boil again. Strain through a napkin or jelly bag, season with salt, color with a teaspoonful of dissolved burnt sugar and remove every particle of grease.

To make the floating custards take three or four yolks of eggs, raw, and mix with them a spoonful of the consomme. Pour into a slightly buttered saucer and steam it until done—10 minutes. Cut the custard in diamond shapes and drop three or four in each soup plate.

Where it is not necessary to be extremely particular good clear soup can be obtained by letting the soup-stock get cold in a jar and after taking off the fat, pouring it off without disturbing the sediment. Strain through a napkin, make hot and add the spoonful of coloring and salt as before.

Cost of material—chicken to be used in salad or patties 0, veal 16, vegetables 5, beef 10, eggs, 6; 37c for 2 quarts, or 3c per plate.

140—Vegetable Soup.

2 quarts of soup stock—8 or 10 cups.
3 cups mixed vegetables.
Seasonings.

Take for the stock the liquor in which any kind of meat has been boiled—be e shank, mutton, heart, tongue, fowl, rab bit, etc., and corned beef liquor does very well. The richer the stock can be, of course the better it is. Strain it into the soup pot. Skim off most of the fat almost every kind of vegetable can be used. Take a piece of each and c ut al into dice shapes, or, if to be very nice, cut vegetables in slices and stamp out little patterns with a tin cutter or the point of a tin funnel. There should be turnips white and yellow, carrot, pumpkin, celery, string beans, green peas, onions, summer squash, cauliflower. If vegetables are scarce, a little parsnip and cabbage and potatoes can be used, but the latter put in late so as not to boil away.

Boil the hard vegetables, such as carrots, turnips, onions, string beans and celery, together in a little saucepan first; then pour the water away and put the vegetables in the boiling stock, and add the easy-cooking kinds, such as cauliflower, asparagus heads and peas—whatever may be on hand. At last add a piece of red tomato, cut small, salt and pepper to taste and a tablespoonful of corn starch mixed in a cup with water.

Cost—about 10c per quart or 8 plates

141—Baked Sea Bass.

Scale and clean the fish; leave the head on if it is to be sent to table whole. Make a stuffing for it of 2 pressed cupfuls of bread crumbs, a small cupful of but-

ter, rind of a quarter of lemon minced fine, parsely, green thyme and marjoram, and pepper and salt, and two eggs mixed with a spoonful of water to moisten it. Sew up the fish when stuffed. Mark it in slices as if to be carved, on both sides, by cutting down to the bone, and put a thin slice of salt pork in each incision. Bake in a long pan, with soup stock and salt and pepper in it, about 30 or 40 minutes, or according to size. Put a little strained tomatoes and brown gravy into the fish pan, and water if necessary; let boil up, skim and strain for sauce.

Cost of material—3 lbs fish 36, pork slices for insertion and scraps in baking pan 6, stuffing and sauce 15; 57c for 8 to 12 orders or 5 or 6c per plate.

142—Small Potatoes.

Scoop out balls size of cherries from large potatoes with a potato spoon. A cupful will make enough for a dozen plates of fish. Make $\frac{1}{2}$ cup of butter and $\frac{1}{2}$ cup of lard hot in a very small saucepan and drop the potato balls in and let them stew slowly. As soon as the butter gets down to the frying point and the potatoes and sediment begin to brown on the bottom pour off all the grease and set the potatoes in the oven a few minutes to acquire a handsome color. Sprinkle salt and chopped parsley among them. Serve a tablespoonful with each plate of fish. These are not the same as fried potatoes and when first put into the boiling butter and lard they must be stirred from the bottom once or twice lest they scorch and acquire a bad taste.

143—Boiled Corned Tongue, Caper Sauce.

Fresh tongues put in a jar and covered with the brine or pickel No. 106, will be of a good pink color and nicely salted in from a week to ten days.

Wash off the corned tongue and boil it three hours. Plunge it in cold water and pelt off the skin then set in a hot place. In carving cut slantingly to make long slices that will not run out too small at the thin end. Serve with caper sauce, which is butter sauce with a little of the caper vinegar mixed in and the capers—about a teaspoonful—dashed on top of the sauce on the meat.

Cost of material—tongue 35, sauce 5; 40c for 8 to 12 orders or 4c per plate.

144—Roast Rib Ends of Beef.

Take the ends of the ribs that are sawed off the rib roasts, and put them in to cook early, while breakfast is still going on. Let there be in the baking pan, which should be a deep one, a handful of salt, 2 or 3 ladlefuls of sweet fresh drippings from the previous day's roasting, and about as much water or soup stock, and let simmer in the oven, never getting quite without water in the pan till very nearly time to serve dinner. If other meats have to be crowded into the same pan let these rib ends be at the bottom, they will be so much the richer and keep on cooking in the gravy till tender and glutinous. At last, the water being all evaporated out of the pan, roll these rib ends over and over in the natural glaze that remains on the bottom and take them out brown and shining before they likewise get dry. Serve cuts of 2 or 3 ribs with gravy.

Cost of material—3 lbs beef rib ends 18, seasonings and gravy 2; 20c for 8 or 10 orders.

145—The Side of Lamb.

The dainty dish of spring lamb may easily be spoiled, or at least made very unsatisfactory by careless cutting. If you take off the shoulder it will scarcely make two good orders when roasted, and the ribs underneath it will amount to nothing. Nearly all who choose their cuts ask for the ribs and the carver needs all that the cook can furnish.

Instead of taking the shoulder off, bone it where it is, beginning at the throat. Cut along on both sides of the blade bone and pull it out. There will not be much time for careful boning, nor is it necessary, five minutes or less will do. Saw the ribs across the middle, hack through the back bone with the point of a sharp cleaver at two ribs apart and hack the brisket through ready for carving in the same manner. Then pull the meat of the shoulder well over the brisket and fasten it with a skewer or two. When carved, the ribs will carry a good, meaty slice of the shoulder with them, and with a little management the brisket ends of the ribs can be equally well portioned off.

The side thus prepared should be roasted in one piece, loin and flank included, but the leg requiring more time to cook, should be made a separate cut. The loin should likewise be carefully hacked through the back bone ready for carving into slices like loin chops.

146—Roast Lamb—Mint Sauce.

It cooks in from 30 to 45 minutes. Should be fairly done through and no more. Needs to be in a pan by itself.

Having prepared the meat as directed above, wash it in cold water, dredge both sides with salt and flour, by pressing both sides down into a pan of flour and shake off the surplus. Place it with the outside upwards in a baking pan already hot and containing a little salt water and drippings. When the upper side has cooked so that the flour will not wash off begin to baste it and repeat frequently. If a quarter pound of quite fresh butter can be had melt it and baste the lamb with it at the finish. The butter froths upon meat and gives it a fine color.

Cost of material—fore-quarter of lamb, or 4 lbs, 60, mint sauce 5; 65c for 12 dishes or 5 or 6c per order.

147—Mint Sauce for Roast Lamb.

The conventional lamb sauce. No

other sauce or gravy is needed when this is used;

2 tablespoons green mint.
1 tablespoon sugar.
½ cup vinegar.

Pick the leaves of mint from the stems, wash and chop fine, and mix with the sugar and vinegar in a bowl. Serve cold, a spoonful to each plate.

148—Roast Green Goose.

Singe and pick the young goose free from pin-feathers and draw it. If to send the table whole, the pinions should be cut off before cooking and the main wing joints skewered to the back, and the legs held compactly to the side either with skewers or twine. Fry a minced onion in butter, light yellow, and not at all dark and strong, and mix it with some dry mashed potatoes; add an egg and the butter that the onion was fried in and a seasoning of white pepper. Stuff the goose with the seasoned potato, sew up, bake it in a pan for about one hour, or more, if large. Dredge the goose over with flour when nearly done, and baste it with butter, which will produce a fine crust and brown color.

If to be sent in whole, bake some small apples in a pan covered with greased paper and place them around the goose in a dish.

Cost of material—the same as spring lamb, about 6 or 7c an order, according to market price.

149—Cucumber Salad.

Slice the cucumbers two hours before they are wanted and sprinkle the slices plentifully with salt. Set the dish in the refrigerator. Just before dinner drain away the salt liquor from the cucumbers and shake them about with oil first, and then with vinegar and pepper. Serve on a very cold dish.

150—Turkey Salad.

Take the remainder of a cooked turkey or half a boiled turkey, if cooked for the purpose, pick all the meat from the bones and remove the thick fat and skin, cut the meat into long shreds and then across, making the smallest, possible dice shapes. Cut celery, if in season, the same way, about two-thirds as much celery as there is turkey, or if that is not in season use crisp lettuce or a mixture of lettuce and finely chopped white cabbage, and add celery salt or extract or celery vinegar. Mix meat and the vegetables together, season slightly with pepper and salt. Pour in a little salad oil—say a quarter cupful, stir about and then stir in as much vinegar. Heap and smooth over the salad in a large platter—it will adhere and keep shape well—then pour and spread over it a well-seasoned mayonaise.

After spreading the mayonaise over the turkey salad, ornament with quarters of hard boiled eggs or with chopped yolks and parsley, olives, cut lemons or shapes stamped out of cooked beets.

Cost of material—2 lbs turkey meat or chicken 40, oil, vinegar and seasonings 10, celery and garnishings 10, mayonaise 15; 75c for 2 quarts, or from 8 to 16 orders; or, 40c per quart or 5c per hotel dinner dish.

151—Mayonaise Salad Dressing.

2 raw yolks of eggs.
½ teacup olive oil.
About half as much vinegar or lemon juice.
A level teaspoon salt.
Same of made mustard.
Pinch of cayenne.

Put the two raw yolks in a pint bowl, add two tablespoonfuls of oil, set the bowl in ice-water or otherwise make it cold, and beat with a Dover egg-beater about a half a minute. Then add more oil and whip, and then throw in the salt, and on whipping again the mixture will at once thicken up, looking like softened butter. Then add a spoonful of vinegar, then oil and so on alternately till all is in. Add the mustard and cayenne for seasoning. The best mayonaise is made with lemon juice instead of part of the vinegar, and when it will not thicken as desired the lemon juice invariably corrects the trouble and gives the dressing the desired consistency. It should not be thin enough to run, but should coat over the pile of salad material it is spread upon. The foregoing shows the quickest method of making this important sauce or dressing; the egg-beater or the want of it need not, however, be an obstacle in the way, for simply stirring around in the bowl with a wooden spoon is the way most commonly practiced.

152—Water Cress Salad.

Cut away the rough stems, pick off the root fibers, and wash the cress carefully. Drain, cut it in inch lengths, season in a bowl with a little salt and pepper, and when they are mixed in sprinkle with vinegar. Serve in small salad dishes individually.

153—Lambs' Tongues with Artichokes.

Take for preference, corned lambs' or sheeps' tongues of a good pink color, and boil them not less than 2 hours, which may be done the evening before they are served, if more convenient. Put them into cold water and peel off the outside and split them lengthwise in two.

Having the halves ready in a dish when the roast meat is done, after taking it out lay the tongues in the fat and glaze in the baking pan for about 5 minutes, then take them out slightly browned and glazed and keep hot.

Cook an artichoke for each dish, as directed further on, boiling them, that is to say, like summer cabbage or cauliflower, but cut them in halves instead of quarters; only scoop out the fibrous part before cooking. Drain them well. Serve half a tongue in the small dish and a half artichoke at each end, and a spoonful of brown gravy over the vegetable without covering the tongue. Tongue and spinach may be served the same way.

Cost of material—4 tongues 20, arti-

chokes and gravy 10; 30c for 8 dishes or about 4 cents per order.

154—Spaghetti and Cheese—Romaine.

Spaghetti is maccoroni in another form, a solid cord instead of a tube.

4 ounces spaghetti—2 cups when broken.
1 cup minced cheese—2 ounces.
1 cup milk.
Butter size of an egg.
2 yolks of eggs.

This dish ought to be quite yellow. Throw the spaghetti into water that is already boiling, and salted. After cooking 20 minutes drain it dry, and put it into the buttered dish it is to be baked in.

Put the cheese and butter and half the milk into a saucepan and stir them over the fire till the cheese is nearly melted, mix the yolks with the rest of the milk, pour that into the saucepan, then add the whole to the spaghetti in the pan, and bake it a yellow brown in as short a time as possible. It loses its richness if cooked too long, through the toughening of the cheese.

Cost of material—spaghetti 4, cheese 3, milk 1, butter 3, egg-yolks 3; 14c for 8 orders, or about 2c per dish.

155—Vanilla Puff Fritters—Rum Sauce.

1 cup water—½ pint.
½ cup butter--3½ ounces.
2 rounded tablespoons sugar.
1 rounded cup flour—5 ounces.
3 large eggs.
1 teaspoon vanilla extract.

Boil the water with the sugar and butter in it in a deep saucepan. Drop in the flour all at once and stir the mixture over the fire till you have a firm, well-cooked paste. Take it from the fire and work in the eggs one at a time with a spoon, and beat the paste well against the side of the saucepan. Add the vanilla with the last egg. The more the paste is beaten the more the puffs will expand in the frying fat.

Make some lard hot. It will take half a saucepanful. Drop pieces of the batter about as large as eggs and watch them swell and expand in the hot lard and become hollow and light. Only four or five at a time can be fried because they need lots of room.

The fritters being slightly sweet will be liable to fry too dark if the lard be made too hot; and they may be as much as five minutes in it before they begin to swell and roll over.

Cost of material—butter 8, sugar and vanilla 2, flour 1, eggs 6, lard to fry damaged 4 21c for 12 fritters—rum sauce 11—32 cents for 12 dishes of fritters with rum sauce or about 3c per order.

156—Rum Sauce for Fritters.

1 cup water.
½ cup sugar.
1 rounded tablespoon starch.
½ a lemon—without the seeds.
1 ounce butter.
1 bastingspoon of rum.
Boil the water. Mix the starch with the sugar dry and stir them in. Slice the lemon into it and add the butter and let the sauce simmer at the side until it becomes quite transparent. Then add the rum. Pour a spoonful over each fritter as they are dished up.

Cost—11 or 12 cents.

157—Browned Potatoes.

Pare the potatoes and steam them, and the broken ones being used to mash, or a la duchesse, put the others in a small pan with some of the drippings from the roast lamb pan and a dredging of salt and bake them brown. Cold boiled or baked potatoes are not fit for this purpose—they can be used better for breakfast dishes.

158—Cauliflower in Cream.

Cauliflower takes from half to three-quarters of an hour to cook done. It should not boil rapidly enough to destroy the small flowerets. Try the stems with a fork and take off when tender. A lump of baking soda the size of a bean in the water will hasten the cooking without injuring the vegetable.

Divide the cauliflower into portions of convenient size before cooking, and when drained and dished up pour a spoonful or two of good strained cream sauce over each portion.

159—Stewed Butter Beans.

Throw Lima or butter beans into a sauce-pan of water that is already boiling and has salt in it, and cook about half-hour, if green beans, but if dried they will take one and a half hours, besides a previous soaking in water. Drain away the water, and mix a little cream sauce or butter sauce, or add milk, butter and salt, and thicken when it boils up.

160—Artichokes as a Vegetable.

Let the artichokes lie in a pan of cold water, the same as is the rule for cauliflower, spinach, etc., an hour or two before they are to be cooked. Wash well, and if the tips of the leaves are discolored, clip them; cut the artichokes in 4 and remove the stringy core. Have the water ready boiling, put in a teaspoonful of salt and baking soda the size of a bean, boil the artichokes about ½ hour or until the soft end of the leaf when pulled out proves to be tender. Drain and serve like cauliflower, 2 pieces in a dish, and a spoonful of butter sauce poured over.

161—Indian Fruit Pudding.

3 cups milk or water—1½ pints.
1 cup yellow corn-meal—6 ounces.
1 teacup minced suet—3 ounces.
½ teacup black molasses—3 ounces.
2 eggs. Little salt.
1 cup seedless raisins—4 ounces.
Same of currants.
½ teaspoon ginger, cinnamon, or grated lemon rind.
Make mush with the meal and water and let it cook well with the steam shut

in for an hour or two. Then mix in all the other ingredients, the fruit previously dusted with flour, and bake it in a pan or mold about an hour. Cover with greased paper to keep the fruit from blistering. Three heaping cups of corn-meal mush ready made will do as well. The above makes a quart of pudding.

COST of material—meal 2, suet or butter 3, molasses 2, eggs 4, raisins 5 currants and spices 5; 21c for 8 orders—with sauce 3c per dish.

162—Rich Lemon Pie.

7 ounces sugar—a cupful.
3 lemons.
1 cup rich cream.
6 yolks of eggs and 2 whites.
Place the sugar in a bowl and grate the lemon rinds into it with a tin greater, and then squeeze in the juice. Beat the yolks of eggs light and mix the cream with them; pour this to the lemon and sugar, and just before filling the pie crust with the mixture whip the two whites to a froth and stir them in.
Use puff-paste to line the pie pans. The mixture will fill two pies, or three if small. It is hard to bake without browning the top too much, so they should be under the shelf of the oven. These rich pies do not need frosting, only a dredging of powdered sugar.

COST of material—sugar 5, lemons 6, cream 6, eggs 12, paste 6; 35c for 10 portions, or 3 or 4 cents each order.

163—White Cocoanut Pie.

1 cup milk.
2 tablespoons sugar.
1 rounded tablespoon starch.
2 or 3 ounces grated cocoanut.
3 or 4 whites of eggs.
Small piece of butter.
Pinch of salt.
Boil the milk alone. Mix the starch and sugar together dry and stir them in; then the butter and cocoanut. Set it away to get cold. Whip the whites to a firm froth and mix them with the pie-mixture. Bake in thin crusts of puff paste. Makes two small pies.

COST of material—milk 2, sugar and starch 2, cocoanut 5, butter 1, eggs 4, crusts for 2 pies 5; 19 cents for 8 portions, or 2 to 3c per order.

164—Apricot Ice.

3 cupfuls of apricots cut in pieces.
1 cupful of sugar—8 ounces.
2 cupfuls of water.
The kernels of half the apricots.
2 whites of eggs.
The ripest and sweetest apricots, if the fresh fruit be used, should be kept out, one cupful to be mixed in the ice when finished.
Stew the other two cupfuls and the peeled kernels in the water and sugar for a few minutes, rub the fruit then with the back of a spoon, through a strainer into the freezer along with the syrup. Freeze like ice cream and when it is nearly finished whip the two whites to a firm froth, mix them in and turn the freezer rapidly a short time longer. Stir in the cut apricots just before serving. Canned apricots can be used as well, and if in syrup that can be mixed in also.

COST of material—apricots 25, sugar 5, white of eggs 4, ice and salt 10; 44c for 3 pints or 8 to 12 dishes, or 4c per order.

165—Fine White Cake.

18 ounces granulated sugar—2½ cnds
8 ounces white butter—1 large cup.
½ pint of milk—1 large cup.
5 ounces of corn starch—1 rounde. cup.
12 ounces of flour—3 rounded cups.
2 large teaspoonfuls cream tartar.
1 small teaspoonful of soda.
12 whites of eggs.
Vanilla extract to flavor.
Sift the cream tartar in the flour three or four times over.

Mix the starch in a small bowl with the cup of milk.

Get the whites of eggs ready in a tin pail or large whipping bowl.

Dissolve the soda in two spoonfuls of milk in a cup.

Put the sugar and butter together in the mixing pan, warm them slightly and stir till creamy and add the dissolved soda. Stir in the corn starch and milk. Whip the whites to a firm froth and mix them and the prepared flour in a portion of each alternately. Flavor. Bake as soon as mixed; either in layers for chocolate cake or in mold. If the latter, frost over when cold.

Cost—50 cents for a 2 quart mold or about 3 lbs of cake; with icing 5c more.

166—Tomato Soup.

2 quarts soup stock.
1 cupful stewed tomatoes.
1 small cupful of minced vegetables.
6 cloves.
1 tablespoon minced parsley.
Salt and pepper to taste.
Little flour for thickening.

Tomatoes stewed down after seasoning with salt, pepper and butter, are a different article from the freshly prepared and impart a new richness to soup.

The soup stock may be the liquor in which a piece of beef or mutton is boiled for dinner, with the addition of other raw scraps and pieces, such as the bones and gristly ends of a beefsteak. An hour before dinner time take out the meat strain the stock through a fine strainer and into the soup pot. Cut piece of carrot, turnip and onion into small dice and throw in and let cook till done and add the cloves and cup of tomatoes, pepper and salt, thickening and the parsley at last.

It is generally considered a reproach to say the soup is thin. A proper medium should be observed. A spoonful of flour gives the smoothness and substance required without destroying the clearness of the soup.

Cost of material—stock 4, tomatoes 6, vegetables and seasonings 2; 12c for 12 plates.

167—Middle Cut of Salmon—Boiled.

Take about three pounds of the middle out of a small salmon, and, having scaled and cleaned it, put it on to cook in water that is already boiling and strongly salted. The fish should be placed on the drainer or false bottom of the fish kettle, but where there is no such utensil the precaution should be taken to wrap and pin it in a buttered napkin, that it may come out of the water unbroken. Let it cook very gently at the side of the range for three-quarters of an hour. Take it up, remove the skin, and place it carefully on a hot dish. At the moment that it is sent to table pour over it some of the fresh butter sauce of the next recipe, fill the remaining space around it in the dish with a pint of potato boullettes, and send in some more of the sauce in a sauce-boat.

168—Scotch Fish Sauce.

Set 8 ounces of the best butter, the juice of one lemon, a pinch of cayenne and a tablesoonful of chopped parsley in a bowl in a place warm enough to soften the butter, but not to melt it, and when the sauce is wanted for use stir together until creamy.

Cost of material—salmon 1,00, potatoes 2, sauce 20; $1,22 for 12 hotel orders or 10c per plate.

169—Boiled Bacon and Cabbage.

Cut 2 summer cabbages in quarters and cut out most of the stem part. Let lie in a pan of cold water until wanted to cook. Put on sauce-pan plenty large enough with water and salt and a very little baking soda in it—about the size of a bean for two cabbages—when it boils put in the cabbage and let it cook half an hour.

Shave the smoky outside off a pound

of bacon and boil the bacon in a sauce-pan by itself for half hour. Then drain off both cabbage and bacon and put them both together in one pot, pour in boiling water just to cover, put on a good-fitting lid and let them slowly cook together half hour longer.

The quarters of cabbage, nice and green appearing, should be drained in the spoon as they are taken up without destroying their shape, and placed in the dish with the bacon sliced on top.

Cost of material—24c for 8 orders or 3 c per plate.

170—Roast Beef.

To roast or bake meat so that, how-ever small the piece may be, it will be found full of gravy when cut, it is necessary to have the pan it is baked in hot before the meat goes in, and al-though there must be liquor in the pan while it is baking, that should be added after the meat has become hot enough outside for the pores to be closed and juices retained inside.

The choice roasting piece of beef is the ribs between the edge of the shoulder-blade and the loin—the short ribs. As the butchers have to sell everything, as a matter of business, they take out the ri bs and coil the thin meat of the breast around the choice upper portion, and make a neat cushion-shaped roast, se-cured with twine and skewers. In the places where the highest prices are paid, however, the breast portion has to be cut away altogether and cooked separately, as in our example of last week, and the choice upper portion or entre-cote only is roasted. This is nearly always cooked rare done, and the plentiful gravy that flows from it when cut is caught in a dish and is the only gravy served with it. As to time, the old rule is the only one. Allow a quarter of an hour for each pound of meat, and less, according to judgment, when the roast is of thin shape or required to be very rare done.

Common Roast of beef. To be carved by slicing off the top.

Choice roast, close trimmed and the spine bone removed. To be carved by cutting entire slices off the end.

Cost of roast beef—common roast beef at 12c, loses one-third in trimmings and cooking—1 pound 18c, 6 plates to the pound, 3c per plate. Choice roast at 18c, same proportions, 6 plates to the pound 4½c per plate.

171—Stuffed Brisket of Veal.

The breast or brisket of veal is a low-priced cut, at least when the veal is large, but is most excellent when cooked tender. There is a large proportion of gelatinous bone and tendon good for soups and stews. Take the entire "plate," as the butchers call it, and take out the bones by cutting down the sides of the ribs and along the brisket edge with the point of the knife, without cutting down through. Then chop the bone in pieces and use them in soup, as directed in a previous receipe. Make the bread stuffing the same as for roast turkey, lay it on the broad, boneless piece of veal—which may be made broader and evener by splitting the breast edge part way—then roll up and tie in good shape with twine. Put the rolled veal into a baking pan, with fat skimmed from the soup, a little water and salt and baked with greased paper on top for a time, according to the size of the veal—probably an hour and a half. Baste it with a little drippings, roll it over in the glaze or gravy of the pan when that becomes brown at last, and make pan gravy when the meat is taken out the usual way.

Cost of material—3 lbs veal brisket at 10c loses one half in boning, soup bones pay for the dressing—2 lbs stuffed veal for 30, or 8 to 10 orders, 3c per plate.

172—Ragout of Sweetbreads and Mushrooms.

2 or 3 large sweetbreads, or 1 pound.
½ can mushrooms.
2 ounces butter—size of an egg.
1 tablespoon flour.
Little minced onion and ham for seasoning.
Juice of 1 lemon.
Cayenne and salt.
Fried shapes of bread for the border.
Take the sweatbreads already cooked and cold, and cut them in large dice.

Make the sauce for them in a deep saucepan, first putting in half the butter, a large teaspoonful of minced onion and a very thin slice of ham, and when these are cooked enough for flavor without browning put in the flour and stir the mixture over the fire until it begins to color. Then add gradually the mushroom liquor and a cupful of the liquor the sweatbreads were boiled in, let it boil up and become thick. Add a pinch of cayenne. Next, melt the other piece of butter in a frying-pan, put in the mushrooms and the cup of sweetbreads and shake them about over the fire until they begin to show color; take it off, squeeze in the juice of the lemon and strain in the thick sauce from the other vessel. Dish them heaped up in the center of a flat platter, or of small dishes for individual orders, and place a border of thin shapes of bread fried in lard around the edge.

Cost of material—sweetbreads 30, mushrooms 15, butter 4, seasonings and croutons 4; 53c for 8 orders or 6 or 7c per plate.

173—Macaroni and Cheese—Bechamel.

5 ounces Macaroni—⅓ package.
2 ounces cheese—½ cup.
2 ounces butter.
1½ pints milk, or water—3 cups.
2 eggs. Salt.
Parsley and flour thickening.
Boil the macaroni by itself first, throwing it into water that is already boiling and salted. Let it cook only 20 minutes. Then drain it dry and put it into a pan or baking dish holding about three pints.

Chop the cheese, not very fine, and mix it with the macaroni likewise the butter. Beat the two eggs and the pint of water or milk together, pour them on the macaroni and set in the oven to bake. While it is getting hot boil a cup of milk (the remaining half pint of the recipe), and thicken it with a rounded tablespoonful of flour mixed up with part of it in a cup, add salt and a tablespoonful of chopped parsley, and when the macaroni in the oven is set so that the two cannot mix, pour this white cream sauce on top of it, shut up the oven, and let it bake a yellow brown. This makes a very attractive dish, as the yellow cheese and custard boils up in spots among the white sauce and parsley.

Cost of material—macaroni 5, cheese 3, butter 4, milk 2, eggs 4, seasonings 1; 19c for 8 orders, 2½c per plate.

174—New Potatoes, Maitre d'Hotel.

All articles that are a la maitre d'hotel have an acid and some green in the sauce. Take potatoes that are small and just out of the ground and scrape them, keeping them covered with cold water until time to cook. Put them on in cold water, with salt in it; boil with care, not to let them break when done. Drain off; put in fresh hot water, little salt, lump of butter, vinegar to make taste slightly, chopped parsley, and when these have boiled up, a spoonful of flour thickening. Shake about, without putting a spoon in, until it thickens.

175—Summer Squash.

This vegetable should always be steamed, or at any rate not boiled in water, it being an object to get it as dry as possible so as to allow the addition of milk or cream when it is mashed. Shave off the outside thinly with a sharp knife; cut each squash in six or eight pieces. It depends upon the age and distinctness of the seeds whether they should be cut out or not if large enough to show prominently in the mashed squash take out the entire core. Squash cooks in about half an hour, and may be allowed to simmer and dry out more after mashing and seasoning, in a pan set upon a couple of bricks.

176—Steamed Cherry Pudding.

1 cup pitted cherries.
2 heaping cups flour.
2 teaspoonfuls baking powder.
½ cup water.
Mix the powder in the flour dry, make a hollow in the middle, throw in a little salt, pour in the water and mix up as soft as it can be handled. Work the dough on the table slightly by pressing in flat with the hands and doubling over. Lay a bottom crust of it in a tin pudding pan that holds a quart; spread half the pitted cherries on it, lay another crust on them, then the remainder of the cherries and a third sheet of dough on top. Set in a steamer and steam from 30 to 45 minutes and serve while hot and light, with sauce.

Cost of material—cherries 10, flour 2, powder 2; 14—hard sauce 13—27c for 8 orders or 3½c per plate.

177—Hard Sauce.

1 large cup powdered sugar, ½ pound.
1 small cup fresh butter, ¼ pound.
Grated nutmeg.
Soften the butter but not melt it. Stir it and the sugar together to a cream as in making cake. The more it is stirred (if in a bowl or dish and not in tin) the whiter it becomes. Spread it on a dish and grate nutmeg on top. Keep it cold until wanted.

Good for all kinds of puddings, and can be colored pink by adding while steaming a little red fruit juice.

Cost—butter and sugar 13c.

178.—Sliced Apple Pie, Rich.

Use this way only the best ripe cooking apples. Pare and core and slice them thin across the core hole, making rings. Fill paste-lined pie pans about two layers deep. Thinly cover the apple slices with sugar, and grate nutmeg over. Put in each pie, butter about the size of a walnut and a large spoonful of water. Bake without a top crust slowly and dry. The apples become transparent and half candied.

Cost of material—for 2 pies, puff paste 6, apples 2, sugar 3, butter 2; count 2 per plate.

179—Lemon Sherbet.

1 quart water.
1 pound sugar.
2 large lemons.
3 whites of eggs.
Grate the rinds of the lemons into a bowl and squeeze in the juice. Make a boiling syrup of the sugar and half the water, and pour it hot to the lemon zest and juice and let it remain so till cold, or as long as convenient, to draw the flavor. Then add the rest of the water, strain into a freezer, freeze as usual, and when it is pretty well frozen, whip the whites to a froth, mix them in, beat up and freeze again.

Cost of material—sugar 10, lemons 4, eggs 4, ice and salt 12; 30c for 3 pints or 8 saucers or 12 glasses, or 3c per order.

180—Small Cream Cakes.

8 ounces granulated sugar—1 cup.
5 eggs.
4 ounces butter, melted—½ cup.
½ cup milk.
12 ounces flour—3 cups.
1 teaspoonful baking powder.

Beat the sugar and eggs together a minute or two, add the melted butter, the milk, the powder and the flour. Slightly grease some baking pans and drop the batter by tablespoonfuls to form little round cakes. Sprinkle granulated sugar on top of each one. Bake in a slack oven. The cakes run out rather thin and delicate and should have plenty of room. Take off with a knife when cold and place two together with pastry cream spread between.

Cost of material—sugar 6 eggs 10, butter 8, milk 1, flour 2, powder 1; 28c—pastry cream 8—36c for 36 cream cakes.

181—Pastry Cream.

1 cup milk—½ pint.
2 tablespoons sugar—2 ounces.
1 heaping tablespoon flour—1 ounce.
1 egg.
Butter size of a walnut.
Lemon extract to flavor.

Boil the milk with a little of the sugar in it to prevent burning. Mix the rest of the sugar and the flour together dry, dredge them into the boiling milk, beating all the while, and let cook five minutes. Throw in the butter and beat the egg a little and stir in. Put the lid on and let cook at the back of the range about ten minutes longer. Flavor when nearly cold.

Cost—8 cents.

Compote of Bananas with Rice.

Peel the bananas and cut them in two across. Make a clear syrup like pudding sauce, drop in the bananas while it is boiling, then remove from the fire, as they do not need to cook, but only scald. Stir a little sugar and butter into some cooked rice. Serve rice smoothed over in the dish, and bananas with sauce on top. Rum is the flavoring mostly used with bananas; it may be added to the sauce. A lemon cut up in it does as well.

Banana Ambrosia.

Cut up bananas and oranges in about equal proportions in a glass bowl, add grated cocoanut, powdered sugar, rock candy and wine to make a syrup, and anything else such as gum drops, almonds and crystalized fruits to make a brimming bowlful that may be desired, and mix all together. The ladies all know how to serve it.

Macaroon Ice Cream.

Use the rich kind of macaroons, known as soft macaroons; they are made like egg kisses with plenty of crushed almonds in to make them brown. Allow a pound of them to three pints of pure cream. Sweeten the cream with maraschino, chop the macaroons fine and mix them in. Freeze; put it in a brick mould, pack and freeze again.

HOTEL DINNER.

182—Puree of Bean Soup With Crusts.

The special seasonings that make this soup good are mustard, butter and minced red pepper, to be added at last. A little of the liquor from the boiling corned beef or a knuckle bone of ham will improve the flavor.

2 quarts of soup stock.

1 cupful of navy beans.

1 tablespoon of minced onion.

Butter size of an egg (optional).

1 teaspoonful of made mustard.

Parsley, salt, little minced red pepper.

Make the soup stock by boiling almost any kind of meat and marrow bones in a gallon of water, with the usual soup bunch of various vegetables in it, until the liquor is reduced nearly one-half. Then strain it and skim off the fat.

The trouble with this kind of soup of the bean puree settling to the bottom and leaving the liquid clear is caused through the beans being imperfectly cooked. Steep them in water over night and put a pinch of soda in the water they are cooked in, to help dissolve them, and when perfectly soft, mash them through a seive or gravy strainer. Have the stock boiling; pour it to the puree gradually and stir to mix; throw in the minced onion. Set on the side of the range or on bricks on the stove top, and let simmer 15 or 20 minutes. Season as already indicated. Add a spoonful of thickening along with the mustard. Sprinkle parsely over the surface. Serve with crusts.

Cost—stock 8, beans 3, seasonings 5 crusts 2; 18c for 2 quarts.

183—Crusts for Soup.

It is a common fault to make these large and unsightly. When, in addition, they are burned in the oven, they spoil any soup, however well made. Shave away the dark crust from cold rolls or slices of bread; cut the bread into neat, dice shapes of even size, and roast it in a pan in the oven to a light brown color all over. Pour from six to twelve in each soup plate before the soup.

184—Baked Whitefish.

Split the fish, after cleaning, down the back and take out the backbone. Put some good, clear drippings to get hot in a baking pan. Wipe the fish, dip it in beaten egg, then dip it in flour and then in egg again, lay it in the pan of fat and bake it carefully at moderate heat—perhaps with the oven door open—for about twenty minutes. Baste the exposed surface with the fat. Fish looks extremely rich cooked this way, yellow-brown and semi-transparent, if not allowed to get too hot while baking; yet the fat must be hissing hot when the fish is put in. Serve tomato sauce at the side. Garnish the fish with fried parsley.

Cost of material—fish 2 lbs. 25, 2 eggs 4, seasonings and frying fat 3, sauce 3; 35 cents for 8 orders or 4 to 5c per plate.

Note—Whitefish does not lose much weight in cooking, and for the above method it is best if in thin and broad pieces—it takes less raw weight for a given number than most other kinds.

185—Roast Leg of Mutton.

For plain roast leg of mutton proceed in the same manner as for roast beef. Whether the mutton shall be rare done or well done must depend upon the preferences of those it is cooked for, but in either case the method is the same and the natural gravy should flow from a well-done leg of mutton as well as one under-done, if not in such large quantity. It is best to make it a rule to always put a little salt in the pan the meat is roasted in, and water enough to cover the bottom, and if a made gravy is wanted some scraps and trimmings beside. The reason is that the gravy that oozes from these scraps, and that will escape from the meat, too, to some extent, will be found at the end of the roasting sticking to the bottom of the pan, while the grease is above it is clear it will dissolve as soon as the grease is poured off and water reaches it instead, but if there is no salt it is slow to dissolve. A spoonful of thickening will be needed in it.

Let the leg of mutton have a good brown color on the outside, even if not done through. Turn it over by lifting the projecting bone, and do not pierce the meat with a fork. From 1 hour to 2 will be required to roast it, according to size.

COST—per plate the same as roast beef.

186—Beef Heart, Stuffed and Baked

Boil the heart tender first, allowing about two or three hours, and let the water be nearly all boiled away at the finish, that the remaining liquor may be available for gravy.

When the heart has boiled long enough cut out a portion of the middle and fill the cavity with stuffing. Set the heart in a pan in the oven with the liquor it was boiled in, and salt and pepper and bake brown. Cut the piece of heart into small pieces, put them to the liquor remaining in the pan and stir up with the fragments of dressing and a spoonful of thickening, making a savory thick sauce or ragout.

COST—heart 10, stuffing 5; 15c for 8 or 10 orders, or 2c per plate.

187—Scrambled Brains in Patties.

A good way to serve brains where there is but a small quantity available.
1 set of brains or a cupful.
2 eggs.
1 ounce of butter—small egg size.
Parsley, pepper and salt.
Puff paste for 8 shells.

Simmer the brains in water, with salt and a little vinegar in it, about 20 minutes. Take out, pick them over to remove the dark portions, put them into a frying-pan with the butter, break in the eggs, and a little chopped parsley, pepper and salt, and stir all together over the fire until the eggs in it are soft cooked. Then fill patty shells made of puff paste, put on the lids and ornament with a sprig of parsley.

Scrambled brains as above also make a good breakfast dish without the patties. It is common to put the brains in the pan raw, but not a good way, for it is difficult to get them cooked through without making them too dry, and almost impossible to free them from blood discolorations.

The shells are formed in the same manner as directed for cherry tartlets, but may be oval or any other shape.

COST of material—brains 10, eggs 4, butter 2, seasonings 1, pastry 8; 25c for 8 patties or 3c per plate.

188—Rice Croquettes with Currant Jelly.

½ cup rice, raw,—or 2 cups cooked.
1½ cup water and milk.
Butter size of a guinea egg—an ounce.
1 tablespoon sugar.
2 yolks, or 1 egg.
Nutmeg.

Put the rice on to boil in a measured cupful of water, and when it is half done add ½ cupful of milk. It is an object to have the rice dry when done, and yet well cooked. Keep the steam shut in while it is cooking. When soft enough, mash it slightly with the back of a spoon, work in the other ingredients and a pinch of salt. Make it in shapes, with flour on the hands, like small biscuits, and make it hollow in the middle to hold a spoonful of jelly. Having coated the shapes well with flour, fry them in a saucepan of hot lard. They will do without breading in egg and cracker meal. Put currant jelly in the depression when dishing up.

Cost of material—rice 2, milk 1, butter 2, egg 2, sugar and flour 1, jelly 4; 12c for 8 croquettes with jelly or 1c each with only powdered sugar.

189—Lobster Salad.

Take the meat of one large lobster and cut it as near as may be in large dice shapes, or at least to uniform size, and keep the reddest pieces in a dish separate. Chop two heads of celery. Parboil two or three green leaves of celery to make them a deeper green, and chop them with the celery likewise to color the whole.

Spread a layer of the celery on a flat dish or platter, then the lobster on that with the red pieces around the edge, where they will show among the green, another layer of chopped celery on top, level over the top surface and pour and spread upon it some mayonaise dressing that is almost thin enough to run. The dressing should be sufficiently seasoned to season all the rest.

Cost of material—lobster 20, celery 5, dressing 9; 34c for from 8 to 12 dishes, or from 3 to 4c per plate.

190—Browned Sweet Potatoes.

If the potatoes are of good size pare them before cooking, split lengthwise and steam them until done. Turn them into a baking pan, sprinkle with salt, moisten with spoonfuls of fat from the roast meat pan and bake them a handsome brown. Sweet potatoes will not bake to a rich color and be really good unless they are first steamed or boiled thoroughly done. Thin and stringy potatoes can be steamed first and peeled afterward

Cost—about 1c per plate.

191—Stewed Turnips.

Pare turnips deep enough to remove the rind that contains the pungent flavor. Boil in salted water until tender—

usually about an hour—then pour away the water and add a white sauce instead, and a slight sprinkling of minced parsley for ornament.

192—Lemon Cream Pie, Rich.

2 cups milk—a pint.
4 tablespoons sugar—4 ounces.
2 heaping tablespoons flour.
Butter size of a walnut.
4 eggs—or the yolks only.
1 small lemon, or some lemon extract and cream tartar.

Mix the sugar and flour together dry and grate the rind of the lemon into them; boil the milk and stir the dry articles into it with a wire egg whisk. Add the butter and juice of the lemon and then the yolks of the eggs well beaten, but take from the fire before they cook. Line pie pans with puff paste or tart paste. Pour in the cream and bake in a slack oven. When done meringue over as directed in other cases for lemon pies and meringues, using the whites of the eggs reserved for the purpose.

Cost of material—milk 4, sugar for pies and meringue 6, butter and flour 2, eggs 9, lemon 2, crusts 5; 28c for 2 large pies, or 10 portions or 3c per plate.

193—Custard Fritters Glazed.

A sort of sliced custard, breaded and fried, very rich and very generally liked, made of

1 cup milk.
2 tablespoons sugar.
1 tablespoon corn starch.
1 heaping tablespoon flour.
2 yolks of eggs.
Butter size of a walnut.
Flavoring. Pinch of salt.

Boil the milk with the sugar in it, which prevents burning. Mix the starch and flour in a cup, with a spoonful of old milk extra, and some of that on the fire; pour it when the milk boils and let boil thick. Beat in the butter and yolks and take it off. Flavor with lemon or other extract, and let it get cold like mush, in a buttered pan. Cut in thick slices or blocks, roll in beaten egg and then in cracker meal, fry golden yellow in hot lard. Pour over the hot slices when they are served a thick, transparent sauce that will coat them without running off. It is made so by a spoonful of corn starch added to boiling syrup and allowed to simmer until bright and clear.

Cost of material—milk 2, sugar, starch and flour 3, butter 2, eggs for mixing and breading 8, flavoring extract 1, cracker meal 2, lard to fry 4, sauce 6; 28c for 8 orders or 3 to 4c per plate.

194—Roman Cream.

As it is always easier to make an article if it is known what it should be like when it is finished this may described as a dark yellow boiled custard stiffened with gelatine and whipped to a light spongy condition while cooling.

1 pint milk.
5 ounces sugar.
1 ounce gelatine—light weight.
Small piece stick cinnamon.
½ cup thick cream.
6 yolks eggs.
½ cup curacoa, or a wine substitute.

Set the milk over the side of the fire, with the sugar, cinnamon and gelatine in it, and beat often with the wire egg whisk till the gelatine is all dissolved, which will be at about the boiling point. Beat the yolks light, mix them in like making custard, allow a few moments for it to thicken but not boil, then strain into a tin pail or a freezer and set in ice water; when nearly cold whip the cream to froth and beat it in and add the curacoa or other flavoring. Where there is no cream whatever to be used for the purpose after beating up the gelatine cream quite light as it cools whip the whites of three eggs to froth and mix in by beating.

When the Roman cream has become cold enough in the ice water to be on the point of setting pour it into small individual molds if convenient, or if not dish up by spoonsful like ice cream out of the vessel it is made in. A spoonful of whipped cream poured around it like a sauce is an improvement.

Cost of material—milk 4, sugar 3, gelatine 16, cream 2, eggs 10, curacoa, rum or wine to flavor 15, ice to set 3; 53c for 1 quart or 16 individual molds, or about 4c per plate.

Note—These creams, of which there are several kinds to be made, can be produced for one-half the above cost by the use of sheet gelatine, which is cheap, and the omission of the expensive liquor.

195—Strawberry Meringue.

This is sold extensively at the fine bakeries under the name, generally, of strawberry shortcake. For the cake take

8 ounces granulated sugar—1 cup.
5 eggs.
4 ounces butter, melted—½ cup.
½ cup of milk.
12 ounces of flour—3 cups.
1 teaspoonful of baking powder.

Beat the sugar and eggs together a minute or two, and the melted butter, the milk, the powder and the flour. Bake on jelly-cake pans as thin as it can be spread, or, if preferred, on a large shallow baking pan. The cake is liable to rise in the middle and must be spread on the pan accordingly.

When done cover the top of the cake with raw strawberries and spread a thick covering of meringue on top of them. Set the cake in the oven one minute to bake a very light color on top, but the meringue paste must not be cooked through.

The meringue paste or frosting is made by beating 5 whites of eggs to a firm froth and then mixing in 4 tablespoonfuls of powdered sugar.

Cut in squares to serve.

Cost of material—cake 27, strawberries 2 quarts 50, meringue 10; 87c for 16 plates or 5½c per plate—or, according to size and the price of berries.

THE ICE CREAM SALOON.

196—Ice Cream—Best.

1 quart of good sweet cream.
10 heaping tablespoons sugar.
2 tablespoons extract vanilla.

Put the the sugar and flavor into the cream. Set the pan or tin pail containing it in ice water and whip with the wire egg-beater for about five minutes till the cream is half froth. Put it into a freezer that will hold twice as much, pack with ice and salt and freeze, and either by rapid motion of a freezer having an inside beater, or by beating the frozen cream with a paddle make it fill the freezer before leaving it. Other flavoring extracts can of course be used in place of vanilla.

Cost of material—cream 24, sugar 6, vanilla 4, twelve pounds ice 12, three pounds salt 3—49 cents for 2 quarts of ice cream or 12 plates, or 4c per plate.

197—Cost of Ice Cream.

There are but few things so uncertain as this, so much depending upon the price of ice and salt and so much more upon the method of proceeding to freeze it. We have stated a supposable average with cream at 90c per gallon, sugar at 11c per pound and ice and salt each at 1c per pound. But undoubtedly while the cream is generally considered the most costly item the real expense is the freezing mixture. Ice at the cheapest is about 50c per 100 pounds, yet it generally rules higher and ice cream often has to be made with ice at 3 dollars per hundred, and salt even of the coarsest, on account of the cost of transportation in some places runs up to an equal figure. It is necessary then to pay particular attention to the freezing process, for one person can freeze the cream as well with ten pounds of ice as another may with thirty. One will have it done and off hand within half an hour and another take all the forenoon to accomplish the same thing and may have to replenish the freezer three or four times over.

When custards are to be frozen or imitation cream made by enriching milk with eggs and starch it is obviously the best to let the boiling mixture become cold before putting it into the freezer. Still where ice is very plentiful, as in winter, some time and trouble may be saved by not going through that preparation, but the hot custard is strained direct into the freezer. In summer, however much it may be desired to make the custard cold beforehand it ought never to be made over night without special care to make it thoroughly cold at once, for otherwise it is almost sure to acquire a curious sort of fermented taste, and will even in large quantities, throw up tiny bubbles of fermentation before morning, and all the high-priced flavoring extract that can be added will not quite disguise the spoiled taste. The proper way to do is to make the custard early in the morning, strain it into a freezer or tin pail and set it in ice water or the cold brine that is left in the freezing tub from the previous day, and when made cold by occasional stirring change it into the packed freezer it is to be frozen in.

198—How to Freeze Ice Cream.

Pound the ice quite fine. It seems to take longer at the beginning but it is by far the shorter plan in the end, for the large lumps that are crowded in to save the trouble of crushing do very little good and a person may turn a freezer packed with such large pieces for three hours without accomplishing the freezing. The quickest freezing is done with a mixture of fine ice and snow and salt.

The large establishments that have the huge cog-wheeled freezers turned by steam power have ice crushers, a good deal like the rock crushers at the mines. A good and neat way on the smallest scale is to put ten pounds of ice into a burlap sack and pound it fine with a wooden maul or even with a hammer It is soon learned by practice how to do this without immediately destroying the sack.

The rough and ready way for ordinary hotel work is to throw a fifty pound block into a large box and pound it fine with the head of an axe.

Having your ice ready, place the freezer with the cream in it. Put around it in the freezing tub about four shovelfuls of ice and on top of that one spoonful of the coarsest kind of salt you can get—bay salt like that seen sometimes in the barrels of salted mackerel—then more ice and salt till the freezing tub is full, and let there be salt on top. Turn and keep the fine ice and the salt well mixed with it pressed and packed into close contact with the freezer, and in a short time, running from 20 to 30 minutes, the freezing will be complete.

There is a hole large enough to admit a cork near the top of the freezing tub. That is to let the brine run off before it rises high enough to flow over the lid of the freezer; and another an inch or two above the bottom, which is to let out the brine when it begins to raise the ice from the bottom. But the brine from the melting ice and salt should not be kept too low, but should fill up all the spaces around the freezer which the ice is not fine enough to fill. The brine in such a condition is colder than the ice itself, for salt water will not freeze until the temperature is a long way below freezing point of fresh water. This accounts for the ice cream remaining at the bottom of the freezer becoming so hard frozen after an hour or two in the brine. But there must always be ice present for the brine to act upon, consequently there must not be enough brine in the freezing tub to lift the ice from the bottom while the freezer is full.

One can never calculate the cost of ice cream without knowing whether the art of freezing it expeditiously with the least possible consumption of ice will be well understood.

In some hotels where ice cream is made every day the brine thus made of clear ice and clean salt can be utilized, put in barrels in which the cucumbers and mangoes as they are gathered daily in the garden may be dropped so keep them until they are eventually made into pickles.

199—Corn Starch Ice Cream.

---

4 cups rich milk.
10 tablespoons sugar.
2 rounded tablespoons corn starch.
3 eggs.
1 tablespoon lemon extract.

This is the best and closest imitation of real cream and is most generally in use wherever real cream cannot be obtained. But in order to give it the *beating up* quality to increase the bulk and make it light and rich eating the eggs must be used strictly as directed.

Separate the eggs and keep the whites cold. Beat the yolks with a basting-spoon of milk added in a large bowl. Boil the quart of milk with the sugar in it. Mix the starch in a cup with a little cold milk and stir it in, and when it boils again pour it to the beaten yolks in the bowl. The heat will cook them sufficiently. Then strain, cool, and freeze in a freezer that will hold twice as much.

When frozen nearly firm enough whip the whites to a froth, add them to the ice cream and work it either by rapid turning or with a wooden paddle until it fills the freezer.

Cost of material—milk 8, sugar 6, starch and flour 3, eggs 5; 22c—ice and salt 15—37c for 2 quarts of ice cream or from 12 to 16 plates, according as dished up, or 2 to 3c per plate.

Note—It is very unprofitable to serve ice cream in a half frozen state, in which condition it is as heavy as water and does not go as far. Neither is it good or profitable when allowed to stand and merely solidify or freeze itself without beating. It will seem rich and soft however hard frozen if it is beaten up, although it may be made only of milk. It pays therefore to have a good freezer and sufficient ice to complete the freezing.

200—Frozen Custard—Rich.

4 cups rich milk.
12 tablespoons sugar.
12 yolks of eggs.
Vanilla or other flavoring.

Boil the milk with half the sugar in it—which prevents burning. Beat the yolks in a large bowl with the rest of the sugar in and a half of cup of milk to make them come up frothing. Pour the boiling milk to them, then set on the fire for not more than a minute, as if too much cooked the custard will not come up light and rich in the freezer.
Strain, flavor and freeze.

Cost of material—milk 8, sugar 7, flavor 2, yolks 15; 32—ice and salt 15—47 cents for something less than 2 quarts. About the same cost as pure cream, or 4c per plate.

201—New York Ice Cream.

Known as Delmonico's ice cream, but most people are averse to printing it so in every hotel bill of fare. Nearly the same as the foregoing with gelatine added to produce extreme lightness.
3 cups good milk.
1 cup sweet cream.
10 yolks of eggs.
A vanilla bean.
10 tablespoons sugar.
¼ package gelatine or less than ½ ounce.

Set the milk on to boil with the sugar, gelatine and vanilla bean (or part of one) in it. The kettle should be set at the side of the range where the milk will heat up gradually giving the gelatine time to dissolve, with frequent stirring from the bottom. The sheet gelatine can be used but is liable to curdle the milk if allowed to boil in it, which the package kind does not.

Add a little milk to the yolks in a large bowl to make them capable of being beaten up light. Whip them light as sponge cake. Pour the boiling milk to them and strain into the freezer. Wipe the vanilla bean and put away to be used the same way again. When the custard has become cold and begun to freeze whip the cup of cream to froth, stir it in and finish the freezing as usual, working the ice cream until it is twice its original bulk.

Cost of material—milk and cream 12, sugar 6, gelatine 5, vanilla 5, yolks 12; 40 cents—ice and salt 15—55c for over 2 quarts or, according to the way of dishing up, from 12 to 16 plates or 4c per plate.

Note—The genteel way of serving ice creams in small individual shapes has in it also the purpose of serving as a measure of quantity. Where there is an abundance of good things served and the ice cream is only one among many it may be quite sufficient to make twenty-four dishes of two quarts of ice cream, while on the other hand in a saloon the size of the dish is an object with the customer. There are ice cream ladles made that form the cream in conical and dome shapes to go in the saucers, and these can be had of different measures to suit the particular case.

202—Corn-Starch Ice Cream Without Eggs.

The former corn-starch cream has the cream color; this is pure white and while it answers to make at times when neither eggs nor cream can be obtained it is also valuable for fancy ices where different colors are required, and besides serving for the perfectly white it takes a handsomer red color from strawberry syrup or other coloring than a yellow cream or custard will.
4 cups milk.
12 tablespoons sugar.
½ ounce butter.
2 rounded tablespoons corn starch.

Flavoring.

Boil the milk with the sugar in it. Mix the starch in a cup with a little cold milk and stir it in while the milk is boiling. Take it from the fire and throw in the small lump of butter and beat till it is dissolved. The butter is not so much for flavor as to make the starch cream white, opaque and smooth and not semi-transparent like milk as it would be without that addition.

Strain, cool, and flavor and freeze as usual.

This kind will not rise and increase in bulk much in the freezer as it is, but if 2 whites of eggs can be had whip them light and stir in when the cream is nearly frozen and it will make a difference in the quantity provided rapid turning or beating is resorted to.

COST of material—milk 8, sugar 7, butter 1, starch and flavoring 2;—18 cents—ice and salt 15—33 cents for about 3 pints or 12 plates, or 3c per plate.

NOTE.—As a rule the richer a cream may be the more ice and salt it takes to freeze it, and the less sugar in the cream the sooner it will become solid. The plain cream of the foregoing receipt will freeze in half the time that may be required for a rich yellow custard.

203—Chocolate Ice Cream.

It is never very good when made with any kind of custard or imitation cream and ought to be made only when real cream is to be had.

4 cups cream.
1 ounce common chocolate.
1 heaping cup sugar.
1 tablespoon vanilla.

Chocolate cream is generally too strongly flavored for the majority. The imported sweet kinds are made of half sugar and more of such chocolate can of course be used, but the common unsweet-ened is the kind generally furnished.

The ounces are marked on the cakes. Otherwise use a half cup dry grated.

Boil a little milk with some sugar in it, put in the grated chocolate and beat up over the fire until it is melted then strain it into the freezer, put in the cream and sugar, freeze and beat up well to make it a rich bright color.

The chocolate can also be mixed in the cream by only melting it in a saucepan set in a rather warm place, with nothing added, but it does not do to pour it into the cold cream without previously dilut-ing it with a little thoroughly beaten in

---

COST—Same as best ice cream.

204—Ordinary Frozen Custard.

---

1 quart of milk.
3 eggs.
1 small cup sugar.
½ a peach tree leaf for flavor.

Boil half the milk with the peach leaf and the sugar in it; beat the eggs in a bowl, pour some boiling milk to them, set on the fire again and in one minute, or as soon as it shows signs of boiling up again take it off and add the cold milk to stop the cooking. Strain into the freezer, flavor and freeze.

NOTE—There is a point in cooking custards when they are at the richest and that is exactly at the boiling point. The custard is then creamy and as thick as it will ever be. A few seconds more of the fire may spoil it or at least make it thin and full of grains of curd. This is a great point to know in making all such sauces and soups as are thickened with eggs as well as sweet custards. A pint or two may thicken almost as soon as it touches the fire but a gallon may require several minutes.

The ordinary custard made as above being less trouble to prepare than the one thickened in part with starch is oftenest made where no particular interest is felt in the quality of the cooking, and earns abuse often bestowed upon hotel ice cream, nevertheless if half cream or even a quarter can be had and the custard is carefully cooked it may prove to be equal to that made with all pure cream.

205—Bisque Ice Creams.

Ice creams with a proportion of the pulp of pounded fruit or nuts added are termed bisques.

206—Bisque of Pineapple Ice Cream.

1 can pineapple or ¾ pound.
2 cups sugar.
4 cups cream.
Chop the pineapple small and put it in a bright pan or kettle with the sugar and a few spoonfuls of juice or water to dissolve the sugar to syrup. Simmer at the side of the range a short time.

Whip the cream till it is half froth, then freeze it first by itself, because the pineapple added before freexing has a tendency to curdle it. Pound the pineapple and syrup through a colander, mix it with the partly frozen cream, and freeze again.

It can and ought to be managed to have the pineapple in syrup prepared beforehand to be cold. In making these bisques it is not best to pound the fruit perfectly fine but the small pieces about like grains of wheat should be perceptible and show that the creams are mixed with fruits and not merely flavored.

Cost of material—pineapple 20, sugar 10, cream 24; 54 cents—ice and salt 20—74 cents for 2 quarts or about 6c per plate.

207—Bisque of Preserved Ginger.

½ pound of either preserved or candied ginger.
1 cup sugar.
Juice of 1 lemon.
4 cups cream.
Cut the candied ginger into very small pieces. Make a hot syrup of the sugar with a few spoonfuls of water and squeeze the lemon into it, then put in the ginger and let it soften and impart the flavor to the syrup. Put the cream and ginger and syrup all together, freeze and beat up.

Cost of material—ginger 30, sugar 6, lemon 2, cream 24; 62 cents—ice and salt 20—82c for 2 quarts or 12 plates or 7c per plate.

208—Italian Bisque Ice Cream.

1 cup sugar.
2 cups milk.
2 cups cream.
8 or 10 lady-fingers (pairs).
3 yolks of eggs.
¼ cup madeira.
Boil the milk with the sugar in it, crumble in the lady fingers, add the yolks and stir over the fire a minute. Put it into the freezer with the wine and cream, freeze, and beat up.

Cost of material—milk and cream 16, sugar 6, cakes 5, eggs 4, wine 10· 41 cents—ice and salt 20—61c for 2 quarts or 12 plates or 5c per plate.

209—Bisque of Almonds.

¾ pound almonds.
4 cups cream.
1 heaping cup sugar.
Scald the almonds and take off the skins. Pound them a few at a time in a mortar with a little sugar and teaspoonful of water. They need not be a perfectly smooth paste, for the reason stated under the head of bisque of pineapple, but when all are pounded mix them with the cream and sugar and pass it through a coarse strainer into the freezer. Freeze and beat up as usual. This is perfectly white.

Cost of material—almonds 30, cream 24, sugar 8; 62 cents—ice and salt 15— 77c for 2 quarts or 12 plates or 6 or 7c per plate.

210 — Brown Bisque of Hickory Nuts.

¾ pound of hickory nut kernels.
1 heaping cup sugar
4 cups cream.
Pick over the kernels to free them

from fragments of shell, and pound them like almonds in a mortar with a little sugar and a few drops of water added. Only a few can be effectually pounded at a time. They should be like meal, to go through a coarse strainer. In order to make the cream about the color of light coffee and cream and to give it a good flavor put two tablespoons sugar in a very small saucepan without water and melt it over the fire and let it burn to the color of molasses, then add a little water let it boil up and dissolve. Put the cream into the freezer, strain in the caramel and pounded nuts and freeze.

Cost—6 or 7c per plate.

211—Fruit Ice Creams.

These have the fruit mixed with the cream either whole or in large pieces.

There is one rule to be observed all through, and that is to add the fruit late, when the cream is already frozen and it is nearly time to serve it, for the reason that fresh fruit freezes easily and some kinds become as hard as rocks and tasteless and useless. The exceptions are the very sweet fruits which will not freeze solid at all, and those made very sweet like pineapple stewed in syrup.

212—White Cherry Ice Cream.

4 cups cream.
2 cups sugar.
5 cups California white wax cherrie
½ cup water.
Make a boiling syrup of the sugar and water, drop in the cherries and let them simmer in it about 15 minutes, without stirring or breaking. Then strain the flavored syrup into the freezer and set the fruit on ice, to be mixed in at last. Add the quart of cream to the syrup in the freezer, freeze and beat up well, then stir in the cherries and pack down with more ice and salt.

Cost of material—cream 24, cherries 24, sugar 10; 58 cents—ice and salt 20—68c for 2 quarts—about 6c per plate

213—Red Cherry Ice Cream.

4 cups cream.
2 cups sugar.
5 cups red cherries.
½ cup water.
Use only the light red cherries for this purpose, for the dark kinds make an unpleasant color.

Boil the water and sugar together and drop the cherries in. Let simmer at the side of the range a few minutes without stirring or breaking them. Then strain the syrup into the freezer and set the fruit on ice to be mixed in at last. Add the quart of cream to the syrup in the freezer, freeze and beat up well, then add the cherries and cover down till wanted.

214—Pineapple Fruit Ice Cream.

1 can pineapple, or a pound.
2 cups sugar.
4 cups cream.
½ cup water
Cut the pineapple in small dice. Make a boiling syrup of the sugar and water, stew the pineapple in it, then strain the flavored syrup into the freezer and set the fruit on ice to become cold. Add the cream to the syrup, freeze and beat up and stir in the prepared pineapple at last.

Cost—pineapple 20, sugar 10, cream 24, ice and salt 20; 74 cents or 7c per plate.

215—White Grape Ice Cream.

Make the same as directed for white cherries.

216—Strawberry Fruit Ice Cream.

1 quart strawberries—red, ripe and sweet.
2 cups sugar.
4 cups cream.
½ cup water.
The fruit need not be cooked as in the case of the preceding kinds, cover the strawberries with the sugar and let them remain some time to form a thick red syrup.

Pick out half of them to be added after the freezing, and rub the remaining half with their syrup through a strainer into the freezer. Add the cream, freeze and beat up and at last stir in the whole strawberries.

Cost—About the same as the other fruit ice creams, varying with the price of fresh fruit.

217--Peach Fruit Ice Cream.

4 cups of peeled and cut peaches.
4 cups cream.
2 cups sugar.
Peach extract to flavor.
Make a peach-flavored ice cream. Mix some of the sugar with the cut peaches and mix them in after the cream is frozen.

218—Ice Cream With Strawberries.

Make any kind of plain ice cream or frozen custard according to directions already given and dish up a spoonful of berries on top in the saucer. Ice cream with rasberries or cut peaches the same way.

219—Frozen Puddings.

Sometimes called ice puddings. Some are as cheap as the commonest ice cream, others are quite expensive. They make a welcome variation either to serve alone like ice cream or for two kinds together.

220—Frozen Cocoanut Pudding.

4 cups milk.
1 cup sugar.
4 yolks of eggs.
½ pound of grated cocoanut.
Make the custard as usual and stir in the cocoanut while it is still warm after straining. Freeze and beat as usual. A little lemon or orange flavoring can be added.
The ordinary ice cream or starch custard can be used the same way as well.

Cost of material—25c per quart or 8 plates or 3c per plate.

221—Frozen Tapioca Pudding.

3 cups milk.
6 tablespoons sugar— 5 oz.
2 tablespoons pearl tapioca.
Butter size of a walnut.
2 eggs.
½ cup cream to whip in at last.
Flavoring.
The pearl Tapioca is the most suitable. If the large grained sort is used crush it on the table with the rolling-pin and then sift away the dust.
Steep the tapioca 2 hours in a cup of milk cold, but set in a warm place. Boil the rest of the milk with the sugar in it, then add the steeped tapioca, cook for 15 minutes. Stir in the butter, then the eggs, and take the custard immediately off the fire, cool, flavor with vanilla or lemon, and freeze like ice cream, and when nearly finished add the ½ cup of cream whipped to a froth, and beat well.

Cost of material—milk 6, sugar 3, tapioca and flavoring 3, eggs 4, butter and cream 4; 20 cents—ice and salt 15— 35c for 3 pints or 8 to 12 plates, or 3 to 4c per plate,

222—Frozen Rice Pudding.

3 cups milk.
2 tablespoons rice.
6 tablespoons sugar.
6 yolks of eggs.
½ cup of cream.
Piece of stick cinnamon.
Wash the rice; put it in the milk and the sugar likewise, and an inch length of stick of cinnamon, and let simmer slowly at the side of the range until the grains are tender—about ½ hour. Beat the yolks with a spoonful of milk, pour some of the boiling rice-milk to them, then set all over the fire again about a minute to nearly boil. Take out the cinnamon. Cool, freeze, add the cream whipped, and finish freezing.

Cost—same as tapioca pudding preceding.

Note.—These as well as all other custards and puddings are richer both in taste and color when made with the yolks of eggs than with whole eggs, and when there is no cream to be had the whites whipped to froth may be added instead just before the freezing is finished. This addition not only increases the volume but gives the frozen custard a soft and creamy taste.

223—Frozen Sago Pudding.

3 cups milk.
6 tablespoons sugar.
2 tablespoons best white sago.
Butter size of a walnut.
2 eggs—or 3 yolks.
½ cup cream to whip in.
Flavoring.

Put on the milk with the sugar and sago in it, stir from the bottom once or twice lest the sago stick at the first heating, and let simmer until the grains are transparent—about 20 minutes. Then add the beaten eggs and the butter, cool, flavor and freeze and beat in the whipped cream.

Cost—same as tapioca and rice puddings.

Note.—The reason for using butter in these preparations of starch, tapiaco and sago is to whiten them. Without it they have more or less of a bluish, semi-transparent appearance that is not rich, but the addition of butter well beaten in makes the fluid portion white as milk and leaves the grains distinct to show up the compound for what it is. This is especially useful to know when eggs are dear and scarce and large quantities of these puddings are needed for hotel use.

224—Frozen Apple Pudding.

Freeze the following compote of apples in one freezer and either of the three or four kinds or frozen pudding of the foregoing receipts in another, and dish up a half portion in the saucer with the spoonful of apple ice in the centre.

2 or 3 ripe, mellow apples.
6 tablespoons sugar.
1½ cups water.
½ a lemon.

Put on the sugar and ½ cup water to boil, and pare and cut the apples in small pieces of even size. Put into the boiling syrup a piece of the lemon rind shaved off thin and more or less of the lemon juice, and then stew the pieces of apple in it, taking them out before they get too well done. Set the pieces on ice. Add the remaining cup of water to the syrup, strain and freeze—it makes a whitish sort of ice—and add the apples to it at last and cover down with more ice and salt to finish the freezing.

Cost—About the same per quart as the rice pudding.

225—Frozen Nesselrode Pudding.

Glace Nesselrode or iced pudding. A frozen custard made of pounded chestnuts, with fruit and flavorings:

1 pound of large chestnuts—about 40.
1 pint of rich boiled custard.
1 cup sweet cream.
2 ounces citron.
2 ounces sultana raisins.
2 ounces stewed pineapple.
½ cupful of maraschino.
1 teaspoon vanilla extract.
Pinch of salt in the chestnut pulp.

Slit the shells of the chestnuts, boil them half an hour, peel clean, and pound the nuts to a paste, and rub it through a coarse sieve, moistening with cream. Then mix it with the boiled custard. Freeze this mixture, and when firm whip the cup of cream, and stir it in and freeze again. Then add the citron cut in shreds, the stewed or candied pineapple, likewise the raisins, maraschino, and vanilla extract. Beat up and freeze again, and either serve in ice cream plates out of the freezer, or pack the cream in a mold, and when well frozen send to table whole, turned out of the mold on to a folded napkin on a dish.

COST of material—chestnuts 20, custard (2 cups milk, 4 yolks, 4 tablespoons sugar) 13, cream 6, raisins 3, citron 5, pineapple 3, maraschino 20, vanilla, 2; 72 cents—ice and salt 23—95c for 1½ quarts.

NOTE.—The foregoing makes about enough to fill one of those brick molds that have a large and deep stamped fruit pattern in the lid and when frozen firm it can be sliced into from 12 to 16 portions. If dished up by spoonfuls out of the freezer and made a little less heavy with fruit it is practicable to make 2 quarts of the same material. When chestnuts are not convenient some of the large cafes use the ready prepared pounded almonds or walnuts that may be bought by the can at the confectioners' supply stores, and various additions or substitutions of green candied fruits are employed to make a handsome appearing compound without changing its general character.

226—Tutti Frutti.

2 cups milk.
6 tablespoons sugar.
4 yolks eggs.
¼ cup curacoa.
½ cup thick cream.
1 pound of French candied fruits of different colors—or else use a mixture of cut figs, sultana raisins, dates and green candied citron and blanched almonds.

Put a spoonful of sugar in the smallest saucepan and burn it to caramel—not too dark—and add a little water to dissolve it. Make a yellow boiled custard of the milk, sugar and yolks, color it with the caramel, add the curacoa for flavor, strain, add the whipped cream when cold and freeze and beat up. Cut the fruits to the size of cranberries, mix them in and cover down the freezer with a fresh relay of ice and salt. May be

served by spoonfuls out of the freezer or packed in a brick mold, turned out and sliced.

COST of material—The same as Nesselrode, or about 60c per quart, depending somewhat upon the cost of the candied fruit and curacoa or their substitutes.

227—Neapolitan Ice Cream or Occhi Pocchi.

Make 3 colors of ice cream or 2 creams and 1 water ice in different freezers, and when they are frozen medium hard place them in layers as even as possible in a brick shaped neapolitan mould. Let the first layer, about an inch deep be of rich yellow frozen custard made with yolks of eggs and milk as already elsewhere directed; having smoothed that over spread another layer an inch deep of pink strawberry ice cream or red cherry water ice or other red kind, and on that spread another layer of white ice cream, either pure cream frozen or a corn starch cream made without yolks of eggs, or else a white orange or lemon ice. Three colors of cream are to be chosen, however, in preference to any water ice when they can be had, because they freeze of even density. A chocolate or caramel cream will answer instead of red.

228—Neapolitan Molds and How to Manage Them.

Properly made molds have a bottom lid as well as top. They can be bought at the furnishing stores. The large establishments, however, find it less trouble to use plain tin boxes almost identical in size and shape with the common wooden cigar boxes. They have a tight fitting top lid, and before being filled are lined with manilla paper, by means of which the brick of ice cream after being firmly frozen can easily be withdrawn It is an advantage to use a paper lining in whichever kind of mold may be employed. Where ice is plentiful, when the freezers have been emptied into the molds these may be placed in the same freezers, well covered down and allowed to remain there two or three hours to become firm. If there is the least risk of the inside not being cold enough, however, immerse the molds in a tub of pounded ice and salt by themselves. Before doing so the joints of the lids should be closed, if not made tight enough with paper, by brushing with melted butter to fill up the spaces where salt might get in.

When the molds have remained in the freezing mixture 2 or 3 hours wash off the outside, take out the shape of cream and wrap it in dry manilla paper and put it back in the freezer, well packed, to remain until it is to be sliced and served.

All kinds of ice creams and frozen puddings in single colros are thus frozen in bricks and served in slices. When to be served at a party table whole the stamped ornamental lid may have the fruit or flower form filled with a colored ice that will show in relief upon the plain form. These forms are served upon a folded napkin in a dish, in some cases, but are better placed in a silver dish having a drainer bottom on the plan of a butter dish.

Among the labor-saving expedients to secure the ornamental tri-colored brick of cream without making different kinds the principal is the employment of the prepared vegetable colors, to be obtained of the manufacturers of flavoring extracts, by which one large freezer of ice cream may be made to take as many different hues as may be desired.

Cost of molded creams—This is quite out of proportion to the cost of ingredients. The extra time and labor and consumption of ice probably will be found to double the expense.

229—Sherbets

Sherbets are water ices with either calf'sfoot jelly or gelatine or white of eggs, or dissolved gum added to make them smooth and capable of being beaten to a light and foamy condition. We give examples only of the use of white of eggs, it being the simplest and most generally available, A remainder of table jelly of the kind usually made for hotel dessert can be used in the same way.

230—Lemon Sherbet.

2 lemons.
1½ cups sugar—12 oz.
3 cups water.
2 whites of eggs.

Grate the rinds of the lemons into a bowl and squeeze in the juice. Make a boiling syrup of the sugar and half the water and pour it hot to the lemon zest and juice and let remain so till cold. Then add the rest of the water, strain the lemonade into a freezer, freeze as usual, and at last add the whites whipped to a firm froth, beat and freeze again The scalding draws the flavor of the lemon; it should never, however, be boiled and fewer lemons should be used when they are large. The sherbet is perfectly white.

Cost—lemons 5, sugar 7, whites of eggs 3; 15c—ice and salt 15—30 cents for 3 pints (if thoroughly frozen and beaten) or 12 plates; or 2 or 3 cents each.

231—Orange Sherbet.

2 or 3 oranges—according to size.
3 cups water.
1 large cup sugar.
1 lemon—juice only.
2 whites of eggs.

Grate the yellow rind of one or two of the oranges into a bowl, squeeze in the juice of all, without the seeds, and the juice of half the lemon. Make a boiling syrup of the sugar and half the water and pour it to the grated rind in the bowl. Let remain until cold. Strain it into the freezer, add the rest of the water, freeze, add the whipped whites, beat up and finish freezing.

This sherbet is cream white tinged with the orange zest and juice.

Cost—same as lemon sherbet.

232—White Cherry Sherbet.

4 cups white cherries without stems.
1½ cups sugar.
2 cups water.
2 whites of eggs.

Mash the fruit raw and thoroughly so as to break the stones, and strain the juice through a fine strainer into the freezer. Boil the cherry pulp with some of the sugar and water to extract the flavor from the kernels, and mash that also through the strainer, add the other pint of water and the sugar and freeze. Then add the whipped whites and finish freezing. This sherbet is not distinguishable from cream as long as it remains frozen. It is a good plan to drop in a few whole cherries that have been simmered in syrup, to show what kind of ice it is. Canned cherries are good enough.

Cost of material—cherries 25, sugar 7, white of eggs 3; 35 cents—ice and salt 15—40c for 3 pints, or 3 to 4c per plate or glass.

233—Grape Sherbet.

Only the kinds of grapes that yield a colorless juice can be used this way. The others turn to a very bad color.

5 cups sweet muscat grapes.
1 cup angelica or other sweet wine.
1 cup water.
1 cup sugar.
1 lemon—juice only.
2 whites of eggs.

Stew the grapes with the sugar and water, then rub them through a strainer into the freezer, with the lemon juice and syrup, and add the wine and freeze. When nearly finished put in the whipped whites beat up and finish the freezing. Some ripe grapes of any kind, not cooked, may be dropped into this sherbet as suggested for white cherries.

Cost—According to locality and cost of grapes and wine—average 5c per plate.

234—Pineapple Sherbet.

1 can of pineapple—or ½ of a pineapple.
1 cup sugar.
2 cups water.
2 whites of eggs.

Make a boiling syrup of the sugar, the pineapple juice and part of the water. Chop the fruit, simmer it a few minutes in the syrup then mash through a strainer into the freezer, using the remainder of the water to help it through. Freeze, add the whites whipped and beat up and finish freezing.

Note.—The canned pineapple is generally riper and sweeter than the fresh fruit that is sent to Northern markets. When the latter is used it should be cut up, have hot syrup poured over and allowed to steep till cold. Two cans contain about 1½ pounds of pineapple. The juice of a lemon is sometimes added to a pineapple ice when the fruit is very sweet.

Cost of material—about the same as cherry sherbet, or 25 to 30c per quart or 4c per plate.

235—Peach Sherbet.

3 cups of sliced mellow peaches.
1 large cup sugar.
2 cups water.
The kernels of half the peaches, or ½ a peach leaf.
2 whites of eggs.

Make boiling syrup of the sugar and water stew the peach kernels and put in it a few minutes to extract the flavor, pass through a strainer into the freezer, freeze, add the whites and freeze again.

Cost—Same as lemon sherbet, 2 to 3c per plate.

236—Water Ices.

The same as the sherbets with the white of eggs or gelatine left out, except that as a rule they cannot be well made with cooked or scalded fruit as sherbets can, but should have the expressed juice of the raw fruit mixed with water and sugar. Some kinds of fruit, especially cherries, grapes and peaches have the gummy property that causes them to become light and white in the freezer if beaten much, precisely as if eggs or jelly had been added; consequently when water ices are desired to serve almost as beverages at evening parties they are better frozen in an old fashioned freezer, scraped down from the sides with a palette knife and not beaten too much.

237--Strawberry Water Ice.

1 quart strawberries.
2 cups sugar.
3 cups water.

Cover the strawberries with the sugar and let them remain some time to form a thick red syrup. Pick out a few of the berries to be mixed in the ice at last. Rub the rest through a strainer into the freezer with the syrup and add the water. Freeze without much beating if a crimson ice is wanted, and add coloring if necessary. Throw the reserved berries on top of the strawberry ice in the freezer and mix them in when the ice is to be served.

COST of material—strawberries 25, sugar 10, ice and salt 15; 50c for 3 pints or from 8 to 16 plates or glasses, or 3 or 4 cents each.

238—Lemon Water Ice.

The same as lemon sherbet without the white of eggs. A good strong lemonade made in the common way answers as well to freeze; the difference is that it takes three times as many lemons as by the other method of scalding the grated rind to draw the flavor.

239—Raspberry Water Ice.

3 cups raspberries.
1½ cups sugar.
2 cups water.

Mash the berries and sugar together and rub them through a strainer into the freezer using the water to help when the pulp is dry. Freeze without much beating.

COST—same as strawberry water ice. Three pints.

240—Pineapple Water Ice.

Scald the the sliced fruit in syrup as in making pineapple sherbet and force a portion of it through a strainer that will not let the fibrous part pass through. It is the same as the sherbet without the white of eggs, but will not make so much in bulk.

241—Orange Water Ice.

Same as orange sherbet without the white of eggs.

242—Cherry Water Ice.

4 cups sweet red or black cherries.
2 cups water.
1½ cups sugar.

Mash the fruit raw and thoroughly so as to break the stones, and strain the juice through a fine strainer into the freezer. Boil the cherry pulp with some of the sugar and water to extract the flavor from the kernels, and mash that also through the strainer, add the other pint of water and the sugar and freeze. Beat the ice only enough to make it even and smooth.

COST of material—cherries 20, sugar 8, ice and salt 15; 43 cents for 3 pints or 12 glasses or 3 to 4c each.

243—Peach Water Ice.

Is best made with soft, raw yellow peaches. Use the same proportions as for sherbet; rub the pulp through a strainer with most of the sugar mashed with it, and make a syrup of the rest and stew the peach kernels or half a peach leaf in it for more flavor. Same as peach sherbet without the white of eggs.

244—Grape Water Ice.

Any kind or color of grapes can be made into water ices if not cooked. Canned grapes will not do. Proceed as for raspberry water ice. Use no white of eggs.

245—Frozen unch es.

These are sherbets and water ices with spiritous liquors added and are of two classes. They are (according to the French usage) Roman punches when they are beaten up with meringue or white of eggs like the sherbets of the preceding receipts, and plain iced punches when not so whitened and are in a semi-transparent condition.

Some of these punches cannot be frozen quite solid and must be served in glasses in a half fluid condition as beverages, on account of the spirit and sugar they contain and all of them take more ice and salt to freeze them than any mixture without liquors. The stronger they are made the harder they are to freeze.

246—Roman Punch.

1 pint water—2 cups.
10 ounces sugar—1½ cups.
1 lemon—juice and rind.
1 orange—juice only.
2 whites of eggs.
Few spoonfuls of rum or chablis.

Dissolve the sugar in the water, hot; grate the rind of the lemon—the yellow part only—into a bowl, and squeeze in the juice and that of the orange and pour the hot syrup to them. Let stand awhile, then strain into a freezer. Freeze, and when nearly finished whip the two whites and stir them in and beat up well. Add the rum, or the mixture of rum and wine, or the wine substitute for rum, at last. Serve in glasses.

Cost of material— sugar 7, lemon and orange 4, white of eggs 3, rum ¼ cupful 6; 20 cents—ice and salt 15—35c for 1 quart or 8 to 12 glasses according to size.

NOTE—Those who aim at making these punches as smooth and delicate as possible will put the 2 whites in a bowl and whip them in a cold place to a firm froth, then add two tablespoons of powdered sugar and beat them together about one minute, making a smooth cake icing, and stir it into the punch when it is first frozen instead of the whipped whites without sugar. The difference is not very marked and those who are in haste will not care to stop to make the icing, still others insist upon its superiority.

247—Kirsch Punch Romaine.

2 cups water.
1½ cups sugar.
1 lemon—juice only.
⅓ cup kirschwasser—small.
2 whites of eggs.
Mix the punch materials together cold, strain into the freezer. When nearly frozen whip the 2 whites firm, mix in and freeze again.

Cost of material—sugar 7, lemon 2, eggs 3, kirschwasser 20; 32 cents—ice and salt 18—50c for 1 quart or 4 to 6c per glass according to size.

248—Maraschino Punch—Romaine.

2 cups water
1 cup sugar.
½ a lemon—juice only.
½ an orange—juice only.
⅓ cup of maraschino—large.
2 whites of eggs.
Mix all, except the whites, together cold, strain into a freezer, freeze as usual, whip the whites firm and stir in and beat up well and freeze again. It is a snow-white ice, rich and tenacious like pulled candy, The fruit juices are not essential, but an improvement.

Cost of material—sugar 5, lemon and orange 4, eggs 3, maraschino 25, 37 cents—ice and salt 15—52c for 1 quart, or 6c each person.

249—Strawberry Punch.

3 cups ripe red strawberries.
1½ cups sugar.
1½ cups water.
½ cup angelica or any sweet wine.
Cover the strawberries with the sugar
and let remain some time to form a thick
red syrup. Rub them through a strainer
into the freezer with the syrup and add
the water and wine and freeze without
any extra beating.

Cost of material—strawberries 18,
sugar 7, wine 12; 37 cents—ice and salt
18—55c for something over a quart, or
about 5c per glass.

Note—In counting the cost observe
that the addition of white of eggs or
meringue increases the bulk of the material in the freezer according to the degree to which it is beaten and a punch
a la Romaine heaped in a glass like ice
cream may cost less each person than a
punch plain frozen of much less volume.

250—Raspberry Punch.

Make the same as strawberry punch.
Stronger wines can be used in it.

251—Regent's Punch.

½ cup gin.
½ a lemon.
½ cup sugar.
½ cup maraschino—or half as much
kirchwasser.
1 cup water.
1 bottle soda water (aerated lemon
mineral water or "soda pop")
Grate the rind of ½ a lemon into a
bowl, pour in a spoonful of gin and rub
with the back of a spoon to extract the
flavor. Add the lemon juice and rest of
the ingredients except the soda; strain
into the freezer and freeze as firm as the
spirit in it will allow, add the soda—
which should be ice cold—and finish the
freezing.

Cost of material—gin 12, lemon 2,
sugar 3, maraschino 20, soda 10; 47
cents—ice and salt 18—65c for 1 quart or
6 to 8c per glass.

252—Victoria Punch.

2 oranges.
4 lemons.
2 cups sugar.
2 cups water.
½ cup angelica or other sweet wine.
¼ cup rum.
2 whites of eggs.
Grate the rinds of 2 of the lemons into
a bowl, add the rum and rub with the
back of a spoon to draw the flavor.
Squeeze in the juice of all the fruit, add
the other ingredients and freeze. Then
whip the whites, stir in and beat up.

Cost of material—oranges and lemons 14, sugar 10, wine 10, rum 6, eggs
3; 43 cents—ice and salt 17—60c for
over a quart about 6c per glass.

253—Imperial Punch.

1 cup sugar.
1½ cups water.
½ can pineapple, or 6 oz fresh.
1 orange.
1 lemon.
½ a nutmeg.
3 whites of eggs.
2 tablespoons each of maraschino, no-
yeau, kirschwasser and curacoa.
½ cup of champagne.
Make a hot syrup of the sugar and
water with the nutmeg broken in it.
Grate the rinds of both lemons and one
orange into a bowl. Grate or mash the
pineapple and put in and pour the hot
syrup upon them. Squeeze in the juice of
the fruit and let stand till cold. Strain
and freeze, then put in the liquors and
after freezing again add the whipped
whites.

Cost of material—about a dollar a
quart.

254—Cardinal Punch.

2 cups port or other red wine.
1 cup water.
1 cup sugar.
1 orange.
12 cloves.
1 cup wine jelly (calfs foot or gelatine).
Bake the orange light brown on a plate in the oven. Make a boiling syrup of the sugar and water with the cloves in it, drop the baked orange into it, add the wine and let remain until cold. Then cut the orange and press it for the juice and strain the punch into the freezer. Add the jelly and freeze. If in the season add red strawberry or raspberry juice to heighten the color.

Cost of material—wine 40, sugar 5, orange 3, jelly 15, 63 cents—ice and salt 20—83c for over a quart or about 7c a glass.

255—Champagne Punch.

1 cup sugar.
½ cup water.
1 bottle champagne.
2 whites of eggs.
Dissolve the sugar to syrup with the water, pour it and the champagne into the freezer. When frozen add the whites whipped up with sugar until like cake icing, and finish the freezing. Serve in glasses.

Cost—The price of the champagne, and freezing mixture added—probably 25c a glass.

256—Fine Bakery Lunch

There are some large establishments in the cities doing an immense business in serving lunches of breads, rolls, coffee-cakes, pies, pastries and cakes with coffee, tea, and milk and no meats beyond a small reserve of ham sandwiches. The lunches of this description are cheap but where the goods are fresh made and of the highest possible excellence and the surroundings clean the extraordinary numbers of customers that avail themselves of it make the business one of great importance. Bread in every form is very cheap diet and cheapest of all when raised with yeast. The dough once made, a very considerable number of different articles such as raised cakes can be made from it easily. The first requisite is good yeast and as the compressed article is not everywhere to be obtained, it often becomes necessary for the baker to make his own, both stock and ferment.

257—Stock Yeast.

Boil a handful of hops in a quart of water about 30 minutes, strain the liquor and put it into a quart bottle. Let the bottle be only two-thirds full. When cool put in a handful of sugar and a handful of ground malt. Cork and tie it down. Set the bottle in a moderately warm corner and let remain about 48 hours. Then boil ½ pound of hops in a gallon of water. Put 4 cups flour in a pan, pour the boiling hop-water through a strainer on to it and mash to a sort of thin paste. When cool add 2 heaping cups of ground malt and 1 of sugar then draw the cork of the bottle, mix in the contents set the stock away in a jar to ferment and in two days it will be ready for use. Strain it into a jug and keep it cold. It will keep good to start ferment with for a month or more.

258—Common Yeast or Ferment.

Stock yeast is not used to make bread with but to start ferment or common yeast such as the bakers sell in most towns.
Take about 24 potatoes.
2 pounds of flour.
4 ounces sugar.
1 quart stock yeast.
Wash the potatoes thoroughly, using a brush for the purpose, and boil them in a kettle of water. When done pour off what remains of the dark water and fill up again with fresh. When that boils turn out potatoes and boiling water on to

the flour in a large pan and mash all to a smooth paste. Throw in the sugar. Thin down with ice water till like thick cream. Set the large colander over your 6-gallon stone jar (just fresh scalded out) and strain the yeast into it. When it is no more than about milk warm mix the stock or other yeast to start it. Let stand in a moderately warm place, undisturbed, for from 12 to 24 hours--according to weather, activity, and need of using. It will then be ready for use, and should be kept cold.

Cost of material—potatoes 4, flour 6, sugar 3, stock yeast or yeast cakes to start with 10; 23 cents for 4 gallons.

Note—The dry hop yeast cakes answer very well to start the ferment above described if used plentifully—a whole package for 3 or 4 gallons—but are not equal to stock in making articles good and profitable to sell. Yeast also is sold and is a source of profit where the demand is such that not much is left to throw away, for ferment will not keep long. The most of the cost is in the labor of making it.

259—Common Bread Dough.

As a rule one-fourth yeast to three-fourths water.

The good potato yeast with no germs of sourness in it, such as we have already directed how to make, does no harm in still larger proportions when the weather is cold or time of mixing late. But the whitest bread is made when the dough can have long time to rise, not hurried up.

1 pint yeast.
3 pints warm water.
1 heaping tablespoon salt.
8 pounds flour.
Makes 8 loaves of convenient size.

Cost of material—There are 12 pounds weight of material which make about 10 pounds of bread after baking and the cost per pound is according to the price of flour, with flour at $3\frac{1}{4}$ this small quantity costs 3c per pound loaf.

260—Cream Rolls.

For about 60 split rolls.
3 large cups milk.
1 large cup yeast.
1 ounce salt. (A heaping tablespoon.)
2 ounces sugar.
2 ounces lard or butter.
4 pounds flour—16 cups.

Strain the yeast and the water into a pan and mix in half the flour. Beat the batter thus made thoroughly. Scrape down the sides of the pan. Pour a spoonful of melted lard on top and spread it with the back of the fingers. This is to prevent a crust from forming on top. Cover with a cloth and set the sponge in a moderately warm place to rise 4 or 5 hours.

This having been commenced at about 8 in the morning beat it again about one, add the salt and make up stiff dough with the rest of the flour. Knead the dough on the table, alternately drawing it up in round shape and pressing the pulled-over edges into the middle and then pressing it out to a flat sheet, folding over and pressing out again.

Brush the clean scraped pan over with the least touch of melted lard or butter—which prevents sticking and waste of dough—place the dough in and brush that over, too. Where economy reigns the strictest a little warm water in a cup, and teaspoonful of lard melted in it will do for this brushing over and insures the truest saving and smoothest bread. Let the dough rise till 4.

At about 4 o'clock spread the dough on the table by pressing out with the knuckles till it is a thin uneven sheet. Double it over on itself and press the two edges together all around first. This imprisons air in the knuckle holes in large masses. Then pound and press the dough with the fists till it has become a thin sheet again, with the inclosed air distributed in bubbles all through it. Fold over and repeat this process several times. Then roll it up. Let it stand a few minutes before making into rolls. Persons in practice find it quickest to pull off pieces of dough of right size and mould them up instantly. Others cut off strips of dough, roll them in extended lengths and cut these up in roll sizes. Mould them up round with no flour on the board and only a dust on the hands, and place them in regular rows on the table—the smoothest side down. Take a little rolling pin—it looks like a piece of new broom handle—and roll a depression across the middle of each. Brush these over with the least possible melted lard or butter, using a tin-bound varnish brush for that purpose. Double the rolls, the two buttered sides together, and place them in the pans diagonally, with plenty of room so they will not touch. Brush over the tops of the rolls in the pans with the least possible melted lard again and set them to rise about an hour—less or more according to the temperature. Bake in a hot oven, about 10 minutes. Brush over with clear water when done.

Cost of material—flour 14, yeast 3, milk 6, sugar 2, lard 6; 31 cents for 4 or 5 dozen, according to size or 6c per dozen. They sell 2 or 3 for 5c with a chip of butter added—about ½ oz, 1 cent.

261—Graham Rolls.

This is for fifty rolls of small size.
2 pounds graham, not sifted.
1 pound white flour.
1½ pints warm water.
½ pint yeast.
½ cup reboiled molasses—small.
1 teaspoonful salt.
Set sponge with the graham at 9 or 10 as directed for cream rolls, at about 1 add all the rest of the ingredients and make it stiff dough. Let rise till 4. Then work the dough by spreading it out on the table, with the knuckles, folding over and pressing repeatedly. Make into little round balls slightly flattened, and if not plenty of room in the pans grease slightly between each one with a brush dipped in melted lard or butter. Brush over the tops with the

same, and set the rolls to rise about 45 minutes. Brush over with clear water on taking them from the oven.

Cost of material—flour 10, yeast 3, molasses 3; 16 cents for 4 dozen or 4c per dozen—sold same as cream rolls.

262—Coffee Cakes.

2 pounds light dough.
4 ounces sugar.
4 ounces butter.
4 yolks eggs
Large half cup milk.
Flour to make it soft dough.
Take the piece of common bread dough, already light and fit to be made into a loaf, 6 hours before the coffee cakes are wanted to be baked, place it in a pan with the butter, sugar and milk. Let all get warmed through and the butter softened, then mix them thoroughly. Next add the eggs and flour by littles, alternately, beating the mixture up against the side of the pan, to make it smooth and elastic. Spread the last handful of flour on the table, knead the dough as for rolls, pressing and spreading it out with the knuckles, and folding it over repeatedly. Set it in a warm place for 2 or 3 hours. Then knead it the second time. Every time the dough is doubled on itself the two edges should be pressed together first. When the dough is good and finished it looks silky, and air will snap from the edge when it is pinched. After this second kneading the dough should stand an hour and then be kneaded once more and made into shapes. The best shape is a twist made by taking as much dough as would make a cream roll—size of an egg before raising, roll it under the hands to a long rope, pinch the ends together and make a long twist. Rise in the pans 1½ hours. Bake in a slow oven 15 minutes. Brush over when done with sugar and water mixed, and flavored with vanilla, and dredge granulated sugar over. If to be made overnight without light dough for a start, all the ingre-

dients can be mixed at once by taking a pint of yeast and a half pint of milk—or nearly all yeast—adding all the other articles and flour to make soft dough.

COST of material—dough 5, sugar 3, butter 7, yolks 6 milk, flour, flavor 3; 24 cents for 30 cakes—sell at 2 for 5c with ½ oz butter.

263—French Coffee Cakes.

The plain coffee cakes described in the preceding receipt are the same that hotel pastry cooks call rusks. They are not so easy to raise and bake perfectly as plain rolls, but where they are made in perfection and nicely brushed over with syrup when done they are extremely popular as a lunch with coffee or milk; but still more of a favorite is this variety, called French. The same dough answers; the difference is in making out, as these have the dough brushed between with a very little melted lard and rolled up so that the cakes when baked will pull apart in flakes and strings. The same as in making split rolls. Wherever the butter touches, the roll will come apart after baking, these cakes having the whole sheet of dough slightly brushed over with lard or butter and folded upon itself without further kneading, will produce the layers and flakes in the cake. These are made in the shape of a large pretzel, raised, baked, brushed over with syrup and one, weighing about the same as one and a half of the others, served to an order. When a still richer kind is wanted use the following ingredients:

1 pound light dough—2 heaping cups.
6 ounces butter—nearly a cup.
4 tablespoons sugar.
6 yolks and 1 whole egg.
½ cup milk.
5 cups flour.
Flavoring.

If for ladies' luncheon or afternoon tea take the dough from the breakfast rolls, and, six hours before the cakes or rusks will be wanted place it in a pan with the butter, sugar, and milk and proceed ac-

cording to the directions given already for coffee cakes. The best flavoring to put in this dough is the grated rind of a lemon and half the juice.

COST of material for the richest variety—dough 3, butter 10, sugar 3, eggs 8, flour 3, milk and flavoring 3; 30 cents for 3 pounds or about 24 rusks, buns, twists or coffee cakes, according to size.

264—Cheapest Coffee Cake.

2 pounds light bread dough—4 cups large.
4 ounces sugar—½ cup.
4 ounces butter or lard—½ cup.
1 egg.   (Not essential.)

Take the dough at noon and mix in the ingredients all slightly warm. Knead it on the table with flour sufficent. Set to rise until 4 o'clock. Knead it again by spreading it out on the table with the knuckles, folding over and repeating. Roll it out to sheets scarcely thicker than a pencil, place on baking pans, brush over with either water or melted lard or milk. Rise about an hour. Score the cakes with a knife point as you put them in the oven to prevent the crust puffing up. Bake about 15 minutes.

One of the attractions of this plain cake is the powdered cinnamon and sugar sifted on top after baking, the cake being first brushed with sugar and water. Cut in squares if not baked in sheet cakes of right size for sale already.

COST of material—dough 5, sugar 4, lard 5, egg, flour, cinnamon, 4; 18 cents for 3 pounds—enough for 8 five cent sheets or 36 round plain buns.

265—Stollen or Picnic Bread.

1½ cups water or milk.
½ cup yeast.
1 teaspoon salt.
4 tablespoons sugar.
½ cup butter.
2 eggs.
1 nutmeg.
1 cup raisins

1 cup currants.

Flour to make soft dough—3 pounds.

Set sponge same as for bread with part of the flour, yeast and water at 8 in the morning. At twelve make it up into dough and work in all the other ingredients. Let rise until 4. Work it on the table, cut in 6 pieces, mould them up into round loaves, make a depression like a trough with the wrists along the middle, brush one side with butter and fold the two sides together like a large split roll of elongated shape. Rise an hour. Bake in a slack oven. Brush over with syrup when done. The same may be made by taking 4 or 5 cups of dough from the bread, already light and mixing the other ingredients in as for rusks and coffee cakes.

Cost of material—dough 5, flour to work in 3, sugar 3, butter or lard 6, eggs 4, fruit and nutmeg 20; 41 cents, or 8c per pound. May be made in all sorts of shapes and baked in pans or molds to serve as a cheap sort of fruit cake.

266—Cheapest Gingerbread, Yeast-Raised.

4 cups light bread dough—2 pounds.

1 cup black molasses—10 oz.

1 cup, small, lard or butter—6 oz.

1 heaping teaspoon ground ginger.

Flour to make it soft dough.

An egg improves it but is not essential.

Work the ingredients all together at about six hours before baking time. Let rise 4 hours, knead it on the table, taking care the molasses in the dough does not cause you to take in too much flour and make the cake tough. Roll it out in sheets, take up on the rolling pin and unroll on the baking pans. Brush over the top with water that has a little melted lard in it. Rise in the pans about an hour, bake 20 minutes. Brush over with syrup. Cut in square blocks for sale.

Cost of material—dough 5, molasses 3, lard 8, ginger 2, flour 3; 21 cents for 4 pounds. Size of cakes according to lightness. Usually cut into 12 five cent blocks.

267—Currant Buns.

No eggs required. Favorite sort and quickly made. This makes 20.

4 cups light dough—2 pounds.

1 small cup currants.

½ cup softened butter.

½ cup sugar.

It is soon enough to begin these 2 hours before baking time or before supper. Take the dough from the rolls say at 4 o'clock. Spread it out, strew the currants over and knead them in. Roll out the dough to ¼ inch sheet. Spread the butter evenly over it and the sugar on top of that. Cut in bands about as wide as your hand. Roll them up like roly-poly puddings. Brush these long rolls all over slightly with a little melted lard so that the buns will not stick together in the pans. Then cut off in pieces about an inch thick. Place flat in a buttered pan, touching but not crowded. Rise nearly an hour. Bake 15 minutes. Brush over with sugar and water. Dredge sugar and cinnamon over.

Cost of material—dough 5, currants 3, butter 8, sugar and cinnamon 4; 20 cents or 1 cent each.

268—Cinnamon Buns.

The same as the preceding with the currants left out, and some ground cinnamon mixed with sugar that is spread over the sheet of dough instead. The buns can be uncoiled after baking on account of the butter being rolled up in them.

269—Plain Doughnuts.

4 cups light bread dough—2 lbs.

½ cup sugar.

2 ounces melted lard.

Lard to fry.

Take the dough from the breakfast rolls, say at 9 in the morning, in Winter. In Summer the dough worked up at mid-day will do. Mix in the ingredients, let stand half an hour. Work up stiff with flour sufficient, and set to rise about 4 hours. Then knead, and roll it out to a sheet. Brush over the whole sheet of dough with a very little melted lard.

Cut out with a large biscuit cutter and cut the middle out with a small one. This makes rings, which must be set to rise on greased pans about ½ hour, then dropped in hot lard. Sift sugar over when done. They cook in about 5 minutes.

Cost of material—dough 5, sugar and lard 5, lard to fry 8; 18 cents for about 24.

270—Bread Doughnuts.

Only plain dough, or French roll dough. Cut out biscuit shapes, let rise, and fry. These are very often found at railroad lunch stands; nearly as cheap as bread and butter, and very saleable.

271—Bismarcks.

Sort of doughnut with stewed fruit inside.

4 cups light dough—2 pounds.
1 bastingspoon molasses.
1 bastingspoon sugar.
1 egg.
1 bastingspoon melted lard.
½ cup stewed apple or other fruit.
Lard to fry.

Put the light dough in a pan with all the other ingredients except the fruit, and work them together, and let stand ½ hour. Then add flour sufficient to make a soft dough of it and set it to rise about 4 hours. Then roll it out to a very thin sheet and brush over with water. Put a teaspoonful of fruit at the right distances apart on one half of it, fold the other half over and cut with a large biscuit cutter so that the inclosed spots of fruit will be in the middle. Rise on pans like rolls nearly an hour, then drop in hot lard and fry to a fine brown color.

Cost of material—dough 5, molasses and sugar 3, egg 2, stewed fruit 3, flour 2; lard to fry 8; 23 cents for 20.

Note—The mixture of molasses and sugar makes a better color on the doughnut than sugar alone. Always, when making any kind of fried cake take care to have the sugar dissolved before it goes into the flour, for mixing dry sugar in is one of the main causes of such things soaking up grease. It is an improvement to dredge them with powdered sugar when done.

272—Fried Pies.

A very good and saleable sort is precisely like Bismarcks except the shape. Cut out large flats, wet the edge, put a spoonful of fruit in the middle and double the side over like any other sort of turnover. Rise an hour and fry. Another sort of fried pie is made of common covered pie paste, in shape like a turnover, with a little fruit inside. Close the edges well. Fry as soon as made, light colored, in hot lard. The others are a kind of fried bread and light. These are fried pie paste, yellow and crisp.

273—Scotch Seed Cake.

Takes five hours time to make, raise, and bake, using dough to begin with.

2 pounds light-bread dough—5 cups.
12 ounces sugar—1½ cups.
12 ounces of butter—1½ cups.
4 eggs.
1 teaspoon caraway seeds.
8 ounces flour—2 cups.

Weigh out the dough at 7 in the morning. Set it with the butter and sugar in a warm place. At about 9 work all together and beat in the eggs one at a time, and add the carraway. Give it another half hour to stand and become smooth, then add the flour and give the whole ten minutes beating. It makes a stiff batter—not dough.

ut it in two buttered cake moulds. Rise about an hour. It should not be too light, bake as you would bread, in a slack oven, less than an hour.

Cost of material—dough 5, sugar, seeds, and flour 10 butter 24, eggs 9; 48 cents for nearly 4 pounds or two 2-quart molds, or 12c per pound.

Note—These raised cakes are like fresh bread, cannot be sliced till a day or two old without waste.

274—Scotch Tea Cakes.

2 pounds light-bread dough.
8 ounces sugar.
8 ounces lard.
1 teaspoonful carraway seeds.
1 pound flour.

The difference between this and the preceeding kind is that this makes a soft dough, to be handled and kneaded like bread. It is less rich and requires no eggs. Make it up the same way or like the cheapest coffee cake and let rise in thin cakes on jelly cake pans. Brush over with melted lard when setting to rise. Score the tops with a knife point when they are light and bake about 15 minutes. If for sale brush over with syrup and dredge with sugar.

Cost of material—25 cents for nearly 4 pounds—equal to about 3 dozen buns or 6 jelly-sheet cakes to cut. Good hot for supper.

275—New England Cake.

Make the Scotch seed cake but with 1 pound of seeded or seedless raisins and half cupful of brandy and flavorings, and omit the carraway seeds.

276—Yeast-Raised Plum Cake.

The slowest to rise. Use the liveliest dough, and in winter it had better be saved over night and mixed up with the main part of the ingredients; add the fruit next morning, and bake after dinner.

2 pounds light bread dough.
1 pound black molasses and sugar, mixed.
1 pound butter.
6 eggs.
12 ounces flour.
1 ounce mixed ground spices.
1½ pounds seedless raisins.
1 pound currants.
8 ounces citron.
Brandy, and lemon extract.

Warm the dough and all the ingredients slightly. Mix well, except the fruit and brandy. Beat the batter, and set to rise in the mixing pan about 3 hours. Beat again and add the fruit, previously floured. Line the moulds with buttered paper, half fill and set to rise again about 2 hours. Bake from one hour to two, according to size. Large cakes should have a coating of paper tied outside the moulds to protect the crust during the two hours baking.

These cakes should not be turned out of the moulds till at least one day old.

Cost of material—dough 5, molasses and sugar 11, butter 30, eggs 12, flour and spices 8, raisins 30, currants 10, citron 20, brandy and extract 12; $1, 38 for about 8 pounds or two 2-quart moulds, or about 18c per pound.

Note—All of the foregoing articles are made light with yeast and all are made by taking a piece of dough that is already light either from the family bread pan or bakers trough. A very good sort of apple dumpling is cheaply made in the same way of the same dough as for doughnuts, the dumplings allowed to remain in the pans long enough for the dough to become light before baking. The dumplings like the doughnuts and all other varieties must have a slight brushing over of melted lard to prevent a crust forming on them and cracking open while set away to rise.

277—Rusks.

These are slices of various sorts of cake dried in the oven something like dry toast

The coffee cakes previously described, if baked in loaves and sliced when stale make the best of rusks and for this reason perhaps, have gained the name of rusks when hot and in fancy shapes. But the name is not correct. They are then cakes or buns. The following are special sorts:

278—Marlborough Rusks.

Make the common sponge cake—called eight-egg sponge cake in the index—and add to the mixture along with the flour one ounce carraway seeds. Bake in long narrow moulds. When a day old, slice and brown the slices in the oven. These crisped slices can be kept a long time, and serve much the same purpose as sweet crackers.

Cost of material—32 cents for 32 slices, or according to size.

279—Anisette Rusks.

8 ounces granulated sugar—1 cup.
10 eggs.
4 ounces almonds.
6 ounces flour.
¼ ounce anise seed.

Mince the almonds as fine as possible, without removing the skins. Mix them and the anise seed with the flour dry. Beat the sugar and eggs together about 20 minutes or until quite light, as if for sponge cake, and lightly stir in the flour etc. Bake in long and narrow moulds and when a day old slice and brown the slices on both sides in the oven.

Cost of material—39 cents.

280—Russian Wine Rusks.

Make with the same care in beating the eggs and cutting in the flour lightly that is needed to make sponge cake good.

14 ounces granulated sugar.
12 eggs.
8 ounces almonds.
8 ounces graham flour.

1 teaspoon almond extract.

Crush the almonds with the rolling-pin on the table without removing the skins, and then mix them with the graham flour, which should have the coarsest bran sifted away before weighing. Beat the sugar and eggs together in a cool place about 20 minutes or until light and thick. Stir in the flavoring and flour and almonds. Bake in long, narrow molds and when a day old slice and brown the slices in the oven.

Cost of material—sugar 10, eggs 25, almonds 20, flour 2, extract 1; 58 cents for 2½ pounds.

Note.—Rusks of the preceding sorts may be seen in the windows of many of the best confectioneries. They are as expensive as cakes and are sold accordingly.

The way of mixing the sponge cake batter for the two foregoing is for one person working alone. The eggs and sugar can be made perfectly light by sufficient beating. If it is preferred to separate the eggs and have the whites and yolks and sugar beaten separately by two persons, observe to mix in the whipped whites last of all, after the flour and all else.

281—Sponge Cake Squares.

14 ounces sugar—2 cups.
8 eggs.
1 cup water.
18 ounces flour—4 rounded cups.
1 heaping teaspoon baking powder.

Separate the eggs, put the sugar and water with the yolks and beat up until light and thick. Mix the powder with the flour. Whip up the whites. Stir the flour into the yolk mixture and then the whites. As soon as they are fairly mixed in out of sight it is ready. Spread it ½ inch deep in a greased baking pan. Dredge a very little powdered sugar over the surface and bake about 10 minutes. When cold cut it into 10 or 12 square blocks.

Cost of material—30c.

282—Small Sponge Cakes.

Either the foregoing or the other sponge cake mixture baked in any sort of gem pans or small oblong molds. They are among the articles that sell in large quantities when well made, and being light are profitable. They may be varied by being frosted on top or in squares in the pans.

283—Wafer Jumbles

14 ounces sugar—2 cups.
14 ounces butter—2 cups.
11 eggs.
18 ounces flour—4 rounded cups.
Cream the butter and sugar together, beat in the eggs 2 at a time, add the flour, beat well. Put into a lady finger sack or paper cornet. Make rings on baking pans very slightly greased, and bake in a slack oven. They run out to a flat and thin shape and become crisp and brown. Need careful baking. If the first tried loses the ring form altogether add an ounce or two more flour.

Cost of material—sugar 10, butter 30, eggs 22, flour 4: 66 cents for 3¼ pounds.

284—Drop Cakes.

1 pound sugar—2 cups.
10 eggs.
10 ounces butter—1 large cup.
½ pint milk or water.
4 teaspoons baking powder.
2 pounds flour—8 level cups.
Beat the sugar and eggs together a few minutes, in a good sized pan, as if baking sponge cake. Melt the butter in a little saucepan, beat it in and the milk, powder and flour. Beat up well. Drop spoonfuls on baking pans very slightly greased and bake in a moderate oven. They rise in the middle cone shaped. For variations sprinkle currants on top, or a shred of citron, or gravel sugar. The latter is crushed loaf sugar sifted through the holes of a colander and the dust sifted away.

Cost of material—sugar 10, eggs, 20, butter 20, powder 4, flour 6; 60 cents for 4¼ pounds plain—about 80 to 100 according to size and lightness.

285—German Almond Cake.

A cheap and simple sort of lunch cake to be cut in square blocks Only good while fresh.
8 ounces sugar—1 cup.
4 ounces butter—½ cup.
6 eggs.
1 pint milk or water—2 cups.
3 large teaspoons baking powder
1½ pounds flour—6 cups.
2 ounces almonds.
Little salt.
Mix up like pound cake by creaming the sugar and butter together, adding the eggs two at a time, the milk and then the flour with powder and salt. Spread it ½ inch deep in a greased baking pan and bake about 30 minutes in a slack oven. Mince the almonds fine, after scalding and peeling them. When the cake is done brush over the top with syrup and sprinkle the minced almonds upon it. Cut in 16 square blocks.

Cost of material—40 cents for 3½ pounds.

286—Corn Rolls.

The bakery name for them. Also known as corn gems and muffins. They are in demand like cream rolls and graham with coffee or milk.
8 ounces white corn meal—1½ cups.
2 ounces butter or lard—large egg size.
½ pint boiling water—1 cup.
1½ cups cold milk.
4 ounces flour—1 cup.
1 tablespoon sugar.
2 eggs. Salt.
1 teaspoon baking powder.
Sift the meal into a pan, place the butter or lard in the middle and pour in the boiling water and mix up Throw in the salt and sugar. Add cold milk and flour, then the eggs and powder and

beat up with the egg whisk. The mixture is thin like batter cakes. Make deep gem pans hot without greasing them, so that they hiss when the batter is poured in then there will not be any black marks on the rolls. Bake about 15 or 20 minutes.

Cost of material—12 cents for 24 to 36 according to size—sell same as wheat rolls, 3 for 5c with ½ oz butter.

287—Macaroon Cake.

A thin sheet of cake baked first, then either spread or striped with cocoanut macaroon mixture, baked lightly and finished with spots of jelly.

For the cake:
8 ounces sugar—1 cup.
4 ounces butter—½ cup.
3 eggs.
½ cup milk or water.
1 large teaspoon baking powder.
Flour to roll out, or about 4 cups. Warm the butter and sugar slightly, stir them together, add the eggs, milk, powder and flour. Work the dough on the table and roll it out thin. Bake on a shallow pan to a light color.

For the macaroon paste:
8 ounces sugar—1 cup.
2 whites of eggs.
4 ounces desiccated cocoanut.
Little lemon extract.
Stir the sugar and whites together in a small bowl rapidly for about 5 minutes. Add the extract and the cocoanut. When mixed place it in cords across the sheet of cake and bake again in a slack oven until the macaroon on top has a light brown color. Place fruit jelly in the hollows between the ridges.

Cost of material—43 cents plain—with jelly 5 cents more—for nearly 3 pounds. Cut in 18 or 20 squares.

288—Boston Cream Puffs or Cream Cakes.

Common in the baker's shops, consisting of two parts, the hollow shell made with a cooked paste not sweetened and a thick custard for filling. This makes about 20.

½ pint water—1 cup.
4 ounces lard or butter—½ cup.
4 ounces flour—1 cup.
5 eggs.
Little salt when lard is used.
Set the water on to boil with the lard in it. Put in the flour dry as it is and all at once, and stir the mixture over the fire about five minutes or until it has become a smooth, well cooked paste. Take it off and add the eggs one at a time and beat in each one well before adding the next. Give the paste a thorough beating against the side of the pan for finish.

Drop portions size of an egg on baking pans very slightly greased and bake in a moderate oven about 20 minutes. Let the puffs bake slowly at last and dry so they will not fall when taken out. Cut a slit in the side and fill with pastry cream by means of a teaspoon

Note.—The eggs must be added to the cooked paste before it becomes cold, otherwise they will be a failure. It is better to use light weight of shortening and full weight of flour, than to risk disappointment by making them too short to retain their hollow form.

It will be found when the first pan of puffs do not rise perfectly that the paste can be much improved by more beating. Make them small for profit but large for show if you want to please the party.

289—Pastry Cream or Custard For Cream Cakes.

1 pint milk or water—2 cups.
4 ounces sugar—½ cup.
2 ounces flour—½ cup.
2 eggs. Very little salt.
1 tablespoon lemon extract, or vanilla.
Boil the milk—a spoonful of the sugar in it will prevent scorching—mix the sugar and flour together dry and very thoroughly, drop them into the boiling

milk and beat rapidly with an egg whisk. When it has thickened add the eggs and let cook slowly at back of the range about 10 minutes longer. Flavor when cool.

The foregoing quantity is right for filling the 20 puffs of the preceding receipt.

Cost of cream puffs—eggs 14, butter 8, sugar 3, extract 3, flour 2; 30 cents for from 15 to 25 according to size. Large ones sell at 5c each.

290—Corn Starch Cream Puffs.

Lightest thinest shells and in other respects the finest.

1 cup milk—$\frac{1}{2}$ pint.
$\frac{1}{2}$ cup butter—3 ounces.
4 heaping tablespoons starch—four ounces.
5 eggs.

Boil half the milk with the butter in it. Mix the starch free from lumps with the other half. Pour both together and let cook to a smooth paste. Add the eggs one at a time after removing it from the fire—and beat thoroughly. Drop spoonfuls size of guinea eggs on baking pans very slightly greased and bake in a moderate oven about 20 minutes. This makes 20 to 25. Fill with the following:

291—Corn Starch Pastry Cream.

1 cup water or m'lk—$\frac{1}{2}$ pint.
3 tablespoons sugar—3 ounces.
1 heaping tablespoon starch —1 ounce.
Butter size of a walnut.
1 egg, (2 yolks are better.)
Lemon or vanilla flavoring.

Boil the water or milk with the sugar in it. Mix the starch with a little water extra; pour it in the saucepan and stir up. Then before it has boiled again, add the egg and butter and stir until the mixture becomes quite thick—perhaps ten minutes. Flavor when cool. Fill the puff with it by means of a teaspoon, the puffs being cut open at the side.

Note—The preceding kind of pastry cream makes a good lemon cream pie if a small lemon is added to it. Grate the rind and squeeze in the juice.

Cost of corn starch puffs and cream filling—27 cents for 20 to 25.

292—Transparent Puffs.

1 cup water—$\frac{1}{2}$ pint.
Butter size of an egg—$1\frac{1}{2}$ ounces.
3 tablespoons starch—3 ounces.
2 whole eggs and 3 whites.

Make the same way as other cream puffs. The use of them is to make puffs different from other peoples and for the following sort.

293—Cocoanut Eclairs.

Make 20 cream puffs of either of the three mixtures above directed and take care not to have the paste too soft through the eggs being very large or the flour scant, as these should rise round and hollow, and not run out wide on the pans.

When baked have some grated cocoanut mixed with granulated sugar ready on a dish and roll the puffs in it, giving a good coating. Set them in a warm place to dry. If you use desiccated cocoanut, mix it with syrup hot.

294—Cream Puff Tarts.

Line 20 common patty pans with a very thin bottom of good pie paste or sweet tart paste and put in each one a spoonful of cream puff mixture—the same as for Boston cream puffs—spread it evenly, then bake about 20 minutes. Have some syrup ready and brush over the tops and dredge with either cocoanut or chopped almonds. They are risen high and hollow like cream puffs in the baking and this surface dredging is to be done while they are hot. After that raise one end with the point of a knife and insert a teaspoonful of any kind of pastry cream.

Cost of material—about 2 cents each.

295—Chocolate Pastry Cream.

2 cups milk— 1 pint.
½ cup sugar—4 ounces.
2 heaping tablespoons flour-2 ounces
½ cup grated chocolate—1 ounce.
Butter size guinea egg—1 ounce.
1 egg (2 yolks are better).
1 teaspoon vanilla extract.

Boil the milk, butter and grated chocolate together, stirring with an egg-beater to prevent burning. Mix sugar and flour together dry in a pan and when well mingled beat them into the boiling milk, then set the saucepan on the side of the range. Mix the yolks well with a spoonful of milk, add them to the other and let cook until well thickened. Flavor with vanilla when cold. Use it to fill chocolate cream puffs same way as plain pastry custard.

Cost of material—13 cents for cupfuls.

Note-The foregoing chocolate cream makes excellent cream pies or tarts, the pie crust to be baked first then the filling put in and frosting over the top. The common unsweetened chocolate is intended. When the sweet chocolate is used a larger proportion will be needed.

296—Chocolate Eclairs.

Bake cream puffs in long or oval shape, put in a small amount of cream filling, then dip the tops in a chocolate icing made of

1 cup sugar.
4 tablespoons water.
2 ounces common chocolate.

Grate the chocolate and set it on with the sugar and water to melt gradually in a place not hot enough to burn it. When it has at length become boiling hot beat it to throroughly mix, and dip in the articles to be glazed while it is hot. May be used also to spread upon cakes.

297—French Cream Puffs.

All three of the puff mixtures preceding are unsweetened and cook light colored; this contains a little sugar and is consequently easy to burn.

1 cup water—½ pint.
½ cup butter—3½ ounces.
2 tablespoons sugar—1½ ounces.
1 cup flour—5 ounces.
3 eggs.
1 teaspoon extract vanilla.

Boil the water with the butter and sugar in it, in a deep bowl-shaped saucepan large enough to finish the paste in. Put in the flour all at once and stir until you have a stiff, smooth paste, or about 5 min. Take it from the fire, drop in one egg at a time and beat it in thoroughly before adding another. When all are in give the paste a very thorough beating against the side of the saucepan. Drop pieces in either round or egg shapes on a baking pan very slightly greased. Bake them about 20 min. in a moderate oven. They rise rounded and hollow. Cut a slit in the side and fill with any sort of pastry cream or with fruit jelly.

298—Coffee Pastry Cream.

1 cup clear very strong coffee,
1 cup cream.
½ cup sugar—4 ounces.
½ cup flour—2 ounces.
2 eggs—(4 yolks make it better.)

Set the coffee and cream on the boil. Mix the sugar and flour together dry then drop them into the boiling liquid and beat up rapidly with an egg beater. (This is the quickest and easiest way of thickening all flour custards and pudding sauces.) When it has thickened add the eggs slightly beaten and cook 5 min. more. Use to fill cream puffs or cakes or tarts, or make coffee cream pie with frosting on top.

Cost of French cream puffs—the paste 16, coffee pastry cream 16; 32 cts for 16. With jelly for filling about the same. Large puffs sell 5c each. May be brushed over the top with sugar slightly wetted, and then dried.

299—Cream Cake or Washington Pie.

Consists of two layers of cake with pastry cream spread between—like jelly cake—and either powdered sugar or plain icing on top. For the cake take

1 cup sugar—8 ounces.

5 eggs.

½ cup butter—4 ounces.

½ cup water—large measure.

2 teaspoons baking powder.

3 cups flour.

Put the sugar, eggs and water into a pan and beat them together a minute or two. Have the butter melted and stir it in, then the powder and flour. Beat all well together. Bake thinly spread on jelly cake pans or on a large baking pan to cut in squares. There are cheaper mixtures that can be used for the same purpose but this if well made with sufficient powder rises very light and makes a large amount. Spread the same pastry cream between that is directed for cream puffs.

Cost of material—cake 26, pastry cream 13 39 cents.

300—Napoleon Cake.

Consists of two layers of puff paste baked separately, pastry cream spread upon one the other placed on top, and icing sugar slightly wetted spread upon that.

Make puff paste with three quarters of a pound of butter to a pound of flour. Roll it and fold it only 6 times instead of 7 as for tarts. Cut in two, roll out thin, place the sheets of paste on two baking pans and after baking light colored place one on the other prepared as above directed. The corn starch pastry cream may be used. The glaze for the top is the same as pearl glaze for angel food. Cut in squares when finished.

Cost of material—puff paste 24, pastry cream 13, glace 3; 40 cents, or same as Washington pie. Can be cut in 8 or 10 ten-cent squares, according to lightness.

Note—In order to handle sheets of puff paste without breaking it is necessary to roll up the raw paste on the rolling-pin and unroll it on the pan it is to be baked on, never touching it with the hands. Take up the sheet of paste after baking by sliding two broad knives under, or paddles made of shingles.

301—Saratoga Cake.

Bake two sheets of puff paste the same as for Napoleon cake. Spread fruit jelly, preserves or some good fruit stewed down rich upon one sheet, place the other sheet on top and cover that with frosting, the same as for lemon pies. Cut in squares.

Cost of material—about 40c, or according to kind of jelly or jam used.

302—Florentine Pastry.

Consists of a bottom crust of rich pie paste in a broad baking pan with jam or good fruit stewed down with sugar, baked in it, and a covering of frosting the same as for lemon pie or strawberry meringue well sprinkled over with shred almonds and slightly baked.

303—English Fruit Pies.

These sell well at the bakeries. Take deep dishes such as are used to dish up vegetables in at dinner, but about 6 or 7 inch size, nearly fill with any kind of berries in season, cover with sufficient sugar and put on a thin top crust of good short paste. Cut around the edges, make a small hole in the middle of the lid. Bake about 15 minutes. There is no bottom crust and all the fruit juice is retained in full flavor.

Cost of material—crust each 1½ cents, berries average including strawberries 4c. Sell at 10c each.

304—Iced Coffee.

Served in a tall glass like lemonade, with two straws and shaved ice in it.

For a single glass take

2 large teaspoons powdered sugar.

4 tablespoons rich milk.

A small cup coffee.

Some shaved ice.

Shake up with a tin punch mixer over the glass (bar-keepers fashion) and serve with the foam on top. The foaming appearance may be increased by one raw egg to a pint beaten up in the milk that is used, and gives it a cream color.

Cost of material—2 cents per glass.

OYSTER BAY.

305—Raw Oysters—Half Shell.

Open the oysters as they are called for, loosen from the shell, serve in the best shell with as much of their own liquor as can be saved, ranged on a plate with half a lemon in the center. Shred cabbage, crackers, butter and table sauces go free.

306—Raw Oysters—Bulk.

"Counts" are the largest—same thing as "Saddle Rocks." "Selects" next largest. Serve a dozen on the plate. Lemon, if called for, in a small glass dish at the side.

Cost—according to the price of oysters—with oysters at $1,00 per 100—oysters 12, lemon $\frac{1}{2}$, crackers 1, butter 2, tomato ketchup etc., $1\frac{1}{2}$; 17 cents a dozen. Small oysters only half the price.

307—Oyster Stew

It is a dozen medium oysters with a pint or less of milk and perhaps a small allowance of butter; with crackers, butter and pickles on the table. Cook the oysters and milk in separate saucepans. Dip the oysters from the saucepan into the bowl, add a ladleful of milk and a small piece of fresh butter. Serve crackers, butter and shred cabbage separately with the stew.

Cost of material—oysters 7, milk 3, table extras 4; 14 cents.

Note—Oysters do not always curdle the milk when boiled in it, but there is always a danger that they may, so the rule is not to run any risk. Besides, to cook the oysters in the milk although good for flavor, always makes a dingy looking stew with a scum on top. To obtain the best quality and appearance boil some oyster liquor separately and keep it ready for orders. As it reaches boiling point the scum on top can be skimmed off and after that pour it through a fine strainer into a clean saucepan, and you have the oyster essence clear and ready for use without detriment to the appearances.

308—Plain Stew.

The oysters cooked as above with the liquor only served with them, and no milk.

Note—It is with cooking an oyster as with cooking an egg. It may be either soft boiled or hard boiled, only there is a difference that an oyster boiled hard is spoiled. To cook oysters for stews set some of the liquor that has been previously boiled and strained as directed above, on the range in a little saucepan and drop in the oysters with a fork. Add a pinch of salt and pepper, shake them back and forth while heating and as soon as the liquor fairly boils they are done. Time about 3 minutes for one stew.

309—Dry Stew.

The same as plain stew but served without the liquor. Have a spoonful of fresh butter ready melted at a convenient place and pour it to the oysters in the bowl after they have been dipped up out of their liquor with a strainer.

310—Boston Fancy Stew.

Make a milk stew in the same style, and a thin slice of buttered toast. Use a broad and shallow bowl. Put the buttered toast in the bowl, dish the oysters (soft cooked) on the toast and pour the liquor in at the side, enough to make it float.

Cost of material—12 large oysters 12, milk 4, buttered toast 1, table extras 3; 20 cents.

311—Box Stew.

The richest stew that can be made and with the very largest oysters, called Fulton Market box oysters.

Prepare a square of buttered toast the same as for Boston fancy and put it in a hot bowl. Take a bastingspoon of cream and put it into a bastingspoon of clear oyster liquor that has been boiled before, and add an ounce of best butter. Cook the oysters in another saucepan. When soft done dish them on the toast in the bowl and pour the cream liquor around.

Cost of material—12 extra fine oysters 24, cream 2, butter and toast 4, table extras, lemon etc., 5; 35 cents. Sells at 60 cents.

312—Oysters Sawteed in Butter.

Not necessary to use eggs. Drop the oysters into a plate of cracker meal and give them a good coating. Be careful not to rub it off as it will not stick a second time. Drop an ounce of butter in the frying pan, and when melted lay in the oysters close together. Cook over a brisk fire to get brown on one side without hardening them. Lay a small plate upside down on the oysters, turn over the pan, then slide the cake of oysters from the plate into the pan again without letting them break apart, and brown the other side. Serve on the plate set in another plate. Ornament with lemon and parsley. There are oval shaped pans for such *sautees* as this, to be in shape for a platter.

Cost of material—12 medium oysters 7, butter 2, cracker meal 1, lemon and parsley garnish 1, table extras 4, 15 cents.

313—Fried Oysters.　Single Breaded.

Dry the oysters by pressing with a napkin. Drop them into beaten egg, in which is a little salt, and out of that into craker meal. Give them a good coating by pressing, with care not to rub, or leave a bare place for the grease to get in. Drop them singly into a frying pan of hot lard. Fry brown in 2 or 3 minutes. Dish neatly in the middle of a hot platter with a piece of lemon and sprigs of parsley

Cost of material—oysters 12, eggs 3, meal 1, lard to fry 2, lemon and parsley garnish 1, table extras 4; 23 cents.

Note—The way of frying oysters successfully without the use of eggs has been fully explained in a former receipt. It needs more care than when eggs are used, but may effect a great saving in the season when eggs are dearest. Even with that fried oysters are expensive over the other methods of cooking because of the lard destroyed. At the end of a meal the craker sediment will have made the lard used dark and unfit for further use, and if clarified of that there still remains a sort of mucilage from the oysters that makes the lard boil over like butter melting, and almost useless. Consequently the charge for fries is, and has to be, higher than for other styles.

314—Fried Oysters.　Double Breaded

Out of their own liquor into cracker-meal, coat well, dip in beaten egg and then in cracker-meal again. Fry 4 or 5 minutes. Oysters look twice as large as they really are, when double breaded.

Cost.—They take up more egg but the expense is made up in the apparent increase in the size, and when they are carefully cooked of a light color and crisp the double breading is preferred by most customers.

315—Broiled Oysters, Bread-Crumbed

The original meaning of breading has nearly been forgotten, so much better for most purposes is the meal of crushed and sifted crackers than grated dry bread. But the smallness of the demand for breaded oysters broiled—a way that over the water is considered most delicate—is proof that cracker-meal is not the thing for it.

Oysters breaded in cracker-meal, then broiled, unless they are deluged with butter, are more like discolored pieces of buckskin than anything eatable.

Grate a stale loaf of bread or else mince the thin slices extremely fine with a knife. Shake the oysters about in a little beaten egg, dip them in the bread crumbs and gently press a coating on both sides. It is better to let them lie in the crumbs awhile if there is time.

Brush the wire oyster broiler with a brush dipped in butter, place the oysters, shut down the other side and as soon as the egg is set with the heat of the bright coals baste the oysters on both sides with the same brush in butter. Get a toast-brown on both sides without cooking the oysters too much. Serve on a dish the same as fried oysters, with a piece of lemon.

Cost of material—oysters 12, bread 1, egg 2, butter 3, table extras 4: 22 cents.

Note.—Where silver-plated griddles and silver wire broilers are used it is practicable to dispense with the butter basting altogether, and prevent sticking by rubbing the bars with chalk. Some of the greatest restaurants of the two continents have had a sort of specialty in this line, and probably proved not only the desirableness but the real economy of the mode.

316—Plain Broiled Oysters on Toast.

Take the largest oysters obtainable. Brush the wire oyster broiler with softened butter, lay in the oysters and broil over a hot fire 2 or 3 minutes, basting once on each side with the butter brush. Dish side by side on one long slice of buttered toast in a dish. Garnish with lemon and parsley.

Cost.—Largest oysters one dozen 24, butter 2. toast 1, garnish 3, table extras 5; 35 cents—Sells at 50c, or according to grade of oysters. There is no satisfaction in plain broiling small oysters.

317—Oysters Broiled in Bacon.

Dredge some large oysters with pepper and squeeze the juice of a lemon over them.

Cut large slices of fat bacon as thin as possible. Roll up two oysters together in each slice, run a skewer through diagonally and put six such rolls on each skewer crowded together to allow for shrinkage. Bake in the top of the oven for a few minutes, the skewers resting on the edge of a pan with the oysters raised above the drippings. Finish on the broiler. Serve on the skewers on buttered toast in a dish, and if common skewers are used slip a ring of fringed paper on the end.

Cost of material—12 large oysters 15, 1 ℔ bacon 15, toast 2, lemon 2, table extras and potatoes 6; 40 cents.

318—Steamed Oysters. Shells.

Scrub the oysters clean in water. Place the deep shell side down in the steamer and steam them about 5 minutes. Take off the top shell and save as much of the liquor as possible with the oyster in the lower one. Serve on a platter without seasoning or any addition, except lemon in quarters.

319—Oysters--Shell Roast.

A bright and glowing charcoal fire is requisite for this. The oyster ranges are nearly all broiler and the bars are near the coals. Scrub the dirt from the shells of the oysters before cooking, with a brush in water. Lay them on the broiler, flat side down, and endeavor to get the shell so hot as to slightly color the oyster. When the shell begins to open turn it over. Dish up in the deep shell, the other removed entirely, and if too dry pour over each one a small spoonful of hot oyster liquor and butter mixed. Serve a dozen on a platter, a half on a fish plate, with lemon.

Cost—12 oysters 12, lemon 1, table extras 4; 17 cents.

320—Oysters—Fancy Roast.

Cut two slices of buttered toast to fit a medium sized platter, when placed end to end, or cut fancy shapes of toast that when placed together will form a star shape,
Roast the oysters in the shells. Take them out when done and place them on the toast and pour some hot oyster liquor mixed with cream over the toast in the dish. Garnish with parsley.

Cost—oysters 12, toast 2, cream 2, table extras and garnishing 4; 20 cents.

321—Oysters—Pan Roast.

An imitation of the shell roast.
1. Put 12 or 13 oysters in a bright pie pan, with their liquor. Dredge with salt and pepper very sparingly. Drop in some small lumps of butter and bake on the top shelf of a hot oven from 3 to 5 minutes. Slide them right side up into a hot dish, and garnish with 1 or 2 quarters of lemon.
2. A very common way in restaurants is to merely stew the oysters in a bright tin pan holding only about a pint, slightly season, and serve them in the same pan set in a plate. And, further, in the same style neat lids are used that fit the pans, to be placed when the oysters are done and sent in so. There is no difference, except in the imagination, betwixt that and a dry stew.

322—Oysters in a Loaf.

Take a loaf that has been baked in a tin mold, such as the bakers sell; cut off the top crust and lay it aside, remove most of the inside crumb, then cut the edge into ornamental notches or saw tooth fashion all around. Spread a little soft butter inside with the back of a spoon and set the loaf in the oven to toast. The top generally gets browned enough by the time the butter inside is hot. Make an oyster stew in the usual way but dredge in a few fine bread crumbs to partially thicken it. Pour into the hot crisped loaf on a dish, no cover.

323—Scalloped Oysters.

In a small deep dish or pan. Mince some slices of good bread extremely fine with your large knife and mix in about a third as much cracker meal. Cover the bottom of the individual dish with these mixed crumbs, and on them lay a dozen oysters. Dredge with salt and pepper, and drop butter in small bits. Cover thinly with crumbs. Have it slightly rounded up in the middle. Bake on the middle shelf one minute, or until a light toast brown, then draw it to the front and baste the top with oyster liquor hot and with a little butter melted in it.
Bake a few minutes. The object is to get a good bake on top without cooking the oysters too hard. Serve in the same dish set in another one.

Cost of material—oysters 12, bread 1, butter 2, table extras 4, 19 cents.

Note.—The appearance is much improved if the oysters are scalloped in metal shells made for the purpose, either stamped heavy tin or silver plated. Proceed the same as with dishes.

324—Scalloped Oysters on Half Shell.

Oyster shells of good shape have to be selected and kept for the purpose.   One large or two small oysters in each may be scalloped this way.   Dredge fine bread crumbs in the shell, put in the oyster, cover with crumbs and bake set in a baking pan on the top shelf.   When lightly browned moisten the tops with melted fresh butter and seasoned oyster liquor.   Serve the moment they are done, or the hot shells will make the oysters cook too much.

There is another way of scalloping them in sauce as directed for clams.

325—Scalloped Oysters for a Party.

Baked on a platter of a size according to number.

Put a border of mashed potato forced like a thick cord through a paper cornet all around the inner rim of the platter to hold in the liquor.   The inside scooped out of baked potatoes is often the available thing for this.

Cover the bottom of the dish with finely minced or grated bread crumbs. Scald the oysters slightly in a saucepan and then place them close together on the layer of crumbs.   Continue until the dish is piled up in the middle and rounded, with the butter, salt and pepper as in the preceding receipt, then mix the oyster liquor with a little milk and strain over the top.   Wipe the edges of the dish dry.   Bake to get a quick brown on top, on the top shelf of the oven.

Cost of material—each dish of one dozen 18 or 20 cents.

326—Scalloped Oysters for Hotel Dinner.

The thing to be guarded against is the getting it all bread and dry and hard and for that reason uneatable   These proportions make it right.

8 dozen oysters and their liquor.
12 ounces 2—cups butter.

2 pound fine bread and cracker crumbs mixed.
1 pint milk.   Pepper and salt.
Use a shallow 4-quart milk pan. Spread a little of the butter all over the bottom and cover that with a layer of the mixed bread crumbs.

Scald the oysters in their liquor just enough to make them shrink a little and place half of them close together on the layer of crumbs.   Then more crumbs, butter dropped about in small pieces, pepper and salt; then the rest of the oysters and cover with the remaining bread crumbs and butter.   Mix the milk with the oyster liquor, strain into the pan, moistening the top all over.   Bake from 20 to 30 minutes.

Cost of material—with oysters at $1, per 100—$1,40 for 16 dishes, or about 9 cents per plate.

327—Oyster Patties—White.

The meaning is that the oysters are in a white sauce, for they may be either white, yellow, or brown.   The same care that is needed to make a good stew is necessary also to make patties delicious, that is, not to cook the oysters long before they are wanted and not to let them get done too much.   If the rich liquor of cream or milk and butter described for the "box stew" were thickened with flour just to the right point, then the oysters lightly cooked in another saucepan, dipped up and put into the sauce the result would be reached of preparing the oysters to fill any kind of patty cases with the white preparation.   If thickened by adding raw yolks of eggs it makes the yellow sauce, if with butter and flour baked brown together and the oysters lightly cooked, stirred in at last it makes the light brown kind.   To begin at the beginning take for 12 patties.

1 cupful of oysters.
1 cup milk.
Butter size of a guinea egg.
1 taplespoon flour.

Cayenne, salt.

1 teaspoon minced parsley.

1 pound of puff paste.

Make the puff paste shells first by rolling out to a quarter inch thickness, cutting out with an oval cutter and marking the inside lid, with a smaller cutter as previously directed for cherry tartlets, bake carefully in a brisk oven and when done lift out the center with a knife point.

Set the oysters over the fire to scald in their own liquor, shake about until they are set, but take off before they boil.

Mix the butter and flour together in a saucepan big enough to hold all the rest, and when it bubbles up on the range begin stirring in the milk, thus making a thick white sauce. Let it boil up, stirring constantly. Season with cayenne and salt. Take the oysters out of their liquor and put them in white sauce, and then stir in a little chopped parsley. Fill the patties, put on the lids and serve.

Cost of material—oysters 10, milk 1, butter 2, seasonings 1, puff paste 10; 24 cents, or 2 cents each.

328—Oyster Patties—Yellow.

Read the foregoing directions. When the thick cream sauce has been made beat up the yolk of an egg with a spoonful of clear oyster liquor and stir it in, and add the juice of a quarter of a lemon.

329—Oyster Patties—Brown.

Put an ounce of butter and an ounce of flour together in a small saucepan or pint cup and stir them over the fire until they are light brown, like the crust of a well baked loaf of bread in color, or else, if time cannot be spared to continue the stirring, set it in the oven, for none of it should be burnt black. When done stir in gradually ½ cup oyster liquor and about half that quantity of milk, and salt and pepper to season, and at last a tablespoonful of essence of anchovies. Pass the sauce through a gravy strainer.

Scald the oysters separately and put them in the brown sauce. Use to fill the *vol-au-vent* patty cases of the foregoing receipts.

NOTE.—The exercise of judgment is required to have the sauces for such patties as are made by filling pastry shells as above of just the right thickness not to run out and leave the oysters bare and dry inside, and yet not so thick as to make the mixture a lump of paste. The addition of the juicy oysters to the sauce often thins it down to a degree that is a source of disappointment to an inexperienced person. Moreover, the addition of yolks of eggs to the yellow kind will not thicken them unless the boiling be stopped immediately after.

330—Oyster Patties, Household Style.

Provide 12 deep tin patty pans holding each about ½ cup;

1 cupful oysters.

1 cup milk.

1 large tablespoon flour.

Butter size of a walnut.

Pepper and salt.

1 pound short pie paste.

Boil the milk, thicken it with the flour mixed up with a little milk cold, add a little salt and the butter and beat until the butter is melted.

Roll out the common pie paste very thin, cut out with a large biscuit cutter and line the patty pans, put a few raw oysters in each, sprinkle with pepper and salt, nearly fill with the thick white sauce previously made, cut out more flats from the sheet of paste and put them on as lids. Brush over with mixed yolk of egg and water and bake. Serve hot with a sprig of parsley on top for ornament.

Cost of material—from 1½ to 2 cents each, according to size and richness.

331—Oyster Soup—Common Lunch.

To make to order have ready some boiling milk and serve in a bowl.

1 pint milk.

6 oysters scalded in their own liquor, and the liquor strained into the bowl first. Crackers and table sauces go free. Price in restaurants 15c.

Cost of materi·¹—Oysters 5, milk 3, table extras 3; 11 cents.

332—Oyster Soup—Good Hotel.

1 quart "solid meat" oysters.
1 quart clear soup stock.
1 quart milk.
Butter size of an egg.
1 teaspoon each of salt and pepper.
2 heaping tablespoons crushed oyster crackers.

The stock is used on the principle that the liquor that meat has been boiled in is better than water. It should be chicken or veal broth slightly seasoned with celery and parsley and other vegetables, and should be taken from the top, clear without sediment.

The things to be guarded against are, not to get the milk curdled by boiling it with the oysters, and to avoid having the scum from the oyster liquor floating on top of the soup. To get out of the trouble shiftless cooks sometimes throw the liquor away and wash off the oysters; of course that makes the soup poor.

Half an hour before dinner time set the quart of stock on the range in one saucepan and the milk in another. Pour the oysters into a colander set in another saucepan on the table and when the soup stock boils pour a few ladlefuls into the oysters, stir them and let them drain. Then set the oyster liquor thus obtained over the fire, when it boils skim it, then strain it into the soup stock. Next throw in the oysters and when they begin to shrink, showing they are fairly hot through take the vessel from the fire. Stir in the rolled crackers, (not cracker meal from the barrel,) the salt, pepper and butter, then at last add the boiling milk and pour the soup into the tureen. Sprinkle a little chopped parsley over the top.

Cost of material—oysters 40, stock 4, milk 8, butter 5, seasonings 2; 59 cents for 3 quarts or 12 large plates, or 5c per plate. It should be observed in comparing cost that the previous receipt for the common lunch soup of the oyster houses supposes a pint or more to each person with crackers etc., on the table. A large soup plate is only half a pint.

333—Oyster Soup—French Way

This is for 25 or 30 persons at a restaurant party, or hotel dinner for 50.

2 quarts of oysters—or 3 cans.
4 quarts of seasoned fish stock.
1 quart French white wine.
3 or 4 anchovies.
18 yolks of eggs.
1 pint of cream.
Salt, pepper, and white butter-and-flour thickening.

Make the fish stock by boiling a 5 pound fish, or some eels, in plain broth, with a head of celery, a handful or two of parsley, salt, white pepper, the wine and anchovies. While it is boiling pour a few ladlefuls into the oysters and then drain them in a colander and add the liquor to the stock. When the fish has boiled slowly about three quarters of an hour strain off the stock into another kettle, add a little thickening, (*roux,*) let it boil and skim it; put in the oysters and while they are nearing the boiling point again beat the yolks and the pint of cream together and stir them in. Draw the kettle to the side of the range and watch till the soup becomes smooth and creamy but take care not to let it boil. Taste for seasoning.

Cost of material—oysters $1,50, fish stock 25, wine 50, yolks 25, cream 15, seasonings 5; $2,70, or about 10 or 12 cents per plate.

334—Brown Oyster Soup.

Take the preceding receipt for quantities. While the fish stock is in preparation fry a small carrot, turnip and a piece of onion, all chopped small, in a little butter till brown, then put them in the boiling stock and let them cook in it some time longer.

Make some brown butter thickening (roux) by stirring together a cupful of butter and the same of flour in a frying pan and letting it bake brown in the oven.

Strain off the fish stock into another kettle on the fire. Add the brown thickening, stirring lest it sink and burn on the bottom. Add the oyster liquor and draw the soup to the side of the range to slowly boil and clear itself by throwing up scum. Put in the juice of a lemon mixed with a little cold water and skim when the soup boils up again. A few minutes before dinner time put the oysters into the soup and take off as soon as it once more begins to boil. If no anchovies have been used in the fish stock to heighten the flavor a spoonful of essence of anchovies may be added to the finished soup. Season with salt and cayenne.

Cost of material—oysters $1,50, fish stock 25 butter for browning 15, flour 1, lemon 2, seasonings 5; $1,98 if made without wine or $2,50 with wine, for 25 or 30 plates, or anywhere from 6 to 10 cents per plate.

335—Clams Raw—Half Shell.

Wash the clams in water using a brush, and wipe dry. Open and loosen the clams from both shells. Serve a dozen on a plate or dish with half a lemon in the center. Oyster crackers, butter and a dish of finely shred cabbage at the side.

Selling price, generally the same as oysters.

Small or "Little Neck" clams only are served raw.

336—Clam Stew.

Make as directed for oyster stew. The smallest clams are the best for the purpose. If the large kind are used cut them in pieces after trimming and bearding.

337—Clams—Shell Roast.

Same as oysters.

338—Scalloped Clams—Half Shell.

Prepare the clams precisely as directed for oysters in patties, by making a white sauce of half clam liquor and half milk thickened and seasoned. Put in the scalded clams. Then put a spoonful, or about two clams with the thick sauce adhering into each clam shell. Dredge cracker meal over the top and bake on the top shelf in a hot oven. Moisten the tops with the back of a spoon dipped in melted butter. When brown serve. About two to a dish for hotel dinners, or by the dozen at a restaurant.

Cost—About the same as scalloped oysters.

339—Scalloped Clams—Party Dinner.

Take the clams out of the shells and scald them slightly in their own liquor. Replace them in the half shell, pepper and salt, and then cover with fine bread crumbs, and bake quickly. Make a little white sauce of the clam liquor mixed with cream and a little butter and spoonful of flour thickening, and pour a spoonful of it over the clam in the shell when it has become browned. Serve same as oysters, on a small fish plate, with a piece of lemon.

340—Fricasseed Clams on Toast.

12 large thin slices of buttered toast.
4 dozen clams and their liquor.
6 yolks of eggs.
1 pint milk.
2 ounces butter.
1 ounce flour.
1 lemon, cayenne, salt.
Boil the milk. Take the clams from their shells and scald in their own liquor, drain them from it and cut them in pieces. Strain the clam liquor into the milk, add a spoonful of thickening, the

butter, and the yolks slightly beaten, and salt and cayenne to taste. Squeeze in the juice of the lemon. Then put in the cut clams. Dish spoonfuls on toast cut in neat shapes, or on fried crusts.

Cost of material—clams 35, yolks 6, milk 4, butter 4, lemon and seasonings 3, buttered toast 8; 60 cents for 12 dishes, or 5 cents per dish—or depending on price of clams.

Note.—The foregoing dish can be made cheaper if desired by several little omissions, and the breakfast or lunch dishes contemplated will be large enough for two at dinner where it is only a side dish.

341—Clam Patties.

The same as oyster patties, or, with the clams prepared as for scalloped or for fricasseed clams on toast put into pastry shells instead.

342—Soft Shell Clams Fried.

This is a large kind of clam with a brittle shell. Cut off the leathery dark portion that projects from the shell and remove with knife and fingers the beard and string from the inside. This leaves the clam in the ring shape in which they come to market sometimes strung on twine. Throw them as they are taken out of the shell into a pan of cold water When wanted dry them between two towles, dip in beaten egg with a little water in it and then in cracker meal and fry in hot lard the same as oysters. Drain in a colander. Serve piled along the middle of a large dish with a quartered lemon and curled parsley for garnish.

Cost of material—Clams at $1,50 per 100 15c, eggs 4, cracker meal 2, lard to fry 4, lemon 2, table extras 3; 30 cents per dozen. Usual charge 50 cents.

Note.—Soft shell clams on account of their large size and open shape when cooked as above make a large and plen-

tiful dish, and a very popular one. One-third as many are sufficient for an ordinary breakfast dish for one person. The lard required is not all used but allowance has to be made for the damage as, after two or three fryings the lard remaining is unfit for further use.

343—Scallops.

The small, soft, white shellfish bearing this name may be cooked in all the same ways as oysters and clams, but is generally preferred breaded and fried.

344—Clam Chowder—Coney Island Style.

The clam chowder so popular in the restaurants as a lunch dish is more of a stew than a soup, being thick with clams and potatoes; a large plate of it makes a hearty meal for a person. It is consequently unsuitable to serve as soup at hotel dinners. The Coney Island chowder contains tomatoes and herb seasonings. Take 1 quart of clams and their liquor—or a large can.

1 quart soup stock (or water).
1 quart raw potatoes cut in pieces.
1 large onion.
Butter size of an egg.
A slice of ham—or knuckle bone.
1 pint tomatoes chopped.
1 teaspoon mixed thyme and savory.
6 cloves, 1 bay leaf, parsley.
1 teaspoon each black pepper and salt.

The different articles should be made ready separately and placed conveniently for use. Have the clams scalded and then cut in pieces and the liquor saved. Cut the potatoes in large squares and slice the onions. An hour before dinner put the butter and ham in a saucepan together, and the onions on top and set over the fire. Put the cloves inside of a little bunch of parsley and tie it and the bayleaf together and throw in on top of the onions, and also the powdered or minced thyme and savory, and put on the lid, and let stew slowly. In about 15 or 20 minutes or before the ham and onions **begin** to brown put into the same saucepan the quart of soup stock, the clam liquor and potatoes, tomatoes, pepper and salt and let cook until the potatoes are done, then put in the cut clams. Take out the soup bunch and piece of ham, let boil up once with the clams in.

It is expected that the potatoes will sufficiently thicken this chowder without the use of flour but they should not be allowed to boil so much as to disappear altogether.

Cost of material—clams 40, soup-stock 4, potatoes and onion 2, butter 4, ham 2, tomatoes 5, seasonings 2, 59 cents for 3 quarts or 20 cents per quart or 5c per ordinary plate of ½ pint. The first-class restaurant price per pint plate or bowl with table extras added is 25c.

345—Clam Chowder—Boston Style.

This is what is called the old-fashioned sort, having no tomatoes in it. Make the same as the foregoing but leave out the cloves, the bayleaf and the tomatoes, and put in a pint of milk instead and a handful of broken crackers.

346—Baked Clam Chowder—Hotel Side Dish.

1 cupful clams.
1 cup of the clam liquor.
1 cup salt pork cut in dice.
2 cups sliced raw potatoes.
1 small onion.
1 teaspoon mixed salt and pepper.
1 cup milk.
½ cup crushed crackers.

A deep pan or crock that holds 2 quarts is needed to cook this without boiling over.

Cut the pork in dice, put it into the pan and bake it light brown. Take the pan out and strew some of the thin sliced potatoes all over the pork scraps and fat. Shave some slices of the onion over them, then half the clams, cut in small pieces, then more potatoes, onion, and the rest of the clams. Potatoes on top and the crushed crackers over all. Mix the quart of milk with the clam liquor, add the pepper and salt and pour it over the crackers. Brush a sheet of thick paper with a little meat fat, lay it on top of the chowder and bake in a moderate oven about 2 hours. It will be partly browned on top.

More liquid may be needed if the chowder boils away fast. It is done whenever the potatoes in the center are done. Dish out spoonfuls on flat dishes

Cost of material—clams 15, pork 6, potatoes 1, seasoning 2; 24 cents for 3 pints or 8 to 12 orders, or 2 or 3 cents per plate.

347—Clam Soup—Hotel.

1 can of clams or 1½ dozen.
1 quart clear soup stock.
1 cup raw potatoes in dice.
½ cup crushed crackers.
1 slice raw ham.
1 heaping tablespoon chopped onion.
2 cups milk.
1 tablespoon minced parsley.

The soup stock should have been already flavored with vegetables in the stock boiler. Strain the required amount and set it over the fire.

Fry the piece of ham at the side of the range brown on both sides, put it into the stock, without the grease and let boil in it for flavor, also, add the onions. Scald the clams in their own liquor a minute or two; take them out, pour the liquor to the soup through a fine strainer, and cut the clams in small pieces. Thirty minutes before dinner throw in the potatoes and seasoning of salt and pepper and take out the ham which is no more needed in the soup), and skim a it begins to boil again. Add the clams and boil a few minutes, and the cupful of crackers and chopped parsley and the milk which should be already boiling.

The care required is to have the potatoes done and not boiled away, and the crumbled crackers just dissolved in the soup without making it too thick.

Cost of material—clams 20, soup stock 4, milk 4, seasonings 4; 32 cents for 2½ quarts or 2 or 3c per plate.

348—Clam Cream Soup.

Cut the clams in four and make the same as directed for oyster soup with milk, and add a cupful of crushed crackers at the finish for thickining.

349—Mussels—Steamed.

Steam them in the shells until they open, then pull of the beard and take out the mussel with a knife into a saucepan or dish. The way to steam them is to first wash the outside thoroughly and pack them in a kettle with only a little water on the bottom to start the boiling. Put on the lid and set over the fire.

350—Mussels—Water Sauchet.

The mussels having been steamed as above and taken out of the shells into a saucepan, strain the liquor they were steamed in into another saucepan. Put in a tablespoon of chopped parsley, a little butter, salt and pepper and let it boil, then thicken slightly with flour mixed in a teacup with water. Put in the mussels and serve with crackers, brown bread or toast.

351—Mussels Stewed.

Having steamed the mussels and taken them out of their shells make a milk stew the same as for oysters, by boiling a cup of milk and adding half cup of liquor from the steamed mussels with butter and pepper. Taste for salt; add a sprinkling of parsley.

Cost—Count about the same as oysters.

352—Lobsters to Boil.

Have a kettle of water with plenty of salt in it boiling briskly and drop in the live lobster. If small it will be done in 20 or 30 minutes, but a large one takes three quarters of an hour. Cool and keep it on ice.

353—Lobster in the Shell.

Split the Lobster lengthwise and serve the half, the meat side up. Take off the large claws and crack them and place on the dish along with the half if it is a restaurant order. Garnish handsomely with curled parsley or endive and cut lemons. When served at hotel dinners they should either be small lobsters or be divided by chopping through the shell.

Cost.—According to locality. Lobsters alive can be bought at one dollar per 100 pounds in some places; in the interior they cost ten or twelve times as much. Usual restaurant price with garnishings and table extras 40c per whole lobster or 25c half.

354—Canned Lobster in Vinegar.

Empty a can of lobster into a bowl and pour plain vinegar over. Serve in place of salad cold for dinner.

Cost—Lobster 20, vinegar 4; 24 cents for 8 dishes or 3 cents per dish.

355—Lobster in Mayonaise—Pastry.

1 lobster.
1 cup minced celery.
1 cup mayonaise dressing.
1 cup shred lettuce.
2 tablespoons olive oil.
3 tablespoons vinegar.
1 teaspoon made mustard.
Salt and cayenne.
2 hard-boiled eggs.
Take the meat out of a large lobster and keep the handsomest pieces of red meat separate after trimming all to a uniform size. Shake them about in a pan with a little oil and vinegar to moisten them. Cut the other portion of the lobster meat small, without mincing it, but mince the celery fine and mix both together along with a little oil vinegar

and mustard, and pinch of cayenne and salt, then press it slightly into a melon mould or some kind of deep bowl.

Prepare the dish with a border of lettuce or endive very finely shred (like slaw) with a sharp knife. Turn out the shape of mixed lobster and celery in the center and cover it all over with thick mayonaise (No. 151). Place the red pieces of lobster around the base and ornament further with quarters of hard-boiled eggs.

Cost of material—lobster 25, celery and lettuce 4, mayonaise 15, oil and vinegar or lemon juice 5, eggs 5; 54 cents for over a quart or 4 restaurant orders for 15c per dish, or 8 individual dishes for 7c per dish.

356—Lobster Mayonaise—Hotel Dinner.

1. The same as the preceding except in shape. Instead of the dome shape or melon shape spread out the mixed lobster meat and celery in a flat platter so that it will be an inch deep and spread the mayonaise all over it. Keep it very cold. When to be served place a little freshly shred lettuce in the small dish, a neat spoonful of the salad in the middle and pieces of red lobster meat around.

2. The dishes can be made to look very neat and attractive by the way above described of taking up spoonfuls from a mass ready spread in a dish, (and it is quick to dish up,) but another way is to dish the lobster salad out of the pan it is mixed in into the individual dish with or without a border of green, then on top drop a tablespoonful of mayonaise, without spreading or smoothing it, and garnish with quartered eggs or or olives or a slice of lemon.

Cost—About 5c per individual dish.

357—Salad Cream Without Oil.

1 cup vinegar.
½ cup water.
¼ cup butter—2 ounces.

½ cup yolks of eggs—5 or six yolks.
1 tablespoon made mustard.
1 teaspoon sugar.
Salt, cayenne.

Boil the vinegar, water, butter and salt together in a bright saucepan, beat the yolks, and add to them some of the boiling liquid, then pour all into the saucepan, stir rapidly, and in a few seconds, or as soon as the mixture becomes thick and smooth, like softened butter, take it from the fire. Add the mustard and cayenne, and make it ice cold for use.

Cost of material—20 cents a pint.

Note.—The foregoing is extremely useful for making a salad of almost any material; it should be practiced a few times until the proper point at which to remove it from the fire is well understood. It is generally thickest and smoothest in half a minute after the yolks are poured into the boiling liquid, and it becomes thicker when cooled by being set in ice water. It will keep a considerable time.

358—Salad Cream—Not Cooked.

The vinegar is boiled but not the eggs and it is somewhat different from the preceding kind.

½ cup vinegar.
¼ cup water.
¼ cup butter.
½ cup raw eggs—3.
Mustard, pepper-sauce, salt.

Boil the vinegar and water together; beat the eggs up a little in a bowl and pour the boiling liquor to them, beating at the same time, then put in the butter either previously softened or in little pieces and stir until it is melted. Add a little mustard thinned down in a cup first with some of the dressing.

359—Lobster Salad Made With Celery.

1 can lobster.
Same measure minced celery.
1 cup salad cream.

Shred lettuce endive or cress.

Mince the celery very fine, but cut the lobster into pieces size of beans. Put the lobster in a bright pan, the celery on top and the salad cream poured over and mix up lightly without mashing the lobster to a paste Garnish the dishes first with shred lettuce and dish the lobster salad in the middle.

Cost of material—30 cents per quart or 3 to 4 cents per individual dish.

360—Lobster Salad made with Lettuce.

Pick out the hearts of lettuce and pu two or three of the smallest leaves in each dish. Chop the rest only a few minutes before it is wanted and mix with lobster and salad cream the same as directed for the preceding kind.

361—Substitute for Celery.

Use tender white cabbage finely minced and flavor it with celery seed, celery vinegar, or celery salt. or mix in a few green celery leaves. It is good also unflavored and seasoned with oil and vinegar.

362—Lobster Salad made with Potatoes.

1 can lobster
Same measure of cold cooked potatoes.
2 hard-boiled eggs.
1 cup salad cream.

Cut the cold potatoes in dice shape and the lobster as near as possible in the same form and eggs likewise. Put all in a pan pour the salad cream over them and mix by shaking up.

Cost—lobster 20, potatoes 2, salad cream 10, eggs 4; 36 cents or 3 to 4 cents per individual dish.

363—Buttered Lobster on Toast.

Take the large and solid pieces of lobster, cut them to an even size but not very small. Put a piece of butter size of an egg in a frying pan and chop it apart with a spoon while it is getting hot over the fire and when melted put in the lobster, dredge with pepper and salt, squeeze in the juice of half a lemon and shake it back and forth. As soon as hot through it is ready. Serve on thin broad slices of buttered toast.

Cost—34 cents for 8 portions or about 4 cents per dish.

364—Lobster Patties.

See directions for oyster patties of the different varieties, white, yellow, brown, in puff paste shells and in household style and make lobster patties the same way, but remember to season lobster with a dash of lemon juice and cayenne.

365—Lobster Cutlets.

So called because made to imitate a lamb chop or cutlet breaded.
1 heaping cup lobster meat—8 oz.
1 cup fine bread crumbs—2 oz.
Butter size of a guinea egg.
1 teaspoon mixed salt and pepper.
2 tablespoons vinegar.
8 lobster claws.
1 egg and one cup cracker meal.
Lard to fry.

Mash the lobster meat and the seasoning ingredients together in a pan to a paste, divide into 6 or 8 portions, take them up with flour on the hands and make into the shape of small pears, then flatten them, stick a lobster claw in each one to look like the bone of a lamb chop. Dip them in egg beaten up with a little water and from that into cracker meal and fry light brown by immersion in plenty of hot lard. Better if you have a wire basket to dip them and not break. Serve with sauce, either tomato sauce or tomato and cream sauce mixed, or parsley sauce.

Cost—of material—lobster 12, butter 3, bread and seasonings 1, egg and cracker meal 3, lard to fry 2; 21 cents, or with sauce from 3 to 4 cents per dish, according to size made up.

366—Lobster Croquettes.

Instead of mashing to a paste as in the preceding case, chop the lobster small and stir in the bread crumbs, melt the butter and pour in, add a little chopped parsley and make up in pear shapes or in any other shape, and bread and fry as before.

367—Shrimps and Prawns.

The small sea shrimp is generally eaten in the shell, the head and tail only removed, being more delicate flavor than the prawn but too small for most culinary purposes. The prawn is twice as large. It is the pink colored large shrimp of southern waters and is now readily obtainable put up in cans ready trimmed and shelled for use.

Shrimps of all kinds are first cooked by dropping them in boiling salt water. It is said to show that they were dead when put in the boiler if they come out lying straight at full length; and it is considered they ought to be dropped in alive and consequently quite fresh, when they come out in the doubled form as they are seen in the market. Ten minutes boiling is enough.

368—Shrimps in Mayonaise.

Put the shrimps—already picked from their shells—in a pan or bowl, add a spoonful of vinegar and the same of olive oil, a pinch of salt, and cayenne and shake them about until they are moistened all over. Then heap them neatly in a dish. Put a border of minced celery or shred lettuce around and a spoonful of mayonaise dressing on top of the shrimps.

Cost—A cupful of prepared shrimps costs 25 cents, or twice as much as lobster. The ways of preparing lobsters serve equally as well for shrimps but the cost should be counted double—or the 25 cent restaurant dishes be about half the cost of lobster salad.

369—Shrimp Salad.

Put the prepared shrimps in a bowl with salad cream enough to almost cover them. Prepare individual salad dishes with a border of fresh shred lettuce and dish up a spoonful of the shrimps and sauce in the middle.

Cost—shrimps 25, salad cream 5, lettuce 1; 31 cents for 6 or 8 dishes or 5 cents per plate.

370—Buttered Shrimps.

Warm up the prepared shrimps in a frying pan with a little butter, pepper and salt and serve them as soon as hot through on a broad thin slice of buttered toast.

371—Shrimp Toast.

Pound the shrimps to a paste, season pleasantly with salt, pepper, a slight grating of nutmeg, a teaspoonful of lemon juice and half as much best butter as there is shrimp, and spread it upon thin slices of toast. A breakfast or luncheon dish.

372—Crabs to Boil.

Boil the same as lobsters. The large deep-water crabs take the same length of time. Soft shells are done in ten or fifteen minutes. Use the large ones if possible for salads and to dress cold.

373—Soft Shell Crabs, Boiled.

As served in the restaurants every part of a soft shell crab is eaten, shell, claws and all, except the sand pouch on the under side, but the small claws should be taken off when the crabs are to be cooked by boiling.

Drop the crabs into boiling water already well salted, cook 10 or 15 minutes, drain, and serve with a sauce at the side.

Tomato ketchup, mayonaise sauce, hot cream sauce or butter or parsley sauce are suitable kinds.

374—Soft Shell Crabs, Fried.

Bread it in the usual manner by dipping in egg in which a small proportion of water has been beaten, then in cracker meal. Drop two or three at a time in a saucepan of hot oil or lard and fry light brown in about ten minutes. The claws should be crisp enough to break. Garnish with fried parsley and serve mayonaise at the.side separately.

Cost—soft-shells bring from 10c to 20c each in the markets when hard shells are but from 2c to 5c—according to where the market may be located. Two soft-shells fried, with sauce and table extras constitute a restaurant dish at 50 or 60 cents.

375—Crab Salad.

6 boiled crabs, common size.
1 cup finely minced white cabbage lettuce, or endive.
½ cup salad cream.
Pick the meat out of the crabs, cut all that can be cut into pieces of even size and rub the rest smooth in salad dressing, adding a little mustard. Mix cabbage and dressing thoroughly, and the crab meat mix in lightly without breaking the pieces. Fill the crab shells with the salad and place them on a dish previously prepared with a bed of cress or other green.

Cost of material—6 crabs 25, salad cream 5, green 2; 32 cents for 6 shells of salad or 5 or 6c each.

Note.—Crab salads may be made in all the same ways as shrimp and lobster salads; particularly good with mayonaise dressing.

376—Dressed Crab.

Pick the meat from the shell and claws, cut the solid part into small pieces, dry the soft part with the addition of a spoonful of fine bread crumbs, mix all with a little oil, vinegar and mustard. Wash and dry the shells and serve the meat in them, placed on a bed of something green—lettuce, cress, young celery plants or parsley.

377—Devilled Crabs.

Boil the crabs in salted water 20 minutes, open and crack the claws and take out the meat, measure it with a spoon into a bowl and add half as many spoonfuls of fine bread crumbs. For each crab add a teaspoonful of softened butter, same of vinegar mixed with a small teaspoonful of made mustard, a pinch of salt and cayenne. Pack the mixture in the crab shells and cover the surface with cracker meal, bake brown in a brisk oven and baste the tops once with butter to moisten the breading. Serve in the shells.

Cost—about 5 cents each.

378—Canned Crabs Devilled.

1 can of crab.
½ cup butter sauce.
4 hard-boiled yolks of eggs.
Salt and cayenne.
Crab shells or paper cases.
Have the butter sauce made the same as if for boiled meat, mash the yolks and sauce together and stir into the crab. Season to taste. Oil the crab shells inside with salad oil, fill up, smooth over the top, bake about 6 minutes and serve hot.

Cost—can of devilled crab 20, yolks 7, butter sauce 3; 30 cents for 6 or 8.

Note.—The canned crab is called devilled crab as it is, simply meaning that it is minced and cooked. It is usually dryer than the meat taken out of the shells, being composed of selected meat—hence the difference between the two foregoing receipts, bread being needed in one case to dry it up. Crab shells may be saved over and used many times for the same purpose. When a number are to be served at once, dish them on a folded napkin and ornament the dish. Paper cases may be purchased to answer the same purpose as shells.

379—Buttered Crabs.

Devilled crab from the cans made hot in a frying pan with a little butter, pepper and salt and served on toast.

QUAKER DAIRY LUNCH.

Farinaceous and milk food; such dishes as mush and milk, bread and butter and fruit and buttermilk are the specialties of some lunch houses. These are all cheap and healthful dishes and many customers avail themselves of the opportunity to avoid meat eating altogether. A large variety of pastry, puddings and cakes, however, gets into the bill of fare of most of the "dairies" eventually, such as have been enumerated already under the head of fine bakery lunch, and a few more will be found following these simpler dishes.

380—Oatmeal Mush and Milk.

1 cup oatmeal.
4 cups water.
2 teaspoons salt.

The coarsest oatmeal is the best and the least liable to burn. It is the dust in oatmeal that sticks and scorches on the bottom, if that is washed away the tendency will be very much lessened. A double bottomed kettle can be used if steam enough can be kept up, but generally mush seems better when cooked in a pot on a part of the range that is not very hot.

Boil the water two hours before the meal, put in the oatmeal, cover down

and let simmer at the side. Watch to see that it does not boil dry but only stir it up when nearly done. Serve warm, with cold milk in another bowl.

COST—with oatmeal 6c per pound—oatmeal mush 3c per quart or 3 large cups, milk 6; 3 cents each person.

NOTE.—This being such a cheap dish and the usual price ten cents, some restaurants serve a platter with an unstinted amount of mush and a pint of milk for that charge.

381—Cracked Wheat Mush and Milk.

The same as oatmeal but the wheat needs longer boiling—say 3 hours. It is better for a previous soaking in water.

382—Hulled Corn or Home Made Hominy.

Steep a quart of white corn in weak lye for two days, wash in two waters and boil it about 4 hours or until tender. The lye from the leach of wood ashes is the kind generally used, but a weak solution of concentrated lye will answer and if that is not available mix a handful of baking soda in water enough to cover the corn twice over and let steep in that. Wash well before cooking, eat with salt and milk.

COST—the same as mush and milk, rom 1 to 3 cents each person.

383—Soda Crackers and Milk.

10 crackers and a pint bowl of milk. Usual charge 10 cents.

384—Graham or Oatmeal Crackers and Milk.

Same as the preceding.

385—Doughnuts and Milk.

Prepare the dough as if for French rolls or cream rolls, roll out thin, cut out like small biscuits, brush over the tops with the least possible amount of melted lard and let stand in pans to rise for an hour. Take them up singly and drop in a kettle of hot lard and fry light brown in about 5 minutes.

Cost of material—these small plain doughnuts 6 cents per dozen. Usually one with a glass of milk, 5c.

386—Baked Pork and Beans.

Wash and pick over a large heaping cupful of navy beans and steep them in water over night. Put them on next morning with fresh water to more than cover, and baking soda the size of a bean and let boil about an hour. Then carry them to the sink, pour all into a colander letting the water run away and put back into the saucepan with cold water enough to come up to a level. Boil again and in a few minutes they will be soft. Season with a little salt and table-spoon of molasses. Put them into four pint bowls or tin pans, lay an ounce slice of salt pork on each and bake half an hour.

387—Boston Brown Bread.

1 pound corn meal—about 3 cups.
1 pint boiling water—2 cups.
¼ cup black molasses.
1 cup cold water.
1 cup yeast or yeast cake in water.
¼ pound of either rye or graham flour.
½ pound of white flour—a heaping pint.
Salt.
Pour the boiling water over the corn-meal in a pan and mix, throw in a tea-spoonful of salt, add the molasses and cold water, then the yeast and then the two kinds of flour. Line two sheet-iron brown bread pails with greased paper, put in the dough and let rise from one to two hours, then bake or steam for five hours. If steamed, bake the loaves afterward long enough to form a light crust.

Cost of material— corn meal 3, flour 3, molasses and yeast 2; 8 cents for two 2-pound loaves.

Note.—A good sort of bread is made as above with a pound of graham sifted through a common flour sieve to remove the coarse bran, and the white flour omitted; or with all rye flour and no graham or white. Care should be taken not to scald the yeast by adding it to the hot meal before the cold water. When this kind of bread is sticky when sliced it shows it was made up too wet. When the loaves come out hollow or caved in it shows too much fermentation.

Cost of material—beans 4, pork 4; 8 cents for 4 dishes

388—Sour Milk Cheese or Smearkase.

Set a pan of clabbered milk on the stove when there is not much fire, and let it heat slowly without burning on the bottom. When it shows signs of boiling it should be taken off, as actual boiling makes the curd tough. Pour it into a piece of muslin, tie and hang on a nail to drip until next day. Chop up the ball of curd and mix with salt, pepper and cream to taste, or cream or sweet milk and sugar.
Sells well at the dairy lunch houses When for sale in that way it is not necessary to add any seasonings but a little salt. Serve in saucers.

Cost of material—one gallon sour milk value 20 cents will yield 12 ounces of cheese, which chopped and moistened with milk makes 3 half pints, or 6 of the little cheeses done up in tinfoil that we find for sale in the stores.

389—Cream Cheese.

Take a quart of cream that has become sour and thick, mix in a tablespoonful of salt and pour it into a piece of thin muslin (butter wrapping) placed in a sieve or basket bottom. Leave it in the milk house or other cold place three days, to drain and ripen, pouring away the whey from the dish it stands on every day. Lift the cheese out by taking hold of the corners of the cloth; invert it on to a plate. These are sometimes inverted on to a large cabbage leaf on the second day and taken to market on the leaf the next day by those who make them for sale.

Note.—The above is the "slipcote" cheese of English dairies and country markets, and is the same in the main as the imported *fromage de Brie*, the differences consisting in the use of a proportion of goats milk in the laster, and peculiar skill in manipulation learned through practice among the English producers.

390—Baked Bread Pudding.

4 heaping cups bread—1 pound.
4 cups water or milk.
1 cup finely minced suet.
2 tablespoons sugar.
2 eggs.
1 nutmeg, or minced lemon peel.

Bread being such a cheap article there is no economy in trying to use the dark crust of the stale pieces that are required, but they should be pared until there is nothing but white bread left. Cut into thin slices and then across in dice, and put it in a pan having the minced suet first strewn over the bottom. Mix the milk, sugar, eggs and nutmeg together and pour it over the bread. Set in the oven without stirring it up, bake until set in the middle. Serve out of the pan and pour sauce (No. 70) over in the saucer.

Cost of material—bread 4, suet 2, sugar 2, eggs 4; 12 cents for near 2 quarts—sauce 8—20 cents for 8 orders or 2½c each—or 1½c for hotel dishes.

Note—It is the genteel way in most places to bake the puddings in bowls holding a pint and serve the sauce in small individual pitchers. Usual charge ten cents.

391—Baked Rice and Milk Pudding.

1 cup rice
1 cup sugar.
6 cups milk.
Cinnamon or nutmeg.
A pinch of salt.

Wash the rice in three or four waters, put it into a tin pudding pan, and the sugar, milk, salt and piece of stick cinnamon with it, all cold, and bake in a slow oven for three or four hours. It may be best to use only five cups of milk at first, and add the other if the time allows the pudding to boil down dry enough. Cover with a sheet of greased paper so keep the top from scorching. Sauce not necessary, but generally a glass of milk served with it.

Cost of material—rice 4, milk 8, sugar 5, seasoning 1; 18 cents for 3 pints, or 6 or 8 orders, or 3 cents each person.

Note—The preceding is a favorite kind of pudding everywhere and in some of the finest hotels is nearly always offered as an alternative from the richer kinds. Its good quality arises from the slow boiling down and condensation of the richness of the milk. When it is to be baked in individual bowls it becomes necessary to boil it first in a kettle and in that case the milk should be boiled down partially, with the sugar in it to prevent burning, before the rice is put in. Then when done dip it into bowls, wipe off the edges and bake until top is brown.

392—Cracked Wheat Pudding.

4 large cups cracked wheat mush.
Small half cup black molasses.
1 cup minced suet—3 ounces.
2 eggs.
1 cup milk or water.
1 rounded teaspoon ground cinnamon.

Mix all the ingredients together and bake about an hour. If wanted to make it better add a cup of raisins, but strew them over the top, for if stirred in they all go to the bottom.

When this pudding is to be made extra, wheat should be put on for the breakfast mush, to secure the benefit of the three hours cooking. When the mush happens to be cold, mash it with the milk made hot, so as to have no lumps.

One laige cup of cracked wheat raw will make the above amount. The mush is expected to be dry, else use less milk or more eggs, The pudding has to be apparently quite fluid when put in the oven but comes out firm enough.

Cost of material—mush 3, suet 2, molasses 2, eggs, 4, milk and cinnamon 1; 12 cents for 3 pints or 6 or 8 orders or 2 cents each, with sauce 3 cents.

393—Lincoln Pie.

1 pound broken crackers or bread.
1 pound brown sugar or molasses.
½ pound currants.
1 ounce mixed ground spices, chiefly cinnamon.
1 pint cold water.
½ pint hard cider, or vinegar and water.
1 pound suet chopped fine, or lard.
Soak the crackers or bread in the fluids awhile. Mix everything together. Cover the bottom of a baking pan with a very thin sheet of common short paste. Pour in the mixture to be 1½ inches deep. Cover with another very thin sheet of paste. Brush over with milk. Bake to a light color in a slow oven about three-quarters of au hour. Cut out squares either hot or cold.

Cost of material—bread 3, sugar 8, currants 5, spice 5. cider 2, suet 10, pie-paste 11; 44 cents for 6 or 7 pounds or 14 squares.

394—Baked Custard in Cups.

1 quart milk.
6 eggs.
½ cup sugar—4 ounces.
Flavoring.
Break the eggs into the sugar and pour in the milk while beating. Grate in a quarter of a nutmeg. Fill five ½-pint cups with the custard, wipe off the edges and outside, set in a pan and bake in a slack oven about 20 minutes.

Be careful not to let the cups remain in the oven longer than till the custard is just set in the middle.

Cost of material—milk 8, eggs 13, sugar and flour 3; 24c, or 5 cents per cup or according to price of eggs. These are restaurant cups that sell as pudding at 10c. Common custard cups only half the size.

395—Blackberry Meringue.

Make the same as strawberry meringue at No. 195.

396—Peach Meringue

Pare ripe peaches (not cooked) and cut them to size of strawberries and make the same as strawberry meringue at No. 195.

397—Peach Shortcake.

The same thing as strawberry shortcake, using chopped ripe peaches instead. It is a cake of short paste, not sweet, as large as a plate and thick as a biscuit, split in two after baking, peaches and sugar spread on the lower half, the other placed on top with the split side upward and more peaches spread upon that. It is eaten with cream. The ingredients required are:
1 cup lard or butter—8 ounces.
3 cups flour—12 ounces.
½ teaspoon salt.
1 cup ice water.
1 quart cut peaches.
1 cup sugar.
Pare the peaches, cut them small and shake up with the sugar before making the paste, and set them in a cool place. Rub the butter into the flour thoroughly with the hands. Salt is needed only where lard is used. Make a hollow in the middle, pour in the water, mix up soft, roll out on the table in flour reserved for the purpose. It makes the cake flaky and part in layers to roll it and fold it a few times like pie paste.

Then make it up round, let stand five minutes, roll out thick as biscuit and bake on a jelly-cake pan. Finish with fruit as above stated.

Cost of material—peaches 20, crust 13, sugar 5; 37 cents for 2 shortcakes, to be cut in quarters.

398—Apple Shortcake.

Use mellow apples of fine flavor and make the same as peach shortcake, the apples not to be cooked, but mixed with sugar and chopped and used immediatly.

399—Peach Cobbler.

A peach pie made in a baking pan to be cut out in squares. Make common pie paste, roll out the larger half of it to a thin sheet and take up off the table by rolling it up on the rolling pin and so unroll it on the pan. Put in pared and cut peaches an inch deep, dredge a little sugar over them, cover with the top crust and bake at out half an hour.

Cost—each person about the same as fruit pie or apple dumplings, or 3 to 5 cents per plate.

400—Apple Cobbler.

Same as peach cobbler. Other fruits same way. With apples use cinnamon or nutmeg for flavor.

401—Boiled Rice and Milk.

1 cup rice—½ pound.
2 cups water.
1 cup milk.
Salt.

Wash the rice in three or four waters, rubbing it between the hands to remove all the flour there may be about it. Set it on to boil in the water and when half done put in the milk. Keep the lid on and never stir it, but simmer at the side of the range and it will not be apt to burn.

Serve like oatmeal or cornmeal mush, in a bowl with another bowl full of milk.

Cost of material—rice 4. milk 2; 6 cents a quart or 3 or 4 portions—with milk 4 cents each person.

402—Batter Cakes with Syrup.

No eggs needed, and raised with yeast
3 cups flour—12 ounces.
2½ cups water and yeast.
1 tablespoon melted lard.
1 tablespoon syrup.
½ teaspoon salt.

The yeast may be either ½ cup of potato yeast or ferment, or ½ a yeast cake in so much water. Sift the flour into a pan, make a hollow in the middle, strain in the yeast and water, stir around to mix in the flour gradually and when all melted without being lumpy add the other ingredients and beat thoroughly. Let stand in a warm place to rise 6 hours, beat up again and bake. When the cakes are for breakfast mix the batter over night with cold water according to the weather.

Cost of material—flour and yeast 3, lard and syrup 2, 5 cents for 3 pints, 24 cakes or 8 orders. See remarks about buckwheat cakes. The cakes cost nothing relatively, it is the syrup, butter, and made of baking that make the expense.

403—Flannel Cakes—Best.

4 cups flour.
4 cups warm water.
½ cup yeast.
1 tablespoon syrup.
Lard size of an egg.
2 eggs. Little salt.

Mix the flour into a batter with the yeast and water either over night, if it is for breakfast, or 6 hours before supper. An hour before it is time to bake add the other ingredients—the lard melted and beat well. Bake when light again.

Cost of material—flour 3, yeast and syrup 1, lard 2, eggs 4; 10 cents for 2 quarts or 30 cakes—1 cent each person. add for syrup and butter

404—Baking Powder Batter Cakes.

Same ingredients as "flannel cakes," but no yeast. Put in two large teaspoons of baking powder and beat up with an egg beater.

405—White Bread Cakes.

2 pressed-in cups bread crumbs.
1½ cups flour.
3 cups water.
2 eggs. Salt.
1 teaspoon baking powder.
Remove all dark crust from the bread, and then soak it in a pint of the water several hours, with a plate to press it under. Mash smooth and add the flour, the cup of milk or water, eggs and powder. It always improves batter cakes to beat the eggs light, before mixing them in. No shortening nor syrup needed for the above.

Cost of material—bread 2, flour 5, eggs and powder 5; 8 cents for 3 pints or 24 cakes.

406—Graham Bread Cakes.

Make like the preceding, with part graham flour, and the crumbs of graham bread.

407—Corn Batter Cakes.

1 heaping cup white corn meal.
1 cup flour—4 ounces.
1 tablespoon melted lard.
1 egg. Little salt.
2 cups water.
1 tablespoon syrup.
1 teaspoon baking powder.
Mix gradually to avoid having lumps in the batter. Add the powder last and beat up well. When you have milk leave out the syrup as the cakes will brown well enough without it.

408—Corn Cakes Without Flour.

2 cups corn meal 12 ounces.
2 cups water.
Lard size of an egg.

2 eggs. Little salt.
1 teaspoon baking powder.
Boil half the water (or milk) and scald the meal with it, add the other ingredients, the powder last.

Note.—Buttermilk and soda can be used instead of baking powder in the several kinds of batter cakes, the proportions are 1 teaspoonful soda to 2 cups butter milk—which should be sour enough to counteract that amount.

409—Rice Batter Cakes.

1 heaping pint dry cooked rice.
1 large cup milk or water.
6 ounces flour— 2 level cups.
2 eggs (or 5 yolks for best quality).
2 tablespoons syrup.
1 teaspoon baking powder. Salt.
The amount of rice to be cooked specially for this is one teacupful, boiled in a pint of water, with the steam shut in. If ready cooked cold rice, warm the milk and mash the rice with it free from lumps, adding flour at the same time. Then mix in the other ingredients; the eggs well beaten first. Bake on a griddle. Buttermilk and soda can be used instead of the powder and sweet milk.

410—Sugar Tops or Cookies Without Eggs.

1 cup butter or lard—8 ounces.
1 cup sugar—8 ounces.
1 cup water.
2 teaspoons baking powder
6 cups flour—1¼ pounds
Mix butter and sugar together, then the water (not too cold) then the flour with the powder in it. The softer the dough can be handled the better the cakes will be. Roll out thin, sift granulated sugar over, run the rolling pin over again to make the sugar stick; cut out and bake.

Note.—In the bakeries baking-powder means pulverized *carbonate of ammonia*. It is the most effective agent for raising cakes because it all evaporates with great rapidity and great force when the substance it is incorporated with is exposed to the action of heat

In making sugar cakes or cookies some practice is necessary to produce them properly for the reason that the softness of the butter or lard used makes a difference in the amount of flour that will be taken up in making them out, and if too much flour the cakes come out like common biscuits, so that with the same receipt to work by one person will make a sugar cake twice as good as another. Another thing to be watched is the amount of baking powder—whether the common household baking powder or ammonia it all ac s the same—because too much destroys the cakes by making them too light, full of holes and spread all over the pans, while with too little or with weak powder they remain harder than crackers.

411—Cookies—Good.

2 cups sugar—1 pound.
1 cup butter—8 ounces.
6 eggs,
1 cup milk.
4 teaspoons baking powder.
8 cups flour—2 pounds.
Soften the butter and rub it and the sugar together until well mixed, add the eggs one at a time, then the milk and flour with powder in. Sift flour on the table, turn out the lump of dough and pat it smooth and compact, keeping it quite soft. Thn roll it out thin as the edge of a dinner plate, dredge granulated sugar over and cut out the cakes. Place with plenty of room between on the baking pans and bake.

The dough when it has been sufficiently pressed or kneaded together should be allowed to rest on the table a minute or two before rolling out which will prevent the cakes drawing up out of shape when cut out.

412—Cookies—Richest and Best.

1 pound of sugar.
1 pound of butter.

12 eggs.
3 teaspoonfuls of baking powder.
Flour to make soft dough—3 pounds.
Cream the butter and sugar together the same as for pound cake. Beat the eggs and mix them in, then the powder, add some flavoring, then flour. Let the dough, after it has been worked smooth, stand a few minutes before rolling it out. Sift sugar over the sheet of dough before cutting out the cakes.

413—Hard Cookies or Sweet Crackers.

To cut in fancy shapes. They do not spread or lose form.
12 ounces of powdered sugar.
6 ounces of butter.
6 eggs.
Half cup full of milk.
1 teaspoonful of baking powder.
2 pounds of flour.
Lemon or cinnamon extract to flavor.

414—German Sugar Tops.

Rich cookies sprinkled with grave sugar.
1 cup sugar—8 ounces.
½ cup butter, large—4 ounces.
3 eggs.
½ cup milk.
2 teaspoons baking powder.
4 cups flour—1 pound.
Work the softened butter and sugar together to a cream, the same as for pound cake, beat the eggs and mix them in, then the milk, and the flour with the powder mixed in it. Keep the dough as soft as it can be handled. After it has been pressed and worked smooth on the table let it alone a few minutes before rolling out, then the cakes will not draw out of shape when cut.

While they are baking mix an egg and some syrup together in a cup. add some flavoring extract, brush the hot cakes over with it and dredge gravel sugar on top.

Gravel sugar is loaf sugar crushed and the dust sifted away, then again sifted in a colander. The sugar that passes through the holes of the colander is gravel sugar.

415—Jumbles.

These are cookies in ring shapes of various degrees of richness. The proper shape is ribbed by being forced out of a tube with a saw tooth aperture. Commonly, however, they are only rings made with a ring cookie cutter. Either of the foregoing mixtures for sugar cakes or cookies may be used or this, which is rich and contains no powder.

1 pound sugar.
12 ounces butter.
8 eggs.
Flavoring extract—either lemon, orange or cinnamon.
2 pound scant of flour.

416—Ginger Snaps—Rich Kind.

8 ounces of butter.
8 ounces of white sugar.
8 eggs.
1 to 2 ounces of ground ginger.
1 teaspoonful of baking powder.
1½ pounds of flour.
Make same way as cookies. Sift granulated sugar over the sheet of dough and run the rolling pin over to make it adhere before cutting out the cakes.

417—Ginger Snaps—English, Richest.

1½ cups sugar—12 ounces.
1 cup butter—8 ounces.
8 eggs.
½ cup milk.
2 tablespoons ground ginger.
2 teaspoons baking powder.
6 cups flour—1½ pounds.
Mix up in the usual way for cookies. Sift sugar over before cutting out the cakes. These will keep for years.

418—Brown Ginger Cookies, Good Common.

8 ounces butter—1 cup.
8 ounces sugar—1 cup.

8 ounces black molasses—a small teacup
4 eggs.
2 ounces ground ginger—2 tablespoons.
Half cup milk or water.
4 teaspoons baking powder.
2 pounds flour, or enough to make soft dough.
Mix the ingredients in the order they are printed. Roll out and cut with a small cutter.

419—Ginger Nuts without Eggs.

8 ounces butter—1 cup.
8 ounces of sugar—1 cup.
8 ounces of molasses—small teacup.
2 teaspoons ground ginger.
2 teaspoons baking powder.
Flour to make soft dough.
Warm the butter, sugar and molasses together and mix them well, when nearly cold again add the ginger, powder and flour. Roll pieces of the dough in long thin rolls and cut off in pieces large as cherries. Place on buttered pans with plenty of room between. Bake light.

420—Brandy Snaps.

1 pound flour—4 cups.
8 ounces butter—1 cup
8 ounces sugar—1 cup.
2 ounces ground ginger.
Lemon extract flavor.
1 teaspoonful soda—rounded measure.
1½ pounds light molasses—2 cups.
Rub the butter into the flour as in making short paste, and add the ginger. Make a hole in the middle of the flour and put in the sugar, molasses and extract; dissolve the soda in a spoonful of water and add it to the rest. Stir all together, drawing in the flour gradually while stirring.

Drop this batter with a teaspoon on baking pans—they need not be greased—and bake in a slack oven. The snaps run out flat and thin. Take them off before they get cold and bend them to round or tubular shape—on a new broom handle.

421—Soft Ginger Nuts—Without Eggs.

Make the dough as for brandy snaps, and add to it 8 ounces more flour. Roll it out to a thick sheet and cut out with a small cutter.

422—Sponge Gingerbread—Best Kind.

8 ounces molasses—a teacupful.
3 large tablespoons sugar—3 ounces.
4 ounces butter—½ cup.
1 cup milk or water.
3 eggs.
1 large teaspoon ground ginger.
1 large teaspoon baking powder.
1 pound or quart of flour.

Melt the butter in the milk made warm, and pour them into the molasses and sugar, mix, add the eggs, the ginger and powder, and lastly the flour.

It is a great improvement to beat the cake thoroughly with a spoon. It is too soft to be handled. Spread it an inch thick in a buttered pan or mold. Bake twenty or thirty minutes.

Cost of material—molasses 3, sugar 2, butter 8, eggs 7, ginger 1, powder 1, flour 3; 25 cents for about a two quart mold or about 20 cuts in a thin sheet for hotel supper.

423—Common Gingerbread.

12 ounces black molasses—a coffee cup.
4 ounces butter or lard—½ cup.
1 egg.
1 tablespoon ground ginger.
1 small teaspoon soda.
1 pound or quart flour.
1 cup hot water.
Salt when lard is used.

Melt the butter and stir it into the molasses and then the egg, ginger and soda.

The mixture begins to foam. Then stir in the flour, and lastly the hot water, a little at a time. Bake in a shallow pan.

Cost of material—molasses 5, lard 4, egg 2, ginger and soda 3, flour 3; 17 cents for a two-quart pan.

Black-Pudding a la Francaise.

Chop fine a few large onions, and boil them in salt and water, with a little thyme and bay-leaf. When done, strain them and remove the seasoning herbs. Next cut up in small dice one pound of inside fat of the pig or "flare," and mix it with the chopped onions and a quart of pig's blood; season with salt, pepper, and some ground spice, and fill up some skins cleaned and prepared for the purpose. Tie the skin with string, so that each pudding may be the length of an ordinary sausage; care being taken to allow a little loose space between each individual pudding, or the skin will burst during the process of cooking. Plunge the puddings in water at boiling-point, and let them remain at the corner of the stove, but without boiling, stirring them occasionally with a wooden spoon.

White-Pudding a la Parisienne.

Pound in a mortar twelve ounces of raw chicken with four ounces of leaf lard; season with salt, pepper, and a little grated nutmeg. When well pounded, add gradually four whites of egg and three-quarters of a pint of double cream. Remove the meat from the mortar, and pass it through a wire sieve. Then work it in a basin with a wooden spoon, and add to it three ounces of truffles cut in dice, and the same quantity of ox-tongue also cut in small dice. Next put this forcemeat into a biscuit-bag fitted with a long tin pipe, and with it fill up the skins, which you tie as in the foregoing recipe, and poach in water at boiling-point for fifteen minutes, taking care that the water does not boil.

FINE CONFECTIONERY GOODS.

424—Peanut Bar.

1 pound granulated sugar.
¾ pound shelled peanuts.
Make the peanuts hot in the oven. Set the sugar over the fire in a kettle to melt without any water. Stir it a little. When it is all melted and of the color of golden syrup or light molasses mix in the peanuts, pour the candy into a buttered shallow pan and when nearly cold cut into strips and blocks.

425—Mint Drops.

1 pound pulverized sugar.
1 heaping teaspoon powdered gum-arabic.
5 tablespoons water.
1 tablespoon essence pepperment.
Put the water on in a small saucepan or cup and the gum in it and let warm up. When the gum is dissolved put about a quarter of the sugar in, let boil up and then add half the sugar that remains putting it in gradually without stirring. When it boils again take it to the table and stir in the remaining sugar and after that the flavoring. Drop portions the size of quarter dollars on sheets of paper. They slip off the paper when cold. It may be necessary to add another tablespoon or two of sugar to give the drops consistency enough not to run on the paper, yet it is better it be too thin than too much the other way.

426—Wintergreen Drops.

The same as the preceding, but make them pink with a few drops of cochineal or vegetable red coloring and use wintergreen extract for flavoring. These drops have a smooth surface but are slightly granulated inside. Clove drops, cinnamon drops etc., same way.

427—Honey Nougat.

A moist candy to be sliced, wrapped in wax tissue paper.

4 tablespoons strained honey.
2 ounces almonds, blanched.
1 pound flour of sugar, or icing sugar.
Make the honey hot without boiling, stir in the sugar a little at a time until it becomes too firm, then turn out on the table and knead in more sugar and also the almonds, which must be dry. When the nougat is firm enough to keep its form in a square bar like a brick split lengthwise, sugar the outside, roll it in wax paper and keep it a day before slicing it up for sale. Wrap the little cuts likewise in wax paper.

428—Tutti-Frutti Candy.

Take the preceding receipt and add to it a teaspoon of vanilla, two figs cut small and an equal amount of raisins seeded and cut; work up into a bar with all the fine, powdered sugar necessary to make it firm, cut in slices and wrap in wax tissue paper.

429—Burnt Almonds.

1 pound shelled almonds.
1 pound sugar.
½ cup water.
1 level teaspoon cream tarter.
Set the almonds in a round-bottomed candy kettle over a moderate fire and stir them until they begin to parch.
Boil the sugar, water and cream tartar together, making a clear syrup, pour a little over the almonds in the kettle and keep them moving while it dries to sugar on them, then pour on more and so on till the syrup is all used and the almonds are thickly covered. A little red coloring can be added to the syrup near the last to make the outside coating of that color.

430—Almond Taffy—Brown.

1½ pounds brown sugar.
8 ounces best fresh butter.
1 teacupful of vinegar and water—about half and half.
8 to 12 ounces almonds.
Scald and peel the almonds, split them

and spread them evenly on two large dishes slightly buttered. Boil the other ingredients together about 15 or 20 minutes. Shake them together at first but do not stir. When a drop of the candy sets quite hard and brittle in cold water take it from the fire and pour it evenly all over the almonds, only just deep enough to cover them. This kind cannot be stirred nor pulled, as the butter separates from the sugar which then turns grainy. Mark it off with a knife while cooling, and when cold cut in strips and wrap them in wax paper.

431—Almond Candy—White.

½ pound almonds.
1 pound granulated sugar,
1 small cup water.
1 rounded teaspoon powdered gum arabic.
1 level teaspoon cream tartar.
Little extract of rose.

Dissolve the gum in the water-made warm, add the sugar and cream tartar and boil without stirring 15 or 20 minutes. When a drop in cold water sets nearly hard so that it can only just be pressed flat between the finger and thumb take the kettle off the fire. Drop the flavoring by spots over the surface, give the candy only one or two turns with a spoon to mix it in, then pour it into slightly buttered pans, in thin sheets. Push the split almonds into the warm candy with the fingers. Mark it before it gets cold for breaking by rolling over it the thin edge of a thin dinner plate. Sliced cocoanut can be used instead of almonds.

432—Cocoanut Cream Squares.

1 pound granulated sugar,
8 ounces cocoanut either fresh grated or desicated.
A small half cup water,

Set the sugar and water over the fire in a small bright kettle and boil about 5 minutes, or till the syrup bubbles up thick and ropes from the spoon, and do not stir it. Then put in the cocoanut,

stir to mix, and when it begins to look white pour it immediately into a shallow tin pan. As soon as it is set solid mark it off, and cut in little squares when cold. The same kind may be colored red, and also be made with chocolate.

433—Chocolate Cream Drops.

½ pound fine icing sugar.
1 teaspoon powdered gum arabic.
2 tablespoons water.
1 teaspoon extract vanilla.
½ pound common chocolate.

Cut up the cake of chocolate into a tin cup and set in a shallow pan of hot water to melt by heat alone without adding any water.

Dissolve the gum arabic in the two tablespoons of boiling water in a small bowl, then stir in fine powdered sugar enough to make it a stiff dough, adding the vanilla at the same time. Turn it on the table, roll into a cord, cut off in balls size of hazel nuts and dip these in the melted chocolate. Set on a pan or dish to harden. Makes 75 to 100.

434—Chocolate Creams—Best.

Make the white inside the same as for the preceding and make the balls up in any shape desired. Instead of common chocolate merely melted dip them in this chocolate icing:

1 cup sugar
4 tablespoons water.
2 ounces common chocolate.

Grate the chocolate and set it on with the sugar and water to melt gradually in a place not hot enough to burn it. When it has at length become boiling hot beat it to thoroughly mix, and dip in the articles to be glazed while it is hot.

435—Chocolate Cream Dominoes.

The white cream candy same as for chocolate drops. Roll it out thin and pour a layer of melted chocolate upon it. Cut when cold.

436— Walnut Creams.

1 pound fine icing sugar.
2 heaped teaspoons powdered gum arabic.
5 tablespoons water.
8 doz walnut kernels.
1 teaspoon extract vanilla.

Put a little sugar in the water to make a syrup, and the gum in it, stir over the fire until the gum is dissolved. Take it off and work in the powdered sugar gradually with a wooden paddle. Add the vanilla. The more it is stirred and beaten with the paddle the whiter and finer the candy becomes. At last turn out the lumps on to the table—it is like soft white dough—and roll it in one long roll, cut off slices, stick a half of a walnut kernel in each piece and pinch the paste up to hold it, by shaping it in the hollow of the left hand. Lay the finished creams on a tray to dry. This makes about 6 dozen. The sugar is not boiled, only the hot gum syrup is used.

437—Date Creams.

The same as the preceding kind with dates cut in pieces to use instead of walnuts.

438—Fig Creams.

Cut each fig in six or eight and proceed as for walnut creams.

439—Angelica Creams.

Flavor the cream candy with extract of strawberry instead of vanilla. Cut green angelica or any other French candied fruit of a rich color and use as directed for walnut creams.

440—Cocoanut Cream Balls.

1 pound pulverized sugar.
1 teaspoon powdered gum arabic.
5 tablespoons water.
2 tablespoons cocoanut, minced.
2 tablespoons currants, minced.
1 teaspoon lemon extract.

Dissolve the gum in the water hot and stir in the sugar gradually, flavor, fruit and cocoanut. Work the paste on the table with sugar until it is firm enough, roll into one long cord half an inch thick, cut off pieces and roll into balls a little larger than cherries. Sugar well outside and let dry. The same can be made with candy colored pink. The foregoing kinds are all easy to make because there is no boiling of sugar.

441—Fine White Sugar Candy—Pulled.

1 pound white sugar.
½ cup water.
½ teaspoon cream tartar.
1 ounce butter.
Oil of peppermint or lemon or other flavoring.

Boil all together, except the flavoring, about 15 minutes. Try by dropping a little cold water. It must set hard to be done. Do not stir it at all, but pour on a buttered dish and flavor when cool enough to handle. Pull it till it is quite white.

442—Lemon Candy—Clear.

1 pound granulated sugar.
1 teacup water.
1 rounded teaspoon powdered gum arabic.
½ teaspoon cream tartar.
Oil of lemon, few drops.

Dissolve the powdered gum in the water made warm for the purpose. Then add to the gum-water the sugar and cream of tartar and set on to boil. Do not stir the syrup after it is once well mixed. It should boil about 15 minutes. Then try it by dropping a little in cold water. When the lump retains its shape pretty well and can be worked between the fingers like gum paste it is ready. Pour it into the buttered plate or in little molds of fish shapes and the like or into a thin sheet to be used broken for mixed candies. The flavoring may be dropped in spots in the kettle just before turning out, and stirred around once.

443—Lemon Cream Candy.

Take the same ingredients as for the lemon candy preceding and boil to the same degree—that is, when the drop in a cup of cold water sets brittle around the thin edges but still can be pressed to any shape between the thumb and finger—then add the flavoring and begin to stir it rapidly with a spoon. In from 10 to 20 turns it will begin to turn white and creamy. Then pour it quickly on to a buttered pan, or into cream bon-bon molds made of plaster paris or formed in a tray of starch.

444—Rose Candy—Clear.

1 pound granulated sugar.
1 teacup water.
1 rounded teaspoon powdered gum arabic.
½ teaspoon cream tartar.
Red coloring, few drops.
Rose extract to flavor.
Dissolve the gum in the hot water, put in the sugar and cream tartar and boil. When it has boiled about ten minutes try a drop in a cup of cold water. When it sets hard around the edges but still so that the entire drop can be pressed to any shape between the finger and thumb it is ready. Take it from the fire, drop in the flavoring and cochineal and stir around only once or twice to mix. Pour it into the buttered plate, or shapes, or into a shallow pan, to be broken and used for mixed candies.

445—Rose Cream Candy.

The same ingredients and proportions as the preceding receipt. Boil to the same degree. Then take the kettle from the fire, let it stand 5 minutes to lose some of its heat, add red coloring enough to make it pink, and a few drops of rose extract. Have a buttered dish ready, stir the candy rapidly with a spoon till it begins to change its bright appearance to a dull color, that is a sign of setting, then pour it immediately into the dish, or into

cream bon-bon molds made of plaster paris, or formed in a tray of starch.

446—Butter Scotch.

1½ pounds light brown sugar.
½ pound best fresh butter.
½ teacup vinegar.
½ teacup water.
Put all on to boil in a candy kettle, stir at first to mix well but not afterwards. When it has boiled 10 minutes try a drop in a cup of cold water. When it sets hard and brittle so that it breaks between the thumb and finger, pour it in a thin sheet in a buttered dish to cool. This kind cannot be stirred nor pulled, as the butter separates from the sugar, which then granulates. Cut in squares when cold and wrap the squares in wax tissue paper.

447—Caramels—Lemon.

1 pound granulated sugar.
½ cup water,
1 ounce butter—guinea-egg size.
4 drops oil of lemon.
Boil all together, except the flavoring about 10 or 15 minutes. Try by dropping a little in cold water. It must set hard and brittle. Do not stir it at, except two turns to mix in the oil of lemon. Pour into a buttered shallow pan, mark off while cooling, and cut in square caramels. Wrap in wax paper.

448—Chocolate Caramels.

1 pound sugar—either brown or white will do.
1 ounce butter.
Half cup milk.
2 ounces grated chocolate.
Vanilla flavoring.
Set the milk, butter and sugar on to boil, and stir in the grated chocolate and flavoring. After that do not stir the mixture again or it will go to sugar in the dish. Boil about 10 minutes. When a drop in cold water sets rather hard but not brittle pour the candy into a dish

well buttered.   Mark in little square blocks when set.   Warm the dish or tin tray a little if the candy sticks.

449—Molasses Candy to Pull.

1 large coffee cup molasses.
12 ounces sugar, either brown or white.
One-third cup vinegar.
Half cup water.
1 ounce butter.
Put all in a kettle and boil 15 or 20 minutes· Try in cold water. It must boil till the drops set brittle and fairly snap between the fingers. Then pour it on buttered plates. Pull.

Molasses candy if not pulled but merely allowed to set on dishes is improved by having about half a teaspoonful of soda stirred in after it has been taken from the fire and before it is poured out. Flavorings may be added at the same time.

450—Chocolate Candy to Pull.

8 ounces sugar.
8 ounces light colored molasses or syrup.
Half cup cream.
1 ounce grated chocolate.
Vanilla to flavor.
Boil the cream, molasses and sugar together for about 15 minutes, then throw in the chocolate and boil till the candy sets brittle in cold water. Pour on dishes, flavor when cold enough to handle and pull.

451—Fig Paste.

3 pints water.
1½ pounds sugar.
3 ounces corn starch.
Juice of half a lemon.
6 ounces glucose.
Boil sugar and water together and thicken with the starch same as in making a thickened pudding sauce, then put in the glucose and lemon juice and cook at the side of the range about 15 minutes. Color a portion of it pink. When

nearly cold mould it into any form and roll in powdered sugar.

452—Frosted Grapes.

Take grapes of two colors as red Tokays and white Muscadels and pull the bunches apart into clusters of three or four grapes each. Prepare a platter with the sort of pulverized sugar known as fine granulated, and make it warm. Whip some white of eggs in a shallow bowl, dip the grapes in it, lay them on the sugar and sift more sugar on top. Lay them on sieves to dry.

453—Grapes Glazed with Sugar.

Divide some bunches of grapes into small clusters.
Put into a deep saucepan.
1 pound sugar.
A large cup water.
½ teaspoon cream tartar.
Stir to dissolve the sugar, then set it on to boil, as if for candy.
When the syrup has boiled 10 minutes try a drop in cold water. When it sets so that it is hard to press between finger and thumb and the edges of drops are hard and brittle it is ready.
Take it from the fire, dip the clusters of grapes in (without ever stirring the candy) and lay them on dishes slightly greased to dry. Should the candy become set in the kettle it may have a spoonful or two of water added and be made hot again.

454—Frosted Oranges.

Make plain white icing and use it to dip orange slices in just when it has become too thick with beating not to run off, and yet thin enough to settle to smoothness. Or, if so good that it has already become too firm, thin it by adding the white of another egg or part of one.
Prepare the oranges by peeling and separating by the natural divisions, without breaking the covering or getting the pieces wet. Have a long splinter or

thin skewer ready for each one, and fill a large bowl with sugar or salt and stick them in. Stick the point of a skewer into the edge of the orange section, dip into the frosting, push the other end of the skewer into the bowl of salt, and let the pieces hang over the edge of the bowl in a warm place to dry.

456—Oranges Glazed with Sugar.

Oranges divided and put through the same course as grapes glazed with sugar.

There has been no calculation of the cost of the articles in this division which come under the head of candies, because they are not necessary in counting the cost of meals and, further, because they can be purchased cheaper than they can be made in small quantities. For the manufacturers have learned now to use large proportions of glucose instead of sugar and honey, and likewise make savings in their flavorings and in buying large quantities. There are times, however, when it is desirable to have a candy party in the house and, as people say, "it is nice to know how."

457—Almond Macaroons.

8 ounces granulated sugar.
4 whites of eggs.
8 ounces almonds.
1 teaspoon lemon juice or pinch of cream tartar.
Put the sugar and two of the whites in a deep bowl together, and beat with a wooden paddle about fifteen minutes, then add another white and beat again, then the lemon juice and then the last white. Crush the almonds by rolling them with the rolling-pin on the table. They need not be blanched (freed from the skins) unless so preferred. When they are reduced to meal mix them with the contents of the bowl. This mixture, as well as cake icing, should always be started with bowl and ingredients all cold, for if warm they cannot be beaten to the requisite degree of firmness.

Drop portions size of cherries on baking pans previously greased and then wiped dry. Bake in a slack oven, until light brown. Too much heat in the oven will cause them to melt and they should be little more than dried pale brown.

Cost of material—sugar 5, almonds 20, white of eggs and acid 6; 31 cents for 4 dozen. Turn to star kisses, No. 5, and note the difference in cost made by the almonds.

458—Common Boxed Macaroons.

12 ounces almonds.
8 ounces granulated sugar.
4 ounces flour.
4 eggs.   Pinch of salt.
1 teaspoon ammonia.
Crush the almonds without taking off the skins, with a rolling-pin upon the table. Mix them and the powder, sugar and flour together in a bowl. Drop the eggs in the middle and mix the whole into a rather soft dough. Place in lumps size of cherries on baking pans very slightly greased. Bake in a slack oven light brown. A few bitter almonds or peach kernels mixed in improves them.

Cost of material—45 cents for 2 pounds or about 6 dozen.

459—Meringue Paste.

This in various forms has to be mentioned often in these columns. It is always white of egg and sugar, but is sometimes soft meringue as on lemon pies, and some times nearly all sugar as in cake icing and "kisses."

460—Meringues a la Cream.

1 pound of granulated sugar.
6 whites of eggs.
Flavoring extract.
3 drops of acetic acid, or a pinch of tartaric, or a little lemon juice.
Put half the whites in a bowl without beating, and all the sugar with them

and beat together with a wooden spoon or paddle. It may save half the labor and insures success to have all the utensils and ingredients quite cold to begin with. It quickens the process if the beating can be done with two paddles, using both hands as regular workmen do. The bowl should be a deep one holding two quarts.

The sugar and egg at first are as stiff as dough. Beat rapidly and constantly for about 15 minutes, when it should be white and rather firm cake icing. Now add the remaining 3 whites of eggs, one at a time, and beat a few minutes between each one, but before the last one is added put in the acid and the flavoring.

The whole time of beating is about 25 minutes. An essential point is to beat the icing after the addition of each white until it will again draw up in peaks after the paddle is lifted from it, except the last white which should not be beaten much as it forms the gloss and smoothness on the meringues when they are baked.

Have ready some strips of writing paper two inches wide and pieces of boards (not pine) to bake the meringues on. Place spoonfuls egg-shaped on the strips of paper, not too close, smooth them with a knife, place the strips on the boards and dry-bake them with the oven door partly open. They need to bake nearly or quite half an hour. They can be lifted off the paper when cold. The boards prevent a crust forming on the bottom and the soft remainder inside can be scooped out. Fill the meringues with whipped cream sweetened and flavored, or with wine jelly, and either place two together side by side with melted candy or icing, like an open walnut shell, and pile whipped cream or chopped jelly upon them. These meringues likewise look well singly as cups filled with bright jellies of different colors and with ice creams.

Cost of material—20 cents for 30 single meringues or "kisses." Place two together with whipped cream, sweetened and flavored, inside, cost of filling 10 cents; 30 cents for 15, or two cents each on an average. But the time and labor are more than the material.

461—Rose Meringues.

Having made the meringue paste according to the preceding directions, color it, or a part of it a delicate pink and flavor with rose extract. Drop with the sack and tube, pieces like large marbles on baking pans previously greased and then wiped dry, and bake slowly without color. These rise rounded and nearly hollow and have a gauzy appearance when rightly baked.

Note—Sometimes the first panful of any of these varieties put into the range will run together and melt and come out worthless, and the next came out perfect meringues, or one side of the pan will be spoiled and the remainder good. This shows that the baking is the critical part of the making, and that is what we never can teach by word of mouth. At a certain gentle heat the egg in the meringues cooks and dries in shape, but at a higher degree the sugar melts and runs to candy in bubbles. At an insufficient degree of heat the meringue dries as it would in the sun and does not swell and change its appearance. In the brick oven after the bread has been withdrawn is the proper place to bake meringues.

462—Chocolate Meringues.

There is nothing of the kind choicer or more fragile than these Only a slight change in the ingredients from the foregoing varieties.

1 pound granulated sugar.

6 whites eggs.

3 ounces grated common chocolate—a heaping cupful.

2 teaspoons vanilla extract.

Beat up the icing as directed for meringues a la creme, and when it is finished mix in the chocolate thoroughly. Drop round portions with the sack and tube on baking pans and bake at a very gentle heat. These rise rounded like a mushroom, and nearly hollow. They slip from the pans easily when cold.

Cost of material—see star kisses and meringues a la creme.

463—Almond Rings and Fingers.

Make the same as the preceding with 8 ounces of blanched almonds minced very small instead of chocolate. Put a smaller tube in the forcing sack, and form finger shapes and rings of the almond meringue paste on baking pans, and bake them in a very slack oven. These all bake light and nearly hollow and have a fine glazed surface.

Note—The foregoing varieties, which can all be made out of one large bowl of meringue paste, form a handsome assortment for the cake stands, to build pyramids, to place around glass bowls of fruit, to decorate cakes and to fill icing or nougat baskets with.

464—Icing and Ornamenting Cakes.

Fruit cakes always need two coats of icing. Common glaze or sugar only, melted with white of egg, may do for the first, and if to be very nice, mix some minced almond in it. The first coat will dry in an hour in a warm place.

Cake icing is the same as the star kiss mixture or meringue, at No. 5, only it is surer to beat sugar and whites together in a bowl, and powdered sugar makes the smoothest icing. Put into a deep bowl two whites and a cupful of sugar, which makes a stiff paste, and beat them with a wooden paddle fifteen minutes. Add some flavoring extract. To smooth over the cake cut a strip o writing paper an inch wide and, stretching it between the hands, draw the edge over the top of the cake.

To make a border put some of the ing into a cornet made of writing paper and pinned. Clip of the point, and the pipe of icing that is pressed out can be laid on the edge of the cake like a braid Leaves and flowers can be bought ready made.

465—Wine and Fruit Jellies.

To make the brilliantly clear, many-hued, and delicately flavored jellies that are found on the tables of the best hotels and at the confectioners, the simple lemon jelly has first to be made in perfection. It is technically called stock jelly, because, when finished, it can be mixed with wine or other liquors and cordials, or be flavored and colored to make as many varities as may be desired.

It may be as well to explain that these jellies are transient and will not keep over two or three days, not like the boiled fruit jellies, but of the same nature as the old-fashioned calf's foot jelly, made now with gelatine.

Once making stock jelly should serve either for a large party or two or there meals.

For 3 quarts of jelly take:
$3\frac{1}{2}$ quarts of water.
$1\frac{1}{2}$ pounds of sugar.
4 ounces of gelatine
5 lemons—juice of all, thin shaved rinds of 2 or 3, according to size.
1 ounce of whole spices—cloves, mace and stick cinnamon.
5 whites of eggs to clarify it.

Put the water in a bright brass kettle, add all the other ingredients—the lemon juice squeezed in without the seeds, the yellow rind pared very thin, and the white of eggs beaten a little with some water mixed in first. The clean egg shells may be put in also to assist in the clarification. Use the sheet gelatine that floats, for preference. Then set the kettle on the side of a range and let it slowly come to a boil with occasional stirring.

Let it boil about half an hour, and above all, to avoid the trouble and waste of having to boil it again, be sure that the white foam of egg on top becomes thoroughly cooked so that it will go down and mix with the jelly again like so much meal. Sometimes, to accomplish this, as a lid cannot be kept on without its boiling over, it is necessary to set the kettle in the oven, a few minutes to get heat enough on top.

Then run it through a jelly bag suspended from a hook. The boiling having been properly attended to, there should not be the slightest difficulty in getting it to run through not only clear but bright and transparent as glass. The first pouring coats the inside of the filtering bag with the coagulated white of egg, and each succeeding running through brightens the jelly.

It may be set down as a rule that this kind of jelly cannot be successfully made without more or less lemon juice, or some acid equivalent—it will not run through a filtering bag without. A cheaper quality can be made with less sugar and lemons.

The stock having been made, it can now be divided into as many kinds as may be wished. But the stock jelly is already good and mildly flavored and care should be taken not to over season it, or injure its bright appearance.

Lemon extract cannot be put into jelly because it makes a milky appearance and dims its brilliancy. Orange extract the same. Most of the other extracts can be used to flavor. Use wine in small proportion to mix with some of the stock, and color deep red, but run through the jelly bag again while it is yet warm. Flavor some with vanilla, and color it either amber or brown with burnt sugar. Flavor some with strawberry and color it pink, and leave some plain, pale yellow.

Cost of material—sugar 15, gelatine average 40, lemons 10, spices 10, whites 10; 85 or 90 cents for 3 quarts or 50 saucers or glasses for dessert.

466—One Quart of Jelly.

The rule is for good quality.
1 quart of water,

1½ ounces of gelatine.
8 ounces of sugar.
1 or 2 lemons.
1 teaspoonful of whole mixed spices.
2 whites of eggs and the clean shells.
But a cupful of water must be added to allow for evaporation and loss, unless it is intended to add ½ pint of wine to the stock jelly produced.

Note,—There are different kinds of gelatine and some that is imported will if bought at retail cost nearly double the above estimate for that ingredient, while some of the sheet gelatine can be bought at a dollar a pound or one third less than our count.

467—Soda Mead.

A "health drink" for summer.
Make a syrup with:
1 quart water.
2 ounces of whole spices consisting of equal quantities of cloves, stick cinnamon, ginger, coriander, seed and cardamons.
1 tablespoon powdered gum arabic.
4 pounds honey.
Boil the spices in the water about half an hour, strain into another saucepan, put in the honey, boil up and skim, dissolve the gum in it. Use same as soda syrup, about a gill to each glass of soda. The gum is to produce foam and white of egg answers the same purpose but not to keep long.

468—English Mead—Small Quantity.

A fermented beer of the "root beer" sort.
To make five gallons procure either a keg that size from the liquor stores or a stone jug. Take:
4 gallons water—(a pail and a half.)
16 pounds honey—(20 large cups.)
1 ounce hops.
1 ounce of coriander seeds.
Rind of 2 lemons.
½ cupful of yeast—or yeast cake softened (with water.) Boil the honey and water together about an hour, skimming

frequently, until no more scum rises.
Tie the hops in a piece of muslin, and the
coriander seed and shaved lemon rind in
another, put them in a tub or large stone
jar and pour the boiling liquor upon them.
When it is no more than milk warm,
spread yeast upon both sides of a piece
of toast and set it floating. Cover and
let stand in a warm place to ferment for
three days, then draw it off without sediment into your five gallon keg, stone jug
or demijohn. Let stand six hours longer,
full to the brim, so that whatever rises
may run over, then cork down and keep
cool. The longer it is kept the better.

469—Wine Mead in Small Quantity

4 pounds of honey—6 cups.
2 gallons nearly of warm water—30
cups.
½ cupful of yeast—compressed, dissolved will do.

Mix the honey, warm water and yeast
together and fill up a two- gallon jug or
keg with it. Set it in a warm corner to
ferment, and as the yeast rises and runs
over the mouth of the jug keep it filled
up with the quart that was left over.
When the fermentation stops cork it tight
and keep cool.

It becomes better with keeping for
several months, and ought to be in bottles.

It is recommended to improve the flavor to put in two lemons sliced, and half
pint of brandy, both to be put in the keg
or jug after the fermentation has ceased.

470—Home Made Beer.

It helps the understanding of what is
to be done if you have never made beer
before to remember that any kind of
sweetened liquor with a little yeast added will ferment and become "pop" in
three or four days. The difference in
strength of beers is according to the difference of amount of sweetening in the
liquor used, strong beer or ale being
made with plenty of malt and other
sweetening added and small beer made

by adding more water to the same malt
for a second drawing. Once the method
is understood it is only a question of different flavoring to make spruce beer, ginger beer, or any other variety as they all
go through the same process.

471—Molasses Beer.

Procure a 10 gallon keg and another
holding 5 gallons, or a jug or two, as
there will be about 15 gallons of beer.
Take

8 ounces hops.
4 quarts coarse ground malt.
6 pounbs brown sugar.
3 pints reboiled Cuba molasses.
1 pint brewers yeast or a quart of
baker's stock.

Boil the hops in a kettle with 2 pails
of water about half an hour, then pour it
boiling hot over the malt, sugar, and mo-
asses in a tub, stir up, let stand an hour,
then strain the liquor without stirring up
the sediment into a keg. Boil 2 pails
more of water, pour it to the malt etc.,
remaining in the tub to extract the remaining substance and when it is settled
strain it into the keg along with the first,
then use another pail of water the same
way but it need not be boiled, only have
the yeast added and when the large lot
is no more than milk warm strain this
yeast water into it.

Let ferment in the kegs 2 or 3 days,
according to the temperature, keeping
them full to the bung so that the yeast
may work over and run off. Then cork
tight and keep a week or a month as
may be desired. If drawn off clear after
ermenting and bottled it becomes very
strong after a few weeks.

472—Ginger Pop.

8 quarts water.
2 ounces raw ginger pounded to pieces.
2 lemons.
3 heaping cups sugar.
2 tablespoons cream tartar.
½ cup of yeast.

EIGHT WEEKS

AT A

SUMMER RESORT.

OUR DAILY BILL OF FARE

AND WHAT IT COST.

THE SECOND PART OF

"COOKING * FOR * PROFIT."

Originally Published in the "San Francisco Daily Hotel Gazette"

BY

JESSUP WHITEHEAD

CHICAGO.

1893.

Eight Weeks at a Summer Resort.

This is my diary of a time when I went out to gain experience at a small place, as compared with our hotel magnitudes, but a first-class summer boarding house, nevertheless, situated on the shore of that beautiful sheet of water called Uintah Lake in the State of Cornucopia. A great number of interesting questions concerning the business of boarding people for profit are to be answered in this way as will be seen as we go along, but more especially the object I have in view is to stop once for all the ceaseless inquiries of a lady friend who keeps a boarding house and is very economically disposed. This lady knows that I have been cooking for profit all my life and is aware that I have become quite indifferent in regard to the state of the market, the state of the larder, or the state of the storeroom, having learned that a good meal can be made out of very slim materials if one knows how to manage, and therefore seems to expect that I can answer the hardest kind of questions off-hand on all sorts of unexpected contingencies.

"Oh," she said one day when I was going out just after breakfast, "before you go do tell me what I can have for dinner?" and she put her hand to her head in the same old state of perplexity she· was so well used to.

"Well, Mrs. Tingee, a suitable soup would be—"

"The weather is too warm for soup," she broke in with, "and besides, I have nothing to make it of, and Anne would not have time."

In this respect I think she was wrong. In warm weather people take liquid food all the more readily and the soup is seldom too hot. I find that the only two dishes that are invariably eaten out clean with no remainders are the soup and ice cream. However, I went on:

"If it is too warm for soup, you might get a fine bluefish and stuff and bake it with about a pound or less of slices of pickled pork laid under and over it, or a pompano or two of them, broiled, with softened butter and lemon-juice, and roast some young chickens, and get some of that early summer squash and corn that has come from the South, and a half gallon of thick, sweet cream and a dozen boxes of strawberries and then if you ·have some sponge cake and delicate cake ready made and frosted and make your coffee strong and clear, you may get through this dinner time very well and you have all the afternoon and night in which to plan for to-morrow."

"I don't want to know that," the lady snapped out, half cross. "Do you know that I have had to drop the price of day board from four dollars a week to three dollars and a half, because the boarders teased me so to do so; they said they could not stand it to pay more and I had to do it, and I should like to see myself buying strawberries for them at thirty cents a quart and cream at twenty-five. Anybody can go to market and buy the best of everything and make a good dinner; what I want to know is what you do when you have no pompano, no chickens, no fresh vegetables, no fruit, no cream, no cake, no nothing—now tell me that."

"Can't tell you, Mrs. Tingee, but I will write out what it costs to give first-class board, plentiful, reasonably rich, but not extraordinary nor extravagant and perhaps you will pick out some items that will be useful to you."

So the knotty question of "What do you do for a good meal when you have nothing that you want to make it with?" recurs continually. How, for instance, can we serve mint sauce with roast lamb in Senator Sawmill's town, where not only no mint is to be bought, but none of the inhabitants apparently have ever heard of any other mint, but Uncle Sam's, where money is made? And here is another instance :

500—A Little Party Supper.

June 25. The proprietor of the Hotel D'Arlington came out with a cigar in his mouth and stood by smiling for a few minutes while I was cutting meat for supper. There was something coming. Presently he said :

"I can't let you go to Uintah Lake for two days yet. Does it make much difference?"

"What has happened?"

"Melnotte, the actor's troupe disbands here to pass the vacation at the summer resorts, and he wants to give a little farewell supper to-night, and to-morrow night the college graduates have a strawberry and ice cream party in the dining room."

"It is after four o'clock now; not much time to get up a supper when our regular supper runs till eight."

"But they don't want this till eleven and it is just a little cold supper nicely set on the table, nothing elaborate. I don't want it to cost much—what can you give them?"

"There are plenty of things, I suppose that can be given for such an occasion, but one can't say in a minute. It is a bad time of year for a cold party supper —no oysters. Will there be any ladies; that is, shall we want any sweets—ice cream?"

"Miss Ophelia will be in the party."

"That is the star actress?"

"Yes, and one or two others, and two newspaper men, but I would not go to the trouble of ice cream—there will only be seventeen all together."

"We must have some chickens."

"I m afraid we can't get any. I have not seen a chicken in this town since the frost broke up."

"Turkeys, then"

"Harder yet. I saw one old gobbler at the butcher's three weeks ago, but it is a thousand chances to one against finding one now."

"We have the best of all sorts of butcher's meats for every meal, but you don't want to sit your actors down to dishes of the same meats cold that they have had hot three times in the day already. Cold roast fowl would be a rarity, and then there must be a salad and it ought to be of turkey or chicken. Perhaps you can find canned chicken at the stores, and if it is not very good for salad alone it can be made better by mixing with white veal which we can get at the butchers. It may be that you can find boneless roast turkey in cans, too, and one or two will suffice. And get some canned Baratana shrimps and let the boy try once more for parsley."

"No use; the people in this town don't know what parsley is, but I will telephone to the stores about the other things—do you want any lobster?"

"I think not. Canned lobster is an abomination. Take shrimp instead, and lettuce and lemons."

The telephone having been employed and yielded nothing, a boy was sent out who returned in an hour with the intelligence that in all this town of 15,000 inhabitants there was no poultry either fresh or canned, but one merchant sent word that he had some nice canned crab and with each two-pound can, eight crab shells were furnished to bake in; that he supplied some of the same to Mrs. Congressman Windmill's party and they were much pleased. So this following was the bill-of-fare that resulted:

Devilled Crab in Shell.
Sardines with Brown Bread.
Garnished Pickles.
Corned Tongue.
Shrimps in Mayonaise.
French Rolls and Butter Bread, Swiss Cheese.
"Maids of Honor" Tartlets.
Strawberries and Cream.   Cake.
Coffee.

Wine, extra.   Cigars, extra.

Of course there was no menu card; a long table was set suitable for farewell speech-making and those things were set on it; and, the waiters out of pure good will went out in the twilight and despoiled somebody's garden of large bunches of lilac and snowballs for decoration.

Cost of material:

3 cans crab @ 33⅓		$1 00
3 cans shrimps @ 30		90
6 small cans sardines @ 20	1	20
6 heads lettuce		15
1 pint salad oil		50
6 lmons for dressin g and garnish		15
½ a cold corned tongue		15
1 bunch red radishes for garnish		5
9 eggs for salad dressing		15
6 quarts strawberries @ 15		90
1 quart cream		25
24 tartlets		25
Rolls, bread, butter		26
Cheese, pickles, condiments		25
2 pounds of cake		25
20 cups coffee (½ ℔ Java)		18
2 pounds sugar		16

$6 75

501—A Dish of Devilled Crabs.

Opened the 3 cans. They proved to be solid packed and good, only a little too salty. It is the common way, to mix fine bread crumbs with the crab meat, but there being rather more than enough of this, the only addition made was a cupful of rich butter sauce made with melted butter, to avoid adding the salt dregs, and some pepper. Buttered the insides of the shells; filled 20 of them, rounded up, and on top pressed some very fine minced bread crumbs; baked to a toast-brown in the oven and basted with a table-spoonful of melted butter.

Ready an hour before supper time.

To serve: Covered each one of three large platters with four of the handsomest lettuce leaves, the curled green edges coming around the edges of the dishes, and arranged the crabs in star form upon them with quartered lemons between the points.

502—Sardines With Brown Bread and Butter; or, en Canape.

Shook out three boxes of sardines on to a dish, took up the unbroken sardines with forks and laid on paper to drain. Chopped a green pickle extremely fine and a hard boiled egg and mixed them together. Cut long, thin slices of graham bread about width of two fingers, buttered them, sprinkled the minced garnish down the middle of each with a tea-spoon, and laid a sardine upon it. Arranged these diagonally on two small platters with radishes scraped in stripes laid between.   The other three boxes of sardines were opened and served in the boxes as they were, for those who might prefer them, on platters having a border of shred lettuce.

503—Cold Corned Tongue.

Red tongue sliced slantwise, extremely thin, enough for two small platters. Minced green radish tops in little heaps around the edges for ornament, and a thin, round slice of lemon in the middle.

504—Shrimps in Mayonaise.

This is only another term for shrimp salad and it is not necessary that the mayonaise dressing (No. 151) be used every time.

Took 5 hard-boiled yolks and 3 raw.
½ cup olive oil.
1 table spoon sugar.
2 teaspoons salt and 1 of pepper.
1 teaspoon made mustard.
Juice of 2 or 3 lemons.
A small cup vinegar.
Whipped whites of 3 eggs.

Rubbed all the yolks to a paste with the back of a spoon and added oil, sugar, mustard, salt, pepper, lemon juice and vinegar, all a little at a time. Kept the lettuce in cold water till the last, then shook and dried between two napkins. Shred the white hearts fine, like slaw, and mixed the shrimps with it. Whipped the whites, added to the salad dressing, poured over the salad, stirred up lightly, dished in two deep glass dishes and garnished with the boiled whites in rings and little round cuts of radishes. Set salad plates handy and silver forks for the waiters to serve it from the dishes if required.

505—Maids of Honor.

This is the old-fashioned name of some sorts of cheese cakes or tartlets. As it is often to be met with in English and old Virginia bills-of-fare it is necessary to use the term, if only for explanatory purposes. Maids of Honor are different from ordinary patty-pan tarts in, being made of fine puff paste, which rises high in the pans.

Took puff paste, left over from dinner pastry, rolled out thin, cut out with a fancy scollop-edge cutter, large as the top of a coffee cup, and pressed the flats into shallow gem pans. Put a teaspoonful of lemon honey (506)—called lemon cheese cake by the English—in each; baked in a slack oven; took out just before the "cheesecake" began to boil over the edges and spoil the appearance. Served on small pastry plates, four in each set, at intervals down the table.

506—Lemon Butter; or Paste; or Cheesecake; or Lemon Honey.

A world-wide favorite made of—
1 cup sugar—8 ounces.
3 lemons.
Butter, size of an egg—2 ounces.
4 to 6 yolks or 3 whole eggs—not particular.

Put the sugar, butter and grated rinds and juice into a saucepan and boil, add the yolks and stir until it becomes thick.

It looks like cold honey when it is cold. May be kept for weeks. Is good to spread jelly cakes with and to fill tartlets and eclairs. It is seldom worth while to make less than double the above amount.

507—Fresh Strawberries.

Washed them in a large jar of cold water to free them from sand. Picked and heaped them in three glass bowls with individual pitchers of cold cream and bowls of powdered sugar at hand, and piles of glass sauce dishes. Cake of two or three varieties in the usual cake baskets on folded napkins.

It was not, then, a strictly cold supper after all, since the devilled crabs were fresh and warm, but what was of more consequence than that, the entire party expected, did not come. There was a moonlight excursion by steamboat that night and Miss Ophelia, and the two ladies and the two newspaper men went off on the boat and only twelve remained; still, the inroads these made upon the eatables showed plainly that had all been there, there would only have been just provisions enough.

The Art of Charging Enough.

June 26. This morning I asked the proprietor of the Hotel D'Arlington:

"Have you any objection to telling me what you charged for last night's supper?"

"What would you have charged?" he returned, with the complacent smile of one who knows how.

While I was figuring on a dollar a plate and not knowing what was to be done about the odd number and the absentees, he added:

"I charged them twenty dollars for the supper and there was a profit on wine and cigars, and they were pleased and satisfied. If it had been a party of our town boys from the college I might have had to take seventy-five cents a plate, but these actors would have gone away thinking they had been treated in a second-class manner if I had charged them less—and I do not work for nothing."

"A very close friend of mine lost his chance of a fortune in the restaurant business some years ago through not knowing how to charge enough."

"It is a very essential thing to know in our business."

"Yes. He took a place and went on serving the best that was to be obtained in a superior style on a sort of ten-percent profit plan until all the one-horse eating houses around him closed, one after the other and he had all the trade."

"And then he raised his prices!"

"No."

"He was a fool."

"Yes. And went on doing more business and working harder and making less money, until—"

"He took sick?"

"No. But a man who knew how to charge five dollars for a two-and-a-half supper came along, bought him out easy, stepped in and made a few thousands without ever taking his gloves off, as it were."

"Now, that is not the way to look at the matter. The man who charged five dollars for a two-and-a-half supper did quite right and just what a portion of the public wanted him to do. They that paid it paid two-and-a-half for exclusiveness. They paid a price that Tom, Dick and Harry could not pay, purposely that those three objectionable persons might be kept out; and, they paid it for better table-wear, finer furnishings and better service.

There is a vast amount of working for nothing in the ordinary boarding business. Great apparent profits would turn out to be dead loss in many cases if all the principals were paid as exactly as the hired helpers are. Summer boarding-house keepers will tend a garden four months in advance, turn the products into the boarding-house and count so much more made because they have no vegetables and fruits to buy when if they paid themselves for their gardening they would come out in debt.

Such might even be the case with such an apparently renumerative supper as that previously detailed, and this will explain why persons never become suddenly rich by setting up to furnish parties to order, and why they cannot afford to be cheap in their charges, and why, moreover, hotel-keepers themselves seldom make any profit on any suppers or banquets that are beyond the easy capacity of their own establishment without outside help. If a little extra supper in a hotel requires the attendance until a late hour of three waiters, a pantryman or girl, and a dishwasher, the proprietor is not ordinarily expected to pay extra for such service, because, hiring by the month some accommodation is looked for from the help as an offset to the times of dull business when there is little to do, but the pay goes on all the same. But if these had to be specially hired for the occasion the cost would be one dollar each in most places, and half that amount in the very cheapest. A first-class cook in New York or Saratoga, if called in to prepare a private party can generally obtain ten dollars a day for his services. Ordinarly, a first-class caterer in any city, having such cooks in his employ charges for their services when they are sent out about \$5 a day, and about such a rate the hotel-keeper would have to pay if he had not his own cook to command. Add then the cost of gas, of fires, the hire of dishes and tableware, hire of express wagon and a hand to go to and fro, pack and unpack, the washing of napkins and table cloths and other like incidentals and the anticipated profits from even the finest ball supper may delusively vanish before you know how it all happened—unless you rush in slowly and know how to charge enough.

508—A School Commencement Strawberry and Ice Cream Supper.

June 26. The supper ordered for to-night is a very different affair from that of the actors. It is for some professors and teachers but mostly for girl graduates who are not hotel boarders. It is condemed in advance as an affair that will be more bother than it is worth; that will not pay a cent; but, that must be accepted for the sake of popularity in the town. Perhaps it will turn out more profitable than is anticipated. It is to be fifty cents a plate for all who eat except five musicians who are free. There is a guarantee of forty persons with a possibility of seventy-five. Orders to provide for fifty and take the chances on more or less; to make nothing expensive and not lose any more on the party than was absolutely unavoidable

The bill-of-fare:

Thin sliced baked ham 5 dishes.

Thin sliced corned tongue, 5 dishes.
Thin sliced bread, 10 plates.
Ham sandwiches, 2 dishes.
Butter; the usual dishes and individual chips.
Cream rolls (No. 260) 10 plates.
Pickles cut in thin strips, 10 plates.
Coffee cakes, (No. 262) 10 plates.
Lemon tartlets (like No. 134) 15 plates.
Angel Food cake (No. 2) frosted, 4 stands.
Butter sponge cake (like No. 299) 4 stands
Strawberries, 5 glass bowls.
Vanilla ice cream (No. 196) served individually from a side table.
Lemonade, an unmeasured quantity well iced.
Coffee; cream; powdered sugar.
Cost of material:

Ham, 4 ℔s @ 15	60
Corned tongue, two, @ 30	60
Bread, 6 loaves	25
Curled lettuce for garnish	5
Devilled ham for sandwiches	25
Butter, 4 pounds @ .25	1 00
Pickles, 1 qt.	10
Cream rolls, sixty	50
Coffee cakes, seventy-two	90
Lemon tartlets, seventy-two	90
Angel Food with thirty whites, etc.	70
Butter sponge cake, frosted	80
Strawberries, 10 qts. @ .12	1 20
Ice cream, 5 qts. cream, sugar,etc	1 60
Lemons, 3 doz	75
Sugar for lemonade, four ℔s	35
Cream for table, two qts.	50
Powdered sugar, two ℔s	18
Coffee, one-half ℔	20
	$11 43

Sixty-nine persons partook of the supper of whom sixty-four paid fifty cents each—$32. There was quite enough of everything, and nothing left; the only thing requiring to be eked out by a plan of dishing up light was the ice cream. The only freezer in the house held nominally eight quarts. Five quarts of pure cream put in increased to seven quarts in freezing and was all the freezer would hold. Among the best things to make for such an occasion are the coffee cakes referred to. These were made like split rolls in shape, then the edges notched with a knife to make what the boys call "dog-toes," then set to rise. They open up in baking, are rich looking and when brushed over with syrup and dredged with sugar are the showiest things on the table.

509—Sandwiches of Devilled Ham.

A twenty-five cent can of the devilled ham sold in the stores will spread 50 thin sandwiches. Sandwiches are never good unless they are thin. There should be a very sharp knife used and an effort to try how thinly the bread can be sliced. Spread one slice with butter the other with ham, put them together and cut off the edges smooth and even.

UINTAH LAKE,
STATE OF CORNUCOPIA,
July 1.

Came over with Mr. Farewell and his family of boys to commence the resort season. It will be a good opportunity to note the cost of first-class family living, with a regular bill-of-fare.

Mr. Farewell has invented and manufactures the only successful fire escape and in the course of the business has learned a good deal about hotels. He formerly had a "shooting box" at the lake where he would pass an occasional week, then as the lakeshore became settled up he built a house to bring his family to for a few days. Then he built another in which they could live all summer. Then came all the relatives and friends and business acquaintances who respected Mr. Farewell, and he built still another house, wherein they could pass the summer, too. But it is very likely that at the end of last summer's pleasure the hostess quit pretty tired. I don't know what she said, but the fact is, that this year Mr. Farewell starts in with a regular hotel register a regular manager, a regular housekeeper, a regular cook and a bran new omnibus. I am afraid it will not pay him in cash, but he will get peace, rest and pleasure for his family at a less cost than heretofore.

So, this is the kitchen; a summer kitchen, truly; not ceiled, with plain boards for a floor. I am glad it is so, for there are no hotel advantages to be counted. I'll bet it is just like all the rest of the summer boarding house kitchens, on both sides of the lake, just like the Trulirural House, over on the point; just like Swibob's on the right and Barnacle's on the left. Yes, it is good enough.

And this is the stove, a number 14 or 16, or thereabout; and this is the cook's hot water tank—a big tin teakettle—the reservoir being for soft-water for the dishwashing. I suppose there has been many a fine meal cooked for a hundred or more on smaller stoves than this, and teakettle cookery is not so bad in some places. Anyway, it is as good as all the rest and the stove has an immense oven. The Palmer House at the depot has a fair-sized range and a new 30 inch broiler arrived for it on the last train, but we are not a large house like that.

510—The Question of How Many Fires.

There is a wonderful disproportion in some hotels between the size of the furnishings and appliances and the results they are intended to secure. One of the best fitted-up, most city-like country hotels I know of, is the Devereux House in the city of Pandora, State of Cornucopia, but it is also keeping up one of the silliest pieces of extravagance in running seven fires in the kitchen for the cooking for generally forty and never more than fifty persons; the proprietor at the same time paying $6 a cord for wood and fifteen cents a bushel for charcoal and pinching and saving in all other ways to make both ends meet. As some readers will be puzzled to see how so many fires can exist in one small kitchen at once, we will give a diagram to show:

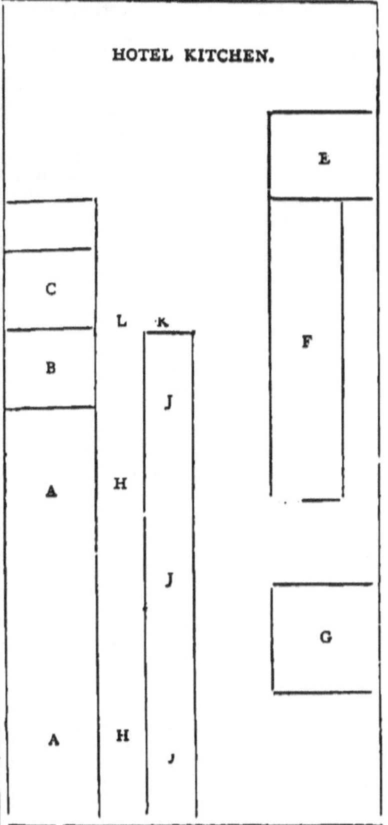

AA—12-foot range, steam chest and hot water tank—fire sixteen hours a day.

B—30-inch broiler—fire six hours a day.

C—No. 10 cook stove for batter cakes, private tea-pots, milk for toast, soft water in reservoir—fire eight hours a day.

D—Charcoal toast range — fire six hours a day.

E—Two-story zinc oven dish-heater with furnace—fire ten hours a day.

F—Carving table with furnace, for keeping rolls and corn bread warm and for dinner—fire ten hours a day.

G—Pastry cooks oven, zinc, with furnace—fire ten hours a day.

HH—Hot place for the cook.

. I—Hard place for the hand that keeps up all the fires.

JJJ—Kitchen table; K meat block; L dead line for help.

The reason why they use so many fires to feed 40 or 50 people is that once upon a time, long years ago, the house used to contain 150 people and the fires were not too many; the trade went away but still, like the Aztecs, they keep up the sacred fires.

Now here is the other extreme:

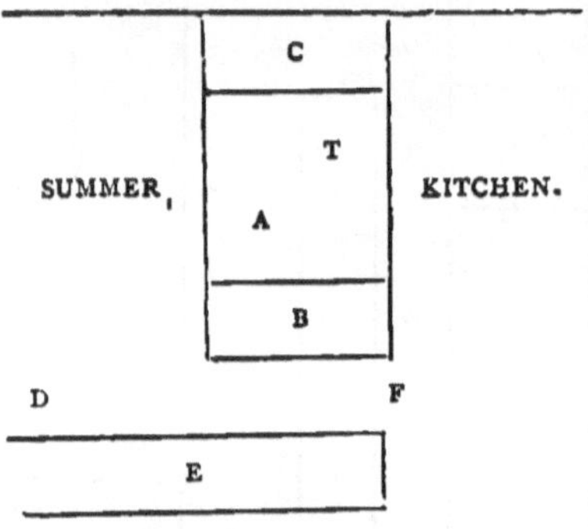

A—One large cook stove.

B—Big broiling hearth and gridiron to same.

C—Hot water reservoir and tin dish-closet under.

D—Meat block.

E—Kitchen table.

F—Dead line for help.

T—Tea kettle.

We all like plenty of conveniences, a place for everything, and I am not going to make an argument against plenty of range room. There must be a medium, however, somewhere between these two pictures. This stove is to serve for some number unknown except that it will never exceed fifty. How well I remember the splendid and plentiful dinners that used to be cooked for as many as from 150 to 300 people on those little up-river steamboats at this very low-water time of year, on light six-foot ranges that we could almost carry around. More than half had to be done by steaming, because the ovens were so small. Half-a-dozen entrees would be well cooked over the ash-pan full of coals with the gridiron upon them. Right now, there is the *City of Fremont* of the Lake Superior line setting a magnificent table for large numbers, though her kitchen (caboose) is little more than a cupboard; the range one of the smallest; the pastry room positively too small for a man to stretch his arms to pull off a coat. And still they prepare all sorts of delicacies in it. "There is more in the man than there is in the land."

Supper.

Only been here an hour or two and boy clamorous for pie already. "It aint good for you, honey." No provisions but some fragments of the janitor's and contents of lunch basket.

Ham, cold boiled, sliced thin ½℔	10
Salt pork, fried 1℔	10
Potatoes, German fried	4
Tomatoes, 1 3-℔ can, seasoned	14
Bread and butter	11
Coffee, tea, milk, sugar	10
Baked custard, 2 quarts	21
	80

Fourteen persons; 6 cents a plate.

511—German Fried Potatoes.

This is the name the restaurant keepers have given to the family style of cooking potatoes. Boil potatoes with their jackets on then peel and cut in thick slices into a large frying pan. Put in drippings, or butter, or the fat from fried pork enough only to well grease the pan; let the potatoes have plenty of time to brown on one side then shake them over till they are nicely colored all through. Sprinkle with salt.

512—Plain Baked Custard.

Quickest and easiest of all puddings.
Took 6 cups milk (4½ cents)
10 eggs (12½ cents)
1 cup of sugar (4 cents)
Grating of nutmeg.
Beat all together with a wire egg beater, pour into an earthern dish and bake. Be careful to take it out as soon as it is set, as too long baking causes it to break and turn watery. Should be eaten cold. No sauce needed.

Breakfast.

July 2nd.

Minced ham on toast	20
Cold ham, thin sliced ½ lb	10
Poached eggs, 8 orders, 16 eggs	21
Potatoes baked in milk	13
Baking powder biscuits, 40 large	72
Butter, 15; bread, 3; cream, 10; milk, 6; coffee and tea, 4	38

$1 38

Fifteen persons; 9 cents a plate.

513—Minced Ham on Toast.

It is best when freshly made. The ham should be sliced and then minced and served up as soon as it is hot, before it turns to a dark color. Took the last lean trimmings of the boiled ham that would not make slices, 1 lb, 18 cents, minced fine. Put in saucepan, butter, 1 cent, and large spoonful water, put in the ham and let get hot but not fry. Season with black pepper only. Made 12 thin slices of toast of one-half loaf bread, 2½ cents. Spread a spoonful of minced ham evenly on the toast as called for.

514—Potatoes Baked in Milk.

A third of a peck of potatoes, 4 cents, pared and cut in thick slices raw into a tin baking pan. Added part of a green onion, a teaspoon salt, butter, 1 cent, and two quarts milk, 6 cents, and put in when the fire was first made, baked slowly until the milk was dried down like cream and brown on top.

515—Baking Powder Biscuits.

The lady before referred to, who keeps a boarding house under difficulties, did not take kindly to my way of making biscuits, it seems too dear; but, I should like to talk it over with her. In the first place, there is so much difference between the cheapness of all sorts of bread and vegetable food and the dearness of meat, that we cannot take too much pains to make the breads good in order that they may be eaten and the meat saved. Then in places where one man cook has to do as much as four of Mrs. Tingee's girls put together and be ready every time without excuses, the difference in time saved between our method of pouring in the butter or lard in a melted state and adding the milk or water to it and so getting them mingled with the flour instantly, and the other slow way of rubbing the cold shortening into the dry flour with the hands, becomes quite an object. But I do not recommend anybody to make baking powder bread or biscuit anyway, only for convenience. It is dear and not nearly so good as yeast-raised bread and rolls. This is the way:

2 quarts or pounds flour (7 cents)
6 teaspoons, rounded up, baking powder (4 cents)
½ cup soft butter or laid (4 cents)
Little salt
2 cups milk (2 cents) or water.

Mix the powder in the flour by rapid stirring around. Pour in the shortening in a hollow made in the middle and the milk (not too cold, else it will set the shortening in lumps) and mix up soft. Press the dough together on the table and when worked tolerably smooth let it stand a minute or two and it will roll out better. Makes about two dozen biscuits, according to size.

516—The Round of Beef for Steak.

We are going to get our meats from Basswood City by express twice a week or as needed, and our fresh fish from Whitefish Bay the same way. There are some fishes in Uintah Lake, but they will not come out when wanted, so we have to send further. When I was at Basswood I found the steward of the new Memphremagog House at that place was buying selected round of beef instead of loin for steaks. Not the common round steaks which the butchers cut straight along good and bad together, but the tender side only, cut off the bone as neat and trim as a ham. I had previously written up and advocated the use of the tender side of the round instead of the most expensive short loins, but had in view the case of such hotels as Black's, the other rival house here at the depot, where they have ninety summer boarders, at $10 a week, and still buy their beef by the entire side at a time, hind-quarter, fore-quarter, neck, shanks and everything. But the getting the butcher to cut out the best piece of round for a house every day was new to me. The tough side of the round, of which there is a portion in every whole round steak, is about one third of it. How the butcher disposed of that does not concern us, but he charged the steward for the other 13 cents a pound. The choice cut of the loin at the same time was costing 15 cents and one-fourth of it was bone. Twenty pounds of loin at 15 cents comes to $3. Take out the bone and you have fifteen pounds of meat that has cost 20 cents, a clear difference of $7 on every hundred pounds of beef bought. This meat is not as good as the best parts of the loin but it ranks second best, and is better than the flank part which every loin cut carries. The drawback is a piece of the sinewy end of the round, about three or four pounds that become tough and dry and has to be cut off to make either corned beef or soup.

There are plenty of people to whom one beefsteak seems as good as another, they are so hungry it makes no difference; but, at the same time there are others whom we like to pamper with choice bits, and besides, we are loth to lose the rich loin bone for soup, so I called on the butcher and arranged that he shall send a round and a loin alternately, and that promises to be good enough. While that is on the way we shall have to pick up something at "The Glen," where the village butcher kills something once or twice a week, or whenever he has nothing else to do.

517—A Meat Block.

There is as yet no meat block in the kitchen, but one must be procured soon. The block, the same as all butchers have, but small, is the first sign of the difference between professional cookery and poor Mary Jane's fried victuals. It is all Greek talking about selecting choice parts of meat to those who don't know the use or see the need of having a meat block. It is part of a cook's trade to know how to select and he must have a block to saw and chop upon, to trim and

shape and divide the tender from the tough and cut out the superfluous bones for the soup boiler. There is no real economy in the use of meat possible without selection. Our manager has been over to "The Glen." He does not know one piece of meat from another and is proud to say so, because he is a college graduate and is going to be a lawyer, and he has brought back some beefsteak that nobody can eat. It would require a person to have cast-iron jaws. Round steaks cut low down on the leg of a very tough old ox. But we must do something with it and the woodman must saw off the butt of a tree for a block.

Dinner.

Beefsteak stewed in gravy	20
Potatoes (4 cents) mashed with butter	7
Green peas from garden	15
Corn, 1 2-lb can	15
Bread custard pudding (No. 113 doubled)	16
Rhubarb pie, 3 large covered	30
Milk 4 quarts	12
Coffee and tea	5
Bread and biscuits from breakfast	5
	$1 25

Fifteen persons; 8⅓ cents a plate.

518—Beefsteak Stewed in Gravy.

Took 1½ pounds the toughest part of steaks, cut thin and stewed two hours in water with small bits salt pork, salt and pepper. Put a spoonful butter in large frying pan, dipped out pieces of steak and simmered in the butter till all light brown, added heaping tablespoon flour, stir to mix, then the reduced liquor this was stewed in, poured through a strainer. Let stew together ten minutes longer to become thick smooth gravy. Served like steak in individual dishes.

519—Covered Rhubarb Pie.

Took 8 cups flour (2 pounds, 7 cents.) 2 cups butter (1 pound, 19 cents.)

Rubbed together dry and wetted with two cups water (No. 20.)

Lined three pie pans, dinner plate size, cut up into them raw rhubarb in very small pieces (4 cents) and spread over it a pound of sugar (8 cents). Covered with very thin crust, cut off by pressing the paste against edge of plate, baked light colored. One-third the paste left over. Cut pies in five each; 2 cents each plate.

520—A Bill of Groceries and the Cost.

We are now to make out an order and send to Lakeport for a store-room stock of groceries. The great expenses are going to be for perishable provisions, for meat, butter, eggs, cream, milk, fruits and such things as people go to the country expecting to enjoy in abundance. Besides those there is a bewildering lot of articles to be always on hand and it saves a great deal worry and a good many forced journeys to get them together all at once. The hostess laughs when this is mentioned, saying she has always been in the habit of looking through a cook book when this ordering was to be done, to be reminded of things that would be wanted. This time, however, we will dispense with the cook book lest it lead us to order articles that would not be needed once in a year. The following is what we ordered and the prices they cost. The calculation was for one month's supply with the expectation of a big business to be done— for a house of this size:

Sugar, granulated, small barrel, 221 @ 7		$15	47
Sugar, cut loaf, for table, 35 @ 8		2	80
Sugar, powdered for fruit, etc., 20 @ 8		1	60
Flour, 550 lbs	@ 3½	19	25
Coffee, 30 lbs, Java	" 28	8	40
Table fruits in syrup case	" 25	6	00
Apples canned 8 gals.	" 25	2	00
Vegetables assorted 36 cans	" 15	5	40
Maple syrup 6 gals	" 1 25	7	50
Crackers, 3 kinds, 30 lbs	" 7	2	10
Cheese 10 lbs	" 11	1	10
Baking powder 7 lbs	" 37½	2	62
Raisins stoneless cooking 14	" 10	1	40
Nuts assorted 18 lbs	" 15	2	70
Tea 2 kinds 2 lbs	" 70	1	40
Pickles 5 gals.	" 30	1	50
Chow-chow 2 qt bot's	" 60	1	20
Rice 12½ lbs	" 8	1	00
Currants 10 lbs	" 7		70
Vinegar 5 gals	" 20	1	00
Cocoanut 5 lbs bulk not sweet @ 20		1	00
Gelatine 4 packages	" 15		60
Codfish, boneless, 12 lbs	" 9	1	08
Sardines 3 half boxes	" 16		48
Prunes 5 lbs	" 12		60
Citron 4 lbs	" 20		80
Black pepper 2 lbs	" 25		50
Tapioca 1½ lbs	" 8		12
Cornstarch 2 lbs	" 10		20
Beans, navy 10 lbs	" 4		40
Beans, dry Lima 1½ lbs	" 7		11
Macaroni 7 lbs	" 7		49
Soda, baking, 1½ lbs	" 10		15
Cracker meal, 4 lbs	" 6½		26
Honey, 8 lbs comb	" 12½	1	00
Oatmeal, 50 lbs	" 5	2	50
Cracked wheat 10 lbs	" 5		50
Corn meal, 33 lbs	" 2		66
Graham, 8 lbs	" 3		24
Pie fruits, 2 doz, 2-lb cans		2	50
Raisins table layer ¼ box			75
Cayenne pepper			5
Worcestershire sauce 1 qt for cruets			90
Chocolate 1 lb			40
Mustard 1 lb			50
Salt, table, 8 sacks			80
Salt, rock, for freezing, ½ bbl			75
Vanilla extract, ½ pint			75
Lemon extract, ½ pint			65
Nutmegs, 2 ozs			10
Spices, 5 sorts, 5 ozs			12
Ginger, 2 ozs			5
Cream tartar ½ lb			25
Molasses, 1 gal			50
Mustard, French, 2 bot's			25
Barley, 1 lb			6
Lobster, 1 can			25
		$106	46

Freight charges on above $3 06 cents, which in round numbers we tack on to the sugar, making all the sugar cost 8 cents a pound.

521—Cooking Tough Steaks.

Supper. Cooked the better part of

handsome young manager's tough beef-steak. First cut in two ounce pieces; pounded it both with back of cleaver and side until beaten out thin (it draws up thick again in cooking) drew out coals in front of fire and made the gridiron hot. Brushed both sides of steaks with brush, dipped in melted butter to prevent sticking to bars, broiled over the coals about three minutes. Ours are all "well-done" people, but must cook the steaks rare to be eatable, and then disguise them with gravy.

522—Beefsteak Gravy.

Put in a pan, butter size of an egg, level teaspoon black pepper, little more of salt and two tablespoons water; drop in the rare-cooked steaks and set the pan over the coals a minute or two. The gravy that runs from the meat mingles with the rest and makes a rich gravy that many will like better than the meat itself.

Oatmeal, 1 heaping cup when raw (½ lb, 2½ cents.)

Beefsteaks twelve (1½ lbs, 19 cents; gravy, 2½ cents.)

Codfish in cream (½ lb codfish 5, milk and butter 2—7.)

Potato cakes (mashed left from dinner, 2 cents.)

French rolls, thirty-five (3 lbs flour, etc.. 15 cents.)

Milk (4 qts, 12 cents.)

Butter (½ lb, 10 cents.)

Coffee and tea (8 cents.)

Cream to coffee and oatmeal (1 pint, 10 cents.)

Eggs, 1 order 3.

96 cents. 16 persons; 6- cents a plate.

523—Potato Cakes or Pats.

All cold mashed potatoes can be used by pressing them into little pats like biscuits with plenty of flour on the outside and browning first one side and then the other in a frying-pan with very little drippings or butter. It is one of the most popular ways of serving potatoes.

524—Why the Codfish was Dark.

"It is a pretty good supper bill-of-fare, but what makes the codfish in cream so dark?"

That is what the chief cook of the New Hebrides Hotel wanted to know when he stopped one night on his travels —not at this house where cream is plenty but at the Sapolio City House. No doubt but he makes it so himself and thinks it is quite a luxury, but very few do. One trouble was, the milk was skimmed milk and half water, besides, and wouldn't look like cream under any circumstances, and, to make it worse the codfish had never been steeped to freshen and whiten it. If the fish has been forgotten over-night put it in a large pot of cold water as soon as you remember it and let it slowly get warm over a slack fire. Before it becomes hot enough to cook it pour away that salt water and fill up again with cold and do as before, and the third time let it boil up. Pick it apart in cold water and it will not only be fresh enough but quite white. Put it in a saucepan with good milk, a little butter, add a very little flour, thickening when it boils.

525—Pickerel Fried in Butter.

July 3. Breakfast.

The early boys caught something this time: rose at four and coaxed two 4-lb pickerel out of the lake. There is as yet no lard, no meat fat, bacon nor pork to fry them in; might be broiled, but conclude to fry in butter sparingly. Cut in thin slices crosswise of the fish, pepper and salt well, dip both sides in flour. Put into the frying pans only a little butter and fry the pieces on both sides. The pieces are cut thin to cook this way because butter browns and burns too easily to let thick slices get done through. Take up on a hot pan to drain. Send in as soon after cooking as possible.

Oatmeal (2½ cents.)

Pickerel (3 lbs net @ 10 cents; butter, 5—35 cents.)

Beefsteak (remainder of h. y.- m.'s tough, 12 cents.)

Potatoes, baked, (3 cents.)

Biscuits (21 cents.)
Milk and cream (22 cents.)
Butter (10 cents.)
Coffee, tea, bread. sugar (16½ cents.)
$1 22. 18 persons; nearly 7 cents a plate.

—

526—The Refrigerator Question.

—

"Our first expressed lot of meat will arrive at noon; what is to be done with it to keep it? The cellar is as warm as out of doors and a good deal worse. New milk put down there at night sours before morning. A ham of the janitor's is covered with blue mold and is sticky to the touch, and salt and saltpetre on the shelf are trickling away in moisture, besides, the floor is muddy and the steps are broken down—are the other summer resorts around Uintah Lake no better fixed—Swibob's and Barnacle's and the Trulirural House?"

"Oh, that's all right; we are going to have a good refrigerator."

"What, right away, to be built now, in July?"

"Why, yes; as quick as the Fourth is over the men are ready to come. We waited for you to show them what is wanted. You chalk out the plan for an ice house and we can get plenty of ice to fill it."

The greater number of refrigerators put up for hotels and similar houses are failures through so few people understanding really what is needed until they have learned by dear experience. A refrigerator must be dry as well as cold, not steaming and with the clammy moisture of a cellar. It is often a good scheme where such a humid vault has nearly spoiled the meat in one day to take the meat out and hang it in the open air wrapped in a sheet and so keep it a week longer. Such a failure of a refrigerator as that, is a positive damage instead of benefit.

It should be conveniently located where it can be entered every few minutes, if necessary, without a long journey or a climbing of steps each time, if it is not, a great part of the benefits of having a perfect refrigerator are lost. And then it should be so constructed that the very frequent opening and shutting of the door will not have the effect of driving a warm blast through the mass of ice and unduly wasting it besides keeping the interior of the refrigerator always warm.

To meet all requirements some houses have several refrigerators, each for a special use. There is the Tremont House at the other end of the avenue with perhaps a dozen, of all sizes, from the large storing rooms opened only once or twice a day to the handy little box holding cut meats close to the kitchen range.

ICE.		ICE.	
Fruits and Vegetables.	Milk and Butter.	Meats.	Beef.

Plan of a large hotel's cold store rooms, front view

These are rooms of good size, say 6x10 and 6 feet high divided from each other; doors opening in front, with one large ice room above; all ventilated and drained and forming one great ice house with double walls filled with pulverized charcoal. This is built in a dry basement.

Out at the Bubbling Springs House they have a good ice house that is made to serve for many purposes, and it is built out of doors, just four steps from the kitchen door and therefore quite handy. It is good because it is well constructed with thick double walls well filled in and is roomy, perhaps 10 x10 inside. It is a two-story building, the ice chamber being above; the ice blocks resting upon a frame of oak scantling. A zinc-covered floor leads off the water; the communication with the room below is by apertures along the sides of the floor. The roof is flat and covered deep with gravel. A spreading cedar tree partly protects it from the sun's rays. The defects of this ice house are these: It is but one room and it is the one refrigerator that must be used for everything. When the door is open the entire refrigerator is open and the hot summer air rushes up into the ice chamber—and the door is opened every few minutes through the day. Then it has no window, and the cook having excellent reasons for keeping his meat block within it and cutting the meats there must keep the door open while at work. It is more than probable that several hundreds pounds of meat and tons of ice are lost every summer through the general unhandiness and incompleteness of the refrigerating arrangements. A very bad break of this sort exists at the Balbriggan House, where the arrangements are generally very good, and a seemingly perfect square room refrigerator, with ice chamber above, as in the preceeding specimen, stands conveniently at one end of the kitchen. But when the carpenter work on this one was nearly finished, it happened that no sawdust could be obtained. As it was winter time there was no immediate need experienced; the refrigerator was finished up without either sawdust or charcoal being filled in the double wall and it remains so still, serving as a receptacle to melt away from two to three tons of ice each week with very little effect in cooling anything in the heated season.

These one-room refrigerators are, however, not the sort to have unless there can be more than one or two of them in a house, each devoted to a different purpose.

The great International Cafe had to undergo two changes of proprietors and be partly remodeled within before it ever became the successful restaurant where elaborate little meals made up of the most diverse orders of viands could be obtained in a reasonably short time after the order was given. There being no room and no calculations made in the building for a convenient refrigerator a number of small ice boxes were first resorted to, set in all sorts of out of the way corners, one holding one thing and another something else, and it often happened that every one of them would have to be visited before the required articles were put together. A cook can perhaps travel twelve miles up and down stairs in twelve hours or sixteen miles through several halls and passages and back again in sixteen hours if he is required to do so, but he cannot cook many dinners at the same time.

Thus it was when the waiters would come rushing into the kitchen singing: "Hey; where's my order? Where's the cook?" The vegetable woman would answer: "The cook? he's gone a traveling down to the big ice box and when he gets there he'll go excavating through the ice to find something, but I guess he'll be back in half an hour."

When the source of trouble at length became fully understood at the International Cafe, something was pulled down and a refrigerator half as long as the kitchen was built along the wall opposite the range with so many compartments that it was hardly possible for an order to come that the material could not be found in one of these drawers. Since that time, instead of one cook and a losing business, the cafe has kept six or eight busy, and had a profitable career.

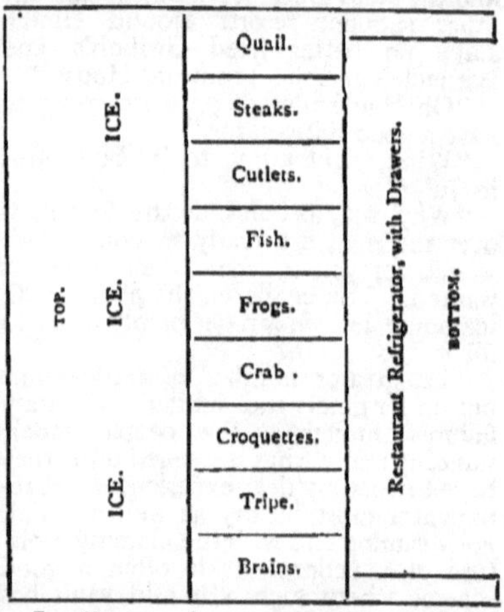

In all cases the construction ought to be planned in view of the fact that cold air descends and warm air rises In the specimen above marked out the provisions do not come in contact with the ice. The long box at top is filled with broken ice and has a zinc floor and the drawers slide in and are cooled from above through slits in the zinc so made that the water cannot drip through. Of course, like all ice boxes, the walls are double and the lid which is drawn up by means of a rope and pulley is the same.

The common square ice box filled with broken ice is also a good keeper of fish and similar kinds of provisions that are not injured by water. Put frogs' legs, lamb's fries, brook trout and a few such articles in muslin bags and bury them in the ice and they keep a long time and can be withdrawn easily when wanted; but, with that the usefulness of such a box ends, for meat is injured by being kept wet and by being washed after lying on ice, and pans set on top of ice are set in the wrong place, they should be beneath it.

In order that it may be clearly seen how much is required of a hotel refrigerator for all purposes let us look at the inventory of the contents of one for one day. There are:

Beef loins and roasts—always keeping a supply ahead to allow it to improve by keeping and become tender.

Cut meats and small meats—pans of steaks, chops and sliced ham, loin of veal, mutton, lamb, liver, etc., all carried in warm.

Brine keg for corned beef and tongues —it must stand in a cold place or the pickle will spoil in the course of three hot days and all the newly added meat with it.

Butter—one jar at least, for cooking, and probably the table butter likewise.

Lard—a can put in in a melted state.

Yeast—a jar just made and brought in warm.

Milk and cream—the cans warm from the dairy wagon and the milk pans from the kitchen for the milk to be poured in, all brought in to be made cold.

Fruit and melons—they will not be fit for the table unless cooled.

Ham and corned beef for supper—just out of the broiler and brought in smoking hot.

Roast meats left from dinner—brought in warm from the carving table also gravies and sauces, a dish of fish and plates of croquettes or other side dishes to be saved for another day.

Potatoes cooked to be ready to slice up for breakfast, dishes of peas and corn, half a pudding, some cooked codfish, a dozen bunches of celery, two or three pies.

These things and more brought in for this meal and soon taken out for the next cause the ice house door to be always in motion.

Some reader will say this thing or that shall not be put in, but managed some other way, but it is futile fighting against the inevitable. Perhaps a gallon of boiling hot mush will be stopped at the door and forbidden to be put in; but, will be left on the kitchen table and never be cold enough to slice and fry in the morning and so next night the refrigerator will catch it. That is what it is for. There should be a good one and large, if only one is to be built.

527—A Good Hotel Refrigerator.

The annexed diagram explaining the form and construction of a refrigerator that was found to meet all the requirements at a certain popular hotel, was printed some time ago in "Hotel Meat Cooking" since when I have heard of two or three hotel keepers, who could be named, having built refrigerators in their houses after that pattern and they approve it. It seems advisable therefore to reproduce it here, as it is at least a safe pattern and not like a thing untried. The dimensions might be varied to suit.

This gives a front view as the interior appears when the doors are open. The height inside is six feet; depth, front to back, five and a half; the middle compartment for the ice is three feet wide; the cold rooms on each side three and a half. The drip from the ice is led away by a zinc drainer, and the space below is both dry and cold. The outside walls are, of course, double, and filled in with eight inches of dry sawdust. This refrigerator is built close by the outer door on one side of a cellar basement, the storeroom being directly opposite. It is elevated a step or two from the door.

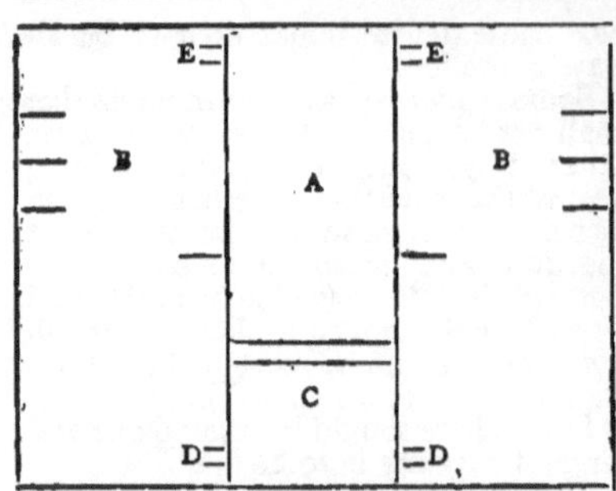

A Place for the blocks of ice, opening in front.

BB Cold rooms fitted with shelves. Front doors.

C Space under ice floor and zinc drainer where milk and butter may be kept. Front door.

DD Small doors opening into the ice box letting the cold air in.

EE Small doors open into a ventilating pipe letting the warm air and vapor out.

—— Shelves.

One of the two rooms can be used to hang joints of meats upon hooks set under the shelves and be opened only at long intervals while the other side used for various purposes may have the door in almost constant swing, and instead of letting a warm blast be forced through the ice every time the door is banged, a self-acting spring door over the aperature D closes with the momentary pressure.

Milk and butter easily take the flavors of other articles of provision such as onions and celery, stored with them; hence, the use of having a special compartment for them in the refrigerator.

It is, unfortunately, a very common supposition that the cellar is the best place for the refrigerator, while, on the contrary, it is generally the very worst. A half-cellar or basement partly above ground and with a free circulation of air, is likely to be the best; and, yet, some of the cooling rooms, which it is a pleasure to enter, where everything has the cool, fresh and solid appearance of a dry winter's day, though the mercury outside has climbed up into the nineties, are built in recesses left for them in the walls of the buildings on the same levels as the dining room and kitchen.

"When I get my refriergator built," says Mr. Farewell, "how much ice will it take?"

"You will require two tons a week, because, out of the same stock of ice the ice-pitchers will be filled, ice cream made, and ice for the various other needs taken. An ordinary two-horse wagon bed full is about a ton of blocks of ice."

528—Potato Cream Soup Without Meat.

Neither meat nor soup vegetables in house. Took:

8 potatoes
1 quart skimmed milk.
1 quart water
½ cup butter
Carrots and onions from garden, very small, about ½ dozen
Salt, pepper, slight grating of nutmeg.

Use two saucepans. Boil the potatoes in salted water in one; the vegetables, cut or chopped, in water in the other. When the potatoes are well done drain them, mash with the milk and butter and stir through a seive or strainer into the other saucepan containing the vegetables The soup should be of the consistency and appearance of cream with the minced vegetables showing plainly. A little flour thickening may be needed or more milk.

Dinner.

Potato cream soup (3 quarts, 10 cents.)
Pickerel, boiled, butter sauce (30 cents.)
Roast loin of mutton (5 lbs, 55 cents.)
Potatoes steamed and browned (3 cents.)
Tomatoes stewed (1 can, 15 cents.)
Bread custard pudding with sauce (No. 113, 9 cents.)
Cherry p es (2 made of 1 can, 14 cents; crusts 4 cents.)
Milk, coffee, tea, butter, bread (20 cents.)
$1 60; 17 persons, 9½ cents a plate.

Meat arrived at noon.

Loin of mutton charged @ 11 cents.
Leg of veal @ 12½.
Beef loin @ 15.
Liver at 12½.
Sweetbreads free.

These prices are too high. They are the prices that prevailed in Spring, but meat becomes cheap in July if ever. Write to the butcher.

Box of fish packed in ice arrived, charged 19 lbs @ 7 cents, and expressage to pay.

So we are to have the refrigerator of the last pattern shown in diagram built in a room back of kitchen, where formerly was a bedroom. The elevation is right for easy drainage. A grove of pine and black oak shades the roof.

Supper.

First meal that caused talk. Superb French rolls; fine creamery butter. Not much besides, but these are a feast by themselves.

Calf's liver, fried, plenty of gravy (10 cents.)

Cold roast mutton from dinner (charged that meal.)

Baked potatoes (18, 3 cents—half left.)

Molasses pound cake, warm (1½ lbs, 14 cents.)

French rolls (30, 12 cents.)
Butter (12 ounces @ 24, 18 cents.)
Milk (3 qts., 19 cents.)
Cream, coffee, tea, etc., (19 cents.)
85 cents; 17 persons, 5 cents a plate.

529—Fried Liver and Gravy.

Only about half the people anywhere will order liver when there is an alternative of cold meat or something else.

Cut about 8 thin slices, which will be little over half a pound. Lay them in a frying pan with some drippings or bacon fat and fry brown on both sides. Season with salt and pepper while cooking. Take up the liver and put into the pan a heaping tablespoonful of flour and when that has been stirred around, a cupful of hot water. Let boil up and strain over the liver.

530—How To Bake Potatoes.

Though there are fifty other good ways there is no better way than baking or roasting either for potatoes that cost five for a cent or large truffles that cost five dollars each. Pick out the largest and smoothest potatoes to bake because any size will do to pare and mash and even if a person should waste part of a too large one on his plate it would still be the cheapest dish of the meal. After washing well cut off the ends of the potatoes. It may not make them any mealier, although some suppose it does; but, it makes them look better, and as if they had been cared for. Put them in the oven as a rule just one hour before the meal. When done instead of sliding them into a hot closet or under the stove to become dry and worthless, take up each one in a damp towel in the hand and press it gently together and after that cover the pan containing them with the same damp cloth and keep them warm.

531—Molasses Pound Cake.

This will be found quite an acquisition to the list of cheap and easy cakes:

1 cup sugar, small—6 ounces.
1 cup butter—6 ounces.
1 cup molasses—12 ounces.
1 cup milk.
2 eggs.
6 cups flour—1½ pounds.
1 teaspoon each of ground ginger **and** cinnamon.

Make the butter soft and mix it and sugar, molasses, milk, eggs, and spices together in a pan. Mix the powder in the flour, then stir that in and beat up thoroughly. Bake in two small cake moulds. Makes 3 lbs @ 9 cents a pound.

This cake can and ought to be made with a cup of sour milk instead of sweet, and a teaspoon of soda instead of the powder—only sour milk is not always at **hand to use.**

532—French Rolls.

As a rule a pound of light dough makes 10 rolls of such a size that most persons take two at a meal; but, as it takes half a pound of liquid to make **dough** of one pound of flour if we have three pounds of dough and make thirty rolls of it they contain only 2 pounds of flour, costing, probably, 7 cents. The cost is increased by a few enriching ingredients and the yeast. To make 10 or 12 rolls out of a pound of dough, however, we must raise them as light and large as it is possible to do, like the best baker's buns for lightness, only better eating, and we have no calculations made for poor Mary Jane's squatty little lumps of dough that she calls rolls. It seems so easy to make fine rolls, especially with the compressed yeast that has of late years come into general use that the wonder is how anybody can make bad ones even if they try. Generally the failure seems to be owing to not using enough yeast, not setting the dough in a suitable place to rise and not giving the rolls time to become as light as they might be in the pans before baking. I think if those who keep boarders could know what an advantage this cheap luxury of fine rolls is to a house—even to the extent of bringing a higher price for board—there would be a general cultivation of the art of domestic bread making. It does no good to make fine rolls only once in a while and miss the mark twice as often; and, perhaps that is where the difficulty lies, the constant care to do always the same way at different times being so hard to exercise.

I am asked "Do you put eggs in the rolls," and the answer is no—not in the every day kind that is good enough for anybody all the year round; but, there are varieties of rolls of different degrees of richness that are made with eggs, such as butter rolls and tea cakes. It is not so much what they contain as the way the dough is managed that makes them good. Take:

2 quarts or pounds, or 8 cups flour.
2 large cups sweet milk (water will do.)
1 cent's worth compressed yeast.
1 tablespoon sugar.
½ tablespoon salt.
Butter or lard size of an egg—2 ounces.

If the rolls are for 6 o'clock supper, any time in the forenoon will do to mix the dough. Noon is a good time in summer. Make a hollow in the flour, dissolve the yeast in the milk and pour it in, add the sugar, salt and half the shortening, stir up into stiff dough, turn it out on the table and work it well with the knuckles. Slightly grease the bottom of the mixing pan which you have scraped out clean, press the lump of dough down into the greased pan and turn the greased side up—which prevents a crust drying on the dough while it is rising and helps the appearance of the rolls. Then set the pan on an upper shelf where it will be warm and let stay there until 3 o'clock. At that time work the dough on the table again and put it back to rise another hour or more.

Work the dough again with the knuckles, roll it out to a thin sheet. Brush over with the remaining butter or lard melted, cut out with an oval cutter, double over, place in a pan far enough apart not to touch, rise an hour and bake in a hot oven about eight or ten minutes. Brush over with clear warm water when done.

Mrs. Tingee looked incredulous when I told her to bake these rolls only 8 or 10 minutes—thought they would not be well baked but they will. Had to explain that the lighter an article is the quicker it bakes—that a souffle or meringue may be done through in three minutes; a perfect sponge cake will bake in 20 minutes because it is light and full of air spaces while a fruit cake of the same size requires 2 hours. Rolls are spoiled by dry baking. Hotel cooks have their ovens hot, hotter, hotest.

There is a patent roll cutter made and for sale, which forms the rolls of the right shape and makes the depression across the middle to fold them over by. The size of the rolls may be governed by the thickness or thinness to which the sheet of dough is rolled. In order that these or any sort of rolls may have a good regular shape it is necessary after the dough has been kneaded and rolled, to let it alone a few minutes while you get pans ready or do something else that it may lose the elasticity which causes it to pull back out of proper form.

533—About Compressed Yeast.

There are but few towns now where compressed yeast cannot be obtained, the express service being so nearly universal. This yeast is a great saver of time and trouble. Although the expense of purchasing it may amount to several dollars during a season at a resort it is money well spent if there is any business done worth counting at all. It comes in cakes wrapped in tin-foil which retail at 2 cents or 5 cents, according to size. Will keep about a week in cool weather or in a refrigerator, but should be obtained from the manufacturers fresh every day or two if possible. It is the quickest kind of yeast, as by using a double quantity good rolls and bread can be made and baked within three or four hours. To use it take half a cake or more, crumble it into tepid milk or water and let it dissolve, then pour all into the flour. Those who cannot obtain the compressed yeast, or who object to the expense of it can find full directions for making yeast of the best and strongest liquid sort at Nos. 257 and 258.

Breakfast.

July 4.
Oatmeal 1 cup raw, 2 cents.
Beefsteak (2 pounds loin, clear, 40 cents.)
Eggs, scrambled (6 orders, 12 eggs, 17 cents.)
Potatoes, stewed in cream (7 cents.)
Biscuits (2 doz., 15 cents.)
Batter cakes (cheapest; 3 pints batter, 8 cents.)
Syrup (12 cents.)
Butter (1 pound for table and steak, 25 cents.)
Milk, cream, coffee, tea, 22 cents.
$1 48; 19 persons, nearly 8 cents a plate.

534—Potatoes Stewed in Cream.

Variously called stewed potatoes, minced potatoes in cream, and other ways, and a favorite way with many people. Take cold cooked potatoes, slice them as thin as possible into a stew pan, pour in good milk to come up even with the sliced potatoes and set over the fire. While it is heating, chop the potatoes small with a knife point, add salt, butter and cream, according as can be afforded. When made as most people like them these are almost as thick as mashed potatoes.

535—Clabber Batter Cakes.

About the easiest, quickest made and best batter cakes, are made with only four ingredients, *viz*: "clabber," or milk curdled by souring, flour, soda and salt.

Take a little sifted flour in a pan, add the "clabber" until it can be stirred to the proper consistency to bake on a griddle, then add a little salt and soda. There is no measure to give only that in a general way 2 cups of sour milk needs 1 teaspoon of soda.

When you make other flour batter cakes, syrup, eggs and shortening are needed—the syrup to make them brown easily—but these "clabber" cakes need nothing but what is named above.

This is the Fourth, the great excursion day. Flags are flying at the large hotels at the depot and at the Trulirural House. There is some danger that a few of the straggling excursionists may come to our house to dinner and we are not prepared. Stores have not arrived; scarcely a thing in the house besides the meat and fish. So much uncertainty it is useless to prepare extra dishes or even ice cream, but it is well enough to make a little larger quantity of such plain things as we must have.

Dinner.

Tomato and green pease soup (4 qts. 28 cents.)
Fillet (leg) of veal stuffed (4 pounds veal, 52, and dressing 5; 57 cents.)
Potatoes mashed and browned (10 cents.)
Corn (1 can, 15 cents.)
Plum pies (4 covered, of two cans plums 28; sugar, 6; crust, 10; 44 cents, 24 cuts.)
Cream curd pudding with sauce (allowing full price for the soured milk, 27 cents.)
Second cooking:
Fish, fried (12 pieces, 2¼ lbs gross, 25; lard, 5; 30 cents.)
Mutton chops (2 pounds, 24 cents.)
Eggs (6, special order, 8 cents.)
Milk (6 quarts, 18 cents.)

Bread (15 cents.)
Cream (1 qt., 20 cents.)
Coffee (one-third pound, 10 cents.)
Butter, sugar, etc. (20 cents.)
Total dinner, $3 26; 30 persons, 11 cents a plate.

In this case it turned out as was half expected for at just about the time that the regular dinner was ended there came two little parties of five and six persons respectively, making eleven more to furnish dinner to. Such little parties coming on the heels of a meal are generally profitable to the hotel keeper. On this occasion there was enough soup, coffee, potatoes, pudding and pie remaining and the fish and mutton chops specially cooked made up a good and plentiful dinner at an additional expense of less than a dollar. The party of eleven contributed 50 cents each, the regular price per meal.

In calculating quantities to be prepared it is never necessary to count one portion of every dish to each person. Perhaps some who take fish will decline meat, or will take corn and not potatoes, and only half the number will call for pie.

536—Tomato and Green Pea Soup.

One of the best looking soups when the pease are green and the soup is rich colored. This day it was the soup of necessity rather than choice for in truth we had a half can of tomatoes (8 cents) and nothing else for soup unless the late and neglected garden would yield some trifles. Found a few green pease, not enough to use as a vegetable, but about two cupfuls (10 cents) are plenty in soup, also some carrots and onions as thick as straws. Where there are no herbs, or cloves, or parsely a very small quantity of the feathery green carrot leaves may be used with advantage, minced and dropped in the soup just before serving. Made tomato soup as directed at No. 166, and let the green pease cook in it about one-half hour. Made four quarts and used one-half can tomatoes. Little burnt sugar to improve the color.

537—Stuffed Fillet of Veal.

The same in the main as the brisket (No. 171) the fillet of veal being the same as the round of beef and solid meat. The dressing is pressed into the cavity left by removing the bone, and inclosed also by the skirt of fat, which should be left on the meat drawn close and tied around with twine. The surplus stuffing may be baked in a small pan and served with the meat and gravy. For best stuffing see No. 62. Half the quantity will serve for veal, and an egg added will make it richer. Drippings, lard or butter can be used instead of suet.

538—Cream Curd Pudding

Our wretched cellar sours the milk with wonderful rapidity. Lucky thing milk is cheap at this place. This morning used some curdled milk for batter cakes and still there remained 4 quarts more, and part of it was cream. It would make good cream cheese or smearkase if it could be spared, but there being none of the usual pudding ingredients in the house this comes in opportunely for a good pudding. Curd from the cheese vats, that has been curdled with rennet and is not sour, is the chief ingredient in the genuine cheesecakes of old Maryland cookery; mixtures made too rich for everyday dinners. This is of the same kind and can be baked without a crust of pastry; it is a pudding and not a tart or pie.

1 pound or little more of scalded curd.
½ teaspoon soda.
½ cup sugar.
½ cup butter.
1 cup fine or minced bread crumbs.
1 cup milk.
Nutmeg or other flavoring.
3 eggs.

It does not make much difference how the ingredients are put together, but it is best to first take the dry articles and pound them smooth and then add the eggs and milk.

To obtain the curd set the pan containing a gallon of curdled milk on the stove when it is not very hot and let come to boiling heat, then pour it into a fine strainer or in a napkin to drain.

There will be nearly a two-quart pan of pudding from the above ingredients. Bake light brown and serve with a sauce.

Supper.

A fragmentary meal. Great rival displays of fireworks getting ready in the shrubbery of all the resort houses around the lake. Nobody caring about eating.

Oatmeal (2 cents.)
Cold veal (8 slices, charged at dinner.)
Fried liver (10 cents.)
Beefsteak (1 pound flank, 13 cents.)
Codfish in cream (5 cents.)
Potatoes baked (3 cents.)
Smearkase (No. 388—of 2 qts. milk, 8 cents.)
French rolls (45, 20 cents.)
Cake (12 cents.)
Butter (1 lb. creamery, 25 cents.)
Milk and cream, (22 cents.)
Coffee, sugar, etc. (10 cents.)
$1 30; 22 persons, 6 cents a plate.

"After the Fourth," says the resort proprietor, "we must begin and get ready for the rush."

"Will there be a rush?"

"Oh, the people have to come sometime—they always do."

"There has nobody come yet—seems to be getting late."

"No, this isn't late, it is early. I never looked for anybody to come until after the Fourth."

"No?"

"They cannot; the schools don't close till now, the weather is cool at their homes all through June; the Government employes do not take their vacation till now and so many people will not leave their homes for fear they may be burned up on the Fourth, or be entered by roughs."

"And yet Black's Hotel over here, has had, so they say, ninety boarders for a week or two past."

"Oh, well, the people he gets would not come here, anyway, and they that will come here would not go there. He lets them fiddle and dance all night if they wish to, and drink beer, and row boats and sail and fish on Sundays."

"They would not stay here a minute"

"I suppose not."

"And still they pay Black about nine hundred dollars a week"

"Well, I don't expect this thing to make any money, but if it pays its own expenses and keeps me and my family pleasantly I shall be satisfied."

"I'm afraid your profits will never compare with Black's profits."

"Well, well; we will be virtuous and we shall be happy."

529—Shall We Have a Bill-of-Fare?

The answer that was reached when this question was discussed at this place was, that a bill-of-fare is a luxury that shonld be indulged in if possible and that in this case it could be adopted for dinner and was necessary, but was not needed for breaskfast or supper to an extent commensurate with the trouble of preparing it

At the Pansyblossom House where I put in one summer they had never before run a bill-of-fare but were quite delighted with the apparent ease, the neatness and economy of the bill-of-fare plan. I heard somebody saying, when the busy season was over, that the proprietor intended to run a bill all through the rest of the year after that "for then instead of setting out a lot of dishes to each person he would only have to give them what they called for." The sequel to that story I never knew, but feel sure the bill-of-fare was not kept up. It is harder for the cook and requires knowledge of tne names of dishes that poor Mary Jane does not possess. Here at Uintah Lake it was allowed that it would be the stylish thing to have one.

"But I don't see how we can" says the landlady.

"Didn't you have a bill-of-fare last year?"

"Why, no, of course not. The girls just called off what we had."

"Were they sweet-voiced German girls, like these who cannot warble out the names of our dishes with any more distinctness than an opera singer might give the words? And if so I don't see how you ever let your guests know what you had for them to choose from. The bills cannot be printed daily in this country place. We can get blanks printed however, and write the dishes in the proper places."

"When I was clerk at the Rushbottom House at Limbertown," says the manager, "we used to have seven different bills-of-fare all printed at once, one for each day of the week so when Monday came around we brought on the Monday bill and so on through the week— why would not that do here?"

"Would not do at all because of the location for one thing, for it will often happen that not a single dish that is on your bill-of-fare can be obtained when wanted; but it would not do for other reasons, because such a way defeats the object of having a bill and makes the hotel like an almshouse or House of Correction where they have a certain fare for each day; their boiled beef day, their suet pudding day, their pork and beans day and so on perpetually."

Then the housekeeper spoke up:

"At the Water Cure Home at Camp-meetingville in the Great Frying Pan Valley we used to get along very well with having the waiters call off what we had, but then we never had but two kinds; still, that seemed to be enough."

"Ah, yes," chimed in the proprietor facetiously, "but this will not be a water cure so much as a sort of hunger cure, and we must have variety. If we don't feed the people well they may be going over to the Trulirural House where they can board cheaper."

"It is impossible," the cook said, "to set a superior table and distance rival houses or to get the full credit of your more liberal providing without a bill-of-fare. Suppose we have but two kinds of meat, there will be and ought to be about six kinds of vegetables, which are cheap and attractive if properly cooked and which make up a good meal, and it would be tedious to call off so many while very few at table would really have opportunity enough to choose what they wished as they do from a printed list. There is just one other way; that is, to call the meats only, and set out the full array of everything else that is ready in small dishes. Plenty of people like that way best, for they get plenty set before them and eat whatever strikes their fancy. The great objection to it is the great waste entailed. The perfection of all plans is to have a new bill-of-fare printed for each meal that comes, breakfast, lunch, dinner, supper, always new. That method leads to the smallest proportion of waste and greatest freshness of cooked dishes. The expense of so much printing and the fact of there being so little to change in the breakfast

and supper *menu* leads nearly all hotel keepers to get the bills for these meals printed once for all, the same bill for weeks or months, while they change the dinner bill every day. Rather than do this I would 'call off' the breakfast and supper and have but few dishes; for dinner, as said before, a written or printed bill-of-fare is indispensable."

Breakfast.

Baked Pork and Beans.
Tea, Coffee and Chocolate.

MISCELLANEOUS.

White Rolls. Muffins. Corn Bread.
Griddle Cakes.
Dry Toast. Milk Toast. Buttered Toast.
Chipped Beef with Cream.
Oat Meal Mush.

BROILED.

Beef Steak, plain or with onions.
Mutton Chops. Pork Chops.
Breakfast Bacon. Ham. Veal Cutlets.

EGGS.

Boiled. Fried. Scrambled. Poached.
Omelet.

FRIED.

Liver and Bacon. Codfish Balls.
Fresh Fish. Mush. Sausage.
Corned Beef Hash.

POTATOES.

Baked, Fried, Lyonaise, Stewed.

In order to point out the the detriment these unchangeable breakfast cards are to the quality of the dishes served, here is a copy of one that was in use at a good two-dollar-a-day hotel. There are so many articles offered to the person at table, there are too many, but no more than rival houses offer and no more than is expected. It was a rule of that landlord that nothing must be crossed off his bills.

"Our list is so small," he would say, "that we cannot afford to drop even one dish from it." Consequently, although the meats might be cooked only as wanted there were many other articles that were necessarily prepared beforehand and by the usual contrariness of the luck when the corned beef hash, the corn bread, codfish balls, or whatever else was fresh made, as good, as bright colored, as rich, as well flavored as it could be there would not be one order for it; but, when it had been put away, brought out again and warmed over, lost its first good quality and looked common and stale, then by the same blessed luck everybody in the dining-room would be seized with a desire to have some. Did we try another way and make only five codfish balls instead of twenty—determined not to have any left over—that very morning at least twenty-five people would call for codfish balls at once.

But here at Uintah Lake we will not have any breakfast or supper bill and you shall see how we will make the cod-fish balls go, each one to its proper plate.

———

Mr. Farewell's consultation, as it seemed to be, with the manager and the house-keeper was only a pretense for the purpose of reconciling them to the daily task in store for one or other of them of writing in the blank *menu* for dinner, for he had long ago decided that point for himself and taken pride in selecting a handsome heading of fine type with flourishes, which announced that this was the dinner, on such a date, at The Eyrie, Uintah Lake, State of Cornuco-pia, John Smith Farewell, proprietor:

Dinner.

———

SOUP.

FISH.

ROAST.   BOILED.

ENTREES.

VEGETABLES.

PASTRY AND DESERT.

Assorted Nuts. Raisins. Tea. Coffee.

That is a copy of our blank bill-of-fare, as simple as could be made, having the headings, and blank spaces for writing in. It seems, at first glance, that a number of stand-by dishes such as roast beef and mashed potatoes might as well be printed in and save so much writing; curiously enough, however, experience shows that your boarders look only at the writing and you seldom get a call for anything that is in print. Let there be stewed tomatoes printed in place under the vegetable heading and one can will last a week, but write stewed tomatoes and you need two cans in one day. It should be all written or all printed.

———

Breakfast.

———

July 5.
No oatmeal in house.
Veal steaks (2 lbs, 26 cents.)
Mutton steaks or rough chops (2 lbs, 22 cents.)
Butter gravy for meats and eggs (6 oz, 7 cents.)
Stewed eggs (22 eggs, 28 cents.)
Potatoes minced and browned. (7 cents.)
Biscuits (14 fresh made, 8 cents.)
Rolls (14 left last meal warmed over.)
Batter cakes (No. 402—1 qt, 8 cents.)
Coffee 5, tea 1, milk 12, cream 10, syrup 10, butter ½ lb, 10, bread baked 15.
$1 69; 21 persons, 8 cents a plate.

———

540—Broiled Mutton Chops.

———

Lay the chops on a plate and touch both sides with the butter brush. Broil over clear coals about five minutes, turning over only once.

Put a tablespoonful of butter into a tin pan, together with as much water and a pinch of salt and pepper. Shake together and when the chops are done let them lie in the pan and form their own gravy.

———

541—Stewed Eggs.

———

These are eggs poached, a large num-ber at once, then partly chopped, seasoned and dished up by spoonfuls.

Drop into a saucepan of water that is boiling gently (See No. 93) about a dozen eggs and cook medium or until the yolks begin to harden, then either drain away the water or dip the eggs into another vessel. Throw in a few small lumps of butter, salt, and if you have white pepper a little of that. Cut each egg in four with the edge of a spoon.

542—Potatoes Minced and Browned.

At No. 82 find potatoes minced and browned in entire dishes for restaurant orders. At No. 534 find potatoes minced. in cream. Another way is to put the minced cold potatoes in a baking pan, mix in a little milk, butter, pepper and salt and brown the surface in the oven. Serve spoonfuls in flat dishes.

543—To Warm Over Rolls.

Take rolls left over from the previous meal, place in a pan and cover with a wet cloth, half a cotton flour sack or piece of old table cloth dipped in water will do. Set in the oven and by the time the cloth is dry the rolls will be as good as if fresh baked—for such as are not critical judges of fresh bread.

Some nights when the bands are playing and rockets flying it is exceedingly inconvenient to stay at home and mix dough, and a pan of rolls left over on purpose may do to satisfy the inexorable breakfast bill-of-fare at such a time.

544—Fine Bread.

If such good bread can be afforded the receipt for French rolls (No. 532) may be used. That quantity makes two loaves. After it has been kneaded on the table the last time, as if for rolls, divide it in two and work up into round shape, then let them remain a few minutes while you grease two long and deep bread tins. Take your loaves, the rough under side up, and press a long depression down the middle with the knuckles. Then fold over one edge into the depression and press that down; then the other edge, and you have a long roll of dough. Place it in the tin and brush over with the brush dipped in a teaspoonful of melted lard and set on a warm shelf to rise. The use of being particular how you fold up the dough is that if done right the loaves rise even and smooth without a break, but if wrong they rise and split open at one end. This is a dainty sort of bread that makes baker's bread ashamed.

Dinner.

Lake trout, baked, gravy, (2 lbs, 20 cents.)

Veal pot pie (meat, 24, crust, 4—28 cents.)

Potatoes mashed, browned (5 cents.)

No other vegetables in house.

No butter in house.

Cherry pies (2 with 1 can cherries, 14; crust, 4; sugar, 2—20 cents.)

Cottage pudding, hot cream sauce (2 lbs, 20 cents.)

Milk, cream, coffee, tea (26 cents.)

$1 19; 20 persons, 6 cents a plate.

That meal used up last of first lot of meat except sweetbreads reserved.

Bought jar fresh butter at neighboring creamery at 20 cents a pound. Bought canned goods at country store.

545—Veal Pot Pie.

Put into a saucepan the pieces of veal that will not slice into neat cutlets, rinse off with cold water, then fill up and boil about half an hour. Take up the meat and cut it all into neat pieces as near one size and shape as can be, put in another saucepan or other pan and pour the liquor it was boiled in to it through a fine strainer. Put in a slice of salt pork, an onion, half blade of mace or half teaspoon of powdered sage whichever may be at hand, for all are good seasonings for veal; boil half an hour longer, add salt and pepper and thicken with flour mixed with water. Then drop spoonfuls of dough on the surface, set in the oven and let cook about twenty minutes. Milk may be added to the liquor sometimes for a change, making a white stew and then there should be a little green parsley in it.

The use of taking out the meat and cutting when half cooked is for the better appearance on the dishes, as the pieces keep their shape and may be placed two in a dish with a light dumling on top. `

46—Pot Pie Dumplings.

To make them, whether dropped far apart as dumplings or close together as one covering of crust, so that they will remain light after cooking and not go down like lumps of lead, it is necessary to mix the dough so soft that it must be taken up and dropped with a spoon. All that is needed is:

2 cups flour.
1 heaping teaspoon baking powder.
Salt.
1 cup water.

But sour milk and soda can be used and save powder. And to make a rich yellow sort an egg, or two yolks may be added. Mix the powder in the flour, pour in the water and stir hard for one minute then drop into the boilng stew.

547—Cottage Pudding.

This, as well as the molasses pound cake is a great acquisition to the list of cheap cakes, for a good sort of cake it is, although served as a pudding. Some of the large city bakeries are selling it now in different forms (See No. 285.) It is good likewise as a sally-lunn for breakfast, being not too sweet or rich, but short, light and wholesome:

1 cup sugar—½ pound.
½ cup butter—¼ pound.
6 eggs.
2 cups milk—a pint.
3 large teaspoons powder.
6 cups flour—1½ pounds.

Make up like pound cake by creaming the butter and sugar together, add the eggs two at a time and beat in well, then the milk. Mix the powder in the flour and stir in. Beat the mixture well with the spoon.

This makes two cakes in the common shallow tin baking pans about ten inches long. Let the batter be less than an inch in depth to bake easily, and sift some granulated sugar on the surface before putting in the oven and the cakes will come out nicely glazed. One will serve to slice for pudding with sauce, the other for cake. About 3½ pounds costs 28 to 30 cents.

548—Cream Sauce for Puddings.

Boil rich milk or cream with stick cinnamon or broken nutmeg in it and sugar to sweeten. Stir in a spoonful of starch mixed with cold milk.

Supper.

No meat in the house, but some fish left yet. Good country lake house supper.

Fried trout (18 pieces, 4½ lbs gross, @ 8, 36; 2 eggs and cornmeal 4; lard, ½ lb, 7—47 cents.)
Potatoes plain boiled (3 cents.)
French rolls (24, 10 cents.)
Cherries (2 cans, 28 cents.)
Cake (No. 547—13 cents.)
Butter 10, milk and cream 20, coffee, tea, sugar 9 (39 cents.)
$1 40; 20 persons, 7 cents a plate

549—Is Fish Cheaper Than Meat?

A few meals back some pickerel, home caught, is credited in our account, to the boys, as worth ten cents a pound, that is net weight. That is what the fish we get by express seems to cost as it is put in the pan. It is bought at Whitefish Bay at seven cents, packed in ice and boxed; but it has to be expressed over two railroads in some way that makes it pay double rate, and twenty-five pounds costs 50 cents, and there is another carriage from the depot. Although they come clean as to the insides, the heads, fins and backbones take away one-sixth of the weight, on an average, of different kinds of fish. Therefore, 25 lbs @ 7 cents and 50 cents added costs, $2 25. Take off one-sixth in trimming before cooking and we have scarce 21 lbs of fish for that sum, it being nearer eleven cents per pound than ten. As there is waste, likewise, in all other kinds of meat, the only fair comparison that can be made is with the solid, boneless round of beef (No. 516) which we buy at thirteen cents. There is then a difference of three cents in favor of the fish, but if we cook it by breading and frying, the cost of fish and meat is about the same and our fish supper with fruit and cake is not one of the cheapest meals. The conditions are, of course, only local but are stated at length because they are likely to be much the same at a great number of resort houses.

550—Fried Lake Trout.

None of these tea-kettle cooks, either in this house or around at the neighbors', I find, have ever seen frying by immersion in hot fat before. Mrs. Tingee, too, I remember, although she had kept house fifteen years and a boarding house ten, had never known that potatoes could be cooked by dropping them raw into hot fat—as French fried, and Saratoga chips—neither did the two ladies who boarded with her, the retail merchant's wife and the photographer's wife, they all thought that in every case potatoes must be boiled first. After thinking it well over I concluded not to mention frying fish that way to her, being afraid to go into her kitchen and take her whole pound of lard at once, if I could ever find so much there, and proceed to make it hissing hot over the fire, because it is dangerous to have a kettle of hot lard on the fire and a lady fainting around, both at one time. We grow reckless of lard where we cook for a number of people every day, who pay a fair price for board and have something good to eat, and generally, besides, have a jar full of roast meat fat and melted suet that helps out without depending upon it except for a few things that must be fried of a good clean color. It does not really consume much lard or fat to fry in it, as the same can be used several times over if care is taken not to let it burn black, still, in counting the cost it has to be remembered that the pound of lard put in the frying pan becomes worse and darker with every frying and at last has to be thrown away.

Cut the fish in pieces across without splitting it, if the full flavor of the fish is desired rather than the fried crust.

Beat one or two eggs with half their bulk of water. Pepper and salt the pieces of fish well, dip them in the egg and then in corn meal, coat well by pressing, then drop into lard that is hissing hot and fry brown, allowing 8 or 10 minutes for the fish to get done to the bone. Dredge a little fine salt and keep hot in a pan in the open oven until served

To fry without using eggs, mix 1 cup of flour and 2 cups powdered crackers together. Dip the pieces of fish in milk, then in the mixture, coat well, dipping twice if necessary, and fry brown. (See Nos. 13, 98 and 314.)

551 Potatoes Plain Boiled.

To go with hot fried fish there is no form of potatoes better than plain boiled. Pare them first and put on in salted water. When done drain off the water and serve the potatoes out of the saucepan as wanted.

———

"Roll on, thou deep and dark blue ocean, Roll!"

Cold day for resort keepers. Fierce north-west gale been blowing all day. This green little two-mile lake has been trying to lash itself into a rage and swamped all the skiffs.

Second lot of meat:
Ham charged @ 15 cents.
Mutton @ 10.
Loin beef @ 12½.
Rib roast beef @ 12½.
Bacon @ 12½.
Salt Pork @ 10.
Liver @ 12½.
Sweetbreads, 1 ℔ free.
Some reduction in prices from former lot, but too high yet, and the loin has over five pounds of suet and waste fat and mutilated kidney in it, and they sent us no lamb.

———

Breakfast.

———

July 6.
Oatmeal (3 cents.)

Ham broiled (6 slices, 11 oz. net, equal to 1 lb gross, 15 cents.)

Mutton chops broiled (11 chops, 2 lbs, 20 cents.)

Poached eggs on toast (16 eggs, 20, and toast buttered 7—27 cents.)

Broiled potatoes (few, and baked 12, 5 cents.)

Batter Cakes (1 qt. with 2 eggs, No. 403, 10 cents.)

Syrup (10 cents.)

Butter (average of many meals, 12 oz., 15 cents.)

Milk and cream (average, 21 cents.)

Coffee and tea (average, 5 cents.)

French rolls (16, 8 cents.)

$1 39; 20 persons, 7 cents a plate.

552- Cutting Up a Ham.

One of the most serious calamities that ever befalls Mary Jane is the sending her a whole ham to cut up, all by herself: it is a calamity to the ham, too, when she has whittled it and hacked and torn it with her little case-knife that she tries to sharpen on the edge of the stove. Her reliance and the reliance of most private families is upon the butcher generally, to slice the ham before sending it, but in that case good ham is never as good as it might be because it is cut too thick and being sawed through the bone from one end to the other many of the slices are of such a sort that a little of it goes a long way. We have in our kitchen a meat block, a meat saw and a small cleaver, besides good knives. These things are indispensable both for economy and good quality of the dishes we cook. Without them our choice ham that costs 15 cents a pound gross, and when the bone and rind is counted out, costs somewhere between 20 and 25 cents, might all have to be whittled away in shreds and shavings without a respectable slice among them. The best and most saving method of dealing with a ham is as follows:

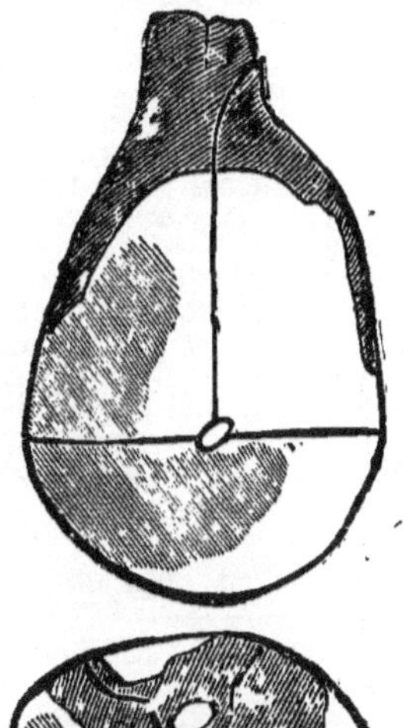

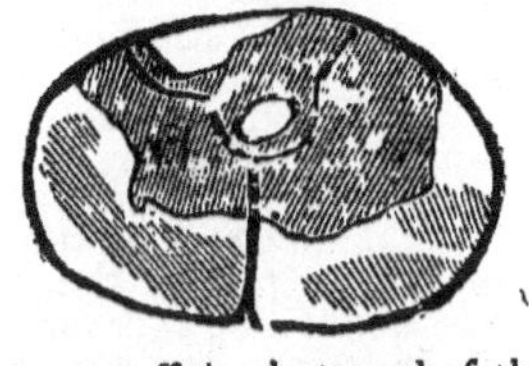

First, saw off the butt end of the ham as shown above, taking the projecting point of bone that is easily found for a guide where to cut. The lower woodcut shows the inside of the butt where it has been cut and the black lines show where the knife must go to separate the meat on both sides from the irregular shaped bone. There are then two pieces of ham, all meat, ready to be cut in slices, the thinner the better, with a sharp knife. Then cut down the large or main portion as the line shows, from the shank to the bottom. There is a bone that guides the knife down that mark. All the piece on the right is solid meat; the best part of the ham, and makes the handsomest slices. The other side can be sliced part way or be used for boiled ham.

553—Broiled Ham.

Strange it seems, but it will not do to make a regular practice of broiling ham over the stove hearth because it ruins the stove for drawing. After broiling a lot of ham where the smoke from the broiling goes into the draught, the fire will go almost out and something generated by the salt in the stove pipe prevents the fire being good again for a whole day. A few slices for a family may be broiled without the bad effect being noticeable but when the house is full of people it may save trouble to resort to frying.

It was thought here that charcoal would have to be provided, but the wood embers drawn out into the ash pan prove to be sufficient to broil over, thus far.

Slice the ham thin and broil—if you can broil it—over clear coals about five minutes, turning it to get a good even brown on both sides.

554—Poached Eggs on Toast.

A neat little way of poaching eggs for a few people is to take tin muffin rings, the kind without bottoms, put them in a frying pan of salted boiling water and break an egg into each one and let it cook. Take up ring and all with a cake turner or shallow perforated ladle and take off the muffin ring after the egg has been placed safely on its piece of buttered toast. We call this good for a few people, because when there are many it takes too long. (See No. 96.)

555—Fancy Toast for Poached Eggs.

Cut for each dish three slices of bread very thin and quite square in form. Toast them, butter them, place one square in the middle of the dish. Cut the other two squares across cornerwise and you have four triangular pieces to place around that in the dish, the points outwards.

556—Broiled Potatoes.

They can be done in two ways, either cold boiled potatoes may be sliced, buttered with a brush, placed in the hinged wire broiler and broiled or toasted over the fire, or raw potatoes may be done the same way. The boiled potatoes are quickest done and are much liked. Should be sprinkled with finely minced parsley and with salt and pepper

and if done before time to dish up can be kept hot in a pie-pan without spoiling.

557—Trouble With the Coffee.

We are having bad coffee, it is poor in taste, worse in appearance; has that dirty color as if mixed with ink and none of the reddish-brown hue of good coffee. People here don't care much, as milk is the principal beverage except for two or three. That makes no difference, however, for the coffee must be not only good but superlatively so. Proprietor good naturedly says it is the fault of that common twenty-cent coffee, that is the only grade the country store can furnish, and we must wait until the good coffee comes with all the other groceries. But it is not that. If they bring coffee that costs fifty cents a pound it will be as bad when made as this is, unless there be some other method of making adopted. I have blamed the coffee pots and tried and discarded three because they have lost their bright tinned inside and allow the iron to act upon the coffee and have taken to a bright tin pail, with some improvement but great unhandiness. There is one remedy for bad coffee but it is a last resort. In hotel work we go a long way around to avoid using eggs to clear coffee with. It is a constant tax to have to use half a dozen eggs every time coffee is made when eggs may be both dear and hard to get, and we make fine coffee without, by dripping through a sack into an urn that has an earthen jar or porcelain lining inside instead of metal. But here the common family coffee pot is the only utensil to use unless we send to Lakeport for an urn.

Tried the egg remedy and it proved satisfactory. Put the ground coffee in a small deep pan with a cup of cold water, broke in one egg and mixed well by stirring, put it into the pot of boiling water and when it boiled up again set it off the fire and poured in a little cold water to make it settle. The coffee is fine now, although of a low-priced sort, but only as long as it remains in that coffee pot. Poured off some into another coffee pot to be clear of grounds and in fifteen minutes it had turned to the same muddy, inky fluid we had before, while that in the pot it was made in remained good and bright the whole day.

The worriment about poor coffee is almost universal. The egg-clearing way is well-known, but there is, even after that, some attention to be paid to the vessel it is kept in. It may be that the good effect of the egg was greatest in coating over the inside of the coffee pot it was cooked in. At this place eggs are cheap and we shall use whatever may be necessary to keep the coffee bright and clear, and not buy an urn.

———

The 'bus has brought a passenger. Put him on the new register, quick! A majestic looking gentleman, and they say he is all the way from Rome.

Later.

The passenger only came to try to contract to deliver us a carload of watermelons every week. The extent of our business will not warrant such a contract at present. I would rather have fifteen cents' worth of onions, ten of turnips and ten of carrots and parsley for my soups. He thinks we might club together with the other houses. After dinner he will go and see them and then he starts back to his home in Rome (Ga.)

———

558—Cooking Sweetbreads.

——— ———

It is the making of sweetbreads to press them to a flat shape between two pans after boiling them, and let them get cold that way. As a rule they are always boiled before being otherwise cooked; not but what they may be cut up and stewed, or split open and broiled without previous cooking if they are calves' sweetbreads, and tender, still it is best to do the other way and the largest and finest that people will naturally select for the best are the very ones that need about an hour's boiling to make them tender.

Sweetbreads are the whitish pieces of soft meat that look like fat, found near the throat and the heart of the animal, the largest coming from the heart. They are used extensively as a fancy meat for little side dishes.

When they first come from the butcher's put them in cold water and after steeping a while set them over the fire in a saucepan of water to cook for an hour. As they have an insipid taste that is not improved by keeping, a little vinegar should be put in the water they are boiled in—about four tablespoons—and some salt. Take them up in a pan or dish, put another on top of them and a heavy weight like a pail of water on that. When cold you can split them into thin slices and trim off the rough edges.

———

Dinner.

———

Roast Mutton No. 185—4½ lbs, 45 cents.

Sweetbreads fried in butter sweetbreads worth 30, and butter 5, 35 cents.

Green pease (small quantity from garden for garnishing sweetbreads, worth 20 cents.)

Tomatoes (1 can, 15 cents.)

Potatoes mashed with milk and butter (6 cents.)

Rhubarb pies (No. 114—3 large, covered; cost 27 cents, 18 cuts; 1½ cents each.)

Cup custard (No. 136—used six eggs to a quart milk, made 3 pints, 18 custard cups, 15 cents.)

Milk and cream average 21, butter and bread average 12 cents.

$1 96; 21 persons, little over 9 cents a plate.

———

559—Sweetbreads With Green Pease.

———

Have the sweetbreads previously cooked and pressed (No. 558.) Split each in two, dredge with a little pepper and salt then dip both sides in flour. Put a lump of butter in a frying pan to melt over the fire and lay the sweetbreads in when it begins to froth. Cook them a nice brown on both sides.

Have green pease ready cooked and season with salt only. Serve one sweetbread to each dish, placed diagonally with a spoonful of pease across each end and a teaspoonful of the butter they were fried in (*beuerre noir*) for sauce.

560—To Cook Green Pease.

Hard water is the best to boil them in as it preserves the green color. If they take more than half an hour to cook it shows that they are not worth the name of green pease. Very few people gather pease young enough to be at their prime or seem to know how great the difference can be. We get pease from the garden, as good and better than the finest French canned pease, by taking them early.

Have the water boiling when you put the pease in, and a little salt in it and boil gently till done. If old pease, put a pinch of soda in the water and keep stewing an hour or more. Drain off the water and season either with butter, or cream sauce. (See No. 50.)

Who's going to scrub the kitchen? Not I, of course. It is getting pretty dirty by this time, the stove, too. Housekeeper comes along casually as it were, and looks, and looks. She does not say anything; she will never say anything, but some people can *look* a whole volume. I suppose she had everything dreadful nice and clean at the Water Cure Home at Campmeetingville in the Great Frying Pan Valley.

When I first came here I was allowed my choice of four of the hired girls to take one to be my second cook. Was fool enough to choose the prettiest and smartest. Guess she will think herself too nice to scrub. Don't like to ask her. Wish I could swap her off for my old Mike or Slim Jim, or Reddy; they were the boys could sling a scrub broom and were not afraid of a kettle of boiling lye —except when they had new boots on, which was about once a month, poor boys, for hot lye is awful hard on boots

Supper.

Beefsteak (16 2-oz steaks, 2 lbs loin net, 40 cents.)
Potatoes baked (15, 3 cents.)
French rolls (30, 14 cents.)
Rhubarb sauce (9 cents.)
Butter sponge cake, warm frosted (No. 561—1½ pounds, 15 cents.)
Milk and cream (20 cents.)

Butter (table and steak, 1 lb, 20 cents.)
Coffee tea (5 cents.)
$1 26; 20 persons, little over 6 cents a plate.

561—Butter Sponge Cake.

One of the best and most useful cakes.
1 cup sugar—8 ounces.
½ cup butter, large—4 ounces.
4 eggs (use 5 if they are cheap.)
½ cup milk.
1 large teaspoon baking powder.
3 cups flour.
Beat the sugar and eggs together a few minutes, melt the butter and beat it in, add the milk, then the powder and flour and beat up thoroughly. Good to bake in a shallow tin and frost over with No. 3 or for layer cakes or with currants and raisins mixed in. About two pounds; costs 10 cents a pound.

Breakfast.

July 7.
Liver and bacon, a la brochette (liver 9, bacon 7, 16 cents.)
Beefsteak broiled (7 steaks, 1 lb common 15 cents.)
Lyonaise potatoes (5 cents.)
Rolls, bread and toast (16 cents.)
Batter cakes (1 qt, 8 cents.)
Syrup (10 cents.)
Butter, milk, cream, coffee, tea (40 cents.)
$1 20; 20 persons, 5½ cents a plate.

562—Calf's Liver a la Brochette.

Take a thin slice of liver and one of breakfast bacon for each person and cut them into little square pieces as nearly of one size as may be and place them on tin skewers, a piece of liver and a piece of bacon alternately till the skewers are full. Dredge with pepper, place them in a dripping pan in the oven, turn them over two or three times while they are cooking and when done place the liver and bacon on long pieces of buttered toast already in a dish, hold in place with a fork while you draw out the skewers, then send it in.

As only about half the people will take liver when there is other meat, and as each slice weighs but an ounce, three quarter pound of liver and half pound bacon serves for 20 persons' orders. Brochette is French for spit or skewer.

563—Lyonaise Potatoes.

Lyonaise potatoes are cold boiled potatoes sliced in a frying-pan, and browned with a little minced onion mixed with the drippings. But, on account of the very general objection to onions, at least among business people, the name of lyonaise is often given to the plain article, that is, to cold potatoes fried more or less brown, in a little fat in a frying-pan without the onions.

In this case, having no parsley I used green onions from the seed bed very sparingly, as much for the green sprinkling as for taste; partly fried the onions in the drippings before putting the potatoes in. Potatoes this way should be sliced small.

But who is going to scrub the kitchen? My gracious! And the housekeeper, from the Water Cure Home has been in since breakfast looking harder than ever. And there is my "sec." A great singer she is, with not the least intention of having a scrub out, singing in chorus with three other German girls, and wiping pans, not at the hotel rate of a mile a minute, but at about the eighth of a mile an hour. It is a very pretty pic-nic, this summer resort business, at present and I hate to break it up.

"Shall we gather at the river
The beautiful, beautiful river."

That is what they are singing but not in the same tongue. They have it:

I

Sammeln wir am Strom uns Alle,
Wo die Engel warten schon,
Und die Wasser wie Crystalle
Fliessen hin vor Gottes Thron.

CHOR.

Ja, wir sammeln uns am Strome,
Dem herrlichen, dem herrlichen
Strome;

Sammeln uns am Lebens Strom,
Der da fliesst von Gottes Thron.

II

Dort, wo an des Strom's Gestade
Sich die Silber-Welle bricht,
Preisen ewig wir die Gnade
An dem Tag voll Glanz und Licht.

CHOR.

Ja, wir sammeln uns am Strome, etc.

III

Ehe wir zum Strom gelangen,
Legen jede Last win hin;
Dort als Sieger zu empfangen
Kron' und Purpur zum Gewinn.

CHOR.

Ja, wir sammeln uns am Strome etc.

IV

In des Stromes hellem Spiegel
Nimmt man Jesus Antlitz wahr,
Und des Todes Schloss und Riegel
Trennt nicht mehr die heil'ge Schaar.

CHOR.

Ja, wir sammeln uns am Strome etc.

V

An den Silberstrom im Leben
Schliesst sich unser Pilgerlauf,
Und des Herzens heilig Leben
Geht in Wonnejubel auf.

CHOR.

Ja, wir sammeln uns am Strome etc.

Dinner.

Nudel soup (4 qts, 12 cents.)
Rib ends of beef (No. 144, but smaller cuts—30 cents.)
Browned potatoes (No. 157—5 cents.)
Baked pork and beans (No. 386—beans 1 lb, 4; pork ½ lb 5—9 cents for 2 quarts or 10 orders.)
Tomatoes (1 can, 15 cents.)
Rhubard pie (cheap short crust, 3 pies, 21 cents.)
Milk 20, butter 5, bread 6, coffee and sugar 6 (37 cents.)
$1 29; 20 persons, 6½ cents a plate.

564—Nudels, Noodles or Nouilles Paste.

There was a rather funny passage of

comment and rejoinder not long since between certain New York and Philadelphia editors, occasioned by the former having seen "Nudels" somewhere for the first time and the latter remarking that his friend would see nudels or noodles very frequently indeed if he would visit the good land of Pennsylvania. It is just barely possible that neither of these had ever recognized "nudels" in the French *nouilles* soup of their several city hotels and restaurants. Undoubtedly German *nudel* is the proper word and the nudel is the original German home-made macaroni.

To make nudels is an extremely simple matter if you start right and there is no real need of the trouble being taken of drying the dough before or after shredding it. Drop the yolks of two eggs in a cup, add flour by the teaspoonful and a little salt and stir together to make it a stiff yellow dough. Then turn it out on to the table and work more flour in as long as the yolks will take up any. Next, roll out the lump till it is as thin as a knife blade, dust it all over with flour, cut it into bands and lay one on top of the other—the flour keeps them from sticking together—and then with a sharp knife cut off the nudels in shreds no thicker than straws and all of one length, which will be the width of the bands of dough. Shake the shreds apart and dust with flour and slide them into a dry pan to keep until the soup is ready to receive them. Any surplus flour may be got rid of by shaking the nudels around in a seive, and if to go in a very clear soup or consomme (139) they can be parboiled separately first and dipped up with a skimmer.

565—Nudel or Noodel Soup.

It has no particular or special flavorings beyond the nudels or *nouilles* paste. Make as rich a broth as the meat and bones at your disposal will allow, by boiling them several hours, with a bunch of the ordinary soup vegetables and a stalk of celery. Strain the broth into a clean saucepan, skim off all the grease, add a spoonful or two of tomato juice or catsup, salt and white pepper and a little flour thickening, and if you wish to make it a prettier color and show up the nudels better put in a tablespoonful of burnt sugar coloring. Let it boil again and fifteen minutes before dinner time throw in the nudels and let cook until time to serve.

At the Monegaw White and Black Sulphur Springs Hotel, I used to make nudel soup almost daily for a poor lady in the last stage of consumption who could eat a plateful of this farinaceous sustenance every day for weeks after she was past every other kind of food.

566—Beans Baked in Jars, or Boston Baked, or Potted Beans.

We see this dish with all these names and others besides in hotel bills-of-fare. This is something that we can never have at this little summer house, for the cooking arrangements are not right. There is a very wide-spread custom among hotel-keepers of having baked beans and brown bread served hot for Sunday breakfast. It is generally thought that a brick oven is an indispensable requirement for the baking, yet at the Rathburn House at the Mountain Gap, we used to bake beans most perfectly in the range in which the night-watchman kept up a slow fire all night. On account of the expense of fuel we only baked once a week and then used two jars of a larger size, than is ordinarily required, that there might be cold beans for several days after. For a gallon jar take:

8 cups of navy beans (14 cents.)
½ cup molasses (2 cents.)
1 tablespoon salt.
½ pound salt pork (5 cents.)

Supposing they are to be baked during Saturday night, put them in water to soak in the morning, and set the pan in a warm corner. At night drain away the water that remains, put the beans in the jar, also the molasses, salt and piece of pork and pour in fresh water enough to be about an inch above the beans. Put on the lid or a little plate and set the jar in the oven. It is a mistake to get up a great fire and keep the beans furiously boiling as some do, that try it for the first time; they have not the taste of baked beans when done; but keep a slow and steady fire and let the jar remain in the oven 8 or 10 hours. They should come out brown on top, yet not quite without water at bottom.

567—Canned Tomatoes as a Vegetable.

Let the tomatoes stew down to dry out the surplus juice if possible, instead of adding bread crumbs to thicken them. Canned tomatoes are vastly improved (in the way of being solid packed) over what they were a few years ago, when they were generally colorless and watery. While they are stewing add salt and pepper and a small piece of butter if afforded. If bread crumbs are added mince them very fine first, or better still, do as they do at Black's, for their 90 boarders; put the cold rolls in a pan of cold water and after a few minutes drain the water off and squeeze the bread dry. This soaked and squeezed bread is called panada. It is used for chicken stuffing as well as to thicken tomatoes.

"When we're rich we ride in chaises,
  When we're poor we walk (or work)
    like blazes!"
    —*Hudibras* (or some other fellow.)

The deuce take this disappointing summer resort business. Here is a week gone and nobody has come yet. Proprietor evidently disappointed; feels like one forsaken; has gone and got a saw and hatchet and is tearing up and repairing the dilapidated cellar steps with his nearly new fifty-dollar summer resort suit on. That's a great way to save expenses. I feel sorry for his suit but not so sorry for him as I should be for a poor man who might have spent everything getting ready for a resort business that never comes after all. One week is nothing if one only knew what is to come. If one week goes by and brings nobody why may not the next and the next? There may be a host of summer tourists on the way who will fill all the rooms and ask for cots and tents, and beds even on the roof of the house, for all we know, but suppose a rainy spell or a cold spell intervene and they never get here. And they say that at this time last year there were over forty

people visiting here. When a man who has been keeping open house for years, at last provides himself with a real hotel register with $2.00 per day printed on the top of every page, it does seem as though by that act he had alienated every friend he had in the world. That's what makes the proprietor tired. He is tired of playing the lone fisherman; tired of sitting on the piazza seeing the 'bus come back and waiting my darling summer boarder for thee; tired of hearing his hired girls sing the beautiful river; tired of seeing his boat boy in the big sailor hat idly sitting on his lone rock by the sea; tired of thinking that somebody's coming when the dew drops fall; tired of resting and gone to work.

568—How to Scrub the Kitchen.

Swish, Bang !

Why, it is a real relief to see the boiling hot suds and lye water dash around and deluge tables, walls, shelves, stove and floor once more, after all these years endurance of that vile, slimy, push-the-dirt-in-the-corners-and-leave-it-there way of mopping the horrible painted, grained and varnished kitchens of the present idiotic fashion. What! let the spiders build webs over the range and stay there the year around because the painted walls are too good to have hot suds thrown upon them?

Now, I hope that housekeeper from the Great Frying Pan Valley will stay away while I scald something. This is my water cure, and my old Mike and Slim Jim and Reddy know it is a good one. I want to scald the winter and spring mouldiness, the bugs and roaches, flies, muddaubers, daddy-longlegs, spiders, centipedes, mice, toads, snails and things, and there will be no reserved seats for spectators for a while. One afternoon, not long since, I went to show an old second of mine who is pastry cook at the Bendebeer House at Bingen-on-the-Bayou, how to make the Kaaterskill flannel rolls, sometimes called German puffs, that are just now the fashion, and while there had a chance to try the efficacy of boiling water. That house, too, has a painted and varnished kitchen with everything as inconveniently placed as all the modern improvements could possibly be, and altogether too nice for cleanliness. There are patent doors with patent springs to shut them up quick to keep the fresh air out; patent windows with nickel-plated fastenings and blinds and screens and shutters to keep the foul air in. The meat block is at the other end of the table distant from the broiler; the pastry room is two rooms distant from the oven; the kitchen floor is covered with oilcloth and a girl slimes it over with a mop at eleven every morning, and the cockroach population of that fine house is over a hundred millions (estimated). Seeing an odd million or so of the abominable insects roosting in a bunch under a low shelf near the range I could not resist the temptation to sling a two-quart dipper of hot boiling water. Brought them all down at one shot. But, as if that was not enough, from some painted and grained little cuddy hole underneath a lot of mice skipped out, for the hot water had fallen into a breeding place that had been undisturbed perhaps since the house was built. It being none of my funeral I left the place before the cook came home.

Swash, Zip!

There's that housekeeper from Camp-meetingville looking again, and I guess she is laughing now. But, for pity's sake, what made her skip away so quick? There was no danger. Guess I can hit where I aim, if she can't, and did not aim her way. Boiling water and plenty of it, is a good thing to fight a mutinous boat's crew with. It is an infallible exterminator. This method of hydraulic scrubbing is new to her. Wants a hose and tank of boiling water to do it up perfectly. She was looking to see where the water goes when it is brushed off the tables and stove and falls from the walls. Where does she think it goes? Where does she think the flies comes from that she spends half her life fighting to death? They come out of the ground, under damp floors where there are crumbs and sweepings and decaying matter. That is where this scalding lye and soap water is going and it will kill more flies in their infancy than her suffocating insect powder ever will. Insect powder does not kill. It is necessary to take up the vermin in their apparently dead state and burn them, otherwise, after a few hours they begin to kick, then get up and look around, shake themselves

and go back to their old haunts.

It is all egregious folly making kitchens too good to stand boiling water. At some hotels that have been rebuilt two or three times and thereby cured of the first follies and made right at last. They have stone floors in the kitchens even when up stairs, and tile drains where the water may flow free. The old and natural style of kitchen had massive oaken beams and rafters, solid oaken tables and walls or wainscot that could be scrubbed. Every time I chop the fins and head off a fish, or strike a broiling chicken with the side of the cleaver to flatten it for the gridiron a spray of animal juices flies and strikes somewhere. It may be scarcely visible at one time yet it coats over the walls after a while. On the river we call the dividing walls bulkheads and we used to scrub these bulkheads as thoroughly as the tables and floors and we found that after scrubbing with brooms dipped in a tub of hot water containing some lye or soap, if the water we rinsed off with was likewise boiling hot the boards dried much whiter than if rinsed off with cold water.

"Oh! how white your tables are drying?

"Yes, of course they're white—did you think I was going to mop them?"

"Housekeeper says we can get a tub of boiling suds and do the pantry that way."

"Ah, wretched hypocrites, you can get awfully enthusastic over it now the work is done. Get out."

———

It is not so mnch of a pic-nic for the waiter girls when these summer houses fill up at last. The reason why the girls at that same Bendebeer House at Bingen-on-the-Bayou looked so pale and powdered and rouged so ridiculously was not because they were dissipated as some thought and said, but because the necessity of keeping their pink gowns starched out as wide, stiff and sharp almost as mowing machines robbed them of hours of sleep. I should like to know if anybody thought they could pay for all that laundry work out of their wages —their linen cuffs and little frilled aprons and white neck gear, fresh ever dinner time. They rose at three in the morning taking turns by squads to have the use of the laundry before the regular laundry hands came on; in the interval between dinner and supper they had to go and do something else to the duds and at night after the dining room doors were closed and the laundry hands had vacated the place they took possession of the starching and ironing tables for several hours at a spell. Misery loves company and they did not seem to know they were suffering as long as all the other girls had to go through the same ordeal. But it did make them pale and gaunt to a degree that the regular day work alone would not have done. Then they piled on the artificial colors.

569—Trouble with Steam Chest and Vegetables.

The caustic concentrated lye we buy in cans has to be used in moderation; the steam from it alone caused a painful ulceration of the breathing apparatus of a lot of us fellows once where we threw it around too carelessly. The old-fashioned ash-hopper lye is doubtless as dangerous if boiled down strong. It was at the Uncomphagre House, out in the Rathskeller Range of mountains, Slim Jim Dalton was my second then. He was the most cleanly boy I ever knew. He had just quit the Quaintuple House at Turtle Key, because he could get nothing but sea water there to scrub with, and it would not make a lather. I doubt whether he would have taken the key as a gift, or a whole bunch of keys in Grouper Inlet if they were without soft water to make soap suds with. But he could never be a good cook for he seemed to be devoid of the senses of taste and smell. A thing might be burning up on top of the range for an hour before ever he would find it out, and then he was indolent. If he scrubbed the floor until it was as white as a table-cloth it seemed to be only that he might have the luxury of rolling down to sleep upon it without soiling his white shirt, and after draining the steam chest dry he often forgot or neglected to fill it again, and the result was that the pipes which take the water down into the fire-backs often went dry and burnt a goodway up, and that makes one of the worst of smells and taints the vegetables that are steamed over the steam chest for days afterwards. Another thing, there was no ice, and the water the pared potatoes were kept in would hardly stay sweet over night.

We have to keep potatoes and other vegetables after they have been pared ready for breakfast covered with water, otherwise they turn black and wilt in a short time, but it is necessary if any are left over to put them in fresh water and let them be the next to be used. This Slim would not always do, and the potatoes at the bottom of the keg acquired a bad smell. We had a lot of awful particular people in that house, and one day after those bad potatoes had been steamed over that badly burned steam chest some of them made a grand kick and the proprietor who did not know what was the matter any more than a child, got clear off his head about the reputation of his house. I promised there should be no more cause for complaint and Slim turned over a new leaf with his potatoes; threw away the wooden keg and got two stone jars and kept them scalded out. But we did not know what to do with the steam chest. The foul smell was caused by the starchy sediment that drips from steaming vegetables going down into the pipes and burning there when the pipes get dry. I suppose the only way to clean them was to take them off, but that we could not do. Slim thought concentrated lye was good for everything and put a can in the steam chest and let it dissolve. The burnt stuff was not the right sort for lye to act upon, but it seemed to eat away by degrees, so we kept it up for days and weeks, drawing the lye water to scrub with and putting in fresh every morning and living in the steam from the boiling lye until it had nearly put the whole of us, seven in all who worked in the kitchen, past working at all, our lungs seemed all on fire and we had not the least idea of what was causing the sickness. The truth dawned upon us at last, and then I banished concentrated lye from the place entirely and drove a wooden plug into the faucet so that Slim could not drain the steam chest dry any more. The cause once understood and removed, we soon recovered from the ailment. But Slim was all broke up. The floors lost their whiteness. He took to looking out of the windows and whistling to himself, and soon left me, to find some other place where the water was all soft and where they made in unlimited abundance their own soft soap.

Five arrivals this evening. They have come for the season. They are either from Paris or Peoria, Pekin or Pewaukee —it's a P, but I did not quite catch the name.

Goods arrived from Lakeport at last. Open them to-morrow.

Supper.

Broiled Mackinaw trout (4 lbs, gross 30, butter to baste 5—35 cents.)
Broiled tenderloin steak (No. 40-7- steaks, 1lb. 25 cents.)
Beefsteak common (8 steaks, 1lb. 16, butter gravy 5-21 cents.)
Eggs (4 orders, 14 cents.)
Potatoes baked (5 cents.)
French rolls (35 and loaf bread, 19 cents.)
Rhubarb sauce (10 cents.)
Cake, frosted (1½ lbs, 18 cents.)
Butter, (average count 15 cents.)
Milk and cream, (average count 28 cents)
Coffee and tea, (10 cents.)
Twenty-five persons; 8 cents a plate.

570—Broiled Mackinaw Trout.

If the fish is of small size, split it lengthwise in halves and remove the bone entirely, by cutting along both sides of it. Dry the halves on a clean kitchen towel, dredge with pepper and salt, dip both sides in flour, place them in the hinged wire broiler and cook over clear coals. When partly cooked, brush over with melted butter and keep it moist until well done through. To serve, turn out of the broiler on to a little board on the table, kept for the purpose and divide each side in four by a sudden chop with a large sharp knife. For a plain family supper like this, no sauce is needed, but have the fish freshly cooked and hot. May also be served like No. 58.

Note.—It is not necessary to cook broiled fish entirely on the broiler, but, when the place is wanted to broil the beefsteaks the fish may be finished in a pan in the oven. Very large fishes are sometimes broiled whole ostensibly, when they are in reality baked except for sufficient broiling at first to give them the marks and appearance. A very nice broil can also be effected over the top of the stove, by beginning a little earlier.

Breakfast.

July 8. Meats all cut and laid ready in a pan are to be broiled as ordered. Where there are so many kinds offered it is sufficient to prepare two or three orders of each.
Beefsteak (6, 12 ozs, net, and seasonnings, 16 cents.)
Liver (4 slices, 8 ozs, 7 cents.)
Bacon (4 slices, 6 ozs, net, 6 cents.)
Ham (4 slices, 8 ozs, net, 12 cents.)
Mutton chops (6 lb, gross, 10 cents.)
Eggs (2 dozen, and butter to fry, 35 cents.)
Potatoes baked and fried (8 cents.)
Rolls and bread (15 cents)
Batter cakes (2 qts, 13 cents.)
Syrup (of 1½ lbs, sugar, 12 cents.)
Butter (1 lb, 20 cents.)
Milk and cream (25 cents.)
Coffee and tea (10 cents.)
Total, $1 89; 25 persons; 7½ a plate.

Dinner.

Not having soup regularly as yet, for no reason of expense but because it makes more work waiting on table, washing plates, and prolonging the meal.
Boiled trout with butter sauce (2 lbs, gross and sauce, 18 cents.)
Roast beef (2 ribs, 4 lbs 50 cents.)
Boiled ham (knuckle with 2 lbs, net, 30 cents.)
Corn (2 cans, seasonings, 31 cents.)
Green peas (from garden, equal 2 cans, 30 cents.)
Potatoes (7 cents.)
Baltimore butter pie (No. 577 increased —3 large, deep, 40 cents.)
Raisins, nuts, cheese, pickles, condiments (average cost 1 cent each person

all counted together, 25 cents.)
Bread, butter (16 cents.),
Milk, coffee, tea (30 cents.).
Total, $2 77; 25 persons; over 11 cents a plate.

571—Boiled Trout.

When we have but a small amount of fish we boil it, because we find that "it goes further" that way than if baked or broiled; whether the reason be that it shrinks less or that there are fewer orders for it. Boiled fish ought not to be considered inferior, for in no other way is the peculiar flavor of a fine fish so well preserved. It is always safe when the preferences of the people to be served are unknown, to boil a trout or salmon in water that is well salted and without other seasonings. At some other time you can try the addition of an onion stuck with four cloves, and half a cup of vinegar to the water, and perhaps a bayleaf and some parsley, besides the salt. Use a bright pan if you add vinegar, or the fish will be dark. As our summer boarders all come to the table at the same minute and want to be served instantly, we prepare the fish for dishing up by cutting it in portions half way through before boiling, being careful to sever the bone at each cut, which is easily done with the point of a large knife. Then the fish must not boil too long, nor too fast; have the water boiling in a deep boiler, pan, or something roomy enough, drop in the fish and simmer not longer than half an hour. Drain off most of the water. Serve on small plates with the sauce at the side of the piece of fish.

572—Taking Unwarrantable Liberties

Whoever serves fish or meat to a number of guests at a public house of whose tastes and preferences he can know nothing, takes unwarrantable liberties with their food if he covers it with a sauce before sending it in. The sauce should be placed under or at the side of the cut. The salmon or the trout may be fine, firm, flaky, pink-fleshed, good to look at, and appetizing, but the sauce may be a dull paste, perhaps tasting of butter of a poor quality; or, if of the very best quality when first made it may have become thick and stringy with waiting, or, it may be a caper sauce, which the person does not like, or eggs, or tomato, or anchovy which many detest—why should the fish or meat be deluged with these peculiar flavors whether the recipient wishes it or not? There is an answer—it is because that it is the custom of French cooks and so the directions read. But it never was intended for general application. One day I happened to be at the Lookover-the-Mountain House (by-the-Sea) when a large number of prominent townspeople were taking dinner there for some complimentary purpose concerning the excellence of the table, and the cook served the fish with wine sauce. The fish was of the finest; probably it was well cooked; but whether it was the wrong wine or no wine at all, but a substitute, the sauce was sweet; it could hardly have been sweeter if it had been molasses; it had the Parisienne potatoes in it saturated and dingy, and each portion of fish served was buried out of sight under a large spoonful of the mess. There are plenty of reasons why sauces may be bad in spite of skill and good intentions, but they are of small consequence in the houses where they are but poured at the side and not over the cut of meat or fish, because then a free choice is left to either take or leave, and the cook's sauce is placed upon its own merits.

573—Butter Sauce—Best.

2 cups clear strained broth or water.
¼ pound butter or more.
2 heaping tablespoons flour.
Salt, if not enough in the butter.

Take half the butter and all the flour and stir them together in a saucepan over the fire. When well mingled and bubbling from the bottom add the boiling water or broth a little at a time, stirring till all is in and the sauce has cooked thick and smooth. Take it from the fire and beat in the other half the butter a portion at a time and do not let it boil again. It looks glossy and smooth as soft butter; may need thinning down for some purposes, as for parsley sauce, etc.

The above makes over a pint of sauce; the cost is whatever the price of the butter used may be.

574—Cheap Butter Sauce Substitute.

2 cups clear strained broth or water.
Flour and water thickening.
1 ounce butter (guinea egg size.)
Salt.

Thicken the broth or water by stirring in the mixed flour and water. Take it from the fire and beat in the lump of butter until it is melted. Do not boil after the butter is in.

575—Family Roast Beef.

Each **'** of beef weighs on an average 2 pounds 'hen it has been shortened and trimmed ready for roasting. Our 2-rib roast weighs 4 pounds and takes an hour to cook well done. Roasted meat is at its best when it is but just done, when the gravy flows freely, as soon as it is cut. I make it an invariable practice to hold back the roasting until the last; a cut that will take 2 hours goes in just 2 hours before dinner time, and if there is no gravy on hand and the pan is required to make some, change the meat into another pan 15 minutes before dishing up—which gives time for the gravy making.

Some comical wordy encounters take place at times through the difference of menus of quantity between hotel and private house people. "Four pounds of beef for twenty-five people's dinner!" says one, "why, that would not be more than enough for my family at home." "Two pounds of meat to make an entree for a dinner for fifty!" exclaims another—"and even when it is chicken meat nicely fixed up, still only two pounds! Nonsense, you can't tell me, I know that one hungry man could eat up the whole business."

At the same time Mrs. Tingee, who knows far more about saving than ever I can tell her would think we were giving ruinously large rations if she could see.

It is a curious study, this bill of fare plan with its small amount of each of many viands, I have not time to attempt to explain how it is that the one hungry man does not eat up the whole business, nor a dozen hungry men either. These little bills of fare are truthful records of stubborn facts and they may explain it all. If not, we shall find out how well fed all these people have been when we count up the sum total at the end of the book.

576—Brown Pan Gravy or Espagnole.

The brown sauce which in systematic cooking we find so useful, so indispensable, even, is not much unlike the frying-pan gravy that Mary Jane makes very nicely, sometimes, by taking out the fried pork, sausage or chicken and pouring in water or milk and thickening it when it boils, but we are strictly careful to get rid of all the grease. We think over the matter an hour or two ahead of the time for making gravy to see what can be put in the pan to make it richer and to improve the color, and we make it in the roast meat pans, and generally in the oven. The material for making the gravy is the essence of beef or other meat that escapes from the meat in roasting, as already mentioned at Nos. 170, 185, 171, 144 and other places, and settles at the bottom of the pan, and of course the more meat the better the gravy will be. It is well enough, but not strictly necessary to put a piece of turnip, carrot and celery in the pan along with any rough pieces of meat besides the roast, and there must be some salt put in at the beginning. All the time the meat is roasting there is more or less water in the pan and the grease and gravy are mixed together, but when the meat is taken out the pan dries down, the essence sticks on the bottom and turns brown like the outside of roast meat and the hot grease above it is as clear as water and can be poured off into a jar to be used for frying and other purposes. That being done put into the pan a quart, more or less of water or soup stock, let it boil up and dissolve the brown glaze, then add flour thickening a little at a time, making it as thick as cream, let boil and strain it into a saucepan. It is then ready for use; but if allowed to simmer at the side of the range, it will throw up scum and grease which must be skimmed off, and the sauce becomes bright and is much improved.

577—Baltimore Butter Pie or Custard Without Eggs.

Having no eggs left after breakfast,

made a kind of pie that serves in place of pudding and needs none.

At the Kissimmeequick Hotel—a noted resort on the Kissimmee River—they have one of those little customs with which no fault can be found of keeping a standing favorite dish always on the bill of fare, and there it is custard pie, regularly, there being another kind of pie and the pudding and cream to make the changes on. But there the supplies are by no means regular in arriving, and when they have no eggs they make custard this way:

4 cups milk—a quart.
1 small cup butter—6 ounces.
1½ cups sugar—12 ounces
1 level cup flour—4 ounces.

Boil the milk with the butter in it and a spoonful of the sugar to prevent burning. Mix the flour and sugar together dry, stir them into the boiling milk quickly with a wire egg beater, like making mush and take from the fire as soon as it begins to thicken. It will finish cooking in the pies. Line 2 deep custard pie plates with crust rolled very thin and pour the whole 3 pints of mixture into them—if you have people enough to eat so much, if not, of course the receipt can be divided. The butter is the only flavoring needed in this mixture and must be good. Bake in a slack oven until the filling begins to rise in the middle. It will rise and flow over the edge if baked too long. Cost of mixture here 17 cents and crusts of rich paste 10 cents for two. Cut each pie in eight—they are deep enough for that. Can be made richer yet with cream.

Supper.

Beefsteak (10 orders, 20 ozs, 25 cents.)
Mutton chops (9 orders, 24 ozs, 20 cents.)
Cold boiled ham (8 ozs, 10 cents.)
Potatoes (5 cents.)
French rolls (35, 14 cents.)
Batter cakes (2 qts, 14 cents.)
Syrup [12 cents.]
Blueberries [2 cans, and sugar, 33 cents.]
Molasses fruit cake [No. 578, 1½ lbs, 15 cents.]
Butter 15, milk, cream 25 coffee, tea 8.
Total, $1 96; 25 persons, nearly 8 cents a plate.

578—Molasses Fruit Cake, Cheap.

---

3 cups raisins—a pound.
4 cups currants—a pound.
1 small cup sugar—6 ounces.
Same of butter.
1 large cup molasses—12 ounces.
2 eggs.
1 cup sour milk and teaspoon soda—or else use sweet milk and baking powder.
6 cups flour—1½ pounds.
Spices if desired.

Prepare the raisins and currants and dust them with flour. Mix all the rest together and beat well, then add the fruit. May be baked in a shallow pan to cut out squares warm or in deep mold. Makes about 5 pounds, costing 45 cents, or 9 cents a pound.

Divide before baking and you can have one cake and the other half steamed to-morrow for pudding.

There is music on the water to-night—serenading party in boats—fifteen young ladies have come to the Trulirural House to board for a week or two—glee club or seminary class or something of the sort from Basswood City, and they are down at our boat landing singing. Proprietor of the Trulirural has instigated them to that—knows that our side cannot muster even a parlor quartette. If Mr. Farewell would put his hired girls in a boat and tell them to sing their loudest that party would soon be put to flight. I suppose that would not do—it would make what they call a scandal, and, instead, the manager, the housekeeper and 'bus driver are hanging the trees full of Chinese lanterns, and the boat boy with the big hat, is getting out some fire-works.

"For it makes the heart so gay,
  To hear the sweet birds singing
On their summer hol-i-day."

It does put new life into a fellow who is weary of his ill success when duck hunting to see the game come circling around at last.

579—Mrs. Tingee's Custard Pie.

The glory of the custard pie, is in the depth or thickness of it. The distance should be great between the glossy surface wavering between orange, yellow and brown and the substratum, wafer-like in its thinness, of paste. The custard pie, then demands a pie pan of an uncommon depth and spaciousness, with a capacity not frittered away in broad and spreading edges but, rather, with boundaries of an upright character and quite unobtrusive, the necessary wall of crust being of no great moment, so that it be respectably short as all about a custard pie that is worthy of consideration relates only to the filling. Taking this view of the custard pie, which I believe is the popular one. I have been troubled about pie pans. We have none at this place but such as are shallow, almost flat, nothing that is a cross between pie plate and pudding pan, which is what the exigency demands. Thinking to get out of the dilemma easily enough I went over to the country store and explained the matter to the merchant, who would not even stop for me to finish before he went off nodding and smiling, saying he had just what I wanted, some pie plates that were deep and some that were deeper. There never was a man more mistaken in the use of words. All he really had was some that were shallow and some others that were shallower, and I spent some time trying to prove it to him, but as he was German it seemed without much success. Then I had to come home, take a hammer and beat the broad, flat, edges of the pie plates we have into a comparative perpendicularity. They look bad but, "what can't be cured must be endured,"—as the sailor said when he bade his sweetheart, good bye—"so farewell, Susan," etc.

The very last time I had a talk with Mrs. Tingee—we are opposite neighbor's and it is common for me to step in of a morning—just as I was as I thought well out of the house she stopped me on the steps with the usual, "Oh, tell me something, now, what *can* I have for dinner?".

"Why; Mrs. Tingee, why don't you give your boarders some roast lamb? There is nothing better; and as for the price it is really no dearer now than mutton or the other meat you buy." But, wouldn't they eat—" Whatever she may have intended to say, she did not finish the sentence but stopped for a moment and then resumed:

"No; it is not much trouble about the meat part, but it is the something to come after. I ought to make them something. Day before yesterday I gave them pudding; yesterday we had nothing and it seems as though I ought to have something to-day, and it ought to be pie and, oh, I do dread to make pie, so!"

I could plainly see a shiver ran all through the poor lady as she said this; probably she was thinking of lard and the outlay involved in its use.

"Why not make a custard pie," I said, "it does not require much pie paste.'

"I should want some eggs, shouldn't I?" she asked dubiously.

"Yes; perhaps four.'

"Couldn't you make it with two, if it was you?"

"How can I tell when I don't know how much or how many you are going to make."'

She gazed away off into space for a while. There was a mighty argument for and against pie going on in her mind. Then coming close and looking around to see that there were no listeners, she said in a low tone :

"I would not say it to anybody but you, but I have one boarder, a young man, that actually sometimes eats four pieces of pie?"

So that's what made this poor woman shiver. Not the bare reflection upon the expensiveness of lard, but the dread of this young man's calling heartlessly one, two, three, four times for pie; having her in his power; knowing she dared not say no, or, "it is all out," while the other boarders were, yet to be served and would presently be, right before his eyes. I think if he had been in my place and realized what depths of doubt and fear this likelihood of his wanting four pieces had opened before her he would have sworn off from ever going beyond the second order. However, there are extenuating circumstances to be mentioned in his favor.

We fellows who make our custard pies in all that swaggering, arrogant feeling of boundless wealth that is born of having a plethroic store-room and whole barrels full of "stuff" to use out of would feel more like pitying than blaming the young man who would essay to move around after a four-piece *in-vest*-ment of our pies, however good and wholesome, for, as we fill each one to the brim with a pint of milk, four eggs and four ounces of sugar and the crust weighs at least four ounces more it is within an ounce or two of being two pounds weight for each custard pie, and though we cut it in the smallest pieces, that is in eight, the young man who would eat four would almost surely feel such discomfort that a pound of pie at once would bring its own punishment; and I understood Mrs. Tingee to say that she cut her's in only six—so much the worse for the young man. However, in this case I tried to sympathise with Mrs. Tingee and offered her the poor comfort of saying that everything costs and it might as well be custard pie as something else; with which she cautiously agreed.

"But won't it take milk? she asked."

"Yes, of course."

"How much, do you think?,'

Now I verily believe she was thinking spoonfuls while I was thinking quarts, but not wishing to alarm her, I said:

"Oh, about a pint."

"But that's for tea," she replied.

"Maam?"

"That's for tea."

"What, the pie?"

"No, the milk."

"Oh! yes, I understand," and did begin to apprehend her meaning. That is just like a woman. I was thinking of a pint of milk—any pint of milk—from anywhere in the world so that we got it; she was thinking of the pint of milk, the one pint of milk in her cupboard set there to be used for the tea at the evening meal and, to her the only pint of milk in the universe.

"Well, then," I said, "you need not use that; you can make just as good a custard with water."

"Is that so?" she said, brightening up, "have you ever made custard with water?" I nodded an affirmative.

"What ever made you think of trying that?"

"It tried itself, as it were. You see when at the Cloverdale Hotel and cottages in the early part of the season we had more milk than we could possibly use we made custard pie with cream, and of course it was good. As the season advanced and the crowd increased we got down to skimmed milk and to milk mixed with water, and still the custard pies were apparently as good as before;

so when it happened, as it will in every place sometimes, that there was no milk at all it was but an easy step further to make the custard pies with water alone and not care whether the cows come home or not."

"And they were every bit as good?"

"Yes, ma'am—apparently."

"Did you ever hear of anybody using flour or starch or anything to save eggs?"

"Oh, yes; there is a rule for that. If you have need of four eggs you can mix up some flour and water to the consistency of thick cream and each cooking-spoonful of that is equal to one egg, for thickening purposes, but it will be white."

"But if I use three of that and one egg it will look yellow. Well, I must get to doing something, for the morning is half gone."

So then I was released, but only for a short time, for after dinner Mrs. Tingee made me cross the street again.

"I want you to come and try my custard pie," said she.

"No, thank you—I have had dinner."

"But you must—tell me whether I did right or wrong and what you think of it."

But the pie she set before me was none of mine. I disclaim having anything to do with it. My custard pies are big and fat—three big cups of custard in each one, and there is room to dive down deep in them; but this! Oh, Mrs. Tingee how could you! It is only the ghost, the shadow, the skeleton of a custard pie. I hope she will not ever ask me any more questions. Sometimes I feel like pitying her, but am always sure to be taken aback by some such exhibition of the preternatural sharpness she has acquired in the long battle of three-and-a-half-a-week. In this case—to borrow a simile from minister Schenck's book on poker—she has seen the hand I held and gone me one, ten, aye a hundred better. One of us two has been "sold" and it wasn't Mrs. T. Her custard pie is primped and crimped around the edges, but there is nothing of it. It consists of a sheet of bottom crust about as thin as paper, with a yellow layer of custard about as deep as a sheet of blotting paper upon it. Why, three cups of custard would cover "wilds immeasurably spread" of paste of such a depth as that. With a quart of such custard made with no milk but one egg she could fill pies enough to stock up a bakery. I am afraid of her. As for the young man who, sometimes eats four pieces I may envy him his vigorous appetite, but I utterly despise him for his want of taste. Let him go without a lecture. Mrs. Tingee is able to cope with him alone. In some way or other he gets his full punishment, never doubt it.

Breakfast.

July 9.
Ham and eggs (7 orders, 12 ozs, ham, net, 15; eggs 18, 33 cents.)
Beefsteak (8 orders, 1 lb, net, 20 cents.)
Mutton chops (8 orders, 12 cents.)
Stewed kidneys (½ lb, 6 cents.)
Potatoes baked and fried, (5 cents.)
Wheat muffins (No. 102 doubled, 14 cents.)
Batter cakes (2 qts, 12 cents.)
Milk and cream (average count, 25 cents.)
Butter 15, syrup and sugar 16, tea and coffee 6.
Total, $1 64; 25 persons; about 6½ cents a plate.

580—Ham and Eggs, Hotel Style.

The large dish of ham and eggs served at some restaurants as described at No. 76 as costing 25 cents is not the best dish of the kind that can be served. It is quantity in that case rather than quality. Take the best pieces of ham, the right-hand cut shown at No. 552, shave off the outside, cut slices very thin the full size of the piece—they scarcely ever weigh so much as two ounces—and broil over a brisk fire. Lay on a good sized platter up towards one end and two fried eggs partly upon the ham and partly on the dish. If at 18 cents a dozen two eggs cost three cents, and two ounces of choice cut of ham worth 24 cents a pound net costs 3 cents each dish served counts six cents for material.

581—Stewed Kidneys, or Saute of Kidneys.

Kidneys cooked this way are not really stewed, but we have to call them so, because of the dazed looks we meet if we used any harder words.

Slice the three or four kidneys that have been taken from the different meats and steep a short time in cold water. Put them in a frying pan with a little butter, dredge with pepper and salt, and simmer slowly over the fire shaking the pan occasionally. There will be a rich gravy in the pan in a few minutes in which the kidneys become well cooked and remain tender, but if not watched the gravy presently coagulates and the kidneys are hard and tasteless. The cooking should take place only a short time before the meal begins. Add a tablespoonful of walnut catsup to the gravy before serving.

582—Muffins in Haste.

There are no better muffins than the kind made according to the directions at Nos. 102 and 103, but in summer weather and with compressed yeast they can be made of fine quality in a still shorter time with only one rising. Breakfast beginning at half past seven, I mix up the muffins at six. Take a piece of the light dough that was set over-night for rolls or bread, put it in a pan, add four yolks, six tablespoons melted butter, same of warm milk and one tablespoon sugar and pinch of salt. Hold the pan over the stove to warm the ingredients while you thoroughly mix and beat them together. Drop into greased gem pans, set in a warm place to rise about an hour, then bake.

Dinner.

Soup—purée of tomatoes with duchess crusts (5 qts, 25 cents.)
Boiled ham (knuckle, 2 lbs, 20 cents.)
Roast beef (1 rib and cap or shoulder cut, 4 lbs, gross, 50 cents.)
Mutton pie (1 lb, meat 8, 1 lb, paste 7, 15 cents.)
Macaroni and cheese (No. 584, 12 orders, 12 cents.)
Mashed potatoes, (7 cents.)
String beans (2 cans, seasoned, 28 cents.)
Steamed fruit pudding (2 lbs, 20 and sauce 5, 25 cents.)
Rhubarb pie (2 large, rolled thin, 12 cents.)

Cheese, raisins, pickles, crackers, condiments (average count, 25 cents.)

Butter (average, 15 cents.)

Milk, cream, coffee, tea (36 cents.)

Total, $2 71; 25 persons; nearly 11 cents a plate.

583—Puree of Tomatoes Soup.

A puree is a paste or pulp like mashed potatoes and a puree soup is one thickened by having a puree of vegetables or perhaps of fowl or game stirred into it; a plain tomato soup may be thin and clear enough to show up green peas, rice or other additions, but a puree soup is thick, more like tomato sauce. These explanations will do to refer to again.

The butcher over at "the Glen" would sell us a beef shank for 12 or 15 cents, but as that is a distance of four miles we must either say, "can't make soup," or do this way. Take the bone of the short loin of beef, (all the meat for steaks having been cut off raw,) the piece of shoulder off the rib roast, bone out of the veal, shanks of mutton, small piece of ham, all raw. Wash in cold water, and reject every piece that has become stale and dark through exposure to the air. Put them into a large pot with two gallons of cold water and set on to boil between 8 and 9 o'clock in the morning. Skim when it begins to boil. These bones we will count worth 10 cents.

The flavors which "go well" with tomatoes are onions, ham, garlic, cloves, green and red peppers, allspice, clams, lamb, walnut catsup, anchovies. Not to be used all at once.

Into the soup pot you had better put one onion, six cloves, piece of turnip and carrot and a three pound can of tomatoes (15 cents) or fresh tomatoes to that amount and let boil with the meat and bones until near dinner time, them add flour-and-water thickening a spoonful at a time until it seems thick enough, and season with salt and cayenne. The soup is then ready to be strained and freed from grease. Take a clean soup pot and set a strainer over it. A colander-shaped strainer at least as fine as a flour seive should be used, or one of perforated tin, finer still. You can hurry the soup and all such mixtures through by rapidly striking the strainer edge with an iron

spoon—better than stirring around.

There will be five or six quarts. Set it on the back part of the stove and as it slowly boils up at one side all the grease that is in it will collect on the surface at the other and must be skimmed off. Serve with a few duchess crusts, not put in the soup previously, but dropped in the plates as they are taken in.

584—Duchess and Conde Crusts or Croutons.

These are the names given by the French to what English cooks call "sippets of fried bread." Cut bread in thin slices without crust, then in dice no larger than navy beans. If you drop them for a few seconds, into hot clarified butter, oil or lard and fry them light brown they are duchess crusts, if, instead, you put them in a pan in the oven and bake them brown like toast they are conde crusts. They are to eat in soup instead of crackers.

585—Macaroni and Cheese—Ordinary.

This makes 12 orders at a cost of one cent each.

½ pound macaroni.

2 ounces cheese—a small cup grated or minced.

2 ounces butter—size of an egg.

1 cup milk.

1 spoonful flour thickening.

1 egg, salt, cracker crumbs.

Set on a saucepan of water and when it boils put in the macaroni broken in pieces. Cook 20 minutes then drain in a colander. Get a pan or deep dish that holds about three pints, butter it, put in the macaroni, the cheese minced fine and butter in small bits, mix them with a fork.

Break the egg in a bowl, add a cooking-spoonful of flour thickening and beat while pouring in the milk, add it to the macaroni, dredge cracker meal over the surface and bake until the liquid is set and surface brown.

There should be a little mixed flour and thickening, about as thick as cream always at hand when cooking is going on. The use of a spoonful saves an egg in this dish and is better, but do not use enough to make the macaroni solid and dry. For a high-flavored dish of macaroni, see No. 154, which is macaroni in a *fondue*, like Welsh rarebit.

586—Cheap Steamed Fruit Pudding.

Take the molasses fruit cake mixture, No. 578. Put it in a cake mould and steam from one to two hours. The color both of pudding and cake will be from yellow to black according to the kind of syrup or molasses used. Serve with sauce, Nos. 70 or 156.

Supper.

Oatmeal mush, (3 cents.)
Beefsteak (8 orders, 1 lb, net, 20 cents.)
Cold beef and ham (from dinner.)
Potatoes, (enough left from dinner.)
Biscuits (2 doz, 15 cents.)
Fresh wild raspberreis (2 qts, 30 cents.)
Cookies (3 doz, 12 cents.)
Batter cakes and syrup, (14 cents,)
Butter 15, milk and cream 30, coffee, tea 10.
Total, $1.49; 25 persons; 6 cents a plate.

587—Cookies—Good Common.

2 cups sugar—a pound.
1 cup butter—½ pound.
5 or 6 eggs.
1 cup milk or water—½ pint.
4 teaspoons baking powder.
8 cups flour—2 pounds.
Soften the butter and stir it and the sugar together, add eggs, milk, beat well. Mix the powder in the flour; mix all to a soft dough. Press it together on the table, roll out thin, sift granulated sugar all over and cut out the cakes. The softer the dough can be worked the better the cakes will be. Makes 9 dozen, cost 36 cents, 4 or 5 cents a dozen; or twice as many if rolled extremely thin.

Breakfast.

July 10.
Cracked wheat mush (2 cups cracked wheat, 4 cents.)
Beefsteak (7 orders, 1 lb, 20 cents.)
Ham and breakfast bacon (6 orders, 15 cents.)
Buttered eggs (No. 558, 18 eggs and butter, 25 cents.)
German fried potatoes (No. 511, 20 potatoes, 6 cents.)
Corn muffins (No. 286, with 2 cups meal, etc., 20, 12 cents.)
Graham batter cakes (with sour milk, like No. 535, 2 qts, 15 cents.)
Syrup 12, butter 15, milk and cream 30, coffee, tea, sugar, bread 20.
Total, $1 74; 25 persons; 7 cents a plate.

Boarders and children are getting filled up. No longer ravenous and covetous of large portions. Just beginning to have misgivings as to the gentility of large cuts, heaped up dishes and six batter cakes on a plate; willing to have them made small and only three at a time. 'Tis ever thus after a week or two. Out of eggs again, as usual; must make up a dinner without. The big hotels at the depot catch up all that comes to that little country store. Our manager as busy is as a bee from morn till dewey eve playing croquet and has no time to go further to buy. But we are out of meat, too, and somebody must go to the "Glen," which is a few sizes larger than the depot village, and buy some.

588—Trouble with the Oatmeal.

The majority of those who board where the oatmeal or cracked wheat mush is made regularly and made good soon find they cannot make a satisfactory meal without it. It is an article of diet especially desirable for children. I believe, moreover, that more hard work both of hands and head can be done, particularly in hot weather, upon a diet of oatmeal and cream than upon any mixed diet of meat and vegetables. There are two ways of cooking it and the best way is difficult and more or less wasteful. There is no waste in cooking the oatmeal in a farina kettle—as the double kettles are called—but there is a loss of something still. We cooks know by various signs when a dish strikes the peoples' fancy, and know that the oatmeal and cracked wheat that is eaten to the last grain and for which the disappointed "help" after the meal want to scrape the kettle clean for a dish for themselves is not that which is cooked in a farina kettle or steam chest, but that cooked in a thick-bottomed saucepan slowly at the back of the range, where a crust bakes under and around it and the mush gets a baked flavor. I think the best way to cook oatmeal mush would be the same as Boston baked beans, in a jar in the oven, but have never been sufficiently interested to try it. A cup of oatmeal costing two or three cents requires four cups of water to cook it, and makes a quart or two pounds of good food. If we make up our minds that it is cheap enough to throw away the crust that forms in the kettle every time it is made, the best quality can be secured that way, provided there is a slow place on the range for it to simmer for a couple of hours. Such, however, is not the case here. The thin stove fired up with light wood causes the mush to burn at the bottom every other day and the fine baked flavor and the fine theories go up in smoke together. This will never do. So having no farina kettle and there being none to buy at either village, my "sec" and I have hit upon the plan of taking a five-pint milk pail with a tight lid and setting it with the oatmeal, previously steeped in the requisite quantity of water, inside a deep iron pot containing water and so boil and steam it, covered with a lid. These tea-kettle cooks steam many a loaf of brown bread very well by the same plan, and could steam a variety of good puddings in the same contrivance if they only knew how to make them.

589—Buttered Eggs.

Break some eggs—about 6 or 8 at a time—into a bright saucepan and add for each egg a tablespoonful of melted butter and very little salt. Have a pan of water boiling on the stove; set the saucepan in it and stir and beat the eggs until they are cooked as thick as scrambled eggs. Serve sometimes plain in dishes same as scrambled eggs, sometimes on fancy toast.

590—Graham Cakes with Sour Milk— Cheapest.

It is necessary to mix white flour with the Graham, about half of each. Otherwise they are made the same as the other kind, No. 535.

Dinner.

Vegetable soup (No. 140; cost nominal, say 16 cents.)
Roast loin mutton (3 lbs, 30 cents.)
Potted beefsteak (village bought, rough, 30 cents.)
Macaroni with creamed cheese (12 orders, 12 cents.)
Green peas (from garden, worth 20 cents.)
Lima beans (dried, ½ lb, and seasoning, 5 cents.)
Tomatoes (1 can, 15 cents.)
Potatoes (plain steamed, 3 cents.)
Spice pie (No. 593; 3 pies, 19 cents.)
Old-fashioned rice pudding (2 qts, 13 cents; sauce, 3—16 cents.)
Condiments, crackers, nuts, raisins, cheese (average, 25 cents.)
Butter 15, milk and cream 30, coffee, tea, bread 10.
Total, $2 46; 25 persons; nearly 10 cents a plate.

591—Potted Beefsteak.

Beef in pieces baked in a covered jar, like Boston beans. Put two or three pounds of rough cut beef into a gallon jar, with a few cloves, a slice of bacon, a bayleaf, salt, pepper, little vinegar and two cups water. Cover the jar with a lid, plate, or greased paper. Bake 3 hours in a slow oven. Then take out the meat, strain the gravy and skim off the fat. Add a tablespoonful of walnut catsup to the gravy and serve it with shapely cuts or strips of the beef.

592—Macaroni with Creamed Cheese.

No eggs required, costs about 12 cents for 12 dishes.
½ pound macaroni.
4 ounces cheese—a heaping cup minced.
2 ounces butter—size of an egg.
2 cups milk.
Cheese that is good enough for use is generally too soft to grate, but must be

chopped fine.

Break the macaroni and throw it into boiling water, cook 20 minutes.

Warm the butter and cheese in another saucepan and rub them together with a spoon, add milk a little at a time as the cheese becomes hot, and a pinch of cayenne. The mixture must not reach the boiling point. Cheese and butter will combine when warm and the milk gradually diluting them makes a thick, creamy sauce, but they separate if boiled. Drain macaroni and pour the creamed cheese over it. Serve it in flat dishes heaped as much as possible.

593—Spice Pie, Vinegar Pie or Harvest Pie.

No eggs required nor milk.

2 cups water—a pint.

1 cup vinegar.

2 cups brown sugar—a pound.

1 ounce butter—small egg size.

1 cup flour—4 ounces.

1 teaspoon ground cinnamon.

Boil the water, vinegar and butter together. Mix sugar, flour and cinnamon together dry and dredge them into the boiling liquid, beating at the same time. Take it off the fire as soon as partly thickened, before it boils. It will finish cooking in the pies. Bake with both a bottom and top crust rolled very thin. It is necessary to be particular to get just the right proportion of flour.

594—Baked Rice Pudding without Eggs.

Neither eggs nor butter required. It is called by a dozen different names, such as Astor House, poor man's pudding and others and is made daily in many fine hotels as an alternative from the richer kinds, which some cannot eat.

1 cup rice—½ pound.

1 cup sugar—½ pound.

6 cups milk.

Cinnamon or nutmeg.

A pinch of salt.

Wash the rice in three or four waters, put it into a tin pudding pan, and the sugar, milk, salt and piece of stick cinnamon with it, all cold, and bake in a slow oven for three or four hours. It may be best to use only five cups of milk at first, and add the other if the time allows the pudding to bake down dry enough. Cover with a sheet of greased paper to keep the top from scorching. Serve with sauce.

Supper.

Oatmeal (3 cents.)

Beefsteak (6 orders, 12 oz, equal 1 lb, gross, 15 cents.)

Cold mutton (8 orders, 10 oz, net; charged dinner.)

Potatoes (2 ways, 3 cents.)

Graham rolls (No. 596; 30 rolls, 12 cents.)

Raspberry shortcake with cream, (No. 595; 2 dinner plate size; paste 27; berries and sugar 30; 24 cuts 57 cents.)

Cream 40, milk 18. coffee, tea, sugar 14, butter 15.

Total, $1 77; 25 persons; over 7 cents a plate.

595—Raspberry Shortcake.

Boys made a bargain with me that I should make raspberry shortcake for the crowd if they would go and pick the berries. Imposed the condition that they should bring a gallon. Said they would if they could, but it was a week too early yet for berries to be plenty. They came home at four o'clock in disorder. Had been in old Barnacle's woods and the old chap and his hired man came up with switches and wanted to take the berries away from them. Boys called up their big dog to defend them and ran home. I am under solemn promise "not to tell pa." Sorry, for they will be afraid to go to Barnacle's to buy eggs, now. They brought nearly two quarts red raspberries (25 cents.) After looking them over I shook a large cup powdered sugar (5 cents) into them. For the short paste:

8 level cups flour—2 pounds.

2 cups butter—1 pound.

Rub the butter into the flour, after first slicing it thin. When well mingled, wet with two small cups water. Knead the paste smooth, roll out and bake on two jelly cake pans or large pie pans if the others are not at hand. Split the shortcakes when done and spread with berries both inside and on top. Cut in 8. Cost

2½ cents a cut.   Serve cream in individual creamers.

596—Graham Pocket Book Rolls.

Graham rolls are a novelty in most places and very nice if made like French rolls, that is, folded over with a touch of butter between, so that they pull open when baked. It requires more practice, however, to make them of good shape, as Graham dough rises faster than white and the shapes run out flat if kept too warm. Of course the more difficult it is to make such an article the more merit and the more of a specialty it is for the one who can. Some white flour must be mixed with the Graham. The addition of the white of an egg to the liquor the dough is mixed with, is an improvement—Section No. 261. Use compressed yeast. Make half in split rolls, the rest a loaf of Graham bread.

Breakfast.

July 11.
Oatmeal (3 cents.)
Salmon trout, breaded and fried (15 orders, 4½ lbs, gross, 36; 2 eggs to bread 3; cracker meal 2; lard to fry equal to ½ lb, loss, 6—47 cents.)
Beefsteak (8 orders, 1 lb, net, 20 cents.)
Breakfast bacon (4 orders, ½ lb, 6 cents.)
Potatoes German fried (6 cents.)
Corn bread (No. 599; 11 cents.)
Biscuits (24, 15 cents.)
Batter cakes [cheapest, 1qt, 7 cents.]
Syrup 10, butter 15, milk, cream 22, coffee, tea 7.
Total, $1 69; 25 persons; nearly 7 cents a plate.

597—Salmon Trout Fried.

Split the fish down both sides of the backbone and take it out, cut the two sides in two-ounce pieces; salt and pepper, dip in egg and then in cracker meal and fry by immersion in hot lard.

593—Building a House with Bread Crusts.

We have all heard of gingerbread houses or gingerbread work upon them, but the meaning is not half so literally intended as a remark I heard when old Mr. Sticktite was building the fine view four-story Sticktite House at Jimsonvale Junction. It was said he built that house with money saved by drying the broken pieces of bread and crushing them to use instead of cracker meal to bread-crumb fried oysters and fish and other things. No doubt but that particular was but one tangible point seized upon to represent a life full of small saving ways, by which wealth was acquired in the long run. But I don't see where the harm was in that. Mr. Sticktite had the depot eating house and he had a large oyster trade besides and he was not the man to give grounds for the cutting sarcasms which are flung at railroad eating-house sandwiches, bread and rolls. When they became dry—really, dry and hard—he, instead of palming them off upon helpless travelers took them off his counters and tables and even out of his show cases, had the dark crust shaved off and spread them on trays in a warm plac cover the oven to become dry enough to crush; then, to keep the boys and girls out of mishchief between train times, he made them roll and sift the dried bread so that it looked like corn meal or cracker meal. And some of them could easily save their wages that way. It does not take long to use up a barrel of cracker meal where there is a considerable trade in fried oysters or in a hotel where veal cutlets and fried mush are breaded every day. As our price list of groceries shows cracker meal costs exactly the same price as new crackers, or seven dollars a hundred, so a hundred pounds of crushed dried bread is worth just that amount.

But is it as good? is the question.

Yes, if selected and freed from crust before crushing.

599—Fine Corn Bread.

Happily for us all this little company of people contains no distressful hypochondriacs nor people with special aversions. Two harmless hot-water drinking lunatics, that's all. But some of them have intimated that it is essential to their happiness to have corn bread for breakfast constantly, and baked potatoes; orders which make those two dishes fixtures on the bill of fare from this time forth.

For fine corn bread take:

2 heaping cups corn meal.

1 or 2 ounces butter or lard—size of an egg.

2 eggs, salt.

2 teaspoons baking powder.

Milk or water to mix.

Make a hollow in the meal and put in the butter and pour in a little boiling water from the teakettle to scald part of the meal. Thin it down with cold milk, add the eggs and salt and lastly the powder. Beat it well with spoon or egg whip. Have the baking pan hot and not greased, If it hisses when the corn batter is poured in the bread never sticks. Perfect success with corn bread of this fine sort depends on having the batter the proper consistency. It should be like thick batter-cake mixture when poured in the baking pan. If just right it will rise rounded and smooth and cuts like cake. For corn bread without eggs, see No. 626.

Third expressed lot of of meat arrived. Have got prices down to:

Mutton charged @ 10 cents.

Lamb, @ 10.

Beef round boneless for steak, @ 13.

Beef rib roast, @ 12½.

Liver, @ 12½.

Sweetbreads, small lot presented.

Dinner.

Cream of rice soup (No. 600; 4 qts, 15 cents.)

Trout baked, an gratin (No. 601; 3 lbs, 30 cents.)

Roast beef (2 ribs, 4 lbs, 50 cents.)

Roast mutton (2 lbs, 20 cents.)

Blanquette of lamb (No. 602; 12 orders, 14 cents.)

Green peas (10 cents.)

Lima beans (charged yesterday's dinner.)

Mashed potatoes (5 cents.)

Raspberry meringue (No. 604; 24 orders, 36 cents.)

Vanilla ice cream (2 qts, 26 cents.)

Raisins, nuts, cheese, condiments, crackers (average, 25 cents.)

Milk, cream 30, coffee, tea 6, butter, bread 10.

Total, $2 77; 25 persons; 11 cents a plate.

600—Cream of Rice Soup.

Put into 5 quarts of water some soup bones and the neck and shanks obtained from the newly arrived side of lamb, 3 or 4 small green onions, a pinch of thyme and savory; boiled an hour and took out the pieces of lamb to make the blanquette. An hour later poured the stock from the bones through a fine strainer into a clean soup pot, and skimmed off the fat.

Boiled half a cup of rice in a small saucepan. Made a quart of milk hot and mashed the rice with milk added a little at a time; put it into the soup stock, also a half blade of mace, salt, cayenne, a small carrott from seed bed finely minced. Let simmer and skimmed again. Lastly added a spoonful of thickening, half cup of cream and an ounce of butter. Costs 4 cents a quart.

601—Trout, au Gratin.

Au gratin signifies that the fish is gratinated or browned like toast on the surface, and therefore, that it is covered with bread crumbs. It comes handy to express it in that way, as the fish is not exactly breaded as for frying.

Split the fish in halves and dredge both sides with salt and pepper. Put a spoonful of drippings into your baking pan and let it get hot. Dip the skin side of the sides of fish in either milk or egg, and then in cracker meal or crumbs and place in the pan with the breaded side up. Bake it brown and baste once with butter. Divide neatly in pieces with a sharp knife. Serve either sauce, gravy, or potato balls with it.

602—Blanquette (or White Dish) of Lamb with Fried Crusts.

This was the first appearance of the lamb in any form at this table and the little entree was quite sure to be in request; and although but a trifle to fill the bill it served as a premonition to the boarders of more lamb to come.

Took the pieces of lamb cooked in the

soup stock, cut into large dice. Boiled a ladleful of stock with teaspoonful minced onion, put the cut meat in and seasoned with salt and pepper.

Made white sauce of ladleful of the finished soup (to save time) with cream, butter, thickening and scrap broken nutmeg and a tablespoon of mushroom catsup (private stock from the cook's valise) and poured it to the lamb. Serve with cut shapes of fried bread for border and a sprinkling of green peas.

603—Fancy Shapes of Fried Bread.

These may be very ornamental if fried to a clean, bright yellow-brown color in the clear oil of butter or in lard. Cut slices of bread in diamond shapes or six sided and cut out the middle, then divide by a cut across and you have a border for each end of the dish and the filling will be in the middle, or, cut thin slices and then take a scollop-edge cutter and cut out crescent shapes and fry them.

604—Raspberry Meringne.

Bought wild raspberries at 12 cents a quart. Meringne is best made with cake as at Nos. 195, and 295, but having paste left over from shortcake trimmings of previous day used that. Lined two shallow pans with thin crust and baked light colored. Spread them both with one quart berries mixed with half cup sugar. Whipped 8 whites, stirred in 8 teaspoons sugar, spread on top and baked lightly. Made 24 cuts; cost 1½ cents each. Serve with cream.

605—Vanilla Ice Cream.

1 quart milk.
8 yolks (left from raspberry meringne.)
1 heaping cup sugar.
1 pint cream.
Vanilla extract 1 tablespoon.
Made rich boiled custard of the milk, sugar and yolks (No. 200) strained into freezer, added the cream and flavor. Takes half hour to freeze and half hour more to stand and become firm, 3 quarts after freezing, 8 orders to a quart, 1½

cents each.

Supper.

Broiled Pickerel (3 lbs, gross, and butter, 30 cents.)
Beefsteak (6 orders 12 ozs, 11 cents.)
Cold meats (6 orders, charged dinner.)
Codfish in cream (4 orders, 3 cents.)
Baked potatoes (3 cents.)
Butter rolls (No. 607 ; 20 cents.)
Raspberries and cream (2 qts, berries 25, sugar 5, cream 20; 50 cents.)
Plain white cake (No. 609; 2 lbs, 17 cents.)
Butter 5, milk, cream 20, coffee, tea, bread, sugar 15.
Total, $1 74; 25 persons; 7 cents a plate.

606—Broiled Pickerel with French Potatoes.

Pickerel is a firmer fish than Mackinaw trout, less oily than whitefish and preferred by many. Split by cutting down both sides of the back bone. Cut each half in three or four, dip in flour, put in the hinged wire broiler, broil both sides and brush with butter. Serve with a few crisp "Francaise" potatoes in the plate.

607—Butter Rolls.

Sometimes called tea cake, and also Sally Lunn.
2 pounds light bread dough.
1 ounce sugar—a spoonful.
4 ounces butter—½ cup.
3 yolks of eggs.
1 teacup milk or cream.
1 pound flour to work in.
Take the dough, already light, 4 hours before the meal, mix in all the ingredients. Let rise 2 hours. Knead, then make the dough into round balls and roll them flat. Brush over with melted butter and place two of the flats together, one on the other. Press in the center. Rise an hour, and bake. When done, slip a thin shaving of fresh butter inside each and brush the top over slightly, too. Should be made very small if to serve whole, or as large as saucers, to cut. Makes 8 large enough to cut in 4. Cost buttered 20 cents.

608—Raspberries and Cream.

Serve the berries in glass plates or ice cream saucers individually, quite plain, with powdered sugar and cream on the table.

609—Good White Cake.

A great deal of the fuss and labor some people go through every time a white cake is to be made is altogether needless: to prove it try this easy cake and be surprised: that it can be put together so quickly :

2 cups sugar—a pound.
1 cup melted butter—½ pound.
10 whites of eggs.
1 cup milk.
2 teaspoons baking powder.
1 teaspoon cream tartar.
6 cups flour—1½ pounds.

Put the sugar and melted butter into the mixing pan along with the whites, not whipped, then take the wire egg beater and beat them together a minute or two; add the milk, powder, cream tartar and flour and some flavoring extract if you choose, and beat it up with a spoon thoroughly. The more it is beaten the whiter and finer the cake. If there is no cream tartar handy use the juice of a lemon. Makes nearly 4 pounds; costs 34 cents. Ought to be frosted the easy way, No. 3; or, with frosting that will slice without breaking, No. 635.

Breakfast.

July 12.
Fresh black cap raspberries (1 qt, 10 cents.)
Oatmeal (3 cents.)
Fish plain fried (7 orders, 1 lb, and lard, 12 cents.)
Beefsteak (12 orders, 1½ lbs, 20 cents.)
Liver breaded (8 orders, 12 cents.)
Potatoes baked and a la Francaise (7 cents.)
French rolls (25, 10 cents.)
Corn bread and corn batter cakes (16 cents.)
Cream and milk 42, syrup 6, butter 15, coffee, tea 12.
Total, $1 65; 25 persons; 6½ cents a plate.

610—Fish Fried Plain.

Dip the pieces in flour only and drop into a saucepan of lard hot enough to hiss. All the smaller kinds of fish and those most esteemed for their flavor such as brook trout and whitebait are best fried that way, and it is suitable for all kinds if they are cut in thin pieces.

611—Calf's Liver Breaded and Fried

Cut thin slices, pepper and salt them, dip in a little milk in a saucer (not to wash the seasoning away) then in cracker meal in which a little flour has been mixed. To make it a better color the liver had better be dipped twice giving it a double breading, otherwise it comes out dark. Drop into a frying pan of hot drippings or lard, and fry. Serve either plain or with a slice of broiled bacon.

612—Potatoes Francaise.

Cut potatoes raw with a fluted or scolloped knife, (there are knives made for the purpose) in thin strips the length of the potato, and drop them a few at a time into a saucepan of hot lard or drippings. When they rise from the bottom and float, they are done. Take up in a colander set in a plate. Sprinkle with fine salt and a little minced parsely and serve hot and crisp. The fat should not be very hot for these as if fried too quickly the potatoes turn soft after taking up.

Dinner.

Italian soup (No. 613; 5 qts, 20 cents.)
Boiled Mackinaw trout, pickle sauce (2 lbs, and sauce, 20 cents.)
Roast beef (1 rib, 2 lbs, 25 cents.)
Roast lamb (Nos 145, 146; 3 lbs, 35 cents.)
Beet greens (from garden, worth 10 cents.)
Sweet corn (1 can, 15 cents.)
Rice with cream (½ cup raw 2; seasoning 4—6 cents.)
Mashed potatoes (5 cents.)
Steamed raspberry pudding, hard sauce (Nos. 176 and 177; 21 cents.)
Chocolate butter pie (without eggs; No.

617; 3 large, 20 cents.)
Pickles, condiments, cheese, nuts, rrài
sins, crackers average, 25 cents.
Butter 10, milk, cream 22, coffee, tea 10.
Total, $2 44; 25 persons; nearly 10
cents a plate.

613—Italian Soup.

4 quarts soup stock (obtained as at No.
582.)
1 quart milk.
4 ounces macaroni broken small.
1 cup cooked lamb, veal or chicken cut
small.
1 cup mixed vegetables same way.
Chopped parsely or other green herb or
vegetable.
Salt, cayenne, thickening.
It is a white soup with macaroni, etc.,
in it. Strain off the stock, skim free from
grease, put in the vegetables and macaroni and afterwards the cut meat and
milk. . When lamb is boiled the broth
has a milky appearance and it is advisable to make white soup of that material.

614—Beet Greens.

Take the leaves of young beets, throw
away the thick stalks, wash the leaves
and keep in cold water. Shortly before
dinner put them into a pot of boiling
water in which throw a lump of baking
soda size of a bean. The greens cook in
about half an hour. Drain in a colander.
Season with salt and corned beef fat or
butter and cut them small in the pan.

615—Rice with Cream.

Wash half a cup of rice and put it to
boil in a cup of water with a lid on. When
nearly dry add half a cup of milk and
little salt. When done mix in a half a
cup of cream. Serve same as a vegetable
in deep dishes.

616—Puddings without Eggs.

At Cedar Point Cottage on Nipantuck
Island, one day I found Mary Jane in a
state of great perturbation; she was sitting on the edge of a washtub, her face
very red and with her wetted thumb she
was turning over the leaves of a cook
book at a rapid rate.

"I don't know what to g.ve 'em," she
said.

"What's the matter?"

"Pudding: Them fifteen boarders will
be here in less than an hour as hungry as
go-its, and they won't think they've had
any dinner if there don't be pudding
every day."

"Well," I said, "you know there are
some kinds can be made in a few minutes," and I looked to see whether her
fire was good.

"I know," she returned, "yes, I know
lots, but all the dratted puddings seems
to want eggs and there isn't an egg on the
island this blessed day."

"Oh, that's the trouble; then why not
try this," and I pointed out No. 176.

"There it is again," says Mary Jane,
"that's cherry pudding and where would
I get the cherries?"

"Don't you see that what is good for
one kind of fruit is good for any other kind?
That receipt shows the way they make
the steamed apple pudding or apple rolls
as they call it at some high-priced city
restaurants; for never an egg do they use
for puddings at some of those places; they
chop the apples small and use the same
as that says to use cherries."

"And would these blackberries do that
I was going to make pie of and didn't find
time?"

"Of course they will, and it only takes
about five minutes and your pot there is
boiling and there is the steamer hanging
up clean and ready and you must do this
way, use a large pie plate, and be sure
not to have the layers of dough too thick
because they rise so much that the pudding will seem to have too little fruit if
you do. It will be all the better for being
made late and being served as soon as it is
done."

By that time Mary Jane's perplexity
was all over, and when the time came to
change those fifteen plates she had ready
for them as fine a pudding as you would
wish to meet on a summer day. For another class of puddings without eggs see
Nos. 631, 639, 652, 594 and index.

617—Chocolate Butter Pie without Eggs.

The same as No. 577 with a small cup of grated chocolate added to the milk when put on to boil with the butter in it. Chocolate flavor is not good in combination with eggs, but it is with butter and cream. Chocolate custard frozen is not much esteemed, but chocolate with pure cream is one of the favorite ices. So this chocolate butter pie is the best flavored compound of the sort that can be made. If wanted as good as it can be, use a pound of sugar and half a pound of butter to a quart of milk and four ounces flour and the cup of chocolate. Makes three pies large and deep, each to cut in eight.

Supper.

Discouraged landloard. Twelfth of July gone and still "nobody in the house," comparatively speaking.

Some very fine people sure to come soon and there is a party or two talked of but meantime he says there is no use of our doing our best. Cut down expense and take it easy. There is pleasant rowing on the lake and the girls have struck up some new tunes.

Cracked wheat mush (3 cents.)
Lamb stew with potatoes (10 cents.)
Cold roast beef (charged dinner.)
Potato pats and German fried (cold served previous meals.)
French rolls (10 cents.)
Flour batter cakes (cheapest, No. 535; 2 qts, 10 cents.)
Peaches (3 lb, can Cal. in syrup, 25 cents.)
Chelsea buns (No. 619; 22, 16 cents.)
Syrup 8, butter 20, milk, cream 32, coffee, tea, sugar, bread 17.
Total, $1 51; 25 persons; 6 cents a plate.

618—Lamb and Potato Stew, or Gallimaufry.

This is said by one of our French authors to be the ancient dish of gallimaufry a la Languedocienne. It does not hurt anybody to eat it, however, and only costs 10 or 12 cents with all its wealth of name thrown in..

Take some pieces of cold lamb; about 1 pound of clear meat will do and it may be the neck or shoulder that was boiled until just done in the soup boiler. Shave off the dark portions and cut the meat in large dice. Cut an equal amount of raw potatoes the same way and put both on to boil with clear broth or water barely to cover. Put in a small onion cut up and if to be true to name a clove of garlic and sprig of green thyme and little chopped parsley. When it has stewed until the potatoes are done, season with pepper and salt and thicken it slightly if the potatoes have not boiled away and thickened it already. It is a neat looking little stew and good for a family supper.

619—Chelsea Buns, without Eggs.

One of the sweetest warm breads that serve in place of cake when there are no eggs to be had.

Take nearly half the dough that is mixed up for French rolls and work into it a few currants. Roll it out to a very thin sheet, brush over with softened butter, sprinkle sugar all over, then cut the dough into ribbons and coil them into spiral buns. Place with plenty of room between in a buttered pan, rise an hour and bake. Sugar over when done. For exact proportions, see No. 267. That variety is like currant rolls, these are flat coils.

Breakfast.

July 13.
Oatmeal (3 cents.)
Beefsteaks (6, 12 cents.)
Lamb chops (10, 1 lb, net, 1½ gross, 15 cents.)
Ham (4, 8 cents.)
Shirred eggs (No. 94; 18, and butter, 24 cents.)
French fried potatoes (6 cents.)
Corn muffins (No. 286; 24, 12 cents.)
French rolls (8 cents.)
Graham batter cakes (1 qt, 8 cents.)
Syrup, butter 23, milk, cream 32, coffee, tea, sugar 12.
Total, $1 63; 25 persons; 6½ cents a plate.

620—Lamb Chops and Toast.

Lamb chops are tedious, being small, but make a choice dish for a Sunday breakfast. As, in order to make a chop worth having of the ribs it is necessary to cut two ribs to each, take out one bone and leave all the meat on the other, there can be but few, to serve to the most honorably select, the main dependence for quantity is in cutting up the entire loin and perhaps the leg. Flatten with the cleaver. Trim and shape all as near like rib chops as may be. Cut little pieces of buttered toast very thin and in pear shape. Place one in the dish, a broiled chop leaning upon it, another piece of toast and another chop—all on an end aslant in the dish—and garnish with parsley or cress or young seed-bed celery.

Dinner. (Sunday.)

Roast beef (1 rib, 2 lbs, 28 cents.)
Spring lamb (4 lbs, 44 cents.)
Tomatoes (1 can, seasoned, 16 cents.)
Corn (1 can, seasoned, 16 cents.)
String beans (1 can, 14 cents.)
Tomatoes (2 ways, 6 cents.)
Rhubarb pie (1, 9 cents.)
Cocoanut custard pie (No. 621; 2, 20 cents.)
Ice cream with raspberries (No. 218; 3 pts, pure cream 15, 14 ozs, sugar 7, 2 qts, berries 20, freezing 5—47 cents.)
Fine white cake frosted (No. 622; 20 cents.)
Layer cake with raspberry jelly, frosted (No. 622; 22 cents.)
Nuts, raisins, cheese, crackers, pickles, condiments (average, 25 cents.)
Milk (2 galls, 24 cents.)
Cream (1 pt, 10 cents.)
Butter, bread 13, coffee, tea 6.
Total, $3 20; 25 persons; nearly 13 cents a plate.

621—Cocoanut Custard Pie.

2 cups milk—a pint.
½ cup sugar—4 ozs.
3 eggs—or, 6 yolks left as from No. 622.
1 heaping cup cocoanut—grated fresh, or dry.
1 teaspoon lemon extract.
Beat the eggs sugar and milk together, add the cocoanut and flavor. Makes a quart and fills two pies large and deep.
Costs: milk 2, sugar 2, eggs 4, cocoanut 6, extract 1, short crusts 4 or 5; 20 cents for 2. Cut each in 8.

622—Best White Cake, or "Dream Cake."

2 cups granulated sugar—a pound.
1 cup butter—½ pound.
12 whites of eggs—12 ounces.
1 cup milk—½ pint.
2 rounded teaspoons baking powder.
1   do   cream tartar.
Vanilla or lemon extract.
4 large cups flour—a pound good weight.
Sift the flour, powder and cream tartar together three or four times over.
Soften the butter and stir it and the sugar together until white and creamy, gradually stir in the milk, tepid, and a handful of the flour to keep them from separating. Whip the whites to froth and add part whites and part flour until all are in. can be baked in cake moulds or in layers. Makes 1 3-pint mould of cake and 1 shallow tin cake pan an inch deep. When done, spread over them the easy cake frosting, No. 3 and set in a warm place to dry.
Cost: sugar 8, butter 10, whites equal to 8 eggs @ 15, 10, milk 1, powder and c. t. 3, flour 3, frosting for 2 cakes 5; 40 cents for 4 pounds.

Supper.

Beefsteaks (9 orders, 18 cents.)
Codfish in cream (5 cents.)
Potatoes baked and fried (4 cents.)
German puffs (No. 623 trebled; 24 puffs, 18 cents.)
Toast and bread (6 cents.)
White cake, cookies, jelly cake (from dinner.)
Rhubarb stewed for sauce (13 cents.)
Milk, cream 34, butter 20, coffee, tea 12.
Total, $1 30; 25 persons; about 5½ cents a plate.

623—German Puffs, Flannel Rolls, Muffins or Popovers.

It makes a great difference whether any dish or product of skill is the present fashion or not. We have all heard of somebody's popovers and come across remarks in the farmers' papers about somebody else's popovers that wouldn't pop, without wanting any in ours particularly. So when I saw that Mary Jane, at Cedar Point Cottage, on Nipantuck Island had a stove-full of very fine ones ready for supper I admired them, and told her they were splendid and she ought to be proud that she could make them (as indeed she was) without yet caring to get the receipt for my books; having so many good yeast-raised fancy breads already; and, besides, I had heard Mrs. Tingee condemn popovers on account of their using up her eggs too fast and not being very good eating anyhow.

"But that isn't what we call 'em," said Mary Janes, "them's flannel rolls."

"They are popovers, Mary Jane," I persisted; "did you never hear of popovers, and popovers that wouldn't pop?"

"The baker at the Nipantuck House called 'em flannel rolls," said she, "and I guess he knew and he brought me the receipt before he went away." She heaved a little sigh and turned away as if there was nothing more to be said on that question.

Afterwards, upon the very voluminous breakfast and supper bills of fare of a very large summer hotel I found printed "Kaaterskill Flannel Rolls," and in thinking over what they might be, naturally reverted to that stove-full of "flannel rolls" on Nipantuck Island, and learning almost immediately that the Grand Pacific was serving them as "muffins," the Palmer House as "German puffs" and the Matteson as "flannel rolls," I began to feel like a collector of coins, who has heard of a date that is not in his collection, or like one of those Dutch tulip fanciers when they heard of a new color, and started out to catch up with the procession. I soon overtook my friend the steward of the Matteson who, for the good of the public handed me this: take

2 eggs.
2 cups milk—a pint.
2 cups flour—10 ounces.
Salt, a small teaspoon.

Break the eggs into a bowl; beat them light and keep adding the milk to them gradually while your are beating. That takes about five minutes. Add the salt. When all the milk is in put in the flour, all at once, and beat it smooth, like cream. Butter the inside of six coffee cups, divide the batter into them and bake in a moderate oven about half an hour.

It is to be observed there is no powder nor raising of any kind in them and no butter, yet they rise high above the tops of the cups and are hollow inside when done. They are not perfect if made with skimmed milk. When they collapse in the cups and come out tough and heavy it is owing to the baking, the stove being not hot enough on the bottom, or, possibly not having been thoroughly beaten. I have made large batches and baked some for early breakfast and beaten the same batter again and baked it two hours later and found the last to be as good as the first.

Cost, 6 cents. But the cups are not the best for a number, holding too much. There are deep gem pans shaped like small tumblers that suit better to bake in. These are a pleasing kind of bread to make, their remarkable lightness making them always something of a marvel.

Breakfast.

July 14.
Cracked wheat mush (2 cups raw, 3 cents.)
Beefsteak (14 orders, 1¾ lbs, and butter, 25 cents.)
Breakfast bacon (6 orders, 8 ozs, 7 cents.)
Calf's liver broiled (5 orders, 7 cents.)
Potatoes (4 cents.)
Plain rolls (30, 10 cents.)
Corn bread (without eggs, No. 626; 12 orders, 5 cents.)
Batter cakes (cheapest yeast-raised, No. 267; 3 pts, 7 cents.)
Syrup (common, 1 pt, 7 cents.)
Butter 15, milk, cream 30, coffee, tea, sugar 12.
Total, $1 32; 25 persons; 5¼ cents a plate.

624—Plain Rolls.

For 30 rolls dissolve 1 cent's worth of yeast in 2 cups of milk or water, warm but not hot, add a teaspoonful of salt and stir in the flour enough to make dough (2 lbs, 6 cents.) It is just as good made up in dough at first as if a sponge was set, (that is, making a soft-batter first, and working it up into dough afterwards,) the part that makes the most difference in quality, is the proper kneading of the dough which should be as for coffee cakes, No. 262. If made up over night, the dough will be light in the morning. Knead it well, make up in round rolls, touch between each one with a brush dipped in melted butter to cause them to separate easily when done. Rise an hour and bake.

The rolls will have a thin and soft crust and will be much better looking if they are brushed over the tops with a very little lard or butter when they are first placed in the pan. It takes away the rough and floury appearance of common bread.

625—Plain Bread.

The same as plain rolls preceding. That quantity, makes 2 loaves. A particularly sweet home made Vienna bread is made by giving the bread only one rising: mixing with milk, compressed yeast and salt at, say, 3 in the afternoon, making up into loaves at 6 and putting in the oven almost as soon, or in 15 or 20 minutes. Brush over with milk after baking.

626—Corn Bread without Eggs.

It is as light and soft and smooth-crusted as wheat bread.

1½ cups corn meal.
½ cup flour.
1 tablespoon sugar.
½ teaspoon soda; same of salt.
4 tablespoons melted butter or lard.
Sour milk or buttermilk enough to mix it up about as thin as batter cakes.

Beat up well with the spoon. Bake it in a shallow pan. Have the pan hot and greased before pouring it in.

Baking powder and sweet milk can be used as well.

The same can be raised with yeast. Makes 12 to 16 orders; costs about 5 cents.

627—Yeast Raised Batter Cakes Without Eggs.

3 cups flour.
2 cups warm water.
½ cup yeast—or 1 cent's worth--compressed.
1 tablespoon melted lard.
Same of syrup—(to make them brown easily.)
½ teaspoon salt.

Mix all the ingredients together like setting sponge for bread—with very cold water if made over night for breakfast, or else 6 hours before the meal with warm. Beat thoroughly both at time of mixing and just before baking.

Cold weather prevails; "it rains and the wind is never weary." The 'bus will not go to the trains to-day. The driver has started with a wagon to a distant town to buy brick wherewith to build two chimneys in the cottages occupied by the shivering guests of the house, that they may have fires. At present they are huddled around the dining room fireplace. Hope they have some among them "whose smiles can make a summer." for we need one, badly.

Hard Times Dinner.

But it was all good, and nobody would ever suspect that there was a paucity of material or omission of the usual ingredients.

Pearl barley soup (No. 628; 5 qts, 20 cents.)

Roast beef (rib ends, 1½ lbs, 15 cents.)

Roast lamb (brisket, shoulder, left when ribs were taken for chops; 5 lbs, 50 cents.)

Macaroni and cheese (without eggs or butter; No. 629; 9 cents.)

Potatoes in cream sauce (5 cents.)

Tomatoes (1 can, 15 cents.)

Corn (1 can, 15 cents.)

Pumpkin pie (No. 630; without eggs or butter; 3 large; 24 cuts, 24 cents.)

Plain boiled rice pudding (No. 631, without eggs; 3 pints, 14 cents; sauce 4—18 cents.)

Coffee 10, tea 3, milk 4 qts, 12, cream 1 qt, 20, butter average 15, bread 6, cheese 5.

Total, $2 42; 24 persons; 10 cents a plate.

628—Pearl Barley Soup.

4 quarts soup stock.
1 quart milk.
5 tablespoons barley.
1 cupful minced vegetables.
1 ounce butter.
Salt; cayenne.

It is a white soup suitable to be made with mutton or lamb. To obtain the stock boil any spare pieces of meat in 5 quarts of water for 2 hours. Put in a small turnip, onion and carrot, and stalk of celery. Strain, skim, add the milk. Boil the barley separately. A teaspoonful to each quart is enough. Pour off the bluish barley water and put the barley in the soup. Mince a few spoonfuls of different colored vegetables, such as string beans, young carrots, white turnips, green onions, add them to the soup and boil half an hour. Skim while boiling. Season and add butter.

629—Macaroni and Cheese without Eggs.

"I never could understand," said Mrs. Tingee, one day, "how the Italians can be so poor, as the papers say they are, and yet eat so much macaroni as the papers tell us they do: I should think it would break them up buying eggs to cook it with. But then," she added reflectively, "sometimes the papers say things that ain't so. Do you cook macaroni sometimes?"

"Yes ma'am, quite often."

"Do you put cheese in it?"

"Yes."

"And eggs?"

"Yes; and butter and milk and tomatoes and gravy and oysters and chicken and many more things."

"Ah; I had a girl once who wanted to make a dish of macaroni and I kept laying off to get the things together, but, somehow, I never did. Do you know, a friend of mine told me she once knew a hotel cook who never made a dish of macaroni without putting eight eggs in it! Do you think that was true?"

"Yes, ma'am; and I have no doubt but that there are hotel cooks who will even use as many as twelve, or thirteen."

Then Mrs. Tingee said, "O, my!"

It is a singular trait in this lady that she never seems to regard the difference between a dish for two hundred people and a dish for two or three; all she sees is the eight eggs gone at one fell swoop.

I venture the opinion that the Italians eat macaroni alone or in soup or gravy without much thought of cheese and without any thought of eggs, and I doubt very much whether many of them would touch the dry and heavy cake of macaroni and cheese that is seen at many hotel tables in this country. There is a good example of an Italian way of preparing macaroni, spaghetti, lassagnes, ndilini and other such pastes at our No. 65; which requires neither eggs nor butter, and here is another just as good:

½ pound macaroni.
2 or 3 ounces cheese—or a grated cupful.
3 or 4 basting spoonfuls of fat from the roasting meat.
2 cups water or milk.
2 spoonfuls flour thickening.
A handful of crushed crackers.

Boil the macraoni 20 minutes, then pour off the water. Put in the cheese and other ingredients and salt; turn it into a 2-quart pan, strew the crushed crackers on top and bake brown.

The flour thickening added is to form a sort of sauce in it, but not enough to cake to the macaroni together. When there is a suitable sauce or gravy ready at hand it can be used to good advantage in that way. The strained gravy from a chicken stew, for example. Cost, 9 or 10 cents for 12 dishes.

630—Pumpkin or Squash Pie without Eggs.

The bakery pumpkin pie; the pie of the lunch houses and shops.

1 can of pumpkin, or a quart fresh

cooked (which is cheaper.)

1 cup sugar.
2 cups milk.
3 basting spoonfuls flour-and-water thickening
1 teaspoon each ground ginger and cinnamon.

Mash the pumpkin through a colander, stir in the other ingredients. It makes 3 pints, enough to fill 3 deep pie plates lined with thin crusts of common short paste. Pumpkin 14, sugar 4, milk, spice and flour 2, crusts 4—24 cents or 8 cents each.

631—Boiled Rice Pudding without Eggs.

---

1 cup rice.
4 cups milk.
½ cup sugar.
Butter size of an egg.
Wash the rice free from dust and cook it with the milk in a farina kettle or double kettle. If you have none put the sugar and rice both into the milk and let boil in a saucepan at the back of the stove with the steam shut in. Never stir it while cooking and it will not burn. When done stir in the butter. Serve in small pudding saucers with sauce poured over. For the sauce, boil ½ cup sugar and piece of lemon, nutmeg or stick cinnamon in 2 cups water; thicken slightly, add small piece of butter and simmer until it is like jelly.

Two strangers arrived on the five o'clock train. Just the luck. The only time the 'bus failed to go to the train somebody came. But they got a livery rig and came over. Somebody says they are real dukes.

Later: They are real Dukes. Not the European article, but members of the firm of Duke and Diamond, the well-known advertising agents, of Lakeport.

Supper.

Cracked wheat (3 cents.)
Beefsteak (8 orders, 1½ lbs, 20 cents.)
Ham and eggs (8 orders, 36 cents.)
Cold lamb (1 lb, from dinner, charged.)

French fried potatoes (6 cents.)
German puffs (No. 623; 30; 23 cents.)
Plain rolls (few from breakfast.)
Wild raspberries (2 qts, 10 cents.)
White cake (without eggs, No. 632; 15 cents.)
Cream 30, sugar 10, milk 12, butter, bread 20, coffee, tea 12.
Total, $1 97; 27 persons; 7¼ cents a plate.

632—White Cake without Eggs.

---

1 small cup sugar—6 ounces.
½ cup butter—4 ounces.
2 small cups milk—little less than a pint.
2 heaped teaspoons baking powder.
5 cups flour—1¼ pounds.
Warm the butter and stir it and the sugar together until well mixed, then add the milk and a little flavoring of nutmeg, lemon, vanilla or cinnamon.

Mix the powder in the flour, stir all together. It makes a stiff batter. The more it is beaten up with the spoon the better the cake.

To make it as white as if made with white of eggs, one cup of the milk used should be sour, or else add a small teaspoon of cream tartar—the same thing that makes "angel food cake" so white. Brush the top with milk before baking.

633—White Layer Cakes without Eggs.

Bake the white cake of the preceding receipt in jelly cake pans; spread with jelly when done; place two or three together and frost over the top. Should be very thin in the cake pans or they rise too high to make handsome layers.

634—Chocolate Layer Cakes without Eggs.

Put half cup sugar over the fire to boil with a large spoonful of water and add to it two ounces of chocolate. When melted use instead of jelly as in the preceding receipt.

635—Cake Frosting without Eggs.

It is not necessary to have white of eggs to make cake icing or frosting. A better kind of frosting that will not break when the cake is sliced, is made of either dissolved gelatine or powdered gum arabic. They need only be dissolved in boiling water to make a mucilage like the common bottle mucilage in thickness, then beat up sugar in it just the same as with white of eggs. It is quicker to make than the egg kind and is extremely white. If too thick on the cakes, set them in a warm place and this kind of frosting will run down smooth and glossy. There is a powdered kind of gelatine called granulated, that is very good for this purpose.

Breakfast.

July 15.
Cold night. Rolls poor; no place in summer kitchen to keep dough warm. Cold enough for buckwheat cakes—wish we had some. Good time for mince pies —make sausag anyhow.
Oatmeal (3 cents.)
Beefsteak (7 orders, 1 lb, and butter, 15 cents.)
Breakfast bacon (5 orders, 8 oz_s, gross, 7 cents.)
Crepinettes de veau (No. 636; 12 orders, 1½ lbs, one-third raw meat, 7 cents.)
Potatoes baked and French fried (9 cents.)
French rolls (18; 8 cents.)
Corn bread (fine, with 2 cups meal, 2 eggs, 10 ozs, butter, etc.; No. 599; 12 cents.)
Batter cakes (1 qt, 7 cents.)
Butter 20, syrup 8, milk 12, cream 20, coffee, tea, sugar 17, bread 4.
Total, $1 49; 27 persons; 5½ cents a plate.

636—Crepinettes, or Sausages of Cocked Meat.

Take two-thirds cold cooked meat and one-third raw meat with some fat upon it, chop it into sausage meat, season with powered sage, some salt and plenty of black pepper. Make up in little cakes as with pork sausage and fry brown on both sides. Cook only as wanted. They are nice when fresh cooked and hot. Serve without sauce or gravy, but garnish with parsley or seed-bed celery.

Dinner.

Dinner ordered an hour earlier. Two lady boarders arrived. The firm of Duke and Diamond intend to make much of their vacation from city business and will take a sail with all the ladies on board around the lake. Looks like an exploration : Perhaps there is business in it. It may be there is to be no more dependence upon the patronage of friends and acquaintances, but an advertisement to the great pleasure-seeking public of the claims of this place. However, the dinner will not be much regarded and must be short and easy.
Consomme jardiniere (5 qts, 25 cents.)
Roast beef (2 ribs, 3 lbs net 40 cents.)
Spring lamb (5 lbs 50 cents.)
Summer beets in sauce (10 cents.)
String beans (garden 10 cents.)
Corn (1 can 15 cents.)
Potatoes browned, mashed (9 cents.)
Tomatoes (1 can, 15 cents.)
Raspberry pie (open ; puff paste; 3, 30 cents.)
Boiled corn starch pudding (No. 639; pudding 9, sauce 4,—13 cents.)
Vanilla cup custard (No. 136 treble, 22 cents.)
Spice cake (without eggs, No. 640; frosted, 21 cents.)
Nuts, raisins, cheese, crackers, condiments. (average count, 27 cents.)
Butter, bread, coffee, tea, milk ,cream, 63 cents.
Total, $3 50; 29 persons; 12 cents a plate.

637—Consomme Jardiniere.

The words signify a clear soup with vegetables. See No. 139. When the materials recommended are not available make as rich a broth as can be with the shoulder bone of the beef roast and the "cap" or coarse meat that is upon it and a veal shank. Strain, and remove all grease.
Cut string beans in little diamonds, take an equal quantity of green peas, young carrots and turnips cut to the same

size; also two green onions, a summer squash and a small green cucumber; or whatever of the kind can be obtained, all cut small, and about three cupfuls in all to five quarts. Boil the vegetables a few minutes in water. Season the consomme with salt and cayenne, and add two tablespoons of walnut catsup. Drain off the water from the vegetables and put them into the consomme. A heaping teaspoonful of starch may be used to thicken it slightly. Let it boil until clear again.

638—Beets in Sauce.

Boil blood beets in plenty of water from one to two hours. Try with a fork. Put them into cold water and rub off the skin. Cut in quarters or suitable pieces into a saucepan, and fill up with three parts water and one part vinegar. Boil, add salt, a little butter, and flour thickening.

639—Boiled Corn Starch Pudding without Eggs.

4 cups milk—a quart.
2 heaping tablespoons sugar.
4 do corn starch—4 ounces good weight.
1 ounce butter—small egg size.
1 yolk to color it if you like.
Boil the milk with the sugar in it.

Mix the starch with a little cold milk, thin it with some hot out of the kettle, pour it quickly into the boiling milk and stir while it is thickening, which it does immediately.

Throw in the butter and beat up, then add the yolk of egg thinned with milk, and take it from the fire. An extremely easy and simple pudding and excellent. Must not be kept too hot after cooking as that causes it to turn thin. Serve with sauce.

640—Spice Cake without Eggs.

A great favorite: Looks like chocolate cake. Would not be any better if made with eggs.
1 small cup sugar—6 ounces.
½ cup butter—4 ounces.

2 cups milk—a pint.
2 heaped teaspoons baking powder.
5 cups flour—1¼ pounds.
2 teaspoons ground cinnamon.
1 teaspoon each of cloves and allspice.
Warm the butter; stir up the sugar and milk. Put the powder and spices in the flour, mix all and beat up well. Bake in shallow tins and frost over when done. Before baking brush over the top of each cake with milk; it glazes them, and makes smooth crust.

641—A Pastry and Store Room Necessary.

It took about two weeks at this house to get a little room fixed up with a few shelves to keep certain kinds of stores upon and a table in the same room for the bread-making pastry, although I had made temporary arrangements of the kind on the very first day, being allowed to gently pitch a lounge and rocking chair out of the window of a little room adjoining the kitchen for the purpose. If one person with very little help is going to get up a great number and succession of dishes week after week and always "get there" as soon as the clock does, give every guest their orders according to their taste, keep nobody waiting and never omit to prepare every sauce, stuffing, ornament and trimmings which the bill of fare promises, the track must be cleared of obstructions and every thing placed so that it can be picked up in passing whenever it is wanted. Then it is all easy, and, as somebody expressed it here yesterday, "it is fun to cook." But to have things as they had them here last year would make life a burden and take twice as many hands to prepare meals of half the dimensions that we expect to serve; with the meats at the bottom of the house, the sugar at the top, the oatmeal across the way, the vegetables down the alley, the baking powder locked up in a cupboard and the keys running around somewhere in somebody's pocket; the flour in a corner of the kitchen and all the pastry table and work place being a board on a barrel. These are the misarrangements which make Mary Jane seem so inefficient, and she herself does not know what is the matter that she cannot get along without calling upon the whole household to drop their work and come and help her through. I am under the impression that a vast number of fine houses both public and private want a shaking up in their culinary departments and all the loose ends bringing together where hands can be laid upon them without waste of time, and want something better in the way of a work table for the cook than a mere board on a barrel.

642—A Board on a Barrel.

Which reminds me that it is better to be born lucky than rich. How many lucky rascals there are wherever there is a good hotel, not really deserving more than stale bread and butter, who manage to get either by audacity, favoritism or some petty terrorism of influencing trade a living that a king might envy, the first, best and dearest of everything that comes to market; and how many deserving but unlucky rich people there are in private homes who never know what it is to have a really good meal. One such family living in a small city in the Delectable Mountains, on a certain occasion employed me to get up a "Mother Hubbard party" supper for fifty.

These good people had an income from a fortune of two hundred thousand dollars; they were amiable, generous to an extreme; the lady was sunshine itself in spite of poor meals; they deserved really, to live in a good hotel and enjoy the best of cookery and yet in fact they had nothing but Mary Jane and a kitchen, that was little more than a board on a barrel. As for my own three days' work that did not concern me, for I had a separate room and everything needful, but then I could see the gentleman was not happy. He was intended by nature to be a man of a large and portly presence; the frame was broad, but there was not much upon it; his vest was not filled out and could not be with such poor cooking as a board on a barrel affords. I could not see without some concern their Mary Jane trying to broil large and thick beefsteaks over the holes of a stove filled with soft coal, doing the same thing three times each day and sending them in half cooked, half raw, blackened with **coal** smoke, dirty. Carrot croquettes she tried to make and they melted down in the grease, (not hot enough) and were sent in that way, soft and disgusting and a dozen such blunders or more I should have liked to correct but the contract would have been too large, and, besides, there was no convenience. When their Mary Jane made bread she mixed up a pan of dough, using for her table a board set on top of the barrel of flour. When she wanted a handful of flour she had to set the pan over on the dish sink and remove the board, and then set them back again—and it was a fine painted, grained and ornamented kitchen too—and when she made rolls she could not knead the dough, but seized a handful, squeezed it and pinched off the little dumpling shape that rose up out of her fist. Well, they were not very bad rolls, and not very good; just the commonest of the common although the people were rich and might as well have had the finest; and neither Mary Jane nor I could roll out the pastry on a board on a barrel that tipped over.

We may take Mr. Toots' view of such a matter saying, "it's of no consequence," for health and strength may be kept up on very plain food, if one will be an ascetic and philosopher, but that is what very few will be. In this family were four daughters, young ladies for whose pleasure this party was given, and the mischief of the situation is, that having grown up with nothing better before their eyes they will go out to their own housekeeping thinking that a board on a barrel is all that is needed to set up a kitchen, and that the miserable ways of Mary Jane which they have seen are the ways they must remember and carry on as all that is necessary to know about cooking.

Finding these good people inclined to liberality in the matter of expenditure, when sending for some Liebig's extract of meat, wherewith to make their *bouillon* of extra fineness, I sent for twice as much as was needed that some might remain to give them pleasure some other day; the same by the finest salad oil, the walnut catsup to give a new zest to their soups; mushroom catsup to transform their chicken stews and pies; genuine table sauces to help ameliorate those dreadful beefsteaks; some kirchwasser for the ladies' punch; genuine maraschino to implant a new sensation for them in the creams and jellies; a few truffles to cause them to ask questions; Camembert cheese in tiny round boxes; Roquefort cheese in larger bulk; biscuits ot the superfine sorts and choice fruits, all in excess of the needs of the one night. After the supper was over I had the satisfaction of seeing the remainders of the goods and sweets with the unwonted flavors spirited away to secure hiding places by fairy fingers, and then had to leave these poor two-hundred-thousand-dollar people to the maladministrations of Mary Jane with her board on a barrel; but they seemed to deserve a better fate.

Supper.

Cracked wheat (2 cups, 4 cents.)

Beefsteak (7 orders, 1 lb, and butter, 18 cents.)

Lamb chops (11 orders, 1½ lbs, 18 cents.)

Chipped beef in cream (3 orders, 3 cents.)

Cold meats (6 orders, 12 ozs, net, charged dinner.)

Potatoes French fried and baked (6 cents.)

Sally Lunn (20 cents.)

Batter cakes (1 qt, 8 cents.)

Green gages in syrup (1 can, 25 cents.)

Cake and cookies (without eggs, 15 cents.)

Buttermilk, cream, milk 36, bread 6, syrup 6, butter 15, coffee, tea, sugar 16.

Total, $1 96; 27 persons; 7¼ cents a plate.

643—Chipped Beef in Cream.

Shave the dried beef extremely thin with a plane or sharp knife, and parboil it in water.

While it is in preparation, make a cupful of cream sauce; beat in a small lump of butter additional, then drain the water from the beef and pour the sauce over it instead.

644—Sally Lunn Tea Cakes.

If you are making rolls or bread daily, for the evening meal it will be easy to change the dough into sally lunn. Make up the dough at, say, 11 o'clock, the same as at No. 532 and let it rise until 3. Then take nearly all, or 2½ pounds, or 5 or 6

cups of the dough.

½ cup butter, melted.

3 tablespoons sugar

2 eggs and 2 yolks.

½ cup warm milk.

2 cups flour.

Work them all together and beat up very thoroughly. It is like muffin dough or fritters, too soft to handle.

Let rise until 5. Beat again. Divide it in 4 or 5 pie pans previously buttered and rise half an hour, then bake and have them hot and ready at 6. Cut like pieces of pie carefully with a sharp knife not to crush it. Send it in instead of rolls. Makes 24 to 28 cuts; costs 20 or 21 cents.

645—Cookies without Eggs.

1 small cup sugar—6 ounces.

½ cup butter—4 ounces.

2 small cups milk—little less than a pint.

3 heaped up teaspoons baking powder.

Flour to make soft dough—about 6 cups.

Warm the butter and mix it and the sugar together and then the milk (water will do.) Mix the powder in the flour, stir all together. Roll out very thin. Shake some granulated sugar over the sheet of dough, cut out and bake well done. Costs 17 or 18 cents for about 100 cookies.

Breakfast.

July 16.

Fresh raspberries (2 qts, 20 cents.)

Oatmeal (2 cents.)

Beefsteak (8 orders, 1 lb, and butter, 18 cents.)

Mutton chops (11 orders, 1½ lbs, 18 cents.)

Ham (6 orders, 12 ozs, equal 1 lb, gross, 15 cents.)

Omelets and boiled eggs (20 eggs, 25 cents.)

Potatoes German fried (5 cents.)

Corn bread (without eggs, No. 626; 5 cents.)

Buttermilk muffins (without eggs, No. 646; 22, 8 cents.)

Rice batter cakes (10 cents.)

Milk, cream, buttermilk 36, coffee, tea, sugar 20, butter 18, syrup 8, bread 6.

Total, $2 14; 27 persons; 8½ cents a

plate.

646—Buttermilk Muffins without Eggs.

4 cups flour.
1 tablespoon sugar.
1 teaspoon salt.
1 teaspoon soda, small.
2 or 3 tablespoons melted butter or lard.
2 cups butter-milk.

Mix all, beat up thoroughly—the more it is beaten the better the muffins will be—then drop spoonfuls into greased gem pans. Makes about 22 or according to size; costs 7 or 8 cents.

647—Rice Batter Cakes.

2 large cups dry cooked rice.
1 large cup milk or water.
1 cup flour.
2 eggs.
2 tablespoons baking powder.

Mash the rice free from lumps; mix all and beat up well. Butter milk and soda can be used instead of baking powder, and milk. A small cup of rice raw makes the required amount. Costs 10 cents a quart, or 24 cakes.

Dinner.

First bill of fare.
Soup—Macaroni clear (4 qts, 20 cents.)
Corned beef (1 lb, 10 cents.)
Roast beef (1 rib, 2 lbs, 25 cents.)
Roast lamb (3 lbs, 30 cents.)
Broiled Sweetbreads, maitre d'hotel (No. 651; Sweetbreads 19, sauce 5; 24 cents.)
Green peas (garden, equal 1 can, seasoned, 20 cents.)
Corn and tomatoes (30 cents.)
Potatoes mashed, browned (6 cents.)
Tapioca pudding (without eggs, No. 652; and sauce, 12 cents.)
White Mountain ice cream (2 qts, 35 cents.)
Chocolate and other cake (without eggs, 20 cents.)
Cherries, nuts, raisins, pickles, cheese 27.
Butter, bread, coffee, tea, milk, cream 50.
Total, $3 09; 27 persons; 11½ cents a plate.

648—Macaroni Clear Soup.

One ounce of macaroni or less to a quart is enough.

Make soup stock by boiling soup bones and a bunch of vegetables and spoonful of tomatoes in five quarts of water. Strain through a napkin or fine seive. Skim off all the fat. Boil again, season, thicken slightly with a tablespoonful of starch. Boil gently until it again becomes clear and skim well. Boil separately 4 ounces macaroni until half done (10 minutes), drain, and as it lies in the colander cut it into very short pieces all of one size. Rinse it off with hot water to get rid of crumbs and drop it in the clear soup to finish cooking. Lamb should not be used for clear soups as it makes a whitish stock. Use little burnt sugar to color if necessary.

649—Trouble with the Corned Beef.

An old friend of mine went as steward to open the new and splendid Winnipegaway House at Red Lake Falls, and when I arrived there a week or two after and asked "how's everything" he said, rather sorrowfully that everything was all right, "except—blame the luck—!"

I thought he was going to say the drainage or climate or railroad connections or something large, but, after all it is the small troubles that are hardest to bear—he said he couldn't get a bit of corned beef fit to put on the table, and he had all the directors of the new concern there, hawk-eyed and exacting to the smallest particulars; just as is always the case whilst a new hotel is the new toy of a company.

They had salt beef but it would not turn to that pink or scarlet color which you like to see—a streak of pink and a streak of fat—upon a bed of pale green boiled cabbage for your New England boiled dinner; for plain salt beef turns dark, almost black after slicing, and has something of the depressing effect upon the diner of a cloudy day. It was not only their own which they had tried to pickle, but the village butcher's was equally poor.

It is saltpeter that gives the required color. They had both employed saltpeter. They were a good way from a large town, but both had obtained their stores from the same place. Told the steward that I thought I used to know that there are two sorts of saltpeter, but it does not make any difference if you make sure to get the large crystals, size of your thumb, look like washing soda or alum. That which they had used was small like common salt. We obtained the right article the next day, made new brine according to the following receipt; dropped some beef in it while it was warm —almost hot—and in twelve hours thereafter used some of the thin pieces that boiled as red as a painted town.

650—Corned Beef Brine.

6 gallons water—nearly 3 pailfuls.
3 to 6 ounces saltpeter, in water.
1 pint sugar.
10 pounds coarse salt.
Boil the above all together and skim while it is boiling. Pour it into two stone jars or a keg or barrel. The jars are best in places where there are pieces of beef unsuitable for roasting, to be rolled up and tied in shape and dropped in every day, one jar to receive the fresh additions and the other to use out of that which is sufficiently corned.

For this use the larger quantity of saltpeter is needed. Beef dropped in this pickle will be ready for use in a week.

But when a quarter of beef is to be cut up and put down in brine to remain in it a very long time, 3 or 4 ounces of saltpeter is sufficient. The barrel should be kept in a cool, dry cellar. Put a board on top of the meat and a rock upon that. Keep covered.

651—Broiled Sweetbreads, Maitre d'Hotel.

It can generally be relied upon that only two-thirds, perhaps only half the people will order such a dish as this however good it may be. Prepare the sweetbreads by splitting in slices the flat way, dust with salt and pepper, press down in a plate of flour to coat well on both sides; broil in the wire oyster broiler. Turn frequently and baste with a brush dipped in butter.

While they are cooking soften 4 ounces of butter, squeeze in the juice of half a lemon, add a dust of cayenne, a tablespoonful chopped parsley or other green and spoonful of water. Serve the sweetbreads hot from the broiler with sauce poured over and garnish of lemon and parsley or seed-bed celery.

Anything cooked a la maitre d'hotel has a combination of green herbs with an acid; it may be in butter or in thin white sauce.

652—Tapioca Pudding without Eggs.

Costs 10 or 12 cents or 1 cent each order.
1 heaping cup tapioca—½ lb.
4 cups milk—a quart.
2 tablespoons sugar.
Small lump of butter.
Take half the milk and put the tapioca in it to soak in a little pan set in a rather warm place for an hour or two. Boil the rest of the milk with the sugar and butter in it, put in the tapioca, stir up, pour into a buttered pan and bake half an hour. It is, of course, quite white. Serve with any pudding sauce. One egg or two yolks may be added if wished to have it richer. The eggs must not be boiled in the milk, but stirred in just before putting in the oven.

653—Red Raspberry Sauce for Puddings.

Take half red raspberry juice or syrup and half water. To one cup add half cup sugar with a heaping teaspoonful starch mixed in it dry. Simmer over the fire until thick and clear. Good sauce for any white pudding like the preceding.

654—White Mountain Ice Cream.

1 quart cream.
1 pint milk.
1 cup sugar.
2 large tablespoons starch.
Boil the milk and sugar and thicken with the starch. Add the cream cold. Flavor, strain and freeze.

655—Chocolate Cake without Eggs.

1 small cup sugar—6 ounces.
½ cup butter—4 ounces.
2 cups milk—a pint.
2 rounded teaspoons baking powder.
5 cups flour—1¼ pounds.
2 ounces chocolate.

Warm the butter and stir it and the sugar together until well mixed, then add the milk and vanilla flavoring if you have it. Mix the powder in the flour and stir all together.

Melt two ounces of common chocolate in a little pan by warming it with nothing added and beat it into the cake batter.

Bake in shallow tins and frost over when done, with frosting made without eggs, No. 635.

Supper.

Oatmeal and cracked wheat mush (3 cents.)

Beefsteak (8 orders, 1 lb, and butter, 16 cents.)

Corned beef stewed with potatoes (½ lb, meat, etc., 6 orders, 7 cents.)

Codfish in cream (4 orders, 3 cents.)

Cold meats (4 orders, charged dinner.)

Potatoes (from dinner, baked few, 2 cents.)

Plain rusks (without eggs, No. 657; 20 rusks, 10 cents.

Rolls and bread (11 cents.)

Raspberry tartlets and cake (paste trimmings and remainders from dinner, say, 10 cents.)

Fresh raspberries (3 pints, 12 cents.)

Batter cakes (no orders.)

Butter 15, milk, cream, buttermilk 42, coffee, tea, sugar 16.

Total, $1 47; 26 persons; nearly 6 cents a plate.

656—Corned Beef Stew with Potatoes.

Called also hashed corned beef. Make same as the lamb "gallimaufry" No. 618; of equal quantities of corned beef with some fat upon it and potatoes all cut in neat dice shapes.

657—Rusks without Eggs.

Take half your roll dough and work in sugar and butter, set it to rise again and at 4 o'clock make out in round balls or cut with a small biscuit cutter; butter between them when placing in the pan and brush over the tops; place near together but not crowded; rise an hour or longer and bake in a slack oven about 20 minutes.

The difficulty with most people's sweetened breads is that they are clammy like dough not sufficiently baked. There is no need of having them that way for all that is necessary to make them feathery light and dry, is the proper way of kneading fully explained for coffee cakes at No. 262 and elsewhere; and then sufficient time to rise.

The right proportions are:
2 pounds light dough—about a good quart dipperful.
3 ounces butter or lard—½ cup.
8 ounces sugar—1 cup.

Brush over with syrup when done and dredge sugar.

Breakfast.

Blackcap raspberries and currants (2 qts, 18 cents.)

Oatmeal (2 cents.)

Beefsteak (4 orders, 10 cents.)

Lamb chops (10 orders, 20 small chops, 2 lbs, 20 cents.)

Omelets with green onions (No. 89; 4 orders, 8 eggs, 10 cents.)

Eggs poached and boiled (10 orders, 24 cents.)

Potatoes minced in cream (No. 534; 7 cents.)

German puffs (No. 623; 18 large with 6 eggs, etc., 18 cents.)

Corn bread (buttermilk, no eggs, 8 orders, 3 cents.)

Graham batter cakes (no eggs, 1 qt, 7 cents.)

Milk (6 qts, 18 cents.)

Cream (3 pts, 30 cents.)

Butter (1 lb, 20 cents.)

Syrup 4, bread 4, coffee, tea, sugar 14.

Total, $2 09; 26 persons; 8 cents a plate.

658—White Citron Cake w.thout Eggs.

1 small cup sugar—6 ounces.
½ cup butter—4 ounces.
2 cups milk—a pint (part of it should be sour.)
2 heaped teaspoons baking powder.
5 cups flour—1¼ pounds.
½ pound citron cut small.
1 teaspoon lemon extract.

Soften the butter, stir it up with the sugar and the milk not too cold to mix. Sift the powder in the flour. Mix and beat well and add flavor and the citron previously dusted with flour. Bake in round mould or shallow tin and frost over. Fine cake and favorite. If no sour milk use pinch cream tartar or juice of half a lemon to whiten it. Use no soda in any cake that is to be white. Costs, 30 cents for 3½ pounds frosted without eggs.

Dinner.

Soup, beef a l'Anglaise (5 qts, 25 cents.)
Whitefish, Point Shirley Style (2 fishes, 4 lbs, 20 orders, with seasonings, 45 cents.)
Boiled corned beef (½ lb, 5 cents.)
Boiled bacon and greens (trifle, 3 cents.)
Roast loin of beef (2 lbs, 30 cents.)
Roast lamb (3 lbs, 30 cents.)
Veal patties, bechamel, (10 with ½ lb, veal, 12 cents.)
String beans with bacon (garden, 12 cents.)
Green peas (garden, 10 cents.)
Tomatoes and corn (20 cents.)
Potatoes (two ways, 7 cents.)
Sponge pudding, cherry sauce (No. 664; 1½ lbs, with sauce, 19 cents.)
Cherry pie (1 large, with 1 pt, pitted cherries 6, sugar 3, crust 3; 12 cents.)
Raspberries and cream (1 qt, berries, 8 cents.)
Cream 20, milk 12, butter, bread 11.
Crackers, cheese, pickles, condiments, nuts, raisins, average 27 cents.
Coffee, tea, sugar 12.
Total, $3 19; 27 persons, nearly 12 cents a plate.

659—Beef Soup, a l'Anglaise, or English Style.

It is a brown, strong soup with small cut beef and vegetables in it.

Prepare stock over night that the soup may be ready in good time in the forenoon, to allow it to simmer and have frequent skimming to brighten it. The stock may be made by boiling the lower portion of round of beef (2 lbs., 15 cents) with other beef trimmings and a veal bone; a bayleaf and six cloves and an onion. Strain and skim, boil and add a thickening of brown *roux* if you can have good butter, or of baked flour, or common flour-and-water. Cut 2 small cups of different soup vegetables in small dice and the same of the cold boiled beef out of the stock pot. Simmer at least an hour; skim often, season, and at last add a tablespoon of walnut catsup, and half a lemon cut in small slices.

660—Whitefish, Point Shirley Style.

The fish are split in halves, laid open, seasoned, baked in a buttered dripping pan, egged over while baking and spread with softened butter and minced parsley when done. Divide in portions with a broad fish slice; serve on small plates with a spoonful of mashed potato in the same plate.

661—Bacon and Greens.

A small quantity of greens, not enough to serve as a vegetable with every order, fills up a gap in this way and will seldom be called upon when other dishes are numerous. Boil the bacon with the corned beef first, then with the beet, radish or turnip greens. Serve a slice on each dish of greens.

662—Veal Patties, Bechamel.

The term bechamel attached to a dish signifies that it is in cream sauce and consequently white; thus the white oyster patties, No. 327, are *a la Bechamel* in a bill of fare. It is the name of a French steward or cook, who brought cream sauce into notice; but to be genuine the sauce should be but half cream, the other half seasoned broth boiled down strong and clarified. Cut cooked veal in neat dice, put it in bechamel sauce well seasoned and fill patty shells with it same as oysters.

663—String Beans, German Style.

Snap short and boil an hour. Instead of butter or cream sauce to finish cut up some bacon or salt pork quite small, and boil with the beans after pouring off the first water.

664—Baked Sponge Pudding.

Make butter sponge cake, No. 561. Bake in shallow tins. Sift granulated sugar over before baking and it will come out glazed. Cut in small square blocks and serve with red syrup made of cherry juice, water and sugar.

665—Cherry Pie, Country Style.

Roll the paste thin, line the largest pie pan. Put in 2 cups of pitted cherries raw, spread sugar over, cover with a thin crust, bake slowly and well but light colored.

Supper

Oatmeal (2 cups raw, 4 cents.)
Broiled bass (11 orders, 2 fishes, 3 lbs, gross, and butter, 30 cents.)
Beefsteak (3 orders, 7 cents.)
Cold corned beef (4 orders, charged dinner.)
Potatoes (pats and cold fried, charged dinner.)
Biscuits (20, buttermilk, 9 cents.)
French coffee cakes (No. 262; 30, glazed, sugared, warm, 20 cents.)
Cake (2 kinds, for show, trifle used, 10 cents.)
Raspberries (3 pints, 15 cents.)
Cream (3 pints, 30 cents.)
Butter 15, bread 4, coffee, tea, sugar 17.
Mik, buttermilk 24.
Total, $1 85; 27 persons; 7 cents a plate.

666—Broiled Bass.

It will be found that dipping the split fish in flour before broiling secures a better brown color than it will take on without. It is a firm fish and rather dry when broiled, but preferred so by many to whitefish or other oily kinds. Split lengthwise, divide each side in two or three, flour, and while broiling baste with a brush dipped in butter. Small ones may be broiled whole, the head being left on, and larger ones for restaurant orders partly broiled, and finished in the oven or wholly broiled by being wrapped in buttered paper, allowing plenty of time.

Breakfast.

July 18.
Cherries and gooseberries (2 qts, 16 cents.)
Oatmeal (3 cents.)
Fried trout (dipped in flour only, 4 orders, 8 cents.)
Saratoga chips and baked potatoes (5 cents.)
Beefsteak (6 orders, 8 cents.)
Bacon (1 order, 2 cents.)
Lamb chops (13 orders, 26 chops, 3 lbs, gross, 30 cents.)
Fancy twisted rolls (20 rolls, 10 cents.)
Corn egg-bread (6 cents.)
Graham batter cakes (1 qt, 6 cents.)
Cream (3 pts, 30 cents.)
Milk, buttermilk (6 qts, 18 cents.)
Butter 15, syrup 6, bread 4, coffee, tea, sugar 16.
Total, $1 83; 26 persons; 7 cents a plate.

Last evening two of Black's boarders came over to look at rooms—ladies—said to be a banker's wife and daughter—said they could not endure the noise over there had heard good reports of our "Eyrie" from our two friendly Dukes; took rooms in the hill cottage and would move over this morning. They came again for good after breakfast. Gentleman soon after came over in a buggy; a colonel somebody; has been stopping at the Palmer, the other large hotel at the depot. He says they gave him a sour mutton chop for breakfast this morning; that every steak and mutton chop he has had since he has been there has been sour "and a fellow can't stand that, you know." He must have had previous acquaintance with these ladies for after engaging a room and sending for his baggage they three went sailing into the west in the same boat together before they had been here an hour.

On eleven o'clock train arrived another member of the Dukes firm—lady this time. Has been at some neighboring resort.

"What is a lady duke called—isn't she a duchess?"

"Why, certainly she is a duchess—of course. Goodness! girls, you must wait on them splendidly, the best you know how—for now we have a family from Paris, two dukes, a duchess, a colonel and a banker's wife and daughter—you must fold the napkins in beautiful shapes, like this and this, and cut the finest bread in thick blocks and lay one under the fold of the napkin on each inverted plate, this way. The housekeeper will show you more when she comes in, but I hope they will keep her always busy in the cottages now."

———

Arrived at same time two elegant boquets for the cook, viz.: one basket of summer cabbages, 8 cost 40 cents; and one basket summer beets and onions, cost the same.

Have just received notice to prepare a little birthday supper two days hence.

———

Arrived, first lot of meat from a new butcher, one who is used to supplying hotels. Was rather surprised to find by bill everything charged one uniform price, 11 cents a pound.

There is 15-cent ham, 12½-cent loin beef and roast, 13-cent lard, 8-cent mutton and 10-cent lamb and other items all charged at 11 cents all round. Seems novel, but good enough.

667—Trouble with Sour Meats.

———

Noblesse oblige. A gentleman speaks truth about a hotel although he may be seeking reasons for leaving it. When the colonel says the steaks and chops served to him at the Palmer House at Uintah Lake are always sour, there is nothing to be said but to seek the reason why.

Our breakfast and supper bills of fare show that sometimes there will be four beefsteaks ordered and at another twelve tor fourteen; the same with lamb or mutton chops, bacon, fish and other meats; these numbers are to be multiplied by ten a for house like the Palmer, at the depot, and yet if a train should arrive bringing an unusual number of people to a meal, there would be no unusal flurry and the many would receive their fresh broiled meats as soon as the few would have done; and, taking one time with another, there will be no more cooked steaks and chops left over after a meal for a few than for a large number. This is because the meats are always kept ready to be laid upon the gridiron, but are never actually cooked until they are asked for, and this is the great recommendation of the first-class plan of broiling meats to order over the Barnacle way of cooking up a lot of meat large enough to meet expected demands and having to throw away panfuls, blackened, dried or sodden of that which is left, or be thrown into wild confusion by the arrival of five or six unexpectedly. The one disadvantage of the possibility of the cut meats turning sour before they are cooked, is due entirely to carelessness

There should be a tray made purposely to hold the raw steaks, chops and other meats, like this:

Cutlets Veal and Pork	Bacon Ham.
Mutton and Lamb Chops	Tenderloin Common Steak

Broiler's Tray of Cut Meats.

———

This tray is best made of galvanized iron: the compartments are 10 or 12 inches square, the sides are 3 inches deep; there are stout handles on two sides, like a baking pan, to carry and hang up by when not in use. A tray with more or smaller compartments than this is hard to clean, being unweidly, but there might be two used for a large business requiring twice as many kinds of meats to be ready.

The trouble over at the Palmer House is caused by the tray being overstocked. They not only fill it but stack it up with steaks, chops and cutlets; bring it from the refrigerator to the kitchen, keep it there in front of range and broiler for four hours—from 6 till 10 in the morning—of a hot summer day; only use half and carry the remainder back to the meat house where it hardly becomes cool before supper time when it is brought out again. They would not have any sour meats if they would but leave the bulk of them in the refrigerator and only bring out a dozen or two of orders at a time—mere matter of forethought.

Dinner.

Consomme, a la de Stael (No. 668; 6 qts, 35 cents.)
Salmon trout, a la Chevaliere (2 fishes, 4 lbs, and seasonings, 40 cents.)
Nantaise potatoes (3 cents.)
Boiled ham and corned beef (20 cents.)
Roast loin of beef (3 lbs, net, 38 cents.)
Lamb cutlets with puree of green peas (12 orders, 18 cents.)
Scrambled sweetbreads in pasty borders (6 orders, 10 cents.)
Marrowfat peas (15 cents.)
Lima beans (dried, ½ lb, and seasonings, 5 cents.)
Corn and tomatoes (20 cents.)
Potatoes mashed, boiled (6 cents.)
Eve's pudding, raspberry butter sauce (No. 675; pudding 20; sauce 9; 29 cents.)
White cocoanut pie (No. 677; meringued pink with raspberry juice, 2 pies large, deep, 26 cents.)
Vanilla ice cream (32 cents.)
Cherries and currants (2 qts, 16 cents.)
Cake assorted (12 cents.)
Cheese, crackers, pickles, nuts, raisins (average, 30 cents.)
Milk 12, cream 15, coffee 6, tea, sugar 6, bread 6.
Total, $4 00; 30 persons; 13⅓ cents a plate.

The colonel when at table, it would appear, is talkative and full of life and spirits. That's all right. He made the aemark that my consomme was exquisite but, was seasoned too highly with cayenne, and of course I heard of it. No such thing. But that's all right. I'll bet he only said it to lead off to curries and his experiences in hot climates and his "hairbreath 'scapes by flood and field." That's all right too; we all have our parts to play and get our work in when we can. Then, later on, he asked the manager, with whom he is already on terms of the utmost cordiality, why this was called Eve's pudding and the manager, laughing, said he would ask me. Now, a fellow does not want to be bothered with fool questions after scudding around the whole of a hot morning preparing a dinner and then carving and serving it; still I did not tell them to go to thunder as cooks generally do under such circumstances—this house being too small for anybody to be mean in—but replied that the pudding is as old as the hills; one of the best ever was invented; the receipt has been put in rhyme like Sydney Smith's salad dressing; didn't known why it is called Eve's unless because it contains apples, and couldn't even see where that came in. Then the irrepressible colonel took a bill of fare and wrote on the back of it:
Eureka!
"The woman tempted me and I did eat."
The pudding tempted *me* and *I* did eat!
The manager showed it to me after dinner was over. That's all right. I'll keep it to fling at the next one asks me something I don't know. I'll have to save tenderloin steaks for the colonel.

668—Consomme a la do Stael.

It is a clear, rich brown soup with lozenge shapes of fried bread and quenelle forcemeat in the plates.

Make a rich broth of beef and veal boiled down strong overnight with a bunch of soup vegetables and three or four cloves. Strain into a jar. When cold remove the fat, pour off from the sediment. Chop a pound of lean beef and boil up in the beef broth. Strain through a napkin. Set over the fire again skim, season, and add from one-third to one-half of a little white pot of Leibeg's extract of meat (private stock from the cook's valise.) The consomme will then have sufficient color and flavor.

For the quenelles mince a piece of white veal size of an egg, (or; use breast of partridge, quail or chicken if at hand) and then pound to a paste. Season with a pinch of minced herbs or parsley and grated lemon rind (very little), moisten with yolk of egg, flatten out, cut with something like a funnel point or apple corer if you have not the proper cutters, drop the quenelles in boiling water; dip up two to each plate of soup. Cut out bread with the same cutter, fry in the clear part of melted butter and put two in each plate with the quenelles.

These little accessories can be made ready long before they are to be used; perhaps in the intervals between orders while breakfast is going on. The French name was given long ago in allusion to Madame de Stael, of literary and political fame.

669—The Chevalier Style.

One of our French authors writes admiringly of "the chevaliers and abbes" of the last century, and their beneficent influence in advancing and disseminating the art of cookery. The chevaliers, it appears, were men of high social position; a sort of gentlemen soldiers, educated according to the culture of those days; having nothing particular to do but travel and see what they thought was the world; putting up themselves and their steeds at the monasteries when it happened that there was no inn that offered entertainment for man and beast; observing what the fattest of the fat friars ate and thrived upon and telling it at the next table for the edification of the new company; sampling and remembering the best dishes of the different countries and carrying the news in the times when books, papers and readers alike were few and dull. It could not be otherwise than that some *maitres d' hotel* (stewards of wealthy houses) should eagerly name some dish which had been so lucky as to be approved by one of these perhaps temporarily conspicuous personages, *a la chevaliere*, which is impliedly *a la mode chevaliere;* or—as we should write it—in the chevalier fashion; and it appears that there have been many dishes so named, but nearly all were evanescent, having no distinguishment but some trifling accessory or whim of decoration of no permanent value. A comparison of several authorities shows that the only dishes which all agree in designating as a la chevaliere, are those that are egged and bread-crumbed. A chicken breaded and fried is a la chevaliere, a trout breaded and fried is a la chevaliere, too. The decorations vary, the breading is the one permanent feature. There is a refinement in this however, which requires grated cheese —Parmesan—to be mixed with the bre d curmbs used to coat the morsel. It may easily be imagined how some epicurean rover sitting down to breakfast with the sleek abbot found a surprise and a revelation in his first dish of capon breadcrumbed and fried in oil; how he labored to reproduce the dish when he returned come, and how it came to be called the chevalier's.

It should be observed that although the masculine *chevalier* does not terminate with *e*, a peculiarity of the French language requires a terminal *e* to be added and makes it feminine in the *menu*, as are all the words which follow "a la mode." Parisian style potatoes assume the feminine Parisienne; macaroni Italian style becomes Italienne, and so with all designations after "a la" except the proper names of persons.

670—Trout, a la Chevaliere.

Split the fish, remove all bones, season with fine salt, cayenne and drops of lemon juice. Mix together 2 cups cracker meal and 1 cup grated or finely minced cheese (any kind.) Dip the sides of the fish in beaten egg in a shallow pan, then in the cracker dust mixture and let lie in it awhile. Spread a baking pan with soft butter, lay the fish in and bake slowly, basting once with melted butter. The pan should be roomy that the pieces of fish may not be crowded together. Serve hot and crisp without sauce, but with potatoes in the same plate.

671—Nantaise Potatoes.

Scoop out fluted berry shapes of raw potatoes with a potato spoon, put them in a saucepan with a lump of butter and let simmer in it until done, then pour off the butter, set the potatoes in the oven to brown slightly. Sprinkle with minced parsley. Serve with fish. Nantaise has reference to the city of Nantes, in France.

672—Lamb Cutlets with Puree of Green Peas.

Take the best shaped lamb chops, trim nicely and flatten, season, dip in flour and have them ready in a frying pan with very little fat from the roasting meats.

Mash some very green cooked peas through a seive, season with butter and white pepper, drop a pear shaped spoonful of this green puree in each individual dish, shape and smooth it a little, fry (saute) the lamb chops, lay one on top of the puree, press down slightly, pour a spoonful of light brown sauce around the base in the dish.

673—Scrambled Sweetbreads in Pastry Borders.

Small and fragmentary sweetbreads that cannot be sliced can be used this way. Cut them in dice, put in a frying pan with butter and eggs, salt, pepper, scramble same as eggs, not too dry, add a squeeze of lemon juice and little minced parsley.

Roll out scraps of pie paste, cut out crescent shapes with a scolloped cake cutter and bake them. Serve the sweetbreads in flat dishes with pastry crescents at each end.

674—Dried Lima Beans.

The dried are better than the canned. They are not hard to cook either. Soak a cupful in water a few hours and boil about an hour. Drain off and season in the same way as peas, that is, sometimes with cream sauce, sometimes with butter only or, with small pieces of bacon or salt pork stewed in them. Should they prove to be of a sample difficult to boil soft add a small piece of baking soda to the water they are boiled in.

675—Eve's Pudding.

It is a good sort of boiled plum pudding, not so rich and heavy; is cinnamon colored when made right. It is well worth while to weigh the ingredients as they are uncertain things to measure.

½ pound bread crumbs minced fine—about 4 cups.
¼ pound chopped suet—1 cup.
6 ounces raisins or currants—1 cup.
Same of chopped apples.
Nutmeg—about ¼ grated.
Mix the above together dry, then beat up in another bowl:
4 eggs.
6 tablespoons milk or water.
3 tablespoons sugar.
Minced lemon peel, or a little extract if at hand.
Stir all well together; tie up in a pudding cloth and boil 4 hours. Serve with hard sauce or any other plum pudding sauce.

676—Raspberry Butter Sauce.

Make hard sauce in the usual manner (No. 177;) and stir in enough of the syrup from scarlet raspberries to color and and flavor it.

677—White Cocoanut Custard.

There is a most excellent white cocoanut mixture at No. 163; but takes up more time than this to make.

For this proceed as if making custard pie, using all whites and counting 2 whites equal to one egg; which will be:
3 cups milk.
1 cup white of eggs—10 or 12 whites.
½ cup sugar.
1 heaping cup cocoanut.
1 teaspoon lemon extract.
Beat up, fill 2 paste-lined pie pans and bake slowly.

Meringue (or frost) them over when they are nearly done; stirring in a little raspberry syrup to color the frosting pink and dredge granulated sugar on the surface before baking.

678—Trouble with the Ice Cream.

A little party of four ladies from the Trulirural House came over in a boat immediately after dinner. Wanted to know of the manager whether really and truly, you know, we have ice cream every day. Said they never were so disappointed. the Trulirural only makes ice cream once a week, that is on Sunday, and after all when it was made it proved to be only frozen buttermilk full of lumps of butter. These four are the elders remaining of the party that came over serenading about ten days ago. They have taken rooms and will move over before supper. I know how that ice cream trouble occurred; saw the same mishap at Basswood City. There was a young fellow of a too sanguine disposition struggling along with a restaurant that did not pay, buoyed up by the visions of wealth he was going to realize during the approaching summer by making ice cream. Being consulted, I advised the purchase of only one freezer, or, if he must have two, to get a 4-quart and a 6-quart size. Young man thought I was surely jesting and sent off for a 4-gallon and a 10-gallon. On the first balmy day that foretokened the arrival of gentle spring he invited all his acquaintances to a treat of the first luscious ice cream of the season; his own make; the first he had ever made, and after all it proved a delusion and for him a mortification that he never recovered from. It was buttermilk and butter frozen. Such a thing could not happen to a person who might not care whether the ice cream were not good or indifferent, but this party was too solicitous, whipped or churned the cream to make it foamy, and increase the bulk when the temperature was just right for "butter to come" quickly. If the young man had had freezers to buy that afternoon he would have been content with a 1-quart and a 2-quart, for he took a sudden disgust at the ice cream business. Pour your cream into the freezer, sweeten and flavor it and freeze without further preparation, but after it is frozen then the more it is beaten the better it will be and "butter won't come" at that temperature.

Supper.

Oatmeal (3 cups raw, 4 cents.)
Broiled whitefish (4 lbs, net, and ¼ lb, butter, 45 cents.)
Beefsteak (7 orders, 1 lb, loin net, 15 cents.)
Cold meats (8 orders, charged dinner.)
Potatoes (from dinner, and baked, 4 cents.)
French rolls (30; 12 cents.)
Waffles (No. 679; 3 qts, 24, and lard to

bake 6; 30 cents.)
Crackers and milk (crackers, 5 cents.)
Cherries, fresh ripe (2 qts, 20 cents.)
Cocoanut cookies (without eggs, and other cake, 15 cents.)
Cream 30, milk 24, syrup 16, butter 20.
Coffee, tea, sugar 22, bread 6.
Total, $2 68; 34 persons; 8 cents a plate.

679—Waffles--Yeast Raised.

6 cups flour—1½ pounds.
2 large cups milk or water.
2-cent cake compressed yeast.
½ cup melted butter or lard.
4 or 5 eggs, or yolks left over.
Salt.

Dissolve the yeast in the milk (or water) lukewarm; stir up all to a thick batter and beat it well with a large egg whip or spoon. Let rise in a moderately warm place about 4 hours, beat up again half an hour before baking time. If you use potato yeast a cupful will be required. If mixed at 2 o'clock in summer the batter will be ready to bake at 6.

Anyone who has made muffins out of the roll dough as at No. 582; can take the same advantage making waffle batter, using about 4 cups of roll dough, warm milk to thin it down like batter cakes and the enriching ingredients the same as in this receipt. It will be ready to bake in an hour after, if warm.

Any kind of batter cake mixture can be baked in waffle irons if they are in good order and not burnt, and waffles can be made without eggs if the same as batter cakes, but when they stick to the irons the remedy is to add an egg or two, and waffles without eggs cannot be baked in much haste but must have time and dry out of the irons. Syrup or sugar in the batter causes them to bake brown. It is a vast improvement and prevents sticking to beat the batter very thoroughly.

Make the waffle irons hot, put in a teaspoonful of melted lard and turn over, pour batter in each compartment, shut up and bake both sides. Waffles are known only by the name of wafers in some places.

680—Cocoanut Cookies without Eggs.

The same as No. 645; but, before all

the flour is in add a cup (4 oz.) of common bulk, or new grated cocoanut.

681—Good Fruit Cake without Eggs.

1 small cup sugar—6 ounces.
½ cup butter—4 ounces.
2 cups milk or water—a pint.
2 heaped teaspoons baking powder.
5 cups flour—1¼ pounds.
2 teaspoons ground cinnamon.
1 teaspoon each cloves and allspice.
1 or 2 cups raisins and the same of currants. Cut the raisins in halves, dust them and currants with flour. Mix up the cake the usual way by stirring butter, sugar and milk together first. Frost over when baked with frosting made without eggs, No. 635.

Breakfast.

July 19.
Raspberries and cherries (2 qts, 18 cents.)
Cracked wheat (2 cups, 3 cents.)
Beefsteak (9 orders, 1¼ lbs, net, 20 cents.)
Mutton chops (6 orders, 1 lb, 13 cents.)
Liver and bacon (11 orders, 1¼ lbs, 15 cents.)
Ham and eggs (6 orders, 12 egg 15, 12 oz, ham, net 15—30 cents.)
Potatoes, Saratoga chips and baked (7 cents.)
Corn bread (with 3 cups meal, 2 eggs, 2 yolks, etc., 18 orders, 12 cents.)
French rolls (30 rolls, 13 cents.)
Butter 20 oz, 25, syrup 5, bread 6.
Cream 3 pts, 30, milk, buttermilk 2 gallons 24.
Coffee 12, tea 3, sugar 12.
Total, $2 48; 34 persons; little over 7 cents a plate.

682—Saratoga Chip Potatoes.

Shave raw potatoes into the thinnest possible slices, drop a a few at a time into a saucepan of hot lard and let fry to a deep yellow color. Drain them well, keep hot in a colander set in a pan, sprinkle with fine salt. They curl up like shavings if sliced thin enough. Not really necessary to dry each slice on a towel before frying, although it has been done at some places of great repute.

Busy day in the kitchen and dinner must stand back and make itself small. Fruit is very abundant and cheap and the hostess and that one of her hired girls that has the biggest arms are twisting and squeezing currants and raspberries in strong towels expressing the juice to boil down with equal weight of sugar to make jelly. It is a pressing business which makes the girl red in the face, as pressing might be expected to do, and the landlady herself has her lips curiously set as she says she is "afraid somebody will be very much annoyed by their putting up fruit in the kitchen, but—."
I don't know what the final but, was intended to mean, unless it was:
"But when she will she will, you may
    depend on't,
And when she won't she won't, and
    there's an end on't."
However, the landlady is very kindly disposed and interested, as this is Mr. Farewell's birthday, and a little supper is in preparation to celebrate the anniversary. The cakes are already ornamented with initials and dates on them as large as life and wreathed with roses, but carefully hidden away to guard against springing the surprise too soon. The chickens are already boiling for salad, and the manager went to the depot this time under heavy injunctions not to forget the lemons. Mrs. Farewell also, made a special request of me that the frosting on the cakes be of such a nature that it can be sliced evenly with the cake itself, whether the slices be thick or thin; not break off in the annoying way of their town confectioner's cakes as soon as the cake is cut. Requests like these are imperial orders and must be obeyed, and—
"Our praises are our wages."—(Shakespeare.)
But, Mary! It is time now to set your preserving kettle away off the stove until after dinner; it would break my heart to see you all starving to death at one o'clock precisely.

Dinner.

Soup—Scotch barley broth (6 qts, 20 cents.)

Trout a la Bechamel (No. 684; 4 lbs gross, and sauce, 42 cents.)

Boiled corned beef and cabbage (1 lb, beef, 10 cents.)

Roast beef (not in demand, some from previous day enough.)

Spring lamb (4 lbs, net, 48 cents.)

Stuffed shoulder mutton (No. 686; 3 lbs, net, boned, and stuffing, 35 cents.)

Macaroni and tomatoes, Italienne (No. 65; ½ lb, macaroni, ½ can tomato, 2 ozs, cheese, etc., 14 cents for about 14 orders.)

Summer beets in sauce (5 beets and sauce, 6 cents.)

Cabbage (2 heads, 10 cents.)

Onions in cream (5 cents.)

Potatoes browned, mashed (8 cents.)

Baked corn starch pudding, red cherry syrup for sauce (No. 689; 24 cents.)

Raspberry pie, apple pie (used canned apples, 3 pies, 30 cents.)

Vanilla ice cream (3 pts, cream, etc., 40 cents.)

Angel food cake (No. 2; doubled, 25 cents.)

Nuts, raisins, cheese, crackers, condiments, pickles 35.

Butter 10, milk 24, cream 10, coffee, tea, sugar 16.

Total, $4 12; 34 persons; about 12 cents a plate.

683—Scotch Barley Broth.

Take the trimmings of the lamb, tne shank, shoulder bone and neck of mutton, and add spare pieces of other meats; boil them in eight quarts of water from early morning until 10 or 11 o'clock. Boil 6 tablespoonfuls of barley for 6 quarts of soup in a separate saucepan.

Strain off the broth, skim well, put in 2 cupfuls of turnip, carrott and onion cut in small dice, some chopped parsley, salt and pepper, the barley already cooked and rinsed off in hot water; boil till the vegetables are done, thicken very slightly and add a cupful of lean meat from the neck of mutton, also cut in dice.

684—Trout a la Bechamel.

Another name for it is trout baked in cream. As previously stated at No. 662, any dish of fish or meat that is in cream sauce is allowably designated a la Bechamel; because that is the name of the sauce, it is always a cream-white dish.

If you put your fish to bake in plain milk or cream at first, expecting to thicken the sauce when the fish is done, you find that it has been curdled by the gelatine from the fish and has an unsightly appearance. Make the cream sauce first, of rich milk, a little minced onion, butter and flour, pour it boiling hot over the fish in a baking pan; bake about ¾ hour basting twice; at last add a little cream and chopped parsley. Serve in small plates with Parisienne potatoes plain steamed in the same.

685—Corned Beef and Cabbage.

The beef having been well corned, the next requisite to make it a good dish is to give it plenty of time to boil tender. The cabbage should be boiled separately and chopped and seasoned at last with the fat from the beef boiler. If cooked together the beef left to slice cold is too strongly flavored. Serve the cabbage in a flat dish with a slice of beef on top.

686—Stuffed Shoulder of Mutton.

Take out the bone, lay a thin covering of well-seasoned bread stuffing upon the meat; roll up, tie with twine and cook the same as rolled brisket of veal; No. 171.

687—Beets in Butter Sauce.

Beets should not be cut before cooking as they lose their juice and color. Boil about an hour, rub off the skin in cold water, cut up into a saucepan, add 2 cups water, ½ cup vinegar, half as much butter, salt, and flour thickening to make a moderately thick sauce when it boils.

688—Onions in Cream Sauce.

Boil in plenty of water and pour the water away entirely, as it is dark colored. Make sufficient cream sauce well salted in another saucepan and put the onions in.

689—Baked Corn Starch Pudding

6 cups milk—3 pints.
6 heaped tablespoons starch—7 ounces.
3   do   do   sugar.
¼ cup butter—2 ounces.
5 or 6 yolks—(left over from making white cake.)
Flavoring extract, pinch salt.
Boil the milk with the sugar in it—which prevents burning at bottom. Mix up the starch with a little cold milk and then some hot, pour quickly into the boiling milk in the kettle and almost immediately, or, as soon as fairly mixed, take it off the fire. Beat in the butter, the yolks beaten up with a spoonful of milk, flavor then, bake in a pan or earthen dish about 20 minutes. Too much cooking causes starch pudding to turn watery. Serve with sauce made of part fruit juice, sugar, water and starch simmered clear and bright.

Supper.

Oatmeal (3 cups, 5 cents.)
Beefsteak (12 orders, 20 cents.)
Calf's liver breaded (12 orders, 18 cents.)
Broiled bacon (2 orders, 4 cents.)
Codfish in cream (4 orders, 5 cents.)
Cold meats (½ lb, charged dinner.)
Potatoes French fried and baked (8 cents.)
Rolls (30, 12 cents.)
French coffee cakes (No. 262; made 30, 20 cents.)
Pears in syrup (2 cans California, 50 cents.)
Cake, cookies, ginger snaps (15 cents.)
Milk, cream 44; butter 22.
Coffee, tea, sugar 21; bread 6.
Total, $2 50; 35 persons; little over 7 cents a plate.

690—A Birthday Party Supper Prepared without Eggs.

Gotten up without using eggs, to show that it can be done; and that if it be well done the party will never discover any difference.

MENU.

Cold Roast Chicken garnished with Jelly.

Sandwich Rolls with Potted Tongue.

Pickles.   Lettuce.

Lobster Salad.

Calf's Foot Jelly (Lemon and Raspberry Flavors.

Panachee Ice Cream.

Florentine Meringue.   Chocolate Layer Cake

Birthday Fruit Cake, Ornamented.

White Citron Cake. Neapolitan Cake.

Nuts.   Raisins.

Lemonade.   Coffee.

This was for a party of 20 persons who did not really need to eat an extra meal; it was a supper table for a social family gathering and so provided for, the quantities would not be sufficient for a calculation for a paid supper.
Cost of material:
Roasted breasts only of 4 chickens equal 2 chickens, 50 cents.
Savory jelly for decoration, 1 quart, 25 cents.
20 Sandwiches of potted tongue and butter, 20 cents.
Lobster salad, lettuce and pickles, 25 cents.
Calf's foot jelly 3 pints, 45 cents.
Ice cream, 2 quarts, 70 cents.
Florentine meringue, 15 cents.
Chocolate layer cake, 15 cents.
Fruit cake ornamented, weight 5 lbs., 70 cents.
Other cakes small amounts, 10 cents.
Nuts and raisins about 3 lbs., 60 cents.
Lemonade iced, 45 cents.
Coffee, cream and sugar, 15 cents.
Total, $4 65; 20 persons; over 23 cents a plate.

691—Cold Chicken with Aspic Jelly.

The supper being for 20 persons, took 4 large spring chickens and of these used only the breasts to roast cut off raw, and the rest of the chickens reserved for a side dish for next day's dinner. After roasting in a small pan about half an hour set them away to get cold, and at night sliced thinly enough for 16 individual dishes to be set at intervals along the table, ornamented with colored jelly, and the remainder kept in reserve in case of further orders.

692—Calf's Foot or Aspic or Savory Jelly.

Colored jelly in ornamental shapes was the distinguishing characteristic of Careme's system in cookery, particularly as he employed it to produce gorgeous effects of light and color in the elaborately decorated set tables and grand banquets of his time; classic figures in wax, waxen leaves and borders and scenic designs are the distinguishing characteristic of the later system originated (or, rather resuscitated, for there is nothing new) by the court cooks at Vienna, and fostered and encouraged by the emperor and empress themselves, as if they would fain have an original system for their own court and following, not borrowed from the French.

The extent of the impression made by Careme upon the English cooks and confectioners, then, might almost be measured by the frequency of the dishes in aspic and the offers of brilliant sweet jellies among the confections for sale in the shops; the prevalence of the German methods by the frequency of the waxen Neptunes, dolphins, forests and flowers worked on the stands which hold up the dishes at any elaborate exhibition of culinary skill. The essential part of the cookery, that which affects the eatable part of the dishes cannot in the nature of things differ much, it is only a divergence of externals and it has to be said of the dishes in jelly that they are at least all eatable, the savory ornaments even more so perhaps than the meat itself.

If there could be an American distinctive style it would be marked by the use of fruit jellies, cranberry sauce and jelly with game, apples, pears and peaches in compotes and pickles sweet as well as sour, such things as Careme had an inkling of when he built up his "supremes of fruits"—pyramidal forms of fruits preserved whole and decorated with strawerries and green angelica.

But the simple style of individual service now so universally employed while it brings into use a great number of small dishes, glasses and silver-ware almost precludes the use of any method of ornamentation beyond such borders and sprinklings as may be formed in the act of dishing the food.

693—To Make Calf's Foot Jelly.

For reasons named in the preceding article if in England or France we write jelly it is understood first to mean gelatine jelly, whether savory like the jelly o head-cheese or sweet and wine flavored, but in the United States it is taken to mean jellied fruits. So if we find ourselves at some country resort where the landlady and all her maidservants are busy making currant, gooseberry, raspberry and apple jellies to put away for winter use and we have to make at the same time ornamental clear jelly of Careme's own sort with which to decorate a birthday supper table, we must call it calf's foot jelly, lest there be an impression that we have been surreptitiously dipping into the wrong kettles.

To make the jelly really of calves feet as it used to be forty or fifty years ago, you first put on 2 feet in 4 quarts of water, simmer for 6 or 8 hours, and the feet will be so nearly dissolved that the liquor that remains—which will measure about 2 quarts when strained off—will set in strong jelly when cold. It has then to be freed from fat, sweetened, spiced and clarified in all respects the same as the gelatine jelly of Nos. 465 and 466; that is if to be a lemon or other sweet jelly, but if to be savory jelly it will be seasoned something like a savory dish of meat.

694—How to Serve Colored Jellies— Five Ways.

1. Pour the jelly (No. 465;) when made into soup plates or bright pans quite shallow. Set on ice. Cut it in diamond shapes when set, and put one piece of each color in small stem glasses, get three glass cake stands, set one on the other, they being of three sizes; set the glasses of jelly upon them for a pyramid of jelly for the center of the table.

2. Cut the jelly in diamonds or squares and serve in ice cream saucers individually with cake.

3. Pour the jelly into small custard cups, or individual ornamental jelly moulds or other small form, run a penknife around to loosen and shake out the form of jelly on to the individual ice-cream plate.

4. Cool the jelly in the ordinary stamped jelly moulds, dip in warm water when wanted, turn out the shape and place on large dishes along the table, to be served with a spoon or the people to help each other.

5. Cool the jelly in the large ornamental border moulds which have a hollow middle. When perfectly cold turn out the border of jelly—first dipping the mould a moment in warm water—on to a cake stand and fill the center cavity with whipped cream.

695—To Make Savory or Aspic Jelly.

Aspic is the French cooks' name for it. It is the jelly formed by boiling meat down till the liquor will set when cold, the jelly, for example of head cheese, or of boiled chickens when the liquor has nearly all boiled away, and if it is the intention to make jelly of such liquor an extra calf's foot or pig's foot or two will be thrown in at the beginning of the boiling and make the liquor stronger. This being the jelly in the rough state—seasoned as soup would be to make it taste good and relish—in order to change its appearance from dull gray into an article of sparkling transparency it is necessary to clarify it by boiling white of eggs and lemon juice in it and straining it through a flannel jelly bag.

The making of savory jelly is not an abstruse and foreign affair, but anyone who takes pleasure in such things finding at hand some meat liquor that has set in jelly firm enough to cut with a knife can clarify it and use it to set off a luncheon or supper table in a way that is by no means common.

But when there is no meat jelly already formed make some by dissolving an ounce of sheet gelatine in a quart of good soup stock, season it nicely, let it get quite cold to remove the grease, then melt and clarify it as for sweet jelly at No. 465.

Make different tints by adding burnt sugar dissolved in boiling water for amber and brown, and cochineal or beet juice for pink and red.

Extra fine jelly, more brilliant than is ever seen in the restaurant windows, is made by putting it through the clarifying process twice, allowing a little in the measure for the inevitable loss of quantity in the repeated boiling and filtering; and a correspondingly enhanced flavor is obtained by adding a proportion of sherry.

696—Ornamenting with Aspic Jelly

1. Place thin slices of breast of chicken or turkey in individual platters. Chop some jelly quite small, put it in a paper cornet, snip off the end and squeeze the jelly through in a cord around the edge of the dish or in patterns the same as the ornamental frosting of a cake.

2. Chop some of the brightest jelly not very small, and sprinkle about a teaspoonful over the sliced meat or around upon a salad.

3. Cool the jelly in plates quite shallow and when set cut, it in triangular shapes, large or small in proportion to the size of dishes to be ornamented, and set the pieces in order around the edge of the dish.

4. Pour the jelly upon the thin sliced meat in large platter, just enough to cover, set it on ice and when it has become firm cut out the slices with the coating of jelly upon them and ornament the edges with minced jelly and parsley.

5. Take a solid boneless piece of cooked and pressed meat like head cheese, pressed corned beef or tongue, boned turkey or chicken or liver pate and put it in a mould or pan that is a little too large for it, fill up the mould with melted jelly—there should be a quarer inch or more space for the jelly on all sides and underneath—make it quite cold, turn out by first dipping the mould a moment in warm water and then slice the meat with border of jelly adhering to each slice.

697—To Clarify Jelly without Eggs.

Use lean beef chopped fine, about 4 ounces to a quart. This is the way fine consommes are made clear, and it is as good for jelly. Mix the minced beef thoroughly with a little cold water, stir it into the jelly after it has been boiled once, (without any white of eggs) then boil again and strain through the jelly bag. It is the albumen in beef that has the effect in clearing the fluid it is boiled in.

"But won't it make it taste?" somebody says, as the mineed beef goes into the sweet jelly.

"No; only like calf's foot jelly;" indeed it is an improvement, for all gelatine has a slightly unpleasant flavor which the fresh beef removes. Of course if white of eggs can be had as well as not there is no need to resort to the substitute, yet, it is often very convenient to know how to do without.

698—Tongue Sandwiches.

Make dough as for French rolls, after the last kneading roll it out extremely thin, brush the sheet all over with melted butter and double it upon itself; roll it again and when it has stood a minute or two to lose the tendency to draw out of shape cut out with a biscuit cutter, place in pans, brush over with butter, rise nearly an hour and bake. These are flat round rolls that will pull apart when done. Spread one half with butter the other with potted tongue and put them together. Or, use potted tongue with plain sliced bread.

699—Potted Tongue.

Boil a corned tongue 3 hours, if a beef tongue, or until tender. Dip it in cold water and peel off the skin. Cut up and mince small, then pound it to a paste. Melt two large cupfuls of butter and prepare a teaspoonful of mixed ground spices, half mace and the rest cloves, nutmeg and cayenne. Add the spices to the tongue, and a little salt besides, and most of the clear part of the melted butter, and pound it all together. Press it into cups or small jars tightly to exclude the air and pour the rest of the clear butter on top. Keep covered in a cool place.

700—Lobster Salad without Mayonaise.

Cut white heart lettuce in shreds and across quite fine; break about the same amount of lobster in small pieces but without mashing it, season both with celery, celery-salt, salt, cayenne, oil and vinegar enough to moisten, mix together, serve on individual dishes ornamented with cooked beets stamped out in shapes. Can be made likewise with finely minced cabbage with some thick cream, salt and pepper stirred in and the lobster on top.

701—Panachee, or Tri-colored Ice-Cream.

The same as Neapolitan, No. 227; which see for directions and use of molds. The bill-of-fare writers get tired of and having the same thing over and over instead of repeating Neapolitan they call it *panachee*, it being like panachee jelly, which is of three colors in layers, and named after the tri-colored feather which used to be worn in the hat as the sign or badge of the French republican.

To save trouble on the occasion of this party supper, the 2 quarts of white ice cream frozen with the dinner cream in the morning was divided, and half of it colored with caramel and cinnamon and frozen again in a small pail set in a washtub of small ice and salt. The red was cherry juice taken from the preserving kettles and mixed with water, then frozen the same way and all three kinds put in brick moulds and packed down for 3 hours. Cost 67 cents for 3 quarts.

702—Florentine Meringue.

Roll out a sheet of puff paste thin and cover a baking pan bottom with it, spread jelly or preserves upon it and bake. Whip up some meringue and mix in chopped almonds or desiccated cocoanut and spread that on top of the florentine, sift sugar on top and bake. It is like the fruit meringues in a general way but ought to be thin, to cut in large, but flat strips. The meringue can be made with gelatine instead of white of eggs if so needed.

703—Neapolitan Cake.

The new fashion for it is to make layer cakes of three colors, white, yellow, (or pink) and chocolate, spread jelly and build up to 6 layers high; trim the edges and ice it all over. Three kinds can be made without eggs, by using Nos. 655 and 632; and making part of the latter pink with raspberry juice. The old fashion was to make pound jelly cake 6 or 8 layers high and ice it and ornament.

704—Ornamented Fruit Cake.

Cut a pound of citron in strips and add to the mixture No. 681. Bake in a large round mold previously lined with buttered paper. Put on two coats of icing, a border around, and if for a birthday party put up the initials of the person's name in letters of lace-work icing 6 or 8 inches high according to plan to be found described in succeeding pages.

705—Cake Frosting That Will Not Break Off.

Our birthday cake was required to be cut in pieces and sent hither and thither, a piece or two to Basswood City and some more to Lakeport, and it would have been extremely annoying had the frosting all broke away on the first attempt to cut it, and yet that is just what the common raw icing will always do if made with white of eggs alone. But if you dissolve a little gelatine in hot water in a cup, have it like thick mucilage, then use it and one or two whites of eggs mixed in to beat up the sugar with; the frosting will stay on the cake and cut as easy as a piece of cheese. For a rule, take:

2 tablespoons dissolved gelatine.
2 whites of eggs.
2 cups sugar.

Put all in a bowl and stir with a wooden paddle. To making icing or frosting easily it is best to have it as thick as dough at first, it soon turns thin as the sugar dissolves, when it becomes too thick with long stirring it can be reduced with warm water by the teaspoonful, or with white of egg.

A few drops of acetic acid, or lemon juice, or cream tartar added to icing whitens and stiffins it. Add lemon or vanilla extract to flavor.

706—Boiled Icing, That Will Not Break.

1½ cups sugar.
4 tablespoons water.
2 whites of eggs.

Set the water and sugar on to boil, have it just like making candy. Whisk the whites to a stiff froth, pour the boiling sugar into the whites, stir up and spread on the cake immediately. If boiled enough it will set firm as soon as cold, if not set it in a warm place to dry.

707—Chocolate Boiled Icing without Eggs.

1 pound sugar—2 cups.
½ teacup water.
4 ounces common chocolate, grated—1 cup.

Boil all together almost to candy point, flavor with vanilla when partly cooled, beat a short time, spread over the cake.

708—Chocolate Icing Not Boiled

1 pound sugar—2 cups—either granulated or powdered will do.
6 whites of eggs.
4 ounces grated common chocolate—1 cup.
2 teaspoons vanilla extract.

Put the sugar and whites of eggs together into a bowl and beat rapidly with a wooden spoon or paddle, in a cool place for about ten minutes, or until you have good white frosting. Set the grated chocolate on the side of the stove to melt merely by the heat, without anything added to it. Pour it to the frosting in the bowl, add flavor, beat up and use to cover cakes or spread between layers.

Speaking of cake glaze and icings, however, there are two young friends of mine, the head and second baker at the Gondolier-Grand Hotel, at Firefly Grove, who have their ambition aroused even now while I am writing this, trying how many and how choice a lot of small cakes and trifles they can send in, in the silver baskets daily, and are much pleased with the soft glazes or icings of the following receipts, which they found in the *American Pastry Cook*. They find a number of uses for them and are glad of having so many kinds and colors. Another friend, a grizzly bearded old partner up north was using them one day, and he remarked: "Ha! that's what we call *bong dong*, eh?—you know?"

"No—that is not quite *fondant*, al though it is as good for these uses. To make *fondant* you must have a saccharo-meter, kettle and marble slab, etc., but these fondant icings a boy or girl can make with a tin pan, a spoon and an egg whip."

709—Yellow Glaze or Boiled Icing.

This should be the first to be tried as it is of less consequence whether the sugar is boiled to the exact point for yolks of eggs than for whites.

2 cups granulated sugar—a pound.
½ teacup water—6 tablespoons.
6 yolks of eggs.
Flavoring extract.

Boil the sugar and water for 5 minutes, or until a drop in cold water sets in candy so hard it can be hardly flattened between the finger and thumb. Have the yolks slightly beaten ready in a bowl, pour the bubbling syrup to them quickly while you keep beating with an egg beater. Set over the fire for a minute or two and keep beating while it cooks a little more, flavor and pour it over sheets of cake, or dip small cakes in it. If the sugar was boiled enough it will set hard and dry as soon as cold. Is improved by being beaten in the saucepan until partly cooled, and the flavoring should go in the very last thing to avoid loss by boiling out.

710—White Glaze or Boiled Icing.

2 cups sugar.
6 tablespoons water.
4 whites of eggs.
Flavor.

Boil the sugar and water until a drop in cold water sets in brittle candy. Have the whites slightly beaten in a bowl, pour the boiling sugar to them while you beat very rapidly. Set over the fire again until it boils, taking care to keep it from burning. Then set it on ice and beat with an egg beater until it is perfectly white and creamy like *fondant*, and begins to set. Ice cakes with it or dip small cakes in, such as sponge drops, holding them on a fork. This is quick and easy after the first trial; the point is to boil the sugar to "the crack," which takes a little practice. Add flavoring extract when nearly cold.

711—Rose Glaze or Boiled Icing.

The same as the preceding with color-ing to make it pink. Cherry juice or cochineal can be used.

712—Chocolate Glaze or Boiled Icing.

1 pound sugar.
½ cup water—7 tablespoons.
3 ounces grated common chocolate—a cupful.
3 eggs.
Vanilla flavoring.

Boil the sugar, water and chocolate together until a drop in the water sets in candy. Beat the eggs and add the boil-ing candy to them with rapid beating.

Dinner.

July 20.
Soup—Consomme Brunoise (5 qts, 30 cents.)
Fillets of trout, Spanish style (3 lbs, gross, potatoes and sauce, 35 cents.)
Potatoes Brabant.
Boiled meats (no orders, left over for supper, etc.)
Roast beef (2 lbs, 25 cents.)
Roast pork (2 lbs, 22 cents.)
Roast veal with dressing (2 lbs, and dressing, 30 cents.)
Epigramme of lamb, sauce Trianon (2 lbs, and sauce, 30 cents.)
Potato salad (5 cents.)
String beans 5, butter beans 5, cabbage 2 heads 10 tomatoes 15, potatoes 8—43 cents.
Raspberry drop dumplings with sauce (30 dumplings and sauce, 17 cents.)
Custard pie (2 with 1 qt, milk, 8 eggs and sugar, 20 cents.)
Lemon sherbet (No. 179; 2 qts, before freezing, 20 cents.)
Angel food cake (baked thin, frosted and sliced, 22 cents.)
Nuts, raisins, cheese, crackers, con-diments (average, 35 cents.)
Milk (9 quarts, 27 cents.)
Cream 10, coffee 10, tea 3, sugar 4, butter 10, bread 6.

Total, $4 04; 35 persons; 11½ cents a plate.

713—Consomme Brunoise.

5 quarts clear soup stock.
½ lb, chopped lean beef.
2 whites of eggs to clear it.
1 cup green cooked peas.
1 cup carrot and turnip and leek and celery if you have them cut in smallest dice.
1 teaspoon extract of meat.

Draw off the stock free from grease, put in the beef and white of egg mixed with some cold water and set it on to boil. When well boiled strain through a napkin or tammy cloth or jelly bag. Cook the vegetables separately, wash them off, season the consomme with salt and cayenne and add meat extract (or glaze of your own making) to color light brown, and then the vegetables.

714—Fillets of Trout Spanish Style.

Cook the fish this way when you have a lot of small ones, such as brook trout, or lake herring. Run a knife along both sides of the back bone and take it out. Take the two sides, double them, the meat side outwards, lay them in a buttered baking pan one leaning upon the other so as to hold it in shape, and so proceed until the pan has all it will contain, one layer deep, the boned part of the fillets of fish being on top. Before putting in the fish strew some finely minced onion in the pan. After the fish is in, sprinkle salt and pepper, sift over a little cracker meal, and pour in enough light colored veal gravy mixed with strained tomato, or Spanish stock sauce (No. 784;) to half cover the fillets, and bake light brown. Dish out of the pan it is baked in, one fillet to each person, a spoonful of the sauce and a few potatoes of any baked or fried kind like the following in the same plate.

715—Potatoes, a la Brabant.

Cut raw potatoes in dice, medium size and perfect cubes, rejecting the uneven sides and ends. Boil them in water, drain off before they break, then fry in clean lard very light colored. Sprinkle with salt and finely minced parsley. Brabant is the name of a place—a duchy.

716—Epigramme of Lamb, a la Trianon.

Epigramme is the French cooks' name for the brisket or breast of lamb. After cutting lamb chops for breakfast there will be three or four of these briskets on hand. Saw them lengthwise in two, boil for half an hour in soup stock well seasoned, press them between two dishes. When cold bread them by dipping in egg and cracker meal, lay in a pan, pour a little oil, clear butter or drippings over and bake light brown. To serve: divide in pieces about 4 or 5 ribs wide, place a spoonful of sauce in the dish and the meat pressed down in it. It does not do well to fry it after breading, the bright yellow-brown of a careful bake is what makes it a desirable entree.

717—Sauce Trianon.

It is a yellow sauce made of white butter sauce with yolks of eggs stirred in to color, and speckled with minced truffles, mushrooms, shalots and white pepper. Add a spoonful of white wine or little dash of lemon juice. A very small quantity of such a sauce can be made to fill the bill and one small truffle out of a bottle and four or five mushrooms sliced will be all that are needed. Trianon is the name of a place —a French palace.

718—Potato Salad.

Take cold boiled potatoes, slice them thinly so that the vinegar will penetrate. For a bowl of sliced potatoes mince one good sized onion and a bunch of parsley and throw on top, also salt and white pepper. Pour over half cup of olive oil and mix all well. If you mix all with oil this way first the parsley retains its green color, which vinegar used first takes away. Pour over half cup of vinegar and mix by turning from one bowl to another shortly before serving. A pint cupful is enough at such a house as this with no expense worth counting but a few spoonfuls of oil, but where there is lunch served potato salad is a leading dish and not a cheap one because oil must be used‧ plentifully.

719—Raspberry Dumplings without Eggs or Powder.

When rolls are made in the morning instead of making loaves of bread of the dough that remains keep it cold until the middle of the forenoon. Then roll it out on the table to a thin sheet—as thin as the edge of a dinner plate. Cut it all in squares, about 2½ inches, place a tablespoonful of fruit in the middle of each and lap the corners over the top. Pinch the edges together a little, set the dumplings in a greased pan and also brush over the tops with a little melted lard or butter. Let rise about 45 minutes, like rolls. Have a large pan of boiling water—a baking pan will do, drop the dumplings in and cook 20 minutes either on top of the stove or in the oven. Serve with sauce, either No. 70; or, hard sauce or cream.

Dinner.

July 21.
Soup—Green corn (6 qts, 30 cents.)
Boiled muskalonge, egg sauce (3 lbs, sauce and potatoes, 33 cents.)
Potatoes Hollandaise.
Boiled smoked tongue and corned beef (few orders, 12 cents.)
Roast beef (1 rib, 2 lbs, 26 cents.)
Roast lamb, mint sauce (5 lbs, 60 cents.)
Fricassee of chicken, Parisienne (2 chickens, sauce, etc., 65 cents.)
Haricot of mutton, Bourgeoise (13 cents.)
Summer cabbage 2 heads 10, beets plain stewed 2, tomatoes 12, string beans 6, potatoes 8—38 cents.
Tapioca custard pudding (2 qts, 20 cents, with sauce, 25 cents.)
Cherry and raspberry pie (2 pies, 16 cents.)
White Mountain ice cream (36 cents.)
Nuts, raisins, cheese, crackers, condiments (average, 35 cents.)

Bread, butter 10, coffee, tea, sugar 14.
Milk 24, cream 10.
Total, $4 47; 35 persons; nearly 13 cents a plate.

720—Green Corn Soup.

Any good simple soup not specially flavored may have grated corn and some milk added to it and will be generally acceptable. For a rule for 30 to 35 persons take:
5 quarts soup stock.
1 or 2 quarts milk.
1 can of corn or a quart of green corn grated.
1 tablespoon minced onion.
½ lb, salt pork.
Boil a carrot, turnip and onion with the meat, bones and water that makes the stock. Cut the pork in dice and fry it light brown, and then pour away the fat, boil up the milk in the pork pan to obtain the flavor of the frying, and pour all back into the stock pot. Strain into a clean saucepan, add the minced onion, the corn mashed or grated, boil up and season, and sprinkle a little parsley finely minced.

721—Boiled Muskallonge.

The muskallonge is fish like the pickerel. It is convenient sometimes to have another name even for the same fish for the purposes of a bill of fare. Mark off the fish in individual portions. Have the water ready boiling, put in a bay leaf, an onion and 4 cloves and salt and piece of lemon if at hand, drop in the fish, boil gently at the side of the range not over half an hour. Serve with egg sauce or other kinds suitable for boiled fish, and a spoonful of potato.

722—Potatoes, Hollandaise.

Cut raw potatoes in quarters lengthwise as if to be fried, then trim to a rough kidney shape, boil in salted water, take off before they break, drain, and sprinkle with parsley, melted butter, salt and lemon juice. Serve with the fish on the same plate.
There used to be a Dutch kidney potato of small size but much esteemed, which these cut potatoes are intended to imitate

and, like those of Holland, are to be simply cooked.

723—Fricassee of Chicken, Parisienne.

Cut tender chickens in joints, pepper and salt and roll in flour, either fry or bake brown using enough oil, clarified butter or drippings to baste with. Make yellow fricassee sauce—that is, white sauce with yolk of egg added and lemon juice and cayenne, and prepare a pint cupful of Parisienne potatoes. Serve sauce in the dish, piece of chicken in it, potatoes around and, if wished, decorate further with button mushrooms same size as the potatoes.

Fricassee, is the French word for fry, and seems to have meant fried chicken with sauce at first, but fricassees are variously put up. The term "Parisienne," is one of the convenient designations that, like "a la Russe," means but little and does no harm. Two chickens can be cut into 28 or 30 pieces.

724—Haricot of Mutton, Bourgeoise.

Haricot, is the name of a stew of meat with vegetables in it. Bourgeoise signifies that it is common—in family style. Haricots is also the French for beans. Cut up the breast and neck of mutton, brown it first in a pan either in oven or on top of stove, with frequent stirring. Then put in a saucepan with turnip, carrot and onion cut in large pieces. Stew till tender, season plainly with salt and depper and thicken the liquor.

725—Beots Plain.

Boil the beets, peel in cold water, cut them in dice size of cherries, season with salt and one spoonful of roast meat fat shaken about in them to keep them from drying out and serve so without sauce.

726—Tapioca Custard Pudding.

1 heaping cup tapioca—½ pound.
6 cups milk—3 pints.
½ cup sugar—4 ounces.
1 ounce butter—small egg size.
4 eggs, or 8 yolks.

Crush the tapioca, if the large and rough kind, put it to soak in half the milk for 2 hours.

Boil the other half the milk with the sugar in it, stir in the soaked tapioca, let simmer slowly at the side or in a pan of boiling water for half an hour, or until the tapioca is become transparent and well cooked. Then stir in the butter and eggs and bake. Serve with sauce. This makes over 2 quarts, about 24 portions, costs 20 cents; with sauce 1½ cents each person.

Dinner.

July 22.
Soup—Barley, a la Princesse (6 qts, 30 cents.)

Whitefish, a l' Espagnole (3½ lbs, gross, and sauce, 35 cents.)

Julienne potatoes.

Boiled meats (nominal to fill bill, rarely ordered.)

Roast beef (1 rib, 2½ lbs, 30 cents.)

Roast lamb (4½ lbs, 50 cents.)

Fricassee of veal, Francaise (15 orders, 1½ lbs, with sauce, and garnishing, 25 cents.)

Brochettes of liver, Bretonne (10 orders, 1½ lbs, 18 cents.)

Marrowfat peas 20, string beans 8 corn 1 can 15 potatoes 9—60 cents.

Boiled suet pudding, silver sauce (pudding 20 sauce 16—36 cents.)

Covered lemon pie (No. 22; 2 pies, 16 cents.)

Vanilla ice cream (3 pints cream and milk, etc., 35 cents.)

Assorted cake (15 cents.)

Nuts, raisins, cheese, crackers, condiments (average, 35 cents.)

Milk, cream 34, butter, bread 14, coffee, tea, sugar 14.

Total, $4 38; 34 persons; about 13 cents a plate.

727—Barley Soup a la Princess, or Consomme a l' Orge.

Prepare 5 quarts of clear consomme; boil ½ cup pearl barley separately until well done, then wash it in a colander in plently of water. Cut a piece of carrot and turnip in fine dice no larger than the barley grains and boil a few minutes, strain and wash, then put barley and vegetables in the consomme just before time to serve. Orge, is the French name for barley.

728--Whitefish a l' Espagnole.

Anything and everything you may meet with in a bill of fare that is a l' Espagnole is in brown meat sauce, either cooked in it or has the sauce poured over it. Fish cooked in this way is more like meat than in any other form. It is not a good way with a soft kind of fish or when the sauce is too dark. A nice veal gravy and a firm whitefish will make a good dish. Split the fish, as only small portions are wanted to be served, score off the portions, without cutting through. Brush a little fat over the baking pan, lay the fish skin side up; cut carrot, turnip and onion in very small dice and strew a small portion in the spaces in the pan, dredge salt and pepper and bake about 15 minutes. Then pour in enough light colored veal gravy or Spanish stock sauce (No. 784) to come half way up and bake 20 minutes longer, basting the fish with the gravy and having some left in the pan to serve with the fish. Send in some kind of potatoes in the same plate.

729—Potatoes a la Julienne.

Choose the longest potatoes, slice them raw very thinly and then cut the slices in shreds thin as shoestrings. Fry in hot lard, drain well, sprinkle with salt.

730—Fricassee of Veal, Francaise.

Take veal that is not suitable for cutlets and cut it in square pieces, put in a frying pan with a little oil, butter or roast meat fat and fry (saute) over the fire until it is light brown. Put in water or stock enough to cover, add a minced onion and little grated nutmeg and let stew until tender. Take out the pieces of meat into another saucepan so that you can thicken the liquor, which requires about 1 spoonful of flour thickening and 2 yolks of eggs or according to quantity, and add salt, pepper and juice of half a lemmon. Immediately after adding the

yolks, take the sauce from the fire before it becomes rough with curdling of the egg and strain it over the meat. To garnish: Cut out leaf shapes of thin puff paste, egg over and bake and put one or two in each dish when served.

731—Brochette of Liver a la Bretonne.

Make thin slices of liver and equal number of bacon and cut them in squares not much larger across than a silver quater, place them on skewers alternately, have the skewers nearly full. Dip in egg and cracker meal and fry light brown. Serve whole or half one to each order, slipping them off the skewers and placing in the dish first a spoonful of sauce, made by frying minced onion light brown, adding brown sauce, a spoonful of made mustard and same of vinegar. Can also be fried without breading and served on toast.

732—Boiled Suet Pudding.

4 cups flour—a pound.
2 large cups minced suet—6 ounces.
1 cup sugar—½ pound.
1 large cup raisins or currants—½ pound.
1 cup milk.
1 egg.
Pinch of soda and little salt.

The suet should be selected, free from skin and meat and minced very fine. Rub it into the flour. Put in the other ingredients, stir together very thoroughly. Tie up in a pudding bag and boil 4 or 5 hours. Take up only just before it is wanted as it is best when first taken from the pot. Serve slices with sauce. Three pounds costs 19 cents.

733—Silver Pudding Sauce, or Sweet Velante.

1 cup powdered sugar.
½ cup butter.
3 whites of eggs.
3 tablespoons brandy or little flavoring extract.

It is hard sauce (No. 177) improved by having whipped white of egg stirred in while it is still soft. It should be made the last thing before dinner and then kept cold as the whites go down with standing.

734—Pound Cakes, Assorted Kinds.

4 cups sugar—light weight of 2 pounds.
4 small cups butter—1½ pounds.
20 eggs.
8 rounded cups flour—2 pounds good weight.

Warm the butter and sugar to soften, then stir them to a cream, add eggs two at a time and work them in, then the flour. No powder or raising of any kind wanted but a good beating at the last to make the cake fine grained, and pound cake should not be flavored.

Having made the above you can bake part of it in a deep mould for pound cake; spread some on jelly cake pans for jelly cake or any other kind of layer cake; bake one sheet thin on a baking pan and frost over when done for meringue cake, put citron, raisins or currants in some of it, or mix in some melted chocolate.

Dinner.

July 23.
Soup—Puree of green peas, or potage St. Germaine (6 qts, 36 cents.)
Fillets of whitefish with fine herbs (3 lbs, net 30, mushrooms, etc., 15; 45 cents.)
Potatoes, Victoria.
Boiled tongue and corn beef (2 orders, 10 cents counting waste.)
Roast beef (end of loin 2 lbs, 24 cents.)
Roast pork, apple sauce (2½ lbs, and sauce, 35 cents.)
Escalopes of veal, sauce Bearnaise (2 lbs, veals net 30, breading, and butter to baste 10, sauce 10; 28 orders, 50 cents.)
Deviled ham, puree of potatoes (6 orders, 8 ozs, 12 cents.)
Summer beets (3 large and sauce 6 cents.)
Green peas, corn, tomatoes, potatoes (with seasonings, 50 cents.)
Boiled spice pudding, golden sauce (3 lbs, 20, and sauce 9; 29 cents.)
Gooseberry jelly tarts (22 tarts, 20 cents.)
Frozen custard (with milk, little cheaper than cream, 2 qts, and freezing, 34 cents.)
Cake, crackers, cheese, bread, butter 34.
Milk, cream 34, coffee, tea, sugar 14.
Total, $4 33; 34 persons; nearly 13 cents a plate.

735—Puree of Green Peas Soup, or Potage St. Germaine.

Boil 3 pints of dry peas of a good green color, or 5 pints of fresh green peas in 5 quarts of clear soup stock. Put in a piece of salt pork, about half a pound and a handful of soup vegetables. When the peas are thoroughly done take out the pork, which can be used as boiled meat, and pass the soup and peas through a fine strainer or seive into the soup pot. Season, and keep hot without boiling. Serve toasted bread (croutons) cut very small, a few in each plate, or the kind made as follows.

736—Croutons Soufflees.

These are little squares of fine puff paste, cut no larger than white beans, thrown into hot lard and fried of a very light color.

737—Fillets of Whitefish with Fine Herbs.

"Fine herbs" as applied to several dishes and to "sauce aux fines herbes," means mushrooms, shalots or green onions and parsley minced and mixed together in a light brown sauce.

Take whitefish when fresh and firm, cut the two sides from the back bone, then holding them flat on the table slice them the flat way again with a very sharp knife to make thin, broad pieces. Cut these in strips, double them as you place them in the buttered baking pan to have the boned side up and lean one against the other until the pan is full.

Chop half a can of mushrooms, four young onions and handful of parsley together and strew them among the fillets, also, a dredging of salt and pepper, some bits of butter and the liquor from the can of mushrooms. Bake about half an hour, basting twice with a little light colored veal gravy. Serve one fillet and potatoes in some special form on the same plate.

738—Potatoes a la Victoria.

They are balls of mashed potato egged on top and baked.

Boil 4 potatoes, drain off and mash them with the raw yolk of an egg, pinch of salt and slight grating of nutmeg. Make in round balls about the size of walnuts, place in a baking pan, egg over the tops and a few minutes before dinner put them in the oven to bake a light brown. Serve one or two with fish or use to garnish entrees.

739—Escalopes of Veal a la Bearnaise.

The slices must be thin and of a choice cut to look well; scraps and fragments will make other dishes; the leg or best meat of the loin and ribs will make escalopes.

Cut like small thin steaks about half as large as the palm of the hand, season with a dredging of spiced salt, or with salt and pepper only, egg and bread them in cracker meal, lay in a buttered pan, moisten with oil, clear butter or fresh roast meat fat; brown them handsomely in the oven. Place a spoonful of sauce in the individual dish, the veal in that and ornament with either fried bread in fancy form or pastry leaves or lemon.

740—Sauce Bearnaise.

It is a thick yellow sauce that looks like tartar sauce or mayonaise, but hot and contains minced shalots, mushrooms, truffles and parsley.

Put into a small bright saucepan 4 tablespoons vinegar and 1 of minced young onions, and boil; add 2 ounces best butter (large egg size) and then 4 yolks and stir over the fire until it begins to thicken; add 1 tablespoonful each of minced mushrooms and truffles, little salt, cayenne and finely minced parsley. It is to be cooked enough to set the egg yolks to a buttery thickness, but not enough to cause them to break into curds.

There was a king called Henry the Bearnaise. The word refers either to him or his country.

741—Deviled Ham with Puree of Ploato.

Thin slices ham half the size that are used for breakfast will do for this. Spread them with French mustard, largely diluted with oil and vinegar, or with common mustard as if for sandwiches, lay in a pan and cook them in the oven. Dish a spoonful of mashed potato (sweet potato is better) and a slice of the deviled ham pressed down on it.

742—Boiled Spice Pudding.

4 cups flour—a pound.
2 cups minced suet— 6 ounces.
1 cup molasses—½ pound.
1 heaping cup raisins—½ pound.
1 tablespoon mixed ground spices—cinnamon, nutmeg, cloves, alspice or whichever may be at hand.
1 small teaspoon soda, same of salt.
1 cup milk.
1 egg.
Mix the suet and flour together, put in soda, salt, spices; cut the raisins in halves and throw in. Stir together the egg, milk and molasses, mix up the dry stuff with them, stir thoroughly. Tie up in a pudding bag, leaving a little room to swell, boil 4 or 5 hours. Puddings of this sort should be made before breakfast or over night that they may have plenty of time to boil. They are light, rich and cheap, using the surplus suet from the meat.

Costs 19 cents for three 3 lbs. or 2 quarts.

743—Golden Sauce for Puddings.

1 cup sugar.
1 cup water.
1 heaping teaspoon corn starch.
1 yolk of egg.
1 ounce butter.
Lemon peel or nutmeg.
Boil the sugar and water with the flavoring in it. Mix the starch in a cup with water and thicken, beat in the butter then the yolk or two of them. Costs 8 or 9 cents for a pint.

744—Gooseberry Jelly Tarts.

One making of puff paste or a piece kept

on ice from a previous day will do for the fried souffles for soup (No. 738) for leaf or crescent shapes to decorate an entree, and the remainder for tarts. Roll it out thin, cut out with a cake cutter, press into gem pans, a teaspoon of jelly in each and bake.

745—Trouble with the Fruit Jellies

This is about jelly that "wouldn't jell". It was beautifully pink and clear, however, that is the jelly which the lady of the house and her maids made was, while a quart that the cook made in a sort of short order way for present use was not clear and was rather dark; but it was solid enough to slice when cold. Probably the difference was caused in part by the little lot that was made in haste, having plenty of sugar and the large lot that took all the afternoon and evening to boil and all night to stand and get cold and thin "wouldn't jell" and had to go it all over again, had not. They talked about it beforehand and intended to have the jelly as good as could be made (for small fruit is very abundant here, the best costing only 6 to 8 cents a quart,) but came to a wrong decision about the amount of sugar; one said that the rule was to use a pint of sugar to every pint of fruit juice—that is a pound to a pound—but then, they said, that was for jelly to put away in glass jars or tumblers and keep for a year or more, only to bring out for company, and they only wanted this to keep through the winter and use it when needed and it seemed as though three-quarters of a pound of sugar to a pound (or pint) of juice ought to do, so that was what they allowed and the result was the jelly "wouldn't jell." Perhaps it would have "jell'd" if they had boiled it down more; but then there would not have been so much of it and it would have been as dear as if it had more sugar. I think after all that it was the housekeeper who was to blame, but the jelly stayed soft and they put it back in the kettle next day and put in a lot more sugar without weighing or measuring, only being sure to give it plenty and then boiled it all the afternoon and it came out all right, at least so far as setting solid was concerned, but it was not fine jelly after that, the second boiling took away the good color. They had better have al-

lowed pound for pound at first. It is very likely the cook was half-way glad that jelly "wouldn't jell" through covetousness; for he knew that whether good or bad none of it would come to him and there were pound layer cakes made last evening waiting for jelly to spread them with, tarts for dinner that wanted jelly and some white cake layers to come yet with the ice cream, but he went on saying the jell that all are praising is not the jell for me, and took 2 quarts of ripe gooseberries in a small tin pan with a cover and put in ½ cup water and parboiled them with the steam shut in about ten minutes, then rubbed the pulp and juice through a fine strainer, added 2 cups sugar, set the pan on top of a stove-lid to hold it up from the stove, and let simmer without further attention for 2 hours. Produced 1 quart dark red jelly very firm; good for all ordinary uses in pastry; cost: 2 quarts berries 16, and 1 lb. sugar 8—24 cents.

To make really cheap jellies it is necessary to use apples at the cheapest season; proceed the same as above named for gooseberries and either mix the juice of other fruits with the apple juice to get various kinds, or else merely color and flavor it as desired.

Hurrah for fresh vegetables and sea fish! First arrival. Right here in the heart of an agricultural country canned goods are used as much as a matter of course as if it were a mountain camp; find it is about as difficult to buy poultry as it would be to buy a turtle or terrapin; perhaps these could be obtained by express in even less time than it would take to find a farmer with young ducks or chickens so sell. Instead of inquiring whether a resort is situated in a good farming region, people who desire all the luxuries of the season would do better to ascertain if the express companies reach the point in question. Received:

1 bbl new potatoes, 3 bu @ 75.
2 boxes tomatoes, a bushel, 1 20.
1 bu green pease 1 00.
1 bu turnips 60.
25 heads summer cabbage @ 5.
8 lbs fresh salmon @ 12½.
7 lbs red snapper @ 12½.
Calf's head and feet 75.

Dinner.

July 24.

Soup—Consomme Solferino (6 qts 35 cents).

Sliced tomatoes (10 cents).

Fried black bass, tartar sauce (5 lbs gross breaded and fried 50 sauce 8; 58 cents.)

Potatoes, gastronome.

Boiled meats (nominal, left over for cold.)

Roast lamb, mint sauce (3 lbs 40 cents.)

Roast veal with dressing (1½ lbs and stuffing 23 cents.)

Beef a la mode (2 lbs 25 cents.)

Epigramme of lamb, a l'Allemande, (1½lbs 15; sauce 5; dumpling 5—16 orders 25 cents.)

New potatoes 12, cabbage 12, rice 3, peas 10, corn 7—44 cents.

Queen fritters and sabayon (24 fritters 22; sauce 10; 32 cents.)

Apple and cherry pies (3 pies 27 cents.)

Cake and milk (47 cents.)

Nuts, raisins, cheese, crackers, condiments (34 cents.)

Butter 7, bread 6, coffee, tea, sugar, 16.

Total $4 29, 34 persons; 12½ cents a plate.

746—Consomme Solferino.

A clear brown consomme with white quenelles in the plates.

When boiling the strained broth to clarify it (as at No. 139) add a tablespoonful of whole cloves and alspice, giving the finished consomme a spicy flavor, and add a little extract of meat or a well browned roast chicken to color and enrich it. To make the quenelles; boil ½ cup farina in three times as much milk, as at No. 761, making a stiff porridge ot it, add salt, nutmeg and two raw yolks, pound all together, let cool, then roll up in balls, size of cherries; boil them in water a few minutes, drain off and put half a dozen in each plate.

747—Fried Black Bass, Tartar Sauce

Split the fish, divest them of skin, which can be done by cutting close with a sharp knife or else by dipping in hot water; cut in small pieces, salt well, roll in flour only, and fry in a kettle of hot lard. Serve with potatoes in some special form in the same plate, and tartar sauce in a separate dish.

748—Tartar Sauce.

It is mayonaise sauce with minced pickle, capers and onion added.

Put 2 raw yolks into a pint bowl, add a tablespoon of salad oil and stir together with an egg beater, add more oil and continue stirring, throw in ½ teaspoon of salt and it will become thick almost immediately; then add a teaspoon of vinegar, then 2 of oil and continue until you have enough for the purpose constantly stirring the sauce, adding oil twice and vinegar once alternately and always in very small portions, and at the finish or when you have near a cupful, squeeze in the juice of half a lemon. Mustard and cayenne may be added if wished, but are not essential ingredients of mayonaise sauce.

Mince a few capers and piece of green pickle and a young onion or two extremely fine, drain the mince on a napkin, stir it into the mayonaise and you have tartar sauce. Serve cold in individual sauce dishes or large butter chips.

749—Potatoes a la Gastronome.

Cut raw potatoes in shape of bottle corks, which is done by first cutting in thick slices and then with an apple corer or funnel or a column cutter of graded size proper for the purpose. Boil in salted water and then fry in fresh hot lard and drain on a sieve. Sprinkle with minced parsley, lemon juice and a little clear butter, shake up and serve 3 or 4 in each plate with the fish.

750—Beef a la Mode Jardiniere.

Take a lean piece of beef—about 1½ pounds, and ½ pound salt pork and a turnip and carrot. Choose the pork fat close to the skin because it is tough enough to lard with without breaking. Cut it in strips rather thinner than a common pencil and cut the turnip and carrot the same way. Fill the piece of beef full of these strips drawing them in with a larding needle. Put the beef with the fragments of pork and vegetables into a saucepan, add an onion with a few cloves stuck in it, a bay leaf and soup stock to nearly cover and simmer with the lid on or in the oven 2 or 3 hours. Take it up, either make sauce in the same or add some Spanish sauce, (No. 784) and a little wine, strain, skim off the fat and serve in the dish with the meat carefully sliced across the larding and garnish with a few shapes stamped out of cooked vegetables and warmed in sauce. Small larding is necessary to make this a desirable dish; the slices of meat should show spots no larger than French peas.

751—Epigramme of Lamb a l' Allemande.

It is lamb stew with German dumplings, Allemande signifying German. The sauce is light yellow, the dumplings raised with yeast and strained separately. Chop the breast of lamb into strips, then into pieces of 3 or 4 ribs, wash, stew with a few cut vegetables and season. Take out the meat when done —which will be in less than an hour if young lamb, strain the liquor, add a thickening of flour and 2 yolks. Let the yolks be added after the flour has boiled up in it and do not let boil again. Throw in a little minced parsley and pour the sauce over the pieces of meat. Serve one piece of lamb with sauce and a dumpling at one end.

752—German Dumplings without Eggs or Powder.

Leave out a piece of roll dough from the breakfast breads and keep it cool. About 2 hours before dinner make it out in round balls, set them in steamers, taking care not to cover all the holes, grease the tops to prevent drying, let rise an hour, steam about fifteen minutes. Serve as pot pie dumplings or in such dishes as the preceding, or with sweet sauce or fruit or butter and sugar to take the place of pudding.

753—Queen Fritters Beignets Souffles.

1 cup water—½ pint full measure.

2 ounces butter or lard—large egg size.
1 round cup flour—4 ounces.
5 eggs.
Set the water on to boil in a saucepan and the butter (or lard) in it. Stir in the flour all at once and work the paste thus made with a spoon till smooth and well cooked. Take it from the fire and work in the eggs one at a time, beating in one well before adding another, and when all are in beat the mixture thoroughly against the side of the saucepan. Make some lard hot. It will take half a saucepanful. Drop pieces of the batter about as large as eggs and watch them swell and expand in the hot lard and become hollow and light. Only four or five at a time can be fried because they need plenty of room.

If dropped small, say, not much larger than a walnut, the above will make 25 fritters. They show their remarkable lightness better, however, when made larger.

754—Sauce Sabayon.

Boil together 1 cup sugar and ½ cup water and thicken with cornstarch. Beat 2 or 3 yolks in a bowl with 4 tablespoons of wine and 2 of sugar; when it is frothy with beating pour the thickened sauce to it, whisk again and serve as sauce to fritters and puddings. Other flavorings can be used, rum is frequently employed or brandy when for plum pudding. The golden sauce No. 743 is nearly the same thing if whisked to a foam, and does not require liquor or wine—which suits a temperance house like this we are writing of.

Dinner.

July 25.
Soup—Puree of white beans or, potage a la conde (6 qts 30 cents).
Sliced tomato and cucumber (10 cents).
Salmon au gratin, tartar sauce (3 lbs net @15, breading and sauce 53 cents).
Potatoes, mareschale.
Boiled ham with greens (7 orders, 1 lb ham 15, with greens 20 cents).
Roast beef (2 ribs 3 lbs 36 cents).
Veal with dressing (1½ lbs 20 cents).

Entrecote of pork, Dauphinoise (3 lbs net 40, with dressing 45).

Kromeskies a la Russe (8 orders 16 cents).

Green peas 15, string beans 5, rice with cream 6, tomatoes 8, potatoes 12 (46 cents).

Boiled farina pudding, lemon sauce (3 pts 12, with sauce 18 cents).

Coffee ice cream (1 qt cream, sugar, coffee; 2 qts frozen 35 cents).

Cake assorted (20 cents).

Nuts, raisins, cheese, pickles, condiments (35 cents).

Milk, cream, coffee, tea, bread, butter (55 cents).

Total $4 39 : 35 persons; 12½ cents a plate.

755—Puree of White Beans or, Potage a la Conde.

It is bean soup with milk-added—a cream of beans. Take:

4 cups beans.
1 large onion, carrot, turnip.
1 lb lean salt pork.
5 or 6 quarts soup stock
1 or 2 quarts milk.

Soak the beans in water over night; put them in with the vegetables either whole or in large pieces and boil in the soup stock until the beans are quite soft. The pork which is for seasoning need only be boiled in it an hour then taken up and kept for some other use, as for baked beans etc.

Half an hour before dinner take out the vegetables and pass the soup and beans through a sieve or strainer into the soup pot. Boil the milk, add a little thickening then pour through a strainer into the puree of beans. Season and serve with small conde crusts of a very light color—dried instead of toasted. See also No. 182. The French word probably has reference to a Prince de conde who was very popular in his time.

756—Sliced Tomatoes.

While it is quicker and easier to peel tomatoes if they are first scalded in hot water, they are never so good afterwards, and some people take a little more time and patience and peel them with a sharp knife without scalding. That is the best way. Keep cold and serve with pieces of ice upon them.

These belong to the list of cold *hors d' ouevre* or side dishes; their place in the bill of fare is after the soup when soup is the first dish named; but if raw oysters or clams precede the soup, the tomatoes, cucumbers, olives and similar articles will be written after them. Being generally placed on the table before the beginning of dinner some latitude is taken by the guests as to the time of partaking of such relishes and salads according to individual preferences.

757—Salmon au Gratin.

Means that it is browned in the oven—*A gratin* is a baking pan; anything gratinated is toasted or browned.

Take half the salmon and lay it open without quite dividing; take off the skin with a sharp knife, moisten the fish with a little olive oil, pepper and salt, and let lie in the pan an hour or two. An hour before dinner make some fresh roast meat fat hot in the pan and bake brown in about half an hour, basting once or twice with clear butter. Drain away the grease, or move the fish into a clean pan. Serve small portions cut with a fish slice with tartar sauce at the side and potatoes in some special form on the same plate.

758—Potatoes a la Marechale.

The name for the familiar browned whole potatoes with the difference, however, that these must be all quite round and of one size, made so by cutting out with the largest size of potato spoon which forms them large as crab apples or small tomatoes. New potatoes of a round smooth sort-scraped serve the purpose. Put them in a pan with roast meat fat and cook brown in the oven. Serve with fish or entrees.

759—Entrecote of Pork, Dauphinoise.

Entrecote signifies choice piece, middle cut, the cut between the ribs, generally applied to beef. The use of it is to intimate that it is not plain roast pork but something seasoned.

Cut the meat from the back bone of a

loin or rack of young pork in one long fillet and a portion of the flank with it. Make a roll of it that will be quite small; split the meat if too large when rolled and make two. Before rolling up spread upon it a seasoning of finely minced onion, powdered sage or rosemary, bayleaf also powdered, salt and a little cayenne, tie up with twine, cook in soup stock a while without browning, then roll in egg and cracker meal and bake brown. Bake a few small tomatoes set far apart in a pan so that they will dry away from their juice, and also a few small onions and when time to serve put a spoonful of gravy into the small dish, a slice of the roll of pork and baked tomato and browned onion at the ends for garnish. Dauphinoise is equivalent to saying after the manner of the people of Dauphiny.

760--Kromeskies a la Russe.

Kromeskies are a kind of meat fritter or fish or oyster fritter; for kromeskies can be made of anything that will make croquettes. Mince some veal, lamb or chicken very fine; season with spiced salt, or salt, pepper and nutmeg, mix with a little very stiff sauce made by stirring butter and flour over the fire and adding broth or water, taking care not to get in too much liquor. When cold roll up the preparation like very small sausages; dip into thin fritter batter and fry light colored in fresh lard. Serve with a spoonful of good white sauce placed previously in the dish and sprinkle with finely minced parsley. As these are fried they should be laid on paper to drain. Very few are called for at the first time of serving, the name not being familiar to many, and expensive ingredients may as well be omitted. Make kromeskies of game or lobster same way.

761--Boiled Farina Pudding.

4 cups milk—a quart.
1 small cup farina—4 ounces.
¼ cup sugar.
1 or 2 yolks.
Butter size of an egg.
Boil the milk with the sugar in it, beat in the farina with an egg whisk the same

as making mush. When well mixed put a lid on and let it cook an hour; set it on a brick to raise it from the fire, or in a farina kettle. Beat in the butter before serving and the yolks first beaten with a little milk. The pudding need not be baked. Serve with sauce.

762—Coffee Ice Cream.

1 quart pure sweet cream.
1 cup sugar.
½ cup strong clear coffee.
Mix and freeze.
In order to obtain coffee strong enough not to dilute the cream a cup of made coffee can be boiled up with a heaping tablespoon of ground coffee and then strained into the cream. It is not best to make it too highly flavored.

Dinner.

July 26.
Soup—consomme aux pates d' Italie (6 qts 30 cents).
Sliced tomatoes and cucumbers (10 cents).
Salmon a l'Ecossaise (3 lbs gross @ 13, with sauce 48 cents).
Potatoes au naturel.
Braised tongue a la Flamande (tongue 24 cents, la ded, garnished, 30 cents).
Roast beef (2 ribs 3 lbs 36 cents).
Spring lamb, mint sauce (fore quarter 6 lbs 70 cents).
Pork cutlets, sauce Robert (10 orders 1½ lbs net and sauce 20 cents).
Queen fritters requested and double quantity of other day, (40 fritters with transparent sauce 60 cents).
Green peas 15, string beans 5, cabbage 10, tomatoes 12, rice 5, potatoes 10 (57 cents).
Baked plum pudding (No. 29, with sauce, 35 cents).
Custard pie (2 pies 18 cents).
Cherry water ice (No. 242, 30 cents).
Delicate cake (No. 770, 1 lb 10 cents).
Jelly roll (No. 7, 1 lb 10 cents).
Nuts, raisins, cheese, crackers, pickles, condiments, 39 cents.
Milk, cream, coffee, tea, bread, butter, 60 cents,
Total $5 63; 39 persons; 14½ cents a plate.

763—Consomme with Italian Pastes or aux Pates d' Italie.

It is clear consomme made as for royal (No. 139) with some sort of Italian pastes cooked separately, washed free from meal and put in. These are various, such as alphabet pastes of the same material as macaroni stamped in letters or in fancy figures. There is a short kind of macaroni for the purpose, or common macaroni may be cooked and afterwards cut into quarter inches and put in the consomme. Fidelini, spaghetti and lasagnes are other varities of macaroni which can be used in the same ways.

764—Salmon, Scottish Style or a l'Ecossaise.

Have some water boiling ready, throw in salt enough to make it taste, and half an hour before dinner drop in the fish and boil gently at the back of the stove. Stir some butter to make it soft without melting it and mix in lemon juice and parsley. Cook potatoes with the skins on, peel when done and cut in quarters. Take up the salmon (there should be a fish kettle with a drainer or false bottom to boil fish in) serve small portions individually with the prepared butter for sauce and the cut potatoes on the same plate.

765—Braised Tongue, Flemish Style, a la Flamande.

It is corned tongue larded through lengthwise with strips of fat pork, simmered in a covered saucepan with vegetables and seasonings, sliced across the larding so as to show it, laid upon a spoonful of greens in the individual dish to serve. Anything in the style of Flanders or Holland may be expected to come up with a garniture of greens.

763—Pork Cutlets, Sauce Robert.

Cut pork chops or steaks very small and thin, dredge with salt and pepper and dip into flour; lay them in a frying pan ready. Cook on top of the stove a few minutes before dinner, using roast meat fat or butter and get them brown. Serve a spoonful of sauce Robert in the dish and a cutlet in it and a fried bread crouton for garnish.

767—Sauce Robert.

Named after a French restauranteur of the last century who made it known and valued as an accompaniment to broiled pork.

Mince an onion extremely fine and stir over the fire in a small saucepan with a little oil or clear butter until it is cooked and beginning to brown, then put in a little made mustard, a tablespoonful of vinegar, pepper, and half a cup of light veal gravy or Spanish sauce. Skim off the oil or butter as it rises. Serve without straining—it is a yellowish brown sauce with miinced onion in it.

768—Rice Plain, Southern Way.

The object is to get the grains loose and distinct and served dry although well cooked. Wash a cupful of rice in three waters; put in on to boil in four cups of water and shut up with a lid. Never stir it. When done, or in half an hour, drain off the water; wash it in cold water, pour into a colander to drain, put back into the saucepan with a little salt shaken about in it and let get hot again without more boiling; serve dry.

769—Rich Baked Plum Pudding.

Had broken cake and frosting from party supper, crushed and rolled it to crumbs, took

6 heaped cups of cake crumbs and icing.
6 eggs.
1½ cups milk.
¼ cup brandy.
1 lemon.

Mix eggs and milk together, stir in the cake crumbs, add the grated rind of the lemon and the juice, stir up and bake covered with buttered paper to prevent blistering. Cost; cake 2 lb 10, eggs 8, milk 3, lemon 2, brandy 6; 29 cents for 2 quarts. Serve with sauce sabayon or transparent.

770—Delicate Cake.

One of the very best white cakes.
2 cups granulated sugar—1 pound light weight.
2 cups white butter—¾ pound.
13 whites of eggs—¾ pound.
2 cups corn starch. } 1 pound together.
2 cups flour.
1 teaspoon cream tartar.
1 teaspoon baking powder.
Flavoring extract or little brandy if wished, but not essential; ½ cup milk.
Sift the cream tartar and baking powder in the mixed starch and flour.
Soften the butter and stir it and t e sugar together to a cream; add the whites a little at a time, without previous beating, then the flour and starch and beat well; and at last beat in the milk. Bake either in moulds or in jelly cake pans. If lemons are at hand the juice of one may be used instead of cream tartar; but use no soda in white cakes.

Dinner

July 27.
Soup—cream a la duchesse (8 qts 45 cents).
Scalloped salmon, frizzed potatoes (fish, charged previous days, say, 20 cents).
Boiled corned tongue (2½ lbs, 28 cents).
Corned beef and cabbage (1 lb, and cabbage 16 cents).
Roast beef, (2 ribs, 3 lbs net, 39 cents).
Spring lamb (side, 7 lbs net, 80 cents).
Roast mutton (for second table, 4 lbs, 48 cents).
Grenadins of veal, sauce Napolitaine (8 orders, 1 lb select and sauce 24 cents).
Brochettes of kidney, sauce claremont (4 orders, 10 cents).
Mashed turnips 4, hot slaw 9, green peas 15, stewed tomatoes 15, potatoes two days 15 (57 cents).
Steamed pound pudding, wine sauce (2 lbs and sauce, 28 cents).
Apple tarts (24 tarts, 30 cents).
Boston cream puffs (No. 288; 32 puffs half size, 36 cents).
Sultana cake and pound cake (15 cents).
Vanilla ice cream (2½ qts pure cream, sugar, etc., 70 cents).

Nuts, raisins, cheese, crackers, pickles, condiments (48 cents).
Milk 36, cream 20, butter 20, bread 12 (88 cents).
Coffee 10, tea 3, sugar 4 (17 cents).
Total $6 99; 48 persons; 14½ cents a plate.

771—Cream Soup, a la Duchesse.

A rich white soft soup like cream of chicken with egg custards.
Boil either a chicken or white veal in the stock until quite tender; chop in the meat and pound it in a mortar. Boil a cup of rice and when done and drained pound it also with the meat and pass throuh a sieve. Use 4 or 5 quarts of seasoned stock, 2 or 3 quarts rich milk and the puree of chicken and rice to thicken.
Beat 4 eggs slightly, season with nutmeg, salt and pepper; put in a deep pan and cook either in steamer or in pan of water in the oven. Cut out cork shapes of custard with a column cutter and put in the soup just before serving.

772—Scalloped Salmon, Plain or au Vin.

Take cold cooked salmon which may have been left from a previous day and some other fish or canned salmon to make enough, and pick it into pieces of even size without bones. Mix finely minced bread and cracker meal in equal quantities. Butter a baking pan, cover the bottom with the crumbs, place fish enough to cover that, and plenty of crumbs again on top.
Take soup stock and milk if to be in plain style, or soup stock and white wine if that way, enough to thoroughly moisten, season with pepper and salt, pour over the scallop and bake brown. Cut out squares, place on the dishes as neatly as possible, add a border of frizzed potatoes for decoration.

773—Frizzed Potatoes.

The same as Julienne (No. 729) but shred much finer. Slice raw potatoes with a Saratoga cutter, then place the slices upon each other and shred them. Fry almost white in fresh lard. Serve as a garnish.

774—Grenadins of Veal, Napolitaine.

Small selected veal steaks, size of the palm of the hand, larded with a few strips of fat pork, baked in a quick oven, served with sauce in the dish.

Slice the leg of veal for them and use the trimmings in soup or stews. Draw the lardoons through so that a dozen ends will cluster in the middle of each grenadin. Butter a pan, strew a very little minced onion, salt and pepper; place the veal close together; bake light brown. Have some clear soup stock boiled down to glaze and baste them with it while baking.

775—Sauce Napolitaine.

Mix grated horseradish in thin white sauce, made by thickening strong chicken broth with white roux. Butter sauce diluted will answer the purpose ordinarily— the horseradish is the chief ingredient.

776—Brochettes of Kidneys and Ham.

Slice up the kidneys that may have accumulated, and small pieces of ham, cut them to one size as near as can be, and not larger than a silver half dollar. Run them on iron skewers, a slice of kidney and a slice of ham alternately until the skewers are full. Trim off corners with a straight cut, lay in a pan and bake. Serve in a spoonful of sauce in the dish, pushing off the portion from the skewer with a fork.

These may also be fried in hot fat and served for breakfast; also breaded and fried.

777—Sauce Claremont.

Mince onions and stir over the fire in a little oil until cooked; add brown sauce or light veal gravy; skim off the oil as it rises.

778—Hot Slaw.

1 or 2 heads white cabbage.

1 cup vinegar.
1 cup water.
4 yolks of eggs.
1 tablespoon butter.
1 tablespoon salt.

Shred the cabbage fine, mix the yolks well with some water, put everything into a saucepan or into the sink of the steam chest and stir occasionally until it reaches boiling point; then keep it where it will not boil. This makes a yellow sort of cream dressing in the cabbage; but boiling curdles the egg and would make it not so good. Add minced red pepper if you have it; some add sugar.

779—Hot Slaw Another Way.

The common hotel way of making hot slaw is to put the shred cabbage into a large saucepan with roast meat or bacon fat and vinegar and stir it over the fire until the cabbage is partly cooked and the vinegar has dried out, making a sort of imitation of sour krout; it is cheap.

780—Steamed Pound Pudding.

1 pound sugar—any kind.
¾ pound butter.
10 eggs.
1 pound flour.

Stir the butter and sugar together; add the eggs, two at a time, not beaten; when all are in add the flour. Beat up well. Use part to steam in a mould or pan for pudding. It takes from one to one and a half hours to steam; must have a good lid on or paper cover under the lid and plenty of steam. As the pudding is sliced like cake and "goes a good way" there will be some of the batter to spare to bake a pound cake at the same time. Serve sauce with the pudding. If no wine, add some fruit juice to the syrup made of sugar and starch and boil until clear.

781—Apple Tarts.

Made of puff paste and cooked apple put through a colander and well sweetened. Canned apples will answer when fresh cannot be had.

Roll out puff paste, cut flats and line large patty pans or jem pans, put in a tablespoon of apple and bake. A favorite sort of pastry, richer than apple pie and sells well at the fine bakeries.

782—Eclairs a la Creme

The French name for cream puffs No. 288 when filled with whipped cream. In places where pure cream can be obtained, as at this summer resort, instead of using the pastry custard take cream, set in a pan of ice water, sweeten, and then whip with the wire egg-whisk until it is frothy and thick. Flavor with vanilla or lemon; cut the puffs open at top fill with whipped cream and replace the piece. Cream puffs can be made for 15 cents a dozen of small size with eggs at a low price, and cream.

783—Sultana Cake

Make delicate cake, No 770, and add to it a pound of sultana seedless raisins.

784—Spanish Stock Sauce.

When the number of people to be provided for amounts to forty or fifty, it is a saving of labor to keep stock sauces on hand; the most useful is that which has come to be called Spanish sauce, containing a small proportion of tomatoes.

It will have to be made every second or third day and kept cold until all is used. Take a large saucepan, pour into it about a cupful of the clear oil of melted butter and lay in some pieces of raw ham—the rough ends will do but no smoky outside. Throw in 6 or 8 onions or leeks or both, cut in large pieces, as much turnips and carrots, a tablespoon of cloves and some allspice and crushed black pepper, lay on these some soup bones, veal shank and neck, flank of beef and any small pieces that can be spared and set over the fire without any water but with a lid on to stew and slowly become light brown, stirring it frequently with a long wooden paddle. In about half an hour or an hour, according to the heat of the fire, put in a small can of tomatoes and 5 or 6 quarts of soup stock or part water, and a handful of salt. Let cook slowly for 2 hours then thicken with flour to be about like a tolerably thick soup, and presently strain it off through a fine gravy strainer and set it away to become cold. The fat can be taken off when cold. There should not be enough tomatoes used to make everything the sauce goes in taste of them.

The uses of this Spanish sauce are to add to soups of several kinds. Mock Turtle, green turtle and other such soups are half made when this sauce is made, and a number of brown sauces need only certain other ingredients, such as fried minced onion or mushrooms to be added to the stock sauce, to bring them to an easy completion.

Dinner

July 28
Soup—Mock turtle (8 qts, 60 cents.)
Sliced tomatoes and cucumbers (10 cts.)
Fish—Redfish au court-bouillon (4 lbs and sauce 56 cents)
New Potatoes.
Corned beef and tongue (12 orders 22 cents.)
Roast beef (1 rib 2½ lbs 30 cents.)
Roast leg mutton (4 lbs net 50 cts.)
Fricandeau of veal, Italienne (2 lbs veal, lardoons, sauce, 40 cts.)
Small patties a la Toulouse (8 orders 24 cents.)
String beans in espagnole 10, cabbage 10, stewed turnips 5, rice 5, potatoes 15, beets in vinegar 4, (49 cents.)
Apple pie, old style (3 pies 25 cents.)
Boiled cinnamon pudding, hard sauce (3 lbs and sauce 30 cents.)
Vanilla frozen custard (3 qts and freezing 60 cents.)
Cakes and star kisses (No 5; 20 cents.)
Nuts, raisins, crackers, cheese, pickles, condiments, (48 cents.)
Milk, cream, butter, bread, coffee, tea, sugar, (1,00)
Total, $6.24; 48 persons; 13 cents a plate.

785—Mock Turtle Soup

Light brown, rather like a thin gravy with square cut pieces of calf's head in it and chopped hard boiled yolks, wine and lemon.

Boil a calfs head and feet for 2 hours—the head previously split and tongue and brains taken out. Take the calf's head liquor 4 qts and Spanish stock (No. 784) 4 quarts, mix, boil, thicken slightly, strain, skim free from grease. Cut half the calf's head into large dice and add salt, cayenne, little sherry and juice of half of a lemon and chopped yolks of 2 eggs

If no stock sauce on hand, and the soup must be started from the beginning, butter the bottom of a saucepan and lay in 2 slices of lean ham, a handful of onions, same of turnips and carrots and fry them together. Put in half can tomatoes, two bay leaves, cloves, parsley, thyme, the calf's head liquor and strong soup stock made in the usual way, enough to make about 2 gallons. Boil an hour and thicken either with roux or flour and water, Strain, add calf's head, wine lemon juice. sherry, salt and cayenne.

786—Redfish au Court-Bouillon.

This is one of the specialties of New Orleans and all Southern hotels and restaurants. The court-bouillon is not the same seasoned stock for boiling a whole fish in, that is generally known by that name and which contains wine, but is a sort of soup of onions, thyme, garlic, olive oil and tomatoes in which the slices of fish are stewed and both fish and sauce served together. No one of the ingredients named should be in excess, but all in moderate proportions. It is a standing dish on the breakfast bills of fare of the best hotels in the Southern cities, trout, snapper, or other good fish taking the place according to the market. Without expecting it to meet with any particular appreciation in this little community. I let it appear once for novelty, our butcher's little shipment of sea fishes allowing the opportunity.

787—Sauce Court-Bouillon.

½ cup olive oil
½ cup minced young onions.
3 cloves (quartered) of garlic
1 teaspoon thyme—green or dried but on powdered.
½ cup flour.
½ cup tomatoes.
4 cups soup stock.
Salt and pepper
Take a flat-bottom saucepan, put in the oil, onions, garlic, thyme, and let them cook over the fire a few minutes

with constant stirring, put in the flour and stir that about until the mixture (which is a seasoned roux) begins to brown. Add the soup stock (or broth or water) and let boil u p, and then the tomatoes. Season with salt and pepper. Skim off the oil while it is boiling.

Cut fish in slices and cook it in the sauce. Serve fish and sauce together with toast either under the slice of fish or as a garnish at the edge. Rice is also served with this dish the same as with a curry, by way of variety.

788—Fricandeau of Veal, Italienne.

It is a piece of veal larded, cooked and glazed in its own gravy. Take any lean piece such as the shoulder with the bone removed, or part of the flank, or the leg and lard it full of strips of fat salt pork the same as for beef a la mode or larded and braised tongue. Cut the pork close to the skin and it will be found better to lard with than bacon, which is too strongly flavored. The larding finished, put the scraps of pork in a baking pan of small size and depth, also some pieces of turnip, carrot and onion, sweet herbs if at hand, such as thyme and parsley; put in the veal, thin a little broth and wine, cover with a buttered paper and bake in a moderate oven about an hour, basting occasionally.

Take up the meat when done in another pan, strain the remaining liquor, skim it, glaze the meat by pouring it over and letting dry in the hot closet. Slice the meat so that the lardings will show and serve small cuts with Italian sauce in the dish and two or three olives for garnish.

789—Italian Sauce, Brown.

1 cup brown sauce (roast meat gravy skimmed, strained and thickened.)
1 teaspoon minced onion.
2 of minced mushrooms.
Same of parsley.
Juice of 1 lemon.
Cayenne and salt.
Pour half the juice from a can of mushrooms into the brown sauce, add the other ingredients and boil for 15 minutes. A better appeance can be secured if time allows when serving to retain the parsley

which loses color in the sauce and add it in each dish. If Spanish sauce be at hand it can be used in place of meat gravy.

790--Small Patties a la Toulouse.

Puff paste shells filled with a ragout of brains, chicken and mushrooms.

Boil the brains taken from the calf's head used for soup, cut when cold into large dice, cut white meat of chicken the same way and slice a proportion of mushrooms. It does not take much to fill patties, perhaps half cupful of each will be sufficient. Make white sauce, season well, put in the meats and keep hot to fill the patties with as wanted. Toulouse is a part of France where the most mushrooms were found before they were grown artificially.

791—String Beans in Espagnole.

Boil the beans and pour over them rich meat gravy or brown sauce No. 576.

792—Boiled Cinnamon Pudding.

The English suet pudding No. 732, with a teaspoonful of ground cinnamon added has a pink color and forms another variation among the kinds which can be made with suet, saving butter and eggs.

Dinner.

July 29

Soup—Consomme imperial} (8 qts 56 cents.)

Red snapper a l'Indienne (3 lbs and sauce 48 cents.)

Rice au gratin (with the fish instead of potatoes.)

Boiled ham with greens (8 orders 1 lb and greens 18 cents.)

Roast beef (sirloin 5 lbs 65 cents.)

Shoulder of veal stuffed (4 lbs in all 50 cents.)

Calf's head, turtle style (½ head and feet 40 with sauce 55 cents.)

Scallops of mutton a la Provencale (8 orders 1 lb net and sauce 18 cents.)

Baked beans and pork (1 lb beans 4 oz pork 2 qts 10 cents.)

Summer beets 9, cabbage 5, green peas 15, corn 15, potatoes 2 ways 12, (58 cents.)

Cracked wheat pudding with maple syrup (No. 392; with sauce 24 cents.)

Apple cream pie (4 pies 33 cents.)

Lemon ice cream (starch and milk, no eggs, 3 qts and freezing 40 cents.)

Cake assorted kinds (2 lbs 20 cents.)

Nuts, raisins, crackers, cheese, pickles, (average 49 cents.)

Milk, cream, butter, bread, coffee, tea, sugar, $1 00.

Total, $6.44; 49 persons; fraction-over 13 cents a plate.

793—Consomme Imperial.

Almost the same as royal, No. 139. The egg custards can be cut with a round cutter instead of in diamonds, and add a half pint of Madeira or sherry. A liberal allowance of extract of meat should be used when desired to make this consomme of good quality in places where there is no poultry to be had, and the extract makes it unnecessary to use coloring, as it imparts a very rich color itself.

794—Red Snapper a l'Indienne, or with Curry Sauce.

Fish baked in curry sauce with a border of rice baked with it in the same dish.

Any dish that is said to be a l'Indienne may be expected to contain curry powder or curry paste.

Brush a baking pan or dish with butter, skin 3 lbs of fish and cut it into suitable pieces to serve. About half the people will not take fish and this amount will make from 24 to 30 portions. Place them in the dish in close order.

Take some cooked rice, season it with salt and milk and 1 egg or the yolk only and make a raised border of it all around the edge of the baking dish. Use a wet knife to smooth it over. Set the dish in the oven for 15 minutes for the fish to become partly cooked then pour in enough curry sauce to almost cover, and bake again until the surface of both fish and rice border is brown. Serve a portion of rice with each order and the curry sauce belonging.

795—Curry Sance

Mince an onion extremely fine, put it in a small saucepan with butter and stir over the fire until it is cooked without browning; put in three times as much grated cocoanut as there was onion (dry cocoanut will do but not sweet) and a heaped teaspoonful of curry powder. When these are hot add a pint of light brown sauce (No 576) or Spanish sauce or fresh made gravy from the meat pans. Skim off the fat, add a pinch of cayenne and pour it over the fish or chicken or whatever is to be baked in the above receipt.

796—Calf's Head, a la Tortue, or in Turtle Style.

Calf's head previously cooked, cut in pieces in a brown sauce containing olives, mushrooms, wine quenelles or egg balls and mushroom liquor. Cut the half head and the boneless feet reserved from the mock turtle soup, making into pieces of even size and put them in a saucepan of Spanish sauce (No 784) or good bright pan gravy with a seasoning of tomato, add a small portion of each of the ingredients above named, and make hot. The olives should have the stones taken out by means of a small corer out of the column box, or by running a penknife around. It is a great improvement to the appearance to add egg-balls as a garniture. Tortue is French for turtle.

797—Egg Quenelles for Turtle Sauce and Soup.

2 hard boiled yolks.
½ as much hot boiled potato.
1 teaspoon chopped parsley.
Cayenne and salt.
1 raw yolk.
Mash all together. Make up in balls size of cherries, with flour on the hands. Poach them a minute or two in a frying-pan of boiling water. Take up on a skimmer and drop them into the soup.

798—Forcemeat Balls or Quenelles.

½ a calf's tongue, cooked, or some cold veal.
½ the weight of fine bread crumbs.
2 or 3 tablespoons melted butter.
Seasoning of sweet herbs, and nutmeg.
Pepper and salt.
1 raw egg.
Mince the meat small, add the other ingredients, and pound them all together. Make up in little balls, with flour on the hands. Poach them in boiling water and put them in the soup.

The above two mixtures can be used as croquettes, made into shapes, and fried and are good to place as ornamental acessories in the sauces to fish and meats.

799—Scallops of Mutton, Provencale or Creole

A scallop of meat is a thin slice or steak, as is the Scotch collop and the French escalope. Anything a la Provencale in French cookery is the same as a la Creole in American, it implies tomatoes, onions, cayenne, oil, wine and sometimes garlic.

For this dish cut small slices of mutton, saute them first in a frying pan, light brown, then simmer in water, stock or sauce until they are tender and add sufficient strained tomatoes to serve as a sauce. Season the meat and sauce while stewing with onion, salt and pepper, A leaf shape of fried bread is a good ornament to the dish.

800—Apple Cream Pie

2 cups stewed apple—a pint.
1 cup sugar—½ pound.
1 cup milk.
½ cup butter—¼ pound
4 eggs (or 8 yolks if any left over)
½ cup sherry or nutmeg or lemon flavoring.
Have the apples dry by cooking with scarcely any water but the steam shut in, mix apples, sugar and butter together and milk and eggs together, stir up all and flavor. Make 5 cupfuls, enough for 4 pies large family size to cut in 6 or 8, like a custard with no top crust. Cost, with wine 31 cents, without wine 25; crust for 4 pies 8 cents.

Dinner

July 30.
Soup—Potage a l' Andalouse (8qts.-48 cents.)
Sliced cucumbers and tomatoes (12 cts.)
Broiled whitefish, Venitienne (4 lbs and sauce 52 cents.)
Potatoes dauphine.
Boiled corned tongue (28 cents)
Roast beef (1 rib 2½ lbs net 32 cents)
Spring lamb, mint sauce, (6 lbs and sauce 75 cents.)
Veal stew a la Milanaise (1½ lbs and trimmings 23 cents.)
Rissoles of sweetbreads with truffles (28 orders 60 cents.)
Beets in sauce 10, rice 5, green peas 15, string beans 4, corn 15, tomatoes 8, potatoes 12, (69 cents.)
Steamed currant roll (No. 809; 2 lbs with sauce 18 cents.)
Pumpkin pie (No. 810; without eggs, 3 large, 20 cents.)
Rasberry tarts (24 tarts 30 cents.)
Delmonico ice cream (No 201; 3 qts 80 cents.)
Chocolate and rose kisses (No 461; 20 cents.)
Cake, assorted kinds (15 cents.)
Milk, cream, butter, bread, cheese, pickles, coffee, tea, sugar and crackers (1.15)
Total, $6.97; 49 persons; fraction over 14 cents a plate.

The dinner above prepared for 49 persons was partaken of by only 32, the rest being away across the lake. Much provision was left over to be taken care of as best it may, some for supper and breakfast, some for the next day's dinner.

801— Potage a l'Andalouse.

Andalusian or Spanish soup. Make same as directed for Spanish sauce with twice as much tomatoes. It is a brown tomato soup with a light flavor of garlic. Serve a few croutons in the plates.

802—Broiled Whitefish, Venetian Sauce.

Split the fish and cut in small pieces. Broil in the oyster broiler only a few minutes before it is wanted. Serve Venetian sauce and dauphine potatoes in the same plate with the fish.

803—Venetian Sauce for Fish

Make drawn butter (butter sauce) a little thinner than usual for that sauce, with a liberal amount of the best butter beaten in. Add the juice of half a lemon, some minced parsley and minced capers. A cupful of sauce is enough and the expense is small for just sufficient to fill the bill.

804 — Potatoes a l. Dauphine.

They are potato croquettes of a flattened shape.
Take 4 or 5 potatoes out of the steamer and mash them with the yolk of 1 egg, salt and a grating of nutmeg. If very dry a small lump of butter may be added. Make them out in flattened pats, very much like figs as they are pressed in boxes, dip in egg and cracker meal and fry to a fine yellow color in hot lard. Serve with fish or with meat entrees. Potatoes in this form are fine as ornaments but most tedious of any to prepare, requiring three or four separate operations.

805—Veal Stew. Milanaise

Stew pieces of veal the same as for potpie; also, boil 4 ounces of macaroni broken in short lengths and when done drain dry and season it. Dish up macaroni in the individual dish with stewed veal placed upon it. Milanaise means in Italian style, or of the city of Milan in Italy.

806—Rissoles of Sweetb.eads with Truffles.

Sweetbreads cut small in very stiff sauce rolled up in pie-paste and fried.
Boil and then cut small 4 or 5 sweetbreads. Take ½ cup of minced onion and the same of mushrooms and ½ cup butter and stir them over the fire, then put in ½ cup sifted flour and when that is heated through, add a cup of broth or mushroom liquor from the can gradually, stirring it up to a very thick sauce. Sea-

son with salt, pepper and nutmeg and then mix in the sweetbreads. Let the mixture become cold. There will be about 32 ounces, making 32 rissoles. Add a slice of truffle to each one. Roll out good pie paste as thin as card board, cut squares the length of a finger place the sweetbread mixture in the middle, roll up with the ends doubled in and touch the edge with a little beaten egg to make it stick. Drop into a kettle of lard moderately hot and fry light-colored. Serve a good sauce in the dish, or green peas in sauce by way of garnish to the rissole.

807—Corn and Tomatoes.

Cut corn from the cob and instead of the usual milk dressing, mix it with stewed tomatoes, salt and little butter, and serve.

808—Sweet Tomatoes.

Peel tomatoes and put them in a pan with sugar enough to cover and bake in a slow oven. The sugar melts, then dries down to syrup, and tomatoes that way are esteemed a luxury among dinner vegetables by many at the South

809—Currant Suet Roll.

One of the cheapest and best boiled puddings.
3 cups flour—¾ pound
2 large cups minced suet—½ pound.
1 heaped cup raisins or currants—½ lb.
1 cup water.
Salt.
Mix all together. Make the dough into a long roll, solid; tie it up in a cloth, pin or sew in two places, boil 2 hours. It is best when the dough is made up very soft, almost too soft to be handled. Dip in cold water when done to get it out of the cloth, serve with sauce.

810—Sauce Diplomate for Puddings.

Sugar and water boiled and thickened with flour, allowed to simmer until clear, red fruit juice or wine, lemon and mace added.

811—Pumpkin Pie without Eggs—Richer.

4 cups stewed squash or pumpkin—a quart.
½ cup sugar.
¼ cup butter.
2 large basting spoons of flour and water to thicken it.
1 teaspoon cinnamon.
1 teaspoon ground ginger.
Melt the butter, stir all together. Fill two or three pies and bake a long time. Cost; a quart pumpkin 8, sugar 2, butter 3, spice 1; 14 cents. crust 2 cents each pie.

812—Pumpkin Butter for Tarts.

4 cups pumpkin cooked dry.
2 cups sugar.
½ cup butter.
Grated rind of a lemon or some kind of spice flavor. Mash the pumpkin through a colander, mix in the other ingredients, stew down rich and thick. Will keep a long time.

Dinner.

July 31.
Soup—Consomme Milanaise (7 qts 40 cents).
Tomatoes, cucumbers, pickled beets on the table (12 cents).
Fillets of trout a la Morney (6 lbs grass and trimmings 70 cents).
Potatoes au gratin.
Boiled tongue (from previous day).
Roast beef (reserved from previous day.)
Roast pork, apple sauce (3½ lbs and sauce 47 cents.)
Rib-ends beef and Yorkshire pudding (No. 144; 3 lbs ribs 21, pudding, No, 815; 11, 14 orders 32 cents.)
Lamb stew, jardiniere (3 lbs. lamb and trimmings 40 cents)
Green corn fritters, cream sauce (20 fritters and sauce 20 cents.)
String beans 2, beets 4, cabbage 10, tomatoes 12, rice 4, potatoes 14, (46 cents.)
West Point pudding (No, 820; 2 qts and sauce 20 cents.)
Frozen rice custard (No, 222; 3 quarts

and freezing 50 cents.)
　Cake, assorted kinds (20 cents.)
　Milk, buttermilk, cream (47 cents.)
　Nuts, raisins, cheese, crackers, pickles, coffee, tea, butter, bread,(75 cents)
　Total, $5.44; 48 persons; 11½ cents a plate.

The dinner above prepared for 48 was partaken of by only 37, the others being out on excursions, There will be some waste and things available— such as cold meats—for succeeding meals, and pastry-cake and ice cream disappear by mysterious means after meals and at night.

813—Consomme Milanaise.

Clear consomme with short cut macaroni or spaghetti or fidelini in it and red corned or smoked tongue cut in shreds size of Julienne vegetables. Cook the macaroni or spaghetti separately, wash off in cold water and place ready to drop a spoonful in each plate—precaution to avoid spoiling the clearness of the consomme. The shred tongue makes no difference.

814—Fillets of Trout, a la Morny

Small fillets doubled up in order in a dish, a raised border of potato around and all baked brown, with sauce. Morny is the title of a French duke. A large platter such as is used to dish up a whole turkey for a family dinner, should be devoted to the purpose of cooking fish in this way, which is like the rice-bordered dish No. 794, and if it can be a metal chafing-dish of the same shape it, will be the better. If no dish can be had a shallow baking pan can be made to answer tolerably well, but it does not hold the border above the fish gravy.
Cut as many thin slices lengthwise of the fish as there will be orders, which may be about two thirds the number of people, place them, doubled, close together till the dish is full. Mash potatoes with egg-yolk salt and nutmeg same as for croquettes and make a border all around and brush with egg. Mince a small onion, twice as much mushrooms, strew them amongst the fillets. Add half cup white wine to a pint or white sauce

(No. 819) pour over the fish and bake on the bottom of the oven about half an hour. Serve potatoes, a fillet of fish and some of the sauce in the same plate.

815—Yorkshire Pudding with Roast Meats.

A rich egg-batter pudding; can also be served with sweet sauce.
　1½ cups flour—6 ounces.
　3 cups milk—1½ pints.
　1 ounce butter, melted.
　3 eggs.
　Salt.
　½ teaspoon baking powder.
　Mix the flour and milk carefully not to have it full of lumps, add the melted butter, salt, pinch of powder, the eggs well beaten and beat up thoroughly. Butter a small baking pan and make it warm in the oven, pour the batter in only about ½ inch deep and bake 15 or 20 minutes. Water instead of milk can be used, but then a tablespoon of syrup should be added to cause it to brown quickly without drying out. Cut squares and serve with roast beef and gravy.

816—Lamb Stew, a la Jardiniere.

Jardiniere is French for gardener; the made jardiniere always implies the use of a mixed lot of vegetables. There are jardiniere cutters to be bought which cut vegetables in various fancy shapes effecting a great saving of time.
Chop up the breasts and neck of lamb or mutton, stew until tender, let boil nearly dry, skim, season and thicken the liquor that remains. Cut carrots, white and yellow turnips, Kohl-rabi or cabbage-turnips, leeks, onions and string beans, all or any of them, into dice or like peas with a scoop cutter, and boil until done, drain off and pour some Spanish sauce or light brown sauce to them. Serve the vegetables as a border in the dish with stewed lamb in the center.

817—Green Corn Fritters.

　1 heaped cup corn.
　½ cup butter.
　½ cup flour.

1 cup milk or water.
1 egg.
Salt and pepper.
Batter to fry in.

The corn may be either from a can of the dry solid packed sort or else green corn shaved off the cob.

Make white roux first by stirring the butter and flour over the fire, add milk to make stiff sauce, stir in the corn, season, and then put the mixture which is a stiff paste an inch deep in the pan to get cold. Cut pieces two inches long, dip in thin batter (same as if made for pancakes) and fry light colored in hot lard. Have a cupful of cream sauce ready and serve a spoonful under each fritter. Another and easier way may be found by reference to the index.

818—Cabbage au Veloute.

Means cabbage in white sauce, as en Espagnole means brown sauce. Chop the cabbage, season it, serve a spoonful to a dish with sauce veloute poured over it.

819—Sauce Veloute.

Is white sauce but not cream sauce which latter is called Bechamel. The word veloute means velvety or smooth. To make the sauce take some chicken or veal broth boiled down strong enough to be jelly when cold, but, without cooling it strain through a napkin and use it to make butter sauce thinner than is usually made; and after that let it slowly boil and the butter (that the roux was made with) will rise to the top. Skim it off and you have a bright veloute that is not greasy and can be used as a stock sauce for white dishes and for fish. This is one of the main stock sauces in systematic cookery but in point of fact is not so necessary as brown sauce and therefore is not made in every place.

820—West Point Pudding.

Brown cracked wheat pudding with molasses and raisins.

4 heaped cups cracked wheat mush.
½ cup molasses.

1 cup minced suet—4 ounces.
2 or 3 eggs.
3 cups milk.
1 teaspoon ground cinnamon.
1 cup raisins or currants.

Take cracked wheat mush that was left over from breakfast and is well-cooked and dry, mix in the other ingredients, eggs last and well beaten, and bake in a slack oven an hour. Maple syrup is good sauce for it, but hard sauce (No 177) is the favorite.

Dinner.

August 1.
Soup—Croute-au-pot (8 qts. 40 cents.)
Tomatoes, cucumbers, (12 cents.)
Boiled whitefish, parsley sauce (3 lbs. and sauce 34 cents.)
New potatoes browned.
Tongue, corned beef, ham (nominal, 3 orders, rest left over.)
Roast beef (2 ribs cut short, 3 lbs. 36 cents.)
Spring lamb (6 pounds and sauce 75 cents.)
Sweetbreads, au beurre noir (18 orders, sweetbreads 50, butter 10, olives, lemon 11; 71 cents.)
Ragout of veal, a la Julienne (7 orders 16 cents.)
Green peas 15, beets 4, cabbage 10, succotash 15, rice 5, potatoes 12 (60 cts.)
Boiled lemon pudding (No. 827; 3 lbs. with sauce 27 cents.)
Ripe gooseberry pie (3 pies 27 cents.)
Tea, ice cream (2 qts. and freezing 60 cents.)
Chocolate eclairs (No. 296; 24 small 38 cents.)
Cake, ripe fruit, cheese, crackers, (21 cents.)
Milk, buttermilk, cream (40 cents.)
Butter, bread, coffee, tea (38 cents.)
Total $ 5.95; 46 persons, 13 cents a plate.

The dinner above prepared for 46, part taken by only 37; the others away on summer rambles.

821—Croute-au-Pot Soup.

Crust-pot or crust soup; a good soup of mixed vegetables and small toast. Make the vegetable soup No. 140 and add tomatoes, or the tomato soup No. 166, and add more vegetables. Cut some slices of bread extremely thin and then in small pieces and toast them in the oven. Drop a few in each plate when serving.

822—Boiled Whitefish, Parsley Sauce.

Set on the poissoniere or fish-kettle half-full of water, put in an onion stuck with cloves, a bayleaf, salt, a handful of parsley and half cup vinegar. When it boils put in the fish on the moveable drainer bottom and boil gently about half an hour. Slide off the drainer on to a dish. Serve by cutting portions with a broad fish slice. Parsley sauce and new potatoes in the same plate.

823—Parsley Sauce.

Make good butter sauce (No. 573)and add to it a cupful of chopped parsley while at boiling heat.

824—Sweetbreads au Beurre Noir

Some epicures, apparently have discovered an agreeable new zest in butter browned by frying, for it has been employed as a flavoring in sweets as well as in meat sauces. The English call it nut brown butter. Prepare the sweetbreads by boiling and pressing and when cold slice thinly, season and dip both sides in flour and have them ready in a pan. Shortly before dinner make a cupful of butter hot in a frying pan. While it is frothy and beginning to brown lay in the floured sweetbreads and give them time to get brown on both sides. Serve when done with a little of the butter upon them, two or three olives and quarter of lemon in the dish.

825—Ragout of Veal, Julienne.

A ragout is a mixture of meats and ther edibles cut small in a sauce. Elaborate mixtures of this sort are some-oimes served like a sauce to larger meats, and again, are served in this way. Cut a piece of veal into large dice and a kidney and slice or two of salt pork into pieces only half as large. Stir them over the fire in a saucepan with a spoonful of fat or oil until they are slightly browned, then drain off all the fat throw in a few sliced mushrooms, a sprinkling of onion and garlic and pour in enough Spanish sauce to cover, or, if no sauce ready use light brown gravy.

For the border cut Julienne vegetables as if for soup, boil them, drain, mix in a white sauce (some of the same made for the fish) and put a spoonful in each dish, making a hollow with the spoon and the ragout in the middle.

A Saratoga potato slicer is a help in cutting Julienne, which is rather a tedions operation without. The thin slices can be laid together and shreded finely.

826—Succotash.

Corn and beans mixed together is called succotash; butter beans is the kind preferred but all sorts of green garden beans are used. Season as corn alone would be seasoned, with a little sauce made of milk, butter and salt, or, with salt alone.

827—Boiled Lemon Pudding.

A lemon suet pudding; pale yellow, rich.

2 cups flour—½ pound.
2 cups minced suet—½pound.
2 solid cups minced bread—½pound.
½ cup sugar
2 lemons.
2 eggs.
2 cups milk—a pint.
½ teaspoon soda.
Same of salt.

Make the bread crumbs fine by grating or mincing. Grate the lemon rinds into it, put soda in flour, mix dry articles together, wet with the eggs and milk and stir up thoroughly. Tie up in pudding bag or mould and boil 2 hours. Cost of pudding 21 cents for 3 pounds or two quarts.

828—Tea Ice Cream.

Can only be made with pure sweet, cream as it is not good with custard or starch, but fine if made right. Sweeten 2 quarts of cream with 2 cups sugar and add 1 cup strong tea made as for drinking and freeze as usual.

Dinner.

August 2.

Soup—Consomme Calcutta (6 quarts 35 cents.)

Sliced tomatoes and cucumbers (on table; 10 cents.)

Fillets of sole, a la tartare (5 pounds grass and sauce 70 cents.)

Potatoes duchesse.

Corned beef and cabbage (2 lbs and cabbage 21 cents.)

Roast beef (from previous day and 1 lb 13 cents.

Spring lamb, mint sauce (fore quarter 6 lbs 75 cents.

Veal with dressing (shoulder boned, 3 lbs net and dressing 45 cents.)

Scrambled sweetbreads, puree of peas (part charged yesterday; 20 cents.)

Turnips mashed 5, rice 5, string beans 4, corn 12, tomatoes 10, potatoes 12 (48 cents.)

Pineapple fritters (2 cans pineapple 50, batter, frying 10, sauce 7, 30 fritters 67 cents.)

Raspberry tarts (small open pies, puff paste, cut in three; 18 orders 27 cents.)

Vanilla jelly (1 qt 25 cents.)

Chocolate ice cream (3 pints cream, 1 pint milk 2 oz chocolate etc, 60 cents.)

Cakes assorted (1 lb 10 cents)

Milk, cream, buttermilk (40 cents.)

Nuts, raisins, cheese, crackers, condiments (38 cents.)

Coffee, tea, butter, bread, sngar (32 cents.)

Total $6,36; 43 persons, nearly 15 cents a plate.

829—Consomme Calcutta.

Clear consomme with a teaspoonful of pulp of tomato curry, and cayenne (or Tobasco or Chili sauce) in each plate.

Make and clarify the consomme according to directons for royal at No 139 with the difference that either fowls roasted brown or brown glaze made by boiling down meat, or else the prepared extract of meat should be used to make good consomme and coloring substitutes omitted; for a light brown color is to be obtained by some means and meat extract is the best where a choice of materials for soup making is not offered.

The consomme having been prepared rub some tomatoes through a coarse strainer, drain away part of the juice and simmer down the pulp until it is thick; add a teaspoon of curry powder and a good pinch of cayenne and salt. Drop a little into the consomme on serving in the plates, without mixing them.

830—Fillets of Sole, a la Tartare.

The sole is a flat-fish much esteemed in the seaports where it is khown and often represented by some good substitute in the interiors where it is not known. The fillets are the boneless strips of fish left when the broad spine has been cut out and fins removed.

Roll up the thin fillets, trim one end of the roll so that they will stand, dip in beaten egg and cracker meal and allow to pass inside to stick the wrap together, set them in a baking pan, make some lard hot and pour around the fillets and so bake them brown in the oven. But if you have a proper fry-basket you can fry them in the usual manner without their losing shape. When done drain on a sheet of paper laid in a pan, sprinkle with fine salt and serve hot with some special form of potatoes in the same plate, and tartar sauce in a butter chip, separately.

831—Potatoes a la Duchesse.

Take 4 or 5 potatoes out of the dinner steamer and mash them with a seasoning of salt, the yolk of an egg and grating of nutmeg or pinch of ground mace. When perfectly smooth roll it on the flour board, cut off balls larger than walnuts, flatten and pinch them up to a thick leaf shape, mark the tops with back of the knife, set in a buttered pan, wash over with egg and bake to a fine color. Serve with fish or with entrees, as an ornamental garnish.

832—Scrambled Sweetbreads with Puree of Peas.

Cut up cooked sweetbreads into large

dice and put them in a buttered pan into about half the amount of raw eggs, or 5 eggs to a pound of sweetbreads. Grate in a little nutmeg, add salt and pepper and keep covered until time to cook. Mash some green peas—the greener the better, but those left over from the previous day are as good as if newly cooked —and rub them through a strainer adding a little hot broth or white sauce to help pass the puree; season and set it to get warm.

Stir the sweetbreads and eggs over the fire until soft cooked. Place a spoonful of the green puree in the small dish in the manner of a border and the scrambled sweetbreads in the middle.

833—Pineapple Fritters and Sauce

Open 2 cans pineapple, save the juice cut the larger slices in two.

For the batter:

2 cups flour.

1 small teaspoon baking powder.

2 eggs.

1 cup milk or water.

1 tablespoon oil or melted lard.

Pinch of salt.

Put all at once into a small pail or deep pan and beat up with a spoon. Put in the pineapple slices, take up well coated with batter and drop into a kettle of hot lard. Fry light-colored. Drain well and break off the rough edges. Serve with thick sauce in the dish. To have fritters of good shape the batter should be made thin. Too much lightness makes them absorb grease. To have them of very light color use water instead of milk in the batter—but some people must have them well browned, which calls for milk or a spoonful of syrup mixed in.

834—Pineapple Sauce.

Half pineapple juice and half water, a cup of sugar to 2 cups of it, and a tablespoon of starch. Boil and color pink with raspberry or other fruit juice. It should be thick enough to coat over a fritter and glaze it, and when so used the articles are put on the bill of fare as "pineapple fritters glace."

835—Vanilla Jelly.

Sweet jelly of gelatine (No 465) made with a little lemon juice to help in the clarifying but without lemon peel and a flavoring of vanilla instead. Color like golden syrup with few drops burnt sugar caramel. (See No 694.)

August 3.

We have a new boarder this morning but his meals will not count at present. Early breakfast ordered for a doctor who is going away. I hope no sickness has broken out at our resort. My "sec" has an unusual amount of business to talk over with the other girls and has let the Lyonaise potatoes burn up.

At seven o'clock a little three-year-old comes running over the croquette ground to tell me that the doctor has brought her a new brother and I ask her what she'll take, but she says ma won't let her eat anything before breakfast time.

There the nurse comes to borrow my scales without saying what for.

When she brings them back she says "just twelve pounds and only half-a-pound to take off for the wraps."

Now, that must be pretty good weight for the newspaper paragraphs generally quote them at ten pounds. You see, Mrs Tingee, the effects of good cooking and good feeding—everything is sleek and fat around here.

Only 37 is the house-count to-day though it went up with the thermometer and touched 49 during the week, and I expect everyone will be on time to dinner as no person in this house excursionize on Sunday. If there was not something to expect from the advertising that is out it would look as though the past week was the culmination of our season's business and small affair it would be. But the advertising is bound to work a change; it has torn up all our peace and quietness already in one way and made great trouble with the meals, getting them ordered an hour earlier or an hour later or divided in two or three or turned into half meal and half picnic lunch and making dinner small and disappointing by the absence of guests, and supper large and vexatious through their unwonted promptness and inexpressible appetites. For this small but romantic Uintah Lake in the State of Cornucopia is a most interesting locality when its merits are once known. There is no end to the places and objects to be seen if some knowing person will clearly point them out. The Barnacles family will talk about these things well enough if somebody else starts the subject but are the last people to ever think of making any matter of local interest known; and you might as well look at any old and unremarkable building in any old and unremarkable town as to look at the most historic pile in Europe or elsewhere if you have not a guide book or other informant to awaken your imagination and interest by showing wherefore the historic pile is forever famous. So that is about the way that our little company got stirred up to an extent that they cared little for their meals, or at least were willing to forego a dinner or two for the sake of an exploration, after the papers began to drop in, which contained descriptions of "The Eyrie" and the points of interest about Uintah Lake. Over there by the Barnacles point you may see in windy weather when all the rest of the' lake is either yellow or green through shallowness, there is an expanse of water that remains blue almost to blackness; it is the unfathomable place, the well, the bottomless source of the waters of the lake which has an outlet like a mill-race but no other inlet, and as soon as that was known there was an early breakfast, the sailboats were brought into requisition and all went, if only to drop pebbles and look into the depths and imagine, but some went to heave the lead, and finding no bottom; went again next day, and others were led off to a sequestered bay that was covered with a magnificent species of water-lily. There is one remarkable hill on the lake shore called Crystal Cone; it is covered with pine and cedar and would not be observed without being pointed out, yet all the houses in this neighborhood have, as curiosities, some specimens of the brilliant rock crystals that are found there sometimes in large masses, and the Cone is full of diminutive wells that have been dug in search of them. Among the objects of sentimental interest the chief is the half-built and now decayed chateau which a certain singular and melancholy German baron began to build in the wilderness and surrounded it with a maze or labyrinth through which no intruder could find the way unless by chance, part of which still remains; a tortuous thicket of thorny bushes, and near by is the remains of the log house he lived and died in alone. The Barnacles family firmly believe the place haunted and never go to that side of the lake at night, but that of course is nonsense. Our people go in daytime to find some sort of a scarce flower that he planted here and there and as this is the season of its blossoming they sometimes bring home a few specimens and set in glasses on the breakfast table.

When we had a house count of 49, there were some disagreeable people who could not be expected to stay long anywhere. One man and his wife made a specialty of deriding hotels and the entertainment and accommodations they offer. Said he had been trying his powers of endurance of all evils at the Hotel-de Villa-Franca at Cabbageadia, and made much sport of it. He did not seem to find fault with anything here and yet he made people feel uncomfortable and many were glad when he and his wife went away at the end of two days. Three or four of the young people besides went away Saturday evening, as this place is intolerably dull on Sundays.

Ah, but here is worse sorrow; The house and the guests are to lose the Colonel and the banker's wife and daughter to morrow morning. They have been the right sort of guests, evidently, for they seemed always in the lead for pleasure. Btu they have been reading the advertisements of other resorts very closely in their resting spells when the papers lie on the piazzas and in the reading room, and they have found a place that seems to suit their case better. So to morrow they go to the Rosedale house at Purple Lake (it is in the Cashmere Vale, and the nightingales sing round it all the day long —so the advertisements say) but they promise the company to come back again before the season ends.

That is early breakfast Monday morning for the friends who will go to see them off, and at night comes off another birthday supper—this time it is for the lady hostess and must be fine. I have a 13-pound rich fruit cake made some days ago to be old enough to cut to morrow, for fruit cakes of the richest sorts are not good until a week after baking.

836—Rich Fruit Cake or Black Cake.

This is the kind of cake or rather, one of the kinds that can be kept for years without detriment to the cake. Some caterers have had it mentioned among their specialties as "grooms cake, 3 years old"

Prepare the fruit first:

2½ pounds raisins—6 heaped cups,
2½ pounds currants—same.
1½ pounds citron shred fine—4 cups.
2 heaping tablespoons mixed ground spices—cinnamon, cloves, nutmeg and mace.

1 small cup strong black-coffee.
1 Sall cup dark molasses.
Same of brandy.

A small addition of almonds, nuts or cut figs can be mixed in if wished, and a spoonful of lemon extract.

Then mix the cake batter:

14 ounces sugar—2 cups.
14 ounces butter—same if pressed.
10 eggs.
18 ounces flour—4 large cups.

Mix up same as pound cake, the sugar and butter together first, then eggs 2 at a time, then flour. After the flour, put in the 2 ounces spices, coffee, molasses, brandy and lemon extract. The batter is quite thin, but no matter. Mix flour in the fruit to dust it well, then stir up all together.

Take a mould that holds at least 6 qts. or two moulds of 4 quarts each, line them with greased paper, put in the cake and wrap other papers around the outside and tie on to guard the cake against too much heat in baking. Bake from 2 to 3 hours. The raisins ought to be stoned or, if there is nobody to do that, cut them in two, but not mince them small, as that spoils the appearance of the cake.

Cost of large fruit cake, about 15 cents a pound.

Note. The above has been proven a valuable receipt about Christmas and party times but as it makes a cake so nearly all fruit it will bear a little thinning down with more cake batter for most occasions. I make twice the amount of pound-cake mixture, use a little of it as pound or jelly cake and put the specified amount of fruits in what remains or mix them without taking any out; it is a rich cake still, only of diffierent degrees; and if they are temperance people and will not buy brandy put in another spoonful of spices and the cake will be just as good as if the brandy was put in and baked out of it. Cost as above with prices as quoted at this place, 14 pounds including one coat thick icing $1.85.

Dinner.

August 3.
Soup-Consomme, chatelaine (6 qts. 40 cents.)
Tomatoes and cucumbers (on table 10 cents.)
Flounder a l'Italienne (4 lbs. gross and sauce 45 cer.ts).
Potato croquettes.
Boiled ham and tongue (nominal, left for cold).
Roast beef, (1 rib 3 lbs 39 cents.)
Braised brisket of veal, mareschale, (3 lbs. 36 cents).
Lamb cutlets, a la Nelson (14 orders, 2 lbs. and trimmings, 48 cents).
Rissolettes, a la Marseillaise, (12 orders 26 cents).
Baked tomatoes 15, onions in cream 10, rice 4, beans 4, cabbage 8, potatoes 16, (57 cents).
Queen pudding with cream, (No. 845; 3 qts. or 4½ lbs. 35 cents).
Blackberry pie (2 pies large, 20 cents).
Bisque of pineapple ice cream(No. 206; 2 qts. and freezing 65 cents.)
Cakes assorted (15 cents).
Nuts, raisins, cheese, crackers, condiments,(37 cents).
Milk, buttermilk, cream, (46 cents).
Butter, bread, coffee, tea, sugar, 38 cents.
Total $5,57, 37 persons; 15 cents a plate.

837—Consomme Chatelaine

Like consomme royal with minced shalots and mushrooms in the custards.

Make and clarify the consomme as at No. 139; there ought to be a fowl roasted brown and then boiled in it, otherwise add extract of meat for richness and color.

Mince an equal quantity of butto

mushrooms and young onions, about ½ cup of each; break 3 eggs in a pan, add a spoonful of milk or both and the minced ingredients, season, stir up, put in a buttered small pan or mould and cook by steaming. When the custard is done and cold cut out shapes ether like corks or plain squares. Put half a dozen in each plate when the consomme is served.

838—Flounder a' la Italienne.

The flounder is a flat fish about same size as the sole, common and quite cheap in the seaports.

Cut in pieces across the fish and remove the dark skin; cook it the same as at No. 184. Serve with brown Italian sauce and a potato croquette in the same plate.

839—Potato Croquettes.

Take 4 or 5 potatoes out of the dinner steamer and mash them with salt, the yolk of an egg, or two, and pinch of ground mace or nutmeg and if quite dry add a little butter. Roll on the flour board, cut off balls larger than walnuts, roll round, bread them in egg and cracker meal and fry to a handsome light brown same as dauphine. They can be made in other shapes but the round is the quickest.

840—Braised Brisket of Veal Marechale.

To braise or braze meat is to cook in a brazier or covered pot with live coals on top. It can be done nearly as well in deep baking pan in the oven if covered with buttered paper—which will stand a good deal of heat without burning and keeps the steam in the meat. Saw the breast of veal in strips across the ribs, put them in the pan with some soup stock, vegetables and garden herbs and salt and cook with the paper cover on in the oven for an hour and a half. Have it so that the liquor is dried down to glaze that sticks to the pan and to the meat. Take the meat out, pour off the

fat and boil up some Spanish sauce in the pan, if you have it, if not use water; strain and use as gravy to the meat and serve browned potatoes in the same plate.

841—Lamb Cutlets, a la Nelson.

Cutlets spread with a highly flavored mince in stiff sauce, dredged with bread crumbs and baked brown.

Prepare the cutlets (chops) as for broiling, lay in a pan and bake half-done so that they will retain their shape afterwards.

Mince an ounce each of ham, mushrooms, young onions, little parsley and crush a clove of garlic and mince it with the rest. Take a spoonful each of flour and butter, stir them over the fire and add water to make a sauce thick as paste; stir the minced ingredients in. Spread a teaspoonful on each cutlet, round it over and cover with bread crumbs or cracker meal and brown them in the oven. Serve a spoonful of Allemande sauce in the dish and the cutlet in it and garnish with a strip of toast.

842—Sauce Allemande.

Take chicken or veal broth boiled down rich and strained through a napkin and pour it to a roux of butter and flour made hot over the fire as if making butter sauce.

When thin enough let it slowly boil at the side and skim off the butter that rises while the sauce is becoming thicker by reduction. Shortly before it is wanted mix the yolk of an egg with it carefully, without curdling the yolk with too much heat, and add the juice of half a lemon. Allemande sauce is German sauce

843—Rissolettes a la Marseillaise.

Picked fish and cheese pounded together, rolled up in pie paste and fried.

Take cold whitefish or any other that is free from bones, and half as much cheese, mince, and then pound them together to a sort of paste and season with salt and pepper.

Roll out a piece of good pie paste very

thin, cut out with a biscuit cutter, make little turnovers or other shapes such as long rolls with a spoonful of the fish mixture inside and the edges of the paste wetted with egg to make them adhere. Drop the rissolettes into the same kettle of hot lard the potato croquettes are to be fried in. Take out while still light-colored and place on paper in a hot pan to absorb every particle of grease. Serve one or two to each dish with a green border of fried parsley or a green puree, or chopped yolk of egg for ornament. Marseilles is a seaport and great place for fish dinners—hence the names.

844—Baked Tomatoes.

If not intelligently managed, baked tomatoes are sure to be a failure through all dissolving into liquid. Without peeling, cut off a slice of the top and scoop out the inside with a teaspoon into a strainer that will let the surplus juice flow away. Chop the pulp, add bread crumbs on top and bake in a buttered pan.

845—Queen Pudding.

This is known by half a dozen different names—it looks well and is a favorite kind. It is a bread custard with jelly spread over the top after baking and meringue (frosting) upon that like a lemon pie,

1 pressed-in quart bread crumbs—4 cups.
4 cups milk.
½ cup butter, melted.
½ cup sugar.
4 yolks eggs.
1 cup fruit jelly.
4 whites and ½ cup sugar for the frosting.
Have the bread very finely minced, mix the first five ingredients together and bake until the bread custard thus made is set in the middle. Spread the jelly over the top and set in the oven again. Whip the whites firm enough to bear up an egg, add the sugar, spread it on top of the hot jelly and finish baking with the oven door partly open as too much heat spoils the meringue. Costs about 35 cents, but is enough for thirty people.

Use a large pan that the pudding may be shallow and cut out the better for it.

Dinner.

August 4.
Soup—Potage a la Reine (5 qts 40 cents.)
Fillets of trout, a la Chambord (4 lbs, with forcemeat etc. 70 cents.)
Potatoes, Monaco.
Boiled ham with spinach (3 orders ham, 9 spinach 13 cents.)
Roast beef (1 rib, 2 lbs net 28 cents.)
Mutton a la Bretonne (No 849 shoulder 2 lbs and beans 30 cents.)
Chicken pie (5 chickens $1.00, with crust etc, $1.20.)
Green peas 15, mashed turnips 5 rice 5, potatoes 15 (40 cents.)
Birdsnest pudding with cream (No 851; about 28 cents.)
Lemon pie (No 852; 3 medium size 30 cents.
Vanilla ice cream (2 qts pure, and freezing 65 cents.)
Nuts, raisins, cheese, crackers, pickles, (35 cents.)
Cake assorted kinds (1 lb 10 cents.)
Milk, buttermilk, cream (45 cents.)
Butter, bread, coffee, tea, sugar (43 cents.)
Total $5.97; 35 persons; 17 cents a plate.

846—Potage a la Reine.

Reine is the French word for queen, this would therefore be in English "Queen's Soup."
It is a puree soup like the potato cream and puree of beans, but thickened, instead, with the paste or puree of pounded chicken and rice.
Take:
3 quarts chicken broth.
4 solid cups chicken meat.
1 heaped cup boiled rice.
1 quart cream or good milk.
Procure 4 cupfuls of clear chicken meat tender enough to mash to a paste, either from two or three young chickens roasted, or 1 large fowl boiled. Mince it fine, pound it smooth, add the rice while pounding, pour in some of the broth to moisten it, then rub it through a perfor-

ated tin gravy strainer or a sieve.

The chicken (or veal) broth should have a small bunch of parsley, 1 stalk of celery, a small piece of onion and piece of broken nutmeg boiled in it, and if obtainable a sprig of green thyme, and after that be strained. Mix it boiling hot with the puree of chicken and rice; set on bricks or at the back of the stove to keep hot without boiling, and boil the cream separately and pour it in at last. Serve with soufflee crouton, No. 736.

Another way is to make a cream of rice with chicken meat in it cut small, and no croutons.

847—Fillets of Redfish a la Chambord Individual.

Thin fillets spread with a paste or forcemeat containing lobster, rolled up and baked and served with a lobster sauce.

Chambon is the name of a part of France on the sea coast and also a count's title. The redfish is from the Florida coast where it is also called red grouper.

Slice the fish lengthwise into fillets thin and broad like fillets of sole and as small as possible, pound a quarter can of lobster to a paste, add as much panada (soaked and squeezed bread) season it, add a raw yolk. Spread the fillets with the mixture thinly, roll them up, and lay in a pan and bake with butter and water just enough to keep them moist, and baste twice. They will cook in about 30 minutes.

Pound the reddest pieces of lobster meat and rub it through a sieve, mix it with a little good butter sauce; slice in 3 or 4 mushrooms and as many shrimps, if at hand, or a few pieces of lobster cut in dice and season with pepper and lemon juice. Serve a fillet to each plate with sauce and some special form of potato in the same.

848—Potatoes a la Monaco.

Cut cores out of raw potatoes with an apple corer or column cutter, and slice them into thick lozenge shapes like gunwads. Boil first, then fry in a kettle of lard. Before serving, shake them about in a pan with a lump of butter, dredge with salt and fine minced parsley. Serve with fish. Monaco is the name of a german resort, a sort of Saratoga.

849—Mutton a la Bretonne.

Mutton and beans. The French equivalent for our pork and beans. The frequency of the sign in the windows of French restaurants seems to indicate that it is in demand at least for a lunch dish.

Take a shoulder of mutton and remove the bone by cutting close, laying out the meat like a thick steak. To season it mince one onion and crush a clove of garlic with the side of your knife and mix it in and stew over the meat, dredge thyme or sage, salt and pepper, roll up and tie and then braise the meat in a covered pan with broth or water at first, allowing it to dry down and brown like a roast at last.

Boil two cups of white beans in the usual way while the mutton is braising. Take the mutton out of the saucepan and cook a little minced ham and onion in the gravy that remains, then put in the cooked beans and shake up.

Serve beans in the dish with a cut of the roll of mutton on top.

850—Chicken Pie, American Style.

When you make chicken pie cut down the quantities of all other meats and cut down the vegetables and leave out the third entree altogether that there may be afforded enough of this and without having to serve the roughest pieces of chicken. It is one of the favorite dishes alike in the largest hotels and the smallest and it is poor policy to make it a disappointment in either place. Let there be a surplus of the liquor the chicken is stewed in left over to pour into the pie as it dries down while dinner is going on, for the cry is " still they come"—no, not that but "plenty of gravy and more of the crust."

A large chicken can be cut or chopped into 18 pieces for stew or pie but such pieces are not able to make you any reputation. If the back bones and necks are left out to be used in soup or other ways it may take another chicken to make the pie large enough but after all you will not have to work so hard to find a piece of the breast for the few fastidious people who can't eat anything else.

Cut up five chickens making 6 choice cuts of each without counting the back or neck; allow about ½ pound salt pork cut in strips, a heaped tablespoon minced onion, same of salt, a teaspoon of white pepper, some chopped parsley, flour to thicken the liquor and about 3 pounds short pie crust.

Boil the chickens in water enough to cover, time according to age; young chicken's less than ½ hour; old fowls 3 hours; with the seasoning of salt, pork and onions. Thicken the liquor, add parsley, dip the chicken into a baking pan dredge over with pepper and flour and cover with a thin pie crust. Bake ½ hour. Cut in squares.

There should not be gravy enough in the pan to drown the crust before it can bake—the gravy can be poured in afterwards. Baking powder crust can be made good with care but seldom is, for it rises too thick and absorbs all the sauce. A short paste is better.

851--Birds Nest Pudding.

An egg batter pudding with apples. Probably gets its name from its appearance when baked in round pan.

1 large cup flour—5 ounces.
3 cups milk—1½ pints.
2 heaped tablespoons sugar.
Butter size of an egg.
3 eggs. Little salt.
Apples enough for a 4 quart pan.
Sugar, butter and cinnamon or nutmeg for the apples.

Pare and core the apples—enough to cover the pan bottom; fill core holes with sugar and some butter, water to barely wet the pan, cover with greased paper and bake until done and the syrup dried down. Mix the batter smoothly, as if for batter cakes, pour it over the apples and bake about ½ hour more. Pure cream sweetened is a good sauce, any other will answer if cream is not to be had.

852—Lemon Pie Meringued.

Rule: One lemon and two eggs to each pie.

1 cup sugar.
2 cups water or milk.
2 lemons or 3 if small.
½ cup flour.
6 yolks of eggs.

Put the sugar in a saucepan and grate lemon rinds into it, squeeze the juice, add the pint of water and boil. Mix the 2 ounces flour with water and thicken the boiling syrup. Take it off and pour it gradually to the beaten yolks. Fill three pies and bake.

Whip the 6 whites, add 6 tablespoons sugar, spread over the pies while they are still hot in the oven and bake light-colored. A richer appearance may be given by dredging granulated sugar over the frosting before baking; it makes a crust. Too much baking will spoil the frosting, causing it to fall; also, be careful to get about a tablespoon of sugar to each white of an egg.

853—Galantine en Bellevue

A galantine (not gelatine as it often mistakenly appears in printed bills) is a boned fowl or bird of any sort; it is en bellevue when it is encased in jelly and ornamented. Galantines are made the same of either chickens or turkeys, according to the following directions.

Singe and pick over a young turkey or pullet, and without otherwise opening it, cut the skin along the whole length of the back and with the point of a sharp knife go on cutting the meat from the bone on both sides until the hip joints and wings are reached. Chop through these with the heavy end of a carving knife and continue cutting close to the breast bone until the frame is entirely removed without the skin being cut through.

After that, bone the legs and wings half way and chop off the rest. The meat of the legs and wings is to be tucked into the body, which, when done up, will be a smooth cushion shape.

Then wash the turkey in cold water and dry it on a cloth. Spread it out with the skin side down on the table and cover with the forcemeat; draw the two sides together, sew with twine, put it into a pudding cloth previously buttered and tie and pin it securely Boil the turkey in salted broth or water containing the bones and any other trimmings left from the forcemeat besides, for from two to three hours, according to size.

When the boned and stuffed turkey or chicken has been sufficiently boiled, press it, still in the cloth, into a pan or mold, and there let it remain with a weight on top until cold. Into whatever shape it may be, there should be another vessel a size larger precisely like it, and the boned turkey or chicken, being taken out of the first mold, and the cloth taken off and the surface wiped clean with a napkin dipped in hot water, is then to be placed in the larger one; the space is then filled up with aspic jelly, poured in nearly cold, and when set, the mold being dipped a few moments in warm water, the galantine can be turned out onto its dish and decorated.

The way to get a coating of jelly all over the galantine is to stamp out star shapes from thick slices of white turnip or other material and lay them on the bottom of the larger mould. They hold up the galantine from the bottom for the jelly to run under, and show up as ornaments.

Decorate with blocks of colored jelly set around and upon it, and with ornamental silver skewers, with lemons cut like baskets, and with flowers.

Two fair-sized turkeys, prepared as above, either stuffed with forcemeat or with the meat of another turkey or chicken, will slice into fifty plates.

854—Stuffing for Galantines.

Where boned turkey and chicken is served so frequently for lunch that it is no rarity, the easiest and quickest way of stuffing may perhaps be as good as the best; a boned turkey then becomes a fraud, if considered as turkey while it may be very good if regarded as sausage, for the most available material is a common sausage meat to fill up the space formerly occupied by the frame of the fowl. Next to that and perhaps the oftenest used is a mixture of selected lean veal and fat salt pork minced into a sort of veal sausage, well seasoned and served up in the turkey. That can be made by any person without special directions.

Another and better way is to bone two turkeys or a turkey and chicken and put the two in one, being careful to have the inside chicken or small turkey quite young and tender. Season well without cutting or mincing, lay one on the other,

place a few strips of fat pork about as thick as a pencil, lengthwise, and half a dozen hard-boiled yolks, gather up and sew in shape. When cooked, pressed and sliced this will be all turkey or chicken and better liked than the sausage business.

For something more elaborate for a little party supper or lunch the following may be relied upon to make a nice dish, worth ornamenting.

855—Forcemeat for Boned Turkey and Chicken

The quantity of this receipt is sufficient for one medium-sized turkey that will slice into twenty-five individual dishes. For a large chicken the amounts may be one-half. This makes about four pounds of choice meat, in addition to the turkey.

2 hens, boiled tender.
6 ounces fat salt pork—a cup.
6 ounces butter—a cup.
6 ounces white bread crumbs—2 cups.
2 raw eggs.
8 hard boiled eggs.
1 cup broth or water.
1 lemon.
Nutmeg or thyme.
Salt and pepper.

Take the dark meat of the fowls, cut it in very small dice and keep it separate. Take off the white meat, chop fine and then pound to a soft paste. Throw in the fat pork minced, the seasonings and the bread crumbs and mix together, and soften the butter and stir in. Mix the two raw eggs with the cup of broth, add juice of lemon, and with this mixture moisten the forcemeat. It is now ready for use.

Strew over the turkey about half the dark meat mince, and over that spread half the white forcemeat. Cut the yolks of the hard boiled eggs in quarters and scatter some over the layer of forcemeat, then the rest of the minced dark meat, the remaining forcemeat and egg yolks. Do up the boned turkey thus filled as above directed.

When sliced cold the above shows little dark squares set in a white meat, all spotted through with the yellow egg yolks.

Cost of material; 2 fowls 50, pork 5

butter 8, eggs 13, bread, lemon and seasonings 4; 80 cents.

856—Cost of Galantine of Turkey or Chicken.

Twenty cents a pound for material is the lowest that boned turkey and chicken can be expected to cost, and if prices rule' high the cost may be sometimes twice that sum. A 14 pound turkey (plucked but not drawn) may be dressed boned and then done up with 6 pounds of raw veal forcemeat or sausage meat inside and after cooking and pressing it will scarcely weigh 10 pounds altogether —a loss of over half; so that if the turkey be bought at 12½ the galantine will cost 25 cents a pound at the lowest; and we find that our chicken galantine containing one-half the amount of forcemeat, (No. 855) and a 3½ pound fowl bought at 10 cents a pound, making a total of 75 cents, weighs but 3½ pounds at last and has therefore cost over 21 cents a pound for material. The greatest shrinkage takes place in the boiling.

Such is the calculation to be made when contracting for a party.

On the other hand it is to be considered the galantine is subject to no further depreciation In our 3½ pounds are 56 ounces; about 2 ounces make as large a slice as anybody wants, being about 25 plates for 75 cents, or 3 or 4 cents a person. The aspic jelly makes a separate calculation; it is not essential, but to be charged to ornamentation. It is, however cheaper by the pound than the meat and at a large party may be converted to profit by an expert carver.

857—Chicken Salad.

The same as No. 150. Make up the form in a round salad bowl, place a heart lettuce on top, and quarters of eggs in close order around the base.

858—Art in cutting Eggs.

Hold the hard-boiled egg in a napkin in your hollowed hand while you cut it in quarters lengthwise, and avoid breaking the yolks and spoiling the eggs for ornamental purposes. Eggs are turned blue and made to look as if bad by too long boiling; when they are fairly hard-boiled put them immediately in cold water and there will be no discoloration.

859—Art in Mincing Parsley.

Chop parsley very fine, inclose it in a clean towel and wring by twisting it until all the juice is expressed. The parsley is then a green dust which when scattered upon a dish will not fall all in one spot but will divide as easily as grains of colored sugar. For salad ornamentation dip round slices of lemon in the green parsley dust and border the dish.

Birthday Party Supper.

MENU.
Galantine of Chicken en Bellevue.
Pain de Foies-gras.
Toasted Rusks.   Sandwiches.
Chicken Salad.
Ornamented Fruit Cake.
Charlotte Russe.   Orange Cake.
Meringues a la Gelee.
Frozen Bisque of Preserved Ginger.
Lemonade.   Coffee.

There were but 21 or 22 persons to be provided for so the difficulty in such a case is to provide a small enough quantity of each dish and yet make a table that is pleasing to look at, for they that come to the supper are not really hungry and only care to try whatever is new; at the same time you do not like to ask them to a Barmecide's feast of empty plates and nothing else. There is nothing for it but to utilize most of the surplus, such as cakes, for the next dinner table, make as little as possible of liver pate and chicken salad and submit to a little waste in other respects, knowing that the ice cream and meringues will be sufficiently well patronized and the large fruit cake will be wanted to be sent away in presents to absent friends.

Cost of material :
Galantine—fowl 75, jelly 2 qts 55 (1.30)
Pain de foies-gras 45, jelly 25 (70)
Rusks (No. 277) and sandwiches, (25 cents).
Chicken salad, (No. 857), (70 cents).

Ornamented fruit cake (No. 836), (2.00)
Charlotte-Russe of 2 qts Bavarian and
cake, (55 cents).
Orange cake, (No. 867), (35 cents).
Meringues, 25 (No. 460) with jelly
(45 cents).
Bisque of ginger, ice cream, (No.
207), (60 cents).
Lemonade and coffee, (35 cents).
Total $7,25; 22 persons, 33 cents a
plate.

860—Pain de Foies-Gras.

It means loaf or cake of poultry livers,
and is of course, a high-flavored dish of
which a small quantity suffices, to be eat-
en with thin sliced bread as potted tongue
or ham would be. Pain is the French
word for bread or loaf and seems to be
used in the same sense as we use the
word cheese in head-cheese, liver-cheese
and the like. In other words this is a
form of liver paste, or pate-de-foie-gras,
turned out of its mould and incased in
jelly by the same method as for boned
chicken. Take the ingredients in two
parts and it does not seem so formidable.

¾ pound chicken livers.
6 ounces fat hen or salt pork.
2 ounces lean cooked ham.
½ cup sherry.
1 bayleaf, pepper, little mixed ground
spices, salt.

6 ounces panada (bread soaked and
squeezed dry.)
2 raw eggs.
4 hard boiled yolks.
½ a corned tongue cooked.
Some chopped mushrooms and aspic
jelly.

Steep the livers in water to whiten them.
If the poultry livers are short weight use
calf's liver to make the amount. Set all
the ingredients of the first part to simmer in a saucepan with a lid on the back
part of the range and let remain till a convenient time, 2 or 3 hours. Then mash to
paste. The livers should be nearly dry in
the saucepan but not fried or browned.
Mix the raw eggs with the panada and
these with the pounded liver and press
through a sieve. Cut up the tongue,
yolks and few mushrooms and mix them
in the liver paste.
Take a pan or mould that holds over
3 pints and cover the bottom with very
thin slices of fat salt pork, press in the
liver paste, put on top a bay leaf and
slice or two of pork and a buttered paper over that. Set the mould in a pan
of water in the oven and bake about
an hour. Turn it out of the pan or
mould when cold, remove the fat and
it is ready for use, but if to be set on
the table whole, proceed as for a galantine of chicken and encase it in aspic
jelly.
Cost of material [about 45 cents for
2½ pounds or about the same as boned
chicken.

861— Charlotte Russe—Three Ways.

It is an outside casing of cake filled
with a thick cream, which ought to be
real cream thick enough to whip to froth;
if such cannot be had, a thin cream can
be made firm by adding gelatine to it;
and if no cream at all then make the
same thing of milk and whip it up light
as explained at No. 865.
There are many ways of putting up a
charlotte.
1. Procure 3 or 4 dozen lady fingers
(No. 4) and a tin shape, which is nothing
more than a hoop of tin with straight-up
sides, like a three pint milk cup would
be without a bottom. It may be either
round or oval according to the dish to be
used to set the charlotte on the table.
Cut the edges of the lady-fingers straight,
wet them with white of egg and line the
shape with them set upright and the
shape being on the dish. Whip the
cream to firm froth, sweetening and flavoring at the same time; fill up the shape
with it and let it remain in a cold place
till wanted, then carefully lift off the tin
shape and the cream will keep the form
together if it was double cream at the start
—that is cream that has stood on the
milk two days before skimming.
If not sure of the cream being firm
enough, then add gelatine according to
directions for Bavarian cream.
There is no covering of cake in this,
but the surface of the cream may be ornamented with some of the same cream
in a cornet or ornamenting tube the
same as if it were icing.
2. When a shorter way must be
adopted bake a good sponge cake in a
round mould. No. 281 is as good as any

with a liberal allowance of powder. Then cut out the inside to use as cake and take the shell or crust to fill with whipped cream. If the cake is evenly baked of light color this way does very well; and where the charlotte is to be sliced and served individually, as in most hotels, the long and narrow moulds such as loaves of bread are baked in may be found most suitable, as the charlotte can then be cut across.

3. Another way to be adopted when the charlotte-russe is to be set on the table whole, as for a party supper, is to take a deep, plain mould or a tin pan, cover the bottom with the thinnest sliced sponge cake or lady-fingers and line the sides with the same, fill with cream stiffened with gelatine, keep cold and when set, turn it out of the mould bringing the bottom on top and ornament that either with whipped cream piled up and spotted with strawberries or else with only a coat of icing and a border. Cream stiffened with gelatine is called Bavarian cream—see receipts below.

862—Individual Charlotte-Russe. Six Ways.

1. It is best to make individual charlottes where the time allows, for hotel dinners or parties. In some places paper cases can be bought and the charlottes made and served in them. Make the same mixture as for sponge roll, very thin, and cut in bands and pieces that will fit inside; then fill with whipped cream. Some of the largest hotels serve them in these paper cases always.

2. If you have no ready-made cases you can make some of white unruled paper, cutting the first piece to fit inside a small tumbler, and then using it for a pattern to cut the others by. Paste them together, put in a bottom and fringe the edges. Line with lady-fingers made small and cut to fit; fill with whipped cream and serve them in the cases.

3. Small sponge cakes can be baked in the deep muffin pans or gem pans—they are tumbler-shaped—the inside cut out to be made into pudding, and the shells filled with cream, and sent in without a paper case.

4. Another way and a good one is to cut sponge-roll sheets into pieces that will just line the inside of deep muffin rings of the sort that have no bottom. Fill them with cream stiffened with gelatine and set on ice, and when cold and firm slip them out of the rings, and serve with a fine strawberry on top or ornament with pink spots of meringue.

5-6. A good deal of variety can be had with this form of charlotte as, sometimes, white sponge cake can be made and filled with yellow Roman cream (No 194) or with chocolate or coffee cream, and another time the ordinary yellow sponge cake lining can be filled with white cream, or strawberry cream, etc.

863—About Whipped Cream.

Good thick cream, if cold, can be made firm enough by beating with a wire egg whisk to fill charlottes, or even plates lined with a thin sheet of cake, or to spread over a cream pie without the addition of gelatine or anything else, and once so whipped to firmness it will not go down again as long as it is kept cold—provided, however, that there is not much sugar mixed with it. A half-pint cup of good cream will increase in volume, when beaten sufficiently, to fill about eight of the small charlotte cases previously mentioned.

864—Bavarian Cream—Best.

But whipped cream as stated in the foregoing not being capable of carrying much sugar or flavoring, a little gelatine has to be added to give it substance. Half an ounce to a quart is sufficient unless there is to be an addition of some flavoring cordial or fruit juice, when an ounce to a quart will be the rule, and four to six ounces of sugar. No boiling is required, but set the gelatine in half a cup of milk or cream on the shelf of the range where it will gradually get hot. When it is dissolved, place the cream in a deep pan set in ice water and pour in the dissolved gelatine while beating. The cream can then be put into molds, very slightly oiled, and left to become firm, or used to fill cases lined with cake for charlottes.

Cost: 1 qt cream 20, ½ ounce gelatine 6, sugar 3, flavoring 5; 34 cents. Makes 2 qts when whipped light; about 18 cents for each quart mould.

865—Bavarian Cream—Substitute.

This is, in effect, blanc-mange whipped up light while cooling, with the aid of white of eggs, so that when perfectly cold it can be sliced and shows the same spongy texture as fine bread It is good to fill charlottes when pure cream cannot be obtained, and good for dessert in place of ice cream.

4 cups good rich milk—a quart.

1 small cup sugar—6 ounces.

1 ounce gelatine—nearly a package of the shred kind, or 2 or 3 sheets.

3 whites of eggs.

Vanilla flavoring.

Set the milk over the fire with the sugar and gelatine in it and stir it until the gelatine is all dissolved. Better not let it quite boil because sometimes milk is curdled by the gelatine at boiling point; strain it into a pan set in ice water, and when nearly cold beat it up light. Whip the three whites quite firm, and stir in and continue the beating until the cream has become nearly solid, then pour it into moulds or into the charlotte-russe case, which may have been prepared previously. The flavoring extract can be added while beating. A little salt mixed in the ice water makes it colder and hastens the setting of the cream.

Cost: milk 5, gelatine 1 oz 10, sugar 3, flavoring 4, whites 3; 25 cents for 2 quarts.

866—Maraschino Cream.

For filling charlotte-russe **or serving** instead of ice cream :

2½ pints thin cream.

1 teacup maraschino.

7 ounces sugar.

1 package of gelatine—1½ **ounces.**

Put the extra half pint of cream in a small saucepan, and the gelatine and sugar with it, set over the fire and beat with the wire egg whisk till the gelatine is all dissolved—the quicker the better. Pour the maraschino into the cold cream, then strain in the contents of the saucepan, set the whole in a pan of ice water, and whip the cream mixture until it begins to set, when pour it into the pre-

pared mould.

Maraschino is a cordial that gives a pleasant flavor to creams and jellies. It is kept in all first-class bars. Comes in flasks bound in basket work. Is made by steeping the kernels of an Italian cherry in spirits of wine and then adding syrup.

867—Orange Cake.

White cake layers with orange ·icing (frosting). Make the best white cake, No. 622, and bake on jelly-cake pans. Grate the rinds of 2 or 3 oranges into 2 large cups powdered sugar. Take 3 whites of eggs in a bowl, put the flavored sugar in, and beat with a wooden paddle until you have a pale yellow icing firm enough not to run off the cake. Spread some between the layers and the rest over the top and sides.

Dinner.

August 5.

Soup—consomme printanier royal (5 qts, 40 cents.)

Tomato salad (on table, 15 cents.)

Fillets of sheephead a la Horly (fish 2 lbs 24, batter frying, 20; 44 cents.)

Potatoes Julienne, corned tongue and cabbage (25 cents.)

Roast beef (1 rib, 1½ lbs 20 cents.)

Loin of mutton (1½ lbs 18 cents.)

Roulade of veal, Napolitaine (shoulder, 3 lbs 40 cents.)

Cutlets of minced chicken (21 orders, equal to 1 fowl 55, with trimmings, frying 55 cents.)

Poultry livers in potato croustades (filling charged previous meals, 10 croustades, 15 cents.)

Apricots, a la Colbert (30 orders, 1 can 25, rice, breading 26, sauce 4; 55 cents.)

Turnips, beans, corn, tomatoes, potatoes (45 cents.)

Preserved tomato tarts (8 saucer size, cut in three, 2 lbs tomatoes 20, crust 7; 27 cents.)

Lemon frozen custard (3 qts frozen, 60 cents.)

Cakes (charged other meals.)

Nuts, raisins, cheese, crackers, pickles (35 cents.)

Milk, buttermilk, cream (average 1½ cents each person, 44 cents.)

Bread, butter, coffee, tea, sugar (40 cents.)

Total $5 78; 35 persons, 16½ cents a plate.

868—Consomme Printanier Royal

It is consomme royal, No. 139, with a jardinier mixture of vegetables in it—or consomme jardiniere with custards in it, whichever way you may choose to regard it. Make the consomme good with roast chicken, plenty of beef, or meat extract; cut the vegetables as small as peas, with a jardinier cutter if you have one at hand, otherwise in very small dice, and have fresh green peas and asparagus points also if in season.

869—Tomato Salad.

Take small tomatoes not ripe enough to be soft, pare them with a very sharp knife without scalding. Cut in quarters, then in slices, put in a bowl with oil, vinegar, pepper, salt; same as plain potato salad, shake up, serve with border of small lettuce leaves.

870—Fillets of Sheephead, a la Horly.

Strips of fish fried in batter, served with Julienne potatoes and crisp fried onions. The sheephead is one of the best of the Southern sea fishes; in shape and quality it is very much like the black bass, and is generally reserved for boiling. It is so named for its projecting front teeth. To cook it a la Horly, cut it in strips size of a finger, salt well, pepper a little. Make a good frying batter with 2 eggs to a quart of flour, little melted butter or oil, and milk enough to make like thin batter-cake mixture. Dip the pieces of fish, drop in hot lard, fry slow enough to let get well done, but of light color.

Slice 2 or 3 onions in rings, flour them and fry yellow and dry, also fry a few handfuls of Julienne potatoes. Serve a little of each at the side of the fillet in the same dish.

There was a duke de Horly, prominent in the wars of the last century.

871—Roulade of Veal, a la Napolitaine.

Napolitaine is but another way of say-ing Italian style; it means with macaroni when it is not with Neapolitan or horse-radish sauce. Roll up a shoulder of veal after taking out the bone, and braise or roast it covered with buttered paper. Cook a dozen sticks of macaroni, cut short, put in light gravy or Spanish sauce and serve in the dish with a slice of veal on top.

Napolitaine is the French spelling; Neapolitan is the English; it means of the city of Naples in Italy.

872—Cutlets of Minced Chicken, Bordelaise.

2 solid cups chicken meat, or, equal to the meat of one fowl.

1 cup panada.

½ cup butter.

1 tablespoon minced onion.

2 tablespoons minced mushrooms.

2 eggs.

Thyme, parsley, pepper, salt.

Pick the chicken meat to pieces and mince it; there should be over a pound. Make panada by soaking white bread in cold water and squeezing dry. Put the butter in a frying-pan along with the onions and mushrooms, and stir over the fire a few minutes, then put in the panada and when hot add the eggs and after that the chicken and seasonings.

Let get cold in a pan, then make up with floured hands, first in pear shapes, small size and flatten them to look like lamb chops. Get a piece of macaroni for each one and insert it to look like the bone. Dip in egg and cracker dust and fry in lard or oil. Serve with Bordelaise sauce in the dish and for ornament take a small crouton of fried bread, cut heart shaped, dip in tomato sauce, sprinkle with parsley dust and set in the end of the dish.

873—Croustades of Chicken Livers.

The livers of poultry and game being high-flavored should be set apart for special uses instead of being stewed promiscuously with the chicken, or pot-pies to which they give a taste that may not be to the general liking. In some of the most elaborate ragouts of the French order, these livers are used in equal parts with truffles, mushrooms and wine as special flavorings. A simple brown stew of chicken livers in meat gravy makes a good dish served in cases made as directed in the next article.

874—Potato Shells or Croustades.

Make the same mashed potato preparation as for croquettes with one or two yolks in it, take it on the pastry board with a little flour, make a long roll of it, cut off slices like common biscuits in size, dip them in egg and cracker dust twice over, giving them a double coating. Then take a small cutter and mark a lid in each one as you would in a puff-paste tartlet. Put them in the frying basket to fry, and only keep them in the hot lard a short time lest they burst out of shape. When of a good, yellow-brown color take up, lift out the lid with a teaspoon point and scoop out the inside, making a crisp shell of potato to be filled with any kind of savory ragout or mince. After making the round shape once, oval and diamond and boat shapes can be made as well. It is work that consumes a good deal of time—not adapted for crowded houses.

875—Apricots a la Colbert

Half an apricot or peach placed against a like amount of rice croquette mixture, egged and breaded in the form of a ball, and fried in a kettle of lard. When done, light-colored, rolled in sugar and served with sauce in the dish, made of the apricot syrup. Make rice croquette preparation as at No. 188, or light potato croquette with a little sugar added. Some of the canned apricots are firm enough to use for this purpose. Drain them well from the juice.

876—Preserved Tomato Tarts or Pies.

When there are fresh tomatoes around, perhaps already peeled and not otherwise needed it is easy to put them in a pan with a cup of sugar and piece of bruised ginger and let slowly stew down to preserves. Make small open pies of them, the crust made short and the pies or tarts baked to dryness in a slack oven.

877—Trouble in Planning Dinners

The last dinner was not well planned; there were good things in plenty but they ought not to have met in the same bill of fare; there were too many fries; came near being all fried; the fish in batter with potatoes and onions fried, chicken cutlets breaded and fried, croustades the same, croutons too, and then apricots a la Colbert. It was a mistake to have it so, and such mistakes are being made wherever bills of fare are written continually. When we see a bill of fare in print in a newspaper, it generally is a model one or tries to be so; but models there are few or none in actual practice. The cook does not intend to get several dishes of the same nature or appearance in the same dinner and generally does not know it till it is too late to make a change; perhaps his time for reflection was short or he was thinking about the butcher's bill, or had found one thing he intended to use was spoiled, and an unsuitable substitute was put in hastily. While one bill may be all fries, perhaps another time it will be all cream—cream soup, fish with cream sauce, macaroni a la Bechamel, onions in cream, fried cream fritters, cream cakes and ice cream—for if there is a pastry cook he is sure to be lucky enough to come in with his contribution of creams at the same time. Another day the dinner will be all dough, with nudel soup, fish in batter, meat pie rissoles or kromeskies, fritters of some kind or pancakes and a batter pudding, or fruit cobbler. Still again there may be a surfeit of oysters; oysters raw, oyster soup, fish with oyster sauce, oyster stuffing in the turkey and oyster patties. So it goes about planning a dinner. One of Thackeray's novels has a French *chef* for a character, who goes off and plays the piano while composing his bill of fare and seems ludicrous to the reader but there is nothing extravagant about that. Most cooks make up the bulk of the bill of fare for to-morrow whilst carving or dishing up their entrees to-day when their thoughts are upon the subject; but some must go off and smoke or sit alone, and there is no reason why a piano or a banjo might not come in useful at such a time and help to prevent the bad arrangement which makes a dinner be all cream or all dough, or of any one thing more than its due proportion. And we have not touched the still higher consideration of how some dinners are all heaviness and indigestibility, beginning with a heavy soup and stuffed fish running on through dishes that allow no relief by contrast to plum pudding, mince pie and tutti frutti; while others are as uniformly thin and meagre, going from weak consomme through water, and more water to a finale of lemon water ice. If a piano will help theproper planning of a dinner, every house ought to have one.

Dinner.

August 6.
Soup—Mulligatawney a la Manhattan, (4 qts 32 cents.)
Sheephead, a la Dieppaise (2 lbs 24, trimmings 20; 44 cents.)
Potatoes, serpentine.
Roast beef (1 rib steak rare 1 lb 15 cents.
Beef a la mode Pariessene (2 lbs with pork etc 33 cents.)
Veal pie, a la Fermiere (1½ lbs veal 18, crust etc. 8; 26 cents.)
Cutlets of sweetbreads, Victoria (12 orders, 1 lb sweetbreads 25, sauces, breading, frying 20; 45 cents.)
Green peas 10, cabbage 4 string beans 2, corn and rice 15, potatoes 15 (46 cents.)
Indian pudding, hard sauce (3 pts and sauce 26 cents.)
Blackberry—apple pie (2 pies large 20 cents.)
Pineapple ice (made like No. 214 with water and whites instead of cream, 2 qts frozen 50 cents.)
Cake assorted (15 cents.)
Nuts, raisins, cheese, pickles, condiments (32 cents.)
Milk, cream, buttermilk (38 cents.)
Coffee, tea, bread, butter (24 cents.)
Total $ 4.46; 32 persons, 14 cents a plate.

878—Mul igataw y a la Manhattan.

Mulligatawny soup is always a curry soup although it may be changed in other respects. This remark is prompted by the mistake some cooks are making of giving the name to a soup made of tomatoes and vegetables without curry powder. Mulligatawny is from two East Indian words.

The soup above named is a chicken and rice soup with enough curry powder mixed in to give a pale yellow color. It is light and simple. Boil the fowl in the stock, take out and cut it in dice. Strain the stock, put in vegetables cut in dice and the chicken and little rice, curry, seasonings and small amount of starch thickening.

879 --Sheephead a la Dieppoise.

Fillets of fish placed in a deep baking pan, a matelotte (or fish stew) poured over, cracker crumbs on top and baked. Dieppe is a seaport and fishing town. Cut the sheephead or other fish in two-ounce strips, free from bones. Mince an onion fine. Butter the baking pan, strew the onion in and fill with the fish.

For the matelotte make white sauce about 3 cups, and put into it shrimps, oysters and button mushrooms, about ½ cup of each, or if oysters are out of season, use lobster or crab substitutes, pour over the fish in the pan, bake as above stated. Dish up with some of the sauce, and serve potatoes in the same plate.

880—Potatoes Serpentine.

There is an instrument like an auger made for the special purpose of boring out potatoes in corkscrew shapes. When it has passed through a potato you have two spirals of the size and appearance of strands of untwisted rope. Fry light colored in hot lard. Serve with fish and entrees.

881—Beef a la Mode Parissienne.

A piece of beef larded with salt pork only, braised tender, garnished in the dish with large cuts of vegetables in fancy forms, and very green peas, and a crouton. Braise the beef as usual. Prepare an assortment of bright-colored vegetables—carrots, turnips, parsnips, anything that may be at hand, and cut them in shapes like a section of an orange, and some like bottle corks; and for the round ones pick out small onions, size of marbles, and fry them till they are lightly browned, in a frying pan. Boil the vegetables, then put them and the onions in brown sauce; strain in the braised beef gravy and add little wine. Have a bowl of small peas, very green, either garden or French canned. Slice the a la mode beef, place mixed vegetables in gravy around it, spoonful of peas on top and a crouton dipped in sauce at one end.

882—Veal Pie, a la Fermier

Fermier is French for farmer; a la mode fermiere means country style. Make a good veal stew with milk in it as directed for veal pot pie, cover with short pie crust and bake.

883—Cutlets of Sweetbreads, a la Victoria.

Croquette mixture of sweetbreads made in cutlet shapes.

There are two principal ways of preparing croquettes, either with panada as for the chicken cutlets of the last dinner or with roux of butter and flour, which is richer. Prepare the roux and the sauce made of it by putting a cup of flour and large ½ cup butter into a frying pan and stir over the fire until they bubble, hen add 2 cups broth, allowing it to boil with constant stirring; this makes sauce of double thickness. Put in a pound or more of minced sweetbreads previously boiled, and 2 raw eggs. Stir till well cooked, add little nutmeg, salt, pepper, lemon juice, and then cool it in a pan. Make out in shape of mutton chops, stick a length of macaroni to imitate the bone, dip in egg and cracker dust, and fry in hot lard. Serve with Allemande sauce in the dish and garniture of croutons, fancy potatoes or quenelles.

884—Baked Indian Pudding—Richest.

4 cups milk—a quart.
1 heaped cup corn meal—6 ounces.
Butter size of an egg—2 ounces.
1 large cooking spoon molasses—
3 ounces.
4 eggs (8 yolks are better.)
1 small lemon.

Make mush of the milk and meal and set it at the back of the range, or on a brick and with a tight lid on keep cooking slowly for an hour or two. Then grate in the rind of lemon and squeeze in juice of half; add the black molasses, butter and eggs and bake in a 2 quart pan about ½ hour. It makes 3 pints. As only half the people, or probably less will order pudding or any other ordinary dish in a plentiful dinner this amount is enough for a dinner for 30. There are plenty of cooks even in very good hotels who can never make a satisfactory Indian pudding; it runs with them from a hard corn cake to a sort of brown gruel which nobody wants. The only remedy is to weigh or measure the ingredients and follow directions.

885—Mixed Fruits For Pies.

When certain kinds of fruits have been repeatedly used because of their plentifulness some variety may be had by mixing two sorts together. Apples and blackberries are good in any form of pastry when so mixed; in the bakery pies, No. 303, in steamed fruit puddings, No. 176, and in the ordinary family pie—and mulberries which are almost useless alone may be used as well as any other fruit if mixed with an acid variety.

886—Trouble With Captain Johnson.

The trouble with Captain Johnson was, he was too superficial in his methods for his own interests and was not so smart as he thought himself. It was a long way from this place; yet I could not help reverting to one of the extremes of wastefulness, when, by a singular unfitness of season, just as I was deploring the loss of frying fat in making the dinner of two days ago, the woodman, or keeper of this place through the winter time, came with a complaint that he is getting no grease this summer for his wife to make her winter's soap with, as he has been used to do, and that the waste from the kitchen is not sufficient to fatten over half the pigs he has supplied himself with, and his pork crop will be deplorably short. He intimates that his place is not worth much to him if shorn of these perquisites. This is a sad case, but none of us get any such perquisites in this house. The question is here how a good table can be set in a house that charges ten dollars a week when all the saving ways of turning one thing into another and using up everything by the appliance of skill such as the French are credited with in the same line are brought into requisition and carried out industriously, and not how many hogs can we fatten, or how many barrels of grease can we make. Poor John! By the time the little suet that comes on the closely trimmed meats has been used for shortening pie crusts and puddings, and the fat from the roasts and soups is used for frying and sauteing, there is hardly enough left for him to grease his boots with. I know from experience that thousands of meals are sold daily for from 20 to 25 cents that are allowed to cost 40 or 50 cents, not through what the people eat or want, but because of the unnecessary wastes of all kinds and the extraneous expenses, and the sellers of meals on those losing terms are only kept up by their beds, their bar profits, livery or other source of revenue.

John is a young man and was born too late. He would have been happy on Captain Johnson's steamboat on the Mississippi where the cooks made from 7½ to 10½ barrels of grease to sell for themselves every trip the boat made. It will be observed there was always a half barrel—that is where Captain Johnson comes in. He could neither read nor write, but he owned his steamboat and she was a good one—the America—carrying cotton, tobacco and pork from the city of N——, State of T——, to New Orleans, and taking molasses and imported goods on the return trip. But New Orleans was the point the employes considered the beginning and the end of the trip. This used to take about three weeks on the average. On every trip up the boat used to take on a supply of pine knots at the mouth of Red River; that was racing fuel kept ready in case any boat came in sight, that it was necessary to beat; for the America could beat most of them. But before reaching Red River on the return trip, that stock of pine was exhausted; and there being nothing but Tennessee poplar and gum wood on the

boat, it was no uncommon thing for the engineers to seize all the bacon shoulders and hams they could lay their hands on to mix with it to make more steam. The cooks thought that a very poor use to put fat bacon to, and, to prevent it, all they could lay their hands on, they cut up and laid snugly out of the engineers' reach in the bottom of their grease barrels. Captain Johnson, as may well be supposed, was averse to all such proceedings, and instituted a rule which none dared break, that no soap-grease man should take away the "slush" or any part of it before he had examined it. Does the reader think that that placed the boys in a bad fix? Not at all; they knew him well. So every trip on the day of reaching port he went down into the kitchen and rolled up his right sleeve.

"Well, boys, how many barrels of slush have you made this trip?" (This is where the politicians get the word "slush money"). "Only eight and a half, Captain,—been as saving on you as possible —it might have been ten barrels if we hadn't took good care."

"Eight—nine! why you villains— what do you mean, going to rob me out of my boat?"

"Captain, we had a big trip of passengers up, and a long trip, and the meats were some fatter than usual, and this ain't so much as last trip by half a—"

"Let me see it—let me see it—well, why don't you bring me my long flesh fork—here—no, not that, the long one. Oh you infernal rascals, I know you. I began life as a cook myself, and I know you."

And with that Captain Johnson began forking the contents of the first full barrel over into the half-filled barrel that stood ready for it. By the time the full barrel was half emptied the half barrel was, of course, full; and, having no more room, he commenced forking over the next full barrel into that he had just quit, never reaching the bottom of any barrel in the row, but keeping up his talk all the while.

"You can't rob me, boys, I've got eyes and my eyes ain't sheep's eyes that you can pull the wool over—I've been a cook and I know the ropes—and—and I've pulled 'em all—there, now; I've got you, what's this?"

But it always proved to be a bare bone or something worthless; and so the farce was always carried out on every trip during the eight month's season, and the boys received $4 a barrel from the soap men for spending money as soon as the boat reached the wharf.

It stands in proof that human nature—even steamboat human nature—is not wholly depraved; that nobody ever wounded Captain Johnson's self-love by informing him how grossly he was being deceived. Suppose the boys beat him out of a hundred dollars over and above what was right; he must be dead before this; for he was well along in years at that time, and surely it was worth twice a hundred dollars to him to die in the happy belief that nobody had ever been able to pull the wool over his eyes.

Dinner.

August 7.
Soup—Potage a la Bagration (6 qts 36 cents.)
Croaker in batter, sauce remoulade (3 lbs and sauce, 46 cents.)
Potatoes a la Bazaine.
Boiled mutton, caper sauce (boned shoulder, 2 lbs and sauce 27 cents.)
Roast beef (2 lbs flank 22 cents.)
Spring lamb (hind quarter, 6 lbs 70 cents.)
Emince of veal with eggs (6 orders, 8 cents.)
Timbales of macaroni a la Rossini (15 orders 23 cents.)
Rice 5, peas 12, corn 15, cabbage 6, potatoes 15 (53 cents.)
Sliced bread and butter pudding (with sauce, 2 qts, 20 orders 22 cents.)
Apricot pie (2 with one can apricots 25, crust 5, 30 cents.)
Vanilla ice cream (2 qts pure, 3 when frozen 65 cents.)
Chocolate cake (finest, No. 894, 1 lb 12 cents.)
White cake (finest, No. 622, 1 lb 10 cents.)
Fruit, cheese, crackers, pickles (30 cents.)
Milk, cream, buttermilk (38 cents.)
Bread, butter, coffee, tea (28 cents.)
Total $5 20; 32 persons, 16 cents a plate.

887—Potage a la Bagration.

Anything denominated bagration will prove to be a mixture of fish and vegetables. For potage bagration make a white rice soup with mixed vegetables cut in small dice and fish cut small, about one-third of it milk, and flavor with curry or saffron. If in Lent make the stock of the fish by boiling it whole, take out, strain the liquor and cut the fish in pieces to be added after the rice and vegetables are cooked enough. The soup should be rather thick with rice and fish and well sprinkled with parsley at dishing-up time.

Careme was at one period in the employ of the Countess of Bagration; it is probable that the half dozen dishes bearing that designation were named in compliment to her or to the house.

888—Croaker in Batter, Sauce Remoulade.

The croaker is a southern sea-fish, small, something like a white perch—good for frying and broiling.

Split the fish lengthwise, remove the bone, salt well, dip in thin batter same as for a la Horly, or same as fruit fritters, and fry in lard not too hot. Serve with sauce and some special form of potatoes.

889—Sauce Remoulade.

Remoulade is the French name of a favorite kind of salad dressing that is made with cooked yolks in part, has garlic, shalots and parsley added. It is different from mayonaise which is made with raw yolks. Looks like sauce tartare, which is minced pickles and shalots (young onions) in mayonaise. Take:
3 hard boiled yolks.
1 raw yolk.
¼ cup olive oil.
Same of melted fresh butter.
½ cup vinegar.
1 teaspoon salt, pinch of cayenne.
1 teaspoon made mustard.
2 or 3 cloves of garlic crushed and minced, and 2 tablespoons finely minced green onions.
Pound the hard-boiled yolks in a bowl

with the butter; add salt, mustard pepper; then the raw yolk, or two of them, and stir in the oil gradually and alternately with the vinegar. It makes a buttery compound that is a most excellent salad dressing without the garlic and onion, but add those to make the sauce remoulade.

890—Potatoes Algerienne.

Cut raw potatoes in large cubes (dice) same as for Brabant, the more perfect the better; the outside trimmings of potato can be used to mash. Steam or boil first and let get cold, then saute the cubes in a frying pan like Dutch fried. Sprinkle with salt and parsley when done. Serve with fish and as a garnish for entrees. Cold boiled potatoes can be used equally as well as raw, and the outside cuttings cooked a la Lyonaise.

Lyonaise refers to the city of Lyons in France. Bazaine was the name of a general.

891—Emince of Veal With Eggs.

Trim up the remains of cold veal or shave off the outside of cold cooked cutlets; mince the meat small, put in a pan with few spoonfuls of hot gravy, seasoning of powdered thyme or sage or nutmeg, salt and pepper; make hot without cooking. Serve neatly a spoonful heaped in a small dish with a lengthwise quarter or two of hard-boiled egg on top and croutons, fancy potatoes or quenelles for ornament.

892—Timbales of Macaroni, a la Rossini.

A timbale is a shape, mould or form; the term is not often applied to anything but moulds of macaroni, rice and potato.

Cook ½ pound of macaroni, and when cold, cut it in inch lengths, and mix with it a cupful of grated cheese, little salt and pepper.

Slice up ½ cup of button mushrooms, same of cold, smoked tongue, same of truffles or boiled chicken (livers substitute); moisten them with a spoonful of Spanish sauce or gravy; then mix them

with the macaroni and cheese.

Take deep gem pans or patty pans of sufficient number, butter and coat them with cracker dust, press in the macaroni mixture, put a small lump of butter on top; bake brown.

Serve with a spoonful of gravy in the dish, the timbale turned out of the mould, a conical pile of cheese on top.

Named for Rossini, the composer, who is said to have been extremely partial to both truffles and macaroni.

893—Sliced Bread and Butter Pudding.

1 pound bread in slices—about 1 loaf.
½ cup butter.
4 cups milk.
2 tablespoons sugar.
3 eggs (6 yolks are better.)
1 cup currants.
Grated nutmeg enough to flavor.

Have the slices free from dark crust, spread the butter on them, place in two layers in the pudding pan with currants between and on top. Beat eggs, sugar, milk and nutmeg together, and pour over the bread, cover with either buttered paper or crust and bake half an hour. Serve with sauce or sweetened cream.

894—Chocolate Cake—Best.

2 cups granulated sugar—a pound.
1 cup butter—½ pound.
1 cup milk—½ pint.
5 cups flour—little over a pound.
2 teaspoons baking powder.
12 whites of eggs—or 1½ cups.
4 ounces chocolate.
Vanilla extract.

Make up same as white cake, No. 622, melt the chocolate by warming it in a cup with nothing added, and beat it into the cake. Vanilla extract improves the chocolate flavor but is not essential. 4 pounds cost 48 cents.

895—Trouble in Serving Meals.

At a pleasure resort it is the same as on board a steamer or at the first table of a public banquet, everybody sits down to the table at the same instant, and, to all appearances, begins instantly to wish that he were the only guest and all the other people were waiters so that he might be instantaneously served. It may seem somewhat ridiculous in people who have really nothing else to do to become so impatient over a little delay in receiving their meals; but with that we have nothing to do; to be successful in serving meals it is quite as important to get them on the table expeditiously as it is to have them well cooked.

It happened that I was a passenger on two excursion steamers belonging to the same line on the great lakes and saw on board one of the very worst, and on the other the very best method in practice for dealing with this difficulty. The first was the newest, largest, finest, steamer of the line, the pet of the company, and, being too good to adopt common ways, its dining saloon was run on the plan of those high-priced restaurants which get about one customer in every half hour, and keep him reading the paper another half hour, while they cook a meal for him, but it did not work on this steamer, where a hundred people sat down at once, and did not want to wait over a half minute apiece. There was nothing on the tables that people could help themselves to. The waiters were almost invisible; a few ladies at the further end took up all their time putting a little more water in their tea, and changing their beefsteaks for one a little better done, while all the rest at all the other tables sat unnoticed and getting madder the longer they sat. Perhaps a waiter with a tray load of cups full of coffee would be captured by one table, and another with meat or rolls by another, but very seldom did all the parts of a meal meet together at any one place; the service was, therefore, an utter failure, and the quality of the cookery could not even come into consideration, no matter how high the pretensions of the boat to superiority might be. The other boat had two long tables with a large part of the staple articles that go to complete a meal set upon it within easy reach—the individual butters and creams, bread, pickled jellies, mustard, sugar, cheese, salt— there was a saucer as well as a plate at every seat. When the steward's bell taps for breakfast as the passengers filed in and took their places the waiters at the same time came on with their trays ready loaded with the dishes which were surest to be called for—beefsteaks, ham, eggs, chops, hot breads and fried potatoes— and with cups of coffee, and by the time the people were well in their seats, the full meal was before them, and if the waiters were then sent off by a few for chocolate, hot milk, boiled fish instead of fried omelets, or a little more water in the tea, they did not leave the great majority in a state of suffering and suspense.

There is a good deal in having plenty of waiters; and yet that is not all; for often there are so many they are in one another's way, because of the impossibility of getting the cooking or carving done just enough to keep them in motion. It is scarcely necessary to say that all was joy and peace and contentment on this steamer where the passengers found their soup just being set at their place as they reached it and where the ice cream and cake came even before they were ready for them, and the waiters seemed almost troublesome by their frequent offerings of fruit and glasses of water, while the other steamer, the too good one, came into port loaded down to the guards with remains of good intentions, of good things that were provided, but could never be served, and with execrations and maledictions of the dissatisfied. Bestowing some thought on these things before we pull the bell rope at our little summer house, we have the eggs broke and dishes ready for immediate frying, the gridiron chock full of steaks and chops already sizzling over the glowing charcoal and the gravy made ready; and we get the housekeeper to come, like a good fellow, and dish up the stewed tomatoes, potatoes, oat meal and side dishes generally, while we are turning out the omelets and eggs, or carving the roast, and our "sec" is making toast or serving ice cream and fruit.

Dinner.

August 8.

Soup—Consomme with quenelles (5 qts 35 cents.)

Red Snapper a la Joinville (3 lbs and trimmings 60 cents.)

Potato boulettes.

Boiled ham aud tongue (left for cold, say, 15 cents.)

Roast beef (rip ends only, 3 lbs. 24 cents.)

Spring lamb (fore quarter, 6 lbs, 70 cents,)

Veal cutlets, a la Milanaise (8 orders, 1 lb and trimmings, 20 cents.)

Vinaigrette of brains, Provencale (7 orders, brains with trimmings, 25 cents,)

Marrowfat peas 20, beets in sauce 6, rice 4, string beans 2, tomatoes 15, potatoes 14 (61 cents,)

Boiled plum pudding, sauce sabayon (No. 901, with sauce 38 cents.)

Rhubarb pie (2 small garden, 15 cents.)

Peach ice cream (No. 217; Cal. peaches in syrup, 1 can 25, 3 pts cream, etc., 75 cents.)

Cakes, fruit and white (charged previous meals.)

Summer apples, nuts, raisins, cheese, 40 cents.)

Milk, buttermilk, 2 gallons 24, cream 1 qt 20, (44 cents.)

Butter 10, bread 6, coffee, tea, 12 (28 cents.)

Total $5 50; 32 persons, 17 cents a plate.

896—Consomme With Quenelles.

Clear soup like No. 139 with yellow egg balls in the plates. One way of making egg balls for such purposes may be found at No. 797. Another sort is made as follows: Put into a small saucepan a heaping tablespoon of flour, and about the same weight of butter, and stir them over the fire as if to make butter sauce, instead of a full cup of water or broth, which this amount of flour would thicken, pour in only half a cup, stir up, and you have a stiff butter paste. Add the yolks of 4 eggs, one after the other, stirring over the fire until they are cooked in the mixture. Season with salt, if not enough in the butter, cayenne and nutmeg. Make in balls when cool, size of grapes, poach them in water, drop 4 or 5 in each plate of consomme when served. Another way is to pound 4 hard boiled yolks with an equal amount of butter, add all the dry flour needed to make dough of it, make in balls and boil.

897—Red Snapper a la Joinville.

Remove the rough skin of this fish with the point of a sharp knife or by dipping in boiling water, but it need not be split open. Brush over with egg, sift cracker meal upon it, take up and place in baking pan with oil or lard and bake light brown, basting once. Make white sauce (veloute) with fish liquor or oyster liquor and a small portion of white wine. Add to it oysters, crayfish, button mushrooms, very small onions, shrimps and scallops, or such substitutes as may be available to make a good matelotte sauce with wine, salt and cayenne. Serve portions of the fish with plenty of the matelotte poured over, and potatoes in some special form in the same place. Can be served whole for a party as well with the matelotte poured around, sliced lemons on the fish and potato boulettes or Parisienne stacked in groups at ends and sides.

Joinville is the title of a French prince

898—Potato Boulettes.

Potato balls, made of potato croquette mixture with another raw yolk added to make it moist. Roll in flour till they have taken a good coating and without egging or breading; fry them in the frying basket in very hot lard, only a minute or two. They burst open if fried too long. They should be about the size of walnuts or little larger. Serve two in each plate of fish.

899—Veal Cutlets, Milanaise.

Cut 8 cutlets small and thin, but of good shape; dust with powdered herbs, salt and pepper; dip both sides in a plate of flour and let them remain in it until near dinner time. Melt 4 ounces of butter in a frying pan, and, when it froths up, lay in the cutlets and saute them brown. Serve direct out of the pan with the hot, brown butter adhering, and a few olives and a quarter of lemon in the dish.

900—Vinaigrette of Brains, a la Provencale.

French vinaigrette sauce of minced pickles and shalots of olive oil seasoned with salt and pepper; poured over a portion of calf's brains previously boiled.

Parboil the brains first, and pick off all the dark stains, divide in portions and simmer for half an hour in seasoned broth, cut up a lemon in them and keep hot till served. The vinaigrette sauce to be kept cold. It is thick with minced pickles and shalots enough to season—like tartar sauce made of clear oil instead of mayonaise.

901—Boiled Plum Pudding.

1 pound white bread crumbs—4 pressed cups.
½ pound sugar—1 cup.
½ pound minced suet—2 pressed cups.
½ pound raisins—1 heaped cup.
Same of currants.
1 cup milk.
4 eggs, pinch soda and salt.
1 teaspoon mixed ground spices—cinnamon, nutmeg, mace, alspice.

Mix the dry articles together—the bread crumbs chopped very fine; mix the milk and eggs, salt and soda, and, if you use brandy or wine, add a few spoonfuls and pour it over the dry mixture and stir up thoroughly. Tie up in two pudding bags, or put in two moulds and boil or steam them 4 hours. Brandy sauce, or sabayon or No. 733.

Cost, bread 5, sugar 4, suet 4, raisins and currants 10, milk 1, eggs 5, spices, lemon peel or liquor 5; 34 cents for 3½ pounds or 25 orders.

902—Trouble With the Manager.

The trouble with our manager is, he is not making as much money as he expected, and he is looking at the table and at my regularly rendered account of cost per meal to find the reason why. Another of those blue spells has come upon us which often occur early in August when it turns unseasonably cold and there has been two days of steady rain. The people sit and mope and have no appetites for meals, get tired of themselves and want to get up and go, and some do go; many resort houses are almost emptied by the occurrence of two rainy days. Not only that, but those who are free are often curious to try a

number of different places during the season and although the average of goers and comers may be equal in the end, there are times when an hotel is almost depopulated for no reason but that it is the ebb before the flood, and it happens so.

The way it began between the manager and myself was this: You see the manager at such a small place as this has to be a gentleman of all-work; he is required to look sweet, and play croquette and tennis part of the time, but he also acts as host, clerk, cashier, bookkeeper, paymaster and part steward. As long as there was nobody in the house and no bills to collect we will suppose the owner of the place put up the money for expenses, but when there began to be some receipts, the manager was told to go it alone, and I expect he has been counting over his money. Day after to-morrow he has to pay all his help, the tenth being the day of the month almost always observed in that way, for by that time the monthly bills which fall due on the first have been collected and the indebtedness to the butcher and market men has been liquidated, then when the employees are paid he can count over his balance on hand, or at least ask where it is. If our crowd had kept up to about forty-five souls he would have been away ahead and would have asked me no questions; as it is he has been asked on every trip to town to bring back a couple of cans of mushrooms, or a dozen lemons, or a can of shrimps and bottle of oil and so forth and while he always brings them he hesitates and asks first if they are really necessary, with a great stress laid upon the "really." Now, the butcher at the Glen knows we get our meats by express and never go to him except in a case of necessity; consequently, he puts his finger in our manager's eye every time he sells him a piece of meat. This afternoon he sold the manager—who is proud to say he does not know one piece of meat from another—a piece of the neck of beef for a roast, and flour briskets of mutton for racks and loins to cut into chops, and when I explained the manager only laughed, and said it was good enough, and he would like to make some money anyhow, and there was no use of being so particular. Then he went on to ask why the dinners now were costing sixteen and seventeen cents a plate according to my own showing; whereas, for two or three weeks they ran from seven to eleven cents only, and why the same cheap scale could not be always preserved. There is no reason why. He is in the right. Ten-cent dinners such as we had three weeks back could be continued all the season, and give satisfaction. However, I have not been under any instruction or restraint in this matter. If the owner of the place has had any thought about the matter, it has probably been only to see what I would do, and in what ways this summer's style would differ from the household style of keeping up a table. John, the keeper, has been comparing the frugal management of provisions this summer, which leaves him no perquisites with the waste of former years, which gave him a large pork crop, and he thinks it extreme niggardliness.

The manager, who was not here last year, is comparing the seventeen-cents-a-plate of to-day, with the ten-cents-a-plate of last month, and it seems to him a change to extravagance. There is no room for a reasonable doubt that there was much wasted last year through want of knowing what to do with it, and through cooking too much as it takes to make our most expensive meals now. The extravagance of the dinners, such as it is, arises from the use of more meat in the soups and sauces, the use of sea-fish, which the butcher sends according to a custom which prevails, at eleven cents, and which costs 12½, delivered; whereas, the lake fish costs but 9; and the cooking in fillets entails a loss of bulk and requires more pounds gross for a given number of people than if cooked plain, with the bones in. There has been an indulgence in a few cans of pineapple, and other fruits in syrup, a few olives, a bottle of wine, a mincing up of pickles, a rather more lavish use of eggs and crackers for frying, and of lard for the same, a little waste in the matter of potatoes in fancy forms, the new potatoes being dearer than the old, and all the odd cents counted up together have swelled the sum total. There has not been a corresponding increase in the cost of breakfast and supper, the latter, indeed, being half made up of the meats and other remains from dinner, and being quite an inexpensive meal.

But what are we here for? Not alone to see how cheaply one summer hotel can be kept, but to find out how much it costs to live well. The custom mentioned in connection with the butcher is, that one who supplies a number of hotels occasionally get a refrigerator car full of special kinds of provisions, which he sends around to his first-class customers, without waiting for the order, assuming that a novely will be welcome in the height of the season.

Dinner.

August 9.
Soup—Pot au fere (6 qts 20 cents.)
Sliced cucumbers (on table 12 cents.)
Stewed codfish and potatoes (18 cents.)
Corned tongue and cabbage (½ tongue 15, cabbage 5, 20 cents.)
Roast beef (piece loin, 2½ lbs 30 cents.)
Breast of lamb, a la jardiniere (2 briskets, 4 lbs 32 cents.)
Ragout of beef, a la Creole (meat from soup pot 20, with trimmings 30 cents.)
Macaroni au gratin (No. 629; 12 cents.)
Summer beats 5, string beans 3, corn 15, rice 7, potatoes 15 (45 cents.)
Baked Indian pudding (cheap, 20 cents.)
Apple pie, rhubarb pie (4 pies, 28 cents.)
Lemon ice cream (2 qts milk, starch, eggs, etc., 38 cents.)
Cakes (2 lbs 18 cents.)
Nuts, raisins, pickles, cheese crackers (40 cents.)
Milk, buttermilk 24, coffee 10, tea, sugar 6, bread 6.

Total $3 99; 40 persons; 10 cents a plate.

Eight military cadets arrived shortly before dinner—had to add a little here and there but, practicially, the same dinner was sufficient that would have been prepared for 32—it is but a more thorough clean-up of the dishes and a little ekeing out of the corn and ice cream, and a few slices of cake served in place of the departed pudding. In a case like this it is the home folks that go without.

903—Pot-au-Feu or Gravy Soup.

Take 3 or 4 pounds of coarse beef, the

neck will do or the long strings of the flank which some butchers sell attached to the porter house steaks; cut in pieces, put it into a jar or pot with 6 quarts of water and set it in the oven while breakfast is going on or at such a time that it may bake 3 hours. Sometime while baking throw into the jar an onion cut small, a piece of carrot, turnip, celery and parsnip or whichever may be at hand, merely to give a little flavor, but the meat gravy is the characteristic of the soup and not the vegetables. Season with salt and pepper. Take out the meat and reserve it for a side dish. Skim the fat off the soup, add a little flour thickening, boil up and serve with a few squares of toasted bread in the plates.

904—Stewed Codfish and Potatoes.

Chop a pound of salt codfish in pieces size of walnuts, steep them a few hours to freshen, boil in water, throw that away and boil again in fresh water and milk; put in as many potatoes as there are pieces of fish, also a small onion, lump of butter, pepper, and thicken like white sauce with flour.

905—Breast of Lamb, a la Jardinier.

Chop briskets of mutton lengthwise in strips, put them in a deep baking pan with seasonings and vegetables, cover with buttered paper and let cook in the oven until quite tender and the liquor is dried down.

Prepare a bright-colored jardinier of very green peas, white and yellow turnips, string beans, summer squash, cucumbers, carrots, whatever of the kind can be had except beets which would color everything. Cut these vegetables all to one small size, and boil in water till done. Mix them in one saucepan and pour over them the seasoned gravy, made in the baking pan, which should not, however, be of a dark color. Serve cuts of the braised ribs of lamb or mutton smothered with the vegetables and a spoonful of gravy poured under.

906—Ragouts of Beef, a la Creole.

Take the pieces of beef from the soup pot and cut to medium sized portions. Mince an onion, crush a half head of garlic with the side of your knife, and mince that; put them on in a frying pan with a spoonful of the clear fat from the soup and stir over the fire until cooked and beginning to brown; then add a small can of tomatoes, rubbed through a colander; season with salt and pepper, then put in the pieces of beef and keep simmering, set upon a brick until served. If not likely to be a thick sauce by boiling down there should be a little thickening of roux or raw flour added to the tomatoes. Cut a leaf shaped crouton of thin bread for each dish and fry them brown to be placed at the end for ornament and for use.

907—Baked Indian Pudding—Cheap.

1 pound corn meal.
2 quarts water.
Make mush of them, set at back of stove or on a brick and let cook with a lid on a long time. Then add:
½ cup butter or fine minced suet.
1 small cup molasses—the black sort.
4 eggs.
1 teaspoon ground ginger.
Stir up and bake. Serve with any pudding sauce or sugar dip or cream.
Costs 16 cents for nearly three quarts.

Supper For Forty.

August 9.
Oatmeal mush (2 heaped cups 1 lb, makes 2 qts, 5 cents.)
Beefsteak (21 orders, 10 tenderloins 11 common, 3 lbs, 45 cents.)
Broiled ham (6 orders, 12 ounces net 15 cents.)
Cold meats (for chidren, 6 orders charged dinner.)
Welsh rarebit (19 orders 1¼ lbs cheese etc. 22 cents.)
Broiled smoked salmon (8 orders, 12 ounces, 12 cents.)
Potatoes new baked (10 cents.)
French rolls (30 rolls 12 cents.)
Corn muffins (No. 286; 18 deep with 2 cups meal, 1 flour, 3 eggs; 13 cents.)
Canned grapes in syrup (2 cans 50 cents.)
Cakes assorted (2 lbs 20 cents.)

Milk 2½ gal 30, cream 3 pts 30, coffee ⅓ lb 10, butter 1¼ lbs 25, tea 4, sugar 1¼ lbs 10, bread 3 (112 cents.)

Total $3 16; 40 persons, nearly 8 cents a plate.

908—Welsh Rar.bit—Three Ways

A Welsh rarebit is a slice of cheese baked upon a slice of bread; the seasonings are optional.

1. A good and easy way for a family party is to cut a number of thin slices of bread, toast them and spread with butter; cut a very thin slice of cheese for each one, place in a baking pan and bake on the top shelf in the oven until the cheese is melted; serve hot or bake only three or four at a time if the orders come that way.

2. This is more elaborate; it is the restaurant and club style :

1 pound cheese.
4 ounces butter.
1 glass ale.
Salt, cayenne.
10 slices of toast.

Mince the cheese small, put it and the butter in a saucepan, set over the fire and work them together with a spatula or a pestle until the cheese is hot and melted, but take care not to let it reach boiling heat, but keep it cooled by adding ale in small portions until the mixture is smooth and creamy. Add cayenne and perhaps a little salt if not enough in the butter. Place thin slices of toast in the dishes, pour a spoonful of the creamed cheese upon them and set in the top of the oven for 3 or 4 minutes. Pour a little ale upon the edges of the toast and serve.

3. For a large number as in a hotel, the creamed cheese prepared as above may be kept warm without boiling by setting in a vessel of hot water, the toast kept ready and spread with a spoonful of the cheese as called for and sent in without baking.

4. Instead of ale use milk and a milder flavored dish will be the result, which may suit better at a country house.

909—Cheese Fondue.

Is the name of a sort of cheese omelet that is fully half cheese and is a dish much esteemed in some quarters, and does not mean the same as fondu or melted cheese.

Make the creamed cheese as for the Welsh rarebits of the foregoing receipts, and while stirring over the fire break in 6 eggs, one at a time, and finish like scrambled or buttered eggs. Serve on toast or in a dish bordered with toast cut in shapes.

910—Smoked Salmon—Broiled.

Cut smoked and dried salmon in broiling slices and steep in water for half a day. Dry the slices on a cloth, brush with butter and broil about 5 minutes.

Breakfast for Forty.

August 10.
Fresh huckleberries (2 qts 24 cents.)
Summer apples (10 cents.)
Oatmeal and hominy grits (3 cups makes 3 qts, 7 cents.)
Beefsteak (18 orders, 2¼ lbs net and butter 45 cents.)
Mutton chops (9 orders, 1½ lbs, 18 cents.)
Ham (9 orders, 1 lb net, 15 cents.)
Eggs any style (3 dozen 45 cents.)
Codfish balls (18 with 1½ lbs fish etc. 24 cents.)
Fried mush (4 orders 4 cents.)
Potatoes baked, and a la Francaise (10 cents.)
Muffins (No. 582; 18, 14 cents.)
French rolls (30, 12 cents.)
Corn batter cakes (1 qt 9 cents.)
Milk 2 gal. 24, cream 2 qts 40, butter 1¼ lbs 25, syrup 8, coffee 8, tea 2, chocolate 8, bread 4, sugar 12 (131 cents.)

Total $3 68; 40 persons; little over 9 cents a plate.

911—Codfish Balls.

There should be nearly as much fish used as potato, say 1 pound of salt codfish to 8 potatoes. Codfish balls cannot be made very good with cold mashed potatoes; all should be fresh boiled for the purpose and made up hot.

Steep a pound of codfish in water to

freshen it, boil in two waters, pick free from bones, mash it thoroughly in a pan with a potato masher. Turn in the hot potatoes and pound them together, add a seasoning of black pepper, very little butter and, if you choose, 1 egg or 2 or 3 yolks. Make up in balls either round or flattened with plenty of flour on the hands; drop in hot lard and fry brown.

If they do not have a good appearance when done you can change it next time by breading them in egg and cracker meal.

912—Cream Chocolate

There was the Queen and Crescent restaurant enjoying quite a reputation for its chocolate, every cup of which was said to be served with whipped cream on top although, in fact, no cream ever came near it—it was simply made to order and whisked up while on the fire as directed at our No. 56, but with less milk than that, and served with the appearance of whipped chocolate cream upon it. And there was, close by, the Hotel Fantastic, on Fantastic Beach, that was said never to have served a good cup of chocolate during the whole of its unprofitable existence. Such is the difference resulting from the methods of making—the latter using twice as much chocolate, making it hours too soon and spoiling it irrevocably in the detestable, bain-marie can, a miniature mud well.

Dinner.

August 10.
Soup—Consomme Knickerbocker (6 qts 30 cents.)
Lake trout stuffed (3 lbs and stuffing, 36 cents.)
Potatoes a la Colbert.
Boiled ham (shank, 2 orders 5 cents.)
Roast chicken with currant jelly (4 hens, 32 orders 110 cents.)
Beef a la mode Allemande (3 lbs net and trimmings 45 cents.)
Braised mutton with nudels (2 briskets, 4 lbs and trimmings 40 cents.)
Summer squash 14, beets 4, cabbage 10, rice 3, corn 15, potatoes 15; (61 cents.)
Baked prune pudding (2½ qts with sauce 28 cents.)

Custard pie (2 large, deep 24 cents.)
Blueberry pie (1 qt, 2 pies, large, thin 20 cents.)
Lemon ice cream (5 pts pure cream, sugar, flavor, freezing, makes 8 pts for 75 cents.)
Cakes, assorted kinds (2 lbs 20 cents.)
Nuts, raisins, cheese, crackers, pickles (average 42 cents.)
Milk, buttermilk 2½ gals. 30, cream 1 qt 20, coffee 8, tea 4, butter 20, jelly 10, bread 8, sugar 8 (108 cents)
Total $6 44; 42 persons: 15⅓ cents a plate.

913—Consomme Knickerbocker.

It is chicken broth made dark colored with fried vegetables and chopped fresh tomatoes, and a small amount of barley added. When you have fowls that must be boiled before roasting, the liquor they are boiled in makes good soup. Strain and skim it. Cut a mixture of small vegetables in dice and saute them with a little butter and sugar, the same as for Julienne; when lightly colored put them into the broth, and, if you have no fresh tomatoes, use the solid part of the canned cut in pieces, and without the juice. Barley should be boiled separately for it, or rice that is already cooked may be washed off clear and used instead. Season to taste.

914—Fish Stuffed and Baked.

Make a small amount of stuffing the same as for chicken and turkey, and seasoned with either powdered thyme or sage, and add an egg or two yolks. The back bone can be taken out of the fish without quite dividing the two sides, by cutting down inside nearly to the skin, and pulling the bone away. Wash the fish and dry it; spread the stuffing on one side, double over to the original shape; it may be sewed up with thread, but will do very well without. Place in the baking pan and score the upper side with a sharp knife in places where it is to be cut when done. Put a minced onion and some scraps of fat, salt pork in the pan, a spoonful of drippings, water and salt and bake nearly an hour. Serve out of the pan with a spoonful of Spanish sauce or other gravy, and potatoes in the same plate.

915—Potatoes a la Colbert.

Like marechale, largest size of Parisienne, size of crab apples, of raw potatoes, but steamed for this style instead of baked brown, and sprinkle with fine parsley, salt and melted butter.

916—Roast Chicken with Currant Jelly.

Boil old fowls two hours, take out, dredge with salt and pepper, then with flour, which insures a good, rich brown color, and bake about ¾ hour. Carve and serve with gravy and currant jelly.

917—Beef a la Mode Allemande, or German.

Lard a piece of lean beef in the usual way by drawing it full of strips of pork or bacon fat, put it in a jar or pot in the oven, with water enough to cover, and salt, pepper and few pieces of carrot and turnip, and bake about three hours. Take out the meat, skim and strain the liquor, add to it a cupful of white wine, one of raisins and one of prunes, and a small amount of flour thickening and boil up. Put back into the gravy the vegetables that were strained out before and serve this sauce with the cuts of beef.

918—Braised Mutton with Nudels.

Something like mutton with beans, a la Bretonne, but with nudels (noodles or nouilles) cooked separately and in gravy to serve with the cuts of mutton.

The briskets of mutton as well as the shoulders can be used up in this way. Take out the bones, season the meat and roll it up and bake or braise it long enough to make it quite tender, always keeping water enough in the pan to keep it from drying out, and a cover of greased paper on top.

919—Baked Prune Pudding.

Make a bread pudding, either No. 113 doubled perhaps in quantity, or at No. 390. Take three cups of stewed prunes without the juice and drop them in as you would raisins; the prunes are better if pitted and sprinkled with lemon juice.

920—Summer Squash.

This vegetable should always be steamed, or at any rate not boiled in water, it being an object to get it as dry as possible so as to allow the addition of milk or cream when it is mashed. Shave off the outside thinly with a sharp knife; cut each squash in six or eight pieces. It depends upon the age and distinctness of the seeds whether they should be cut out or not; if large enough to show prominently in the mashed squash take out the entire core. Squash cooks in about half an hour, and may be allowed to simmer and dry out more after mashing and seasoning, in a pan set upon a couple of bricks.

Dinner.

August 11.
Soup—Potage Parmentier or potato cream (7 qts 40 cents.)
Boiled pickerel, parsley sauce (3 lbs and sauce 36 cents.)
Potatoes Hollandaise.
Boiled ribs beef with horseradish (15 cents.)
Roast saddle of mutton (5 lbs 55 cents.)
Braised veal with browned potatoes (breast 5 lbs and potatoes, 60 cents.)
Ragouts of giblets en croustade (18 orders 30 cents.)
Green corn fritters, American style (30 orders 45 cents.)
String beans 3, beets, cabbage 10, rice 6, tomatoes 15, potatoes 15 (49 cents.)
New green apple pie (3 pies 21 cents.)
Raspberry pie (2 pies 18 cents.)
Gipsy pudding (24 orders 34 cents.)
Tapioca jelly with cream (jelly 1 qt 8, cream 4, 12 cents.)
Brandy snaps and wafer jumbles (15 cents.)
Nuts, raisins, cheese, condiments (average 44 cents.)
Milk 30, cream 20, butter 20, bread 8, coffee, tea, sugar 18 (96 cents.)
Total $5 70; 44 persons; 13 cents a plate.

921—Potage Parmentier, or Potato Soup.

Named for the man, M. Parmentier, who first brought the potato into France.

Take about 10 or 12 potatoes, steam or boil, mash and mix them with a quart of boiling milk or cream. Have a well seasoned soup stock ready made with beef and veal bones and the usual vegetables and a knuckle bone of boiled ham and a large onion additional boiled in it, and slightly thicken it while boiling, which will prevent the potato puree from settling. Mix 4 quarts of this stock with the potato cream, pass through a strainer or seive, season with salt and pepper, add a sprinkling of minced parsley and keep hot without boiling. Serve crusts or puff-paste croutons (No. 736) in the plates.

922—Breast of Veal with Browned Potatoes, or a l'Anglaise.

Saw through the ribs to make convenient cuts; cook as directed for rib ends of beef and serve new potatoes first steamed and then browned in the oven, and gravy in the dish.

923—Ragout of Giblets en Croustade.

Boil the livers, gizzards, hearts and necks of poultry in water to cover, when done drain them out and cut all into small pieces. Mince an onion and fry it in two ounces of butter or oil, put in two tablespoons flour and stir until it begins to brown, strain in the giblet liquor and a little Spanish sauce, Worcestershire sauce, or gravy besides; cut a slice of ham in small dice, throw that in and then the cut giblets. Season with cayenne and salt and wine, if wanted. Serve in patty shells or croustades like the following.

924—Croustades or Shells of Rice.

Make the same as directed for potato croustades, No. 874, using boiled rice mashed with yolk of egg instead of potato.

925—Corn Fritters or Mock Oysters —Two Ways.

The French way of making corn fritters is found at No. 817. These two ways, one with canned corn and one with roasting ears the cheaper and much more popular.

1. To one can of corn allow 2 eggs, an ounce of softened butter, teaspoon of mixed salt and pepper and about a cup of flour or according to the dryness of the corn. Stir up vigorously. Set a frying pan over the fire with lard in it just to cover the bottom when hot and drop in spoonfuls of the corn mixture flattened and about the size of large fried oysters. Cook brown on both sides and serve hot and fresh cooked. Good for a breakfast dish as well as for dinner.

2. Take ears of green corn and shave off the cob, and every pint count the same as one can above, and proceed the same way. These made with green corn have more of the taste of oysters than the others.

926—New Green Apple Pie.

Apples before they are ripe are best used this way. Steam them as you would potatoes without paring, when done mash them through a colander. Add sugar, butter and nutmeg to the pulp and make open pies with crust rolled thin, same style as pumpkin pie.

927—Gipsy Pudding.

Sponge jelly cake floating in a pan of cold custard.

Make the sponge cake No. 281 and bake on jelly-cake pans, put two together with fruit jelly between. Make boiled custard, No. 136, put in a tin milk pan when cold and the cake in it. Have a cup of cream in a large bowl, flavored with vanilla. Serve spoonfuls of the cake and custard, and whip up the cream and serve a spoonful on top for a finish.

928—Tapioca Jelly.

4 cups water.
½ cup tapioca—4 ounces.

1 heaped cup sugar—10 ounces.

1 cup raspberry juice or syrup, or lemon juice and rind and water.

Steep the tapioca in half the water two hours. The water should be cold but set in a rather warm place. Boil the other pint of water with the sugar in it and the raspberry or lemon syrup. Stir in the steeped tapioca and cook gently at the back of the stove until it is transparent, about half an hour. Pour into wetted cups or moulds; when cold and set turn it out and serve with cream or boiled custard.

Pearl tapioca is the best; the coarse granulated if used should first be crushed.

Cost: 8 cents a quart.

929—Brandy Snaps.

The name of a sort of molasses wafer, but there is no brandy about them.

4 cups flour—a pound.

1 cup butter—½ pound.

1 cup sugar—½ pound.

2 ounces ground ginger.

Lemon extract to flavor.

1 teaspoon soda—rounded measure.

2 large cups common molasses—1½ pounds.

Rub the butter into the flour as in making short paste, and add the ginger. Make a hole in the middle, put in the sugar, molasses and extract, dissolve the soda and put in, stir all together.

Drop the batter with a teaspoon on baking pans, not greased, and bake in a slack oven. The snaps run out flat and thin. Take off before they get cold and bend them to tubular shape on a new broom handle.

Dinner.

August 12.

Soup—Consomme St. Xavier (7 qts 42 cents.)

Lake trout, a la Genevoise (5 lbs and wine 70 cents.)

Potato bignets (10 cents.)

Roast beef (loin and flank 4 lbs 50 cents.)

Spring lamb, mint sauce (5 lbs 60 cents.)

Mutton stew a l'Irlandaise (2 lbs and vegetables 13 orders 20 cents.)

Macaroni a la Palermetane (12 orders

12 cents.)

Peaches a la Richelieu (1 can in syrup, 20 orders 33 cents.)

Stewed carrots 4, squash 6, butter-beans 8, mashed turnips 4, rice 5, potatoes 14 (41 cents.)

Steamed huckleberry roll (No. 937; 22 orders 28 cents.)

Saratoga shortcake (No. 301; 32 cents.)

Floating island (2 qts custard, cakes, jelly, cream 30 orders 26 cents.)

Corn starch jelly (1½ qts and cream 18 cents.)

Nuts, raisins, cheese, crackers condiments (45 cents.)

Milk and buttermilk 3 gallons 36, cream, 3 pts 30, butter 1¼ lbs 25, bread 8, coffee, tea, sugar 22 (121 cents.)

Total $6 08; 45 persons; 13½ cents a plate.

930—Consomme St. Xavier.

A brown vegetable broth with a kind of nudel paste in it.

Make a good consomme as usual, with brown roasted chicken and beef in it if practicable or make good with meat extract, and add to it a small portion of vegetables cut fine.

Make a yellow egg batter about as stiff as for fritters, with 8 yolks, a spoonful of water and flour sufficient and add a small amount of minced parsley and salt. Let some one stir the consomme around while you pour the batter in a colander and let it drip through the holes into the consomme which immediately cooks it in rounded lumps—another form of nudel soup.

There is another way of reaching a similar result, that is by putting the yolks in a pan and carefully mixing flour with them with the finger tips while shaking the pan at the same time, making loose yellow crumbs of nudel dough, soft but separate, and then scatter them loosely into the boiling soup. American cooks call this "riffle soup."

St. Xavier is the name of a place.

931—Lake Trout a la Genevoise.

Fish baked in wine and served on toast in gravy.

Take a 5-pound trout, cleanse and wipe dry; score through the skin on both sides where the individual portions are to be taken off, and also sever the bone by striking the point of a knife through. Dredge salt and pepper in a buttered baking-pan, put in the fish, a pint of wine, an onion stuck with cloves, and bunch of parsley and thyme. Set in the oven and bake and baste the fish while baking very frequently. The gelatinous gravy from the fish makes a glaze with the wine, which is to be coated over it by the basting. When done, which should be in half an hour, take up the fish into a dish, pour a pint of broth in the pan and make gravy, thickening with brown roux, strain, skim, make pieces of toast, serve toast in each dish, well saturated with the sauce and a cut of the glazed fish upon it and round slice of lemon dipped in parsley dust on top.

To serve whole in this style the head should be left on and the fish should be brown and shining, and placed upon a large crouton foundation of fried bread cut to its shape and the wine gravy poured around with garnishments of lemon and special forms of potatoes and small croutons.

932—French Potato Fritters or Beignets.

This makes 25, small size for garnishing:

12 ounces potato—2 cups mashed.
½ cup flour—2 ounces
2 tablespoons cream.
Same of white wine or sherry
3 eggs and 2 yolks
Salt, nutmeg and cayenne.

Take the potatoes from the dinner steamer and mash the required amount through a colander and while still warm mix in the other ingredients except the flour. The mixture should be in a deep pan or saucepan and set in cold water.

While it is cooling whip it light with an egg whisk, then stir in the flour.

Drop small spoonfuls egg-shaped in hot lard, fry light colored, drain on paper, serve one in each plate of fish and with any dish that is a la Dauphinoise.

Cost, about 10 cents for 25 fritters.

933—Mutton Stew, a la Irlandaise.

The half-French bill-of-fare name for Irish stew, No. 60. But there can be beef stew a la Irlandaise as well as mutton; it is beef stewed with potatoes, and a very cheap dish. It is good with tomatoes added, but then these stews have other names, for the original Irish stew has no tomatoes, and some people, driven almost insane through everything that is brought to them in an hotel being flavored with tomatoes against their liking, (the consequence of the indiscriminate use of Spanish sauce), are glad to turn to it for relief, and hope it will always keep its original character. In writing a bill of fare observe that when "a la" comes before a vowel, as in Irlandaise or a l'Italienne or a l'Andalouse— the second "a" is omitted, and the apostrophe takes its place; but the full "a la" comes in before a consonant, like a la Richelieu.

934—Macaroni a la Palermetane.

The special name of the dish at No. 65. Italienne is right, too, for it is a general appellation for any form of macaroni or Italian pastes. Palermetane means of the city of Palermo, in Italy, just as we might say Bostonian or Coloradan.

935—Peaches with Rice, a la Richelieu.

Prepare some cooked peaches in syrup —a compote of peaches—and prepare some rice the same as for croquette or rice cake, that is, slightly sweetened and flavored, and with the yolk of an egg or two in it.

Dish up a spoonful of rice, smooth it around in the dish, place half a peach on top and pour syrup over it. It is a sweet entree like the fruit fritters, etc .

936—Stewed Carrots.

Scrape young carrots, split and divide in quarters lengthwise, boil or steam about an hour. Put them in butter sauce, cream sauce or plain butter only, changing the style on different days.

937—Huckleberry Roll Pudding, or Roly-Poly.

Make biscuit dough by the receipt at

No. 515, which is good for the purpose as it is, but if you would have the dough so that it will peel apart in flakes after cooking, roll it out thin on the table, and spread a half-cup of lard or butter upon it; then fold it up and roll out twice. The last time of rolling out cover the sheet of dough with huckleberries (or other fruit) cut in two or three, roll up, put in pudding cloth, tie the ends and pin or sew the middle, and either drop in a roomy pot of boiling water or cook in a steamer. They cook in an hour or little more. Should be timed as they are not so good if kept long after they are done. Dip in water when taken up and the cloth will leave the pudding easily when unrolled. Serve with hard sauce or cream.

938—Floating Island.

It is a piece of cake floating in a bowl of boiled custard; the cake should be spread with fruit jelly and have a pile of whipped cream on top. Sponge cake and the varieties made out of the same mixture are the best to use. Several other trifles besides are called Floating Islands. Make two quarts of boiled custard and let it be ice-cold for use. Make sponge drops (round lady-fingers same as No. 4.) Spread with currant jelly, drop in the pan of custard; then serve in saucers or glasses with plenty of custard and whipped cream. Costs one cent a dish.

939—Corn Starch Jelly.

This can be made very good, if not spoiled by the use of too much lemon or too much starch.

. 5 cups water—a quart and a cup.
1½ cups sugar—12 ounces.
1 small lemon.
3 heaping tablespoons starch—3 ounces.

Boil 4 cups water with the sugar in it, and juice of the lemon and half the rind cut in small shreds. Mix the starch with the other cup, and stir it into the boiling syrup. Let simmer about 15 minutes to become transparent and almost clear. Pour it into custard cups, or any kind of moulds. Serve in saucers with a spoonful of sweetened cream whipped to froth. Can be colored with burnt sugar or with iced fruit-juice. Cost: 1½ qts 12, cream 5; 17 cents for eighteen portions.

They said they would come again and they are coming. Telegram for Mr. Farewell at 3 o'clock this afternoon asking him to prepare a wedding breakfast for them for to-morrow at 11: they to be married in the parlor of the hill cottage at 10. "Simple and informal; no fuss," the Colonel added at the bottom of his dispatch; they generally say that, but are wofully disappointed if they don't find a fuss being made about their momentous proceedings. This is no way to do; they ought to have given us time to send to the city for the ready-made decorations for the wedding-cake; for floral designs; paper cases for confections; there is no time for anything. Well, this means that somebody in this house will have to work all night, or nearly all, and the bride's cake will not be worth a cent to cut up, so fresh, scarcely cold unless made at once and set in the refrigerator. Wish I knew which is the winner in that match, the colonel or the banker's daughter—suppose a novelist could tell plain enough, but then it is none of our business. Anything for a change; however, I'm glad they chose this place for their breakfast.

From the 11 o'clock train this morning Mr. Farewell brought over their Mary Jane, the one that cooks for them in their city house. He said that as but two weeks of the time now remains of the eight weeks for which I am engaged he should like his home cook to stay in the kitchen and try to catch on—I mean take items, and pick up ideas about cooking for the future benefit of his family and himself, if I was willing as of course I am. Said she is sadly deficient in the styles of putting food on the dishes, does not know how to make a good dish look good, much less how to make a common one look better than it is, and much more. I know what he means, but he could not explain, neither can I—it is the trimming and shaping, flattening and squaring, the clean draining of the fries, the crispness, the gloss, the color, the garnishing. Now I shall tell her that looking on is all very well, but it is not equal to taking hold, and instead of sitting at the door she may take upon herself to pick up something to make supper for the guests whilst I make the wedding-cake.

940—A Picked-up Supper for Forty.

Oatmeal (3 cups raw near 3 qts, 7 cents.)
Beefsteak (cooked 20, small, 2½ lbs 35 cents.)
Mutton chops (cooked 16, small, 2 lbs 30 cents.)
Cold meats (charged dinner.)
Biscuits (made 45; 22 cents.)
Potatoes (baked and saute, 10 cents.)
Cakes assorted (2½ lbs 25 cents.)
Honey in comb (3 lbs 38 cents.)
Milk, 2½ gals 30, cream 20, bread and toast 12, butter, 1½ lbs 30, coffee, tea, sugar 23 (115 cents.)
Total $2 82 : 43 persons; 6½ cents a plate.

941—Wedding Cake.

2 pounds sugar—4 cups.
1½ pounds butter—3 cups.
12 eggs.
2 pounds flour—8 cups.
8 taplespoons wine; same of brandy.
6 nutmegs ground or grated.
5 pounds raisins.
4 pounds currants.
2 pounds crtron.
Stone the raisins, wash and dry the currants, cut citron small, mix them and dust with a cup of flour.

Mix the first four ingredients together as if for pound cake, add the liquors, nutmeg, and then the fruit.

Line the mould with buttered paper, and wrap another paper around the outside and tie it with twine. Bake the cake about three hours.

Made 1 large cake in a 6-qt milk pan, weighs 14 pounds, and 1 small cake 4 pounds. Cost: sugar @ 8, 16; butter @ 20, 30; eggs 15; flour @ 3½, 8; liquors 25; nutmegs 3; raisins @ 11, 55; currants @ 7, 28; citron @ 25, 50.
Total $2 30 for 18 pounds or 13 cents a pound for material.

942—Cost of Ornamented Cakes.

The confectioners and caterers fol-lowing a similar rule to the other employers of skilled labor, charge for the ornamentation of a cake about double the amount that they pay in wages for the time consumed; if a man to whom they pay three dollars a day consumes a whole day in the elaborate decoration of a wedding cake the charge of the ornamenting alone will be about six dollars, and of the cake complete perhaps ten dollars. The same man may perhaps ornament a large number of cakes at Christmas or New Year's on each of which he will spend but half an hour, and the price will be accordingly. The imported ornaments upon a fine cake may very likely swell the cost to twenty-five or fifty dollars.

Wedding Breakfast.

Menu.
Fresh Peaches Sliced.
Boned Chicken with Truffles.
Tomatoes in mayonaise.
Ribbon Sandwiches.

Lamb Cutlets, a la Maintenon.
Potatoes Baden-Baden.
Partridge Souffles in Cases.
Dry and Buttered Toast.
White Coffee.

Ornamented Wedding Cake.
Delicate Cake.   Apricot Ice Cream.

The breakfast was set on the long table in large dishes, family style, though we did not send in all at once and of course the table was set out to the best advantage with the few ornamented dishes, glass and china and a few flowers. The marriage took place at half past ten and the carriages drove up to the door a few minutes later. The two principals in the business took very little lunch and that of the first division of the menu, the *service froid;* the bride cut the large cake in divisions which I had marked previously, to make it easy, and gave away the pieces, and it did not crumble much considering how newly made it was, but I had kept it almost frozen all night that it might cut well. The hostess did up the small cake, the four-pound one, and put it in one of their traveling satchels, then they got into the carriage and two or three others followed and were driven to "the Glen," where they could catch a train at one o'clock. After they were gone the rest of the company went back to the table; we served the lunch in good earnest, and they made a meal of it, and did a little talking, too, I suppose.

Cost of material:

Early peaches, 1 basket	$1 00
Boned truffled chicken	3 00
Tomatoes mayonaise	40
Ribbon sandwiches, 30	75
Lamb cutlets, garnished	1 90
Potatoes	12
Souffles in cases	1 10
Ornamented wedding cakes with 5 lbs icing, 23 lbs in all	3 00
Delicate cake 5 lbs	60
Coffee	30
Apricot ice cream, 2½ qts	75
Toast, butter, trimmings	50
Total	$13 42

25 persons, 54 cents a plate.

The repast was ordered for twenty, but 25 persons, and probably several more, made it their midday meal and it is fairly charged as above, the three-dollar cake included in expense account with the manager.

943—Boned Chicken with Truffles.

Bone one fat young fowl and take the white meat of two more and mince it fine for stuffing. Put the minced chicken in a saucepan with the two ounces of butter, and about a third as much bread panada as there is meat; add a slight seasoning of herbs, salt and white pepper and two raw eggs and stir the whole over the fire until it is cooked to a smooth paste; then put in a small can of truffles whole or only the larger ones cut in two.

Stuff the boned chicken with the mixture, sew up, lined in a cloth in good oval form, boil two hours and press between two dishes. When cold, brush over the outside with melted butter, cut two or three truffles in shapes such as round slices with crescents and dots on each side and decorate the surface of the fowl, place it on a dish ornamented with lemon slices and parsley and keep cold until wanted. Then slice thinly and serve cold. The truffles in the stuffing should show as they are sliced through in every cut.

Cost: 3 fowls, 75; truffles 2 00, seasonings, garnish, 15; $2 90 for 20 to 25 slices.

944—Tomatoes in Mayonaise.

Pare good, smooth tomatoes with a very sharp knife without scalding them and they will retain their crispness, which scalding destroys; then slice each one in three or four. Lay three of these slices in a glass plate and place a teaspoon of mayonaise salad dressing (No. 151) upon each. Serve very cold.

To serve these we covered two large dishes with shred lettuce, set seven plates of tomatoes in each one and bordered them with small lumps of ice; placed them on table last thing before the meal began and removed them early.

945—Ribbon Sandwiches.

Cut thin slices of the finest and whitest bread of close grain and newly baked and remove the crust. Spread with potted ham or tongue, roll them up and tie them around with narrow satin ribbon, making a neat true-lover's knot on each. Fold napkins fan-shaped for two dishes and pile up the rolled sandwiches in pyramidal form.

946—Lamb Cutlets, a la Maintenon.

They are choice rib chops of lamb or mutton the bones scraped, half-cooked in a pan to shrink them, seasoned, spread on one side with a thick, white sauce, sprinkled with cut truffles baked in a buttered pan in the upper part of a hot oven to get a yellow-brown, served with paper frills upon the bones. The garnish for a breakfast dish may be a border of shapes of thin toast and for dinner a bed of peas or other accompaniment. To make the sauce, as good a way as any is to make a white roux of four ounces butter and the same of flour; and when they have been stirred over the fire until well cooked, add but half quantity of liquor (either broth or liquor from a can of mushrooms), which will be about two cups, and cook well with constant stirring. Season with salt and white pepper, set the sauce away to get cold, then use it as ab..ve named, spreading it thickly on the cutlets and smooth over with a wet knife before putting on the trfflues. Small triangles of thin toast are best to border a large dish as these cutlets must lie flat with the frilled ends outwards.

Cost: 20 cutlets 60, truffles 1 00, sauce, etc., 20; $1 80.

Named for Madame de Maintenon, a lady of the French court.

947—Potatoes a la Baden-Baden.

The same as No. 142; simmered in butter first, then drained and carefully baked to a yellow brown in the oven and sprinkled with parsley and fine salt.

To serve them, fry a number of small lettuce leaves in lard or oil as you would fry Saratoga potatoes. The leaves should be of heart lettuce and be shell shaped. Out of the many, which take but a few minutes to fry, select the best, bronze-colored, dry and of good shade; drain them hollow side downward on a sheet of paper spread on a hot pan. Serve the potatoes in them set in individual dishes, and handed to each place as the cutlets are being passed from the large dish. Baden-Baden is a fashionable watering-place.

948—Partridge Souffles in Cases.

Roast three partridges, young guinea fowls or common chickens, pick off the meat without skin or tendons, mince it extremely fine and then pound to a paste and rub it through a sieve. This is a difficult matter to do with any but young and tender partridges or chickens and there ought to be a stone mortar to pound the meat in. However, it can be done without by taking precaution not to try with old birds. A souffle is a puff, and this mixture will not puff if not quite a smooth paste.

Make a thick butter sauce the same as for spreading cutlets a la Maintenon, with mushroom liquor, if convenient. Take 1½ cups of the sauce to four cups of the chicken paste, season with salt, pepper, a slight grating of nutmeg and some of lemon rind, add a spoonful of mushroom catsup and stir over the fire until boiling hot. Then set away to cool.

Separate the whites and yolks of eight eggs, whip them both light, add the yolks to the mixture first, then the frothed whites. Put the souffle in twenty fancy paper cases, bake about 15 minutes, and send them in as soon as they are done, for they fall as they become cool with waiting. Serve in the cases on large dishes with plates of buttered toast to follow.

Cost: 1½ lbs selected partridge meat 60, sauce 10, eggs, seasonings 15, paper cases 25; $1 10 for 20. Paper cases can be bought of confectioners or made at home. They hold about as much as a patty or gem pan and are of various shapes.

949—White Coffee a la Soyer.

Is made with coffee that, instead of being browned is only baked to a slight yellow color and is not ground, or at most the berries are only bruised, and is made with one-half milk and one-half water. It requires twice as much coffee as the ordinary.

For 8 cups take:

2 cups light baked coffee berries.

4 cups boiling water.

5 cups boiling milk.

The berries may have been parched before, but when wanted, heat them over again and throw them hot into the boiling water. Close the lid and let stand to draw for half an hour; then add the boiling milk through a strainer. Drop a tablespoon of whipped cream in each cup as it is carried in.

950—Apricot Ice Cream

5 cups cream.

2 cups canned (or cooked) apricots.

1½ cups sugar.

Pass the apricots without the syrup through a sieve. Freeze the cream and sugar first to guard against curdling by the fruit; then add the apricot pulp and finish the freezing.

951—Four Thousand Meals.

So that couple got safely married and

went away; still the number of guests in the house is steadily increasing. It seems almost a pity there was not a story teller here making a book out of what he saw, for it will be remembered, those young ladies from the Trulirural House never came over here to board until they saw the Colonel sailing around with his best girl; and it stands to reason that there must have been unmeasured mischief in the air, and plotting and counter plotting; and all that is lost. But every man to his trade, as the saying is. The way our part of the play comes in is just this: we have got things down to such a fine point by keeping tally this way that, after a little figuring in the spare hours of the remaining two weeks, we shall all know exactly what it is going to cost that young couple to live, in whichever style, whether in a soup-entree-and-dessert order of existence in a mansion on Euclid or Michigan Avenue or St. Charles or Sacramento street, or on bread and cheese and kisses *a la mode* on laborers' wages in Smoky Alley. Then we shall know how much Mrs. Tingee makes off her boarders and shall see plainly how some people managed to get rich so quickly at the New Orleans Exposition, and, moreover, we shall know how to go about preparing a banquet for 4,000 people.

For, with the wedding breakfast for a finish, the bell has sounded the call 130 times and we have served 4,000 meals. The reasons are cogent for drawing the line at this even number: the stock of groceries laid in on a calculation for one month, which did not arrive until one week was past, has lasted one week over a month and is now exhausted. Marketing is beginning to come in from the farms at all sorts of irregular prices; apples, poultry, vegetables, all getting cheap but impossible to keep track of, and butter and eggs correspondingly advanced; in short we have had a rare opportunity, it has been well improved and now the favorable conditions no longer exist.

952—Review.

In keeping the foregoing accounts of cost of dishes and meals there has been no attempt and no wish to argue that one style of living is better than another; those who must set out cheap meals will look at the comparative cost of dishes, taking notice at the same time of the number of orders that can be served from them, and choose always to make those that are least expensive while others who furnish a complete hotel bill of fare will find an approximate figure to show what the expense ought to be. In this matter of meals and prices, too, instead of ficticiously changing and improving the summer boarding house and its facilities I have studiously represented it as it is with the restrictions as to markets, the lack of proper utensils, the scarcity of "help," and such things as usually furnish excuses for a poor table, because I believe this was a fair average of such houses and I did not want a model place to set up a pattern by. Our advantages lay in having express facilities and in being in close proximity to a creamery and a cheese factory which established low prices for dairy products and at the same time caused the offerings to be plentiful, the whole neighborhood being engaged in the milk business. This it will be seen was an important item, and still the greater number of country houses are as well fixed as we were; it may be by keeping cows of their own, and most of them have far better gardens. In counting the cost of soups I have first added to the price of steaks and roasts the loss of bones and trimmings, making meat that costs 11 cents at first rate at 15 or 20 cents a pound when the net weight was reached, and then have valued these bones and cullings at about 2 cents a pound in soup; vegetables, quenelles, eggs, and all such ingredients have been duly allowed for. It did not prove feasible to show some things in the way of small economies such as every sensible cook puts in practice—how the cold rice left from a previous dinner and the can of peaches opened but scarcely touched, for the preceding supper become the "peaches a la Richelieu" of to-day's dinner; or how the can of corn, too much yesterday, becomes the green corn fritters on a new bill. There has been greater watchfulness over the waste while this record was being kept, than would have been necessary in the ordinary run of work, but otherwise all has been done according to common usage, and the sums total will prove reliable data for future calculations.

953—Groceries for Four Thousand.

Bill at No. 520...............	$109 52
Bought additional:	
Mushrooms, 4 cans..........	1 20
Shrimps, 2 cans retail........	55
Lobster, 2 cans..............	45
Salad oil 1 qt................	1 00
Wine 1 qt....................	90
Brandy for cooking..........	1 00
Catsup, 3 bottles.............	2 00
Gelatine, 4 packages.........	80
Chocolate, 1 lb..............	40
Sundry canned goods........	4 70
Compressed yeast............	2 00
Total......................	$124 52

954—Yeast and Baking Powder.

Bought compressed yeast, used regularly twice a day 5 cents a day, 40 days, $2 00

Baking powder used occasionally cost $2 60

955—Meat, Fish and Poultry for Four Thousand.

Bought meat 888 lbs at average 12 cents, including expressage, $106 56.

Bought fish 232 lbs at average 10 cents, including expressage, $23 20.

Bought poultry 93 lbs @12, $11 16.

Total, $140 92.

A fraction over 3½ cents each person each meal for meat, fish and poultry, and discarding fractions, about 4½ ounces each or 1 lb gross for 4 persons. Meat loses on an average one-fourth the raw weight in bone, and parts with one-fourth more to the soup or gravy pan and in fat and evaporation in cooking; consequently only about 2½ ounces is consumed by each person on an average.

Dinner.

August 14.

Soup—Consomme Colbert (5 qts 24 eggs 55 cents.)

Trout with Chili, Mexican style (4 lbs and sauce 50 cents.)

Potatoes Chilian.

Boiled ham (2 orders 4 cents.)

Roast beef (2 ribs 4 lbs 50 cents.)

Stuffed shoulder mutton, a la Soubise (3 lbs and trimmings 40 cents.)

Saute of chicken with rissotto (4 chickens and trimmings 110 cents.)

Kromeskies, a la Venitienne (16 orders 32 cents.)

New corn 20, string beans 3, onions in cream 5, turnips 3, rice 4, potatoes 15 (50 cents.)

Cream curd pudding (No. 538 increased, 38 cents.)

Potato cream pie (3 pies 30 cents.)

Bisque of pineapple ice cream (No. 206 with twice the cream to same fruit; 3 qts frozen 85 cents.)

Golden cake (20 cents.)

Blackberries and apples, cheese, nuts, pickles (45 cents.)

Milk 10 qts 30, cream 3 pts 30, coffee, tea, sugar, bread, butter 42 (102 cents.)

Total $7 11 : 48 persons, nearly 15 cents a plate.

956—Consomme Colbert.

Clear consomme with small vegetables and green peas in it and a poached egg dropped in each plate when served. Make the consomme same as Brunoise or jardiniere and have the eggs poached nearly hard, ready in a pan of hot water, to dip up as wanted.

Colbert was the name of a French statesman.

957—Trout with Chili, Mexican Style.

The Mexican chili pepper is no stronger than curry powder. It is deep red, and is sometimes called sweet pepper and coloring pepper; is much used in the South and by the Creoles.

Split open the fish, lay it white side up in a buttered baking pan, season with salt, and dredge enough chili pepper to color it red; pour a little broth if necessary to keep the corners of the pan from burning. Bake the fish half an hour and serve with Spanish sauce in the dish or else with veal gravy and little tomato catsup added, and potatoes in some special form in the same plate.

958—Potatoes, Chilian Style.

Mashed potatoes sliced cold, like cold

mush to fry, the slices cut in shapes, floured and sauted in oil or drippings. Season the potatoes when mashing with chili pepper as well as salt, and broth but no butter; rather soft that they may cake together well. The slices cut off can be cut in diamonds or in rounds with a small cutter.

959—Stuffed Mutton, a la Soubise.

Soubise always means with onions either white or brown. Take a shoulder and bone it. Cut 4 slices of bread in dice and throw them in a frying pan; put in also a good-sized onion, cut up small, or a bunch of green onions, a spoonful of roast meat fat and same of water and pepper and salt to season. Stir over the fire till well mingled. Spread this stuffing over the mutton, roll up, and braise tender.

Take 3 or 4 onions from the saucepan where they are cooking as a vegetable for dinner, mince and pass through a strainer and mix in sufficient brown sauce or gravy.

Soubise has reference to a prince de Soubise who made an onion sauce.

960—Saute of Chicken with Rissotto.

Rissotto is rice; this is seasoned the Italian way with salt, cayenne, minced onions, ham and saffron, which makes it yellow. As saffron is not used and not wanted much in this country, a little curry serves as a substitute.

Chop 3 or 4 chickens into small pieces, saute them in a large frying pan and make a thickened gravy to them. Add mushrooms if afforded.

Fry some fat ham, minced onion in the fat, little curry, broth to make gravy and put in boiled rice and stir up.

Dish rice at one side of the dish and chicken at the other, or chicken in the middle and rice pressed into a patty pan to give it a shape and turned out into the dish of chicken.

961—Kremeskies a la Venitienne.

Minced meat rolled in thin bacon, dipped in batter and fried and served with white Italian sauce.

Take the remains of cooked chicken, some of the livers and hearts cooked, and small quantity of lean ham, enough altogether to make two cups pressed, or a pound. Stir a teaspoonful each of butter and flour together over the fire and put in a half cup water or broth. Season rather highly with pepper, mushroom or walnut catsup, thyme and grated lemon peel, add the minced chicken, which makes a stiff sort of sausage meat; set it away to get cold. When cool enough make in shape like corks of champagne bottles. Cut bacon slices as thin as possible; roll up the mince in a slice of bacon, dip in batter and fry light colored. Serve with sauce.

962—White Italian Sauce.

Make butter sauce and use mushroom liquor from the cans instead of water. Let the sauce be rather thinner than the usual butter sauce. Slice button mushrooms, about a dozen to a pint of sauce, and put in, and a spoonful of minced parsley. Same as Venetian sauce except the lemon juice.

963—Corn in the Ear.

Leave a few of the husks on the ears and drop them that way into a boiler of salted water. Boil about half an hour. When to be served take hold with a clean napkin and pull off husks and silk. Take a knife and cut out one row of grains by drawing the point down both sides; then send in the ears.

964—Potato Cream Pie.

2 large cups mashed potato—a pound.
1 cup sugar—½ pound.
Small cup butter—6 ounces.
5 eggs.
½ cup milk.
Flavoring of some kind.

Boil good mealy potatoes and mash them through a sieve; mix the butter in while warm, then sugar, milk and flavoring. Separate the eggs and beat both yolks and whites quite light and stir them in just before baking. Makes three medium pies, open like pumpkin pies. Sift powdered sugar over when done. If you use brandy or wine in any dishes put ½ cup in the above mixture; if not use vanilla or nutmeg and a trifle more milk.

965—Go den Cake.

2 cups sugar—1 pound light.
1 cup butter ½ pound.
1 cup water.
18 yolks—about 1½ cups.
4 teaspoons baking powder.
6 cups flour—1½ pounds.

This cake should be made after white cake or icing has left the yolks of eggs on hand. Beat the yolks and sugar and water together 5 minutes; melt the butter and beat it in, then the powder and flour. Beat five minutes more. May be baked in one mould or in shallow pans. About four pounds costs 39 cents or 10 cents a pound.

966—Flour for Four Thousand.

Bought flour 550 lbs at 3½.......$19 25
Bought corn meal, 33 lbs at 2....   66
Bought graham flour, 20 lbs at 3.   60

Total......................$20 51
Averaging 2⅓ ounces for each person, each meal at cost of ½ cent each.

967--Sugar for Four Thousand.

Bought 276 lbs at 8 cents......$22 08
A little over 1 ounce each person, each meal, used for all purposes, and costing about ½ cent each.

968 –Coffee for Four Thousand.

Bought 30 lbs Java at 28 cents...$8 40
About one-fifth of a cent each person, each meal; but as this was in summer weather, when ice-water and milk were in greater request, the amount will be no guide except under similar conditions.

Dinner

August 15.
Soup—cream of barley (7 qts 40 cents.)
Boiled whitefish, shrimp sauce (4 lbs and sauce 55 cents.)
Potatoes maitre d'hotel.
Corned beef and cabbage (1 lb and cabbage 15 cents.)
Roast beef (flank braised tender, 4 lbs 32 cents.)
Spring lamb, brown sauce (7 lbs 80 cents.)
Young pigeon pie (1½ doz squabs 120, trimmings 20, 36 orders 140 cents.)
Macaroni a la Genoise (20 orders 12 cents.)
Roasted corn 25, beets, 4, summer squash 12, tomatoes 10, potatoes 15 (71 cents.)
Baked sago pudding, lemon sauce (30 orders with sauce 36 cents.)
Sliced apple pie (No. 178, 4 pies 40 cents.)
White Mountain ice cream (3 qts milk to 1 qt cream, etc., 60 cents.)
Sponge cake (common, No. 975, 24 cents.)
Blackberries and apples, nuts, cheese, crackers pickles (50 cents.)
Milk, cream 60, coffee, tea, sugar, bread, butter 48 (108 cents.)
Total $7 58: 50 persons; little over 15 cents a plate.

969—Cream of Barley Soup.

It is puree of barley mixed with half stock and half milk.

Boil 2 cups pearl barley in plenty of water and strain the water away as it is of a dark color. Then put the barley into 3 quarts of milk and cook at the back of the stove or set on bricks for an hour or more. Boil 4 quarts of stock with a cut-up carrot, onion, turnip and bunch of parsley in it. Pass the barley and milk through a strainer (fine or coarse according as you have time, for it is tedious), and mash the barley that remains with some stock to hasten the operation. Strain the seasoned stock into the barley puree, keep hot without boiling, add salt and white pepper and serve with crusts in the plates. A shorter way is to cook the barley tender, mash it to a paste and put it into the stock and milk without passing the barley through a sieve. In that case no crusts need be served as there will be barley grains in the soup.

970—Potatoes, Maitre d'Hotel.

Pick out the smallest new potatoes, scrape or pare, and boil them. Drain away the water, put in a little fresh, and lump of butter, salt and a spoonful of vinegar, and thicken slightly with flour; boil up and lastly shake in a spoonful of chopped parsley. It is a thin, creamy sauce like Venetian, without mushrooms, and only enough to cover the potatoes.

971—Pigeon or Squab Pie.

Young pigeons, called squabs in this country, are pigeonneaux in French. The price varies greatly with locality; we paid 80 cents a dozen. This is a pie with brown gravy instead of white 's in chicken pie.

Take 18 squabs, pick, singe, open down the back, draw, and divide in halves; wash and dry them and flatten with the cleaver. Pepper, salt and flour them on both sides. Melt ½ pound of butter in the baking pan the pie is to be made in, lay in the squabs and bake them light brown. Pour into the pan about 2 quarts of broth or water and continue the baking. When done sufficiently thicken the gravy, add walnut catsup or a little Worcestershire sauce and salt and pepper, cover with a short crust and bake twenty minutes longer. When the crust of a meat pie gives out before the meal, bake a thin crust by itself on a baking pan; cut it in squares and use to finish the meal.

972—Macaroni a la Genoese.

Macaroni plain boiled, served with Spanish sauce or any meat gravy poured first in the dish, the macaroni in that and a dredging of grated cheese on top.

973—Roasting Ears Roasted.

Pull off the outside husks, but leave the ears well covered, throw them in the oven on the bottom, get up a good heat, and they will be done in half an hour. Pull off husks and silk, cut out one row to start the eaters fairly.

974—Sago Custard Pudding.

1 heaped cup sago—½ pound.

6 cups milk—3 pints.
½ cup sugar.
Butter size of an egg.
4 eggs or 8 yolks.
Grated lemon rind or other flavor.

Boil the milk with the sugar in it—which prevents burning—dredge in the sago, push the kettle to the back of the stove, or set on bricks and cook about ½ hour. Beat the eggs, mix all, bake in a 3 quart pan, about ½ hour more. Serve with lemon syrup sauce—the transparent sauce with lemon juice and rind in it. Cost: 20 cents for over 2 quarts or 30 orders.

975—Common Sponge Cake.

2 cups granulated sugar—a pound scant.
8 eggs.
1 cup water—½ pint.
4 rounded cups flour—18 ounces.
2 large teaspoons baking powder.

Separate the eggs, the whites into a good-sized bowl, the yolks into the mixing pan. Put the sugar and water with the yolks, and beat up until they are light and thick. Mix the powder in the flour by sifting together. Whip the whites to a very firm froth, and when they are ready stir the flour into the yolk mixture, and mix in the whipped whites last.

Cost: 24 cents for over 3 pounds.

976—Butter for Four Thousand.

Bought 13 lots butter ranging 25, 20, 19, 15, 12 cents; average 19 cents—lbs 210 at 19, $39 90.
Bought lard 37 lbs at 14, $5 18.
Total, $45 08.

Table butter kept entirely separate; the consumption is a fraction under ½ ounce each person each meal; when part butter and part lard is used for cooking and the whole butter and lard bill counted together, the consumption for all purposes averages a fraction under one ounce each person each meal and the cost is 1⅛ cents each.

977—Eggs for Four Thousand.

Bought 142 doz at 15 cents, $21 30.

That is 1704 eggs; ess than ½ egg for each person; but as they were offered only for breakfast it allowed one egg each for the one-third number and left 374 eggs for the cooking; and when besides that, the individuals who are not expected to want eggs were counted out, it left the usual 2 eggs apiece for proper orders.

978—Potatoes for Four Thousand.

Bought 16 bushels ranging 50, 60, 75 cents.

Total, $9 95.

16 bushels are 960 pounds; about ¼ lb each person each meal at cost of ¼ cent each. Potatoes lose one-third the gross weight if pared raw.

979—Fresh Vegetables and Fruits for Four Thousand.

Bought at sundry times and some from the garden to the amount of $14 00.

980—Canned Fruits and Vegetables for Four Thousand.

Bought vegetables 53 cans.......$ 7 95
Bought fruits, 60 cans........... 11 25
Mushrooms, shrimps and lobster,
  8 cans.......................   2 20

Total......................$21 40

Dinner.

August 16.

Soup—consomme Claremont (6 qts 36 cents.)

Pike, a la Genoise (6 lbs gross and sauce 60 cents.)

Potatoes French fried.

Boiled corned tongue and cabbage (tongue 30, with cabbage 35 cents.)

Roast guinea chicken, currant jelly (8 fowls 2 00.)

Collops of beef, a la Macedoine (2 lbs 22, vegetables 10, 18 orders 32 cents.)

Epigramme of lamb, Bordelaise (2 lbs, 16 orders 24 cents.)

Calf's head in batter, sauce piquante (½ head 30, total 16 orders 45 cents.)

Cut-off corn 20, hot slaw 5, squash 8, tomatoes 10, potatoes 15 (58 cents.)

Baked farina pudding, vanilla sauce (5 pts and sauce 36 orders 32 cents.)

Blueberry shortcake with cream (4 cakes, 32 orders with cream 55 cents.)

Chocolate cup custard (2 qts, 24 custard cups, 20 cents.)

Butter sponge cake (1 lb 10 cents.)

Milk, cream 60, coffee, tea, sugar, bread, butter 52 (112 cents.)

Total $7 19 : 50 persons; 14½ cents a plate.

981—Consomme Claremont.

Clear consomme, like royal, with crisp light fried onions in rings dropped in the plates. Having the consomme prepared and well flavored with meat extract and catsup, cut some onions in slices across and separate the slices into rings; throw these into a pan of flour and dust well; then into clean hot lard, and let fry yellow and dry. Drain free from grease, and put a small proportion in each plate as served. It requires a little practice to fry onions this way successfully just as it does to fry Saratoga chips. Claremont is the name of a place and a palace.

982—Pike, a la Genoise.

Place the fish in the baking pan without splitting open, but scored across where the portions are to be taken off. Slice a small carrot, piece of turnip, an onion and stalk of celery into the pan, and cut a slice of fat salt pork and mix in. Add a bayleaf, salt, pepper and a pint of soup stock. Bake brown with frequent basting for over half an hour. Then take up the fish with a fish-slice carefully into a dish. Pour off the grease from the baking pan and put in a pint of stock again, a spoonful of tomatoes or tomato catsup and ½ cup wine; let boil up till the fish glaze in the pan is all dissolved, thicken slightly and strain for sauce to the fish.

983—Potatoes French-Fried.

The common way. Cut raw potatoes

lengthwise in strips about the size of a little finger and fry in a kettle of lard.

As fried potatoes are generally prepared in haste to order it should be remembered that they rise and float in the fat when done and the color they may take on instantly in fat that is too hot is no sign that they are not still raw and unfit to serve—wait till they float.

984—Roast Guinea Chicken.

Young guinea fowls are more like partridges than like common chickens. Roast them in the usual way with a chicken stuffing, and serve currant or cranberry jelly in small saucers or chips separately.

985—Collops of Beef, a la Macedoine.

Collops are small steaks. Almost any piece of meat will do for this dish but the pieces must be sliced thin and trimmed to be nearly round. Flatten them with the cleaver, salt and pepper and flour them on both sides.

Fry a minced onion in 4 spoonfuls of roast meat fat, and when it begins to color lay in the collops and brown them. Pour in a pint of water or stock, little Worcestershire sauce, salt and pepper and let the collops continue stewing in the sauce until tender, the grease to be skimmed off as it rises.

The Macedoine of vegetables cannot be made to advantage without good green peas, either garden or French canned, as it is the mixture of colors of vegetables that make the dish a good one. Cut pieces of carrot, turnip and other vegetables in dice and boil them; mix a cupful of these with a cupful of green peas—as many peas as of the others altogether—season with salt and butter, or some white sauce, dish up a spoonful of the Macedoine as a border, and a collop glazed with its own thick sauce in the middle.

986--Epigramme of Lamb, Bordelaise.

Divide the breasts of lamb or mutton in strips by sawing through the bones, cook them in a deep baking pan with

broth and seasonings and let dry down until glazed. Serve cuts with Bordelaise sauce in the dish and ornamen. with shapes of fried bread.

987—Bordelaise Sauce.

It is brown sauce with minced garlic, ham, shalot, claret, cayenne and lemon juice. Take a few shreds of lean cooked ham—only enough for a flavoring—and mince and pound it fine, boil it in a pint of brown sauce or veal gravy, or use Spanish sauce if not too much tomatoes in it. Add while boiling a bay leaf, two or three cloves and a piece of mace and pinch of cayenne. In another saucepan put a tablespoon of minced young onion and a clove of garlic crushed and minced and a spoonful of oil, and stir over the fire to cook. Strain the seasoned brown sauce into it, and a cup of claret and let boil down, skimming off the oil and scum as it rises, and add lemon juice and a spoonful more wine to brighten it by causing more scum to rise. Bordelaise means of Bordeaux, the part of France whence claret wine comes.

988—Calf's Head Fried in Batter.

Boil a calf's head and save the liquor for soup. Take out the bones, put the meat in; press between 2 dishes. A calf's head generally requires one hour's boiling but large ones may take two hours.

When the head is cold take half and cut in narrow slices about finger size, salt and pepper them, dip in thin batter same as kromeskies or fritters and fry light-colored. Serve sauce in the dish and the meat in it but not covered.

989—Cut-off Corn.

Boil roasting ears half an hour; then shave the corn off the cob and season it the same as canned corn with butter, salt and milk.

990—Sauce Piquante.

Is brown caper sauce, having capers,

minced young onion and small bunch of seasoning herbs boiled in either brown meat gravy or Spanish sauce and the herbs taken out without straining.

991—Baked Farina Pudding.

---

8 cups milk—2 quarts.
1 heaped cup farina—7 ounces.
Small cup sugar—6 ounces.
½ cup butter—4 ounces.
5 eggs (or 8 yolks.)
Boil the milk with the sugar in it, and sprinkle in the farina dry, beating all the while with the wire and egg whisk as if making mush. Let the farina cook slowly half an hour or more, then mix in the butter and beaten eggs. Serve with sauce. Cost: 30 cents for 5 pints or 35 to 40 orders.

992—Blueberry Shortcake.

Made the same way as strawberry shortcake and others as at No. 397. Pick over the blueberries, mix a cup of sugar in two quarts, and stir them about enough to draw juice to dissolve the sugar. Spread on split shortcakes, made large but thin, cut in eighths and serve with cream.

---

993 -Chocolate Cup Custard.

Make same as boiled custard, No. 136, and add a tablespoon of grated common chocolate. An ounce of chocolate is sufficient for that quantity of custard trebled, and serves for the orders of 40 persons. The surplus chocolate that was too much for breakfast, can sometimes be utilized in this way. A flavoring of vanilla improves it.

994—Milk and Cream for Four Thousand.

Bought milk, regular supply, 40 days, 20 qts. a day, 800 qts @ 3 cents........	$24 00
Bought milk and buttermilk irregularly 6 weeks 140 qts. @ 3 cents..............	4 20
Bought cream 102 qts. @ 20 cents...................	20 40
Total.................	$48 60

Average cost 1 ¼ cents each person each meal; giving half a pint of milk and a gill of cream to each person—some of it used in the cooking and ice cream, however.

995—Total Cost of Provisions for Four Thousand.

Groceries, including canned goods, coffee, flour, meal, yeast, sugar, baking powder.......................	$124 52
Meat, fish and poultry	140 92
Milk and cream...............	48 60
Butter and lard...............	45 08
Eggs	21 30
Potatoes......................	9 95
Fresh vegetables and fruit.....	14 00
Total	$404 37

996—To Save Twenty Dollars a Week.

The above is a fraction—about the ninth of a cent over 10 cents a meal average, including the extravagance of the 16-cent and 17-cent dinners, the 54-cent wedding breakfast and the birth day suppers.

That is an expense of 30 cents a day for each person, or $2.10 a week, for living on the fat of the land and having choice of nearly all the desirable dishes with milk and cream without stint and first quality of butter, coffee and bread. It does not seem very high, not even when the additional expenses are added. Yet as an incentive to carefulness it should be borne in mind that a saving of but one cent a meal on 4,000 will yield 40 dollars; if reduced by 2 cents 80 dollars will be saved and if the meals can be held down 3 cents, or at 7 cents a meal there will be a saving over our figures of 120 dollars, or for 6 weeks a saving of 20 dollars a week on provisions alone. This is why it pays to give good wages to a cook who knows how and is willing to keep down the expenses by avoiding waste and profusion. The dinners can be kept down to 10 cents and breakfasts and suppers to 6 cents and the average of 7 cents all around will easily be maintained; that is 21 cents a day for each person or about $1 50 a week. As a rule supper is the cheapest meal, breakfast a little higher, dinner costs as much as both the other meals put together; where dinner rules at 12 cents breakfast will cost 7 and supper 5; where lunch is served and a 5 or 6 o'clock dinner, the lunch is or ought to be as cheap as the ordinary supper.

Dinner.

August 17.
Soup—Potage Alexandrina (7 qts 40 cents.)
Whitefish a la Cardinal (4 lbs and trimmings, 65 cents.)
Potato crulls.
Cold tongue.
Potato salad (10 cents.)
Roast beef (2 ribs 5 lbs net, 70 cents.)
Roast Pork a l'Anglaise (6 lbs and dressing, 70 cents.)
Veal cutlets a la Maintenon (20 orders, 45 cents.)
Calves brains, sauce remoulade (6 orders, 12 cents.)
Farina fritters, lemon flavor (cold pudding from yesterday, say, 10 cents.)
Fried carrots 6, beets 4, squash 10, grated corn 20, tomatoes 10, potatoes 15 (65 cents.)
Baked cabinet pudding (meringued 2½ qts 30 orders, 35 cents.)
Pineapple cream pie (2 cans, 5 pies open, thin, 65 cents.)
Peach sherbet (No. 235; with can peaches and 2 qts water, etc., 65 cents.)
Queen cakes (No. 1007; 3 lbs 36 cents.)
Nuts, raisins, cheese, crackers, pickles (52 cents.)
Milk, cream 60, coffee, tea, bread, butter 48 (108 cents.)
Total, $7 48; 52 persons; 14½ cents a plate.

997—Potage Alexandrina.

It is a vegetable puree soup spotted with a jardiniere of mixed vegetables cooked separately. Set the strained soup stock over the fire with a cup of raw rice, a quart of green peas, a large turnip, squash, celery, kohl-rabi, leaks and onions, all in smaller quantity than the peas, and a piece of lean salt pork. Cook the vegetables soft, then pass them, the rice, and the stock together through a strainer. It is like green peas soup.

Prepare a small quantity of carrot, turnip and parsnip, or squash or other vegetables cut in small dice, and boiled separately, a spoonful of green peas or flageolets or haricots verts, and mix in and season to taste.

998—Whitefish a la Cardinal.

Lay the fish open in a baking pan, spread over with lobster paste made the same as for lobster croquettes, dredge a small amount of cracker dust on top and bake, basting once with butter. Serve cuts with cardinal sauce in the dish, and some special form of potatoes.

999—Cardinal Sauce.

Anything a la cardinal may be expected to be red or have red ornaments. Cardinal red being the color of the robe worn by the Cardinals on State occasions.

Make butter sauce and make it red or at least pink with pounded red lobster meat and shrimp passed through a seive, add cayenne and lemon juice to this sauce. Lobster coral—the roe—is used for this purpose where it can be obtained.

1000—Potato Crulls.

There are small machines of the apple-parer class, which cut potatoes in spiral shavings called crulls or curls. Fry these in the usual way of fried potatoes, drain, dust with fine salt; serve one with each plate of fish.

1001—Roast Pork, a l'Anglaise.

Pork with sage and onions.
Take the bone out of a shoulder or loin of pork. Mince a large onion, throw it in a frying pan with a spoonful of fat, and stir it over the fire; put in a tablespoonful of powdered sage, some salt and pepper. Spread the minced onion upon the meat and put some in the cavity where the bone was taken out; roll up,

tie with twine, roast in a pan till well done. Take up, pour off the fat and make gravy in the pan with water added to the seasoned glazed that remains, or else pour brown sauce in and let it boil up. Stir in a tablespoon of made mustard, and strain the sauce.

1002—Veal Cutlets, a la Maintenon.

Cut veal steaks from the best part, (using the remaining pieces for stews) very thin and about two and a half inches wide. Make a well seasoned mince like that for kromeskies, No. 961; or chicken croquette mixture. Spread the mince on the cutlets, roll them into a cushion shape, place close together in a buttered pan, pour a few spoonfuls of seasoned broth and minced mushrooms and parsley in the spaces; sift cracker dust on top, and bake about half an hour.

Serve with a brown sauce poured under and garnish with croutons and lemon slices dipped in parsley.

1003—Calves' Brains in Batter, Remoulade.

Boil the brains, perhaps those saved from one calf's head will be enough to fill the bill; and when cold cut in small pieces and put them in a dish of vinegar and water with salt and pepper. When to be cooked again drain the pieces, roll in flour, then dip in thin fritter batter and drop into hot lard. Fry light-colored and serve with remoulade sauce.

1004—Farina Fritters.

Make farina cake or pudding and let it become cold, then slice it in long but narrow pieces, dip in egg and cracker meal and fry brown. Roll the fritters in powdered sugar and serve without sauce. The sugar may be flavored by grating lemon or orange rind into it, or dropping vanilla extract and stirring it about.

1005—Fried Carrots.

Cut in long strips, boil in water, drain, salt well, shake about in a pan of flour and fry the same as fried potatoes.

1006—Grated Corn.

Boil ears of green corn and grate off the cob instead of cutting as for cut-off corn. Season the grated corn with butter, salt and a spoonful or two of cream, and serve as a vegetable same as Summer squash.

1007—Queen Cakes.

Queen cake is the best white cake with sultana raisins, citron and currant; a fine white fruit cake.

Make the best white cake, No. 622; and add about a cupful of each of the fruits. The greenest new-made citron should be chosen as it looks better in the cake than the dark pieces. Can be baked in one mould, or this way:

Having made the cake mixture put it in small muffin pans or gem pans to bake, and frost the tops when done.

Costs a trifle more than other kinds, chiefly because it takes more weight to serve small cakes frosted to each order than in slices.

1008—Baked Cabinet Pudding.

It is made with slices of cake and citron in small slips; custard poured over and baked, and then frosted on top like lemon pie.

Take slices of cake of any sort, but sponge cake is the best, and enough to half fill a three-quart pudding pan.

Place one layer of cake in the pan and drop in bits of butter and shreds of citron, another layer on that and butter and citron again.

Mix three eggs in four cups of milk—no sugar needed—and flavor with grated lemon rind and juice. Pour it over the cake in the pan, cover with a sheet of buttered paper, bake about half an hour. Frost over with four whites whipped up firm, and four tablespoons sugar stirred in. Serve with sweetened cream.

Costs twenty-nine cents for four pints without frosting or sauce, but it uses up dry slices of cake at full value. Brandy is added to this pudding when it is wanted richer.

1009—Pineapple Cream Pie.

1 quart pineapple—2 cans.
1½ cups sugar—12 ounces.
1 cup cream.
12 yolks of eggs.

If fresh pineapple grate it; if cans save the juice for sauces and mince the fruit first and then mash it, and stir it over the fire in a saucepan with the sugar for a few minutes; add the cream and the yolks well beaten and fill into small, open pies, these mixtures being richer than ordinary fruits. The same mixture stirred over the fire after the yolks are added makes a rich pineapple conserve for spreading on layer cakes and filling tartlets. Use the whites of eggs for frosting cabinet pudding and in the sherbet.

Cost, according to pineapple, probably sixty cents for four pies.

1010—How Much They Eat.

To serve four thousand meals required solid food as follows:

Flour and meal 603 pounds made into bread and pastry was, say	800 lbs
Oatmeal and wheat 62 pounds made into mush was say	150 "
Rice, tapioca, starch, beans, 28 pounds made	85 "
Meat, fish and poultry	1213 "
Sugar	276 "
Eggs	170 "
Butter and lard	247 "
Potatoes 960 pounds less ⅓ by paring	640 "
Canned goods 121 average 2 pounds solid	242 "
Green vegetables and fruits, about	170 "
Sundries in grocery bill	234 "
Total	4227 lbs

That is about 1 pound and ½ ounce to each person each meal. Discarding the fractions and leaving the 227 pounds to represent the waste left on the plates, we have one pound of solid food as the requirement for each person three times a day. We are dealing now with averages and these are examples of the average meals.

Average breakfast order:

Fruit or oatmeal	2 ounces
Beefsteak or chop	2 "
Ham and bacon	1 "
Eggs or omelet, 2 eggs	3 "
Potatoes	2 "
Roll, corn bread, toast	3 "
Sugar	1 "
Butter	1 "
Waffle or 2 cakes	2 "
Total	17 ounces

And ½ pint of coffee or tea and the same of milk or water.

Average dinner order:

Soup ½ plate with crackers	4 ozs
Fish with potato or bread	3 "
Roast meat, thin slice	1½ "
Entree, stuffed chicken or veal	2½ "
Vegetables 3 kinds	6 "
Pastry or ice cream	3 "
Bread, butter, nuts, fruit	2 "
Total	22 ozs

And a pint of milk or water.

A large proportion of the people never take soup in Summer and about as many do not order fish, but perhaps take more meat dishes and pastry, and a few make a meal principally of vegetables.

Average supper order:

Fruit or mush	2 ounces
Meat hot or cold	2 "
Roll and muffin	3 "
Baked potato	3 "
Butter	1 "
Sugar	1 "
Cake	1 "
Total	13 ounces

And a pint of coffee, tea or milk.

1011—How Much They Drink.

To serve four thousand meals required:

Milk and cream	1042 quarts
Coffee at 1 lb for 2 gallons	240 "
Tea at 1 lb for 5 gallons	40 "
Total	1322 quarts

Which is ⅓ quart each person each meal. While some drink water exclusively there are others who take double shares in the milk which is one of the most important items in the menu. The best reason that many city people can give for spending the Summer at a country house is the benefit to be derived from an abundant supply of pure milk and cream.

Dinner.

August 18.
Soup—Consomme paysanne (7 qts 42 cents.)
Fried sunfish, a la Margate (string of 30 panfish, 5 lb 40 cents."
Potatoes stuffed.
Sliced cucumbers, potato salad, olives (20 cents.)
Boiled leg of mutton, caper sauce (4 lbs 55 cents.)
Roast beef (loin 4 lbs 52 cents.)
Chicken pot pie (5 fowls 125, with trimmings, 140 cents.)
Small fillets of beef a la **Creole** (2 lbs and sauce, 30 cents.)
Virginia grated corn **pud**ding (25 **cents.)**
Lima beans 7, **mashed turnips** 4, browned **carrots** 5, **tomatoes 12**, potatoes 15 (46 cents.)
Steamed cabinet pudding (36 orders, 50 cents.)
Sweet potato pie (5 pies 43 cents.)
Vanilla ice cream (3½ qts 75 cents.)
Cocoanut macaroons (same as No. 457; doubled, 26 cents.)
Apple, peaches, nuts, crackers, cheese (53 cents.)
Milk, cream 66, coffee, tea, sugar, bread, butter 53 (119 cents.)
Total, $8 13; 54 persons; 15 cents a plate.

1012—Consomme Paysanne.

Clear consomme with vegetables like **j**ardinier and Brunoise but the specialty **o**f shred cabbage in addition. Paysanne **m**eans peasant-county style. For the **v**egetables take the smallest vegetable **s**poon and scoop out carrots, squash, **t**urnips of two colors, or whatever may be **a**vailable in the vegetable line, size of **p**eas, boil them along with a handful or **t**wo of cabbage shred fine as if for slaw; **d**raw away the water when done, and put

the vegetables in the consomme. Have some very small and thin pieces of toast ready and drop two or three in each plate.

1013—Fried Panfish, a la Margate.

Dip small fish in flour and fry in a pan of hot lard.
To garnish, have ready a pint of young green peas, fry them in lard or clear butter, not too hot, until they are dry but very bright green, like parched peas in taste. Shake them up in a little fresh butter and serve a spoonful around the fish. Margate is a pleasure resort and fishing place.

1014—Potatoes Stuffed.

Select medium potatoes all of one size and cut off the ends and bake. When the potatoes are done scoop out the inside, mash and season, then put it back into the shells, set them on end in the baking pan and keep in the oven till wanted. Serve with fish but on a separate plate or dish.

1015—Chicken Pot Pie, Country Style.

Cut up five fowls in joints and boil in water barely enough to cover, and time according to age. Old fowls make good pies if allowed two or three hours to stew tender. Add a seasoning of sat pork and onion, parsley, salt and pepper. When done add milk to make sauce sufficient, thicken till like thin sauce and turn the stew into a pan that will go in the oven. Make up pot pie dumpling batter as elsewhere directed, drop spoonfuls all over the surface and bake twenty minutes or more.

1016—Smal Fillets of Beef, a la Creole.

Small beefsteak pieces sauteed and stewed tender and put in tomato sauce. To saute the meat put in the frying pan first a minced onion and piece of garlic along with butter or oil, and thin pieces of steak on top. When the onion and steaks begin to brown, add soup stock in small quantity and put on the lid and keep it simmering. Fill up with tomato sauce, or Spanish sauce with tomatoes added, just before time to serve. Garn ish with croutons of fried bread.

1017—Grated Corn Pudding.

Grate cooked corn off the cob; to a quart add four yolks eggs, half cup of milk, half cup of butter, salt and pinch of white pepper. Put in a tin pan and bake. Serve as a vegetable, a spoonful in a small dish.

1018—Browned Carrots.

Steam or boil first; put the carrots in a pan in the oven with a spoonful of roast meat fat and bake brown. Dredge salt.

1019—Steamed Cabinet Puddings.

Individual; in custard cups.
Take as many slices of cake as will fill a two-quart pan.
½ cup butter.
½ cup citron shred fine.
6 cups milk.
8 eggs.
½ cup currant jelly.
Spread the slices of cake one side with butter the other with jelly, very thinly; put three or four together cut in dice, mix the shred citron with the cake and fill custard cups or deep muffin pans. Mix the eggs and milk together—no sugar needed—and pour over the cake, press down with a teaspoon after it has soaked a short time, then steam about half an hour.
Turn the puddings out in saucers to serve, and there ought to be either a spoonful of whipped cream or egg meringue on top and the meringue browned with a red hot shovel held over it.

1020—Sliced Sweet Potato Pie.

Steam a few sweet potatoes and let get cold. Roll out four or five pie crusts, slice the sweet potatoes thin and lay in slices enough to a little more than cover the bottoms. Strew in sugar enough to cover the potato slices, and then half a dozen bits of butter size of filberts and one blade of mace broken up in each pie. Pour in a quarter cup of wine, or brandy and water and bake without a top crust slowly and dry.

1021—Cocoanut Ma.aroons.

Make as at No. 457; but use desiccated cocoanut instead of almonds. When you have cake icing left over it can be used to advantage in this way.

How Much to Serve.

It is needless to offer Mrs. Tingee the advice to dish up light as her failing is in that direction already; I have seen her serve portions to her best boarders that I should consider only the scrapings of the dishes, and have seen her boarders, not caring to touch the blackened scraps of meat which she set before them for tea, make the repast of two thin slices of baker's bread and butter and a cup of weak tea with apparent content. I can only account for their staying to board at such a table by supposing that there were other reasons stronger than the love of eating which prevented them from exercising a free choice and going somewhere else. But in nearly all more open and public houses the failing is in quite the opposite way. To hear the waiters in many places trying to cajole or bully the cooks into dishing up two or three pounds to each person one would think their love for those they wait on is stronger than a brother's, and that their sensitiveness at the disgrace of only taking a man just what he can eat and nothing to waste ought to excite our most sympathetic consideration. There are young proprietors and managers, too, working for popularity who make mistakes in this line. It may be good policy in some circumstances to make a show of that sort of liberality which gives three times as much as the average man or woman consumes; in such a case let it be breads and vegetables that are condemned to be thrown away, and always serve the meats small. As some have but little idea of quantities in pounds and ounces, let us observe that ten eggs are a pound and two eggs are three ounces, and enough for nearly every person. If we should set five dishes of eggs each containing two fried, it would certainly look like a profuse allowance, yet there would only be the alloted pound. Take away a dish and replace it with one of meat same weight; take away another and give potatoes or fried oysters, fish, or mush of its weight; take another and give bread, and take the fourth and bring in its place batter cakes and there is but the allotted pound of solids yet, although a good and complete meal. These things are worth considering because they are related to the difficulty there is of living in this world, for it is not what we eat but what we waste that makes board so high.

A man in business ought to have tact enough to relax a rule in economy at the right time but some have not. I stopped somewhere recently where they only served one egg to a dish, with small piece of ham. I have forgotten where it was but as there is no unpleasant impression attached to the remembrance it must have been a good table with enough of other things, where nobody was displeased, and certainly at our Summer house at Unitah Lake, where there was no stint or restraint, about half the orders that came were for one egg only, but eggs are staple and common and that does not excuse the mistake of old Mr. Sticktite at his Union Depot Hotel at Jimsonvale with his asparagus. When the crowd of passengers looked over his bill of fare and saw "asparagus," not printed but written in, they looked around and at each other as if to say, "What a liberal man," and "What an excellent dinner we shall have." But when it was brought in, three poor little infant stalks counted without a miss to each plate the sentiment changed to a dry little laugh and all fell to finding fault indiscriminately with everything on the board. The dinner would have been well enough without the asparagus; it was not expected; why did he have it? For popularity, of course; to make people say he was liberal, but he failed through not giving enough; it did more harm than good. So it was at the Hotel Fantastic at Fantastic Beach, when they tried to give a high-toned Sunday dinner with larded fillet of beef and cooked one

fillet, four pounds, for near a hundred people. Your guests who can afford to pay three or four dollars a day are likely to be aware of the merits of the tenderloin, at least these were, and everybody ordered it, so altogether it was shaved off in slices as thin as card board and all the first half were thereby made as mad as high-toned people dare to get, the other half got none at all and I don't know which end thought they were the worst treated, but probably the hotel lost custom enough to have paid for several fillets. If I were giving spring chicken for breakfast for the first time in the season notwithstanding the two-ounce rule in all else I would give half a pound of chicken to every order, drop off all other kinds of meat for that meal and give the other half pound in the best of breads and sauce and trimmings to the chicken.

Dinner.

August 19.
Soup—Calf's head, a la Portuguaise (6 qts 48 cents.)
Perch, water souchet (6 lbs gross, 48 cents.)
Potatoes a la poulette.
Boiled bacon and greens (16 cents.)
Roast beef (2 ribs short, 4 lbs 52 cents.)
Roast lamb, mint sauce (quarter, 7 lbs 90 cents.)
Chicken giblets saute with rice (16 orders, 20 cents.)
Lobster cutlets, a la Victoria (12 orders, 22 cents.)
Green corn pudding (25 cents.)
Sweet potatoes 20, string beans 3, turnips 3, squash 8, tomatoes 6, potatoes 15 (55 cents.)
Boiled sago pudding (with sauce 12 orders, 20 cents.)
Apple pie (5 pies, 40 cents.)
Lemon ice cream (3½ qts 75 cents.)
Orange butter cake (2 cakes 1½ lbs 21 cents.)
Fruit, nuts, cheese, crackers, pickles (52 cents.)
Milk, cream 60, coffee, tea, sugar, bread, butter 50 (110 cents.)
Total, $6 96; 50 persons; 14 cents a plate.

1022—Calf's Head Soup, Portuguaise.

It is a vegetable soup with barley, and

calf's head cut in dice in it and a small proportion of tomatoes.

1023—Perch Water Souchet.

A water souchet—called "souchy" by English cooks—is fish steaks or fillets stewed in a very little water with herb seasonings and served on toast with some of the broth over the toast.

Slice the fish if large or split and cut in quarters if small, lay the pieces in a bright pan with a small bunch of parsley and green thyme and two or three green onions; add salt and pepper to season, fill up with water enough just to cover the fish and stew gently at the side of the range about half an hour, skimming off the scum that rises. Take out the herbs and onions and serve the fish from the pan on slices of buttered toast moistened with the fish liquor.

1024—Potatoes a la Poulette.

Parisienne potatoes in yellow sauce. Steam or boil the potatoes without breaking. Make butter sauce, add to it the yolk of an egg, salt, white pepper and juice of half a lemon. Put the potatoes in the sauce; serve with fish.

1025—Chicken Giblets Saute, with Rice.

Cut the giblets in small pieces all of one size and steep in cold water. Fry a minced onion in ham or bacon fat, then put in the giblets and fry (saute) them brown. Put in water to nearly cover, season with powdered herbs or Worcestershire sauce, salt and pepper, and let stew with a lid on till quite tender, then skim and thicken the sauce and serve with rice in the dish like a curry.

1026—Lobster Cutlets, a la Victoria.

Take half a can of lobster and pound it to a paste. Put in a saucepan, half a cup butter and one small cup flour and stir them over the fire and when hot and well mingled, add a cup of boiling broth or water. This makes a stiff sauce. Put in the lobster paste and stir all together. Season with a light grating of nutmeg, salt, cayenne and juice of half a lemon. Set it away in the refrigerator. When cold make it in small cutlet shapes, egg and bread them, fry light colored in a kettle of lard. Boil four or five eggs hard and quarter them lengthwise. Serve tomato sauce or cardinal sauce in the dish, the lobster cutlet in it, a quarter of egg and a crouton of fried bread.

1027—Green Corn Pudding.

Shaved cooked corn off the cob, or use canned corn pounded to a half-paste. To a quart add one cup milk, half a cup butter and four eggs and salt and white pepper to season. Bake in a pudding pan; serve as a vegetable entree in flat dishes. This can be made much richer if wanted so, with more milk and yolks of eggs and is a very popular dish.

1028—Boiled Sago Pudding.

4 cups milk.
2 tablespoons sugar.
1 cup sago.
Butter size of an egg.
2 eggs or the yolks only.
Boil the milk with the sugar in it, shake in the sago and keep it stirred up for a few minutes, let cook slowly with the lid on for about half an hour, set where it will not burn on bricks at back of the range. Then beat in the butter and eggs. Serve with sauce.

1029—Work and Wages.

Counting up to the 13th of August we only had an average of twenty-three paying people in the house including the owner and his family. Mrs. Tingee and her two or three girls, and a boy in the yard could take care of that numbe-easily; but it has to be according to style. There is the Summerland House at Unitah running half the time with but seventy-five paying people and eighty-five "help." At this house we are between styles and have nine employes to the average twenty-three guests. and sometimes have ten. There is a fraction of a person somewhere, perhaps that is the baby, but we will not let fractions trouble us when tney are but small, so of the four thousand meals consumed eleven hnndred and thirty-four have gone to the help and the twenty-three guests have to pay for them as well as the two thousand eight hundred and ninety-eight meals for themselves, all at ten cents a meal, discarding the ninth of a cent fraction as usual for the sake of lucidity. Besides this comes the wages paid for carrying on the work of the place to swell the expense account to nearly donble. As most people are sensitive on the subject of the amount of compensation they can command, I will not "give away" anybody but will give the sum total for the bunch of us. There was one whom I have reason to suppose took his light employment as the price of his board during his Summer vacation, and cost the house nothing in cash; another, perhaps, had his compensation contingent upon the amount of the profits; two of the workers were hired by the year at country wages, and the girls who did the table waiting were at the usual house-girl prices. The cook for this short season received as much pay as the chief cook at the best of the two hotels at the depot and a little more than the chief cook at Black's, which was a fancy price for this small house to pay, yet neither of those chief cooks would have taken the situation or done the work because it is mixed, both meat and pastry, and because it is mixed other ways; for there are some things which look natural enough but which it is impossible for a limited and graded, bound and restricted, enthralled and restrained cook to do. I don't know why the French cooks simply say it is impos-*seeble* for them to do so and that is all there is of it—as, for instance, it is quite possible for fishes to fly, I have seen them do it in the tropics, but it is impossible for the chief cook of a full-grown hotel to clean fish, and equally impossible for his second cook to pass dirty dishes over to the next table, however much they may be in his way on his own table,—it isn't his business to gather up dishes.

These impossibilities often cause embarrassment in small houses where perhaps there is not yard-man enough to go droun, or where, it may be, there is no yard man but the proprietor or his clerk, and as they will not clean the fish for the cook and the cook cannot cook it without being cleaned of course there is nothing for that cook and his second to do and they step out. The small houses then hunt up a woman cook, for they are generally more pliable; they either do not know of those iron-clad rules of the kitchen, or, knowing them, with the natural mulishness of woman they choose to do the other way and go right on earning the wages. There are said to be a few first-class female cooks getting as high wages as the same grade of male cooks. Without the least intention of saying what ought to be and only stating facts the highest wages I have ever known a woman to receive for cooking in a small hotel both meat and pastry, was fifty dollars a month. There are thousand of them working in hotels and boarding-houses at five dollars a week, whose work is but little above common labor. There is no doubt but there is a demand for skillful, bill-of-fare, women cooks; such can always secure good situations with sufficient help at about ten dollars a week in any part of this country, board and lodging, of course, in addition. It is on that figure I will base future estimates of the cost of board in country houses. In the present instance, however, I have the actualities to draw from and find that the sum total of wages paid for the six weeks was three hundred and twelve dollars.

1030—Laundry Work.

The washing of table cloths and napkins is an expense large enough to change the grade of the house that cannot afford it from the one that can; it must be paid for by the boarders and consequently affects the price of board. In such a house as the one we write of, however, it is not practicable to make a separate account of it. Good hotel managers expect the money earned by the laundry to pay its way and pay for the laundry work of the house; probably such was the case here and it need not affect our estimates.

1031—Fuel and Light.

This item I could not get with perfect

exactness but can approximate closely. Our John has it as part of his yearly contract that he shall in Winter provide twenty cords of wood for the Summer business. He claims that he had this Spring twenty-two cords, and having but seven cords left we must have used fifteen cords in six weeks. That includes the laundry and dining-room fires, and allowance has to be made for the wood being at least half of it dry and decaying basswood that burns away like paper. Of such wood in six weeks we may have burned enough in the kitchen to be equivalent to eight cords of sound wood worth in the country three dollars a cord or twenty-four dollars.

The house has consumed twenty-five gallons of coal oil of which the dining-room and kitchen cannot have used more than 10, or $2 worth.

1032—Ice.

Mr. Farewell has contract with one of the neighbors, by which he hauls all the ice he needs for the season from said neighbor's ice-house for a compensation of $15. All the ice used for freezing creams has been allowed for in counting cost; for this portion of the season allow for ice otherwise used $10.

1033—Total Cost of Board.

Provisions for 23 boarders 42 days	$290.70
Wages of employes 6 weeks....	312.00
Provisions for employes 42 days	113.67
Fuel, light, ice................	36.00
Total....................	$752.37

This is within a fraction of 26 cents a meal for the paying people and is $5.45 a week each as the actual cost of first-class board and middle-class table service.

1034—How Much Profit?

This house charges $10 a week for board and lodging, transient meals are 50 cents and therefore average half profit, while there is a margin on regular boarders of $4.55 a week each and a total of $627.63 for the six weeks, or over $100 a week out of which to pay the bed rooms

and rent, the laundry and chamber work having already been paid for in this estimate, which includes the help employed. The latter part of the season is the best; there are now in the house 40 boarders to 11 "help," yielding a profit of $182 a week. If a man can have a season of only 10 weeks at that average and these prices he makes $1,820 out of a small house; a sum large enough to tempt many to try the business. The owner of the place and his family are properly counted as boarders in every calculation of expense, having placed the manager and housekeeper in position to relieve them from any active participation.

If the manager and housekeeper were to get married and, with this book for their guide, were to become the landlord and landlady of the house they would have a still better rate of profit to expect than the figures above, for they would have in addition the salaries which they now enjoy, to go a long way towards paying their rent.

The cost of sleeping people consists chiefly in the laundry work involved in changing the bedding after every sleeper. Two sheets, a pillow slip and one or two towels are expected to be washed after every departure, which, put out at schedule rates would cost 35 cents for a bed that only yielded 50 cents. For regular boarders the changes are made only twice or it may be once a week except towels, and reason is found in that for making a difference in rates for regular and transient. The cost of laundry work has also to be reduced to the smallest sum by having it done at home.

Dinner.

August 20.
Soup—Corn and tomato (7 qts 40 cents.)
Halibut, Maryland style (4 lbs 50, trimmings 20, 70 cents.)
Fried hominy.
Boiled chicken with salt pork (5 fowls 1 25, pork 12, and sauce 140 cents.)
Roast beef (3 ribs short, 7 lbs 90 cents.)
Lyonaise of liver with fried crusts (10 orders, 12 cents.)
Queen fritters, vanilla sauce (65 cents.)
Browned sweet potatoes 25, lima beans 6, corn 10, cabbage 6, potatoes 13 (60

ents.)
English suet pudding (29 cents.)
Peach pie (5 pies, 40 cents.)
Blackberry meringue (55 cents.)
Apples, nuts, raisins, cheese, condiments (54 cents.)
Milk, cream 66, coffee, tea, sugar, bread, butter 52 (118 cents.)
Total, $7 73; 54 persons; 14⅓ cents a plate.

1035—Corn and Tomato Soup.

One quart green corn cut off the cob, one quart tomatoes chopped small, one pint mixed vegetables cut small in five quarts seasoned soup stock. Boil up and season to taste.

1036—Halibut, Maryland Style.

Halibut steak cut thin, breaded in corn meal and fried in a small quantity of salt pork fat—not immersed but in a frying pan and turned over to brown. Serve a slice of the dry fried salt pork on top of the fish and a thin slice of fried hominy in a separate dish.

1037—Fried Hominy.

Fine hominy made into mush same as oatmeal. Cut thin slices when cold, divide them in diamond shapes, flour on both sides and fry light colored. Serve with fish and chicken.

1038—Boiled Chicken with Salt Pork.

Boil 5 fowls, time according to age, and a pound of salt pork with them, and make a cream sauce. Serve a joint of fowl with sauce poured over and a small slice of streaked pork by way of garnish.

1039—Lyonaise of Liver with Fried Crusts.

It is liver and onions in brown sauce. Fry a cupful or more of chopped onions, green ones are preferable, in roast meat fat and throw in the liver cut in small blocks; cover with a lid and let them simmer together half an hour. Pour off the grease, shake a basting spoon of flour into the pan and stir until the liver is coated with it; pour in soup stock or water barely to cover; salt and pepper, and let stew half an hour longer. Border the dishes with minced eggs and parsley or croutons or potato balls.

1040—Browned Sweet Potatoes.

Boil or steam first, and then brown in the oven; dredge salt and baste with butter or drippings.

1041—How Many Cooks to How Many People?

My second used to do up her hair one day with blue ribbon and the next day with pink, in the old happy days five or six weeks ago when there was nobody in the house, and singing began and ended the day; now the boat boy never comes to turn the ice cream freezer; nobody has time to help her and she wears no more ribbons; she has soured on the work and gets mad if I call her "sec." All hotel hands are working under a heavy pressure now, at the busiest time of all; there is no getting help when every hand is already at work that can be found. At various times it has fallen to me to take charge of a kitchen for a fixed sum and pay all the other hands myself, when the fewer I had to help me the more money I had left. For such times I had a rule formulated that 1 cook and 1 helper are required for 25 people, and 1 more for every 25 additional, and at this late day I find no reason to change the estimate. This has reference only to the work of hotels or houses where regular meals are prepared after the style of these present. There are places where one man will go into the woods and cook for a hundred wood-choppers or saw-mill hands, and carry his water and split his wood besides, but there is little in that for a comparison. It is the commonest possible mistake to suppose that because there are few people there is but little work; it is the number of dishes made and not the number of people that makes the work. It does not take much longer to make 2 gallons of soup than 1. If I have 5 sauces to make it is immaterial in point of time whether they be 5 cups or 5 quarts. Where the number of people does make a difference is in the duration of meals, breakfast encroaching upon dinner and giving no time to the one cook to begin his preparations at the proper season for the next meal, then another has to take hold of the lagging breakfast orders and give him his opportunity. The time when the paymaster reaps a temporary advantage is when the 25 gradually swell to 40. There is a disinclination to take on another cook or helper, the 2 are in harness and are making the work go on, in part from the force of habit, but it is on a strain and by neglecting the small niceties, by failing to clean up, and by letting things go withount the finishing strokes. It will be found a good rule to count by, that 2 skilled cooks and a pan-washer helper are required to cook for 50.

Dinner.

August 21.
Soup—Puree a la Crecy (6 qts 36 cents.)
Salt mackerel, mustard sauce (4 fish and sauce, 24 cents.)
Potatoes a naturel.
Chicken, a la Bechamel (5 fowls and sauce, 130 cents.)
Roast beef (rib ends 5 lbs 45 cents.)
Stuffed shoulder mutton (4 lbs 50 cents.)
Curry of veal, a la Calcutta (10 orders, 1 lb and trimmings, 23 cents.)
Macaroni, a la Creole (20 orders, 20 cents.)
Fried egg plant 15, turnips 4, corn 10, squash 8, potatoes 12 (49 cents.)
Astor House pudding (No. 594 doubled; 24 orders, 28 cents.)
Covered lemon pie (5 large, thin, 35 cents.)
Frozen buttermilk (5 qts frozen, 25 cents.)
Fruit cake, jelly cake (2 lbs 20 cents.)
Peaches, nuts, cheese, crackers, condiments (50 cents.)
Milk, cream 50, coffee, tea, sugar, butter, bread 48 (98 cents.)
Total, $6 33; 49 persons; 13 cents a plate.

1042—Puree a la Crecy, or Carrot Soup.

Crecy, an old French battlefield, afterwards turned into market gardens became noted again for the production of the carrot, a vegetable more highly valued before the introduction of the beet than it is now, but still one of the mainstays of the French cook. So persistently do these old names cling that but recently a cook contributing a receipt to a New York journal, told his readers to take some Crecy carrots and do thus and so. It is to be hoped they got some.

To make the soup, take soup stock and boil carrots and corned beef in it and a few other soup vegetables for seasoning. Take out the meat and pass the carrots along with the stock through a seive. Skim well, add a small amount of flour or starch thickening to keep the puree (pulp) from settling to the bottom; season and serve like bean soup, with crusts in the plate.

1043—Salt Mackerel Boiled.

There is as much difference between mackerel boiled soft and boiled hard as between eggs similarly cooked. If you would have mackerel tender, as well as of good color, put it on to cook in cold water and take it off as soon as it begins to boil. It is best if it can be cooked to order, or only as wanted, as it becomes hard and curls out of shape with standing long in the water. Mackerel looks best if cut across, not lengthwise, each fish making three portions. Dish the skin side up and a spoonful of melted butter over it.

Mackerel put in water to freshen will hardly keep sweet twelve hours unless ice water be used or the vessel set in the refrigerator. It should remain in water at least twenty-four hours, and be changed once or twice. After that if any are wanted to broil, they should be hung up to dry one meal ahead.

1044—Salt Mackerel Broiled.

Divide the fish lengthwise, and if of

the largest size, again into quarters. Broil over clear coals, or toast before the fire in the hinged wire broiler, browning the inside first. Serve the brown skin side uppermost, with a spoonful of melted butter poured over. It should cook in five minutes.

1045—Mustard Sauce.

Make butter sauce, and mix with ti made mustard enough to give it a pale yellow color, then let boil up again for a moment to thicken, but not to separate the butter.

1046—Potatoes, au Naturel.

Means that they are plain. New potatoes with the skins on, should be steamed and served in a dish separate from the fish.

1047—Chicken, a la Bechamel.

Chickens with cream sauce. Boil the fowls in salted water or broth, and take some of the broth, strain through a napkin, boil, and thicken with flour, then beat in butter and add cream or rich milk and strain again.

1048—Curry of Veal, a la Calcutta.

The specialty of the style is the putting grated cocoanut in the stew; and yet, perhaps, there will be some to say that it is no specialty, but common to all curries if properly made. There is an old sea steward settled down in that haven of rest for old salts, Nipantuck Island, who will talk by the hour about the East Indies and, as he expresses it, there they curry everything and put cocoanut and cocoanut milk in everything.

Pour a little oil or butter into a saucepan, throw in a minced onion, cut any pieces of veal you may have that will not make roast or cutlets into small pieces of one size, put them in with the onion, cover with a lid and let stew in that way without water until the meat begins to brown. **To** a pound of meat allow about a tea-

spoonful of curry powder; shake it about in the stew, then put in water to barely cover and cook half an hour longer. Skim off the grease from one side. Add a heaping tablespoon of grated cocoanut, some salt and pepper, cook a few minutes. Serve with plain rice at one end of the dish or as a border.

1049—Macaroni, a la Creole.

Cook ½ pound of macaroni, cut it in short pieces, fry a little garlic and onion in oil, throw in a minced red pepper, add a pint of tomato sauce, put in the cooked macaroni and shake up.

1050—Egg Plant Breaded and Fried.

See directions at No. 125. Besides that egg-plant can be breaded in egg and cracker dust, and fried by immersion. It is not absolutely necessary to parboil the vegetable, and in places where they are short of help they fry it without that preparation.

1051—Frozen Buttermilk.

A grateful change from ice cream in hot weather. Put buttermilk in the freezer without any addition and freeze with rapid turning to make it foamy, but it should not be frozen solid.

I have had to add sugar before freezing in some places to suit peculiar people, but think it spoils the buttermilk. It is a matter of taste, however.

1052—Boarding the Employes.

In all the preceding estimates and in all the bills of fare the provisions for the help have been counted the same as for the guests and meals charged at the same cost, but the same has not been done in regard to table service and other expenses. This seems the sound way to count the expense: when the bills are to be paid to the butcher and grocer it makes no sort of difference by whom the goods have been consumed. It is but a self-deception for any keeper or manager of a resort hotel to suppose that his help is costing less—speaking of the gross cost of provisions—than his paying guests by the meal or in the aggregate. They eat the same food with the difference that they do not have such a free choice as the guests. They eat what is left over, but not the refuse, only that which the cooks prepare in excess of the demands of the dining room. Of the three classes constituting the community of a large hotel the officers eating at a separate table in a separate dining room are likely to fare the worst as, if the bill of fare allotted them be not satisfactory they have not the opportunities for something supplementary which others below them enjoy. In a large, hotel the early breakfast for the help consists in part of the surplus left from the last nights dinner with enough of fried fresh meat and boiled potatoes to make up the needed quantity; their dinner will consist in part of stews and broiled meats and fish from the dining room breakfast increased as before by broiled or roast second-rate cuts of meat and soup and a cheap pudding. Allow that such a house is well-filled with guests and there is little left; or that the cook is one of the few that can estimate closely how much to cook and the board of the help may cost somewhat less than that of the guests, still the chances are against it, while in a small house the opportunities are such that there is no room for the supposition of a difference unless it be in the helps' favor.

In the house of which I write, I have made use of the help to make a clean sweep of every meal, otherwise there must have been more to throw away and the estimates could not have been so close nor the meals at once so profuse and so cheap. For here as in all small houses the help, what few there are, take their meals immediately after the guests. There is no re-warming provisions from a previous meal, it would be unless, not one of them would even look at them, but if I have broiled 12 beefsteaks and only 8 have been taken in, the help will take the 4. If the guests have taken to corn bread this meal and left the rolls the help will eat rolls; if the guests have taken a notion all to eat baked potatoes then the help will take the fried potatoes that are left or the oatmeal or batter cakes and if, as is more likely than all there is nothing whatever left and we are glad to see it so,

then we will fry a few eggs. After dinner the cook takes a little survey and puts away the solid meats either for slicing for supper or re-roasting; reserves the canned corn and peas, the tapioca pudding if enough for fritters next day, the joints of chicken that will make patties or croquettes or soup, but leaves on the board the mutton, a la Bretonne, the baked beans, the stuffed shoulder of mutton, the haricot, the collops of beef with tomatoes, the stews in general, the macaroni a la Creole, whatever of the sort may unfortunately have been too much, or if none of these, the help will make a good dinner of soup and fish and clean up the pans. With this in view all our dinners are planned with a cheap meat dish.

The guests will eat the Spring lamb and chicken clean and ask at supper if there is any left cold, then the help come in for the beef a la mode Pariseinne, and live high too. If they do not have first choice then they get even between meals by drinking iced milk while the guests are obliged to get along with iced water. Of course we are all honest; would not take a feather's weight out of the house, will not even eat a meal after we are paid off; yet when we are handling the best there is in the house it is but a short distance from one's hand to one's mouth; and does not the cook himself know where the tenderloin steaks are to be found? Look at his rotund form.

1053—Boarding Children

Growing boys and girls consume at least as much food as adults, perhaps more. If there is any difference to be made in regard to children it must be for those of too tender age to come to table. Hotels generally charge full price for children occupying seats at the first table, that is, children who take the napkins, the clean silver, goblets of ice water, the newly filled cruets, the dishes of olives and sardines, the waiter's time at the busy hour; they are charged for all the extras that make meals expensive; as for the amount of food they consume it is but of secondary importance, but it is the same as the adults require. It is often the case that the baskets of fruit and nuts, cakes and candies are untouched during the whole dinner until the childrcn come; the grown people have enough without, but the children will make a clean sweep and carry off what they cannot eat; then it is the children who make the heaviest drafts upon the cans of milk and cream and that, too, between meals. It is good for them and all right, but it ought to be counted at full price if you are going into the business of boarding children on a first-class scale.

Dinner.

August 22.
Soup—Chicken gumbo (1 chicken 25, okra 25, 7 qts 70 cents.)
Red snapper, a la Palatka (7 lbs and trimmings, 100 cents.)
Sweet potatoes fried (12 cents.)
Bacon and cabbage (10 cents.)
Roast beef (flank 4 lbs 48 cents.)
Roast chicken, puree de marrons (8 chickens and trimmings, 220 cents.)
Beef and green peas, a la Turgee (2 lbs meat 22, peas 10, 32 cents.)
Baked beans and pork (20 cents.)
Green corn 20, tomatoes 8, squash 6, beets 4, potatoes 10 (48 cents.)
Spanish puff fritters (No. 155 trebled; sugared, 40 orders, 45 cents.)
Baked apple dumplings (30 orders, 50 cents.)
Frozen buttermilk 6 qts frozen, 30 cents.)
Arabian cake (2½ lbs 25 cents.)
Apples, peaches (25 cents.)
Nuts, raisins, cheese, crackers, pickles, condiments (56 cents.)
Milk 36, cream 30, butter 20, bread 12, coffee, tea, sugar 20 (118 cents.)
Total, $9 09; 56 persons; 16¼ cents a plate.

1054—Chicken Gumbo Soup.

The several sorts of gumbo soup are all named so from being made with okra pods, called gumbo in the South, and used both green and in a dried and powdered state called gumbo *file*. This green powder, a few bay leaves and bundles of sassafras root are offered for sale by Indians in the New Orleans markets and seems to constitute their entire stock in trade. Okra or gumbo. is of too

mucilaginous a nature to meet with much favor at the North. It can be bought in cans like everything else.

Take one fowl, which you can chop into 18 pieces, and an equal amount of veal cut in similar pieces and fry (saute) them in the usual Creole way with oil or clear butter, with a large minced onion and a leak and piece of carrot and turnip cut in dice, and if you use green okra from the garden slice the pods crosswise and let simmer with the meat. When the contents of the saucepan begin to brown add 4 or 5 quarts of soup stock.

If canned okra be used, fry the chicken and veal first then put in 1 or 2 cans and fill up with stock; the okra thickens the soup and the amount to be used is optional.

Tie up bouquet of herb, thyme, parsley, one bay leaf and 6 or 8 cloves—and drop it in the soup, also a pod of red pepper minced, and salt sufficient. Boil until the pieces of chicken are tender, take out the bunch of herbs; have a small saucepan of boiled rice ready at hand, serve a spoonful of rice in each plate and fill up with soup.

1055—Red Snapper, a la Palatka

First make a sauce of the head of the fish, then bake the sliced fish in it. It is a court-bouillon without wine. Split the head, put it to boil in 3 or 4 pints of water with a few green onions cut small and a pod of red pepper. When it has boiled a short time stir it about until it falls to pieces, making the liquor thick like soup. Lay the slices in a buttered pan strewed with finely minced shalots, dredge salt, scatter chopped parsley over; strain the fish sauce into the pan, bake until it is half evaporated and serve the remainder as sauce with each slice.

1056—Fried Sweet Potatoes.

They can be fried raw, or steamed and then sliced raw and fried; are good either way if carefully cooked in lard not too hot, but a little better if cooked before frying. Cut them in slices an eighth of an inch thick and full size of the potato. Serve with fish or as a vegetable.

1057—Roast Chicken, Puree de Marrons.

The words mean chicken stuffed with chestnuts—mashed chestnuts—the dish in reality is chicken stuffed with sweet potatoes. Good sweet potatoes are very much like chestnuts in taste. Mash and season well with butter and salt and pepper, stuff the fowls not too solid and roast as usual.

1058—Beef and Green Peas, a la Turque.

Take any small pieces of beef such as the ends of porter-house steaks, or the shoulder cap, cut all to one size, put them in a saucepan with fat or butter enough to grease the bottom, and a chopped onion, sprig of thyme and parsley; let it fry a while without any water and stir frequently. When it begins to color, add water to barely cover and a pint of green peas to every pound of meat. Stew together until the meat is tender; season with salt and pepper. It will be sufficiently thickened and will be light-brown. Serve in flat dishes and garnish with fried crusts cut in crescents, dipped in bright gravy and sprinkled with minced yolk of eggs.

1059—Arabian Cake—Biscoscha.

There are several grades and varieties of sponge cake to be found in this book, all good in their place, yet the one I used to regard the chief and is so put forward in the *American Pastry Cook* had nearly been set aside here because the boys regard it as laborious and sometimes fail with it in warm weather, until on a recent occasion I found at an "Oriental Cafe"—the Turks who kept the institution were making a specialty of "Arabian cake," selling considerable quantities to the curious passers-by and kept a Turkish woman cook (young, and a real Zuleika, by the way) busy all day making and baking it. As I carry with me the "Open Sesame!" to all the kitchens in the land, I proceeded to investigate and found it to be neither more nor less except the substitution of starch for flour, than our old favorite Savoy cake—fine sponge cake made by beating the eggs and sugar together without separating the whites and yolks, the way alluded to at Nos. 279 and 280 and the note. These Turks beat the mixture about an hour, but in rather a sleepy sort of way and with frequent relays, for Ali, Arabi and Raphael all had to come in turn and work till their oriental arms gave out. Some who read this will be interested in the fact that this notable cook from Constantinople made them always stir the cake one way just like American home folks do. This is the cake:

1 pound fine granulated sugar (light weight.)

12 eggs.

¾ pound of starch (or flour if for Savoy cake.)

Vanilla to flavor.

Have everything cold to begin with; put the eggs and sugar together in a deep bowl or round-bottomed pan or candy kettle, and beat vigorously with a bunch of wire half an hour by the clock.

It should by that time be twice or thrice the volume it was at the beginning. Add flavoring and the flour or starch. Do not beat after that is in but stir around only enough to fairly mix it out of sight. Bake in a deep turban-shaped mold, slightly oiled before the cake is put in.

A large cake of this sort will generally be done in half an hour. Our Turkish woman carried a long straw in her ear—just where a bookkeeper carries his pen—to try her cakes with.

1060—Meals for Ten or Fifteen Cents.

If it be true, as our figures seem to prove, that a pound of food and a pint of drink are the average requirements for a full meal, then if an eating-house keeper offering meals for 10 cents could induce his customers to take a pound of bread, 3 cents, a pound of potatoes, 1 cent, a pound of mush, 1 cent and 3 cups of milk, 3 cents, for the three meals of one day his outlay would be 8 cents and his profit 22 cents; whereas if he should give a pound of meat, 10 cents, a pound of pie, 10 cents and a pound of syrup, butter and batter cakes on one plate 10 cents, for the three meals of one day, he would have furnished no more than the average man could eat, would not have given a full meal and yet would have nothing left for profit. It is by striking a medium between these and not necessarily by using stuff that is unfit to eat that some men manage in every large city to sell meals for 10 cents and make a profit. "Steak, bread, butter and potatoes, 10 cents," is what the sign boards announce. A pound of 8-cent meat, a pound of potatoes, 1 cent, a pound of bread, 3 cents—3 pounds for the three meals of one day costing 12 cents out of 30—add 3 pats of butter ½ ounce each—the regular restaurant size —3 cents more, and the eating-house keeper gives 15 cents and receives 30 cents, serves 300 meals a day and has 15 dollars a day margin out of which to pay his help, rent and wear and tear, etc., could afford even to add 3 cups of coffee to his sign-board inducements, while those who offer meals at 15 cents might afford to set a sumptuous table. There are hundreds of such places in operation : we are only seeking to know how they can do as they do. San Francisco, years ago, was talked about the world over as much on account of her having houses where a good meal could be obtained for 15 cents as for being the chief city of the Golden State.

1061—Country Board at Five Dollars.

It was mentioned incidentally at the beginning of this book that Mrs. Tingee keeps boarders at $3.50 a week, having lately had to make a reduction from her former price of $4, to meet the demands of her boarders and the stringency of the times. Let us see how she does it. Our emals in this small country house up to the 12th of August, counting the small family meals at 5 or 6 cents each person and the more profuse hotel dinners at from 10 to 16 cents, averaged 10 cents each meal each person. Suppose Mrs. Tingee allows her meals to cost 10 cents, either through allowing some things to go to waste, or through want of skill to make good dishes out of cheap materials, or through depending too much on meat and butter to make up her table, then her boarders cost her $2.10 a week each and she has $1.40 each as a margin to meet her other expenses and pay herself; if she has 20 day boarders that leaves her $28 a week.

She will do most of the cooking herself; she has 2 girls, and a boy in the yard, whose wages average $2 a week each, and their meals $2 a week more, making $12, leaving $16 a week for Mrs. Tingee, but out of that she must pay about $4 for fuel, light, ice and incidentals, and she has for herself about $50 a month.

Now, she has house rent to pay and the house she occupies costs her $30 a month but it does not properly come within our scope, as her business is in taking day boarders and letting out rooms enough to pay the rent of the whole house. The only time that she needs and seeks a sympathizing ear is when a young couple or two gentlemen who have been paying a good price for her two best rooms have moved out and left her in fear of having little or no rent coming in. So that, if she sets as good a table as we have been setting here and keeps her 20 boarders she still is able to appear very respectably and send her two children to a good school. In reality, however, Mrs. Tingee does not set any such table. If she would she could set such meals as we have shown in the divisions of this book before the first birthday supper at an average cost of about 7 cents a plate, and, giving a sufficiency, could keep her full quota of 20 boarders. There is a defect in her method, however, which never allows her full success or a full house, for while a pound of food and a pint of drink are required on an average to make a full meal, Mrs. Tingee devotes her ingenuities to make her boarders get along with half a pound, and regards three-quarters as a piece of extravagance only to be indulged in on Sundays. In consequence her boarders, not being well fed, piece out by buying apples, peanuts, candy, cakes and beer, and find when they count up at the end of the week that this sort of desultory boarding around has cost them more than it would to board at a good hotel, and all who are not bound in some way, leave her and she has but 10 whom she can depend on to stay and a transient customer now and then. She does not allow the provisions for these to cost more than 5 cents a meal, 15 cents a day; $1.05 a week, or $10.50 a week total, for which at $3.50 each she receives $35. This leaves her $24.50 instead of $28 as under the other calculation and as the work is less it is a greater proportionate profit. The great difference in the two methods, is that the latter will not stand the test of competition. The landlord and his wife are boarding out the rent; the retail merchant and wife board there because Mrs. Tingee trades with him; the photographer has his gallery next door and his wife finds better employment retouching pictures for him than she would keeping house, so they board there, otherwise Mrs. Tingee would have no boarders at all, poor woman.

It chanced some two or three years ago, I picked up a brief editorial article in an unexpected quarter, considering the argument it contained, for it was the New York *Hotel Reporter*, that said the great want of the people of moderate means of New York and all large cities is good country board for the Summer months at about $5 a week—that is for board and lodging. Well, it would seem there are plenty of places offering board at that price; it may be they do not meet the requirements of the city customers. In a railroad guide book I read of one lake n the State of New York, where there are 8 or 10 hotels but 400 boarding houses; no doubt but there are all grades and prices but still something may be wanting. Nearly all the well-to-do inhabitants of New Orleans and other southern cities leave their homes every Summer for a sojourn at some country place or at the sea side. At Biloxi, Pass Christian, South Pass, there are houses which rent for from $200 to $300 or $350 for the Summer season to be kept as boarding houses and remain closed all the rest of the year. In the New Orleans papers I see an advertisement which reads well, it is of a Summer boarding house at Gobegic Ferry, on the Topinabee, branch of the Tchoupitoulas river, easy to find because exactly 90 miles from New Orleans, and 700 feet above sea level, where there is plenty of milk, eggs, butter and fruit and vegetables, where board is offered at $5 a week, or $20 a month, and children under 12 are taken at half price.

According to the figures that we have devoted to Mrs. Tingee, allowing from 7 to 10 cents a meal for provisions and 50 cents each person as the expense of bed; 20 boarders at $5 would pay $100 a week; the provisions mostly home-raised may be set down at $1.50 or $30 for the whole, which with the $10 cost of lodging them is $40 a week for 20 boarders and $60 remains. Allow $10 for drawback on children and monthly board and there is still $50 a week or nearly $200 a month for the family that keeps the house and does nearly all the work. There will be transient meals enough sold to pay the rent, or boats or carriages let out, or cigars sold or some little side interest to keep the main profit of the house intact. By reducing the cost of meals 2 or 3 cents at this 10-dollar house of ours we could make a profit at $5 even here, where our meats and fish have to be expressed and our fruits and vegetables are nearly all canned goods.

Dinner.

August 23.
Soup—Vermicelli (7 qts 35 cents.)
Catfish stewed with tomatoes (5 lbs net, steaks 60 with sauce, 68 cents.)
Potatoes Hollandaise.
Boiled smoked tongue (25 cents.)
Roast beef (3 ribs short, 6 lbs 80 cents.)
Civet of rabbit, a la Chasseur (8 rabbits 100, with trimmings, 125 cents.)
Chicken giblets, a la Parmentier (20 orders, 20 cents.)
Charlotte of apples, Francaise (36 orders, 40 cents.)
Baked sweet potatoes 20, squash 8, stewed onions 6, rice 6, beets 5, potatoes 8 (53 cents.)
Indian fruit pudding (No. 161 doubled, 24 orders, 36 cents.)
Blanc mange with cream (2 qts and cream, 45 cents.)
Jelly roll, white cake (2½ lbs 26 cents.)
Nuts, raisins, apples, cheese, crackers, pickles (55 cents.)
Milk, cream 60, butter, bread, coffee, tea, sugar 52 (112 cents.)
Total, $7 20; 55 parsons; 13 cents plate.

1062—Vermicelli Soup.

For general directions about making soup stock, or *bouillon*, as the French call it, read No. 115, the quantities to be according to the number of people. The stock having been strained into a clean soup pot a number of simple soups without names can be made by even inexperienced persons by adding a mixturof vegetables chopped or cut small and either rice, barley, macaroni or nudels or the following: Take

6 quarts stock.

5 cups minced vegetables—being cabbage, onion, turnip, carrot, celery, squash, pumpkin, part or all as may suit.

6 ounces or 2 or 3 cups vermicelli broken small.

Boil and season. It will be thick enough if cooked until the vermicelli is well done.

1063—Catfish Stewed with Tomatoes.

Cut fish in slices, each about 2 ounces, and fry (saute) them in a frying pan with very little butter or drippings. When they are partly browned and about half-cooked add a cup of water, a minced green onion or two and pod of red pepper; then strain a can of tomatoes through a colander to the fish and cook together about ½ hour. Serve with strips of dry toast about a finger's length, in the plate.

1064—Civet of Rabbit, a la Cahsseu·.

Chasseur is hunter, a la Chasseur means in hunter's style; it does not signify anything in particular in regard to the dish but is merely an ornamental affix to anything that consists of game. Civet is but another word for a ragout or highly seasoned stew.

Trim off 8 small rabbits by chopping away the breasts, necks and claws, divide each one in 6 or 8 pieces, steep in water a while, saute them brown in a large pan, pepper and salt well and dredge with flour while they are browning, allowing about a cup of flour and shaking till the pieces are well coated. Then put in a can of mushrooms and the liquor and stock enough to barely cover, a bouquet of herbs containing onion, bayleaf and parsley and stew at the back of the range about an hour. Take out the bunch of herbs at last. Garnish with small croutons dipped in minced parsley.

1065—·Chicken Giblets, a la Parmentier.

Giblets with puree of potatoes.

Cut the giblets in small pieces all of one size and stew until tender; strain off the liquor that remains and make a brown sauce of it, or, add to it some Spanish sauce and boil down until it is thick enough, put the giblets in the sauce; dish a spoonful of mashed potatoes, make hollow with the back of a spoon dipped in water and place the stew in the middle.

1066—Blanc Mange.

1 quart milk.

1 package gelatine—1½ ounces.

1 cup cream.

½ cup sugar.

Flavoring.

Put the sugar and gelatine into the milk and set over a slow fire or at the side and stir frequently until the gelatine is dissolved. When it shows signs of beginning to boil, take off and strain into a pan and set away on ice or otherwise make it cold. While it is cooling stir up and flavor it and add the cup of cream cold. It will set like jelly when quite cold; may be set in cups or molds and turned out, or cut in squares and served with sweetened cream. Not essential to have cream but needs rich milk. May be flavored with orange or lemon peel boiled in it or with extracts.

1067—II—A Bundle of Suppositions.

If the colonel and his young wife desire to indulge in meals a little more expensive than their neighbors', as has been the desire of wealthy epicures in all times, they can do so by only eating oatmeal and cream, for if they only take a large cupful each of oatmeal mush requiring 1 cent's worth each of oatmeal to make, and take 2 cups each of delicious cold cream to eat it with, the cream at city price will cost 30 cents for the two and it will be 16 cents a plate or the average of our highest-priced dinners, for a very incomplete meal, and as their one maid servant will inevitably cost them the same rate, they will be at an expense of 24 cents a meal each for provisions alone, and not much provisions either; but if they will take their 1 cent's worth of oatmeal with 2 cents' worth of milk that will be a different affair and much better for their health and temper.

To be extravagant with buckwheat cakes let them have all the cakes they can eat, which if raised with yeast will only cost them 2 cents each, and put between them ½ cup of fine creamy butter at the city price of 40 cents a pound or 5 cents the ½ cup, and ½ cup more of pure Vermont maple syrup at $1.40 a gallon, or 5 cents the ½ cup, and their plate of cakes will cost 12 cents each for material alone, which is higher than the average of any breakfast or supper that we have set out in this book; but if they will take elegant silver drips which can be bought now at 60 cents a gallon or 4 cents a cup and restrict themselves to restaurant allowance of ½ ounce of butter or even forego it altogether, their cake breakfast need not cost more than 4 or 5 cents each person.

It is very likely that the colonel's young wife would be able to prevail on the butcher to cut out tenderloin steaks for her, such as they used to get by favor at our Summer house, but it would be much against his will as it spoils the loin and he would be obliged to charge her at least 40 cents a pound. Taking a quarter pound each and a can of best button mushrooms at 40 cents and ½ cup butter for the sauce, and rolls, butter and coffee, they will have managed to spend 40 cents each for the material for a breakfast and, allowing in a selection of this sort that 10 cents more will feed the girl it is 50 cents each for the meal and $1.50 for the three meals of one day, a sum that with careful management and good cooking might provision them for a whole week at a Summer house after the method which these preceding pages have shown; for if, instead of the 40-cent steak and 40-cent mushrooms or peas, she will take a pound of steak at 10 cents and 10 cents worth of peas—either green garden peas or home canned, and with but half the steak make a stew with peas, a la Turque, the meal need not cost more than 15 cents each, all counted, or 45 cents a day.

There has been plenty of matter contributed to the newspapers at various times in regard to the cost of living, but all partaking more of the nature of arguments in favor of some person's pet scheme than of plain statements of actual trials. What we think this diary of ours proves is that people can live more cheaply and better in numbers together than they can by twos and threes; that a moderate variety of dishes does not necessarily cost more per plate than two or three dishes in larger quantity would if we have the foresight to know how little of some of the dishes will be required and know what to do with the remainders, and that the profit or loss of keeping boarders depends greatly upon the selection of material and the skill to offset one or two expensive dishes with a good many others made of cheap materials, but exceedingly well-cooked and well served—as for illustration; a pound of the breast of chicken costs 25 cents, and you cannot board them on breast of chicken; a pound of baked beans costs 3 cents, and they will not take beans alone; put the two together and you have 2 pounds of the most desirable and most desired food for 14 cents a pound, which you can afford, and it takes more skill and care to cook the beans so that the dish will be sought after than it does to cook the chicken.

Dinner.

August 24.
Soup—Tapioca cream (7 qts 48 cents.)
Fillets of whitefish, a la Normandie (5 lbs 80 cents.)
Potatoes a la Victoria.
Roast ham, champagne sauce (1 lb 20 cents.)
Sirloin of beef, a la Hongroise (20 cents.)
Roast sucking pig, a l'Anglaise (No. 108; 10 lbs and sauce, 210 cents.)
Roast prairie chickens, game sauce (10 grouse, 200 cents.)
Lamb stew with tomatoes (2 lbs 15 cents.)
Stewed khol-rabi 8, browned sweet potatoes 15, corn 10, string beans, a la Turque 10, potatoes 12 (55 cents.)
Lemon soufflee pudding (2 qts 20 orders with sauce, 35 cents.)
Custard and blueberry pies (3 pies, 27 cents.)
Mountain strawberry ice cream (3 qts frozen, 75 cents.)
Almond cream cake, pound cake (2 lbs 25 cents.)
Peaches, nuts, raisins, cheese, condiments (54 cents.)
Milk, cream, butter, etc (106 cents.)
Total, $9 70; 56 persons; 17⅓ cents a

plate.

1068—Tapioca Cream Soup.

Take 3 quarts soup stock and 3 quarts milk, make a white roux to thicken it by simmering a slice of ham in 4 ounces butter and stirring in a cup of flour and add soup to the roux until it is thick sauce; let boil, then strain back into the soup. Put in a small blade of mace, a cupful of minced onion, a cup of turnip and carrot in the smallest dice and small cup of crushed tapioca. Boil slowly until the tapioca grains are transparent and stir in a spoonful of chopped parsley, with salt and white pepper.

1069—Fillets of Fish, a la Normandie.

Cut the fish in thin fillets size of two fingers, double them and place in close order in a baking dish. Prepare mashed potatoes with yolk of egg mixed in as for croquettes and place a border of it round the edge of the dish.

Take the bones of the fish and stew them in water with onion, parsley, thyme, pepper and salt, making a fish stew or sauce, strain it off and use it to make an oyster stew, into which throw a few shrimps, crayfish, lobster pieces, scallops, mussels and button mushrooms, all or part as may be available. Pour this matelotte or fish stew over the fillets, add a cup of white wine, dredge fine bread crumbs and put the dish in the oven to bake.

Serve one fillet, the sauce that belongs and some of the potato border in the same plate. The name has reference to the sea-coast customs of Normandy.

1070—Roast Ham, Champagne Sauce.

Boil a piece of ham, the thick end, and when nearly done put it in the oven to finish and acquire a brown outside. Slice thin, serve sauce under in the dish.

1071—Champagne Sauce.

It is little more than a name for a brown sauce flavored. Take good gravy from the veal or beef pans (No. 576). Put on a spoonful of spices—allspice, cloves and mace—to boil in ½ cup of wine and strain it presently into the gravy. Another way that seems to meet the requirement of a good sauce for roast ham, is to add wine and a little sugar to the brown sauce without the spices. The substitute where there is no wine furnished is vinegar, sugar and water in brown sauce—it is good—nothing wrong about it but the name.

1072—Sirloin of Beef, a la Hongroise.

That is nothing but a name for you to attach to any piece of warmed-over beef on a day when the dinner is such that you know nobody will order beef. Sometimes you can call it a la Demidoff, or Malakoff, or Marco Bozarris or anything; the people will go on ordering pig and paraire chicken with unswerving constancy, just the same.

1073—Roast Prairie Chickens.

Singe them, wipe clean inside and out, skewer through the thighs and body, or else tie the legs in place, put in a salted pan with drippings; roast late and have them come out only just done through. Each one makes 5 dishes by slicing a little off the breast which is the meatiest part, and making 4 quarters besides. Serve with jelly or cranberry sauce or game sauce which is cheaper.

1074 —Game Sauce.

Take two-thirds brown sauce and one-third currant jelly or grape jelly, throw in 6 or 8 cloves and simmer together a few minutes.

1075—Kohl-rabi, or Cabbage Turnip.

It is the light green above-ground turnip or swelled cabbage stalk seen in the markets but not in common use. Pare, cut in large dice, boil as you would turnips and season in the same manner by pouring a white sauce over after straining the water away. It is like cooked cabbage stalk in taste and may be cooked with bacon the same way.

1076—String Beans, a la Turque.

String beans salad, in effect. Cut the beans down the whole length, shredding them, boil till done, drain off, cool, then pour over enough salad oil to make them shine; salt, pepper, vinegar, and shake up well. Serve cold with the vegetables.

1077—Lemon Soufflee Pudding.

It is the pastry cream, same as used to fill Boston cream puffs, No. 289, with white of eggs whipped to froth stirred in and then baked. It rises high in the oven; should be served immediately or at least not allowed to become cold. Use a quart of milk, 8 ounces sugar, 5 ounces flour (a heaped cup) an ounce butter, 8 eggs. The yolks cooked in the mixture which must then be made nearly cold and flavored with lemon, and the 8 whites, then added. A spoonful of sweetened cream in each dish for sauce.

1078—Mountain Strawberry Ice Cream.

Late in the Summer when strawberries in most places are gone and forgotten the mountain gardens send down their crop, as great a rarity in the low country as are peas in January. A few of them may be made to go a long way by making a strawberry flavored ice cream and mixing one quart with it at the finish.

1079—Almond Cream Cake.

Mince a cup of almonds, boil them in a cup of syrup with an ounce of butter, put in a cup of white of eggs (8 whites) and stir until cooked after the same method as lemon honey. Spread between layer cakes.

1080—Keeping Clean Side-Towels.

When a correspondent writes of what she saw at the South Kensington Cooking School, she seems to be the most taken by the ceremoniousness with which the grand high priestess washes her fingers and dries them on a snowy side-towel every few moments. That is all good kitchen form though, as long as there is not much serious work to do. You may hear the boys anywhere, in the Rocky Mountains or at the Gulf of Mexico or the eastern sea-shore mention the Cincinnati House at Gibson City as, a pattern, because every morning every cook whatever his grade, is not only furnished a clean towel, but finds it hung on the hook under the edge of the table at his place when he comes to work. At this small Summer house the towel question seemed to be a knotty one for a while until that good and smart and pretty girl, who was my second, unravelled it. After making the one laundry woman gasp with discouragement at the sight of the jackets, caps and aprons I put upon her according to custom, I was positively afraid to say towels to her; it was the last straw and might have broke her back or raised a rebellion. And yet what was to be done?

There is nothing degardes the kitchen so much as the shameful black rag that lies on the table in contact very likely, with the best and whitest dishes, and when hot baking-pans are to be handled and black-bottomed pots to be carried and table corners to be wiped off as well as one's hands a hundred times, the whitest towel becomes vile in two or three hours. I suppose that last year Mary Jane used to wash her towels out in the afternoon instead of taking her needed half hour's nap, poor thing. Well, I had three new towels with my knives wrapped in, in my valise and out they came and all was well for a day or two while they were new and nice. But my second was one of those extremely clean girls; she used to wash and wipe every egg before they should be used if the lots came in the least off color; she washed the baking potatoes in three waters with a scrubbing brush, washed green peas before she shelled them, picked over coffee grains and beans one by one and never knew trouble or stopped singing until the work increased so that she could not do those things. It was about the evening of the fifth day that she was first struck by the enormity of the dirtiness of those towels,

Dinner.

August 25.
Soup—Bisque of lobster (6 qts 48 cents.)
Baked carp, tomato sauce (4 lbs and sauce, 50 cents.)
Boiled ham with Brussells sprouts (25 cents.)
Roast loin of beef (2 lbs 35 cents.)
Braised young pig, a la Francaise (7 lbs and sauce, 155 cents.)
Salmi of grouse with olives (6 grouse and sauce, 130 cents.)
Egg-plant stew, a la Turque (16 orders, 32 cents.)
Compote of bananas with rice (18 bananas 36 orders, 40 cents.)
Fried cabbage 6, baked pumpkin 8, tomatoes 8, corn 10, beets 4, potatoes 8 (44 cents.)
Baked barley pudding (28 cents.)
Peach meringue (like No. 195; 43 cents.)
Best sponge cake (No. 1091; 25 cents.)
Plums, apples, nuts, raisins, cheese, etc. (44 cents.)
Milk, cream, coffee, tea, butter, etc. (84 cents.)
Total, $7 83; 46 persons; 17 cents a plate.

This morning took place the first break of Summer boarders for their homes; nine went away before dinner; going to prepare their children for school for September.

1081—Bisque of Lobster.

Bisque is paste; bisque soups are soups thickened with a paste or puree or pulp of fish or game, as bisque ice creams are creams thickened with pulp of fruit or nuts. Selected small pieces of the meat are put in at least as a sign of what the soup is made.
Take 6 quarts of soup stock, and boil in it the bones or part of a fish, or perhaps the remains of yesterday's matelotte. Take out half of it and made into butter sauce. Pound a can of lobster to a paste, and mix the butter sauce with it and pass through a seive; strain the rest of the soup stock and mix both portions together. A cupful or two of selected red meat of lobster may be added, and sprinkling of parsley, salt and cayenne.

1082—Baked Carp, Tomato Sauce.

Put the fish in a baking pan without splitting open, with salt and butter or drippings, and bake half an hour. Pour a quart of strained tomatoes into the pan, add an onion and pepper, and bake half an hour longer. Serve by spoonfuls with sauce.

1083—Brussells Sprouts.

They are a small species of cabbage about the size of apples, that grow in rows on a tall stem. All dishes in European cookery that are a la Flamande are with Brussells sprouts. They are met with in only a few localities in this country. Cook and season the same as cabbage or orther greens.

1084—Sucking Pig, a la Francaise.

To make the stuffing; fry a minced onion in some fat, throw in a spoonful of sage, then a quantity of finely minced bread crumbs and ladleful of broth to moisten. Stir around in the frying pan until well mingled, season with salt and pepper, stuff the pig with it and roast it in the oven. When barely done, take the pig and cut it in pieces of the right size to serve, put them in a broad sauce-pan and pour in Spanish sauce to nearly cover, put a lid on and let stew slowly.
Make up the stuffing from the cooked pig into small balls, bread and fry them; serve one such forcemeat ball in each dish with the meat and sauce.

1085—Salmi of Grouse with Olives.

Roast the birds rare done, cool off, cut in pieces ready to serve. Make some Spanish sauce hot, add wine and cayenne, put in the cut birds and a cup of olives stoned and sliced. Serve with crouton ornaments.

1036—Egg-Plant Stew, a la Turque.

Take rough small pieces of beef or the rib ends and cut to one size, put them to stew in water. Choose small egg-plants, the seeds not very distinct, pare and cut up in pieces like apple quarters, and put them with the meat. Add a large onion and two or three tomatoes, salt and pepper. Let stew with a lid on until the meat is tender and the liquor is nearly all boiled out, and the remainder is thickened with the vegetables. It is a sort of gumbo, worth trying a few times.

1087—Compote of Bananas, a la Richelieu.

Make a syrup pudding sauce; cut bananas in halves, put them in the sauce and let be parboiled in it, but not cooked too soft. Make a bed of sweetened rice in the dish, place bananas on the top and sauce.

1088—Fried Cabbage.

Chop, season and saute in a frying pan. A good way to dispose of cabbage left over.

1089—Baked Barley Pudding.

Have the barley thoroughly well boiled then use it to make puddings by the same receipts as cracked wheat.

1090—Best Sponge or Savoy Cake.

Make the cake mixture No. 4; and bake in molds instead of small shapes. May be flavored with lemon rind for lemon Savoy cake.

1091—How Many Fires?—Again.

The one large stove has proved sufficient in all but one particular—we could not fill toast orders with it. If there had been another fire however small there would have been nothing more to be desired. Fortunately as there were no breakfast or supper bills of fare to remind them of "dry, dipped, buttered and milk toast" the boarders seldom remembered to want them, and then if the stove was crowded full with cake griddle, soup pots and broiling meats we had to take the toast to the laundry stove.

They have a portable sort of charcoal stove in the South that would be a boon to all the resort houses elsewhere—a stone pail with a second bottom perforated for draft, put a coal of fire in and fill up the pail with charcoal, and you have the best of fires for broiling, toasting or keeping a boiler on, and one easily started and easily dropped when not wanted. Nine-tenths of all the French market cooking at New Orleans is done on these charcoal burners. That includes the complete work of many restaurants.

Whosever buys a stove such as our number 16, 8 holes, should be advised to take that kind, the old pattern, and not to be induced to get themselves into trouble with a pretty range with doors and closets, shelves and hangers, but no room hardly to cook for a family. If you have a stove that is all top and oven with a good front ash pan to broil over, you may hang a boiling pot upon the very edge and it will keep on stewing just as gently as you want it, and you need not clear off everything and stop everything from cooking in order to get the cake griddle over the only hot place as is the case with a so-called range.

If good and complete bill-of-fare dinners for 50, rolls and bread baking and all can be done on one good stove is it not like taking a steam hammer to drive a nail to furnish a house like the Summerland House at Unitah City, that rarely has more than 75 boarders with:

A 3 oven and 3 fire range.
Two charcoal broilers for steaks and fish.
Two steam jackets for boiling meat and vegetables.
A brick oven.
A hard coal batter cake range.
A hard coal toast range.
A steam closet for steaming puddings.
A steam stock boiler.
A steam boiler for cooking eggs.
A steam carving table.
Steam coffee and tea urns.

A steam "bammeree."
Steam closets for warming dishes and breads.
A steam engine and 2 engineers.
Eighty-five help to seventy-five guests.
A money-losing capacity second to no hotel of its size in the land.

August 26.

1092—A Rich Fruit Cake for the Landlady.

This is an English wedding cake of equal quality with the black cake of the second birthday supper and the bride's cake of the wedding breakfast, but all three are different.

1 pound sugar.
1½ pounds butter.
10 eggs.
1½ pounds flour.
Mix the above like pound cake, then add:

1½ pounds seedless raisins.
1½ pounds currants.
1 pound citron.
8 ounces almonds, blanched.
1 tablespoon mixed ground spices.
Half pint of brandy.
1 lemon, juice and grated rind.

Bake in molds lined with buttered paper. Takes from 1 to 2 hours according to depth. This cake cannot be cut while fresh without crumbling, but becomes moister and firm with a few days' keeping.

Cost: 9 pounds $1 60, or 18 cents a pound; with 3 pounds frosting added $1 90, or 16 cents a pound.

August 27.

1093—Tomato Catsup for the Landlady.

Known to be good.
½ bushel tomatoes.
3 ounces allspice.
2 ounces cloves.
1 ounce cayenne.
1 tablespoon black pepper.
1 cup salt.
2 heads garlic.
2 large onions.
1 quart vinegar.
Take ripe tomatoes slice them up, take out bad spots but not peel them, boil on stone until soft and then strain through a seive. Tie the spices in a piece of thin muslin. Put them in and the remaining ingredients and boil 3 hours or longer, if not thick enough. Use whole spices; keep the catsup in glass, bottles or jars sealed tight.

1094—Chili Sauce for the Landlady:

Known to be good.
24 large ripe tomatoes.
6 green peppers.
4 large onions.
3 tablespoons salt.
8 tablespoons brown sugar.
6 teacups vinegar.
Chop the peppers and onions very fine. Peel the tomatoes and cut up very small Put all into a kettle and boil gently an hour. Keep in glass jars well sealed.

[END OF THE EIGHT WEEKS.]

(Continued from page 166.)

and I went behind a door to watch what she would do. Of course she would not touch them, only walked around the table and viewed them on both sides; nothing further took place that evening. I know the female mind is quick to act, but there was a problem that seemed too much for her, and took all night to consider. But it was all right next morning, for she took a stick and raked them into a gallon apple can, put in a small lump of concentrated lye, filled up with soap suds and let them stew for hours, though I had not a thing but old newspapers to use in the meantime, and every day of the eight weeks since, immediately after dinner that dear girl has put those towels through the same course of treatment, left them stewing all the afternoon and I suppose has washed them out besides, but does it so quickly I have never witnessed the operation; and now if it were not for the burned places the same three towels hanging there are white enough and good enough to begin another campaign.

1095—Banana Ice Cream.

About three good, mellow bananas are enough for each quart of cream. Rub the bananas through a sieve; sweeten the cream as usual, mix in the pulp and freeze. This is a favorite kind when made with real cream, but is not very good in a custard mixture.

1096—Banana Fritters.

Make thin batter, the same as for apple or pineapple fritters. Cut the bananas in halves across, if large, or use whole if small; put them in a bowl and moisten with rum and sugar, dip each piece in the batter, and fry by dropping them in hot oil or lard. At many hotels they are only rolled in powdered sugar when served, but you will find they are liked better with sauce.

1097—Oyster Soup aux Fines Herbes
OR NEW ORLEANS STYLE.

For a hundred people—two gallons of oysters and their liquor, two gallons of milk, two cans mushrooms, one onion, two bay leaves, a handful of parsley, a pod of red pepper, some white roux or butter and flour rubbed together, or common flour thickening.

Set the milk over the fire in one saucepan, the oysters in another; just before the oysters begin to boil drain them from the liquor by pouring in 1 colander, and keep them back till time to serve. Set the oyster liquor over the fire again, boil it, skim, and strain through a fine strainer into the milk, chop the onion, mushrooms and parsley and throw them in and bay leaves and pepper pod whole.

Boil a short time; thicken like cream, add the oysters at last.

1098—Oyster Brochettes, a la Creole.

Run a dozen or more of large oysters on a tinned skewer, drop into hot oil and let fry about three or four minutes to shrink them. Take out and finish them on the gridiron over hot coals. Dust with salt and pepper; serve on toast, withdrawing the skewer, garnish with lemon and parsley.

1099—A Proposal to Rent the Place.

Sept. 7.—As long as the moon shone at night my tent among the bushes on a little point jutting out into the lake was not perceived; there is no path that leads to it from the land side and the boat which I have hired from John is hid under a drooping tree, and having no interruptions the work of transcribing the hurriedly pencilled figures of the summer accounts has been rapid and easy. But now the nights are dark and the tent with a light inside is like a huge lantern and attracts notice. It would be best moved further back if I was not going to leave for good. Mr. Farewell kindly offered me a room in the hill cottage to remain as long as his family remained, and John, too, who has made more pork after all than he expected (for he has two fat hogs that will weigh 250 pounds each) invited me to stay and have a month's hunting with him after the season is over. But I knew that safety from interruption lay only in getting clear away from the house where they could not call on me to help them through sudden troubles.

To-night I have heard the splashing oars of several boats passing the point and there were parties singing on the water the same as during the moonlight nights of last week, and at last commencing on the other shore and coming nearer I heard the familiar sound of

"Ja, wir sammeln uns am Strome,"

And seeing that the promised visit was to take place I threw some oil on a pile of dry leaves and made a fire at the water's edge to guide them. It was John bringing a letter from Mr. Farewell, but he had a pic-nic party with him of young people who filled two boats, and among them was my second and her sweetheart. She wore pink ribbons this time, so the blue that she used to wear may have been for the boat boy. She found an opportunity to tell me that with the money she has earned this summer she has bought a certain handsome young Durham cow that we used to admire sometimes and carry salt and corn cakes to at the fence of the Barnacles' pasture. I don't see what she wants with a cow, unless maybe she is going to set up in business keeping summer boarders. Mr. Farewell's letter says: "Mrs. F. and I have been thinking of making you a proposition to lease our place and run it yourself next year. What do you think of the idea? We think it would be to your interest because you understand the business. There are places in the neighborhood very successful that have not as good advantages as ours, but it needs more attention than I can give it.

We should ask you no rent at first but to accommodate my family with the same rooms we now occupy during the summer season. Come over and let us talk about it.

We have had quite a busy time until yesterday.

The relations who were expected early in the summer arrived the day after you went away. We regretted very much that they had not come sooner. Unfortunately, too, Mary Jane had a spell of sickness in the midst of it. I should have come over to see you if I had known your whereabouts. Do not fail to come and see us before you leave."

———

He would ask no rent but his family's summer board. Let us see how much rent that would be. There are six of them in the family. This summer they have been waited on by the regular "help" of the house, but if this arrangement were made they would have a servant of their own, that would be seven. And under such an arrangement they would stay here twelve weeks. Our figures show that it costs $5.40 per week to keep each person according to the style of the few weeks past. All things considered there would be no need to charge for the servant, who would relieve the house girls of so much work, therefore the expense would be:

6 persons @ $5.40 each $32.40 per week; for 12 weeks, total $388.80.

That is what I shall have to pay them in the way of rent.

If they go to some other resort they cannot get as good as they have here for less than ten dollars per week each and their one servants board free; that will be for 6 persons 12 weeks, total $720, a difference in their favor of $331.20. I had rather pay them a cash rent of $500, on condition that they come and board with me at $10 per week each for 12 weeks; which would cause them to pay me back $220.

———

Another consideration is that they would occupy three of my best rooms, which for at least six weeks of the season I could fill with transients who would pay $14 per week each or even more for choice rooms; and if not transient couples there will be parties like the military cadets who can be put four in a room at special rates which will still make the rooms pay better than having cost-price boarders in them. A man cannot be too careful of his best rooms. I have seen a small hotel-keeper lose money every day in a most prosperous season through his want of skill in rooming people: he had thirty rooms and got thirty single persons in them one in each room, and he could not get them out nor any more in, and the tide of tourists was surging up against his doors. Some people will pay double to keep a good room to their individual use, but that was not the case with his agreements. At the Hotel Fantastic a rich man and his wife occupied three of the best rooms but they paid three hundred dollars per month for them and their board. At the Kennesaw House a banker and wife paid $150 per month for two rooms and their board. At the Bubbling Springs we had 50 boarders who paid $15 per week each. If I take up Mr. Farewell's offer I shall be letting them have three best rooms and board for six for $130 per month of 28 days or $21.60 per month each person. Just about half what it is worth, and my rent on such terms would be too high.

On the other hand it is to be considered, next season will be far better than this has been because the place is now well advertised. Mr. Farewell has put perhaps $200, or $250 in advertising, of which I should reap the most benefit next season, for he began so late, the effects have only been felt during the closing weeks, when many came out of curiosity to see a place they had read about; most people make up their minds where they will spend the summer or winter a good while before the time comes. They may go to a place and it does realize their expectations. While they are dissatisfied they recall the good words they have heard or read in favor of some other place and resolve to go to the other place next time. How often have I heard them, when they were chagrined and humiliated over watered milk, bad butter and coarse meat, say haughtily: "Ah, never mind, we'll go to Saratoga next year!"—as if that was going to be any improvement, the poor innocents! But we have set an excellent table here, and all have gone away praising not only the cooking but the provisions; they will say when they hear their friends complain of places: "Ah, you ought to have gone with us to Uintah Lake!" And they will all come next year.

But, again, there is the consideration that I should not be able to do my own cooking and taking care of provisions. Perhaps I should get cooks who would let the help run away with the kitchen and feast on the best while the guests were served with the worst; perhaps they would carelessly allow every meal served to cost three cents more than it ought to cost; that leakage with the increased number of people would amount to $25 per week and in twelve weeks would be a loss to me of $300. The most serious loss is in the mismanagement of meat. The most successful hotel keeper at Bubbling Springs is one who still cuts and broils and carves the meats himself;

though he has paid for his hotel out of its earnings and has built on to it till its size is double what it was when he bought it and has advanced his rates, too. He has cooks, but he cuts and broils, all or part of the meats and so keeps the chief expense under curb and bridle. He has a wife who can fill his place at the desk when necessary.

There is, however, a great deficiency, of amusement at this house of ours. If there were more pastimes there would be so many more transient visitors that a few hundred dollars rent more or less would not be worth considering. I will see what Mr. Farewell as landlord is willing to do in improving the place as a pleasure resort before deciding.

CONCLUSION.

A few materials have been mentioned as derived from the cook's valise, they are not included in the bills. These are extract of meat, catsups and two or three dollars' worth of canned truffles. Opinions will differ on such matters, but as every cook carries his own knives and larding needles I think it wise and politic under such circumstances as are detailed in the preceding pages for the cook to carry a small stock of such extra helps besides. If the proprietors of the small houses knew everything they would see the advisability of providing all sorts of seasonings at their own expense, as they do not understand the use of them, the cook does well to supply himself and get his pay back in the reputation which he gains for the superior flavor of his dishes and for the unexpected production of a truffled fowl when it may chance there are visitors present who will appreciate the effort. For a good reputation means good pay and choice of good positions, and is worth a little outlay of money as well as a good deal of hard work to secure.

TO MAKE GLAZE.

Extract of meat and the meat glaze made by the cooks are very nearly the same thing. It is an expensive substance when made of the best quality, retailing at about thirty cents an ounce. The cheapest is the Australian extract of beef solid and dry in bladders, which sells at $1.25 per pound. Meat extract added to consommes and gravies gives them a rich flavor which is one of the evidences to the guests at table that there is a professional cook in the kitchen.

There are times when a cook can make his own glaze, which is nearly the same as extract, the difference being that it contains more gelatine from the bones than the extract of lean meat. When there happens to be a great plenty of soup bones and the stock boiler is full of rich stock or *bouillon*, and when instead of using it oyster soup must be made, then the stock should be strained off into a large copper saucepan and be boiled down rapidly until it is nearly dried down to gravy. Then skim off the fat, add some salt, and simmer down carefully until it looks thick and dark and is in danger of burning. Pour it into a jar or can; it will set solid when cold and a slice taken out and added to the soup on a day when the stock is poor will be found the one thing that was needed to bring it up to the first quality. Such glaze or extract will keep for months. The French name is *glace* (Pron. *glarce.*)

The Ballade of "Settle Down."

A printer threw away his stick
 And washed his inky hands.
"I'll go and tempt the Fates," he cried,
 "Far off in Western lands."

And so he landed in Begosh,
 A brand new Kansas town,
And there he built a small hotel
 And named it "Settle Down."

He was the landlord, clerk and cook
 The table waiter, too.
He made the beds and tended bar—
 And had enough to do.

The town grew fast, the hotel throve,
 He hired some extra hands.
His profits quite as fast as got
 He put in Begosh lands.

And as he throve he felt a want:
 Mysterious, dim, obscure,
He could not tell exactly what,
 But there it was, for shure.

"Ha! Ha!" he cried, as sudden light
 Broke on him while at dinner,
"I want a printed bill-of-fare—
 "I do—as I'm a sinner."

There was no printing press in town;
 He sent and bought him one.
It came, with type, he worked—and lo!
 The bill-of-fare was done.

He loaded it with lots of **French**
 To sort of give it style,
And proudfully he set it forth
 His boarders to beguile.

There came six cowboys to his board,
 All armed and fierce and grim.
Each man picked up a bill-of-fare—
 Then hastened out to him.

Then on that pale and trembling man
 Their words fell fierce and hot:
"Why don't yer talk United States?
 "What is this Dago rot?

"Wha's '*A lay-matree D-hotel*'?
 "What's '*pum-mey-D-ter-ree*'?
"What's '*Mack-er-hony-aw-gra-teen*'?
 "What's '*Me-new*'? What's '*Saw-tee*'?

"Who's '*Juli ana*'? Who's '*Tommy T*'?
 "Who's '*Li*' and '*May O'Nass*'?
"Say! is '*Con-Sommy-Printer-near*'?
 "Where is '*Pat.-D.-Foy-grass*'?"

"Yer'r growin' rich! Yer'r gettin' **proud!**
 "Yer want ter be er dude.
"Ther daisies claim yer tender toes.
 "Yer'll du ther grass roots good."

There fell a grave like silence then—
 Each man his cannon drew.
* * * * * * *
The doctor's perforation count
 Came up to forty-two.

EPITAPH.

This man was too advanced for use,
 He had to great a head.
He worked his "Settle-Down" in French—
 His settle-up in lead.
   From the Hotel Register, N. Y.

---

*) Menu should be pronounced *mayne*.

HOTEL CARVING

Cer ain men who practise the same set of duties every day will acquire extraordinary dexterity in their line, and they are the men to watch if one would learn all the sharp cuts in carving. George McG—, a Southern hotel keeper was one of these fine carvers, but rather off-hand and wasteful with it, for he was full of other business and would not dwell upon trifles; he was for rapidity and did not stop to clean all the meat

"Well—that turkey weighed 12 pounds before it was cooked—I suppose I could carve 35 or 40 orders from it if I was trying, and I don't think there are many carvers around here can beat me."

"Mr. McG— I think I can just about double that number for a five dollar bet."

"I'll bet you a ten dollar gold piece against seven days wages you can't beat it over ten dishes"—return-

Philadelphia Capon.

from the carcasses; left them to be stripped afterwards for salad or hash. There was another man employed in his house, a professional carver, Jake Carter by name, and one day he said:

"Mr. McG—, how many orders do you think I can get off this turkey?"

"Oh—I don't know—how much does it weigh?"

"Here it is—you can judge for yourself."

ed McG—and not thinking any more about the matter he turned on his heel and went off to the front of the house. But Jake Carter called witnesses to watch and off that one turkey he carved and sent in 70 passable orders. It was nearly two years before McG—would pay the bet, and then he was greatly in need of Carter's services at a banquet and was obliged to pay it; but that was only one specimen of Carter's skill as a carver which has been so valuable to him that he has had fourteen years constant employment in one city, the time being devided between only two hotels.

The art and the difficulty of it consists in slicing broad but thin, even as thin as paper.

Of course there are two sides of the carving question and the consumer may not see the subject in the same pleasing light that the calculating hotel man does; there must be a medium observed that will result in giving satisfaction to the guests at table, yet it is so true that nearly all hotel dishes contain twice as much as are used for all purposes, and withal, the carver must know where the joints are so well that his sharp knives will pass through them without contending against the bones. With such a keen knife the breast of a small chicken can be laid open so as to top cover four dishes, which would not make any showing upon two dishes in the hands of a clumsy carver, and a large chicken will cover six or eight.

The method is, to place a spoonful of the stuffing in the dish, slice meat off the drumstick and place beside it, or a joint of the wing and on

American Thanksgiving Turkey.

they need and the cost of provisions is needlessly increased in that way that a skillful carver who can make a dish look broad and plentiful without giving it much weight may be the most valuable man in the house.

Some men are not adapted to become good carvers; quick, impatient, irritable men are not. It takes an easy-going imperturbable person who cuts smoothly with long and steady strokes and does not see-saw and scatter the splinters. The knives must be thin and as keen as razors; there can be no good carving with the ordinary kitchen knives which top lay the white meat as broad and thin as the size of fowl will allow.

While such directions may read well enough it will be found the practice is not so easy unless pursued with steady system. Take up the chicken by inserting the fork in the cavity of the neck, where the crop was, and keep the fork there in one place until the fowl is disjointed and the breast is in slices. First take off the legs and thighs, cutting to the hip joint, then with a turn of the wrist throwing it out of the socket and pass the knife clear through, hold up the carcass and strike the knife through the small of the back and the lower part or side bones fall off. Then remove the wings at the sockets. Next take off the first slice —the brown outside—of the breast. If a large fowl you can get a broad slice more of white meat before touching the bone. Next to that is the fowl's shoulder-blade, a bone almost like the wishbone, imbedded in the white meat and very much in the way of the carver who is not posted; but your knowing hand takes hold of it by the projecting knob, which is the wing socket, and gently pulls it off and the white meat that comes with it and covers it, and it makes a slice itself almost as thin and quite as broad as the others. Under that and lying close to the breast bone is another layer to be taken off with the point of the knife and that makes four slices of white meat from one side, eight from the two sides, to make the tops of dishes partly made up of a slice from the leg, or a side bone or split of the upper part of the back.

In carving a turkey the proceeding is the same but less difficult as there is more meat to work on. The usual way, which was the way Mc-G— did, is to place the carving fork astride of the breast bone and keep it there until the turkey is all cut up, but Carter objected that thrusting the fork in there cut through a slice of the white meat in the best part on each side of the bone and he took a hold in the crop cavity as already mentioned.

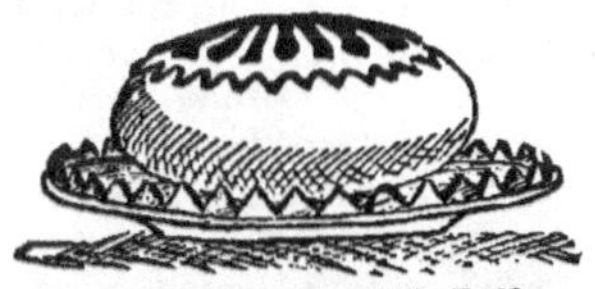

Boned Chicken with Jelly.

ARTISTIC COOKERY

And Notes on the London Cookery and Food Exhibition of 1885.

BY JESSUP WHITEHEAD.

The thousands of intelligent and progressive workers who are now using Whitehead's Hotel Books are reminded of a promise written some years ago in the *American Pastry Cook*, at No. 221, to give at a subsequent time certain illustrated instructions in cake ornamentation, and also some further details of the method of preparing stands and *socles* for meat dishes named at No. 802j. Under the styles of table service at present prevailing, there is not much demand for work of that kind, however beautiful it may be; still, whenever the holiday season approaches, with its banquets and decorated tables, some letters always come with reminders that those promises remain unredeemed. The completion of a new volume in the series now furnishes the desired opportunity.

Had these lines been written a few months earlier, it would probably have been with the impression that a revival of what is called artistic cookery, which is really only ornamental cookery, was taking place; the rather unsatisfactory result of the recent cookery and food exhibition at the Royal Aquarium, London, has a tendency to dispel that idea, however, and seems to show that there is but little recompense to be expected for any efforts in that line, the times being too thorougly practical in their tendency to allow much demand for such fragile and transitory work as the cooks can put upon their cold dishes. A resort hotel in the United States may go through a season's business, entertain ten thousand guests, and pay *a chef* the highest salary, and yet never require a single ornamental dish beyond a turkey in jelly to be sliced before served, or some other such simple dish. Still, as

"BEAUTY IS ITS OWN EXCUSE FOR BEING,"

we must pursue the ornamental branch as a labor of love, because we take pleasure in showing such work, as the cooks of the largest cities yearly make displays of pieces that cost them nights and days of patient toil, simply keeping up the fashions of other times for their own pride and gratification. Numbers of the British aristocracy patronize and encourage the ornamental work that perpetuates old customs, such as boar's head banquets, and the Englishman who eats five meals a day will have the buffet or sideboard, where the early lunch or late cold supper is displayed, decorated in his *chef's* best style, if he can afford it, for there it does not interfere with the newer floral fashions which rule the dinner table. At some American hotels, where a specialty is made of serving banquets to order, this ornamental work frequently comes in place, and on many occasions, such as holidays and anniversaries, the cook can bring in his little surprises for the benefit of his own reputation, if for nothing else.

It was not

THE LONDON EXHIBITION

alone that gave seeming indicatons of a change to a revival of ornamental pieces, for its precursor, a similar exhibition at Berlin a year or two previous, which has already been alluded to in this book (No. 692) where the Emperor and Empress gave their personal attention to the encouragement of such work had the appearance of originating the movement of which the London exhibition with its imposing plan and extensive advertising was a continuation.

The after report shows it to have been principally an advertising exposition of materials and appliances, and in spite of the best endeavors of its promoters, the cooking department attracted less attention than the sideshows and the music. There were about 300 exhibitors, however, and several gold medals and purses were contested for in various departments, that of artistic cookery being the most interesting.

In accordance with the European proprieties, the London exhibition started under the patronage of a dozen titled personages and a jury besides of twenty-six ladies and gentlemen in the artistic cookery department. The motive power of the whole affair seems to have been furnished by three or four firms extensively engaged in the catering and restaurant business, with a hard working honorary secretary who managed all the details, and for whom at last a purse was made up by subscription of the exhibitors in recognition of his untiring exertions. One of these catering firms contracted to furnish meals as follows:

Hot and cold lunches at 50 cents per head.

Dinners a la carte from 60 cents upwards.

The club dinner at 85 cents.

The table d'hôte dinner at $1.25.

The dinner a la carte is the restaurant style where every dish in the bill of fare has the price attached, and a person can order according to what he wishes to spend.

The club dinner is in courses, the person takes all that is offered, in good form but without much choice and pays a fixed price for the repast.

The table d'hote is the hotel plan; the person chooses from the bill of fare whatever he pleases and as much as he pleases, and pays a fixed price for the repast, be it little or much. We give these particulars to show the ideas of the London caterers, of the worth of the different meals.

On certain stated dates they announced they would serve:

The Indian dinner at $1.25 per head.

The American dinner at $1.75.

The old English dinner at 1.50.

Dinner a la Francaise at $1.50.

The Indian dinner was intended to give prominence to East Indian products and dishes of curries, pillaus, kabobs, rice, chutneys and teas, a feature that was instigated by a firm engaged in the East India trade.

The old English dinners we have no particulars about, but doubtless it included roast beef and plum pudding, whatever the side effects may have been, and the French dinner as surely included *bards* and *braizes*, *sautes* and *ragouts*, as well as *sorbets* and *sucres*.

It was certainly atr ibute to the excellence of American fare that the price of the

AMERICAN DINNER

was placed the highest in the list; the plan probably contemplated oysters, turkey, terrapin and canvas back, with hominy or corn, and a pumpkin pie not very far off, and it is to be hoped the caterers were well aware that ice cream, the pure article frozen, is regular American diet. We eat it three times a day and once at night after the theatre.

There was a vast variety in kinds of goods exhibited, ranging from water filters and ranges, electric lighting for dining-rooms, and refrigerators and silver plating to the flexible glass neckties and

FLEXIBLE GLASS WEDDING CAKE

decorations, and from steam machinery for making bread and cake, to "Mrs. Butcher, vegetable flower cutter," who announced: "Flowers carved by hand from carrots and turnips. The process demonstrated." This must have been a very useful old lady to have around at such a time, and her art has some relation to the wax flower work to be mentioned further on. Another oddity among the entries is "Maids of Honour, a peculiar kind of Cheese-Cakes which have been sold at the original shop, Hill street, Richmond, for nearly two centuries." (See No. 505.)

There were

PRIZES OFFERED

for small dishes of sweets, best four by one person, and best two prizes for cold entrees in sets, or for groups of savories and sweets, all by the same maker; prizes for folding napkins and for the best set table, and prizes by the gas stove makers for best things baked in their contrivances; and at certain times there were lectures on cookery which we are led to infer from the reports proved less attractive than the various side-shows which had been admitted to the building.

The two or three days devoted to the

ARTISTIC COOKERY CONTEST

proved the most interesting and drew together the *chefs* and caterers from vorious parts of "the kingdom." Some of the prizes were:

For two grosse pieces, fish, meat, fowl or game, a gold medal and $30; second prize, silver medal.

Four dishes, cold entrees, prizes the same.

Six dishes of meat, poultry, etc., larded and trussed, etc., ready for cooking. Prize, silver medal and $10.

Trophy of birds, animals, fish, flowers, fruit, cascades, temples, or landscapes, any size suitable for buffet. Prize, silver medal and $10.

Four ornamental blocks for sweets or savories made of either of the following: Saindoux, stearine, salt, wood, raised paste, rice, or bread. Prize, bronze medal and $5.

A decorated Christmas cake. Prize, bronze medal.

Twelve varieties of rolls and bread. Prize, silver medal.

Cheap soup for the poor with recipe for making and the cost.

There were about 180 entries in the cookery lists.

The principal pieces entered were:

A cygnet (young swan) in galantine on wax stand.

Boar's head on wax stand.

Peacock a la royale.

Round of beef a l'Ecossaise.

Dinde (turkey) a l'Imperatrice.

Galantine de faisan (**pheasant.**)

Boar's head.

Dish of game.

Tete de sanglier de la Foret noir, sur socle (Boar's head from Black Forest, on stand.)

Capon and tongue, en bellevue.

Poularde a la "Army and Navy" (hotel) on mutton fat stand (a bastion.)

Hure de sanglier (wild boar's head) a la St. Hubert, on mutton fat stand (a fig tree.)

In the section of "trophies" of birds, animals, etc., the pieces entered were castles, temples, windmills and the like made of sugar or gum paste, one temple being made of wood covered with icing, and one consisted of objects representing scenes from operas, in sugar work. There were also entries of—

Two decorated salt blocks, suitable for galantines, tongues, etc.

Two decorated salt blocks, suitable for boar's head, raised pies, hams, etc.

Four carved salt blocks.

Four ornamental blocks of wood, salt and wax.

These selections from a lengthy catalogue will give an idea what the display was made of. The exhibitors were the *chefs* in the employ of certain lords and ladies in most cases, and of the leading restaurants and London hotels. These were the plans before the opening. They were carried out with only partial success. The after report says the exhibitors succeeded in getting a good advertisement of their wares if they did not find many purchasers; and the artistic cookery competition brought together a few good pieces and a great many indifferent and bad ones. This is not to be wondered at. As is the case with the exhibits made at the

COOK'S ANNUAL BANQUETS

in this country the ornamental work is done under great difficulties, usually in the nights after the day's work has been performed, and the cooks are almost all out of practice. If they had the same tasks to perform weekly or monthly they would learn by experience and improve on their former efforts, but if only once a year and they try a new thing each time it is impossible for their works to be strictly works of art or even commonly admirable. Still there are some champions in this line and for their best efforts a

CHAMPION PRIZE

was offered in addition to the other prizes, not to be restricted to any one department, but to be awarded for the best piece in the whole exhibition. It was won by a hotel confectioner for a trophy in sugar work; this *chef d'œuvre* consisted of a double vase of flowers moulded in sugar and colored to imitate the natural tints.

This award gave dissatisfaction to one person at least, this was an exhibitor, a champion, too, in his line, *chef* to a lord, author af a book on confectionery, and who had some admirable pieces on exhibition and he has since challenged the champion prize winner—the hotel man—to another contest for $50 a side. The dissatisfied man is a Frenchman and requires a jury composed of three or four English cooks and as many French to decide upon the result.

Amongst the regrets expressed that this exhibition had not proven richer in fine works of culinary art, it is mentioned that the French cooks in London had made a display of their own some months previous and shown much superior work. As some of the exhibitors have furnished descriptions of their dishes for publication, it is possible to give a very fair idea of what "very best" work consists.

TIMBALES OF TRUFFLES A LA ROTHSCHILD.

By M. Alfred Suzanne, of London.

Choose some large fresh truffles, all of one size and as round as possible. Having thorougly cleansed them by brushing the mould off in water, set them to boil slowly for half an hour in a champagne "mirepoix." When cold, drain the truffles, saving the liquor in which they have been boiled, and with a round cutter scoop out all the inside of the truffles. Next, make a "salpicon" compound of chicken, mushrooms, tongue and truffles; these ingredients must be stamped out with a round cutter, the third of an inch in diameter, and amalgamated together with some Allemande sauce. When ready to serve, warm up the truffles in some of the "mirepoix," the remainder of which is reduced with some Espagnole sauce to pour round the entree. Fill up the truffles with the hot salpicon, and serve.

The season of the London Exhibition was the season also of

THE TRUFFLE HARVEST

in Italy and France. Some exceedingly fine truffles were shown, some, it is stated weighed 1½ pounds each. When absolutely fresh, as these were, the truffle is a thing to raise enthusiasm in the mind both of the gourmand and his cook; it has a rich, nutty flavor that is peculiarly its own and a pefume as pervading as that of a bunch of ripe bananas. It is a tuber that grows spontaneously, just below the surface of the ground; some are nearly white all through but the best are jet black. One recommendation of the truffle in the eyes of the wealthy is its dearness, which keeps it above the reach of "common people." A dish of large truffles prepared as directed in the recipe for a fasionable dinner party fifteen or twenty might perhaps cost fifty dollars. The canned and bottled truffles ranging from the size of a gooseberry up, and which cost about a dollar an ounce, do serve a purpose in furnishing a name for a dish, but their intrinsic value is nothing at all; they are not even the ghost of the real, fresh article.

NECTARINE DE FOIE GRAS A LA MOLESWORTH.

By M. Alphonse Landry, of London.

A cylindrical mould resting on a layer of pounded rough ice is to be lined with a bright aspic jelly, the sides being decorated with cut truffles. Line the mould a second time with white sauce chaudfroid. When set, fill the mould lightly with foie gras mixed with truffles, both cut into small dice. To set the whole, fill up the mould with a good brown sauce chaudfroid, and finish with essence of truffles and aspic jelly of a good consistency. Let the mould remain in the ice until wanted, when dip it into hot water and turn out the contents on a dish. Fill the centre with truffles, and put croutons of aspic jelly round the base.

Foie-gras is liver-fat or fat liver; the French language generally puts the cart before the horse that way; but it specially means the livers of fat geese that come principally from Strasbourg where a great business is made of fattening geese for the sake of the livers.

Pate-de-foie-gras means two things, it is either paste of fat liver, with truffles in it, such as comes in jars from Strasbourg, or pie of fat livers—according to the accent on the word *pate*. The pie or pate made of a crust baked in a raised mould is oftenest lined inside with a coating of paste of *foie gras* and then filled with raw *foies gras* and seasonings covered and baked; to be eaten cold. M. Landry's dish above discribed is of cooked *foies gras* and truffles in jelly, in a border mould, and is a cold ornamental dish.   See No. 860 of this book.

ORNAMENTAL SALT BLOCKS OR STANDS.

A cook having either of the foregoing named dishes in preparation and having to serve them entire at a dinner party will naturally look around for some means to elevate it into a conspicuosness corresponding to the *recherche* character of the composition and brings in little bits of scenery in the way of perhaps a castle carved in salt, with all sorts of ornamental details below while the top with its towers and battlements is so shaped that it holds the dish of timbales, already built up on a double crouton of bread fried brown, or other foundation; or some slender design of figures holding up a stand on which the ornamented "nectarine" is suitably displayed, bordered and brought in contrast of colors.

For salt blocks are carved in selected blocks of rock salt, which is semi-transparent and has a reddish color, and in the finest table salt caked together to the compactness and almost the hardness of stone.   A "trophy of fillets of soles" might find a handsome resting place on top of a rock of rock salt carved into

A SEA CAVERN

below; set upon glass with boats and other accessories of a cavern scene carved out of the pure white fine salt for contrast.

And when any cook or set of cooks have spent more time and pains on the ornamental stands than the edible dishes have cost them, it is but natural for them to carefully mention the stand or *socle* in every catalogue, and name their piece a bastion of truffles, or a "nectarine de foies gras *sur socle.*"   A man does not want people to fail to notice the stand or *socle* that he has been working on of nights for two weeks before, merely because they are eager to sample the contents of the upper story.

Fig. 1.

Dominicaines de Volaille.

By Mr. C. J. Corblet, of London.

Take a dozen tongue-shaped moulds as sold at the principal London coppersmith's. Butter them, line them with thin slices of raw filleted chicken flattened out, and then fill them up with a galantine farce by means of a forcing-bag.

The farce is made as follows: Take the remains of the flesh of the four chickens which have already yielded the fillets for lining the moulds. Put the chicken meat through the sausage machine, with twelve ounces of white of veal, and as much larding bacon; season with salt and spices; and pass through a sieve. Five large raw truffles and five ounces of tongue (red) cut in large short strips are to be mixed in. When the moulds are filled with this mixture, place them in a sauté pan, and put them in a mild oven for half an hour. When cooked, turn them out on a napkin and let them get cold, trimming all the same shape. Sauce them over with a white suprême chaudfroid sauce, with the exception of the thick end, which is to be sauced with a brown chaudfroid sauce. Now cut up in cocks'-comb shape two dozen pieces of very red tongue, and dip them in some aspic jelly half set. Dish the dominicaines up against a wooden stand covered over with mutton fat, spreading the fat with aspic jelly, so that the edible shall not come in contact with the fat. Alternate each dominicaine with one of the pieces of tongue, filling the space between the upper cup and the dominicaines with the cocks'-combs passed in aspic jelly. The upper cup should be filled up with a Russian salad, and at the foot of the stand on either side must be placed four artichoke bottoms filled up with a vegetable salad mixed with mayonnaise and decorated with aspic jelly.

A chaudfroid sauce is one that will set like jelly when cold.

The woodcut representation above gives an idea of the appearance of an ornamental piece—a cold entree that was awarded the prize of a gold medal at the French cooks' own exhibition in London. It is but justice to all concerned to say that these pictures are far less handsome than the reality. It is a piece that illustrates completely the explanations of the methods followed which are found in the salads and cold dishes addition to the *American Pastry Cook*, No. 802j. It was an original design, but employed:

1st. The wooden stand.

2nd. The wax flower and leaf ornaments.

3rd. The figures of swans made of mutton fat by casting in metal moulds.

There are shops in London where a great variety of moulds are kept for such purposes, usually they are of pewter and consist of two parts hinged together. Some are swans, some battle horses, some dragons, mermaids, deer, lions, dolphins, in short anything that would be suitable to place where the swans appear in the cut above can be bought or hired. The process is but to fill them with the whitest fat that can be obtained, in a melted state, open the moulds and take the figures out when cold.

Another sort of mould is also mentioned in the recipe; tongue-shaped moulds, and some London manufacturers advertise that they make any sort of mould to suit new designs and new fashions as they are required.

Another requirement is the wooden stand. The picture shows a wooden stand of two stories, like two cake stands set one upon another, except that these are two bowls or cups instead of flat stands. The whole of the stand is covered with mutton fat so that the wood is not perceivable but it looks like a stand of wax. The edible part is built up in the larger bowl and ornamented also with edibles. It was a symmetrical object and glistening with colored jellies and meats, and colored salads above the waxen wreath that borders the large bowl might well claim attention and admiration.

A few cooks will carry a small assortment of moulds along with them when they travel and if they remain for years in the same city may acquire a large collection; this is not the rule, however, and when a party is to be provided for on short notice the cook must either pick up some such ornamental objects as plaster images or toy birds and animals and make his own moulds in plaster of paris, or else make designs that do not require moulded figures, as can well be done according to the following showing.

The following is the outline of a piece that was put up with a large pattern of ornamentation, suitable for the purpose of these instructions. It is a wooden stand in the first place covered first with a smooth coating of stearine, then bordered and decorated with wax flowers and leaves. On top of the stand is a large platter containing a decorated galantine of turkey.

To obtain the wooden stands apply to a cabinet maker, and have them made of a size to hold the dishes you intend to use. There should be a rim of wooden hooping around the edge both to hold the dish and to give room for the ornaments. These stands will very likely cost about one dollar each. They may be of different sizes, the stems measuring from six to twelve inches in height.

Fig. 2.

Galantine de Dinde sur Socle.

(Boned Turkey in Jelly on Wax Stand, Magnolia Pattern).

By Jessup Whitehead.

Served at a terrapin supper given by Mrs. Robt. J. Lowry (Miss Markham), at Atlanta, Ga.

To cover the stand, melt either some white wax, or parrafine, or stearine, or mutton tallow, or a mixture of wax and tallow. White wax can be and is used in that way and is cleanly, but it is expensive and hard to make a smooth surface with, on account of the high degree of heat required to keep it in a melted state. Mutton fat mixed with wax is a good material, but better still is the same stearine that candles are made of; it does not grease the fingers and has no smell. Wax costs from fifty cents to a dollar a pound while candles can be bougt at eight pounds for a dollar. Melt in a tin pan and pour it over the stand with a spoon. When the wood is everywhere covered hold the stand in front of a fire, turning it about while the surplus fat drips off and leaves a smooth, even surface; then, when the stand has become cold and white take a hot knife and smooth off the edges and ridges that remain.

Fig. 3.

Tree Designs for Game Pieces.

But if the design is to be a tree select a natural bough from a tree or bush, something that branches handsomely like a deer's horns with room in the forks to place a piece of wood as large as a plate or dish. Set the butt of it in a wooden bottom like that shown for the other kind of stand and fasten the upper shelf in the forks where the boar's head is to be, then proceed to coat over the entire stand and branches with stearine as in the other case. Coral branches and sea-weed designs can be prepared in a similar manner. When the stand is thus far prepared proceed to cover it with wax leaves, fruit, berries, flowers or any ornamental shapes that may suit the subject; the tree stand may be decorated with leaves and fruit on every twig.

Wax Leaves and Flowers.

The best material for flowers and leaves is white wax although stearine answers very well for some of the less delicate forms. They are made by carving a flower on a carrot or turnip or potato, dipping it into melted wax and taking off the thin covering of wax that the vegetable shape has taken up. Wax impressions are thinner and finer than stearine, and wax can be pulled gently off of intricate shapes where any other material would break to pieces. Vegetables make the best shapes because wax will not adhere too tightly and they must be kept wet.

Supposing Mrs. Butcher, mentioned in the catalogue as having special skill in such work to have carved a white turnip into the form of a rose and the end of a carrot into the shape and markings of a rose leaf, the next step would be to throw them into a pan of water and then melt some white wax in a tin cup. Take up the turnip rose, dip the face of it in the wax, then immediately in the cold water again and a thin pearly waxen rose can be pulled off the vegetable; dip the leaf-shaped carrot the same way and you have a waxen leaf. The wax must not be very hot. When it is cool enough to be on the point of setting, the leaves and flowers can be made with the greatest rapidity, sometimes dropping from the shape of themselves.

By the same method fan-leaves, palms, bells, grape bunches, cups, thimbles, stars, faces, animals' heads, spear heads, cornices and mouldings can be made in great variety within certain restrictions which will soon be discovered upon trial, such as the impracticability of making a round ball-shaped flower, unless in two halves.

It is best for a beginner to make a large number of very small flowers and leaves at first instead of large and heavy ones, the light ones being easy to fasten in place and less liable to fall off or be broken through projecting too far from the stand.

To Decorate the Stands.

The flowers and leaves are fastened in place by melting a little stearine upon them, hold a rose to its place with the fingers of one hand while the other applies the point of a hot knife to the place of contact. They may also be dipped in melted stearine and pressed in place while it sets. Heavy ornaments require tape stems to be attached to support them on the edge of the stand.

It is scarcely possible to improve upon the appearance of a well exe-cuted wax stand in pure pearly white, yet colored wax can be used and colored flowers made by the same methods. The material of which the colored candles on Christmas trees are made is suitable for the purpose. Wax stands with colored ornaments are suitable for comic designs like pigs in dress coats, and similar notions.

Galantines and Aspics.

Directions for preparing and or-namenting galantines and *apics de foies-gras* have been given at Nos. 853, 860, and 943, and methods of ornamenting with colored jellies at No. 692 and succeeding numbers. Very particular directions for larger operations can also be found in the cold dishes department in the *American Pastry Cook*. The ordinary galantine moulds are tin pans made oval instead of round and of sizes that run about one inch difference in diameter. But any other shape can be used as well if it only corresponds with the stand. A very fine supper with decorated dishes has been set where nothing but the common round glass cake stands were available; but a number of them were covered with melted wax and then smothered in wax flowers till they had not the slightest semblance of a glass cake stand, and they required meat dishes and raised pies to be of round shape to match.

Bread Blocks and Crous-tades.

In order to elevate a galantine into sufficient prominence above the ornaments a bread "block" may be employed or cake of cooked rice, according to the subject. Cut the bread to fit the dish, fry it in a kettle of oil or lard to a handsome light brown color. When cold dip it several times in bright jelly keeping it in ice between each dipping till a good coat of jelly remains upon it, place it in the dish and turn the de-corated galantine out of its mould on top of it.

A very handsome dish or *terrine* of pâte-de-foie-gras can be made in

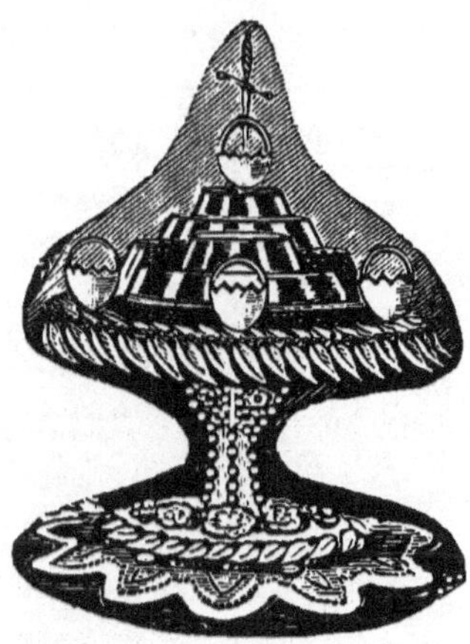

this way. **Prepare** a decorated stand with wax leaves and flowers. Cut three or four blocks of bread of different sizes to make a pyramid and fry them to a nice deep yellow color and place them in their dish. Have some bright aspic jelly ready and chop it quite fine. Take a pan of liver paste (No. 860 will do for the purpose) and cut out pieces with spoons made hot in boiling water. The spoon will shape the liver paste like the half of an egg cut lengthwise. As fast as cut out dredge them with the minced jelly, then place them around on the steps of the fried bread pyramid, covering it very nearly, and between the points insert triangular blocks of colored jelly and decorate with lemon baskets garnished with sprigs of parsley.

Make Allowance for Heat.

Much vexation and trouble overtakes every inexperienced hand who makes no allowance for the effects of a heated supper room upon the jellies which his refrigerator has kept in such a pleasant state of solidity, but after one or two catastrophes caused by the build-up dishes melting down like snow in the sun the workman learns to make his goods doubly firm with plenty of gelatine to withstand the ordeal of a gas-lit and crowded hall.

The Boar's Head.

In the United States we have little or nothing to do with the perpetuation of ancient customs and have little sympathy of sentiment with them that have. We are too ready to throw a wet blanket on every exhibition of the ancient fires by asking and continually asking: "What is the use of it?"

We are so accustomed to looking forward, to "the millions yet to be," to the new, to the cities which are springing up without permission from anybody, that we have forgotten about such things as the ancient granting of city charters by kings and barons with tributary conditions imposed, such as the presenting of a peacock, or a huge blackbird pie, or a boar's head to the suzeraine on a certain day each year; and find it hard to enter into the solemn sort of fun which the very respectable and reverend seat of English learning, Oxford College, enjoys as an annual custom. A little better understanding of the symbolism of some of the designs would make even the exhibition of artistic cookery at the cook's annual banquets far more interesting than they are.

THE OXFORD BOAR'S HEAD DINNER.

The boar's head dinner at Queen's College, Oxford, on Christmas Day is a survival of a custom once prevalent in all England. In 1678, Aubrey wrote: "In gentlemen's houses at Christmas, the first dish that was brougbt to table was a boar's head, with a lemon in his mouth." There is an account of an Essex parish, called Hornchurch, in which the inhabitants paid the great tithes on Christmas Day, and were treated with a bull and a brawn. The boar's head was wrestled for by the peasants on that occasion, and then feasted upon. It would be easy to multiply instances.

At half-past six o'clock in the afternoon of Christmas Day, the Hall of Queens College was filled by persons anxious to witness the time-honoured ceremony of the Boar's Head procession. The hall was liberally adorned with greenery, and a monstrous fire created a welcome temperature. Although the weather was damp and foggy, by six o'clock the picturesque old hall presented an animated appearance, filled nearly to overflowing with a crowd of merry faces; the dark tone of the gentlemen's clothing and the bright bits of colour of the ladies' showed up very effectually against the old oaken wainscoating. The boar's head, which was provided and dished up by Mr. Wm. H. Horn, the College manciple, was a splendid specimen, weighing seventy pounds, and was decorated with the proverbial "bays and rosemary," and surmounted with a crown and flags bearing the College arms. Upon the sound of the trumpet, at the head of the procession of singing men and choristers, marched the Rev. Robt. Powley, M. A., Curate of Cowley, who took the solo part in the "Boar's Head Carol:"

The Boar's head in hand bear I,
Bedecked with bays and rosemary,
And I pray you, masters, merry be,
Quotquot estis in convivio.
CHORUS.
Caput Apri defero,
Redden laudes Domino.

The Boar's head, as I understand,
Is the bravest dish in the land;
Being thus decket with gay garland,
Let us servire cantico.
CHORUS.
Our Steward has provided this
In honour of the King of Bliss,
Which on this day to be served is
In Reginensi Atro.
CHORUS.

Wynkin de Worde's carol (printed in 1521) was, of course, much quainter, especially verse three:

Be gladde, lordes, both more and lesse,
For this hath ordeyned our stewarde
To chere you all this Christmasse,
The Boar's heed with mustarde.

A distribution of leaves which garnished the dish was then made by the Provost (Dr. Magrath). The custom of serving up the boar's head at Queen's College has been observed for about 500 years, one authority quoting 1350 as being the probable year of the first festival.—*London Caterer.*

The man whose office requires him to provide a boar's head in the orthodox fashion for such an occasion as that described, be he "manciple" steward or cook, must feel a greater importance attaching to the task than if it were the most elaborate of transient party dinners. A dozen or more of boar's heads were shown at the London Exhibition. They are equally prominent in continental displays. The narratives of continental history as well as fiction abound in recitals of wild boar hunts, in the Forest of Ardennes, in France, the Black Forest, in Germany. A boar's head a la St. Hubert is among the highest achievements a chef in ornamental work can set himself to accomplish. St. Hubert is the patron saint of hunters. The piece is a boar's head, the bones taken out, stuffed, cooked, set up in the likeness of life, glazed, ornamented, placed upon a stand, set amongst waxen or silver-plated branches of a tree, decorated with bays and hunting horns and spears and heads of hounds. The carcass of a real wild boar from the Black Forest was displayed at the Exhibition, much as a grizzly bear from the Rocky Mountains might be displayed in this country. It was an object of curiosity and interest and was immediately purchased by the steward of a large establishment.

BOAR'S HEAD GALANTINES.

For practice in putting up a boar's head the beginner should bone and cook pigs' heads to serve cold, until he has become familiar with the methods of making them good and of putting them in shape. One or two heads a week would be esteemed a luxury in any hotel among the regular cold dishes. For there was no foolishness about the ancient liking for a hogs head and it is considered as good eating to-day as it ever was, but requires a good deal of the cook. It must be partly salted, it must have the superabundant fat cut out and lean and brawn supplied instead; it must be carefully seasoned and cooked until perfectly tender and the liquor it is boiled in is jelly. Choose a large head for the purpose and a small one to stuff it with. Cut it as far back as the shoulder bones of the hog to get as much of the neck as possible. Begin at the throat and cut the meat from the bone without cutting through the skin; take out the tongue, put them both into the corned beef brine (No. 650) to remain two or three days. Then take them out, wash and trim, and cut away all the fat of the jowls. Sew up the mouth and throat. Place the small head similarly boned and prepared inside the large one, fill in with tongues cut in strips and some well seasoned pork sausage meat,

cover in the neck with the rind of pickled pork, then sew the stuffed head in a cloth, boil it four or five hours, take it up and press it in a suitable mould and set it away to become cold. After that take off the cloth, remove the threads and slice the meat to serve.

TO MAKE AN ORNAMENTAL DISH.

It is not essential that a boar's head shall always be set up with ears erect and mouth open, it may be a smooth rounded dish of meat only having the general outline of the head shape, and to form it that way it is necessary to take the cooked head out of the cloth it was boiled in when it is nearly cold, then take a long muslin bandage and wrap around it, drawing tight in one place and slack in another to give the head the proper form, then set it in the refrigerator to become solid in that shape. Afterwards, take off the bandage, wipe off with a cloth dipped in hot water, then glaze the head by frequent basting with jelly in a cold place until it is covered, or, glazed with meat essence, and ornament with cubes and patterns in aspic.

AS NATURAL AS LIFE.

"Rosemary and bays" always mentioned in connection with the boar's head, belong to that dish by association as holly belongs to Christmas. They are both used for seasoning as well as for green decorations. Rosemary is a herb that looks like pine leaves and has a flavor like a mixture of sage and spruce fir. Season the boar's head that is to be put up in shape with rosemary and bay leaves powdered, instead of the customary sage. To form the head as natural as life and even more ferocious looking it is best to employ a plaster mould which can be made shortly before it is to be used and will serve for many repetitions. It is to be observed that the wild boar carries a high and bristly forehead and the mould is to be managed so as to throw the top of the head into prominence instead of the fat jowls of common hogs. Choose a head of a large porker to make a cast from. It is not advisable to have the mould too large because the cooked head shrinks so much it is difficult to thoroughly fill a large mould. Having the raw head cut off with all the neck belonging, cut off the ears, place it snout downwards and resting on the bottom in a tin pail or five gallon tin lard can. Get half a bushel of plaster of paris, which costs about seventy-five cents at the cement stores, stir it up with water to a thin paste and pour it around the head in the pail. In half an hour the plaster sets and becomes solid, but leave it alone several hours, and then the head can be drawn out and you have a plaster mould of it. Perhaps the mould can be improved in shape by scraping down with a knife, and the bottom of the pail or can should be cut through that the snout of the cooked head may be drawn in.

Prepare a salted head with stuffing as before directed, leave the ears on and lay them flat on the top of the head. Sew up the head in muslin closely wrapped and without any thick folds or knots. Boil four hours, take up and let drain and partly cool off, then place it still in the cloth in the mould, taking care that the ears are in the right place and the snout goes well to the bottom. In that position with the neck above the top of the mould, place weight upon it and leave it in press in a cold place for twelve hours. It can be withdrawn from the mould easily by means of the cloth, which is then to be taken off, the head wiped off with a cloth in warm water, the ears raised up, softened with a hot cloth, shaped as wanted and upheld by a small silver skewer in each; the mouth opened and tusks inserted; bead eyes put in and the head glazed and ornamented.

The tusks finely curved may be obtained from almost any hog's head. Find one with small tusks projecting, boil the jaw bones, then break the bones with a hammer about the roots and the tusks will be found three or four inches long.

Decorated Cakes.

There is evidently a laborious effort to discover something marvelous to put upon a cake when a resort is had to flexible glass, satin sashes, panel paintings and various sorts of millinery in addition to the plaster of paris and gum paste figures and structures which are perennial as cake ornaments. These things come high but they must have them at the London Exhibitions and they do not interest pastry cooks and bakers much because all such methods are outside of their trade. When a cake has to be carried to the glass-blower's, the landscape gardener's, the upholsterer's, the milliner's, the image maker's, and the painter's places, the baker may throw his slipper after it for luck but he need not go with it. It is none of his work to do.

There were prize medals offered for the best decorated Christmas cake and best wedding cake, and Messrs. Newton & Eskell, proprietors of the *Caterer* offered a special prize in that department. This was

awarded to a firm of "country caterers," from Leamington, who came
to the great city and took the premi-
um with a cake that was remarkable
for its elaborate piping in sugar
icing, which is true pastry cook's and
confectioner's work; and the gem of
the exhibition in bride cakes is said
beyond the sphere of the workman
who makes the cake to carry it to
such a completion. It is a trade to
itself to make the gum paste structures with altars and leaves and
flowers which we see exhibited for
sale under glass cases at the confectioners in every large city. Pastry

Cake Decoration in White Icing.

BY JESSUP WHITEHEAD.

(From a Photograph.)

to have been one decorated with
real hot-house flowers relieved by
delicate green ferns, and if the cake
itself was already ornamented in
icing it must have been a beautiful
object and not too far removed from
common ideas of edibility, and not
cooks can make a few flowers on the
spur of necessity. but very few can
make them as perfectly as those do
who never do any other work but
make flowers.

The instructions here to be given
are for designs in pure sugar icing,

practice in which will lead the learner on to a trial of all the additional branches.

The engraving on the preceding page shows the design of cake decorated in the Grecian style that once came under the powerful protection of no less a person than General Grant, whose interference prolonged its existence at least two days. The hand that was extended to make a breach in the upper works was Mrs. Grant's. That serene lady would have broken off one of the white birds which were hovering in the act of sipping the crimson jelly in the glasses. The general put his hand on hers and pushed it aside saying: "Don't break that." "I want to try the confectionery," said the lady.

"There is plenty without—don't break it—," said he again; and it was saved to appear again next day *with sections cut out of both the lower cake and the upper one* on two sides, the cake sliced and part of the slices replaced, and all was done *without breaking the ornamentation,* which

requires but a small foundation to stand upon. The lower cake was made by the recipe No. 836, the upper was a white citron cake.

Over the top of the pyramid, which was all pure white and lace-like, was thrown a long and slender vine of Virginia creeper, much handsomer than smilax because of the finely tapering gradations of the leaf sizes, and these were just turned to vivid colors by the touch of the first October frost.*)

This is a picture of the cake that was made and ornamented in haste and under difficulties for the wedding of the banker's daughter, as hurriedly sketched at No. 941. It took about four hours of a summer night to put up those ornaments in sugar icing. There were, of course, more people concerned in that wedding than it was business of mine to mention at such a hard-working time, and among them was the young lady's father, the banker himself; and when the table was set and the time was right to bring along the wedding presents he walked up and

---

* [That was perhaps the happiest period of General Grant's life. He was spending a week with his family and officers of his staff and their wives at the Manitou House, Manitou Springs, Colorado. He loved that locality, this was his third visit to it; it was in the third year of his first term as President, an office of which he was weary and he delighted the people of Manitou village by declaring his intention of returning and making his home there when his term was ended. He went around the world after that and after all he visited Manitou once more, though only for a day, when on his way to Leadville, where he had thought of investing in the mines.]

Decorated Cake Center-Piece on a Silver Dish.
Height about 3½ ft.

Served at a private supper tendered to General U. S. Grant by Governor Tabor at Leadville, Colo. The baskets and spaces filled up with a various assortment of the lightest Italian cakes, macaroons, meringues, and bon-bons and the whole festooned with smilax.

took out of his breast pocket the title deed to a forty-thousand-dollar house and lot in Lakeport, made out in his daughter's name; he rolled up the document and placed it under the lid of the basket and left it there. The hostess put into the basket on top a silver thimble and the host put in a gold pencil case, then the children climbed on chairs and filled the basket and all the spaces with white flowers which they had been out at sunrise to all the neighbours' gardens to gather. When the bride came to cut the cake she shed tears on the flowers, hung the pencil case on her watch-chain, put the thimble on her finger and tucked the title deed down in the bosom of her dress. And the children ate both the basket and the pedestal because it was all sugar and flavored with lemon.

Cake Decoration in White Icing.

BY JESSUP WHITEHEAD.

From a Photograph.

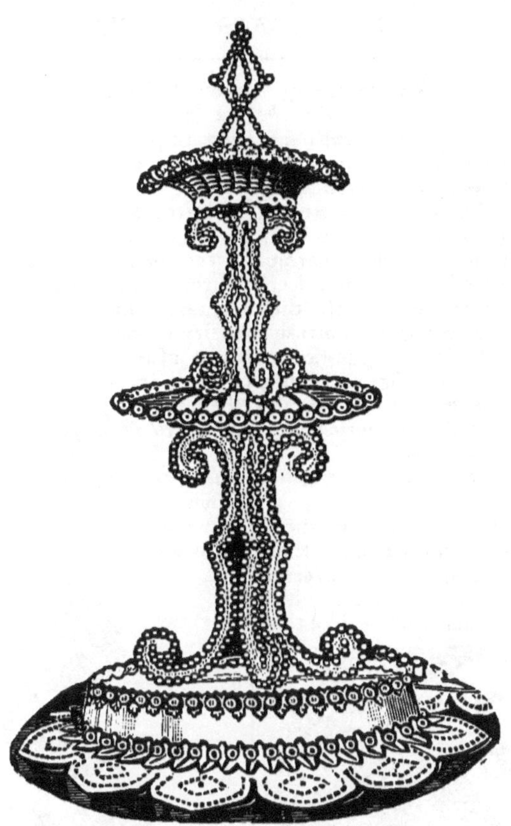

Cake Decoration in White Icing.

BY JESSUP WHITEHEAD.

Cake Center Piece, Stand for Small Sweets, to go with Floral Decorations.   Served at a terrapin supper given by Mrs. R. J. Lowry, Atlanta, Georgia.

This pattern has been redrawn large and distinct to show the details plainly for the purpose of this article. The photographer remarked that "it was a daisy," and he squared himself three or four different ways to get the best expression of it. The pure white and fragile structure was ornamented with bright colored sugar flowers set upon it and around the edges and in the spaces. It was an ornamented cake made to serve as a center piece among some elaborate floral decorations at a party supper given by a lady of Atlanta, Georgia. The design was *finished for the purpose by having the stands and baskets filled up with bonbons, macaroons, kisses, and the lightest kinds of fancy small cakes*, and was hung with trailing sprays of smilax. In such positions these tall pieces harmonize most perfectly with floral decorations, the effect of which they heighten without being too obtrusive and without the least suggestion of children's play-house figures such as attaches to the gum paste temples and pavilions of the ordinary style.

HOW THEY ARE MADE.

For a single stand take two sheets of note paper and keeping them doubled as they are, cut out a scroll pattern with a pair of scissors, which when opened out will be like this:

Fig. 5.

Cut them apart down the back and you have four paper patterns like that on the left side of the cut. Take a tin plate and melt some white wax and mutton tallow in equal parts, dip the paper patterns in it and lay them each one on a separate piece of board or a shingle. Then mix up some stiff icing (directions at No. 464) and lay a piping border on the edge around the outline of the pattern; use a star piping tube and lay a wreath pattern on the waxed paper as shown at the right of the cut, observing that as the extremely light and graceful effect of these designs is largely due to the spaces left between the piping, the icing must not be run together nor placed too close. As fast as they are done place them to dry in some such place as inside an oven after the fire has gone out. When dry turn them over, warm them till the wax begins to melt and then *pull off the paper pattern.* Now *repeat the same pattern of icing on this side where the paper was* and when that is dry and hard on all four you have the four scrolls to set up as a support for the basket.

To fasten them together so that they will stand square and perpendicular it is necessary to procure a small goods box and break off one side with one end attached. Lay two of the pieces on the wood as at figure 5, but a quarter inch space between them, lay some icing on the edges, then place a third one on edge on top of them and all three touching the end piece of the board, which is upright and acts as a square, and set it in a warm place to dry again while you work on another part. When dry set it upright and place the fourth side in place; it will stand with no support but a touch of icing; and when again dry the stand thus far made can be set upon the cake.

To make baskets or brackets use shallow plates or jelly cake pans *waxed over* and cover them with piping, the more open and lace-like the better. Ornament the outer edges as cakes are piped, and when thoroughly dry warm the plate till the thin coating of wax that it was dipped in melts and the shape of icing can be lifted off and placed on its stand. The handle of the basket can be formed on a piece of tin bent to a bow shape. Make it in two pieces with broad foundations, set them up on the basket and fasten the middle with some icing and a rose and leaves.

To build such a design two or three stories high use a sheet of foolscap for the lower pattern and a sheet of note paper for the next, or, let each upper stand be one-third smaller than that below it.

The patterns can be varied and multiplied according to the ingenuity and patience of the operator. The pieces are fragile yet will bear a heavy weight of flowers, cakes and fruit carefully placed. It is said of these objects that they are fresh and new—the people have seen all sorts of ornamented cakes all over the country, but all more or less alike, but never saw any like these, and that is where the advantage is gained, as one can be made for every table in a dining room and each of a different form, without any very great expenditure of time, when we are in practice.

To make icing *tougher* and less liable to break *add gelatine* dissolved, or gum arabic, and for further instructions for such as have had no practice the *American Pastry Cook* should be consulted and directions compared before any work is undertaken that might lead to failure at a time when success should be assured.

PATTERNS ON TINFOIL.

Tinfoil paper such as tobacco and similar merchandise is wrapped in can be used instead of the waxed paper recommended in foregoing directions. Lay a covering of tinfoil on the outside of a bowl turned upside down, lay a piping pattern on it for a basket or other object; let it dry and turn right side up and after removing gently from the bowl the tinfoil can be carefully picked away as the icing does not adhere to it. The learner can practice both ways and decide for himself which he has most success with.

RAISED BORDER ORNAMENTS.

Palisade or garden fence patterns of icing to set around a cake can be made as directed for the bowed basket handles. Make a hoop of tin and wax it with mixed wax and mutton fat, set it on a board and make the pattern upon it in panels or pieces divided at convenient distances. When dry take off the pieces by warming the tin, and set the border around the edge of the cake. The tin hoop must of course be made to fit the cake.

Another way requiring more practice and a steady hand is to take a cake already iced over and quite dry, turn it upside down upon something like a gallon tomato can, then with your piping tube hang a loop or fringe border all round the edge. Dry that and then put on another row of loop border, and continue till you have four or five tiers. Let it get perfectly dry and then turn the cake right side up and if you have no accident you have a raised lace-work border around the cake which raises a wonder as to how it was done.

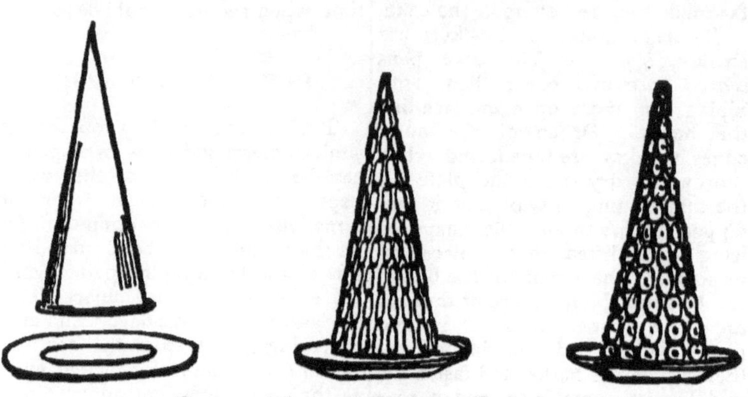

Pyramids of Small Cakes.
Height 20 to 24 inches.

Have a tin shape made like that on the left, with a wired rim on the bottom to keep it firm and several tin circles also rimmed to keep them from yielding and breaking the pyramid, and have them large enough to lift easily without binding on the shape. · Cover the tin circle on the edge with a lace cake paper and slip over the top. Grease the pyramid shape and then build up lady fingers, almond fingers, meringues, cocoanut caramels or anything of the sort by dipping the edges in melted clear candy, or in cake icing. When set lift the pyramid off the shape, still resting on the tin ring and place it on a cake stand. The most beautiful object of this sort is a pyramid of kiss meringues perfectly made, and covered with a veil of spun sugar.

Another Exhibition.

The London managers while yet sore over the unsatisfactory results of this one are asking each other if there shall be another and they are disposed to answer yes. However that may come out there will probably be such an exhibition opened in the United States and it will be successful for it will be arranged and carried out by hotel-keeping men for the furtherance of hotel-keeping interests.

There are two distinct classes of cooks and two different lines of cooking, they are the chefs who cook for my lord the Marquis of Carrabas and his noble compeers on the one side, and the chefs who manage large kitchens and numerous subordinates and who count the meals they send out by the thousands a day on the other, and the American Cookery Exhibition will regard the latter class and their work as the matter of greatest public interest and will stimulate them to seek methods of greater variety and perfection in serving the complete individual dinners of the modern hotel and restaurant system. There were ideas in the London exhibition which will perhaps have to be brought over to this side for development. There was the national dinner idea but too pinched and narrow; the prize table setting, but on a private house basis; the prize napkin-folding, but no waiter's drill nor prize waiter work; there were little dishes made by amateur cooks, but no contests of veterans of the *table d'hôte* system; there were two days of fitful interest over a display of ornamental pieces which resulted in dissatisfaction over the awards of prizes and while even this was being but poorly attended there were a thousand "temperance lunch houses," "coffee taverns," "oyster houses," "railway eating stations," "chop houses," restaurants and hotels of every description where the real cookery exhibitions were going on and in which the public were really interested which had no more part nor lot in the Aquarium exhibition than if it had been in some distant country. They are all interested in the art of cooking for large numbers but not in *pièces montées*. There was one good idea of a hotel cook who entered for exhibition three sauces, but little known; that idea will be amplified in the American exhibition into a show and sampling of all known sauces. There will be a display, for prizes, of the best ways the best cooks have invented of ornamenting the individual dishes of each separate hotel dinner; there will be prizes for the best ten ways of cooking certain specified articles of diet and the requirement of the proper name attached to every dish. There will be exhibitions of rapid waiter-work given at dinners served to members at nominal prices for this purpose, and the specially ornamental cooks who set out very grand banquet tables but never succeed in getting their patrons half waited upon, will have the opportunity to look on and learn how meals are served to hundreds or thousands at once.

THE END.

Suggestions for the Decoration of Small Dishes.

For Restaurant Orders and Course Dinners.

Cases (*caisses*) of various shapes can be made by a simple method similar to that of making a kind of crisp waffle. It is well enough to have the iron or copper shapes but they are not indispensable. Take common tin patty-pans, mix up a pancake batter or the same as used for pineapple fritters, that is rather thin; even flour batter-cake will do. Make some lard hot, dip the patty-pans in, then dip the outsides in the batter, drop into the lard and fry slowly. Soon the batter becomes dry and crisp like a shell. Pull it off, drain on paper, dip the patty-pans again until you have enough. Use these shells or cases instead of puff-paste patties to fill with stewed terrapin or scrambled brains, ragout of chicken liver, etc. Very small ones as thin as paper can be used to set around a dish, some filled with grated horseradish, others with *maitre d'hôtel* butter, with peas or asparagus points. Other shells or cases are made by shaping rice croquettes or potato croquettes in any desired form, egging and breading them either once or twice and frying as usual. When done of a handsome clear brown color cut out the top and remove the inside and fill up with minced chicken, minced kidneys, any curry mixture or ragout, giblets, sweetbreads or brains.

Another resource for small ornamental dishes is the carving of raw potatoes, sweet potatoes and turnips into shapes like cups or tumblers, fry them slowly in lard or oil enough to cover them till done, drain on paper, sprinkle with salt and use them in the ways above described.

Similar shapes may be cut out of bread and fried in the same way.

The common method of ornamenting a spoonful of meat and sauce in an individual dish with a heart-shaped or leaf-shaped *crouton* of fried bread is good with the exception of being too common. The common fault is to cut the shapes too large and out of bread sliced too thick. They should be dipped sometimes in bright sauce and parsley dust and be set up leaning against the meat as well as bordering the dish.

Similar thin pieces of fried bread may be set up on end around a dish, fastened by being dipped in egg and placed while the dish is hot; the meat is then to be dished in the middle. A very handsome border can be made of *duchesse* potato mixture or balls set around, carefully egged over and the top slightly baked by setting on the top shelf.

Another is made by making a firm puree by rubbing green peas through a sieve. Dip a teaspoon in hot butter and with it dip up small egg-shapes and place in order around the dish. Lemons to go with salmon steak or fried oysters may be cut in basket shapes with scolloped edges. Beets may be stamped out with fancy cutters. There should not be too much crowding. One of the most effective ornaments for a salad is a strip or two of blood beet in vinegar cut with a scollop potato knife, small, like a common lead pencil in size, but serrated, and laid on top of the salad.

A little ornamental effect can be given to all the ordinary individual dishes at dinner by placing the meats diagonally in the dish; the rice may be placed slanting across one side and end of a dish and the curry in the same lengthened form in the remaining space just as well as shapelessly bunched up at each end or mixed, and the green peas with a croquette may as well lie in two diagonal lines alongside of it as to be in a promiscous pile. Don't try too many experiments. One new wrinkle a week is enough. But remember that some big reputations and big salaries are made through the assiduous following up of all the advantages afforded by a cultivated taste for ornamentation rather than from any real difference in the cooking that is behind it all.

An Elaborate Dish.
(From the London *Caterer*.)

At the late Cookery Exhibition in Paris the highest award was obtained by M. Charles Poulain for his Bourriche de Gibier à l'Indienne (Basket of Game). We present an illustration, and append some brief descriptive notes of this highly artistic *pièce montée*.

edifice. The projecting flowers were likewise modelled in wax of various colors. The contents of the basket consisted of galantines of pheasants, and ballottines of partridges and quails. These were dished upright, and surmounted by the heads and feathers of the birds. A small silver skewer passing through each bird's head fixed it to the galantine. In

The stand was made of mutton fat, and covered with a mosaic-work composed of diamonds of truffles, tongue, and boiled white of egg. The basket, or *bourriche*, was made of wax, as were also the four modelled Indian figures supporting the the middle of the group rose a high wax vase containing a bouquet of vegetables cut in the shape of different flowers. The hollows between the galantines were filled with aspic jelly.

Trophy of Galantines of Partridges.

This was the work of a French *chef* in London of which the picture only and no particulars were given. borate raised foundation on which they stand, with the borders of aspic and truffles; the truffles, probably, in

Evidently the stand itself is of silver, one of those pieces of "massive family plate" so often mentioned in relation to old and titled families. The cook's work is the four boned partridges finely decorated, the elaborate the two raised baskets at the sides, the waxen bird and basket at top, the waxen figure of the cook himself and his benign angel at the bottom, very likely with a white vax floor and decorations to stand upon.

APPENDIX.

CAMOVITO'S DINNERS.

Because all large dinners in New York are given at Delmonico's, the Brunswick, the Fifth Avenue or the Hoffman House, it is an error to suppose that a really artistic table-spread is never produced outside of those establishments. Steward Camovito, of the Union League club, has arranged some dinners that have never been excelled in this town. The members of the club consider him a genius in his way. President Grant's dinner to Diaz, before referred to, was a case in point. Photographs of the big, round table made especially for the purpose, taken just before the guests set down, give but a faint idea of their magnificence. At the dinner Senator Evarts gave to the French naval visitors and the Bartholdi committee, not long ago, Camovito's model of the statue of Liberty was a triumph of the confectioner's skill. He surrounded Bedloe's Island with natural water clear as crystal, had the Isere and French war ships riding at anchor, and illuminated Liberty's torch with a little incandescent lamp that sparkled like a diamond in a lady's ring. At the Wiman dinner he bridged the Arthur Kill with a towering structure of gelatine and sugar with a train of Baltimore and Ohio cars crossing it, and he set afloat a ferry-boat of white sugar to carry the passengers that Mr. Wiman hopes to capture from the Pennsylvania road if his air castle don't break down. Camovito spends as much time and care over planning a big dinner as some architects do over designing a new house. He told me once that he often laid awake nights thinking over some litte surprise peculiarly applicable to the occasion of the dinner or the guest of the evening. To be sure he gets well paid for it, and he ought to. He is one of the dozen or more *chefs* in New York who can command as high a salary as a successful preacher.

THE tables were appropriately decorated when the Boston Commercial Club gave a dinner to some railroad men. The central piece represented a complete train, with engine and tender two feet high, made entirely of roses, pinks, violets, and other flowers. It extended nearly half across the President's table.

AT a private dinner recently on Brooklyn Heights, where many epicures reside and are not wanting in hospitality, the ice cream, served on a silver platter in front of the hostess, was in the form of a watermelon, and when cut, the deception was excellently preserved.

At a luncheon given by the Viscountess Combermere the table decorations consisted of a carpet of moss dotted with real primroses. In the centre rose a bank of moss, upon which was a gold *épergne* filled with oranges, relieved by little bunches of primroses. The edge of the table was trailed and framed with ivy.

For a ladies' lunch party in a fashionable New York hotel, a novel idea was introduced. Roses were frozen in a large cake of ice, which was placed on a mat of smilax. The effect was as if these were standing in water.

A tiny — very tiny — pig was served at a fashionable dinner, the other evening; and when he was placed on the table a howl went up from the assembled rank and fashion surrounding him. The little beast stood on his own hoofs in the midst of a bed of Marshal Neil roses; in his rosy snout was the customary lemon, and twisted in his small tail was a blue pond lily! How her *chef* accomplished this feat the hostess refused to divulge, and though pork is not usually admitted, in any form, into good society, Mr. Piggy—who was pronounced too sweet for anything—was duly cut up and tasted, and the health of the Chinese cook duly drank in champagne.

A COSTLY DINNER.

Count Horace de Viel - Castel, whose memoirs were recently published, was a decided gourmand. He made a bet once that he would eat a dinner, the cost of which would not be less than 500 fr. The menu, which he prepared for the occasion, was as follows:

Potage a l'essence de gibier.
Laitances de carpe au Xeres.
Cailles desossees en caisse.
Truite de lac de Geneve.
Faisan roti barde d'ortolans.
Pyramide de truffes entieres.
Compote de fruits et stilton.

VINS.

Tokay, johannisberg, glace, clos-vougeot 1819, chypre de la Commanderie.

He won the wager, going about a hundred francs above the stipulated price. He left not a remnant of any dish, nor a drop of wine, and, strange to say, was able to spend the rest of the evening with Earl Granville at the British Embassy.

WINE SERVICE.

The proper service of wines is a study of itself, but we may say generally that sherry should be poured with the soup, white wines with the fish, champagne with the roast and claret all through the dinner. Choice Burgundy comes in with the game, and a glass of fine Madeira finishes the dinner. Liquors and brandy are offered with or after the coffee. It is the pleasant custom now to offer mineral waters with the wine. Appollinaris has been called the Presidential beverage since the days of Mrs. Hayes, and for those who can not drink wine it is a very good substitute.

Kitchen gossips say that $6,000 worth of unused "stuff" was taken from Vanderbilt's house the day after the ball.

In a corner of those magnificent markets of Paris, called Halles Centralles, you may behold a strange sight every morning between six o'clock and noon. Half a dozen large stalls there, bright with gilding and varnish, luxurious with marble, well-furnished, with lusty shop girls, display the remnant of yesterday's banquet—plates of soup; bits of fish half picked, with the sauce still round them; fragments of pates and sweets; liquefied ices; fragments of game; and costly viands formless, heaped together. These are the leavings of a grand restaurant or a ministerial dinner, sold by the officer to whom such perquisities belong. Too proud is he to touch them himself; but round the counter you will see a few workmen, mostly red-nosed and shaggy, the wives of many more, and a crush of threadbare individuals of that class one would rather see by daylight than by dark. It is not that these broken meats, as far as I have noticed, are particularly cheap. Five pennyworth of beef would give more strength than ten plates of melted ice and sauce congealed. But the worn out stomachs of such people crave high seasoning and strong taste, which the beef would not give them. So they take away in bits of newspaper a franc's worth of wretched dainties, and eat them with a scowl and curse against "the rich."

———

Pope Leo XIII. daily dines at a cost of 37 cents, on a simple soup, a little bread, a leg or wing of a chicken, six or seven grapes and one pear, with a big glass of the best Marcia.

———

No. 9 Doyers Street, this city, may aptly be called a hotel for the extremely poor. It is under the management of the Sanitary Aid Society of the Tenth Ward. Boarders are entertained at nominal prices. The three upper floors are full of bunks, similar to those on a ship, covered over with clean white linen. A charge of ten cents is made for each one of these beds a night, including a warm bath, which is made a necessity by the rules of the institution. Breakfast is furnished for three and five cents, and dinner for ten cents. Each lodger is compelled to register his name, give age, occupation, and tell whether married or single before he can get a ticket for a bed. This is the only institution of its kind in the city, but efforts are being made to establish more as soon as possible. As the house is self-supporting money invested is not lost, but pays a good percentage.

———

On the bills of fare in New York Italian restaurant's coffee is 1 cent per cup; steaks, chops and stews, 3 cents; pastry, 3 cents; beer, 2 cents; whisky and brandy, 3 cents. These places are thronged daily by persons of all nationalities.

———

So-called English chop houses are springing up in all parts of the city of New York. Their popularity increases constantly. Three or four years ago there was only half a dozen good chop houses. Now there are a score or more and they are all of them flourishing. The slapbang, greasy, noisy and rushing restaurant, with its dozens of tables, soiled linen, slouchy negro waiters and miserable kitchen, has given way to neat and commodious little chop houses, with well polished tables, quiet waiters and excellent cooks. They sell nothing but chops, steaks, potatoes, beer and ale, and the service is characterized by cleanliness and promptness. The prices are quite reasonable.

THE five-cent lunch places in lower Broadway, N. Y., are getting more numerous and more popular. The proprietor of one of them said to a *Tribune* reporter: "For nearly half a century cheapness in New York, for nearly everything, but especially eating, has been synonymous with dirt. It was my idea in opening this place to make it absolutely clean and neat, the food wholesome and toothsome, and the price so reasonable that I should get not only the multitude who are obliged to buy five-cent lunches, but that other class who pay a higher price to get something clean. I hit it, and so have the other places of this kind. I have enlarged my place twice since coming here, and shall enlarge it again as soon as the present tenants vacate a room next to me."

———

A MOVEMENT is now in very successful operation in Bordeaux to supply workingmen with wholesome, well-cooked and substantial meals at a low cost. To this end a number of restaurants have been started in various parts of the city by a certain company, which is backed by the moral support of the medical fraternity, the churches and the health authorities. In the course of a flying trip to Bordeaux last week, writes a correspondent, I visited one of these restaurants. The bill of fare served and the cost per item were as follows: A large plate of vegetable soup, cost two cents; two large slices of bread, two cents; a plate of red haricot beans, two cents; a plate of roast veal, four cents; a plate of rice, one cent; half a bottle of *vin ordinaire*, four cents. Thus a very fair and liberal dinner — there was no stinting in the amount served—was to be obtained for 15 cents. This

might serve as a hint to New York. What can be made a successful business, where almost every article of food is taxed, ought to pay in New York, where meat and nearly all kinds of food are cheaper. Surely a good warm dinner of this character, served at a comfortable table, is a boon to the artisan.

———

ONE-CENT BREAKFAST.

———

The head master of the Board School at Wallsend, seeing so much distress about, and that many of the children attending his school were badly prepared to face the lessons of the day for want of sufficient food at home, and being, it is said, a firm believer in oatmeal, once the chief of "Scotia's food," determined to do something on his own account without waiting for "a committee." So he ordered a good supply of oatmeal from a mill in Berwickshire, of the finest quality. The cooking operations commenced at 6: 30 A. M., and the porridge is allowed to boil for fifty minutes, and is cooled and ready for serving out at 8: 15. Each child is supplied with about a pint of porridge—more or less, according to size and appetite—and a little more than half a gill of good skimmed milk. About one hundred and twenty children are thus receiving breakfast at a cost of about one-half penny each, and in most cases they are given free. In times gone by oatmeal was also the staple food of the North of England; it will be curious if it comes again into use. Its value as regards nutrition for children is beyond dispute. High wages have conduced to a high class though not better food for the working class. —*London Lancet.*

THE New York *Hotel Reporter* makes the following remarks upon country or seaside boarding.

"As a general thing the city boarder wants the full value of his money when sojourning in the country, and is hard to please. He will criticise the meat and say that it cannot be compared with that which he gets in the city. This may be true, if he really gets first rate city food. Our opinion is that the farmer's wife who takes boarders should confine herself to those dishes which she knows how to cook well—to the stews and the pot-pies. Her deserts should be ample puddings, especially in the season of fruits, the city boarder, who is always hungry in the country, does not care for thin and stingy little slices of cake and a spoonful of sweetmeats. The problem usually is, where can we have still salt water bathing and boating, shade, a quiet farmhouse where the people go to bed early, and where the food is plentiful, without being extravagantly fine, at a cheap price? These questioners always have children, big and little. The busy boarding-house of popular seaside resorts are not suitable for people who are disposed to be quiet and do not wish to be kept awake until after midnight by the banging of a cracked piano, by silly laughter and by noisy dancing. So that the quiet family which should like to be in a farmer's house on a still bay, with both a beach and shady trees, finds itself hard to please, especially when it wishes to pay about five dollars a head. The farmer's wife who has such a place is usually shy of boarders, and looks at them as if they are always dissatisfied, and is not disposed to take them at all. If she is, we have not heard of her at all. But the papers will soon be full of adver- tisements of boarding places and people will be seeking for what they will never get. After all it is a problem. Who will explain?"

THE PREVAILING DISCONTENT.

It was a little country inn
  Without a bill-of-fare.
They simply set forth what they had;
  Variety was spare.

A man of cranky appetite
  Sat at this humble board,
And was no sooner served than he
  Thus started in and jawed.

"Take hence this hammered bit of steak.
  "Remove this old hen's legs.
"Withdraw this bitter chicory—
  "And bring some scrambled eggs."

"Alas!" replied the table girl,
  "To please you much I'd like.
"Some little discontent prevails—
  "The hens are on a strike."

"What is the cause?" the traveler asked.
  "It's simply this," she stated,
"The *plain* glass nest egg's out of style.
  "They want 'em *decorated*."
      —New York Hotel Register.

AU CAFE.

You're a natty little waiter,
  O, Fraulein!
To my wants you always cater,
  When I dine;
And you have no irritating
Way of keeping people waiting,
And your smile is captivating,
  I opine.

You are dressed so nicely,
  O, Fraulein!
All my feelings so precisely
  You divine:
That from soup to *tutti frutti,*
You're acquainted with your duty;
And utility with beauty
  You combine.

You are skilled in fancy cooking,
  O, Fraulein!
You are the maid for whom I'm looking
  For my shrine.
Tho' I have not wealth nor title,
Prithee, list to my recital,
Give my fond love some requital,
  O, be mine!

So you actually are laughing,
  And decline?
And my sentiment you're chaffing,
  And say: "Nein?"
At my proffered love you laugh; eh?
What! you are a better half, eh?
Of the man who keeps this *cafe?*
  O, Fraulein!

             —Chicago Rambler.

TO MAKE AN ASTONISHING EGG.

Labouchere gives the following recipe for a monster Easter egg: Take a dozen eggs, separate the whites from the yolks, which latter you pour into a small bladder well washed and thoroughly cleaned. Shape the bladder like a sphere, close it hermetically and plung it into boiling water. When the yolks are quite hard peel the bladder off; you will find them in the form of a ball, which you must place in a larger bladder, adding the whites. The yellow ball suspends itself naturally in the center of the whites. Close the bladder and plunge it into boiling water. When this monster egg is quite hard peel the bladder off again. When you serve it place it in the center of a bowl of salad; then cut it up and serve with the salad.

THEY had "nudels" at a New York dinner, and Mr. Dana, of the *Sun*, heard of them then for the first time. He describes them, not very accurately, and states how the hostess buys them of a German woman, though they are usually made at home as wanted. The woman started the business, made such nice "nudels" and was so cleanly that she now sells enough to support herself and children. All through Pennsylvania "nudels" are much eaten, particularly in soup. In Lancaster, and other inland towns, they are sold in the market. They are kept by some of the Philadelphia grocers, and are frequently served at Philadelphia tables. They are one of the many excellent dishes to which the New Yorker is a comparative stranger. If Mr. Dana will come to Philadelphia, and let me know of his coming, I will promise him "nudel" soup of home-made "nudels" for dinner. I think he spells the word wrong. It ought to be noodles. It is the custom, when you have noodle soup, to dispose of from four to five plates at least. The chicken, which is boiled in the soup, comes afterwards to table.

MR. BOUCICAULT is said to be such an artist in cookery that he could give points to the best *chefs* in the country. Mr. Jefferson is very fond of griddle cakes; Salvini, of macaroni; Catherine and Jeffreys Lewis, of Frankfort sausage; and Patti has a weakness for onions—but "the weakness is so strong."

"PLANKED SHAD."

The approach of the season when Washington epicures can enjoy the luxury of "planked shad," reminds the correspondent of the St. Louis *Globe - Democrat* of the following story about Daniel Webster: "Webster was an artist in this line, and prided himself greatly upon his gifts. His only rival was an aged slave, a character on the river, called Sam. There were those who said that Sam was the only one who knew how to cook planked shad; others protested that the great statesman was supreme. On sunny spring days, when parties of gentlemen went down the river to watch the fish nailed to their boards, sizzling and browning before the blaze of an outdoor fire, it was arranged to have a trial for the championship between old Sam and Mr. Webster. Each contestant was well backed, and the lights of those early political days were all there. First Sam split the shad, seasoned them as he knew would most suit Mr. Webster's taste, and laid them before the orator done to a turn. "Really, Sam, this is the best planked shad I have ever eaten," quoth Daniel; and applause rang from Sam's adherents. Next Webster laid aside his toga and hovered around the fire, knife and salt-box in hand, watching the shad that he had prepared in the way he knew would best suit Sam's taste. Sam ate three mouthfuls rapturously, and exclaimed: 'Fore God, Mr. Webster, I neber have tasted planked shad before!' Webster yielded gracefully the palm to Sam, outdone by him in compliments as well as in cooking."

"PLANKED" SHAD.

Every little hotel and eating house fronting the Delaware at Gloucester has its specialty of "planked" shad. The fish, fresh from the stream, is cut in twain, fastened by tenpenny nails to a thick oak board, slanted toward a hot wood fire, duly basted and finally served at table on his oak gridiron. That the prince of American fishes, served under these conditions and flanked by asparagus and kindred dainties, is at his best, goes without further saying. Daniel Webster, I have heard, used to plume himself more on his ability to "plank" a shad than on his highest oratorical flights. But if I may venture a personal opinion against so famed an authority, the planked shad is not, after all, decidedly better than the same fish cooked prosaically on the domestic gridiron. He is fresher from the water, he is surrounded by the poetic novelty of odd cookery and service, and appetite is sharpened by the keen, watery air. Take these concomitants away, and the planked shad would lose half his fame.

THE REAL VIENNA BREAD.

Viennese bread is celebrated. It may interest you to know something about it. The excellence of the bread is attributed in Vienna to three reasons—the oven, the men and the yeast. I think another may be added, and that is the dry climate. An ounce of yeast (three decagrammes) and as much salt is taken for every gallon of milk used for the dough. The yeast is a Viennese specialty, known as the "St. Marxner Pressheffe," and its composition is a secret. It keeps two days in summer and a little longer in winter. The ovens are heated by wood fires lighted inside them during four hours; the ashes are then raked out and the oven is carefully wiped with wisps of damp straw. On the vapor thus generated, as well as that produced by the baking of the dough, lies the whole art of the browning and the success of the "semmel."

"YES," said Chef Ranhöffer, of Delmonico's, "we have a great demand for quail. We sold one hundred a day and more before the season ended. We could have given Mr. Walcott a quail cooked differently every day in his match, thus agreeably relieving the monotony of his feat. A person would hardly believe this statement, but quail can be cooked in thirty-four different ways, at a cost to the eater of from seventy-five cents to two dollars for a single bird. We make them into soups, pies, stews and salmis, and add all kinds of sauces. In France a delicious way of cooking them is to wrap them with leaves and a piece of lard, bathe them in wine, and pour tomato sauce over them after they are cooked. Sometimes they are cooked with bay leaves, or they are treated in Spanish fashion and cooked with rice dressing. They can be stuffed like a regular fowl and treated with sauces until they are a luxury to the palate, and the diner will crave for a repetition."

CREAM OR FONDANT.

I presume from your question that the cream you speak of is what we call fondant, which article is the basis of all cream bonbons. This fondant is also used for covering or icing cakes and a great variety of what are called dipped goods. Fondant is made by boiling simple syrup to the forty-fifth degree by the saccharometer; then pouring it on a very clean marble slab between iron bars, and when it has become nearly cold, so that you can place the back of your hand upon it without its adhering to it; it must be worked to and fro with a long-handled spatula until it granulates into a smooth mass, it must then with a knife be loosened from the marble and worked or broken with the hands into a softish mass, and placed in an earthenware pan and covered. When you want to use it for icing purposes place the required quantity in a round-bottomed pan, place it upon a slow fire, and stir constantly with a small wooden spatula until it is thoroughly melted, and there are no lumps in it. Do not on any account allow it to boil, even a little, as that would entirely destroy its creamy texture and change it into hard conserve; when melted pour it over the article to be covered and use a pallet knife to smooth it and facilitate your operation, which must be done quickly, as in a few moments it will begin to set and dry. The cake can then be decorated with ordinay egg-icing, or in any other way to suit your fancy.—*Confectioner's Journal.*

HOW TO PREPARE STUFFED EGG-PLANT.

Mme. C. B. Waite's style is thus described by M. Xavier Wirtz, of the *Société Culinaire Philantropique,* and as fine a chef as ever wore white cap and apron: Cut the top of the eggplant off, also a small piece from the bottom, so it will stand steadily, then cut out all the inside, as near the shell as possible without breaking it. Fill the shell with salt and water (to extract the bitterness) and let it stand until just before dinner time. Stew the inside with a little water, bread crumbs, butter, cayenne pepper, salt, spices and a small piece of onion cut very fine. Before dinner throw the water from the shell and fill it with the hot stuffing. Grate bread crumbs over the top, with a little butter, and put it into the oven for a few minutes to brown.

HOW TO SERVE POTATOES.

A grand international potato exhibition was opened at the Crystal Palace yesterday afternoon by Mr. Alderman and Sheriff De Keyser, in the absence of the Lord Mayor. Ten years ago an association was formed for the encouragement of potato culture, and the introduction and diffusion of improved varieties. An annual exhibition has been held, and the result has been that not only has the number of exhibits increased, but the quality of the potatoes shown has greatly improved. At yesterday's show all the leading growers were represented, and the excellence of the specimens made the task of awarding the prizes no easy one. At a luncheon Mr. Shirley Hibbard remarked that there was still a great deal of ignorance shown in putting potatoes on the table. It was the usual practice to bring them up in a porcelain dish, with a close-fitting cover. In ten minutes the best potatoes, however carefully cooked, were thus utterly destroyed. He recommended that they should be placed in a wooden dish or served in a porcelain dish, with towels above and below to absorb the moisture.

"D. C." wishes to know how to pickle the small red and yellow tomatoes that are brought to market somewhat later in the season. If very small it is not necessary to remove the skin, and you may proceed exactly as if for pickling peaches. Make a sirup of one quart of vinegar and seven pounds of sugar; let this come to a boil, add spices to suit your taste; put the tomatoes in a jar or in a porcelain kettle, having first removed the stems and wiped the fruit carefully; then pour the hot sirup over them. If you wish them for use late in the Spring it is advisable to can them, as then they will keep perfectly. If you can them, put the porcelain kettle over the front of the stove, pour the hot sirup over, and let the fruit boil gently, but do not break it in pieces. If the fruit is very ripe and inclined to be soft, steam it before pouring the sirup over it; then you may can it immediately.

Here is Rossini's receipt for cooking macaroni: Take a pound of macaroni and three parts cook it in salt and water, after which drain it well in a colander, throw away the water, put the macaroni back again into the stewpan in which it has been dressed, pour over it half a pint of good gravy or stock, place the stewpan at the side of the fire where it may keep hot, simmer, simmer, simmer and always simmer, and from time to time shake the stewpan so that the macaroni may be turned about, but be careful not to break it; when the gravy is entirely absorbed by the macaroni, put it in layers on a silver dish (this, of course, is a question of rank, earthenware doing just as well, perhaps better), between each layer spread some grated Parmesan cheese, with sliced truffles mixed with a good Espagnole sauce, and on the top or last layer put the truffles thicker; serve hot with grated Parmesan on a separate plate.

ABOUT TRUFFLES.

Truffles are subterranean in their habits, their position beneath the soil varying from two or three inches to two feet in depth. They have neither root, stem nor leaf, and are of different shades of color, from light brown to black. They are more or less globular in form and vary in size from a filbert to a large hen's egg. Their surface is knotty or warty and covered with a skin of net work which looks like veins. Truffles grow in pastures and on open downs, under trees and sometimes far away from them. They prefer loose soils and affect the neighborhood of oaks, beeches and chestnuts, but they do not thrive well in thick woods. They are common in Central and Southern Europe, particularly in this country, where the Poitou and Perigord districts are most prolific, and Italy, where Piedmont carries of the palm. The French truffles are decidedly superior to those of any country, but they vary in flavor according to locality. Up in the neighborhood of Nancy or Bar-le-Duc they are grayish in color and nearly tasteless; down near Grenoble, Valence and Avignon they have a musky taste; in Burgundy they are smaller, dry and have a flavor of resin, but the Perigord truffle is the kind that makes one's mouth water to think of it. Did you ever eat a Perigord pie? Well, without the presence of the thin slices of the Perigord tuber that delicious *pate de foie gras* would lose half its value. I have a loving remembrance of the *plat de resistance* of our national Thanksgiving Day, for a truffled turkey is quite a different bird from that stuffed with bread crumbs, sausage meat, boiled chestnuts and many other things. In the northern woods they are hunted for with dogs, but down in Perigord they train pigs for this purpose. It seems that pigs have better noses than dogs for this work. This is because the one likes truffles better as an article of food than the other, and a good truffle-hunting hog will fetch as much as $50. Of the same fungi family as truffles are the cham-

pignons, which are now also in season, but which are not so plentiful in France as in some parts of Russia, where they are said to form the principal staples of food with the peasantry.

A BATTLE WITH WILD HOGS.

An Arkansas correspondent writes: Few people are aware that there are such things as wild hogs in this country, but such is the case, however little the fact may be known. Not long since James Reynolds and myself were on a deer hunting expedition on one of the numerous bayous that jut into Red river in the southeastern part of Arkansas. We had with us two dogs, and were trailing along the bank of the bayou —the dogs some 200 or 300 yards in advance. All at once the dogs began to bark, and there arose the greatest consternation imaginable. It did not take us long to determine the cause of all the commotion, as the dogs soon hove in sight, fighting and retreating toward us. Attacking them was a drove of wild, infuriated hogs, some of them so large and ferocious that a grizzly bear would be little more formidable. To say that they would strike terror to the bravest heart is but to make an assertion that would receive immediate credence of the reader should he ever be brought face to face with them.

What was to be done? Here they came with a deafening and unearthly noise, their every bristle projecting forward, eyes maddened with rage, froth dripping from their mouths, and their long tusks ready to rip open any one or anything that offered combat.

I suggested to Reynolds that we give them a volley from our four barrels at once, and perhaps it would so discomfit them that they would retreat. This we did when they were about two rods from us, and although we felled some three or four to the ground and crippled others, they seemed more enraged than ever and were on us before we could reload our guns. The only thing left for us to do was to take to the water (and very fortunate for us that we had water to take to) which we immediately did. Abandoning our guns' we plunged in and swam to the opposite shore, the live dog taking kindly to our example.

Some little time after they had disappeared among the thick timber of the bottom, we swam back to our guns. After making an examination of the hogs we had dispatched, we concluded that we had all the bottom hunting that we desired that day, and struck out for the uplands.

We learned that these wild hogs abound in considerable numbers along the bottoms of Red River and tributary streams in this locality.

The tusks of the largest one that we killed (an old boar) projected fully four inches from the jaw, curving outward and upward from their base on the upper jaw, and upward and outward on the lower. They are frequently hunted in the fall and winter after the mast has fallen and they have become fattened on it and make, it is said, fair bacon.

ABOUT TERRAPIN.

Sam Ward, during his reign at Washington as king of the Lobby, used to delight in treating epicurean foreigners to a thoroughly American dinner. His bill of fare was iced clams, fish chowder, stewed terrapin, canvas-back ducks, oysters on the half shell, hominy and Albany celery, with Chateau Yquem, dry champagne, and old madeira from the Gadsby stock. In purchasing terrapin, Mr. Ward would turn with disdain from the yellow-bills and the sliders, and purchase the diamond backs at twenty-five dollars a dozen. Having sent them to Welcher's, he would go into the kitchen and superintend their preparation after the following formula: Immerse the terrapin in pure spring water, boiling hot, for five minutes, to loosen the skin. The skin is then removed with a knife, thoroughly polished first to free it from any foreign substance, with a piece of chamois leather. Then replace the terrapin in the boiling water, the temperature of which should be regulated by a thermometer. When the claws become so soft as to pinch into a pulp by a moderate pressure between the thumb and forefinger it is sufficiently boiled. Take them out and remove the bottom shell first, as the convexity of the upper shell catches the rich and savory juices which distinguish the terrapin from the mudturtle and the slider. Cut off the head and claws and carefully remove the gall and sand bag. A little of the gall does not impair the flavor of the terrapin, but the sand bag requires the skilful touch of a surgeon, and the heart of a lion, the eye of an eagle and the hand of a lady. Cut up the remainder into pieces about a half an inch in length. Be careful to preserve all the juice. Put in a chafing dish and add a dressing of fine flour, the yolk of eggs boiled so hard that they are mushy, *quantum sufficit* of butter fresh from the dairy, salt to taste, red pepper, a large wineglass of very old Madeira (to each terrapin) and a small quantity of rich cream. The dish, like everything else fit to eat, except Roman punch and Stilton cheese, should be served smoking hot; some persons have been known to season with spices, but this, like the rank perfume which exhales from the handkerchief of under-bred people, is apt to arouse suspicion. Terrapin should be eaten only at night and then only by very honest men. To slightly paraphrase Dr. Boteler: "A better shell fish than the terrapin might have been made, but one never was made."— *"Perley" in Boston Budget.*

EFFORTS rather to preserve terrapins than to propagate them have not yet been very successful. Terrapins may be kept in an enclosure from Summer to Winter, but it is at the sacrifice of their delicacy as food, penned terrapins losing their fine flavor and becoming tough and stringy. Some years ago a discovery was made as to a new method of feeding terrapins. In Washington, where some terrapins had been put in a pond, a neighboring field of clover had been cut. Some of the clover having fallen from the scythe into the pond, the terrapins were seen to eat it with the same avidity as would a cow.

TERRAPIN - FISHING.

"Boil your terrapin for two hours, until the skin on the legs peels off; the pick the terrapin out of the shell and remove its gall-sac; then stew, by adding a quarter of a pound of butter, a taste of red pepper and the squeeze of a half lemon; put as much water as will stew, pour in a dash of sherry, and leave the rest to *nature.*"

Thus "Tommy" Boylan, of Guy's, in Baltimore, to the artist and the writer, and there is no better authority on terrapin from Savannah to the Patapsco River.

Turtle may be fit for aldermen, but terrapin is food for princes, and a terrapin-stew might be served by Hebe to the immortal gods in high Olympus.

Terrapin are caught from Savannah and Charleston up to the Patapsco River at Baltimore, while the genuine "diamond-back" is only to be found in the upper Chesapeake and its tributaries. A diamond-back never measures less than seven inches in length on the under shell, a seven-inch being known as a "count terrapin," while anything under the length of a "count" does *not* count. Ten inches long and eight pounds in weight is reckoned a very large terrapin, the seven-inches weighing, on an average, four pounds.

During the season, terrapins sell for $30 to $38 per dozen; while "sliders" — common river turtles, principally caught in the James River—which sell at from $6 to $8 per dozen, are palmed off by skillful *restaurateurs* as genuine diamond-backs on unwary but ambitious guests, at a dollar and a half the dish.

The male terrapin is known as the "bull," the female as the "cow," the lady being more in request on account of her thirty eggs, which are used to garnish the delectable dish.

The artist and I having consigned our lives and limbs to the custody of the darkest darkey my eyes ever alighted upon, and to the most rickety of crazy skiffs, were paddled up a small tributary of the Chesapeake Bay, situated at about six miles from Annapolis, on a terrapin-searching expedition. Having quitted the sanctuary of the boat for the more genial atmosphere of the mud, our darkey, who was armed with a long, thin pole, commenced to probe the bottom—he was wading waist-deep—or, to use the technical term, to "sound" for terrapin. His practiced sense of touch tells him when he taps terrapin, and if they are numerous, he marks his prey, and returns to grab them with a net.

On this occasion the "birds" — as *bon viveurs* love to call them, although terrapin is used as fish by the most devout Catholics in the severest or Lenten time—were plentiful, and our darkey, having put us ashore, very soon returned with a boat containing his mate, nets, sounding-poles, rakes and other *impedimenta* of his calling, a business that pays the catcher, according to luck, from $5 to $50 a week.

The haul, which was watched by a luckless fisherman with considerable envy, proved a good one, the ground being literally cut from under the feet of the terrapin, and there were vast expansive grins, accompanied by chuckles loud and deep, as the well-laden boat rowed back with its precious freight to the quaint old capital of Maryland.

Terrapins are jealously guarded by the law, and a stringent Act exists which protects diamond-back terrapin in the waters of the State of Maryland. The fishing opens on the first of November and terminates on the thirty-first of March. It is unlawful to catch any terrapin of a size less than five inches on the bottom of the shell, or to interfere with or destroy the diamond-back terrapin's eggs. It is stated that thirty years ago the dealers found it difficult to sell terrapin at $6 a dozen, and now the difficulty lies in obtaining them at any price. Their numbers are rapidly decreasing, and unless some effective protective means are forthwith taken, a terrapin will indeed prove a *rara avis in terris*.

Sliders are plentiful in the tributaries of the Chesapeake, as also are "snappers." Turtles are fished for in this way: The fisherman plants poles, sometimes a hundred, in the middle of the stream; to each pole he fastens a line, to which is attached a hook baited with salted eel. The snapper grabs bait and hook, and is hauled up, always vicious and desperate.

The fishermen around these tributaries take a thousand pounds' weight of turtle a week, which they sell at ten cents a pound. The snappers' eggs, about the size of marbles, are considered a great delicacy.

Apropos of turtle and terrapin, the following is the *menu* of a perfect Maryland dinner, as arranged by "one of the knowing ones":

"Four small oysters from Lynhaven Bay; terrapin *a la* Maryland; canvas-back ducks; a small salad of crab and lettuce. Vegetables—baked Irish potatoes; fried hominy cakes and plain celery."—*Magazine.*

THE CONSUMPTION OF ICE CREAM.

Enormous quantities of ice cream are consumed every day in New York city in warm wether. On the Fourth of July the supply, though unusually large, was nearly exhausted by ten o'clock at night. Ice cream, like ice, in old times used to be considered a luxury in New York instead of a necessity, and old Gothamites recall with pleasure the memories of Vauxhall Garden, Niblo's, Castle Garden and other open-air resorts where ice cream, ices and Roman punches were served during the dog days. In those days a quarter of a dollar was considered a fair evening's investment for a young man treating a single fair friend, as the highest price for ice cream was "sixpence" a plate, and an ice was thrown in for a "shilling." A first-rate Principæ cigar for two cents would top off the treat.

The old times have changed and the cool gardens have vanished. Ice cream is now considered as much of a necessity as ice, and is served as regularly at the tables of private families as at hotels and restaurants. Gardens have given place to "saloons," where ice cream, ices and cakes are exclusively served. Some of the most aristocratic of these saloons are elegantly and expensively furnished, and some are in the rear of bakeries and confectionary stores. From Fifth avenue to Grand street, however, all are alike in having marble-top tables and one or more gilt mirrors. It is a singular fact that every ice cream saloon, whether of high or low degree, has a gilt-framed mirror and marble-top tables, and palm-leaf fans are also much affected.

It is not merely the wealthy or those in moderate circumstances who eat ice cream. From the costly pist-ache or Neapolitaine brick there is a gradual descent to ice cream at ten cents a plate on the extreme east and west sides. Then by a sudden bound an open-air tariff of one or two cents a plate is reached, so that the cooling cream is within the means of every street urchin. The plates are small and no spoons are furnished, and the ice cream is sometimes a trifle gritty, but still it is ice cream.

A large manufacturer said: "You might as well try to find out how many cigars are smoked or how many cups of coffee or tea are used every day as try to find out how much ice cream is consumed. I can tell you how much I sell daily, but there are several other large manufacturers. We supply a good many hotels and restaurants, but many other hotels and restaurants make their own ice cream. We supply hundreds of private families, but hundreds more have their own ice cream freezers. You see it's a big business. What are the prices? Well, the regular standard price for ice cream is forty cents for a single quart, but church fairs, picnics and excursions are supplied in large quantities at twenty.five cents a quart. The regular retail price is fifteen cents a plate, but many fairs and picnics sell small plates for ten cents. Ours is a good, pure article of cream; but, of course, fancy ice creams are sold at wholesale and retail for more than double our rates. We sell to customers outside of the city, and have now an order for five hundred quarts to go some distance out on Long Island.

"The sale of ice cream varies, of course, with the weather, but it is a staple article of consumption all the year round. Some families use twenty to thirty quarts a week, and even then their youngsters will come and buy it in boxes. Healthy? Why, there is nothing more healthy than pure ice cream. Many people actually eat it at breakfast. Vanilla is the standard flavor, but we sell large quantities of strawberry, chocolate and other flavors."

ANALYTICAL INDEX.

ENTREES AND RESTAURANT ORDERS.

ARTICLES RELATING TO THE COST OF BOARD.

WHITEHEAD'S
HOTEL COOK BOOKS.

No. 1.—"THE AMERICAN PASTRY COOK."
PRICE, POSTPAID, $2.00.
EMBRACES THE FOLLOWING:

PART FIRST—The Hotel Book of Fine Pastries, Ices, Pies, Patties, Cakes, Creams, Custards, Charlottes, Jellies and Sweet Entrements in Variety.

PART SECOND—The Hotel Book of Puddings, Souffles and Meringues. A handy Collection of Valuable Recipes, original, selected and perfected for use in Hotels and Eating Houses of every Grade.

PART THIRD—The Hotel Book of Breads and Cakes; French, Vienna, Parker House, and other Rolls, Muffins, Waffles, Tea Cakes; Stock Yeast and Ferment; Yeast raised Cakes, etc., etc., as made in the best hotels.

PART FOURTH—The Hotel Book of Salads and Cold Dishes, Salad Dressings, with and without oil; Salads of all kinds, how to make and how to serve them; Boned Fowls, Galantines, Aspics etc., etc.

☞ The above parts are all comprised in the "AMERICAN PASTRY COOK," together with a large amount of valuable miscellaneous culinary matter.

No. 2.—"HOTEL MEAT COOKING."
PRICE, POSTPAID, $2.00.
EMBRACES THE FOLLOWING:

PART FIRST—The Hotel, Fish and Oyster Book; Showing all the best methods of Cooking Oysters and Fish, for Restaurant and Hotel Service, together with the appropriate Sauces and Vegetables.

PART SECOND—How to Cut Meats, and Roast, Boil and Broil. The entire trade of the Hotel Meat Cutter, Roaster and Broiler, including "Short Orders," Omelets, etc.

PART THIRD—The Hotel Books of Soups and Entrees, comprising specimens of French, English and American *Menus*, with translations and comments. Showing how to make up Hotel Bills of Fare, with all the different varieties of Soups and Consommes in proper rotation, and a new set of entrees or "made dishes" for every day.

PART FOURTH—Creole Cookery and Winter Resort Specialties.

PART FIFTH—Cook's Scrap Book—A Collection of Culinary Stories, Poems, Stray Recipes etc., etc. Index of French Terms, an explanation and translation of all the French terms used in the Book, alphabetically arranged.

☞ The above parts are all comprised in "HOTEL MEAT COOKING," together with a large and varied selection of matter pertaining to this part of the culinary art.

No. 3.—"WHITEHEAD'S FAMILY COOK BOOK."
PRICE, POSTPAID, $1.50.
A PROFESSIONAL COOK'S BOOK FOR HOUSEHOLD USE.

Consisting of a series of *Menus* for every-day meals, and for private entertainments, with minute instructions for making every article named.

The Recipes in all these books are properly headed, numbered and indexed, for handy reference.

The author of this series of Hotel Cook Books is a professional Cook of Thirty Years' Experience, and every recipe has been tried and practically proved.

The above books will be sent postpaid on receipt of price: "American Pastry Cook," $2.00; "Hotel Meat Cooking," $2.00; "Family Cook Book," $1.50.

Adress all orders to

Jessup Whitehead & Co.,
PUBLISHERS OF HOTEL COOK BOOKS,
....CHICAGO, ILL.

WHITEHEAD'S NEW BOOK,
NUMBER 5,

THE STEWARD'S HANDBOOK

AND GUIDE TO PARTY CATERING.

BY JESSUP WHITEHEAD.

PRICE, POSTPAID, $3.00.

EMBRACES THE FOLLOWING:

PART FIRST—HOTEL STEWARDING. Showing the Internal Workings of the American System of Hotel Keeping. The Steward's Duties in Detail, and in Relation to Other Heads of Departments. Steward's Storekeeping, Steward's Bookkeeping, and Management of Help. Also, Composition of Bills of Fare, the Reasons Why, and Numerous Illustrative Menus of Meals on the American Plan.

PART SECOND—RESTAURANT STEWARDING. Comprising a Survey of Various Styles of Restaurants and their Methods, Club Stewarding and Catering, Public Party Catering, Ball Suppers, Base Ball Lunches, Hotel Banquets, etc.; How to Prepare and How to Serve Them, with Numerous Pattern Bills of Fare Carried Out to Quantities, Cost and Price per Head.

PART THIRD—COMPRISING CATERING FOR PRIVATE PARTIES. A Guide to Party Catering. Wedding Breakfasts, Fantasies of Party Givers, Model Small Menus, and Noteworthy Suppers, with Prices Charged. Also, Catering on a Grand Scale. Original and Selected Examples of Mammoth Catering Operations, Showing the Systems Followed by the Largest Catering Establishments in the World. Also, a Disquisition on Head Waiters and their Troops.

PART FOURTH—WHITEHEAD'S DICTIONARY OF DISHES, Culinary Terms and Various Information Pertaining to the Steward's Department, being the Essence of all Cook Books, Telling in Brief what all Dishes and Sauces are or what they should Look Like. What Materials are Needed for and what They are. How to Use to Advantage all Sorts of Abundant Provisions, or How to Keep Them. Comprising, also, a Valuable Collection of Restaurant Specialties, Distinctive National Cookery, Remarks on Adulterations, and How to Detect Them, Treatment and Service of Wine, and a Fund of Curious and Useful Information in Dictionary Form, for Stewards, Caterers, Chefs, Bakers, and all Hotel and Restaurant Keepers.

PART FIFTH—HOW TO FOLD NAPKINS. Abundantly Illustrated with many Handsome Styles and Diagrams which Show how It is Done.

ADDRESS ALL ORDERS TO

Jessup Whitehead & Co.,

PUBLISHERS OF HOTEL COOK BOOKS,

CHICAGO, ILL.

www.ingramcontent.com/pod-product-compliance
Lightning Source LLC
Chambersburg PA
CBHW051116120726
47905CB00005B/1298

9 783744 785044